D0918330

THE FAITH ONCE FOR ALL

Contend for **the faith** that was
once for all entrusted to the saints (Jude 3).

THE
FAITH
ONCE
FOR
ALL

Bible Doctrine For Today

JACK COTTRELL

Copyright © 2002
College Press Publishing Company

Printed and Bound in the
United States of America
All Rights Reserved

Unless otherwise noted, all scripture references are taken from the
NEW AMERICAN STANDARD BIBLE®, © Copyright 1960, 1962,
1963, 1968, 1971, 1972, 1973, 1975, 1977, 1995 by
The Lockman Foundation. Used by permission.
www.Lockman.org

Cover design by Mark A. Cole

International Standard Book Number 978-0-89900-905-6
Previously catalogued by the Library of Congress as follows:

Library of Congress Cataloging-in-Publication Data

Cottrell, Jack.
  The faith once for all: Bible doctrine for today/by Jack Cottrell
    p.   cm.
  Includes bibliographical references and index.
  ISBN 0-89900-905-0
  1. Theology, Doctrinal.   2. Bible—Theology.   3. Restoration movement
(Christianity).   I. Title.
BT75.3 .C68 2002
230'.66—dc21

2002035090

ABBREVIATIONS

AG   Arndt, William F., and F. Wilbur Gingrich. *A Greek English Lexicon of the New Testament*

ANF   Roberts, Alexander, and James Donaldson, eds. *Ante-Nicene Fathers*

ASV   American Standard Version of the Bible

CD   Barth, Karl. *Church Dogmatics*

EDNT   Balz, Horst, and Gerhard Schneider, eds. *Exegetical Dictionary of the New Testament*

ESV   English Standard Version of the Bible

GC   Cottrell, Jack. *What the Bible Says about God the Creator*

GRe   Cottrell, Jack. *What the Bible Says about God the Redeemer*

GRu   Cottrell, Jack. *What the Bible Says about God the Ruler*

KJV   King James Version of the Bible

LXX   The Septuagint (Greek) version of the Old Testament

NASB   New American Standard Bible

NEB   New English Bible translation

NIDNTT   Brown, Colin, ed. *The New International Dictionary of New Testament Theology*

NIDOTTE   VanGemeren, Willem A., ed. *New International Dictionary of Old Testament Theology and Exegesis*

NKJV   New King James Version of the Bible

NRSV   New Revised Standard Version of the Bible

NT   New Testament

OT   Old Testament

RSV   Revised Standard Version of the Bible

TDNT   Kittel, Gerhard, and Gerhard Friedrich, eds. *Theological Dictionary of the New Testament*

(For fuller titles and publishing information on books, see the bibliography.)

TABLE OF CONTENTS

AN INTRODUCTION TO THEOLOGY

At one time theology was called "the queen of the sciences," and any good scientist will seek to clarify and justify his task and his method of inquiry before beginning his actual work. A comprehensive study of theology thus usually begins with an introductory section (sometimes called "prolegomena") that discusses the nature and purpose of theology as such. That is the burden of this chapter, which discusses the concept, possibility, sources, method, and importance of theology.

I. THE CONCEPT OF THEOLOGY

The term "theology" does not appear in the Bible, but it is a perfectly good word for something most Christians do quite frequently and should do even more often. The English word comes from two Greek words: *theos*, meaning "God," and *logos*, meaning "word, statement, speech, discourse." Literally, then, theology is *God-talk*, i.e., the act (or product) of studying, discoursing, or writing about God.

In general the term refers to any deliberate effort to learn and/or to teach about God and his relation to his creation. We offer the following as specific definitions: (1) As an *act*, theology is the study of God, and of everything else in its relation to God, for the purpose of formulating a body of truth thereof. (2) As to its *content*, theology is the body of truth about God and about all creation in its relation to God.

A. Connotations of the Term

The term "theology" is used in a number of ways in the religious world, especially in the academic setting. The following are four common connotations, proceeding from the broadest to the narrowest in meaning.

First and most generally, the whole scope of religious studies can be called theology. Many seminaries include the word "theology" or "theological" in their name, e.g., Princeton Theological Seminary. A seminary curriculum usually includes courses in a number of related fields and areas, such as biblical languages, biblical exegesis, church history, archaeology, Bible doctrine, apologetics, Christian education, preaching, and missions. These courses are usually grouped under four major divisions: the biblical field, the historical field, the theological field, and the practical field. In the broadest sense all are appropriately called "theology."

Second, the term "theology" is used in a narrower sense to refer just to the theological field itself as distinguished from the other three. This field may be subdivided into areas such as systematic theology, history of theology, apologetics or philosophy of religion, and ethics.

Third and most commonly, the word "theology" is used to refer to the specific area of doctrinal or systematic theology, which is usually a study of the Bible section by section or subject by subject (as distinct from book by book or verse by verse). It may involve a systematic study of a specific topic, e.g., the doctrine of sin ("what the Bible teaches about sin"). Or it may be an attempt to set forth the Bible's teaching about *every* major subject in a systematic and orderly way. The latter describes the nature of this book; thus it is a "systematic theology."

Finally the term "theology" is used to refer to the study of the doctrine of God specifically, as distinguished from topics such as anthropology (the study of the doctrine of man) and soteriology (the study of the doctrine of salvation). Sometimes when this precise meaning is intended, the expression "theology proper" is used to avoid confusion.

In this book the term will be used most often in the third sense above.

B. Theology and Doctrine

A biblical term closely akin to theology is the word "doctrine." This English word comes from the Latin *doctrina*, "teaching," which comes from *docere*, "to teach, to show." (In Latin a *doctor* is simply a teacher.) In the Greek NT the nouns most equivalent to "doctrine" are *didache* and *didaskalia* (derived from *didasko*, "to teach"), both of which mean "doctrine, teaching." They can mean either the *act* of teaching (e.g., Mark 4:2; Rom 15:4; 1 Tim 4:13; 2 Tim 4:2) or the *content* of teaching, i.e., that which is taught (e.g., Rom 16:17; 1 Tim 1:10; Titus 2:10; 2 John 9,10).

Whereas the KJV almost always translates the Greek words as "doctrine," most modern translations use the word "teaching" instead. Doctrine and teaching are essentially the same thing. Thus we should not hesitate to use the word "doctrine," nor should we cringe when others use it. It simply means "the teaching" in the sense of "what is taught, the content of the teaching."

How are doctrine and theology related? Sometimes these words are used interchangeably, but more specifically we may distinguish them as follows. "Doctrine" refers to the whole scope of Christian teaching (cf. Acts 2:42; 2 Tim 3:16), which may be divided into the categories of *theology* and *ethics*. Theology is that part of Christian doctrine or teaching that sets forth what is *true* (e.g., Acts 5:28; 13:12; 2 Tim 4:3; Titus 2:1; Heb 6:2; 2 John 9,10), while ethics is that part of Christian doctrine that sets forth what is *right* (e.g., 1 Tim 1:10; 4:1,6,16; Titus 2:1). The former deals with true ideas or concepts, and the latter deals with right actions and attitudes. Thus theology is one branch of Christian doctrine, and ethics is another.

This shows that it is appropriate to use the term "doctrine" in the context of theology; indeed, it is inevitable. This is true especially when we are referring to a specific teaching, e.g., the doctrine of the Holy Spirit, the doctrine of sin. All theology is doctrine, even though not all doctrine is theology (i.e., some of it is ethics).

II. THE POSSIBILITY OF THEOLOGY

The ultimate subject of theology, by definition, is God himself, in the sense that he is the reality about whom or in reference to whom all theological statements are made. But now the issue is this: is it really possible for us to have access to divine reality, in order that we may have true knowledge of him? How is it possible for us to make true statements about God, and about any part of creation in its relation to God?

Here we come face to face with the whole problem of truth, since the possibility of theology presupposes the possibility of truth itself. Theology is nothing less than sound doctrine, i.e., *true teaching* about the works and nature of God and about the whole of creation in its relation to him. Is such truth possible? We will now seek to answer this question under three headings: the definition of truth, the denial of truth, and the defense of truth.

A. The Definition of Truth

Pilate is famous for asking the question, "What is truth?" (John 18:38). This was probably not a request for a list of true statements, but a query concerning the very *nature* of truth. What do we mean when we use this word? What determines whether a statement is true or not?

A common false answer to this question is associated with the philosophy called pragmatism. It says that a statement is true if it *works*, i.e., if it accomplishes its purpose, if it brings about the desired effects. For example, to motivate his soldiers for a coming battle, a lieutenant may tell them of an act of astounding bravery on the part of one of their fallen comrades. Though the officer knows it never really happened, it is considered to be truth because it does indeed inspire the soldiers to win the victory.

The only really valid answer to Pilate's question, however, is known as the *correspondence* concept of truth. That is, a statement is true if and only if it corresponds to reality. A proposition can be called true if it describes what actually exists in reality. This is the common-sense approach to truth and the one assumed by most people even if they have not thought about it formally.

Richard Bowman (9-11), a conservative Disciples of Christ minister and co-founder of Disciple Renewal, shows why it is crucial that we be aware of this distinction. He tells how his liberal seminary professors denied the actual reality of such things as the virgin birth, revelation, and heaven; but they taught that ministers should continue to affirm that such doctrines are *true*—not in the sense that they correspond to reality, but in the sense that they serve such purposes as giving people hope and keeping them committed to the church. (Of course, ministers need not disclose the fact that they are using a definition of truth totally different from that of most church members, who would probably be a bit upset if they knew it!) Thus ministers may confidently affirm that the doctrines of the virgin birth and the resurrection, for example, are *true*, while denying in their hearts that they actually happened!

This is in complete contrast with the Bible, which throughout assumes the correspondence concept of truth. For example, the resurrection of Jesus Christ is affirmed as an objective historical event, with the risen Savior appearing to hundreds of people in his recognizable bodily nature (1 Cor 15:5-7). Paul declares that preaching the resurrection, if it did not really happen, is empty and vain and makes one a false witness. He says that believing the resurrection really happened, if it did not, is a vain and worthless faith that leaves one still in his sins (1 Cor 15:14-17). In other words, claims to truth *work* (pragmatically) *only* when they correspond to *reality*.

B. The Denial of Truth

Probably the most pervasive and far-reaching feature of 20th/21st-century western thinking is the *denial* of absolute truth. This is a characteristic of our culture in general and is called by many names, e.g., situationalism, multiculturalism, pluralism, diversity, inclusivism, and postmodernism. The generic name for such a denial is *relativism*, which simply means that the so-called "truth" of any given statement is relative to the circumstances in which it is made. A particular statement may be true for you, now; but it may not be true for someone else now, or even for you later.

Most major philosophies developed in the twentieth century are philosophies of relativism, including analytical philosophy, process philosophy, existentialism, pragmatism, and postmodernism. Pragmatism, for example, says an idea is true only if it works. William James, one of the founders of this philosophy, said, "'The true'. . . is only the expedient in the way of our thinking, just as 'the right' is only the expedient in the way of our behaving." For example, "On pragmatistic principles, if the hypothesis of God works satisfactorily in the widest sense of the word, it is true" (145, 192).

The most recent relativist fad is postmodernism. It says that any and every viewpoint on any subject is allowable and must be tolerated (i.e., allowed to be valid) except one: the view that there is such a thing as absolute, objective truth. For example, one defense of postmodernism bears the title, "There's No Such Thing as Objective Truth, and It's a Good Thing, Too" (Kenneson, 155-170).

In surveys taken during the mid-1990s, George Barna found that about *three-fourths* of the U.S. population did not believe in absolute truth. The same was true of almost two-thirds of those who called themselves Evangelical Christians.

Of course when the possibility of truth in general is denied, this will also include the denial of the possibility of theological truth and the espousal of doctrinal relativism. When this is applied consistently, it leads to the rejection of the absolute and exclusive truth of Christianity as such, and the acceptance of all religious viewpoints as equally valid. Even among those who are committed to the Christian faith, the influence of relativism has led many to declare, "There is no one right way to interpret the Bible!"

Among numerous examples is William Baird, a Disciples of Christ scholar. He scolds anyone who supposes he "has the true plan and program for the body of Christ" based on biblical teaching. The problem with this is that, even if such a person "can cite chapter and verse, human interpretation is involved. Interpretation of the divine wisdom is necessary, but the factor which turns this wisdom into folly is the notion that one particular understanding is true" (57).

Another example is a statement by Fred P. Thompson: "The spirit of the Campbellian movement is one of openness and generosity toward all. We have never claimed to be the only Christians. We have refused to sit in judgment on the legitimacy of another's faith. . . . No doctrinal tests are applied within our fellowship (at least none should be) to determine each other's orthodoxy" (15).

A final example of doctrinal relativism—even doctrinal irrelevance—is the following by J. Stephen Lang (6-7):

> . . . The apostle Paul himself gathered up all his doctrinal dissertations, logic, teaching, and advice in one dynamic punch line in the first letter to the Thessalonians: "You know how we lived among you" [1:5, NIV].
>
> . . . He wanted them to recall him—not Paul the theologian, but Paul the living witness.
>
> This testimony from Paul challenges us with an overwhelming question. We must ask ourselves not, *What are your beliefs?* but *How are you living?*
>
> Our Heavenly Father does not call us to systematize spirituality into strait jackets of our own concepts and ideas, but to express our terms in a manner of life. Doctrine is important, indeed, but lives are not turned upside down because the theologians wrangle over this doctrine and that. . . . All the great doctrines taught by all the great Christian thinkers can be condensed into one human's Christlike life.

What is the philosophical basis for such skepticism and indifference toward sound doctrine? It is rooted ultimately in the fact that each individual is inherently limited by what is called the "egocentric predicament." Our ego (our self, our consciousness) is encased within a single small space (our skull) and is encaged within a single point of time (the now). This is the perspective from which we view everything and from which all learning takes place.

In general, all the ideas in our minds have entered therein from our own unique perspective and have been filtered through our fallible senses. Thus what exists in our minds as "knowledge" is only our own *perceptions* of things, not the things themselves. This means we can never really know to what degree our perceptions actually correspond to what exists "out there"; nor can we know to what degree our perceptions correspond to *others'* perceptions of the same things. Another limitation on our perspective is the fact that the future is not accessible to us at all, except by projection and guess. Also, the certainty of death puts an unyielding limit on all our searches for truth.

Kenneson sums it up by saying that there is no such thing as a "view from nowhere" (156, 167).

Given this "predicament," it is literally impossible for finite beings to know all there is to know about any specific thing, much less to have a complete knowledge of the whole picture. But how can we make an absolute statement about something, unless we know how it fits into the whole picture, which is impossible without infinite knowledge? Thus it would seem impossible for anyone to have absolute, 100% certainty about any matter of fact, including the facts of theology.

One implication of the egocentric predicament is skepticism regarding the adequacy of human language to communicate ideas. Since each individual sees everything from his own unique perspective, no one will ever experience anything in exactly the same way anyone else experiences it. This means that the one who *makes* a statement always formulates it from his own particular viewpoint. That is, the way he understands and uses words is determined by his own predicament. It is all relative to his culture, his experiences, and his immediate situation. But the one who *receives* the statement receives it from within his own particular framework, relative to his own cultural and experiential perspective. Such "cultural relativism" means that we can be only relatively sure that we have communicated our own ideas correctly, or that we correctly understand what was intended to be communicated to us.

This skepticism is applied even to any attempts that God may make to communicate with us in our own language, i.e., through word revelation. For one thing, how can such a limited thing as finite human language adequately convey the infinite perfection of divine thoughts? Also, even if God words his thoughts with infinite care, must not each individual receive these words from within his own egocentric predicament, thus precluding any absolute agreement as to what they *mean*? Doctrinal relativism would thus seem to be unavoidable.

C. The Defense of Truth

In order to establish the possibility of theology in the sense of sound doctrine, we must show the fallacies involved in relativism. In general, relativism contradicts itself from the beginning, since its dictum "There is no absolute truth" is itself intended to be taken absolutely. Also, as Elton Trueblood points out, the existence of objective truth is clearly established by the abundant and universally recognized existence of *error*. Newspapers print corrections and retractions; students give wrong answers to exam questions; we have all had errors of memory. Even the most ardent denier of truth complains when someone picks up his briefcase or her purse by mistake. But as Trueblood explains, "We cannot be wrong unless there is something to be wrong *about!*" Unless there is truth, there can be no such thing as errors or mistakes (47-50).

In our defense of truth we must first point out several myths regarding "100% certainty." The first such myth is that the lack of 100% certainty is the same as relativism. Finite human beings can have 100% certainty only on formal matters of math and logic; the egocentric predicament prevents such certainty about all matters of fact. This is just the nature of human knowledge. We are limited to *probability* in all matters of fact. It is a serious error, though, to equate probability with uncertainty, and to think that probability is somehow equivalent to relativism. There are different degrees of probability; and where evidence and logic show that a statement is true with a high degree of probability, it is both irrational and immoral to deny it. We can indeed establish that some things are true "beyond reasonable doubt."

A second related myth is this: "We *need* 100% certainty before we can act decisively or commit ourselves to certain beliefs." People usually invoke this myth when they want to reject something even when the evidence for it is for all practical purposes overwhelming. ("You cannot prove beyond a shadow of a doubt that smoking causes cancer!" "You cannot prove with 100% certainty that Jesus rose from the dead!") But the lack of 100% certainty often is usually just a technicality and is not a legitimate barrier to belief and action. We do not need absolute certainty in order to have high probability and thus *moral* and *practical* certainty.

A third myth is the belief that 100% certainty about matters of fact is forever and absolutely impossible under any circumstances whatsoever. This is the idea that there is no such thing as a "view from nowhere." Why is this a myth? Because 100% certainty—and thus absolute truth—*is* possible, if there is someone who is not bound by the egocentric predicament. And such a being does exist: God. The reality of absolute, objective truth is grounded in the fact that a transcendent Creator-God exists.

The existence of God is thus the fundamental basis for truth. Man is finite, bound by an egocentric predicament; but God is not. God is infinite in every respect, including his knowledge. He is omniscient. He knows all things, and he knows them absolutely. His knowledge is complete and perfect. Absolute truth does exist: it is the contents of the mind of God.

This difference between God and man is rooted in the fact of creation. Man is in every respect a creature and thus is limited by nature. God alone is the Creator, the eternal one who brought man and everything else into existence out of nothing—*ex nihilo*. The distinction between Creator and creature is fundamental; it is the most important of all distinctions. The uncreated Creator is a unique kind of being. He transcends all the limitations by which creatures are inherently bound.

The existence of the transcendent Creator-God is the basis of absolutes of any kind. The mind of God is the prototype of all reason and logic. His very essence is *logos*: "word, reason, logic" (John 1:1); he invites us to come and reason with him (Isa 1:18). His infinite consciousness includes all possible knowledge about all things without gaps or errors. Thus everything he says about himself, about the nature of man, about right and wrong, about sin and salvation, about heaven and hell—is true. Thus God and God alone is the source of absolute truth.

The question still remains, is this truth available to finite human beings? Even if an omniscient God exists, unless he chooses to reveal the contents of his mind to us through word revelation, we would still have no access to absolute truth. But God has spoken truth to us, in language we can understand, in the words of the Bible—the *Word* of God. The fact of word revelation is thus the ultimate basis for the possibility of theology.

But what about the claim that human language is inadequate to communicate truth without ambiguity and uncertainty of meaning? Even if we have a perfect message from God in the Bible, can we presume to be able to understand it? Yes. Here we confidently affirm that ordinary human language is an adequate vehicle for the communication of truth, even God's truth.

A general reason for this affirmation is the simple fact that language communication is a universal phenomenon, and it works. Our confidence that the Bible is understandable is based on the simple observation that all verbal discourse *presumes* the understandability of language as such and of the particular words being used. Whenever anyone speaks or writes, he is assuming that his language should be and can be understood in the meaning intended. I am assuming that the readers of this book can understand what I am writing. Even those who write serious treatises on the inadequacy of language are using ordinary human language to tell us this, and they expect us to understand what they are saying!

What makes language communication successful, despite the egocentric predicament, is something called the phenomenon of agreement. By mutual consent we *agree* to let certain symbols (words) stand for certain objects or concepts. It is a matter of *agreed-on definitions*. The evidence that language can communicate via such agreement is the very existence of dictionaries and lexicons.

A specific reason for affirming that ordinary human language is an adequate vehicle for the communication of God's truth is the fact that God himself has used it for this purpose. Would the infinite God bother to speak to us if it were impossible for us to receive and understand what he is saying? But he *has* spoken (Heb 1:1-2) because he knows that the creatures he made in his own image *can* understand his message.

Surely if the ubiquity of language communication among finite creatures presumes its understandability, the fact of divine revelation shows it to be all the more so. It is a simple argument from the lesser to the greater. If we presume understandability in ordinary discourse, we have infinitely greater reason to presume it regarding *God's* communication. This is true because God himself is the creator both of language and of the minds with whom he intends to communicate.

Because God made us with minds that are *able* to understand, we do not hesitate to affirm that theology is possible and that sound doctrine is a reasonable goal. To deny this is to call God's own wisdom and power into question.

We know that God expects us to formulate a body of theological truth because of the Bible's strong emphasis on truth and sound doctrine, and because of its strong condemnation of error and false doctrine. Regarding the availability of truth, Jesus succinctly says, "You will know the truth" (John 8:32). Paul says that God specifically "desires all men to . . . come to the knowledge of the truth" (1 Tim 2:4). Those who lack "faith in the truth" and "love of the truth" will not be saved (2 Thess 2:10,13). John says that nothing gives him greater joy than hearing that Christians are "walking in the truth" (3 John 4). When Philip found the Ethiopian reading from Isaiah, he asked him, "Do you understand what you are reading?" (Acts 8:30). This very question presupposes that there is one right and true way to understand the Bible.

On the importance of sound doctrine, Paul says it is the Christian's nourishment (1 Tim 4:6). He urges Titus to "speak the things which are fitting for sound doctrine" (Titus 2:1), and to personally be a good example of "purity in doctrine" (Titus 2:7). He condemns those who "will not endure sound doctrine" and who "turn away their ears from the truth" (2 Tim 4:3-4). On the other hand false doctrine is condemned as demonic (John 8:44; 2 Thess 2:9-12; 1 Tim 4:1-2). The Bible condemns *teaching* false doctrine (Gal 1:6-9; 1 Tim 6:3-5; Titus 1:9-14; 2 Peter 2:1-3; 1 John 4:1), *believing* false doctrine (2 Thess 2:10-12; 2 Peter 3:16-17) and *supporting and encouraging* false doctrine (2 John 9-11; 3 John 8).

All such teaching is meaningless unless we are truly able to distinguish between truth and falsehood. It leads us to the reasonable inference that true knowledge of God and true theology are possible.

III. THE SOURCES OF THEOLOGY

If God is the ultimate subject of theology, then he is also the ultimate source of theology. Every theological statement must be traceable back to the reality of God himself; this is the only way to ensure its truth. This raises the question of the *sources* of theology, i.e., *how* is it possible for us to have access to the reality of God and thus to true knowledge about him?

Here we must distinguish between the reality itself, and our consciousness of it. Precisely speaking, theology is the reflection upon and analysis of something within our own consciousness. But what are the sources of the content of our consciousness? Exactly what interfaces with our consciousness and feeds content into it, content upon which we can reflect and from which we can produce this stuff called "theology"?

In answer to this question, many possible sources have been suggested, from which we are flooded with an overwhelming amount of ideas about God, many of which are contradictory. Thus it is necessary to inquire whether one of these possible sources may be the *normative* source, in the sense that the content it provides can be accepted as true without having to be measured or tested by the content from some other source, and in the sense that its content serves as the norm or test for truth against which the content from every other possible source must be measured. If so, then this normative source alone deserves to be called *the* source of theology, or at least the one *primary* source. As we shall see below, there is indeed such a normative source for theology, namely, the Bible.

At the same time it may be true that other possible sources of theology bring true data about God into our consciousness, but those same sources may also provide us with much irrelevant material and even false content as far as God is concerned. When any ideas about God come to us from such sources, though they profess to be true and even if we suspect them to be true, they must be measured and judged by the one true, infallible source, the Bible. When their data are thus filtered through the normative source, some of these other sources may prove to be valid secondary sources of theology. That is, they may yield supplementary material in the sense of illustration, example, and elaboration.

A. Possible Sources of Theology

A great many sources for our knowledge of God and his relation to the creation have been suggested. Although in the final analysis not all of them will prove to be valid or useful, in this section we shall attempt to list and explain them as *possible* sources. They fall into four basic categories: revelation, experience, reason, and tradition.

1. Revelation from God

One possible source of theology is revelation from God himself. In an event of revelation God takes the initiative and acts in such a way that data about himself and his world are made available to us and come into our consciousness. Theological knowledge is thus communicated directly from God to human recipients. Such revelation may come to us *objectively*, from outside ourselves, or *subjectively*, from within ourselves.

Objective revelation may take several forms. Sometimes it is nonverbal, i.e., conveyed without the use of words; sometimes it is verbal, given through human language. From another perspective sometimes objective revelation is general, in the sense that it is available equally to the whole human race in general; sometimes it is specific, being given only to specific people at specific times and places.

Given these variables, three forms of objective revelation are possible. First, we may receive revelation that is general and nonverbal. This is the witness God bears to himself through his acts of original creation and ongoing general providence; it comes to us through the world of nature all around us: "The heavens are telling of the glory of God; and their expanse is declaring the work of His hands" (Ps 19:1; see Rom 1:18-20). This is part of what is usually called "general revelation."

A second form of objective revelation is also nonverbal, coming in forms other than words; yet it is given through specific events at specific times and places. Such events may include acts of special providence, e.g., God's orchestration of nations (Isa 14:24-27; Hab 1:5-6) and the infliction of droughts (Amos 4:6-8; Hag 1:3-10). They may also include miracles performed by the hands of God's messengers. Finally, nonverbal specific revelation may include God's mighty acts of salvation such as the deliverance of Israel from Egypt and the redemptive works of Jesus Christ. These are all a part of what is often called "special revelation."

A third form of objective revelation is both verbal and specific. This is the possibility that God may speak to specific human beings in human language, either directly "in his own voice" (Exod 3:1-10; Matt 17:5), or indirectly through a prophet. In the latter case a prophet sometimes may speak orally (1 Kgs 16:1-4) and sometimes may give the message in written form (Jer 36:27-32; 2 Tim 3:16). Many volumes claim to be in this last category, including the Islamic Qur'an and the Book of Mormon, and of course the Christian Scriptures, the Bible. (Even though everything in the Bible is not *revelation* in the strict sense of the word, everything in it is *inspired* by God, thus giving every part of it an authority equivalent to revelation.)

In addition to these objective forms of revelation are several possible subjective forms, in which data is supposedly given by God directly to the inward consciousness of an individual apart from external sense perception. This may include the universal, built-in knowledge of God's moral law (Rom 2:15), and perhaps also an innate awareness of God himself in every heart. (The term "general revelation" applies here also.)

Other possible forms of subjective revelation include God speaking to individuals through dreams, visions, and other kinds of "inner light." Many Protestants also believe in an inner "witness of the Spirit" by which the Holy Spirit communicates to Christians that they are truly saved and that the Bible is true. Further illumination by the Spirit allegedly enables believers to understand what the Bible means.

2. Experience

The second potential source of theology is human experience. As one writer puts it, "Theology comes from experience." He continues, "I, as a Christian, must continually draw from my own Christian experience the raw materials of theology" (C.W. Christian, 29, 95). "Theology thus crystallizes out of experience," says another (Ditmanson, 17).

This can be true in a number of ways, as primarily seen in the following distinction. On the one hand, some level of experience will always be involved even when the primary source of theological data is revelation. This is true because the revelation has to be received in some way. In this case the main focus of theological reflection will be the revelation as such, with experience serving only as a vehicle for the revelation. In other words, theological truth will be drawn from the *object* of the experience, with the experience itself being of only *secondary* impor-tance. Possible examples of such secondary experiences are the observation of the mighty acts of God in nature and in history, the reading of his word in the Bible, and listening to the voice of God speaking within one's heart. For example, any-one who observed the mighty acts of God at the time of the plagues upon Egypt and the crossing of the Red Sea surely had some marvelous experiences, but for purposes of theology the important factor was the divine works themselves and not an observer's experience of them.

On the other hand, an experience in itself may sometimes be the main focus of theological reflection. That is, theological truth may be drawn from the experi-ence as such insofar as it is discerned as a pointer to God. In this case the experi-ence itself will be *primary*, and theological data will be drawn from the *subject*, i.e., the person who had the experience.

Examples of such primary experiences are numerous. Some we might call *in-tuitive*. For example, the philosopher Immanuel Kant discerned within himself and in all men a sense of moral rightness and wrongness. By reflecting upon this "moral experience" he concluded that there must be an afterlife and a God who will judge us. Another example is the pioneer of liberal theology, Friedrich Schleiermacher. He said that all human beings have an innate feeling of being ab-solutely dependent—on something; this feeling as such is the basis for our belief in God and the exclusive source for theology.

Another example of primary experiences are those called *mystical*. The subject of such an experience claims to have had a direct and immediate experience of God himself, an experience of unity with the divine. However, the mystic usually declares that the divine being is itself ineffable, i.e., inexpressible in words; thus the experience as such becomes the only thing he can verbalize about and the main source for his "theology."

A more familiar kind of primary experience is what most people think of as *re-ligious* experiences wherein the hand of God is discerned. Perhaps the most com-mon is the subjective experience of regeneration or conversion, similar to John Wesley's feeling his heart being "strangely warmed." For example, Charles G. Finney reports that on the evening of his conversion "he had several hours of in-tense fellowship with the Lord Jesus Christ in which it seemed to him as if he saw the Saviour face to face. The Lord seemed to be looking at him in such a way that Finney wept like a child." The Holy Spirit came upon him so strongly "that he could feel the Spirit going through him 'like waves of liquid love'" (Wenger, 22).

Another common type of religious experience is involvement with the miracu-lous or the supernatural, either as a participant or as an observer. Those who have spoken in tongues, those who have witnessed or received miraculous healing, those who have been delivered from demonic spirits, those who have had an "out of body" or "life after death" experience—all are usually quite eager to draw defi-nite theological conclusions based on such experiences themselves.

A final category of primary experience is what may be called *life* experience. As C.W. Christian says, one's "theology emerges from his reaction to life as he experiences it" (29). Life experience can be thought of as general or specific. John Macquarrie says (6), "In the broadest sense . . . it is the experience of existing as a human being that constitutes a primary source for theology." More specifically, life experience includes all our interrelations with other people, especially those within the fellowship of the Christian community. It also includes one's own private inward experiences: one's yearnings, pangs of conscience, sufferings, and perceived needs. For example, feminists often declare that the primary source for their theological conclusions is "women's experience," defined as the experience of being oppressed by men and the struggle to be liberated from such oppression (Cottrell, *Feminism*, 182-188).

At this point we are not asking which of these types of experience, if any, are *valid* sources of theology. We are presenting them rather as *possible* sources. The question of their validity will be discussed below.

3. Reason

A third possible source for theology is human reason. We may begin by noting that human reason has three main functions or uses. First is the speculative or *inferential* use, wherein reason serves as the very origin of truth. Here the mind begins with an already accepted truth, and then reasons its way to further truth, using rules of deductive and inductive logic. The beginning point (the already accepted truth) may be an *a priori* innate idea, or an *a posteriori* fact established by sense perception or received by divine revelation. Second is the analytical or *instrumental* use, wherein reason analyzes and organizes already-accepted truth, with the goal of understanding it and explaining it to others. (This is in essence the main task of theology.) Third is the *evaluative* use, wherein reason examines the various propositions that claim to be true and determines which of them may actually be accepted as truth by applying to them the accepted rules of evidence. (This is the main function of reason in apologetics.)

With reference to the question of the sources of theology, only the inferential use of reason is relevant. Also relevant is the distinction between *a priori* and *a posteriori* beginning points.

Some have suggested that certain truths of theology can be attained in a purely *a priori* manner, beginning only with ideas existing in the mind prior to any sense experience. The best example of this is Anselm's ontological argument for the existence of God, which begins only with the *idea* of God defined as the being than which nothing greater can be conceived. It is alleged that we can argue from this concept of God as the greatest conceivable being to the actual existence of God by using human reason alone. Descartes argued that we can arrive at the existence of God by beginning only with an inner awareness of the reality that we are in fact thinking. If we are thinking, we must exist: "I think, therefore

I am" (*cogito, ergo sum*). If we finite beings exist, we must ultimately have an infinite cause, who is God. (This is an *a priori* version of the cosmological argument for God's existence.)

The other possibility is that theological truth can be derived by reason in an *a posteriori* manner, i.e., beginning with truths that have come to us from outside ourselves and through some involvement of our senses. For example, by simply observing the existence of the finite world around us, we may ultimately infer the existence of an infinite first cause, a Creator God. This is another, more common form of the cosmological argument. Or we may observe that certain elements of the natural world are of such a nature that they could not have come into existence by chance, but must have been designed by an intelligent mind, which many would equate with God. This is called the teleological argument for God's existence. More generally, by simply observing various features of the physical universe—its immense size, its intricate detail, its variety and beauty—we may infer the omnipotent and glorious nature of its Creator.

In the examples just given, reason begins with certain aspects of general revelation and infers further truth about God. It may also be possible to begin with the truths of special revelation as given in the Bible, and through the use of inferential reason ("good and necessary inference") to derive further truth not specifically asserted in Scripture. This principle was set forth in the Westminster Confession of Faith (I.vi) thus: "The whole counsel of God . . . is either expressly set down in Scripture, or by good and necessary consequence may be deduced from Scripture." Thomas Campbell, in his famous "Declaration and Address" (¶6) stated that "inferences and deductions from scripture premises, when fairly inferred, may be truly called the doctrine of God's holy word." Though such inferences may not become conditions for accepting the repentant into the church, they "do properly belong to the after and progressive edification of the church." For example, although abortion is not specifically mentioned in the Bible, we may infer that it is wrong based on the sixth commandment and on the biblical teaching concerning the personhood of unborn children.

4. Tradition

A fourth possible source for theology is tradition, which literally means that which has been handed down from previous generations. This can be understood in different ways. In the Roman Catholic Church, "tradition" refers primarily to the teachings of the apostles that were passed along to others orally rather than in writing. To this body of teaching have been added such things as official pronouncements by the Catholic Church through the Pope or through formal ecumenical councils. In Catholicism such tradition is seen as having an authority equivalent to that of Scripture itself, and is a primary source for theology.

Though not agreeing with the Catholic approach, every Protestant denomination or fellowship is heir to its own formative creeds, writings, and practices, which constitute a body of unofficial traditions. While these are not regarded as having normative authority, they still may function as a very influential source of theology from generation to generation.

In a sense, all the theological thinking throughout Christian history, as it is passed along to us through the study of the history of the church and the history of doctrine, can be considered as a general kind of tradition that may help us to shape our theology today.

B. The Normative Source for Theology

We have explored four categories of possible sources for theology: revelation, experience, reason, and tradition. As we shall see, some aspects of these are not legitimate sources, while others are valid sources when used properly. The main question, though, is whether any one of these sources may be regarded as the *normative* source, i.e., the source whose data is accepted as true just because it is from that source, and the source that serves as a measure of the truth or falsity of the data that comes from every other source. Our conclusion is that, because of its very nature as the revealed and inspired Word of God,[1] the Bible is this normative source.

But why should the Bible be so regarded, rather than one of the other possible sources of theology? The following is the procedure that leads us to this conclusion. First, if we have a source that is from God rather than man, we must choose the former as the norm. Human beings are finite creatures who are bound by the egocentric predicament, and thus forever limited in knowledge and liable to error. We are also fallen creatures, whose need to justify our unbelief and excuse our sinful ways makes us likely to exchange the truth of God for a lie (Rom 1:25).

Thus because human beings are both finite and fallen, we cannot trust ourselves to come up with absolutely true and authoritative knowledge of God and his relation to the world. In one broad stroke, then, we must rule out experience, reason, and tradition in all their forms as legitimate norms for theology. The norm must come from God, not from the finite resources of creatures. Thus the norm must be something in the category of revelation, which indeed we do have.

Second, within the category of revelation, if we have a source that is objective rather than subjective, we must choose the former; that is, it must be a form of revelation that comes from outside ourselves rather than from within. This is true because anything subjective is inherently ambiguous with regard to its origin and its meaning, especially in a fallen world. We can never be sure that our inner feelings, experiences, or "voices" are from God, from Satan, or from our own subconscious; and we can never be sure that we have interpreted or even remembered them correctly. The Bible warns us about such ambiguities inherent in all personal experiences (Matt 7:21-23; Luke 13:25-27), and this especially applies to subjective ones. Thus anything subjective, including subjective general revelation (Rom 2:15), is ruled out as a normative source for theology. The norm must be something in the category of objective revelation, if such is available. And it is.

Third, within the category of objective revelation, if we have revelation that is verbal (in the form of words) rather than nonverbal, we must choose the former as our norm. The adages that "a picture is worth a thousand words" and "actions speak louder than words" may have a limited application, but they are simply not true when it comes to sorting out truth from error in the constructing of theologies and worldviews. Theology deals mainly with thoughts and concepts, and well-formulated verbal communication will always be more precise and unambiguous than nonverbal events such as actions (e.g., the game of charades illustrates the difficulty of communicating without words).

Thus even though God has performed and is still performing mighty acts in the world of nature and in the dramas of human history, these acts cannot be normative for theology. Even the great redemptive acts of God have to be explained in words. Even the truth available to us through general revelation in the created universe cannot be a final norm for our theological thinking if verbal revelation is available. And it is.

Fourth, if we have anything in the category of objective verbal revelation that is written rather than unwritten, that must be our norm for theology. Written revelation (or anything written under the power of divine inspiration) takes precedence over a one-time oral revelation because of its finality and continuing availability in dependable form. Thus even objective verbal revelation cannot be a norm for theology unless it has been recorded dependably through the inspiration of the Holy Spirit. This rules out oral tradition as the norm.

We should note, though, that other sacred writings besides the Bible purport to be objective written revelations from God (e.g., the Qur'an, the Book of Mormon). Are all equally legitimate? If not, how do we select among them? Here it is necessary to call upon Christian apologetics in order to establish the exclusive validity of the Bible as God's written Word, and it does accomplish this.[2] The Bible, and the Bible alone, is our only rule of faith and practice.

Fifth and finally, the *whole* Bible is our norm for theology, and not just a part of it. The OT, rightly interpreted in terms of covenantal distinctions, is just as normative for God's truth as is the NT. All parts of both testaments are normative, contrary to a doctrine of limited inspiration or limited inerrancy that would limit the dependability of Scripture only to the so-called doctrinal or didactic materials.

Also, the whole Bible, and not just the life and teachings of Jesus, must be our theological norm. It was never Jesus' purpose simply to be a source and norm for truth, knowledge, ethics, or theology. The main purpose of Christ's incarnation and work was to redeem mankind from sin through the atonement and resurrection. This is contrary to a serious but common fallacy (the "christological fallacy") that says that Christ's primary purpose was to be a unique source of doctrinal truth. Such an error leads to a "What Would Jesus Do?" approach to ethics. It leads to seriously erroneous statements such as this: "If Christ is truly to be preached, then every doctrine and ordinance of the faith must be dependent on

Him, His nature, character, and deeds, for meaning." Or the following: "If you have a theology, let it be Jesus. If you want someone to guide you in your conduct toward others, let it be Jesus."[3] To avoid such errors we must not think that the red-letter sections of the gospels have some unique significance for theology. The entire Bible is God's inspired and authoritative Word.

Without apology, then, we conclude that the Christian Bible in all its parts is the one and only norm for theology.

C. Valid Secondary Sources for Theology

Does this mean that when we do theology, we must keep our heads in the Bible alone, as if everything we will ever want to say about God and his relation to the world will be found there and nowhere else? Does it mean that there are *no* other legitimate sources for theological data? Not at all. True knowledge of God is indeed available by means other than the Bible; many of those excluded above as a norm are still valid as supplementary sources of data that clarify, expand upon, or illustrate the truths found in the Bible. Such sources, however, must be reliable in themselves, and their data must always pass the test of consistency with biblical data.

This applies even to forms of revelation other than the Bible. Without a doubt both objective and subjective general revelation, though nonverbal, gives genuine knowledge of God as Creator and Lawgiver (Rom 1:18-32; 2:14-15). For those who have no opportunity to know God's special verbal revelation, the general revelation by itself is an adequate guide for worship and ethics. We know this because Paul tells us that such people are "without excuse" when they reject such knowledge of God (Rom 1:20; see 1:32; 2:15). Nevertheless, nonverbal general revelation is inherently incomplete, since it does not provide any knowledge about Christ and redemption. It is also inherently lacking in detail, just because it is nonverbal. The knowledge of God that comes through special verbal revelation is so much more clear and complete that it alone can be the norm.

Still, general revelation, especially as known in and through the created universe, is a valuable secondary source of theology. The Bible tells us about the power, wisdom, and love of God; but the universe around us gives us concrete demonstrations and examples of these every day (Ps 19:1; Acts 14:17). Every detail about the size of the universe, the abundance of galaxies and stars, the amazing variety of life on earth, the complexity of a living cell, and the intricate orderliness of the atom "declare their Maker's praise." The more we know about such things, the more our theology will come alive with detail.

What about experience? Can it function as even a secondary source for theology? Here we must be much more cautious because of the inherent ambiguities of all our experiences, especially those that are subjective. Private experiences that seem to have something to do with God are typically ambiguous as to their origin. Many modern cults had their beginning in such experiences. If we believe Joseph Smith, the founding of Mormonism was preceded by separate experiences in which the brilliantly shining Father and Son, and the similarly illumined angel Moroni, appeared to him and instructed him on how to begin this new religion. Sun Myung Moon founded the Unification Church ("the Moonies") after Jesus appeared to him and told him to do it. Victor Paul Wierwille founded the cult known as The Way International after a similar experience. If these experiences happened as described, they were no doubt the product of Satan (2 Cor 11:14), and these men were deceived as to their origin.

A similar ambiguity applies to the meaning or interpretation of one's experiences. In Matt 7:21-23 Jesus speaks of those who have manifested miraculous powers while wearing his name, and have assumed that such experiences are evidence that they were "right with God." Jesus shows us that such an interpretation of unquestionably "religious" experiences is not necessarily correct.

The general rule is this: truth is not derived from experience, but experience is properly evaluated and interpreted by truth as known from Scripture. Thus it is wrong to begin with some experience and use it to interpret God or use it as a sure and certain measure of God and his will. We cannot begin with some vague "women's experience" and validly conclude that distinctions between male and female gender roles are wrong. We cannot begin with the experiences of the "pious unimmersed" and validly conclude that baptism has no role in the reception of salvation. We cannot begin with contemporary experiences of tongue-speaking and miraculous healing, and validly conclude that the Holy Spirit must be giving such gifts today.

The fact is that experience follows belief. Whatever we already are inclined to believe as true will actually affect the kind of experiences we have, as well as the interpretations we give to them. Russell Byrum (34) has said it well:

> The Mohammedan's religious experience differs much from that of the Buddhist because their beliefs differ. Likewise the experiences of the Roman Catholic and Protestant are not the same; and as a result of varying belief, experience differs between Calvinists and Arminians, and between Unitarians and Trinitarians. Even with those holding the same general creed, experience varies according to their particular individual interpretation of their creed. Evidently, therefore, the law of Christian experience is that such experience is the *result* of Christian truth, or the individual conception of it, and not its cause; it is the offspring of theology and not its source.

Nevertheless experience may still function in a limited way in the construction of our theology. If we begin with Scripture and use it as a means of measuring and interpreting experience, then the latter may at times be a secondary source. We should remember that theology by definition is the study of God *and of everything else in its relation to God.* Thus we must have some knowledge or experience of all the kinds of things that exist in the world.

For example, experience may at times help us to clarify our understanding of difficult Bible teaching. To illustrate, someone who in his prechristian life was a practicing spiritist (such as Ben Alexander) may use his experiences to explain and illustrate the reality and nature of the occult practices condemned by the Bible. Also, those who have been involved in deliverance ministry are able to use their experiences to clarify the biblical teaching about the role of Satan and his demons in the world today.

Most important, though, is the fact that experience functions as a source of theology, not by providing answers to life's questions, but simply by helping to raise the questions with which theology must deal. This applies to all types of experience, including intuitive, mystical, and religious. It especially applies to the general category of "life experience." The Christian theologian must be aware of what is happening in the world: scientific developments, cultural trends, international affairs, politics and economics, and certainly the world of religion. As C.W. Christian says (98-99), "There is no dimension of modern experience that can be overlooked and no question which can be evaded." A theologian "must seek to be knowledgeable in many areas. He must read drama, poetry and literature; he must know in general what is happening in biology, physics, astronomy; he must have an acquaintance with sociology and psychology." In other words, we must have a thorough knowledge not only of the *Word* but also of the *world*, and we must use the former to interpret the latter.

Finally human reason, when properly submitted to the lordship of Christ, has a valuable role as a secondary source for theology. It is a serious error to scorn reason and to assume that it is somehow unworthy of God or is inadequate to deal with divine truth. Reason is an aspect of God's own nature and is a part of our nature as created in his image.

The following distinction is necessary, however. On the one hand, we must reject the role of reason as an *a priori* source of theological data. (The ontological argument is thus rejected as invalid.) On the other hand, we affirm that reason has a valid and even necessary role when used *a posteriori*, namely, when used to draw proper inferences from data given through general and special revelation. For example, we may begin with information learned from observations of the physical world, and validly infer the existence of its Designer and Creator (via the cosmological and teleological arguments). Also, beginning with biblical teaching, reason enables us to infer from it a number of unstated yet valid implications and applications. As mentioned earlier, rational reflection on the sixth commandment and on biblical teaching about the personhood of the unborn causes us to infer that abortion is wrong. Or, reflection on the resurrection of Jesus on the first day of the week as the beginning of the New Creation, and on passages about first-day worship (Acts 20:7; 1 Cor 16:2), and on the implied frequency of the Supper in 1 Cor 11:20-34, leads to the inference that the Lord's Supper should be observed on every Lord's Day. For another example, Acts 5:29 shows us how to limit the application of Rom 13:1-2 and Eph 5:22 and 6:1.

Finally there are ways in which tradition can and should function as a source of theology. This does not apply to tradition in the Catholic sense, where it is given normative authority equal to that of the Bible. One should also avoid uncritically absorbing the theological position of his own denominational or brotherhood heritage without first subjecting it to the normative standard of biblical teaching. Still, the study of what others have believed and taught can be a valuable resource in the construction of our own theology.

It is especially important to have a working knowledge of the history of doctrine. This can help us to explain the origins of false doctrines that still persist today. For example, a knowledge of the history of baptism reveals that Huldreich Zwingli, the predecessor of John Calvin in the 1520s, was the first influential thinker to separate baptism from salvation. Also, historical knowledge can help us to avoid repeating errors that have already surfaced and have already been refuted in the past. For example, practically every possible false view about the divine and human natures of Christ was proposed, examined, and condemned in the first few centuries of the church.

In summary, while Scripture is our primary and only normative source for theology, valid secondary and nonnormative sources include some aspects of nonverbal revelation, experience, reason, and tradition.

IV. THE METHOD OF THEOLOGY

Having settled the questions relating to sources, we are now prepared to begin the actual work of theology. Viewing the Bible as our primary and normative source simplifies our task in some ways, since we are no longer *searching* for truth, but simply trying to *understand* it. This is still a formidable task, given the nature of the Bible. It is not just one long, organized doctrinal essay. It is rather a collection of 66 separate units, written over a span of about 1,500 years, by nearly 40 different people, in 3 languages and in several types of literature. All of these units are intimately related to God's historical works of redemption. They are all firmly imbedded in specific historical circumstances, while at the same time they are weaving together a transcendent picture of God's universal plan of redemption.

Thus the data conveyed to us from the Bible at first seem to be absolutely overwhelming, as well as very complicated and obscure. This raises the question of the *method* of theology. That is, using analytical or instrumental reason, how can we understand and organize this mass of biblical data? What is the best way to study it and teach it?

Such study must actually progress through several stages before it reaches the level of theology. Most basic of all is the study of the *canon* of the Bible (how can we be sure these 66 units, and no more, belong in the Bible?) and the *text* of the Bible (how can we be sure that we have the original text of these writings?). Then comes the work of Christian apologetics (how can we be sure that these writings, and these alone, are truly the inspired Word of God?). This is followed by the study of basic introductory issues concerning each writing: Who wrote it? To whom? When and why was it written? How does it fit into the overall scope of re- demptive history? Next comes Bible exegesis, or the work of interpreting each biblical unit verse by verse in an effort to understand its meaning.

This is where theology enters. At the same time that we are studying the Bible verse by verse, we must also be trying to construct an overall view of its contents, or trying to tie it all together into a comprehensive and coherent worldview. This raises the question of the best way to organize the doctrinal content of the Bible as a whole. There are three basic approaches, all of which are possible and all of which have some value.

The first approach is to arrange the biblical data *period by period*. This is viable in view of the underlying historical drama of revelation and redemption reflected in the Bible. Given the historical development of this drama from the Garden of Eden to the apostolic era, we can trace the progress of God's revelation of truth to mankind period by period. This method is developed in Vos's book, *Biblical Theology*. What is unique about it is that "its principle of organizing the biblical material is historical rather than logical." It seeks "to exhibit the organic growth or development of the truths of Special Revelation from the primitive preredemp- tive Special Revelation given in Eden to the close of the New Testament canon" (5). Vos discusses the pre-Fall revelation in Eden and the redemptive revelation in Eden after the Fall; he then discusses the revelation in Noah's era, in the patriar- chal era, in the Mosaic era, in the prophetic era, and in the Jesus era.

Such a method has value for understanding the historical development of God's purposes and for understanding how specific books of the Bible fit into this history. It cannot be considered as the final step in the theological process, however.

Another approach is to arrange the biblical data *section by section*, a method which is also often called biblical theology. This may be done testament by testa- ment, i.e., "Theology of the Old Testament" and "Theology of the New Testa- ment." In this case the contents of the respective testaments may be broken down into smaller sections. For example, George Ladd's *A Theology of the New Testa- ment* is divided into six parts: the synoptic gospels, the fourth gospel, Acts, Paul, general epistles, and the Book of Revelation. Principal themes are then discussed within these sections.

Section-by-section theological studies may be more narrow in scope, e.g., the theology of the prophets, the theology of the Pentateuch, Pauline theology, the theology of Luke, the theology of the Psalms.

This method of theology is common in both liberal and conservative circles. It is very compatible with the liberal approach to the Bible, since liberalism as such rejects the orthodox concept of the inspiration of the Bible, and thus rejects the idea that the Bible derives ultimately from one divine mind and thus possesses unity and consistency of thought. As a consequence liberal theologians see con- tradictions within the Bible and cannot comfortably talk, for example, about "*the* biblical doctrine of the atonement," since they usually see several different such doctrines which are not necessarily consistent with each other.

Conservative theologians also use this approach, and it is indeed a valuable method of theology. But in my judgment it can never be the final step in the theological process, specifically *because* of the phenomenon of the unity of the Bible. As ultimately the product of one mind, the mind of God, the Bible simply must be studied as a whole. Even though it is necessary to study the Bible verse by verse, and extremely useful to study it period by period and section by section, we cannot be satisfied until we have discovered what the whole Bible says about any given subject.

This leads to the last method of arranging the data of the Bible, namely, a study of the whole Bible *subject by subject*. This is usually called systematic theology. Though not exclusive, it is the best and climactic approach to theological study. This is true first because of *who God is*. He is a God of order, rationality, and consistency. Reason and logic are a part of his nature and are fundamental characteristics of his thinking. The idea that the logic of God's thoughts is inherently different from that of finite human beings is based on a false understanding of Isa 55:8-9. In this passage the contrast is not between divine and human thinking as such, but between divine thinking and *sinful* human thinking, as verse 7 shows.

The second reason why systematic theology is the crowning approach is because of *what the Bible is*. Since it is the revealed and inspired Word of the rational God, the Bible must partake of his rationality. Since it is inspired by the omniscient God, it must also be infallible and thus totally self-consistent and without error, as the mind of God is. Without such complete inerrancy the systematic method becomes much more difficult. Also, the fact that the Bible in its entirety is inspired by God means that there is ultimately only one author and one mind behind it all; thus it is a coherent unity. Such a unity requires a systematic approach to theology.

The third reason why the subject-by-subject method is preferred is because of *what man is*. Since we are made in God's image, we too are rational beings, and it is the nature of our minds to think in an orderly way. Thus there is nothing unusual or artificial about a subject-by-subject study of the Bible. A.H. Strong has well said that the necessity of theology is grounded in "the organizing instinct of the human mind. This organizing principle is a part of our constitution. The mind cannot endure confusion," but naturally seeks "to harmonize and unify its knowledge." This is true in all areas of human inquiry, "but it is peculiarly true of our knowledge of God. . . . Theology is a rational necessity. If all existing theological systems were destroyed to-day, new systems would rise to-morrow" (15-16).

Even though systematic theology is committed to explaining biblical doctrine subject by subject, we must still decide the order in which to arrange and present these subjects. A traditional arrangement has been developed over the centuries and is still used by most. The following is typical:

Prolegomena: Introductory matters

Bibliology: The doctrine of the nature of the Word of God (the Bible)

Theology proper: The doctrine of the works and nature of God

Angelology: The doctrine of angels, unfallen and fallen

Anthropology: The doctrine of man, sin, and death

Christology: The doctrine of the person and work of Christ

Pneumatology: The doctrine of the person and work of the Holy Spirit

Soteriology: The doctrine of personal salvation

Ecclesiology: The doctrine of the church

Eschatology: The doctrine of the end times and the eternal states

This arrangement is inclusive, and is perfectly reasonable in that it presents the data in an order that is roughly chronological in terms of universal history.

Sometimes these same subjects are retained but are arranged in a slightly different order, based on some specific organizing motif. For example, some have suggested that the material may be arranged under three major headings corresponding to the three persons of the Trinity: the doctrines of God the Father, the doctrines of God the Son, and the doctrines of God the Holy Spirit. In my judgment this method is less than satisfactory; the proposed subject arrangement is usually arbitrary and unnatural.

This book is definitely a work of systematic theology, and the biblical data are presented subject by subject. Sometimes when I present this material I arrange it under two separate but related motifs that hold the Bible together from beginning to end and that at the same time reflect the historical progression of the plan of redemption. These motifs are *old creation/new creation*, and *life/death/resurrection*. They surface occasionally in this work.

The old creation/new creation motif is suggested by the NT references to salvation as the new creation. The term "old creation" refers to the original creating work of God in Genesis 1 and 2, and to the universe in its unfallen state; it also refers to the ongoing universe as it has been cursed by sin and death. The term "new creation" refers to everything that relates to the saving work of Jesus Christ, beginning with the figurative creation of Israel as the preparation for Christ's coming. It applies most appropriately to the literal new creation that began with Christ's works of atonement and resurrection, that continues in the event of an individual's personal salvation (2 Cor 5:17; Gal 6:15; Eph 2:10), and that will be completed in the final resurrection and the creation of a new heavens and new earth (2 Pet 3:13; Rev 21:1).

The theme of life/death/resurrection is woven throughout the old creation/new creation motif. The original creation was the work of the living God and was itself characterized by *life*: angelic life, animal life and human life. With the entrance of sin, the curse of *death*—physical and spiritual—was imposed upon the entire human race, with unrepentant sinners being destined for an eternal death in the lake of fire along with the fallen angels. God's remedy to this situation takes place in terms of *resurrection*, beginning with the resurrection of Jesus Christ, continuing with the resurrection of spiritually dead sinners to new spiritual life in Christ, and being completed in the final resurrection of saints into glory.

V. THE IMPORTANCE OF THEOLOGY

In his book *No Place for Truth*, David Wells laments "the disappearance of theology from the life of the Church" (95). Failure to understand just how important it is has indeed led to a considerable neglect of theology among Christians.

A. The Neglect of Theology

Some of the reasons for this neglect are cultural. For example, the increasing influence of relativism makes doctrine seem less significant. Henry Thiessen (23) says the reason for the "great prejudice against doctrine" is "the present-day doubt as to whether we can reach any conclusions in this field that can be regarded as certain and final." Anyone who believes that everything is relative and in flux "holds that it is unsafe to formulate any fixed views about God and theological truth. What if he does so today: tomorrow he may be obliged to change his opinions." The fallacies of relativism have been discussed above.

Another cultural reason for the neglect of theology is the spirit of anti-intellectualism, a distrust of reason as such. We have been conditioned by television to prefer pictures rather than words, to be passively entertained in brief bytes rather than to actively concentrate on serious subjects in sustained study. We prefer to focus on the experiential and the mystical rather than the intellectual. We want to "know Christ personally" rather than to worry with doctrinal issues about him. The result? "Say the word 'doctrine' from the pulpit or in any gathering of Christians and you can count on a response of yawning, nervous coughing, and glassy-eyed stares almost before the sound of the word has died in the air. The adjectives most folks would pick to describe 'doctrine' are also found in the dictionary under 'D'—dull, dry, dreadful, dreary" (Greenlee, *Basics*, 15-16).

Some of the reasons for neglecting theology are, ironically, theological. A low view of Scripture, for example, makes the theological enterprise less urgent. When one denies word revelation or biblical inerrancy, it is difficult to get excited about sound doctrine. As J.W. Montgomery once said, when theology is no longer sure of its data, it becomes superficial and faddish.

Over against this trend, we must train ourselves and others not to be afraid of theology. Ben Merold (5) says, "I view doctrine as a skeleton. A skeleton is a rather scary thing." But this does not mean we should avoid it; the solution is to do a better job of teaching doctrine in a clear and relevant way. "Remember, while a skeleton without flesh on it is a scary thing, a body without a skeleton is flabby and useless."

Another theological reason for neglecting theology is a misunderstanding of the concept of *sola scriptura* ("The Bible alone is our only rule of faith and practice"). According to this reasoning, if Scripture is sufficient in itself, why do we need anything in addition to it? This superficial objection confuses the *result* of theology with the *norm* for theology. *Sola scriptura* means that the Bible is our only *norm* for truth. It does not rule out helps and instruments in addition to the biblical text, when these are used simply as a means of understanding and teaching. In principle there is no difference between theology on the one hand, and sermons and commentaries and Sunday school lessons on the other hand. Theology is simply another way of studying and teaching the contents of the Bible. It becomes problematic only when its results take on a normative authority, such as Calvin's *Institutes* often does with Calvinists.

A similar objection to theology arises from a misunderstanding of the common Restoration slogan, "No creed but Christ." In an article by this title in *Christian Standard* Stan Paragein says, "The test of orthodoxy today should not be what a man thinks about the creation of the world, the doctrine of original sin, the resurrection of the dead, congregational cooperation, instrumental music, charismatic gifts, the eldership, or the millennium. If we follow the examples of Christ and the apostles, we can only ask *what a man thinks of Christ.* . . . 'Not what, but WHOM!'" (8). Other such comments from articles in *Christian Standard* include the following: "We are committed to Christ, not doctrine." "Faith is directed not to Scripture but to Christ." "Truth is personal, not doctrinal." "Our faith is in a person—Jesus the Christ—not in a series of propositions." As a would-be preacher put it, "The *only* essential is that Jesus is the Christ, the son of the living God. *Everything* else is up for grabs."

Contrary to such ideas, the only valid application of this slogan is that no man-made theological system or statement of faith can be elevated to a norm for truth or a requirement for salvation. The slogan was surely not meant to exclude systems or summaries of faith—even creeds—when these are used only as teaching instruments and means of bearing witness to the truth. (See Gresham, "Creeds," 1, 4, 8.) Also, we must beware of the christological fallacy when trying to implement this slogan (see pp. 24-25).

Some objections to theology are cultural, some are practical, and some are just pragmatic. In this last category is the common excuse of preachers that they just want to concentrate on people, not doctrine. David Wells tells of a student in a required theology course who complained of having to spend so much time and money "on a course of study that was so irrelevant to his desire to minister to people in the Church" (*Truth*, 4). *Christianity Today* (10/24/94) reported on a poll that asked preachers the top five benefits they hoped to get from their professional training. Theological knowledge came in fifth, topped by relational skills, management abilities, communication skills, and spirituality. Church members who were asked the same question in reference to their ministers also put theological knowledge in fifth place (75).

Wells (*Truth*, 95) refers to the "strident pragmatism" that sacrifices doctrine for the sake of more culturally appealing worship and preaching, in the interest of numerical church growth. A famous evangelist has been quoted as saying, "I've never been strong on doctrine. I've just preached soul-winning." Greenlee quotes Carl Henry as saying that many Evangelicals may be too busy with "soul-winning" to grow the theological roots capable of sustaining tomorrow's churches ("Roots," 15). The attitude seems to be that we can win more people, and have a broader ecumenical fellowship, if we "go easy on the doctrine."

Such an approach commits the fallacy of false choice. Do we have to choose between doctrine and church growth? No! Some numerically large churches are known for their emphasis on sound doctrine. Also, a church that grows numerically without growing doctrinally is immature and not pleasing to God and vulnerable to "every wind of doctrine" and "trickery of men" (Eph 4:14).

Do we have to choose between teaching doctrine and ministry to people? No, this is another false choice. For one thing, every possible means by which the church ministers to people's needs (e.g., evangelism, counseling, edification) presupposes a sound theological base. Trying to minister to people's needs without a knowledge of theology is like a would-be doctor who wants to skip medical school and get straight to the business of healing people. For another thing, putting people ahead of doctrine demotes the greatest commandment to second place (Matt 22:34-40). It puts love for neighbor above love for God himself. We cannot love God without loving his truth with all our minds. If we love him, we will be zealous for upholding and proclaiming the whole body of truth he has given to us.

In the final analysis, the theological and the practical cannot be separated. "The Trinity Manifesto," issued by the Trinity Foundation in 1978, speaks of "the primacy of theory":

> It is a fundamental theoretical mistake of the practical men to think that they can be merely practical, for practice is always the practice of some theory. The relationship between theory and practice is the relationship between cause and effect. If a person believes correct theory, his practice will tend to be correct. . . . It is a major theoretical mistake of the practical men to think that they can ignore the ivory towers of the philosophers and theologians as irrelevant to their lives. Every action that the practical men take is governed by the thinking that has occurred in the Academy, a home in Basel, Switzerland, or a tent in Israel.

Thus "it is the first duty of the Christian to understand correct theory—correct doctrine—and thereby implement correct practice. This order—first theory, then practice—is both logical and Biblical."

B. The Need for Theology

Over against this widespread neglect of theology, we assert instead its *necessity*.

Here we offer several reasons why it is important and even necessary to study the Bible systematically.

First, theology is an aid to sound exegesis. Verse-by-verse exegesis and subject-by-subject theology stand in a dialectical relationship. Each progresses with the help of the other. Just as good exegesis gives us the proper data for theology, so also does theological knowledge guide exegesis and give depth to commentaries and expository preaching.

Trying to exegete a difficult text without being aware of the overall teaching of Scripture on the issues addressed therein can lead to distortions and outright false interpretations. For example, trying to understand the description of Christ as "the Beginning of the creation of God" (Rev 3:14) without being aware of the general teaching of Scripture on the person of Christ could cause one to decide that Christ was simply the first created being (cf. Arianism, Jehovah's Witnesses). Or, trying to interpret Hebrews 6:4-6 without a broader, systematic understanding of apostasy could lead to the false conclusion that those who fall away from Christ can never return.

Second, theology is necessary as an overall safeguard against error, heresy, schism, and cult-building. False systems of thought usually begin with a failure to understand *all* that Scripture says about certain subjects (see the previous paragraph). Thiessen (28) remarks, "The man who has no organized system of thought is at the mercy of the one who has such a system." In Klaus Bockmühl's words (45),

> A lack of doctrine leaves the preaching of the Church . . . without re-examination and therefore without possible correction. Since the lack of theology also entails a lack of tradition and relation to the Fathers of the Church, so the corrective given with the history of Christendom is lost, too. The Church must surrender to the reign of subjectivism. It is likely to fall victim to strong individual personalities, to heresy and division.

Third, theology provides a proper foundation for valid Christian experience. As noted earlier, experience is molded by beliefs more than vice versa; proper theology will yield proper, valid experience. People often experience what they *expect* to experience, based on their prior beliefs. Sound doctrine on such things as baptism, the Holy Spirit, and demons will eliminate a lot of experience-based errors and will pave the way for genuine Christian experience.

Fourth, theology provides the foundation for growth in spirituality and character. Does theology deaden the spiritual life, as some claim? No, says Thiessen; this is true "only if the subject is treated as mere theory. If it is related to life," theology will instead be "the guide to intelligent thinking . . . and a stimulus to holy living" (29). "The strongest Christians," says Strong, "are those who have the firmest grasp upon the great doctrines of Christianity" (16).

For example, the more we know about God, the greater will be our awe and reverence for him, and the more meaningful our worship will be. The more we know about Christ, and especially the meaning of his death, the deeper our love for him will be. Doctrine is nothing less than food for the soul, nourishing and strengthening us within (Heb 5:11–6:2). James Edwards says, "Engagement with Scripture and the great doctrines of the Christian faith is the greatest source of health for Christians. Nothing makes sick theology and morality healthier than being exposed to healthy theology and morality. Spirituality thrives on right belief" (25).

Fifth, theology is necessary as the only sound basis for morality or ethics. What is *true* determines what is *right*. Knowledge of the truth precedes right action; true doctrine precedes right doing; orthodoxy precedes orthopraxis; creed precedes deed. For example, what one believes about the ethical issue of abortion depends on his belief about the nature of human life. Or, what one believes about capital punishment depends on his beliefs about the nature of God, the purpose of Christ, and the purpose of government. Or, what one believes about animal rights depends on what he believes about creation. In general, one's overall approach to ethics depends on what he believes about the nature of God and the nature of the Bible. As Thomas Beasley says, "It does make a difference what you believe, because what you believe determines how you behave" (12).

Finally, theology is necessary simply because the Bible commands us to give attention to doctrine. Much of Christ's own ministry was devoted to teaching; his great commission commands his followers to teach new Christians "all that I commanded you" (Matt 28:20). The earliest Christians "were continually devoting themselves to the apostles' teaching" (Acts 2:42). Church leaders are exhorted to concentrate on teaching doctrine (1 Tim 3:2; 4:13-16; 5:17; 2 Tim 2:2). The very purpose of the Bible necessitates theology: "All Scripture is inspired by God and profitable for teaching, for reproof, for correction, for training in righteousness" (2 Tim 3:16).

Surely we can require no further justification and motivation for the study that follows.

NOTES ON INTRODUCTION

[1] We accept this conclusion as the valid result of Christian apologetics, without attempting to set forth or summarize the procedure here.

[2] See McDowell, *Evidence*; Craig, *Faith*; Gardner, *Christianity*.

[3] See my treatment of the christological fallacy in *GC*, 163-191, especially 166-171, 175, 186-191.

CHAPTER ONE
THE EXISTENCE OF GOD

"The LORD lives!" declares David in Ps 18:46. That God is the *living* God is a frequent theme in the Bible (*GC*, 388-389). For example, "My soul thirsts for God, for the living God" (Ps 42:2). "We have fixed our hope on the living God" (1 Thess 4:10), the one who "has life in Himself" (John 5:26). That God is alive includes more than just the fact of his existence. It refers to his existence as Spirit, as a personal being who is dynamic and active. It means that he exists *for his people*, ready to come to their aid, to act in their defense, and to bless them for his name's sake.

The biblical emphasis on God as the *living* God affirms the fact that he and he alone exists; all the so-called gods of the nations are just idols, lifeless nothings (Ps 115:5-7; Jer 10:5; Hab 2:18-19). The God of the Bible is "the only true God" (John 17:3), the one who creates and the one who redeems. "For You are great and do wondrous deeds; You alone are God" (Ps 86:10). His mighty works are sufficient evidence for his existence (*GC*, 390-419).

In one sense the existence of God is self-evident and intuitive: the entire creation declares his power and glory (Ps 19:1; Rom 1:20). But in another sense we are able to begin with our observations of the existence and nature of the world around us, and then to construct arguments that prove the existence of God by using human reason alone. These arguments are called "theistic proofs," and they are summarized below.

I. THE ONTOLOGICAL ARGUMENT

The ontological argument (*GC*, 420-423) for God's existence is the only purely demonstrative proof. It is strictly logical, being based on the law of non-contradiction. It is an *a priori* proof, which means that it does not depend on the observation of any particular reality. It begins only with the concept of God as defined in a certain way. Given that particular concept, it argues that a denial of God's existence is self-contradictory. The very concept of God necessarily entails his existence.

The basic form of this argument was set forth by Anselm (c. 1033–1109). It proceeds thus: (1) God is a being than which nothing greater can be conceived, i.e., he is the greatest conceivable being. (2) God can be conceived of in different ways. For instance, we can conceive of him as existing *only* in the mind, only as an idea. But we can also conceive of him as existing in *reality* as well as in our minds. (3) The latter is obviously greater than the former, i.e., it is greater to exist in reality than to exist only in the mind. (4) Therefore since God is the greatest conceivable being, he must exist in reality as well as in our minds. Otherwise he is not the greatest conceivable being. By a similar argument Anselm offered proof not just for God's existence but for his *necessary* existence.

Others since Anselm have defended versions of the ontological argument, notably Descartes (1596–1650) and twentieth-century philosophers such as Charles Hartshorne and Norman Malcolm.

In my judgment this argument fails to prove God's existence for a number of reasons. Most significantly, Immanuel Kant (1724–1804) long ago rightly argued that it is impossible to argue simply from the *concept* of a thing to its *reality*. We may argue that the concept of God necessarily entails the *concept* of his existence, even the concept of his necessary existence. But we are still within the realm of concepts. The fact that there is a necessary connection between certain ideas in no way requires a transition from idea to reality. Logical necessity does not imply ontological necessity. The most that can be concluded from the ontological argument is this: *if* God exists, he exists necessarily. But *whether* he exists must be determined on other grounds.

Thus we conclude that the ontological argument has no validity.

II. THE COSMOLOGICAL ARGUMENT

The cosmological argument (*GC*, 424-433) is an argument from causality. It begins with an observed reality and therefore is an *a posteriori* type of proof. It regards this observed reality as an *effect* that requires an explanation or a *cause*. Thus it argues backwards from effect to cause, not stopping until it arrives at an original, ultimate, primary cause—which is God.

The form of the argument varies considerably, and the observed reality varies from version to version. But in every case the cosmological argument includes three basic premises and a conclusion. The first premise is that *something exists* as an observed effect. The observed reality that thus serves as the beginning point for the argument can be almost anything. Here we may consider that reality to be the cosmos as a whole.

The second premise is that every effect must have a cause that is sufficient to explain it or bring it into existence. The cause may be conceived of as an *originating* cause in a temporal causal chain, such as the first domino to fall in a row of dominoes-on-end. Or the cause may be conceived of as the primary *sustaining* cause in a simultaneous chain of interlocking causes and effects, such as a locomotive which pulls the car behind it, which pulls the car behind it, etc.

The key to the entire argument is the third premise, that there can be no infinite regress of causes, which then leads to the conclusion that the cosmos as an effect must have an ultimate or primary cause, which is understood to be God. If the causal chain is regarded as temporal, as in the domino illustration, this means that the universe must have had a beginning, the cause of which was God.

The key question is whether the third premise (no infinite regress) is valid, and many have so argued. One of Thomas Aquinas's famous "five ways" of proving God exists is the argument from contingency. To say that something is contingent means that it is possible for it not to exist. Now, says Thomas, whatever may possibly not exist at one time did not exist (otherwise it would be eternal and necessary, not contingent). But if everything were contingent, then at one time nothing at all would have existed, and therefore nothing would exist now, since from nothing comes nothing. Therefore some noncontingent, eternal, necessary being must exist, which has caused the existence of all contingent beings. Everyone calls this being God.

In modern times William Craig has offered further philosophical proof that an infinite regress is impossible (*God*, 39-51). First, he says, there are different kinds of infinites; and an *actual* infinite cannot exist. But a beginningless series of events in time is an actual infinite. Therefore, a beginningless series of events in time cannot exist. Second, a series of events in time is a collection formed by adding one member after another. A collection formed by adding one member after another cannot actually be infinite. Therefore, the series of events in time cannot be actually infinite.

To these philosophical arguments may be added two scientific arguments that also show that an infinite regress is impossible. One, the scientific principle called the second law of thermodynamics requires that the universe must have had a beginning. This law says that processes taking place in a closed system tend toward equilibrium, i.e., they run down. The universe is a giant closed system and thus in time will run down. But if the universe has existed forever, it would already have run down. Thus it must have had a beginning (Craig, *God*, 63ff.).

The other scientific argument against infinite regress is the phenomenon of the expanding universe, which can be explained only by some kind of abrupt beginning in the nature of a violent explosion, i.e., a BIG BANG (see Jastrow). The "big bang" concept of the beginning of the universe, as presently understood, is thus a significant modern component of the cosmological argument. "If the universe arose out of a big bang," says Hugh Ross, "it must have had a beginning. If it had a beginning, it must have a Beginner" (14).

In my judgment the cosmological argument is generally sound, but it is limited. The argument does indeed establish a beginning for the cosmos, and even a beginner; but the argument in itself does not require that this beginner be the God of the Bible. The First Cause may not necessarily be just one being; Plato thought there must have been at least two. Also, the First Mover is not necessarily all good; after all, are there not a lot of flaws and evils in the world? But in spite of this weakness, the cosmological argument does bring us a long way toward establishing God's existence.

III. THE TELEOLOGICAL ARGUMENT

The next proof for God's existence is the teleological argument. It is like the cosmological argument in that it is *a posteriori* and is an argument from causality. But here is a major difference: whereas the cosmological argument begins with the simple *fact* of something's existence, the teleological proof begins with a certain *quality* in existing things, i.e., apparent design. The name itself is taken from the Greek *telos*, which means "end, goal, purpose." Certain things in the universe seem to be designed for a specific purpose or end; e.g., insect wings seem to have been designed for the purpose of enabling flight. They did not happen just accidentally.

From this kind of observation the argument is formulated as follows. Premise A: Whatever is designed must have a designer. Premise B: Some things in the natural world are designed, i.e., they are obviously the product of intelligent design. Conclusion: Therefore a designer exists, namely, God. This conclusion is required by the principle of sufficient cause.

One of Thomas Aquinas's "five ways" was the teleological argument, but the most well-known traditional example is that of William Paley's "Natural Theology" (1802). Paley reasoned that if one were crossing a meadow and found a watch, he would immediately recognize it as something which did not just happen to be there by an accident of nature. Even if he had never seen such an object before, he would be able to tell that it had been manufactured for a certain purpose, i.e., that it had a maker. In a way no less certain, said Paley, many of the natural phenomena of the universe give evidence of having been designed by a Maker to accomplish a specific end.

> Every indication of contrivance, every manifestation of design, which existed in the watch, exists in the works of nature; with the difference, on the side of nature, of being greater and more, and that in a degree which exceeds all computation. I mean, that the contrivances of nature surpass the contrivances of art, in the complexity, subtilty, and curiosity, of the mechanism; and still more, if possible, do they go beyond them in number and variety; yet, in a multitude of cases, are not less evidently mechanical, not less evidently contrivances, not less evidently accommodated to their end, or suited to their office, than are the most perfect productions of human ingenuity ("Natural Theology," 390-391).

Most modern statements of this argument benefit greatly from advances in modern science. The better our understanding of the natural world, the more the evidence of design shows through. Common examples are the complexity of the human eye (Paley, 332-333), the unique properties of water as an enabler of life (Ramm, *View*, 20-21), and the amazing all-or-nothing survival equipment of many living things, e.g., the bombardier beetle (Behe, 31-36).

One of the most remarkable evidences of intelligent design is the amazing complexity of a living cell. This advance in the teleological argument was made possible by the 1950s invention of the electron microscope, which is able to magnify objects up to a million times and more. Prior to this discovery cells could not be studied in great detail. It was easy (especially in Darwin's time) to assume that cells are simple blobs of jellylike stuff which could easily have evolved from a nonorganic chemical soup. But now the cells of living creatures can be seen and studied down to the smallest molecules—with amazing results!

The complexity of a living cell has been well described by the nontheist Michael Denton in his book, *Evolution: A Theory in Crisis*. Denton emphasizes the abundant evidence for design in the organic realm, especially on the cellular and molecular levels. "To common sense it does indeed appear absurd to propose that chance could have thrown together devices of such complexity and ingenuity that they appear to represent the very epitome of perfection" (326). Denton's description of the complexity of a cell's interior is breathtaking (328-329). He emphasizes the cell's capability "of replicating its entire structure within a matter of a few hours," the capacity of its DNA to store information, its capacity to synthesize organic compounds, its "fully automated assembly techniques which are perfectly regulated and controlled," and its miniaturization (329-337).

This and other such evidence, he says, shows that Paley was right (339-341). Everywhere we look we find a "sheer universality of perfection" that mitigates against the idea of chance. "Is it really credible that random processes could have constructed a reality, the smallest element of which—a functional protein or gene—is complex beyond our own creative capacities, a reality which is the very antithesis of chance, which excels in every sense anything produced by the intelligence of man?" (342). Such an idea, he says, is "an affront to reason" (351).

Denton's work is all the more significant when we remember that he writes as a nontheist, i.e., he himself does not believe in God. Even after his marvelous defense of intelligent design, he declares that he does not know how to explain it!

A more recent work along the same line is Michael Behe's book, *Darwin's Black Box*. A "black box" is any device that functions superbly but cannot be opened in order to understand *how* it functions. Darwin's "black box" was the biological cell. To him it was compatible with evolution because he could not "open" it and thus had no concept of its incredible complexity. But the cell is no longer a "black box"; modern science has revealed its irreducible complexity and shown it to be incompatible with chance origins. To function at all, the cell must have been designed and brought into existence all at once, in its totality. Thus "the simplicity that was once expected to be the foundation of life has proven to be a phantom; instead, systems of horrendous, irreducible complexity inhabit the cell. The resulting realization that life was designed by an intelligence" has shocked many in the twentieth century (252).

What is significant is that this conclusion about intelligent design is being drawn not from religious beliefs but from the hard work of biochemists. The result of their "efforts to investigate the cell—to investigate life at the molecular level—is a loud, clear, piercing cry of '*design*!' The result is so unambiguous and so significant that it must be ranked as one of the greatest achievements in the history of science" (Behe, 193, 232-233).

Thus once again modern science has provided information that serves to strengthen a traditional theistic proof. The current evidence of intelligent design makes the existence of a designer all the more certain.

Our overall assessment of the teleological argument, though, is the same as that of the cosmological argument. It is valid up to the point of showing the existence of a designer for this natural world, but it does not require us to identify this designer with the God of the Bible.

IV. THE HISTORICAL ARGUMENT

As we have seen, even if the cosmological and teleological arguments succeed in their main point of proving the existence of a Creator-God, we still need something more to establish his identity as the God of Israel and the God of our Lord Jesus Christ. This "something more" is historical proof (Cottrell, *Solid*, ch 7; *GC*, 440-442).

In brief, this historical proof centers around the historical claim that Jesus of Nazareth was raised from the dead by the God of Israel, who is also the God of the Christian Church. This is a historical argument and not a biblical one as such, because its methodology deliberately excludes any presupposition about the inspired nature of the Bible. For the sake of the argument it approaches the biblical writings as a historian would approach any other ancient documents, with a view to assessing their claims rationally, i.e., using only the accepted canons of historical research. The argument moves through two stages: first, what proves the resurrection? and second, what does the resurrection prove?

In the first stage the point is to establish the fact that the resurrection of Jesus actually occurred. The key factor in the proof is the principle of sufficient cause. The contention is that there are certain established historical facts for which the only sufficient cause is the bodily resurrection of Jesus Christ. These facts are as follows: the disciples' report that Jesus' tomb was empty; the disciples' report that Jesus appeared bodily to them after his death and burial; the unshakable faith of the apostles; the conversion of Saul of Tarsus; the establishment and rapid growth of the Christian Church; and the transition from Saturday to Sunday as the Church's special day. No other historical explanation can satisfactorily account for these indisputable facts; the resurrection must indeed have occurred.

But this is only the first half of the historical argument. So Jesus rose from the dead: what does that prove? It proves basically the integrity of Jesus as a teacher and the truth and authority of his teaching. This includes among other things his implicit and explicit acceptance of the Old Testament's testimony to the exclusive reality of the God of Israel, as well as his own teaching concerning the reality and nature of Yahweh. The fact that the resurrection occurred in this particular historical context and in connection with these particular teachings establishes the validity of this specific view of God. Thus the historical argument supplies what the cosmological and teleological proofs lack. When taken together, these three proofs establish the rational probability that the God of the Bible truly exists.

CHAPTER TWO
OUR KNOWLEDGE OF GOD

Some may deem it presumptuous for finite human beings to claim to be able to know the infinite God. Zophar the Naamathite rebuked Job thus: "Can you discover the depths of God? Can you discover the limits of the Almighty? They are high as the heavens, what can you do? Deeper than Sheol, what can you know?" (Job 11:7-8).

There is certainly some truth to this. Because he is infinite and transcendent, God would forever be beyond our ability to discover him and to know him if he chose to keep himself hidden from us (*GC*, 306-312). But this has never been his purpose; God wants us to know him, thus he has revealed himself to us. Though we will never have a *complete* knowledge of God,[1] we can indeed have *true* knowledge of him thanks to his own gracious initiative. As Isa 11:9 says, "For the earth will be full of the knowledge of the LORD as the waters cover the sea."

The purpose of this chapter is to examine the means by which we may have true knowledge of God. The process begins with the fact of revelation, through which God makes himself, his truth, and his will known to human beings. It continues with the fact of inspiration, which is the divine influence through which God guarantees that those who receive special revelation can pass it along accurately to the rest of us. It culminates in the production of a collection of written documents that are absolutely accurate and divinely authoritative—a collection we call "The Bible."

The contents of this chapter are basically that section of systematic theology sometimes called *bibliology*, or a study of what the Bible teaches about itself. Four topics will be explored: revelation, inspiration, inerrancy, and authority.

I. REVELATION

Our knowledge of God begins with the divine action of revelation. Revelation as an act or process is represented by many biblical terms, including *galah*, "to disclose, uncover, reveal, appear" (e.g., Deut 29:29; 1 Sam 3:21; Isa 40:5); *apokalypto*, "to uncover, reveal, unveil, bring to light" (e.g., Matt 11:25,27; 1 Cor 2:10; Eph 3:5); *gnorizo*, "to make known, reveal" (e.g., Luke 2:15; Eph 1:9; 3:3); *phaneroo*, "to reveal, manifest, make known" (e.g., Rom 1:19; 3:21; Titus 1:3); and *propheteuo*, "to prophesy, proclaim a message from God" (e.g., Matt 11:13; 15:7; 1 Pet 1:10). Corresponding nouns that refer to revelation as the product of the act include *apokalypsis*, "revelation, disclosure" (e.g., Rom 16:25; Gal 2:2; Rev 1:1); and *propheteia*, "prophecy, message from God" (e.g., Matt 13:14; 1 Pet 1:20-21; Rev 1:3).[2]

These terms are important, but the doctrine of revelation is based on more than just these and other related words. The reality of divine revelation is a theme that permeates all of Scripture. There is no attempt to justify it or to explain it; the fact that God communicates with his creatures is just assumed and is presented as something natural and expected.

A. Forms of Revelation

God makes himself known to human beings in a variety of ways that fall into two main categories: *general* revelation and *special* revelation. The former is called general revelation for two reasons. One, it is by nature available to all mankind in general. Two, it is the source of only a general knowledge of God.

This revelation comes to all human beings in two ways. First, the created world around us testifies to the power and glory of the Creator. "The heavens are telling of the glory of God; and their expanse is declaring the work of His hands" (Ps 19:1; see vv. 2-6). Paul and Barnabas declared to the idolaters at Lystra that they should have known the true God, because "He did not leave Himself without witness, in that He did good and gave you rains from heaven and fruitful seasons, satisfying your hearts with food and gladness" (Acts 14:17). In Rom 1:19-20 Paul declares that even pagans must answer to the true God, "because that which is known about God is evident within them; for God made it evident to them. For since the creation of the world His invisible attributes, His eternal power and divine nature, have been clearly seen, being understood through what has been made, so that they are without excuse" (see *GC*, 324-329).

In addition to the revelation from creation around us there is also an element of general revelation in the heart of every man. Romans 2:14-15 tells us that even the Gentiles who have no access to biblical revelation know God's law and will be held responsible for it. "For when Gentiles who do not have the Law do instinctively the things of the Law, these, not having the Law, are a law to themselves, in that they show the work of the Law written in their hearts." This means that by virtue of the fact that we are created in God's image, we instinctively know that certain acts are right and others are wrong. This is an innate knowledge of the basic moral law of God (Rom 1:26-32). (See *GC*, 329-336.)

The result of this general revelation is that all normal adults have a true knowledge of God as Creator, Ruler, and Lawgiver, and a true knowledge of his basic will for his human creatures. To deny God and flout his law in the face of general revelation is an act of will, a suppression of known truth (Rom 1:18-32).

General revelation is a marvelous gift that Christians should honor and treasure, but it has its limitations. It is limited in its *form* in that it is nonverbal and therefore less precise than revelation that comes in the form of words. It is also limited in its *content*. It tells us of the power of the Creator, but it does not tell us that the Creator is a Trinity—three persons in one nature. It tells us that we must answer to God as our Lawgiver and Judge, but it does not inform us that he is willing to be gracious to sinners. Though some think otherwise, there is nothing in general revelation about salvation, about the Savior, and about how a sinner can be saved.

Finally, general revelation is limited in its *effectiveness*. This is true because sin blinds our eyes and hardens our hearts against it, and causes us to suppress its clear message (Rom 1:18-25). As sinners we cannot trust ourselves to be objective in the moral intuition that derives from the law written on our hearts. General revelation has limited effectiveness also because sin has corrupted the natural world, causing it to send mixed signals (Rom 8:18-23). The presence of natural evils in the world, such as killer tornadoes and killer viruses, seems to nullify the positive testimony found there. But even apart from these factors, general revelation is limited in its effectiveness because it does not provide knowledge of God as Redeemer and knowledge of redemption itself, and thus is unable to lead sinners to salvation. This means that those who have no access to the special revelation of the grace of God, such as that found in the gospel, cannot be saved.[3] This is a major point Paul is making in Rom 1:18-32; 2:14-15; 3:9-20.[4] This is why missionary work is so imperative.

This is also a major reason why God goes beyond general revelation and gives us the second kind, namely, *special* revelation. This is revelation that is not available to all people in all times in the same way, but is given rather in specific instances, at specific times and places, to specific people. It also gives us knowledge about God and about the human condition that is more specific than what is known through general revelation alone. Especially, it provides us with all we need to know about salvation from our sins.

Special revelation is given in many ways (Heb 1:1-3; Num 12:6-8). Here we will distinguish three main forms: the mighty acts of God in history, the spoken words of God, and the personal presence of God within the world.

First, God reveals himself (nonverbally) in deeds or acts or events. These include those occasions when God miraculously intervenes in history in order to perform a specific work or accomplish a specific purpose. Sometimes this intervention does not result in an actual event but comes in the form of a dream or vision presented to someone's mind apart from his senses. Ordinarily such mentally visualized events are symbolic, e.g., Nebuchadnezzar's dream of the statue crushed by a stone (Dan 2:25-35), Peter's vision of animals on a sheet (Acts 10:10-11), and probably many of the scenes shown to the Apostle John and recorded in the book of Revelation. The sole purpose of such dreams and visions is revelation.

Other special revelatory events occur in open history and are observable through the senses of those present at the time. Some are solely for revelation, e.g., the Urim and Thummim (Exod 28:30; Lev 8:8; Num 27:21) and the guiding of lots (Jonah 1:7; Acts 1:24-26); others are primarily for redemption (or even judgment), and are only secondarily for revelation (e.g., the Exodus events, the cross). Some of these mighty acts of God in history are primarily for evidential value, i.e., miracles such as the ten plagues sent upon Egypt and the raising of Lazarus from the dead. These are often called signs (e.g., Acts 2:22; 2 Cor 12:12; Heb 2:4), i.e., they are signs or evidence of the truth of God's prophetic word. Thus they provide a specialized kind of revelation (see *GRu*, 323-240).

All such revelatory acts, mental or historical, are effective up to a point, but they are incomplete without some accompanying explanation given in the form of words. For example, Daniel had to interpret Nebuchadnezzar's dream (Dan 2:36-45), God had to interpret Peter's vision (Acts 10:13-16), and even the cross must be interpreted through the words of the gospel.

This leads to the second form of special revelation, namely, God sometimes reveals himself in words: *God has spoken*; he speaks verbally in human language. Sometimes these words come to the mind only, as in prophetic dreams (Num 12:6) or instructions in dreams (e.g., Matt 1:20; 2:13,19-20). Sometimes the words are spoken orally, aloud, so that anyone present may hear them. Sometimes this spoken revelation is given indirectly, through angels (Luke 1:13-20,26-38; 2:8-14) or prophets (Num 23:4–24:25; 2 Sam 12:7-12; Isa 37:21-35). Sometimes God himself may speak directly, as from the burning bush (Exod 3:4–4:17), in the giving of the ten commandments (Exod 20:1-21; Deut 4:10-13; 5:4-27), and at the baptism of Jesus (Matt 3:17). Sometimes the words are spoken orally, and sometimes they are written, either by God himself (Exod 31:18; Deut 5:22; Dan 5:24-28) or more commonly by prophets and apostles (Jer 36:4; 1 Cor 14:37).

The third way in which God gives special revelation is through his personal visible presence, which has occurred in two ways. First of all God's presence may take the form of a *theophany*, in which he manifests himself directly through visible phenomena, clothing himself with the form of a creature. This may involve a temporary human form, as when God walked in the Garden of Eden with Adam and Eve (Gen 3:8) or dined and talked with Abraham (Gen 18:1-33). Or it may involve a permanent humanlike form, such as the appearance of God in the angelic realm seated on a throne (Exod 24:9-10; Rev 4, 5). Sometimes a theophany may take a nonhuman form such as a pillar of fire (Exod 13:21-22; 19:18-20), a cloud (Exod 40:34-38; Matt 17:5), or a dove (Matt 3:16).

The second form of God's visible presence is the *incarnation*, the unique act in which the Logos (God the Son) became present in this world in and as the person Jesus of Nazareth (John 1:1,14). This is different from a theophany in that Jesus was an actual human person, and not just a human body or form. The incarnation is undoubtedly a form of revelation (Matt 11:27; John 1:18; 18:37; Heb 1:1-3), and it is surely the highest and clearest form. Kenneth Kantzer (76) has rightly said, "The consummating mode of revelation in all of Scripture . . . is the person of Jesus Christ. Jesus Christ differs from other modes in that He is not so much a mode of the divine communication as He is the divine being Himself, communicating to man directly in and through His incarnation in the human race." He reveals God in both deeds and words. When he acts, he is God acting; "and when He speaks, He is, in turn, God speaking with divine authority and divine infallibility."

Two important cautions must be observed regarding the incarnation as revelation, however. First, the main purpose for the incarnation was redemption, not revelation. Jesus came to redeem sinners; the accompanying revelation was secondary to this main work. Interpreting Jesus primarily as a revealer of God leads to the serious error of the christological fallacy, as discussed in the introductory chapter (see *GC*, 371-381). Second, even though Jesus is the highest form of revelation, he is not the *only* revelation, nor is the incarnation as such the *final* revelation. God reveals himself in many ways, from Genesis 1 through Revelation 22. Other revelation from God is just as authoritative as that given by the incarnate Christ. In summary, we should not limit Jesus' work to revelation, and we should not limit revelation to Jesus.

B. The Cruciality of Word Revelation

Of all the forms of revelation, the most crucial for our knowledge of God is *word* revelation. But herein lies one of the most serious points of separation between conservative and liberal theology: Whereas the former affirms word revelation, it is characteristic of the latter to deny it. As Leon Morris points out, "In recent times many scholars have attacked the whole idea of verbal or propositional revelation. They prefer to think that God reveals himself in the mighty deeds that are recorded in the Bible, while regarding the words in which these deeds are recorded as not of primary importance. . . . The revelation is in the deeds themselves and not in the record" (*Revelation*, 43-44).

A good example of this view is John Baillie's book, *The Idea of Revelation in Recent Thought*. Baillie says that revelation does not convey information, knowledge, propositions, or truth (28, 33, 49). God does speak, of course, but he "speaks" through events (51). "All revelation is given, not in the form of directly communicated knowledge, but through events occurring in the historical experience of mankind" (62).

The main reason for denying word revelation is the assumption that God's transcendence—the qualitative difference between the Creator and his creatures—makes it *impossible* for him to express divine truth in finite human language. The finite cannot contain the infinite; relative history cannot contain absolute truth. God can no more reduce his thoughts to human language than Einstein could have explained the theory of relativity to ants. And even if he could, how could man's culture-bound mind hope to comprehend such truth about the transcendent God?

This objection, however, misses one of the main implications of the transcendence of God. Rather than constituting a barrier to communication with mankind, his transcendence and infinity are the very divine attributes that make it possible. In his infinite wisdom, God knows how to cross the Creator/creature gap with meaningful communication. The language of revelation is not man's finite and feeble groping for God; it comes from the infinite, omniscient God himself. And we are able to understand it because, though we are finite, God has made us in his own image; we have been designed for the very purpose of receiving God's spoken word.

Word revelation is not only possible; it is actually necessary, especially now that mankind has sinned and needs redemption. It is true that redemption is accomplished by God's mighty acts in history, but how could we understand their significance apart from word revelation? For these works of redemption to be accessible to us, God's spoken word must explain them and tell us how to respond to them.

In fact, that God has revealed himself in human words is one of the plainest teachings in the Bible. In the very beginning God is pictured as speaking to Adam and Eve (Gen 1:28-30; 2:16-17; 3:9-19). He spoke to Noah (Gen 6:13ff), to Abraham (Gen 12:1ff), to Moses (Exod 3:4ff), to Samuel (1 Sam 3:10ff), and to many other prophets. The messages delivered by prophets to others are described as words from God; "thus says the LORD" is their cry (e.g., Isa 10:24; Jer 8:4; Amos 1:3,6,9,11,13). Isaiah began his prophecy thus: "Listen, O heavens, and hear, O earth; for the LORD speaks. . . . Hear the word of the LORD" (1:2,10). David said, "The Spirit of the LORD spoke by me, and His word was on my tongue" (2 Sam 23:2).

The very concept of "prophet" implies word revelation. The Greek *prophetes* comes from *phemi*, "to speak," and *pro*, "before"; a prophet is basically a spokesperson, one who speaks for someone else. A prophet of God is one who delivers God's message to others, almost always in the form of words.

The NT's testimony to word revelation is clear: *God has spoken* (Heb 1:1-2). Since Jesus himself was God incarnate, every word he spoke while on earth was divine revelation. After he returned to the Father, he continued to speak through the Holy Spirit to and through his appointed apostles and prophets (John 16:13-15; Eph 3:5). Romans 3:2 describes the OT as "the very words of God" (NIV). The very term "Scripture" (*graphe*) means "writing"; it is taken from *grapho*, "to write." The fact that this term is applied to divine communication (2 Tim 3:16) implies its verbal nature, since what is written down must take the form of *words*.

Because revelation often comes through words, it may indeed take written form. Those who deny word revelation must disagree; thus they do not view the Bible as literal revelation, but consider it at best to be a *witness* to the *events* through which God has revealed himself. But when we see that revelation does indeed come through words, it is clear that it can be written down (as in the Bible) without compromising its nature as revelation.

II. INSPIRATION

Our knowledge of God and indeed the whole enterprise of theology are grounded in the revelation God has freely given to us, especially that which has come to us in the form of words. But this is not the whole story; our knowledge of God is also dependent upon something called "inspiration." Thus revelation and inspiration are almost always considered together.

A. What Is Inspiration?

When God uses a spokesman or prophet to deliver a message to other people, this process takes place in two distinct steps. First, God places the message in the prophet's mind in some way. This is the act of revelation. Second, the prophet delivers this same revealed message to others, either orally or in writing. In this way the content of revelation given to us in the Bible originates with God but is mediated to us by other human beings.

This raises the question of the accuracy of the mediated message. Certainly we can trust God to have revealed the message correctly to the prophet in the first step, but how can we trust the prophet to have accurately passed it along to us? More importantly, how can God himself trust the prophets to remember everything he has told them and keep everything straight and make no mistakes as they transmit his message to others? After all, even though God is infinite in his knowledge and power and is infallible in all that he says, human beings are finite and limited and are capable of memory lapses and mistakes. How can God be sure that his words are mediated accurately?

The answer lies in what is commonly called *inspiration*. We usually say that the Bible is inspired, or given by the inspiration of God. This is something quite distinct from revelation. Whereas revelation is God's action in the first step of communicating his message through spokesmen, inspiration is his action in the second step. In this second stage, when the spokesman is in the process of passing the message along (either orally or in writing), God is exerting a power or an influence upon that person in a way that guarantees that what he says will be what God wants him to say. This influence is what we call inspiration.

At this point a formal definition of inspiration may be offered: inspiration is the supernatural influence exerted by the Holy Spirit upon prophets and apostles which enabled them to communicate without error or omission those truths, received through revelation or otherwise, which God deemed necessary for our salvation and service.

We should note that not everything communicated to us by the writers of the Bible can be called revelation (see the words "or otherwise" in the definition). Large portions of the Bible are revealed by God and could not have been known in any other way. But some parts of the Bible consist of data not revealed by God but known to the writers by some other means, such as existing documents, personal experience, and personal investigation.

For example, Josh 10:13 relates something "written in the book of Jashar" (see 2 Sam 1:18). Luke says that he wrote his Gospel after "having investigated everything carefully from the beginning" (Luke 1:3). Since he accompanied Paul on some of his missionary trips, many of the events Luke records in the book of Acts were things he experienced personally (see Acts 20:6-7,13-15). In his writings the Apostle Paul sometimes included references and greetings to his personal friends (see Rom 16:1-23).

The fact that this sort of data is included in the Bible leads us to ask once more, how can we trust this material to be true and trustworthy? The answer again is inspiration. It really does not matter whether the material in the Bible came to the writers by revelation, by experience, or by some other means; all that matters is that when they wrote it down, they were writing under the divine influence of the Holy Spirit. This is what guarantees that their message was exactly what God wanted it to be, and it is the basis for our accepting it as accurate and trustworthy.

In short, some parts of the Bible are revealed and some are not, but *all* of it is inspired. Because of inspiration every word of the original writings of the Bible is of divine origin and thus has God's "stamp of approval."

B. The Biblical Teaching about Inspiration

Sometimes revelation and inspiration occur together, as when a prophet speaks a message from God at the very moment it is revealed to him. Thus sometimes the biblical data on inspiration cannot be clearly distinguished from revelation; in such a case we may say that the biblical reference is to the *divine origin* of Scripture. Such references are abundant. Whatever must be said about the fact and manner of its human authorship, the Bible speaks naturally and frequently of its divine authorship. God is the ultimate origin of Scripture and is ultimately responsible for its content.

In setting forth this biblical teaching we shall begin with the NT's witness to the OT. Over fifty times the NT cites an OT text and refers to God as its author. Some of these references are found in the recorded words of Jesus. On one occasion he refers to a certain teaching from the Law of Moses (Exod 20:12; 21:17; Lev 20:9) and calls it "the Word of God" (Matt 15:6; Mark 7:13). Even though Moses said it (Mark 7:10), because of revelation and inspiration God also said it (Matt 15:4); thus it is the Word of God.

When tempted by the devil to turn stones into bread, Jesus cites the words of Deut 8:3 thus: "It is written, 'Man shall not live on bread alone, but on every word that proceeds out of the mouth of God'" (Matt 4:4). Where is this word to be found, if not in Scripture? This is the only reasonable inference from Jesus' statement.

Citing Ps 110:1, Jesus declares that David said this "in the Holy Spirit," or while under the influence of the Holy Spirit (Mark 12:36).

In Matt 19:4-5, as part of his answer to a question about divorce, Jesus cites Gen 2:24 and attributes it to God. "He who created them from the beginning" is the one who said these words. This is significant because in the text of Genesis itself these words are not attributed to God; they are simply a part of the narrative. Thus even the words of the narrator (i.e., Moses) are of divine origin, because of inspiration.

In John 5:32-39 Jesus equates the testimony of the OT with the testimony of God. He says, "There is another who testifies of Me, and I know that the testimony which He gives about Me is true" (v. 32). This testimony is not from man (v. 34), but is from "the Father who sent Me" (v. 37). Then after referring to "His Word" and "the Scriptures" (vv. 38,39), Jesus says, "It is these [the Scriptures] that testify about Me" (v. 39). Thus the testimony of the Scriptures is the testimony of God.

The Apostle Paul likewise confirms the inspiration of the OT writings. In Rom 3:2 he calls them "the very words of God" (see Rom 9:6, NIV). In Rom 9:17 and Gal 3:8 he says that *Scripture* spoke to Pharaoh and *Scripture* spoke to Abraham. Strictly speaking, Scripture did not speak to either of these men; God spoke to them, and his words are recorded in Scripture. These texts show that in Paul's mind Scripture is so firmly regarded as the Word of God that it can be personified and used interchangeably with God.

Paul's grandest teaching about the divine origin of the Bible is 2 Tim 3:16, "All Scripture [*graphe*] is inspired by God and profitable for teaching, for reproof, for correction, for training in righteousness." Some claim that this should be translated "every inspired scripture" (e.g., the NEB), thus creating a distinction between inspired scripture and uninspired scripture. The presence of the word "and," linking "inspired" and "profitable," is against this claim. Unless both adjectives are part of the predicate, the word "and" has no useful function in the sentence.

The main reason for maintaining the translation "all Scripture" is the comparison with the "sacred writings" (*hiera grammata*) in verse 15, which are undoubtedly the OT as a whole. Is the *graphe* in verse 16 equivalent to, less than, or more than the *hiera grammata* of verse 15? It can hardly be something less; "Scripture" in verse 16 must be at least equivalent to the "sacred writings" of verse 15. Surely Paul would not say that only *some* of the *sacred* writings are inspired. In fact, it is likely that *graphe* in verse 16 is meant to include *more* than the OT writings, namely, the NT writings as well. In other words, it was not just the sacred writings known to Timothy in his childhood that are inspired; the Bible as a whole is inspired.[5]

Exactly what is this verse saying about the Bible? What does the word "inspired" mean? Actually this is a poor translation of the Greek word in verse 16, which is *theopneustos*. This word literally means "God-breathed" and is so rendered in most modern translations. The NIV accurately says, "All Scripture is God-breathed." The reason why this does not literally match the word *inspired* is that this English word means "to breathe in," while *theopneustos* or "God-breathed" means "to breathe out." Thus even though we will all no doubt continue to speak of the Bible as "inspired," we should remember that we mean by this that the Bible is "God-breathed" or breathed out by God.[6]

In view of the literal meaning of this term, 2 Tim 3:16 is usually recognized as making one of the most profound biblical claims regarding the nature of the Bible as a whole. To say that "all Scripture is God-breathed" means that when the human authors of the Bible were engaged in the process of writing their message, whether revealed or otherwise, the Holy Spirit was so guarding their minds and their hands that the result was as if their message had come from the very heart and hand of God. When they were putting their words down on the original parchments or paper, the Spirit was in such control that whatever they wrote was as accurate and trustworthy as if it had been breathed out of the very mouth of God.

The Apostle Peter likewise testifies to the divine origin of the OT. Acts 1:16 records his words, that "the Scripture had to be fulfilled, which the Holy Spirit foretold by the mouth of David" (see Acts 4:25). Also, what "God says" in Joel 2:28-32 was spoken "through the prophet Joel" (Acts 2:16-17). The sufferings of Jesus are "things which God announced beforehand by the mouth of all the prophets" (Acts 3:18). Indeed, the prophets spoke of these things through "the Spirit of Christ within them" (1 Pet 1:11).

Another of Peter's strong affirmations of inspiration is 2 Pet 1:20-21, which says that "no prophecy of Scripture is a matter of one's own interpretation, for no prophecy was ever made by an act of human will, but men moved by the Holy Spirit spoke from God." "One's own interpretation" is sometimes wrongly interpreted as referring to how the *readers* of the Bible interpret or exegete it. This is not Peter's meaning, however. He is actually referring to how the *writers* of the Bible came up with their material. The NIV makes the meaning clear: "No prophecy of Scripture came about by the prophet's own interpretation." In other words, Isaiah's prophecies are not just his own interpretation of things; nor did David and Amos just decide on their own to write part of the Bible. Rather, the Holy Spirit was in control of the writing process. Peter literally says that "men spoke from God as they were carried along by the Holy Spirit" (NIV).

In this passage Peter refers to every "prophecy of Scripture," and to "the prophetic word" (v. 19). He is certainly referring to the OT predictive prophecies about Jesus, but it is likely that he intends to include all of the OT in these phrases. In a real sense all Scripture is "prophetic," since "to prophesy" basically means "to speak on behalf of another, to proclaim or declare a message for someone else"—in this case, for God. Thus every "prophecy of Scripture" may mean "every declaration of Scripture" inclusively. Gottlob Schrenk (755) says it is "impossible" to take *graphe* here "in any other way" than "the unified totality of Scripture."

Other NT testimony to the inspiration of the OT includes Matthew's reference to "what was spoken by the Lord through the prophet" (1:22; see 2:15,17), and Zacharias's reference to the way God "spoke by the mouth of His holy prophets from of old" (Luke 1:70). The letter to the Hebrews attributes OT prophecies to the Holy Spirit (3:7; 10:15; see 1:5-13; 4:4,7; 7:21; 8:8).

We now turn to NT testimony to its own inspiration,[7] beginning with Christ's promises to his apostles.[8] Concerning their preaching in difficult circumstances Jesus made this promise: "Do not worry about how or what you are to say; for it will be given you in that hour what you are to say. For it is not you who speak, but it is the Spirit of your Father who speaks in you" (Matt 10:19-20; see Mark 13:11; Luke 12:11-12). Concerning their general teaching Jesus promised that the Holy Spirit "will teach you all things, and bring to your remembrance all that I said to you" (John 14:26). Here the first promise refers to new revelation; the second means that they would have infallible memories of what Jesus had already taught them. In John 16:13 Jesus specifically promises the apostles (not Christians in general) that "when He, the Spirit of truth, comes, He will guide you into all the truth." Jesus declares that this truth would ultimately be coming from himself through the Spirit (see 16:12-15).

The Apostle Paul affirms the divine origin of the messages given through God's "holy apostles and prophets in the Spirit" (Eph 3:5; see 2:20; 4:11). This includes all the NT writings. In 1 Cor 2:7-13 Paul refers to the divine mysteries revealed "to us" (apostles and prophets) "through the Spirit." In verse 12 he speaks of revelation: "Now we have received, not the spirit of the world, but the Spirit who is from God, so that we may know the things freely given to us by God." Then in verse 13 he affirms the inspiration of the apostles and prophets when they are delivering these revealed messages to others: "Which things we also speak, not in words taught by human wisdom, but in those taught by the Spirit, combining spiritual thoughts with spiritual words."

Even as he wrote his NT letters, Paul was conscious of the divine origin of his teaching. "The things which I write to you are the Lord's commandment," he says (1 Cor 14:37; see 2 Cor 13:3). In 1 Thess 2:13 he declares that his oral message to the Thessalonians was not just the word of a man, but "the word of God." Then in 2 Thess 2:15 he declares that his written words are just as authoritative as his spoken words. See Gal 1:11-12; Eph 3:1-5; 1 Tim 2:7; 4:1.

Some use 1 Cor 7:10-12 in an attempt to weaken the authority of Paul's writings. Here he contrasts *the Lord's* instructions ("not I, but the Lord," i.e., Jesus) with *his own* instructions ("I say, not the Lord"). But this is not a contrast between levels of authority, but rather between what Christ taught in person during his earthly ministry (e.g., Matt 19:3-9), and what he is now teaching in a supplementary way through the Holy Spirit working in his servant Paul (see v. 40). Both are of equal authority.

The same applies to the contrast between the Lord's "command" and Paul's "opinion" in 1 Cor 7:25,40. The translation "opinion" is too weak and is misleading. A better translation is "I give a judgment," i.e., I give a judgment as one chosen by the Lord himself to give true and authoritative teaching (see 1 Tim 2:7). The point is that Jesus gave no teaching on this subject while he was on the earth, but he is doing so now through his inspired apostle.

All in all, the NT puts apostolic writings on an equal level with OT writings. In 2 Pet 3:2 the teachings of the apostles are bound upon the church equally with the teachings of the OT prophets, which Peter has already attributed to the Holy Spirit (2 Pet 1:20-21). See also 1 Pet 1:10-12. In 2 Pet 3:15-16 the letters of Paul are compared with "the rest of the Scriptures," implying that Paul's writings are *Scripture*. In 1 Tim 5:18, after saying "the Scripture says," Paul gives two citations; one is from Deut 25:4, the other from Luke 10:7 or Matt 10:10.

C. The Scope of Inspiration

We have said above that even though all of the Bible is not revealed, it is all inspired; and this divine inspiration is the ultimate source of the Bible's authority. But attempts are sometimes made to limit the scope of inspiration itself. For instance, some say that inspiration applies to the *messengers*, but not to their *message*; the effect would be that the message is somehow flawed. But according to the Bible's own teaching, inspiration applies to both the messengers and to the message. In 2 Pet 1:20-21 the prophets themselves are the ones to whom the Holy Spirit directs his divine influence. But this is only a means to an end, the end being the inspiration of their writings, which themselves are declared to be God-breathed (2 Tim 3:16).

Another attempt to limit inspiration is the view that it applies only to the *thoughts* of the prophets and apostles, and not to the *words* they used to communicate these thoughts. This is not consistent with biblical teaching, however. In 2 Tim 3:16 inspiration is applied to "Scripture," i.e., the *written* product. What is written? Not just thoughts, but *words*. Galatians 3:16 indicates that even the form of a word (singular rather than plural) is significant; Jesus says that even the "smallest letter or stroke" is important (Matt 5:18). In 1 Cor 2:13 Paul specifically includes the words of God's messengers within the scope of what is "taught by the Spirit." Psychologically it is difficult if not impossible to separate thoughts from words.

Since it applies to the very words of Scripture, we may say that inspiration is *verbal*. Here is a very important point, however: verbal inspiration does not imply that every word of the Bible is *dictated* by the Holy Spirit;[9] it means only that he guards and approves every word. Thus verbal inspiration allows for variation in reporting the same event (as in the Gospels) or in stating the same thought, and it allows the writers to use their own vocabularies and styles of writing.

In the final analysis, if inspiration is not verbal, it is irrelevant, since its very purpose is to secure the accuracy of the verbally communicated message of truth.

A third attempt to limit the scope of inspiration is to say that it applies to the *didactic* or theological parts of the Bible, but not to its historical and geographical *details.* This limitation must also be rejected; inspiration applies to all parts of the Bible and to all the kinds of writing it includes, including historical, geographical, scientific, and personal. Since the Holy Spirit guided the writers, then everything they wrote must have the Spirit's approval. Inspiration is thus called *plenary*, i.e., complete and all-inclusive. As 2 Tim 3:16 says, *all* Scripture is God-breathed.

This affirmation of the verbal, plenary inspiration of the Bible applies directly only to the original text as it was first written down. Copies and translations are inspired in a real but indirect sense insofar as they accurately represent the content of the original text.

D. The Mode of Inspiration

Sometimes this conservative view of inspiration is disparagingly called "the dictation view," as if the human writers were just machines that the Spirit used like tape recorders. But such a label is erroneous and irresponsible. No doubt the Holy Spirit was the divine agent in inspiration: see 2 Sam 23:2; John 16:12-15; 2 Pet 1:21. But the exact mode or method of inspiration—*how* the Spirit worked to influence the writers—is not explained in Scripture. It no doubt varied all the way from dictation to general supervision. Dictation would be appropriate where revelation of totally unknown or new information was needed. General supervision would be sufficient to guard against error or omission where the information was already personally known to the writer (e.g., Luke 1:1-4; Rom 1:1-15). Either way, it is the *fact* of inspiration, not the mode, that matters. Our concern is not with the nature of the process but with the nature of the product.

Whatever the manner of the Spirit's participation, the inspiration of the Bible did not rule out the genuine, conscious participation of the human writers. Their full natural personalities were operative even while they were under the divine influence. They were not passive and mechanical instruments, nor were they in a mediumistic, trancelike state. They spoke or wrote in their own vocabularies and styles, often voicing their own thoughts. The Spirit and the human writers thus worked together, with the Spirit having the final say as to the words that were recorded. An illustration would be a person learning to drive in a car with dual controls. The learner is given free rein as long as he is going where he is supposed to go, but the instructor can take control of the process if a problem is about to arise.

E. The Result of Inspiration

What is the result of inspiration? What kind of book is the inspired Bible? It is God's own Word. God was in full control of its production; what was written down was what he wanted to be written. Thus it is fully proper to call the Bible the *Word of God*.

Paul knew the difference between the mere words of men and the word of God. He said to the Thessalonians, "For this reason we also constantly thank God that when you received the word of God which you heard from us, you accepted it not as the word of men, but for what it really is, the Word of God" (1 Thess 2:13). Thus Paul knew his own message to be the Word of God, just as he knew the OT to be "the very words of God" (Rom 3:2, NIV). Jeremiah knew his writing to be the words of God (Jer 36:2). Jesus referred to certain OT texts as the Word of God (Matt 15:6).

That the Bible is inspired means that it is the Word of God; that it is the Word of God means that it is completely true and trustworthy, and completely authoritative.

III. INERRANCY

To say that the Bible is completely true and trustworthy in the fullest sense is to say that it is inerrant. Whether or not the Bible is inerrant has been vigorously debated by Evangelicals over the past few decades. In the process the concept of inerrancy has often been seriously misunderstood and misrepresented. Thus it is necessary to explain exactly what is at stake in this issue.

A. The Meaning of Inerrancy

When one person defends inerrancy and another denies it, exactly what are they arguing about? First we must explain what the issue is *not*. For one thing, the issue is not *terminology*. What is at stake is not any particular word (such as "inerrancy"), but the *concept* of the absolute truth and trustworthiness of the Bible. Once the word "inspired" all by itself conveyed this meaning, as did the word "infallible." But critics have so redefined and watered down these terms that it is now necessary to use the more specific term "inerrancy" to assert what these terms once unambiguously meant. In any case we do not argue from the term to the concept. The concept is the basic point, and the concept is what is found in the Bible even if the term itself is not found there.

Second, the issue is not *copies and translations*. Those who argue responsibly for inerrancy are not saying that any particular translation is inerrant (e.g., the KJV or the NIV). Inerrancy, like inspiration, applies only to the original text of the Bible as first produced by the authors themselves.

Third, the issue is not *laboratory precision* in the use of language. To say the Bible is inerrant does not require some artificial, "heavenly" standard of grammar or numerical precision. Inerrancy allows language to be used in ordinary, everyday ways. It is consistent with such things as approximate times, round numbers, paraphrasing, and grammatical freedom.

Fourth, the issue is not *literalism* in interpreting Scripture. To argue for inerrancy is not to argue that every word, every statement, every prophecy in the Bible must be taken in its most literal sense. Inerrancy takes full account of symbolism in prophecy, of parables, and of the figurative use of words.

One distinction should be made here, however. There is a difference between *linguistic* literalism, which inerrancy does not require, and *historical* literalism, which inerrancy does require. That is, even though inerrancy does not mean that we must interpret all the words of Scripture in their most literal sense, it does mean that we must accept the literal existence of all the historical characters and events described in the Bible as real (e.g., Adam and Eve, the Fall). Thus the issue is not the nature of the Bible's language, but the historicity of the people and events intentionally affirmed therein.

Fifth, the issue is not a particular theory of the *mode of inspiration*. Inerrancy does not require a mechanical dictation or mediumistic type of inspiration. To connect the two, as critics often do, is unwarranted and irresponsible. Inerrancy depends only on the fact of inspiration, not on any certain mode.

Sixth, the issue is not *church history*. Whether or not the church through the ages has espoused inerrancy is beside the point. What Augustine, Luther, Calvin, or Campbell said about the subject is not decisive. The only real issue is what the Bible claims about itself.

Finally, the issue is not *Christian fellowship*. Even though biblical inerrancy is very important, it is wrong to say that those who deny it are for that reason not Christians or do not have a sincere and saving faith in Jesus Christ.

What, then, *is* the issue regarding inerrancy? It is simply this: *are there errors in the Bible* that can be traced to the original text itself? When the biblical writers originally wrote the books of the Bible, did they make some assertions that are *not true*? Did they intend to affirm something as true which in fact is false?

Those who deny inerrancy are saying that, in fact, the Bible in its original text is in error in some of its claims. To affirm inerrancy is to say that whatever the Bible declares to be true *is true*. It makes no errors or mistakes; it makes no false or misleading statements. As one statement of faith says, "All Scripture, as first written by the authors themselves, was produced under the direct inspiration of the Holy Spirit. Scripture is therefore the Word of God in written form, and is infallible and inerrant in its entirety when taken in the original meaning of its authors. Thus it is the sole and sufficient rule for faith and practice."

The terms "infallible" and "inerrant" go together, but they are not synonymous. "Infallible" properly defined means "incapable of error; unable to err, to lie, or to make mistakes."[10] This is a much stronger term than "inerrant," which simply means "absence of error, actually not containing any errors." A statement or document may be inerrant without being infallible, but it can never be infallible without being inerrant. The Bible is inerrant *because* it is infallible, and it is infallible because it is the inspired Word of God.

B. The Biblical Basis for Inerrancy

Our goal in this book is to give a systematic presentation of what the Bible teaches, including what it teaches about itself. A major element in the Bible's self-attestation is its claim to be completely and totally true, i.e., inerrant. Thus the Bible's own teaching on the subject compels us to affirm it.[11]

We may begin by simply stating that inerrancy is a reasonable implication of the fact and purpose of inspiration. Because of inspiration the Holy Spirit is the ultimate author of all Scripture, making God ultimately responsible for the text. Given the omniscience and faithfulness of God, we cannot escape the conclusion that his word—Scripture—must be inerrant.

We may state this in a more formal and detailed way by presenting the biblical data in the form of a syllogism. Major premise: every word breathed out by God is true in the sense that it is without error. Minor premise: every word of Scripture is breathed out by God. Conclusion: every word of Scripture is true in the sense that it is without error.

Such a syllogism necessarily yields a true conclusion, but only when its premises are true. Here is where the biblical teaching about inerrancy is most prominent. It not only directly affirms the conclusion (as we shall see shortly); it also clearly and unambiguously affirms the truth of the premises, thus laying the foundation for the necessary conclusion that the Bible is inerrant.

The major premise, that every word breathed out by God is true and without error, is first of all inferred from biblical teaching about the nature of God. God "cannot lie" (Titus 1:2); thus there can be no *deliberate* errors in his words. Also, God "knows all things" (1 John 3:20), i.e., he is omniscient; thus there can be no *accidental* errors in his words. Therefore every word he speaks must be true.

This premise is not only inferred from the nature of God; it is also specifically affirmed in biblical teaching. Psalm 12:6 says, "The words of the LORD are pure words." They are as pure "as silver tried in a furnace on the earth, refined seven times," or until it is perfectly cleansed from all impurity (see Ps 19:7-10). Proverbs 30:5 declares, "Every word of God is flawless" (NIV; see Ps 18:30). The Hebrew word for "flawless" means "to test, refine, try, purify." In other words, when challenged or put to the test, "every word of God proves true" (NRSV). This is reaffirmed in the words of Jesus' prayer to the Father, "Your word is truth" (John 17:17). In Rom 3:4 Paul declares, "Let God be found true, though every man be found a liar, as it is written, 'That You may be justified in Your words, and prevail when You are judged.'" "Justified" means to be declared righteous; thus Paul is saying that whenever God speaks he will be proved right and his words will be found true.

The minor premise of the syllogism, that every word of Scripture is breathed out by God, is likewise an inference from other biblical teaching, namely, its teaching about revelation and inspiration as explained earlier. The very purpose of the Holy Spirit's involvement in the teaching of apostles and prophets is to guide them into all the truth and guarantee their accuracy in all things (John 14:26; 16:13). If inspiration does not result in inerrancy, then it has no purpose; if there are errors in Scripture, then inspiration is irrelevant and futile.

In short, any concept of inspiration that does not result in inerrancy is not the inspiration of which the Bible teaches. As E.J. Young has said, "There is no such thing as inspiration which does not carry with it the correlate of infallibility. A Bible that is fallible—and we speak of course of the original—is a Bible that is not inspired. A Bible that is inspired is a Bible that is infallible" (*Word*, 109).

The premise that every word of Scripture is breathed out by God is not *just* an inference from other biblical teaching; it is also specifically affirmed in the Bible. Paul unequivocally asserts that *all* Scripture is *theopneustos*, which literally means "God-breathed, breathed out by God" (2 Tim 3:16). Also, all references to the Bible as the word or words of God are asserting this premise. Jesus' reference to "Your word" in John 17:17 at the very least includes Scripture; see Rom 3:2 where the phrase "the very words of God" (NIV) refers to the OT. See Jer 36:2; Matt 15:6; Heb 5:12.

These two premises, both inferred from other biblical teaching and both specifically affirmed by the Bible, *necessarily* lead to the conclusion that *every word of Scripture is true in the sense that it is without error*. By the very nature of logic, this conclusion is a necessary inference from the premises. If one accepts both of these premises, then he must accept the conclusion.

Is inerrancy, then, "merely an inference"? NO! It is also specifically affirmed in Scripture, by no less than our Lord Jesus himself: "The Scripture cannot be broken" (John 10:35). The word for "broken" is *lyo*, which means "to break, loose, destroy, dissolve." That Scripture cannot be broken means that it cannot be destroyed, refuted, found faulty, found untrue, or disproved. Jesus' statement occurs in the context of a dispute with the Jewish leaders concerning his divine nature. In support of his own deity Jesus quotes a rather obscure statement from Psalm 82:6. He then declares that Scripture as such cannot be broken, in order to reinforce the truth and authority of this specific text. In other words, the appeal to Scripture is final, since Scripture cannot be broken. If Scripture can be cited—*any* Scripture, the argument is settled, since Scripture cannot be challenged, disproved, or denied.

We should note that Jesus' statement is an affirmation about the nature of the written word [Scripture] as a whole. It is a deductive argument. One does not have to examine each individual statement in the Bible to establish its truth or falsity. The implication is this: *just because it is in Scripture*, we know it cannot be broken.

The same conclusion, that Scripture cannot be broken (i.e., is inerrant), can also be established inductively by examining the Gospel records to see how Jesus refers to the Jewish Scriptures, the OT (see Cottrell, *Solid*, ch 1, 9-17). The way he (and NT writers in general) use the OT shows that he accepted the historicity of its events and characters in an unqualified way. All are accepted as true, as having happened or existed as described. He also treats OT prophecies as inerrant, as being necessarily fulfilled (Matt 26:54; Luke 22:37; 24:44). Likewise he affirms the infallibility of its ethical teaching (see Matt 4:4,7,10; 5:17-19; Luke 10:26; 18:20). Even in Matt 5:21-48 Jesus is not correcting and replacing OT ethical teaching as such, contrary to a common assumption; rather, he is correcting false Pharisaical interpretations and applications of certain OT teachings.

To those who object that the concept of biblical inerrancy is a "mere inference" or the result of "mere human logic," we make two comments. First, there is nothing wrong with human logic, since it is patterned after the logic of God himself, in whose image we are made. To disparage logic is to set oneself above the very mind of God. The fact is that Jesus himself was using the same form of the syllogism being used here—major premise, minor premise, conclusion—in his argument against the Jewish leaders in John 10:35. Here is the force of his argument: *No* Scripture can be broken (major premise); Ps 82:6 is Scripture (minor premise); therefore Ps 82:6 cannot be broken (conclusion). Jesus' implicit use of syllogistic reasoning shows the futility of questioning the validity of such logic, especially as it is applied to the nature of Scripture.

Second, we again stress the fact that the concept of biblical inerrancy is not *just* the conclusion of a valid syllogism, but is also specifically affirmed by Jesus' statement in John 10:35.

C. Denials and Objections

The doctrine of inerrancy as described above has been the traditional doctrine and belief of the church from its beginning. It is the consistent witness of history. Opponents of inerrancy sometimes try to discredit it by saying it is a "new view" that did not exist until at least the seventeenth century and perhaps not until the modern "fundamentalist" movement of the early twentieth century. Critics within the Restoration Movement often assert that early Restoration leaders, especially Alexander Campbell, did not hold to such a view.

All such claims, however, are shown to be completely false when the facts of history are examined without prejudice.[12] For example, Clement of Rome, the earliest Christian writer, said that the Scriptures "were given by the Holy Spirit," and thus "nothing unrighteous or counterfeit is written in them" ("To the Corinthians," 45 [*Apostolic Fathers*, 53]). Augustine declared that the authors of the books of Scripture "were completely free from error" ("Letters," 82:3). Martin Luther often affirmed inerrancy, e.g., "The Scriptures cannot err"; "The Scriptures have never erred"; "It is impossible that Scripture should contradict itself."[13] Though Alexander Campbell distinguished two kinds of inspiration, he unequivocally affirmed that both kinds yield an inerrant product. Even in the historical sections of Scripture, the writers were "prevented from committing errors" ("Response," 499). They were given "such a superintendency of the Spirit of wisdom and knowledge as excluded the possibility of mistake in the matters of fact which they recorded." The Apostles wrote "without the possibility of error" (*Millennial Harbinger*, 1846:15).[14] The liberal Harvard scholar Kirsopp Lake has put it this way (61):

It is a mistake often made by educated persons who happen to have but a little knowledge of historical theology, to suppose that fundamentalism is a new and strange form of thought. It is nothing of the kind; it is the partial and uneducated survival of a theology which was once universally held by all Christians. How many were there, for instance, in Christian churches in the eighteenth century who doubted the infallible inspiration of all Scripture? A few, perhaps, but very few. No, the fundamentalist may be wrong, I think that he is. But it is we [liberals] who have departed from the tradition, not he; and I am sorry for the fate of anyone who tries to argue with a fundamentalist on the basis of authority. The Bible and the *corpus theologicum* of the church is on the fundamentalist side.

Modern denials of inerrancy began in earnest in the second half of the nineteenth century, especially after the publication of Darwin's *Origin of Species* (McDonald, 196-203). Such denials were part of the essence of both classical Liberalism (late nineteenth, early twentieth centuries) and Neo-Orthodoxy (early and mid-twentieth century). Around 1960 a new wave of denials began, this time within Evangelicalism itself, including the conservative branches of the Restoration Movement.

Typical objections to biblical inerrancy include "Scripture makes no such claim for itself," and "This is a new view created by Protestant Orthodoxy (17th century) or Fundamentalism (20th century)." These objections have been addressed above.

Another objection is this: "Inerrancy requires a mechanical dictation view of inspiration, and thus ignores the human side of Scripture." Though frequently voiced, this objection is totally without foundation. We have already seen that inspiration is not limited to a single mode, and here we affirm that the inerrancy of the biblical writings does not depend upon any particular mode or mechanics of inspiration. The Holy Spirit does not have to "possess" the writers or turn them into machines in order to guarantee the accuracy and truthfulness of their messages.

A main problem with this objection is that it assumes that inerrancy and humanness are incompatible. That is, if the human authors had a genuine part in the writing of Scripture, there must necessarily be errors in it. This is a monstrous fallacy, however. Its most obvious disproof is Jesus Christ, who had a fully human nature but was guilty of neither sin nor error.

Basically this objection confuses the *possibility* of error with the *necessity* for error. It falsely assumes that whatever is by nature human must necessarily err, that humanness requires imperfection.[15] But this is not so. We can grant the possibility of error on the part of fallible men without assuming its necessity. In fact, the possibility of error is the very reason for inspiration. If errors were not possible, inspiration would not have been needed. But if errors were inevitable, then inspiration would have been futile. The very purpose of the Spirit's involvement was to keep men who *could* err from doing so.

Another common objection to inerrancy is this: "The whole issue is irrelevant, since the original autographs have not been preserved." Inerrancy supposedly applies only to the original manuscripts, but these original manuscripts no longer exist. The only Bibles we have are fallible copies and translations, yet they seem to accomplish their purpose quite well. Why, then, should we argue over allegedly inerrant originals which do not even exist?

The basic problem with this objection is that it confuses the original *manuscripts* of the Bible with its original *text*. Although we do not have the original manuscripts, the fact is that we do not *need* them in order to know the content and the nature of the text that was written upon them. Thanks to the science of textual criticism, with relatively few identifiable exceptions we do have the original text of the OT and the NT, and thus we know what the original text of the Bible claims about itself, e.g., in 2 Tim 3:16 and John 10:35. We do not need the original manuscripts in our hands in order to know that these claims appeared in them. Thus we do not need these manuscripts in order to draw conclusions about the nature of the Bible. This applies also to "the Bibles in our hands," since the claims in the original text (as determined by textual criticism and confirmed by Christian apologetics) apply also to copies and translations insofar as they are equivalent to this original text.

D. The Importance of Inerrancy

Why is it important to defend the traditional doctrine of biblical inerrancy? A principal reason is that it is crucial to the whole theological enterprise. If we deny inerrancy, we give up our one objective reference point for truth and sound doctrine. When we accept the Bible as inerrant, it stands before us as an objective standard of truth. The only requirements for sound doctrine are good textual criticism, correct translation, and proper exegesis. But if the Bible is not inerrant, then a more basic requirement intrudes: one must decide which biblical statements are true and thus authoritative for doctrine, and which are tainted with error and thus useless for doctrine.

A practical illustration of this problem is given by Donald McGavran (10-11). He tells of an experience he had as a missionary in India, as teacher of a men's Sunday school class. The men

> . . . were mostly workers in the mission press with an average education of seventh or eighth grade. My predecessor . . . had been a flaming liberal, a graduate of Chicago Divinity School. He had taught this Bible class for the previous seven years.
>
> A turning point in my theological pilgrimage took place one Sunday morning when I asked the class of some fifteen or twenty men, "When you read a biblical passage such as we are studying this morning, what is the first question you ask?" One of the most intelligent workers in the mission press replied immediately, "What is there in this passage that we cannot believe?" What he

meant, of course, was that when we read the passage about Jesus walking on the water, we know instantly that He could not have done that. Consequently, we must understand the passage as an exaggerated or perhaps poetic account of what happened.

I had never before been confronted as bluntly with what the liberal position means to ordinary Christians in multitudinous instances. It shocked me, and I began at that moment to feel that it could not be the truth. Despite all the difficulties, I began to feel my way toward convictions concerning the Bible as infallible revelation. It was God's Word. It was entirely dependable. It was the rule of faith and practice of every true Christian.

The problem is clear. If one denies inerrancy, he is saying there are errors in the Bible—*somewhere*. But how does he know where? There is no comprehensive way to answer this question. Whatever criterion one uses for making such a decision will be subjective; he will wind up believing what he wants to believe, and rejecting what he does not want to believe. The results of such subjectivism will be doctrinal relativism and mystical faith, and for some, agnosticism.

Inerrancy is important because it is, ultimately, the keystone of biblical authority. A keystone is the topmost stone in an arch, the one that holds the others in place. If the keystone is removed, the arch collapses. Inerrancy is like a keystone since without it, the whole structure of biblical authority becomes problematical. History and experience have shown that once inerrancy is surrendered, biblical authority continues to erode because there is no logical stopping place. Denying inerrancy is thus likened to a hole in a dike. The hole keeps getting bigger and bigger as the pressures of unbelief get stronger, until ultimately the whole dike gives way.

If the Bible were no more important than any other book, then it would not really matter whether it is inerrant or not. The need for accuracy in any communication is directly related to its importance. Vacation postcards could contain errors of fact, and little would depend on it. If a road map is wrong it may be inconvenient but not fatal. On the other hand, mistakes in medical prescriptions or in military communications could be matters of life or death. And the biblical message is obviously the most important communication of all, since it is a matter of *eternal* life or *eternal* death. It is a message of such importance that God has not entrusted it to fallible memories and understandings. He has personally made sure that it reaches us without error.

IV. THE AUTHORITY OF THE BIBLE

When we speak of the Bible's *authority*, exactly what do we mean? Authority as such includes the following three elements. 1) It is the right to establish the norms for truth and conduct, i.e., to say "This is true! This is right!" 2) It is the right to demand that others conform their minds, hearts, and lives to these norms, i.e., to say "Believe it! Do it!" 3) It is the right to enforce conformity via the punishment of wrongdoers, i.e., to say "Or else!"

Authority in its fullest sense is a *personal* concept. Persons have authority; objects do not. Those in authority usually assert and implement their authority through words. Words are not impersonal objects; they are extensions of the person who speaks them. They are intimately related to the person. Submission to authority can be measured by the degree to which one respects and accepts the word of the one in authority.

Authority can be either delegated or mediated. It can be delegated by appointing someone to make decisions in the name of the one in authority, or it can be mediated by appointing someone else to bear one's words. Mediated authority is identical with the original authority.

All authority is ultimately in and from the trinitarian God of the Bible—Father, Son, and Holy Spirit. It is grounded ultimately in his very nature as the infinite, eternal, omnipotent, omniscient Sovereign; and it is grounded practically in his work of creation (Ps 24:1-2; 100:3). The authority of Jesus Christ is grounded also in his victorious work of redemption, which establishes him as Lord and King (Matt 28:18-20). In the final analysis God alone has the right to say what is true and what is right.

God chooses to implement his authority through his words. In so doing he may speak directly, or he may mediate his authority through chosen spokesmen, i.e., his prophets and apostles. Here is where the authority of the Bible enters the picture. God exercises his own authority over us through his own words as mediated through inspired apostles and prophets; these authoritative words of God are given to us in the form of an inerrant Bible.

We must remember that mediated authority is equal in every way to the original authority itself. Thus the authority of the Bible is in every way identical with the undiluted, unqualified, absolute authority of God. There is no dilution of authority in Scripture, because God himself is speaking through his spokesmen (see 2 Pet 1:20-21). The written word is a *vehicle* for divine authority: "It is written . . . ." Anything we can say about the authority of God or of Jesus Christ, we can also say about the authority of the Bible. This is why we do not hesitate to say that the Bible is our *only* rule or norm or authority for faith and practice.

Some try to separate the authority of the Bible from the authority of God or of Jesus Christ, declaring that authority is not in a book but in a person. Here is an example: "The New Testament which we accept as our norm does not ask us to accept it as our final authority. It speaks of Jesus the Christ. It proclaims Him as *the* authority. Jesus is Lord" (Norris, 1). We agree, of course, that authority belongs only to God, including God the Son; but we cannot separate his authority from his Word (see Luke 6:46-49). Thus the Bible, being "the very words of God" (Rom 3:2, NIV), carries the full weight of divine authority. The alleged distinction between the personal authority of God or Christ and the authority of the

Bible is a false choice. There is no distinction between them. The only way to deny this is to deny that the Bible is indeed the Word of God.

NOTES ON CHAPTER TWO

[1]This is true because God is *incomprehensible* (*GC*, 312-319).

[2]For a complete list of Greek words related to revelation see Ramm, *Revelation*, 162-163.

[3]Some Evangelicals try to make a case for the availability of saving knowledge through general revelation alone. See Pinnock, *Wideness*; Sanders, *Name*. On the other side see Ronald Nash, *Jesus*; Erickson, *Destiny*. See my treatment of this in *GC*, 340-353.

[4]See my treatment of these texts in *Romans*, 1:131-170, 199-205, 233-245).

[5]See 1 Tim 5:18 and 2 Pet 3:16 for other references to NT writings as "Scripture."

[6]The reason we do not change the English word is that the term that literally means "breathed out" is the term *expired*, which we usually associate with dying or passing away. We simply do not care to say that "all Scripture is given by the expiration of God," or that the Bible is "expired." Thus we stick with inspiration.

[7]We should not forget that "all Scripture" in 2 Tim 3:16 probably includes the NT as well as the OT.

[8]These are good examples of texts which refer to both revelation and inspiration occurring simultaneously.

[9]Some parts of the Bible are dictated, though, notably its predictive prophecies, e.g., Isa 7:14; 9:6. In fact the very concept of word revelation implies dictation; but word revelation should not be confused with verbal inspiration, which applies even to words that are not revealed or dictated.

[10]Recently some have tried to dilute the term "infallible" by redefining it as "certain to accomplish its purpose, competent to accomplish all God intended for it." This may be one connotation of the term, but it is not the only or even most basic one.

[11]Of course, we do not affirm it *just because* the Bible itself teaches it; that would be arguing in a circle. We affirm it, 1) because the Bible does claim it, and 2) because Christian apologetics shows that there is sufficient evidence to prove this claim to be true.

[12]See the excellent treatment of the historical data in Woodbridge, *Authority*. See also my study, "Inerrancy," 70-97.

[13]For these and other quotes from Luther, see Cottrell, "Inerrancy," 79-81. How, then, could Luther say that James contradicts Paul? Because he excluded James from the canon of Scripture!

[14]For these and other references to A. Campbell, see Cottrell, "Inerrancy," 84-89.

[15]This objection assumes that "to err is human" implies "to be human is to err." It thus commits the common fallacy of the false conversion of an A proposition: "All P is Q; therefore all Q is P."

CHAPTER THREE

THE NATURE OF
THE CREATOR-GOD

There are many false gods, but only one true and living God, the God of the Bible (1 Cor 8:4-6). We know much about him from the general revelation present in the natural world, but most of our knowledge of him comes from Scripture. Therein we learn the details of his nature, his works, and his will.

In this chapter we are focusing on the *nature* of God. Who is God? What is he like? What are his *attributes* or characteristics? (GC, 34 43) Asking this question is the same as asking about the *essence* of God, because there is no distinction between his essence and his attributes. God *is* his attributes. We cannot strip away all the attributes of God and wind up with some neutral, attributeless substance. In fact, we cannot take away even one of the divine attributes and still be talking about the true God. For example, a "god" who is not omnipotent or omniscient or gracious is not God at all.

Sometimes the *incommunicable* attributes of God are distinguished from the *communicable* ones. The former are those which belong only to God and in no sense to creatures (e.g., self-existence, infinity). The latter are those which the Creator has shared or communicated in a finite degree with his moral creatures (e.g., love, wisdom). In this context the word "communicate" does not refer to the imparting of information about the attribute, but to the imparting of the attribute itself.

In presenting and explaining the many divine attributes I have grouped them into four categories. First are the attributes which describe the nature of God as he exists in himself, with no necessary reference to any external actions or relationships with his creatures. These are called his nonrelational attributes. Second are the attributes which come to manifestation primarily in his relationships with his creatures as such, both personal (angels, human beings) and nonpersonal. Third are those moral attributes of God that come to manifestation only in relation to his personal or moral creatures, apart from the presence of sin. Fourth are those attributes that are manifested only in response to sin.

I. GOD'S NONRELATIONAL ATTRIBUTES

God's nonrelational attributes are sometimes called his absolute, primary, internal, or passive attributes. They are primary in the sense that they explain the essence of God as he exists in himself. That is, their expression and meaning do not depend upon the existence of created beings, or God's interrelationships with created beings. This does not mean, however, that these attributes can be understood apart from a comparison with creatures. For example, we know the significance of infinity and immutability mostly because of our familiarity with the finite and the mutable. Also, though these attributes apply primarily to God-in-himself, they also in significant ways come into play in God's relations with the world. Thus we confess that the categorization is to some extent arbitrary.

A. God Is Spirit

God in himself, God in his absolute essence, is *spirit*, says Jesus (John 4:24; see *GC*, 222-240). To our understanding God's spirituality means both something positive and something negative. On the positive side spirituality is associated with *life*. The biblical words for spirit can also mean "breath," the breath of life. God is described in Scripture as "the Living God" about 30 times (e.g., Ps 42:2; Isa 37:4; Matt 16:16; Heb 3:12), as the one who "has life in Himself" (John 5:26). This is in contrast both with all false gods, who are lifeless nothings (Deut 4:28; Ps 115:3-7; Jer 10:5,14); and with living creatures, whose life is a gift from God. (See *GC*, ch. 8.)

The other positive aspect of God's spirituality is the fact that he is *personal*. This is probably the most significant thing we can say about the essence of spirit: spiritual beings are persons. Angelic and human spirits are persons; the very idea of spirit implies personhood. Thus to think of God as impersonal or as anything less than personal is a denial of Jesus' affirmation that God is spirit.

Personhood involves four things, all of which apply to the personal God. First, as a person God has *rational consciousness*; he is a thinking being. Thus we can speak of his mind, his knowledge, his understanding, his logic. Second, as a person God has *self-consciousness*, or an awareness of his own conscious existence and identity. His very name is "I AM" (Exod 3:14). Third, God's personhood involves *self-determination*, or free will. This means that anything God does will be freely chosen by him and not imposed upon him from outside himself. Finally, personhood involves *relationships with other persons*. This certainly points to relationships outside himself, both with angels and human beings; but even if other personal beings had never been created, this aspect of personhood would have been expressed within the divine nature itself, since the trinitarian God is actually three persons in eternal interrelationship.

God's spirituality can also be described in negative terms, i.e., as spirit he is *nonmaterial* and *invisible*. The former means his essence is entirely different from anything physical. He does not have any of the innate limitations of material stuff, and should never be thought of as having a physical body (contra Mormonism). Biblical references to God's bodily parts (e.g., face, eyes, ears, feet) are anthropomorphic. This means that God is spoken of figuratively in human terms in order to make his actions and attitudes concrete in our minds.

God as spirit is also invisible (1 Tim 1:17; Col 1:15). This means that his true essence cannot be seen by the eyes of created beings (1 Tim 6:16). God appears to angels in a humanlike form in a kind of permanent theophany (Rev 4), and he has appeared and will again appear to human beings in visible form (e.g., Exod 24:9-11; Rev 22:3-4). But these are deliberate *manifestations* of God, not his true essence (*GC*, 229-233).

God's spirituality is a good example of the point made above, i.e., even though it is an attribute of God as he exists in himself and not in relation to creatures, it is still something that we can *understand* properly only in connection with created beings. This is true especially of its negative aspects.

B. God Is Self-Existent

The second nonrelational attribute of God is his *self-existence* (*GC*, 245-250). This is also called his *aseity*, from the Latin expression *a se*, meaning "from himself, of himself." It literally means that God derives his existence from himself and not from any outside source. His being is not derived from anything and is not dependent on anything; he just *exists*. He is self-sufficient, immortal, indestructible, and independent. He cannot die, he cannot disappear; he cannot self-destruct. All this is in sharp contrast with all created being, which by the very fact of creation owes its existence to something outside itself, namely, the Creator-God. Thus all created being is contingent, whereas God's existence is necessary.

The biblical teaching about God's self-existence begins with his self-revealed name in Exod 3:14, "'I AM WHO I AM.'" Here God tells us the most basic fact about himself, that he is the one who *is*. The verb "to be" serves quite appropriately as his name. In the NT God is described as "incorruptible" (Rom 1:23); he "alone possesses immortality" (1 Tim 6:16). He "has life in Himself" (John 5:26). He does not rely on human hands, as though he needs anything (Acts 17:24-25).

The critical importance of God's self-existence is expressed in Isa 43:12-13, "And I am God. Even from eternity I am He; and there is none who can deliver out of My hand; I act and who can reverse it?" Here we see the total freedom of God to act as he chooses. Because he is not limited by any power or being outside himself, he is free to carry out his purposes without fail. Those who trust in him do not trust in vain, and those who foolishly attempt to oppose him will be crushed.

C. God Is One

At the very heart of the biblical teaching about God is his *oneness* or *unity*. "Hear, O Israel! The LORD is our God, the LORD is one!" (Deut 6:4). This is true in two senses. First, he is one in the sense that he is one indivisible being, not composed of parts. This is the unity of *simplicity* (*GC*, 37-40). He is simple as opposed to compound. Unlike created matter, his essence is not composed of a lot of little parts (atoms) joined together in a divisible whole. He cannot be dissected or divided as if his love were a characteristic of one part of his being with his wrath

being located in another part. All of God's attributes apply equally to his whole being. Nor can he be divided in the sense that somehow one part of his being can be "cut off" and spatially separated from the rest, as in the case of those who have adopted the pagan idea that the human soul is a little "part" of God.

At the same time we must avoid another pagan idea, i.e., the philosophical concept of the *absolute* simplicity of God. This is the idea that God is *one* in a totally undifferentiated sense. Some Christians have uncritically accepted this idea and have wrongly concluded that there are no real distinctions among the various attributes of God. As they see it, in our minds these attributes may differ, but in God's nature everything is one indivisible and indistinguishable essence. His righteousness is his goodness; his mercy is his omnipotence; his wisdom is his sovereignty; his love is his wrath. This often leads to the merging of all of God's attributes into just one main attribute, usually love.

But this is a false view of God. The unity of simplicity rules out divisions within God's nature, but not distinctions. In fact, as we shall see later, there are times when certain attributes of God stand in practical opposition to one another. Specifically, the entrance of sin into God's creation causes his holiness and his love to exist in tension within himself. Also, as we shall see, in the next main section, the unity of simplicity does not rule out distinctions among the three persons of the Trinity.

The other sense in which God is one is the basic truth that there is but one and only one God; this is called the unity of *singularity* (*GC*, 390-419). This is no doubt the main point of Deut 6:4, the words of which are echoed by Paul: "There is no God but one" (1 Cor 8:4); he is "the only God" (1 Tim 1:17). There is no one else in the category of deity at all, whether equal to or inferior to him. This is the basis of the first commandment: "I am the LORD your God, who brought you out of the land of Egypt, out of the house of slavery. You shall have no other gods before [besides] me" (Exod 20:2-3). "I am the LORD, and there is no other; besides Me there is no God" (Isa 45:5; see Deut 32:39; Isa 43:10-11; 44:6,8; Joel 2:27). The practical application is stated by Jesus in Matt 4:10, "You shall worship the LORD your God, and serve Him only." It is the purpose, the duty, and the privilege of every creature to honor the Creator and worship him and glorify him as the one true God. We should make it our life's sole aim to do just this.

D. God Is Three: The Trinity

God is *one*, but he is also *three*. He is one and three at the same time. This is the doctrine of the *Trinity* (*GRe*, ch. 3). There is no biblical term that actually means "trinity"; e.g., this is not the connotation of the KJV word "Godhead" nor of the Greek terms which it represents. We do find the *concept* of the Trinity in Scripture, however.

Exactly what is this concept? The classical Christian doctrine is usually summed up thus, that God is *three persons* who share *one essence* or substance.

Christians have been explaining the Trinity in terms of three persons ever since Tertullian in the early third century. Though some disagree, it is best to understand "person" as a thinking, willing center of consciousness. That God is *three* persons means that within the one divine nature are three individual centers of consciousness. Each of the persons is fully conscious of himself as distinct from the other two and as existing in eternal interpersonal relationship with the other two. We call these three persons the Father, the Son, and the Holy Spirit.

Though they are three, these persons are nevertheless one God. We have already explained that God possesses the unity of simplicity, in that he consists of one undivided essence. Whatever the concept of the Trinity means, it does not mean that the essence of God is somehow divided into three distinct units. Also, God possesses the unity of singularity, meaning that no other God exists besides the one true God; this is monotheism. Whatever the concept of the Trinity means, it does not mean that there are three separate Gods; this would be tritheism.

Within the context of the Trinity, that God is one means that the three centers of consciousness share one and the same divine essence or being or substance. Note: this is not just saying that they share the same *kind* of essence (which they do), but that they also share the same specific essence. Some think it is improper to speak of God's "essence"; but the very fact that God *exists* means that he is a *being* and thus has a kind of essence or substance. To say that Father, Son, and Spirit are one in essence means that the totality of divine substance, the whole of "whatever it is to be God," belongs to each of them. The main implication of this is that each is equally divine. In whatever sense the Father is divine, so also are the Son and the Holy Spirit. All the attributes of divinity belong equally to each of the three. It cannot be otherwise since they share the *same* essence.

Upon what is the doctrine of the Trinity based? It is not revealed in general revelation, but only in the special revelation of the Bible. Within the Bible, it is not derived from the OT, but from the NT. The OT has some hints of the Trinity, such as the plural "Let *Us* make man" in Gen 1:26 (see 3:22; 11:7), the angel of Yahweh phenomena, the incident regarding Abraham and Sodom in Gen 18:1–19:21, and the plural form of the OT word for "God" (*Elohim*). But only in the NT does the doctrine of the Trinity become an inescapable conclusion.

The one specific fact that makes it impossible for us to avoid the doctrine of the Trinity is the NT teaching about the deity of Christ. If Scripture did not portray Jesus as both distinct from the Father and yet as himself God in the flesh, the question of the Trinity may never have arisen. The same is true to a lesser extent of the Bible's portrayal of the Holy Spirit as a divine person. (This data will be examined later.)

In addition to the teaching about the deity of Jesus and of the Spirit are several passages linking the three persons together in a formula-like way that emphasizes their essential equality. The baptismal formula in Matt 28:19 is the most well known and most influential of these: "Go therefore and make disciples of all the nations, baptizing them in the name of the Father and the Son and the Holy Spirit." Another is the benediction in 2 Cor 13:14, "The grace of the Lord Jesus Christ, and the love of God, and the fellowship of the Holy Spirit, be with you all." Another is the reference to the threefold source of spiritual gifts in 1 Cor 12:4-6, "Now there are varieties of gifts, but the same Spirit. And there are varieties of ministries, and the same Lord. There are varieties of effects, but the same God."[1] See also 1 Pet 1:2, which says that the saints are chosen "according to the foreknowledge of God the Father, by the sanctifying work of the Spirit, to obey Jesus Christ and be sprinkled with His blood." All of these passages show that Christians are redemptively related not just to an abstract deity but to the three persons who are the one true and living God.

Other trinitarian texts are Rom 15:30; 1 Cor 6:11; 2 Cor 1:21-22; Gal 4:6; Eph 2:18; 3:14-17; 5:18-20; 1 Thess 5:18-19; 2 Thess 2:13; 1 John 4:13-14; Jude 20-21; Rev 1:4-5.

It is obvious that most of our knowledge of the Trinity is based on God's relation to the world, especially in connection with the work of redemption. So why are we discussing this subject under the heading of God's *nonrelational* attributes? Is God's threeness something that manifests itself as he relates to the world, or is it a real aspect of God-in-himself? Actually it is both, as Christians have long affirmed.

This is seen in the common distinction between the *ontological* Trinity and the *economic* Trinity. The so-called economic Trinity involves the various relationships and works of the different persons of the Trinity toward the world. For example, God the Father foreknows and chooses (Rom 8:29; 1 Pet 1:1-2). The Father also sends the Son and the Spirit; he is never the one sent (John 5:37; 14:26; 20:21). On the other hand, only God the Son became incarnate, lived among us as a human being, died on the cross, was raised from the dead, and is seated at the right hand of the Father as our only High Priest and mediator. In turn, God the Spirit is responsible for regenerating and sanctifying work (1 Pet 1:1-2), beginning on the day of Pentecost (Acts 2:38). He also is the agent of inspiration (2 Pet 1:21), including speaking in tongues (Acts 2:4).

But in addition to the distinct redemptive works through which the three divine persons relate themselves to the world, the threeness of God also exists in the divine essence in and of itself totally apart from such relationships. This is the ontological Trinity. This intradivine threeness is the basis for satisfying and loving relationships among the three persons from and for all eternity.

Do we know any details about the relationships that exist within the ontological Trinity? How much of what we are told about the three persons' relationships to the world can be projected back into God-in-himself? Traditional trinitarian theology concludes that the Father-Son relationship is part of the eternal divine essence, and thus speaks of the eternal Sonship of Christ. That Jesus is the "only begotten Son" (John 3:16) has led to the notion that the Father eternally begets the Son (though no one really knows what this would mean). That the Holy Spirit "proceeds from the Father" (John 15:26)—and perhaps also from the Son—has also been regarded as a mysterious eternal relationship. This has led to the further conclusion that the Son is eternally *subordinate* to the Father, and the Spirit is eternally subordinate to the Father (and perhaps to the Son).

In my judgment all of these ways of speaking should be applied to the economic Trinity only. In other words, the Logos (the second person of the Trinity) is not eternally begotten and not eternally the Son, but is begotten and becomes the Son in the incarnation. The Spirit "proceeds" from the Father and Son when he is sent on Pentecost (Acts 2:33). The relationships of subordination apply only to the roles of the three persons in their work of redemption. The Logos, though eternally equal with the Father in essence and authority, voluntarily and uniquely takes on a subordinate role in his office of Redeemer. This is how we explain passages such as John 4:34; 14:28; and 1 Cor 11:3.

We must be on guard against heretical denials of the doctrine of the Trinity. Some deny the oneness of God and affirm polytheism. This is common among pagan religions and is true of Mormonism and the original Armstrongism. Others deny the threeness of God, saying there is only one truly divine person. An example is fourth-century Arianism, which taught that Jesus is not truly God but is a created being. Jehovah's Witnesses are modern-day Arians. Another denial of God's threeness is any form of unitarianism, which says there is only one divine person. One kind of unitarianism is called modalism, which says that in his inner nature there are no distinctions within God. Only in his external relations with his creatures does God *assume* different modes or roles in order to make himself known and accomplish his purposes among men. These modes are successive, not simultaneous. For example, In OT times the one divine person revealed himself as Father; then he became incarnate as the Son; now he relates to his creatures as the Spirit. A modern example of modalism is the "Oneness movement" among certain Pentecostal bodies, also known as the "Jesus only" Pentecostals.[2]

The doctrine of the Trinity is filled with mystery. That God is one and three at the same time is beyond our ability to understand completely. We should never think it is absurd or contradictory, however. That would be true only if we think that God is one and three *in the same sense*. But this is not the case. He is **one** in one sense, i.e., one essence; and he is **three** in another sense, i.e., three persons.

E. God Is Infinite

Another attribute of God-in-himself is *infinity* (see *GC*, ch 6). To say that God is infinite means that he is nonfinite, unlimited, unbounded. This is not meant in a physical or mathematical sense, as if God were infinitely large or as if he extended infinitely into space. It means basically that God is not subject to the built-in limitations of created beings. Finite beings, for example, are by nature subject to certain restrictions of time and space; the infinite God is not. Finite beings are capable of inconsistencies, errors, and moral imperfections; the infinite God is not. Finite beings are limited in their knowledge and power; the infinite God is not.

As these examples illustrate, infinity is an attribute that qualifies other attributes of God. God is holy, and his holiness is infinite; God is love, and his love is infinite. Likewise we may speak of his infinite wisdom, his infinite mercy, and his infinite glory.

This does not mean that God's infinity is absolute. Two kinds of limits apply to him. First, though God is not limited by anything *outside* himself, he is limited by his *own nature* in the sense that he cannot do anything that is inconsistent with his attributes. For example, since he is a loving God, he cannot do anything that contradicts love. The second kind of limitation is self-limitation, which exists not by nature but by God's own free choice. For example, when God makes a promise he limits himself by binding himself to keep that promise.

The idea of an infinite God is not found outside the teachings of the Bible. All false gods are finite gods. A modern example is the god of process philosophy, who is pictured as being in the process of maturing and developing along with the world as he is influenced by the world. Some find the concept of a finite God to be comforting since it helps them to explain the existence of what they consider to be flaws in the creation. If God himself is imperfect, how can we expect his world to be perfect? But such an easy explanation of the world's ills is too heavy a price to pay for the loss of God's infinity. How can we trust a finite God for salvation? How can we consider him to be a worthy object of worship? But we do not have to pay this price, because the true God, the God of the Bible, is indeed infinite.

F. God Is Eternal

An aspect of God's infinity is that he is unlimited with regard to time: he is *eternal* (see *GC*, 250-264). He is "the Everlasting God" (Isa 40:28), "the eternal God" (Rom 16:26), the eternal and immortal King (1 Tim 1:17). As eternal God he transcends the limitations of time in two senses: quantitatively and qualitatively.

The first and most obvious way in which God is eternal is that by his very nature he has no beginning and no end; he always has existed in the eternal past and always will exist in the eternal future. That is, God's eternity involves endless quantitative duration. This is simply a corollary of his self-existence; since it is his very nature to exist, he always has existed and will always continue to exist.

Some are reluctant to apply this kind of eternity to God because it seems to involve what can be called "eternal time," or eternal endurance along a time line. They say that time in the sense of a duration of successive moments involving past, present, and future is part of the created order and thus does not apply to God himself. Thus they reject a quantitative concept of divine eternity.

I disagree with this approach to God and time, basically because the Bible frequently portrays God's eternity in terms of endless quantitative duration. He has existed "from everlasting" (Ps 93:2), and he "lives forever" (Isa 57:15; see Rev 4:9-10; 10:6; 15:7). He is "from everlasting to everlasting" (Ps 41:13). "Before the mountains were born or You gave birth to the earth and the world, even from everlasting to everlasting, You are God" (Ps 90:2; see Ps 102:25-27). God is the one "who is and who was and who is to come" (Rev 1:4,8; 4:8). He is the first and the last, the Alpha and the Omega, the beginning and the end (Isa 44:6; Rev 1:8; 21:6). This is why "with the Lord one day is as a thousand years, and a thousand years as one day" (2 Pet 3:8; see Ps 90:4). This does not mean that all moments of time are the same or simultaneous with God. It just means that to one who is eternal, one finite period of time is no more significant than any other finite period.

The second way in which God is eternal is that his relation to time is qualitatively different from that of created beings. All creatures exist in an ever-changing "now," and the immediate consciousness of personal creatures (angels and human beings) is bound to this now-moment. We can remember some of the past and make predictions about the future, but we are bound by the flow of time in that our consciousness is locked into the now. This is not true of God, however. In a significant way he is outside the flow of time and is not bound by its limitations.

I say "in a significant way" because I do not believe that God is outside the flow of time in every sense. I have already suggested that God *exists* in an eternal duration of successive moments, which means that in some sense the passing of time is part of the divine nature in and of itself, totally apart from creation. In saying this I am rejecting an aspect of classical theism and even of much Christian theology known as the *timelessness* of God, or the eternal simultaneity of the divine nature and works. This is the idea that with God there is no succession of moments or even a consciousness of succession of moments. According to this view God's being, all of his acts, and all of his knowledge coexist as one eternal **Now**, in a single, simultaneous present. There is no past or future, before or after with God. Though his acts appear on a historical continuum from our perspective, for God himself all his acts, as well as the contents of his consciousness, are frozen in a single, unvarying, eternal simultaneity.

In my judgment this idea of God's eternity is an extreme view based on pagan philosophy rather than on biblical teaching. Everything Scripture tells us about God indicates that he does experience the passing of time in an eternal succession of moments. He exists and acts in the present moment. From God's own perspective some of his acts (such as the creation) are in the unalterable past, while some (such as the final judgment) are yet to come and even God waits for their time to arrive.

What *do* we mean, then, when we say that God is eternal in a qualitative sense? In what sense *is* he outside the flow of time, and therefore not bound by its limitations? Biblical teaching shows that this is true in the sense that his *consciousness* (his knowledge) is not bound by time. Though he exists and acts in the ongoing present (not in a single eternal present), and though he is conscious of existing and acting in this ongoing present, in his consciousness he stands *above* the flow of time and *sees* the past and the future of his creatures just as clearly and certainly as if they were present.

Exactly how this can be true we may never understand. We must not deny it, however, simply because we cannot understand it. Do we suppose we can understand everything about the infinite God? Sometimes, as in this case, we must simply *affirm* that something is true, just because the Bible affirms it. In this case the fact that God's knowledge transcends time is taught in Isa 40–48. Over and over God's claim to be the one true God is here based on his exclusive ability to know the whole scope of history at once, to see it from beginning to end in one and the same moment. See Isa 41:21-26; 42:8-9; 44:6-8; 46:9-11; 48:3-7.

In summary, God is eternal in the sense that his existence has no beginning and no end, and in the sense that his consciousness transcends the now-moment of time and embraces the whole of creaturely history in a single act of knowing.

G. God Is Righteous

The theme of God's righteousness is found throughout the Bible (*GRe*, ch. 4). "The LORD is righteous" (Ps 129:4); "the LORD is righteous in all His ways" (Ps 145:17). "For the LORD is righteous, He loves righteousness" (Ps 11:7); "the heavens declare His righteousness" (Ps 50:6). Jesus is the "Righteous One" (Acts 3:14), and he himself prays to his "righteous Father" (John 17:25).

In biblical terminology "justice" and "righteousness" are synonyms. This can be confusing to those who use the English language, since these two English words have quite different connotations. We tend to equate righteousness with holiness, and justice with fair treatment before the law. But in Scripture the relevant Hebrew and Greek nouns can be rendered as either "righteousness" or "justice," and the adjectives as either "righteous" or "just."

Considered as an attribute of God, what is divine righteousness? A common traditional approach is that the righteousness (or justice) of God is that stern aspect of his moral nature that demands obedience to his law and that requires him to judge people impartially in accordance with their response to the law. Since all have disobeyed the law, his righteousness requires him to punish them. Righteousness is thus viewed mostly as something negative and punitive.

A more recent view, popular especially in liberal circles, is that righteousness is actually a positive and saving aspect of God's nature. It is equated with God's faithfulness to his covenant relationships with his people, the main emphasis being not on the demands of his law but on his keeping of his promises. Thus the main expression of God's righteousness is the salvation and deliverance of his people from bondage and oppression.

When we examine the way in which the Bible uses the terms for righteousness/justice, we see that both of these views are wrong in their exclusiveness and in their failure to express the precise meaning of the biblical terms. This precise meaning can be stated thus: righteousness as such is *conformity to the appropriate norm or standard*. An object (such as a weight, Lev 19:36) or a person is called righteous if it or he conforms to the relevant norm. For human beings the proper norm is the will or law of God; thus a person is called righteous if he is innocent before the law, if his life conforms to the standard of God's law.[3]

The concept of righteousness as conformity to a norm does not disappear when the biblical terms are used for God. In fact, it means exactly this. That God is righteous means that all his actions conform perfectly to the proper standard or norm. What is this norm? It is not external to himself, but consists of his own eternally perfect nature. Thus divine righteousness is that consistency or constancy in God by which all his actions are faithful to the eternally perfect norm of his own nature. Anything God does will automatically be in accord with his own perfections.

A key word is *consistency*: that God is righteous means he is always consistent with himself; he is always true to himself or in perfect harmony with himself. Another key word is *faithfulness*: that he is righteous means that he is always faithful to himself and to his own purposes (Deut 32:4; Ps 143:1). He is not fickle in what he wills to do as if somehow his will were detached from his nature. One implication of this is that God will always be true to his word, i.e., to his announced purposes, promises, and warnings. Thus it is true that the righteous God will always be faithful in his covenant relationships, both to bless and to punish in accord with the terms of the covenant.

Thus we can see that neither of the two views of the righteousness of God explained above can stand alone. Both are implications of divine righteousness. God as righteous must be true to his nature. Because he is by nature holy, he must punish sin; because he is by nature loving, he must save sinners. Because he is righteous, he must do both!

We must note, though, that the punishment of sin does not come from God's righteousness as such; it comes from his holy wrath. But he *must* apply his holy wrath and retribution *because* he is righteous (see Deut 32:1-43; Ps 7:11; 9:3-6; 11:4-7; 97:1-6; Isa 10:21-23; 41:1-2). Likewise, salvation from sin does not come from the righteousness of God as such; it comes from his loving grace. But he *must* provide this loving grace just *because* he is righteous. See Ps 24:3-5; 31:1; 36:10; 40:9-10; 51:14; 71:2; 82:3-4; Isa 1:27; 30:18; 41:10; 45:21-25; 51:5-6.

Knowing that God is righteous is very important to us creatures who are asked to trust him. Because he is righteous, i.e., because he acts with perfect consistency, especially in keeping his word, we *can* trust him; we *can* rely on him and put our utter confidence in him. We know that whatever he does will be right.

H. God Is Immutable

The final nonrelational attribute of God is *immutability* (GRe, ch 8). To say that God is immutable is to say that he does not and cannot change. This is what we would expect of a being who is self-existent and eternal. He is the great "I AM" (present tense, Exod 3:14), the one whose identity remains eternally the same. The heavens and the earth "will perish, but You endure; and all of them will wear out like a garment; like clothing You will change them and they will be changed. But You are the same, and Your years will not come to an end" (Ps 102:25-27). "For I, the LORD, do not change" (Mal 3:6). Hebrews 13:8 says of God the Son, "Jesus Christ is the same yesterday and today and forever."

Some do not include immutability in their concept of God. For instance, process philosophy posits a deity who is in the process of development and growth along with the world. On the other hand, some go too far in the other direction and think of God as absolutely unchanging in every possible way. This is true of classical theism, a view that has been adopted by many Christians.

In classical theism the assumption is that any movement or change in God would have to be toward perfection; and since God is by nature already perfect, no change or movement is necessary or even possible. This view excludes any changes in God's knowledge and in his emotional states, resulting in the idea that God feels no emotions of any kind, such as anger or grief or suffering or joy. In other words, God is *impassible* (literally, incapable of suffering).

This view goes hand in hand with the extreme view of God's eternity discussed above, i.e., the concept of a completely timeless God. If everything is an eternally "frozen present" to God, then not only his being but also his knowledge and even his actions are in fact eternally the same. God is thus seen as static, immobile, rigid, impassive, apathetic, and nonreactive.

Many rightly believe, as I do, that this extreme view is contrary to the biblical picture of God as a living and loving being who enters into this world's history in mercy and judgment. Rather than interpreting immutability in an absolute sense, we should say that God is unchanging in some very important ways, but not in others. In summary, he is unchanging in his essence and character, but may change in his states of consciousness and in his activities.

Most would agree that God is unchanging in his essence and character. He is eternally enduring (Ps 102:25-27), incorruptible (Rom 1:23), and immortal (1 Tim 6:16). As Packer sums it up, "He does not grow older. His life does not wax or wane. He does not gain new powers, nor lose those that He once had. He does not mature or develop. He does not get stronger, or weaker, or wiser, as time goes by" (69). He always has been and always will be holy, loving, and truthful. He is unchanging in his purposes and his commitments; he will ever be true to his word and to his promises. Thus the bottom line of immutability is the *faithfulness* of God (Ps 33:4; 119:90; Lam 3:23; Heb 10:23). He is our *Rock* (Deut 32:4; Ps 18:2; 62:2; Isa 26:4).

But if we take biblical teaching seriously, we must say that changes do occur in God's consciousness and activities. Regarding his states of consciousness, God experiences the succession of moments taking place in his own history and in ours; he acts, is acted upon, and reacts. He experiences different feelings or emotions in response to events in the history of his free-will creatures. Especially he experiences *suffering* in response to our sin and in the events of his incarnation, particularly the cross. God the Father suffered to see what the Son had to endure, and God the Son suffered in the enduring of it.

Also, changes occur in God's activities. This simply means that God's actions upon our world are time oriented, and that he is not doing all of them at the same eternal moment (contra the concept of simultaneity). For example, for a period of time God was engaged in the work of creation, but at a particular point he ceased this activity (Gen 2:3) and began something else. His revealing work with Moses began and ended long before he began and ended the same work with Jeremiah. There are works which God has not even begun yet (e.g., the final judgment). God varies his works according to his purposes and according to the "fullness of time."

These points about the immutability of God are all exemplified in the incarnation. When the Logos became flesh (John 1:14), God's essence and character did not change. The divine Logos, in becoming Jesus of Nazareth, did not undergo alterations in his nature; he did not give up any of his divine attributes or "divest himself of his deity." But God the Logos did experience other kinds of changes in the incarnation. He began to experience firsthand what it means to live as a human being. He performed mighty miracles at specific points in time. He experienced the emotions that come from being rejected both by men (Isa 53:3) and by God (Matt 27:46). He experienced all the sufferings of Calvary, and all the joys of triumph over sin, Satan, death, and hell.

II. ATTRIBUTES SEEN IN GOD'S RELATIONS WITH CREATURES AS SUCH

We turn now to God's relational attributes. Most of these are present within God-in-himself even apart from his relations with his creatures, but they all become manifest primarily through such relations. These attributes are manifest in God's relations to created beings in general, whether animate or inanimate, personal or nonpersonal, sinful or not. They are manifested especially in connection with God's works of creation and providence, which will be discussed in the next chapter.

A. God Is Transcendent

The word "transcendent" comes from a Latin term meaning "to climb over, to go beyond." It describes a relationship between two entities, one of which "transcends" or goes beyond the other. In theology it describes the most basic relationship between God and his creatures. God as Creator transcends all created beings in the sense that he is distinct from them in the very essence of his being. God is "beyond" the universe and every created entity.

This "beyondness" of God is an ontological concept, not a spatial one; i.e., God's transcendence does not mean he is somehow spatially "up yonder" or "outside" his creation, as if theoretically we could travel to the far distant edge of the universe, take one step beyond it, and find God. Rather, it has to do with the essence of his being, which is not only spirit but *uncreated* spirit. The fact that God alone is uncreated makes him qualitatively different from all created reality, both spiritual and material. His essence is different not only from created physical stuff but also from created spirits (human and angelic). There is an ontological gulf between God and his creatures. God is *transcendent* (*GC*, ch 5).

This distinction between the Creator and his creatures is the most basic of all distinctions. As the incorruptible and immortal God (Rom 1:23; 1 Tim 6:16), he alone is worthy of worship. The height of folly and the depth of sin are to worship and serve some creature rather than the Creator (Rom 1:25). Because of this ontological distinction between God and creatures, there is no sense in which any human being can ever be thought of as divine or can ever become divine, sharing the very essence of God.[4]

The biblical term for "transcendent" is "holy," which in the original languages means "to be separate, distinct, set apart." It is used of God in two senses. First, God is separate from sin and from sinful creatures; this is his *ethical* holiness. Second, God is separate from the creation as such; this is his *ontological* holiness, which is seen in Isa 6:3, "Holy, Holy, Holy, is the LORD of hosts, the whole earth is full of His glory" (see Rev 4:8). Likewise Moses declared, "Who is like You among the gods, O LORD? Who is like You, majestic in holiness, awesome in praises, working wonders?" (Exod 15:11). He is "the Holy One of Jacob" (Isa 29:23). See Rev 15:4. This latter sense is what we are calling transcendence; in this book we are using the word "holy" only in the ethical sense.

B. God Is Sovereign

A second relational attribute is divine *sovereignty* (*GRu*, ch. 7), which has to do with the way God rules over his creation. God's sovereignty may be concisely summed up as *absolute lordship*. It is equivalent to kingship or dominion: God has absolute dominion over all things; he is the God of gods, King of kings, and Lord of lords (Deut 10:17; 1 Tim 6:15-16; Rev 19:16). He is "the LORD Most High over all the earth" (Ps 97:9), the "great King over all the earth" (Ps 47:2). He rules over all flesh (Jer 32:27), all mankind (Dan 4:25,32), and all nations (Ps 22:28). "God reigns over the nations, God sits on His holy throne" (Ps 47:8).

A biblical term specifically equivalent to sovereignty is "kingdom," the basic meaning of which is "king*ship*, lordship, rule, dominion." God's sovereignty is naturally and properly understood in terms of kingship. "The LORD reigns!" (1 Chr 16:31; Ps 93:1-2; 96:10; 97:1; 99:1; Isa 52:7). "The LORD has established His throne in the heavens, and His sovereignty rules over all" (Ps 103:19).

Sovereignty is the same as lordship. Basically the term "lord" signifies the owner of something (e.g., a land*lord*). An owner has the inherent right to control and to use his possessions as he sees fit. To say that God is the sovereign lord over all things means that he owns everything, which gives him the right to do what he chooses with it all. Moses says, "Behold, to the LORD your God belong heaven and the highest heavens, the earth and all that is in it" (Deut 10:14). Psalm 24:1 echoes this: "The earth is the LORD's, and all it contains, the world, and those who dwell in it." "All the earth is Mine," says the LORD (Exod 19:5). "Whatever is under the whole heaven is Mine" (Job 41:11). This includes all people as well as all things.

God's sovereign rights of ownership are based on the fact that he alone is the Creator; all else is his creation and thus his possession, including the whole human race (Ps 24:1-2; 89:11; 95:5). The fact of creation is the ground of divine sovereignty.

There is a serious disagreement in the Christian world as to the exact meaning of divine sovereignty. Some, especially Calvinists, equate sovereignty with *causation*, and say that the only way for God to be sovereign is if he is the sole, ultimate cause or originator of everything that takes place, including events in the natural world as well as human decisions. Since God must be the ultimate cause of even human decisions, there is no truly free will. If a creature were truly free in the sense that he were able to originate an action, then God would not be the sole originator of all things and therefore would not be sovereign, says this view. He would be placed in the position of having to *react* to something outside himself. But a sovereign God must always act, and never react. Nothing about God—his knowledge, his decisions, his acts—can be conditioned on anything outside himself. Thus everything that comes to pass is part of God's one original plan, his eternal decree, which is both all-embracing and efficacious. The history of creation is simply God's sovereign enactment of this plan or decree. (See *GRu*, ch. 5.)

In my judgment, equating divine sovereignty with omnicausality is arbitrary and antibiblical. Instead of causation, the key word for sovereignty is *control*. God is sovereign in the sense that he is *in control of* every event that takes place among creatures, whether he actually causes it (which is often the case), or simply permits it to happen (instead of preventing it, which he could do if he so chose). Either way God is "in charge"; he is in full control over his creation; he is sovereign.

C. God Is Omnipotent

To say that God is *omnipotent* (*GC*, 292-305) is simply to say that he is all-powerful, that he is infinite or unlimited in his power. This attribute of God is abundantly emphasized in the Bible. "God is exalted in His power" (Job 36:22). "Power belongs to God" (Ps 62:11); "the LORD on high is mighty" (Ps 93:4). "Be exalted, O LORD, in Your strength; we will sing and praise Your power" (Ps 21:13). One OT name for God is *Shaddai*, which is translated "the Almighty" (e.g., Gen 49:25; Num 24:4; Job 40:2; Ps 91:1). Nine times it appears as *El*

Shaddai, "the all-powerful God" or "God Almighty" (e.g., Gen 17:1; 35:11; Exod 6:3; Ezek 10:5). The NT equivalent is *pantokrator*, "the Almighty" (2 Cor 6:18; Rev 1:8; 11:17; 15:3; 16:7,14; 19:6,15; 21:22).

Omnipotence basically means that God has an unlimited reservoir of power by which he is able to do anything he could ever want to do, even if he does not choose to do it. As Jesus said, "With God all things are possible" (Matt 19:26; see Gen 18:14; Luke 1:37). God declares, "Behold, I am the LORD, the God of all flesh; is anything too difficult for Me?" (Jer 32:27; see Num 11:23). After being thoroughly chastened by God, "Job answered the LORD and said, 'I know that You can do all things, and that no purpose of Yours can be thwarted'" (Job 42:1-2). "Our God is in the heavens; He does whatever He pleases" (Ps 115:3; see Ps 135:6).

We do affirm that the power of the omnipotent God is unlimited, but there is one qualification: Omnipotence does not mean that God can do any *conceivable* thing, since there are some things the Bible itself says God *cannot* do. For example, he "cannot lie" (Titus 1:2; see 1 Sam 15:29; Heb 6:18); he "cannot be tempted by evil" (Jas 1:13). But is God's "inability" to do such things an expression of *weakness*? Hardly! In fact, the opposite is true: the *ability* to do these things would be an expression of weakness. These are negative acts, not positive ones; to do them would imply a lack of strength. That he cannot do them is actually an affirmation of his power.

Another way to approach the things that God cannot do is to point out that they are contrary to the very nature of God, and obviously omnipotence does not include the requirement that God must be able to contradict his own nature. God cannot sin or annihilate himself, since this would be contrary to his very nature. This is also the point with pseudoproblems such as whether God can make a square circle, or make a rock so big that he cannot move it. Such problems involve logical contradictions[5] and are contrary to the nature of God as a rational being.

We have included God's innate omnipotence in the category of relational attributes because it comes to manifestation in his relationships with the world. It was first manifested in the mighty act of creation itself: "Ah Lord GOD! Behold, You have made the heavens and the earth by Your great power and by Your outstretched arm! Nothing is too difficult for You" (Jer 32:17). God's "eternal power" is "clearly seen, being understood through what has been made" (Rom 1:20). Also, God's omnipotence is shown to us every day in his ongoing providential preservation and care of the creation. He "upholds all things by the word of His power" (Heb 1:3). Finally, he has shown us his power by being able to work out his plan of redemption, from preparation through Israel, to accomplishment by Jesus Christ, to application through the church.

D. God Is Wise

Having power, even absolute power, is not necessarily a virtue if one does not know how to use it for good purposes. To do this, one must have *wisdom*.

Wisdom is the ability to choose the best possible end, and then to choose the best possible means of achieving that end. That is, it is the ability to make the right decisions when judging between two different courses of action.

The Bible teaches that God is all-wise (*GRu*, 285-289). He is "the only wise God" (Rom 16:27); "wisdom and power belong to Him" (Dan 2:20). "Oh, the depth of the riches both of the wisdom and knowledge of God! How unsearchable are His judgments and unfathomable His ways" (Rom 11:33). "He is mighty in strength of understanding" (Job 36:5; see Isa 40:14; Rom 11:34).

God's wisdom is manifested in his work of creation. "O LORD, how many are Your works! In wisdom You have made them all" (Ps 104:24). "The LORD by wisdom founded the earth, by understanding He established the heavens" (Prov 3:19; see 8:27-31). "It is He who made the earth by His power, who established the world by His wisdom" (Jer 10:12).

God's wisdom is seen also in his works of providence, especially in his ability to use the forces of nature and the free decisions of human beings to carry out his purposes. This enables him to bring good results out of bad circumstances, and to make us this promise: "And we know that God causes all things to work together for good to those who love God, to those who are called according to His purpose" (Rom 8:28). This gives us complete confidence in the wisdom of God. It indicates that God is not frustrated or thwarted by any contingency, either from sin-corrupted nature or from the evil hearts and hands of men. Even pain and suffering may be harnessed for good results by the all-wise Ruler.

God's wisdom is supremely made known in his works of redemption. Jesus Christ and his cross are "the power of God and the wisdom of God" (1 Cor 1:24; see 2:7-9). The gospel proclaimed by the church demonstrates "the manifold wisdom of God" (Eph 3:10).

If we truly believe God is wise, we will trust his purposes in creation; we will believe that a world with free-will creatures is the best possible world, even though such creatures have the ability to sin. If we believe that God is wise, we will not attempt to criticize or judge what he brings to pass or allows to happen, especially in view of Rom 8:28. Only someone who is wiser than God has a right to sit in judgment upon his providence.

[The only wise response to an all-wise providence is complete trust in the God who makes all things work together for good.] His wisdom, even more than his power, engenders such trust. If God were merely omnipotent, we would have more reason to be afraid of him than to put our confidence in him. But he is both powerful and wise (Dan 2:20). Packer says, "Wisdom without power would be pathetic, a broken reed; power without wisdom would be merely frightening; but in God boundless wisdom and endless power are united, and this makes him utterly worthy of our fullest trust" (81).

E. God Is Good

A childhood prayer begins, "God is great, God is good." Scripture indeed testifies that *goodness* is part of the very nature of God (*GRu*, 289-295; *GRe*, 322-323). When Moses made his bold request to see God's glory, God replied, "I Myself will make all My goodness pass before you" (Exod 33:18-19; see Mark 10:18). "Good and upright is the LORD" (Ps 25:8). "The LORD is good" (Ps 100:5; Nahum 1:7). "You are good and do good," declares Ps 119:68.

What does it mean to say "God is good"? For one thing, it means that he meets the standards of *excellence*; he is absolutely perfect in every way. Also, it means he is *morally* good. Third, it means that he is *desirable*, the proper object of desire ("O taste and see that the LORD is good," Ps 34:8). But mostly, that God is good means that his basic attitude toward his creation is one of *benevolence*, kindness, and good will. He is kind and friendly toward his creatures; he wills and desires to bless them and to do good for them. He is good *to us*. He has a generous spirit, a spirit of giving and sharing and blessing, a spirit of affection and good will. He cares for the welfare of his creatures.

God's goodness (kindness, benevolence) is directed not just toward human beings but toward the whole of creation. He supplies rain just "for His world" (Job 37:13; 38:25-27). "The LORD is good to all, and His mercies are over all His works. . . . The eyes of all look to You, and You give them their food in due time. You open your hand and satisfy the desire of every living thing" (Ps 145:9,15-16). God cares for birds and flowers, says Jesus (Matt 6:26,28; 10:29).

Though the whole universe basks in the goodness of God, the bulk of his kindness and caring is poured out upon mankind. When directed toward human beings, it is called *love*. In his love the Father sends sunshine and rain on both good and evil men (Matt 5:43-45). "He did good and gave you rains from heaven and fruitful seasons, satisfying your hearts with food and gladness" (Acts 14:17). He "richly supplies us with all things to enjoy" (1 Tim 6:17). While the promise of Rom 8:28 is a special display of God's goodness, its ultimate expression is seen in everything he has done to save us from our sins. In this context his goodness takes the more specific forms of mercy, patience, and grace. Truly "He has satisfied the thirsty soul, and the hungry soul He has filled with what is good" (Ps 107:9). "How great is Your goodness, which You have stored up for those who fear You!" (Ps 31:19).

Without this confidence in the goodness of God, it would be very difficult to love him and trust him. If God were not good, his attitudes and actions toward us would be characterized either by cruelty or by indifference. Such a sovereign, omnipotent ruler would be unendurable. This is why, if forced to choose, most people would rather have a *good* God than an omnipotent one. But we do not have to choose; our God is both all-powerful and all-good.

F. God Is Omniscient

To say that God is *omniscient* is to say that he is infinite in his knowledge (*GC*, 273-292; *GRu*, 280-283). "The LORD is a God of knowledge" (1 Sam 2:3) is true without limits. He knows everything there is to know, and he is always conscious of all that he knows. His knowledge is total and perfect; he "knows all things" (1 John 3:20). "Great is our LORD and abundant in strength; His understanding is infinite" (Ps 147:5). "There is no creature hidden from His sight, but all things are open and laid bare to the eyes of Him with whom we have to do" (Heb 4:13). "Oh, the depth of the riches both of the wisdom and knowledge of God!" (Rom 11:33).

Scripture assures us that God knows every detail about the world he has created. He keeps track of all the stars and birds (Ps 147:4; Matt 10:29). He has a total knowledge of all the needs and deeds of every human being, including the number of hairs on every head (Matt 10:30). "His eyes are upon the ways of a man, and He sees all his steps" (Job 34:21). "The LORD looks from heaven; He sees all the sons of men; from His dwelling place He looks out on all the inhabitants of the earth" (Ps 33:13-14). "The eyes of the LORD are in every place, watching the evil and the good" (Prov 15:3). See Ps 139:1-18.

God's knowledge is so complete that he knows even the deepest contents of our hearts. "God is greater than our heart and knows all things" (1 John 3:20). "I, the LORD, search the heart, I test the mind, even to give to each man according to his ways" (Jer 17:10). "God sees not as man sees, for man looks at the outward appearance, but the LORD looks at the heart" (1 Sam 16:7).

Thus we must say that God has an intimate knowledge of every detail in the entire universe, large and small. He keeps a constant surveillance of every passing event; he monitors the cosmos.

Perhaps the most amazing aspect of God's omniscience is his complete *foreknowledge* of the entire future history of his creation, including the free-will decisions of human beings. His perfect knowledge of the past is not difficult to understand, since he has already observed it all and forgets nothing. But can God really know every detail of the *future*, including all contingent events and free-will choices? The answer is yes. Though we cannot understand how it is possible, we must affirm it is true because the Bible teaches it.

God tells us that the sure mark of deity is the ability to declare what is going to take place, to announce what is coming (Isa 41:21-23). This is exactly what God has done: "I am God, and there is no other; I am God, and there is no one like Me, declaring the end from the beginning, and from ancient times things which have not been done" (Isa 46:9-10). See also Isa 42:8-9; 44:7-8; 45:20-21; 48:3-7; Ps 139:4,16. In all these texts God asserts his exclusive possession of knowledge of the future.

The NT specifically affirms that God's foreknowledge is a crucial factor in predestination: "For those whom He foreknew, He also predestined" (Rom 8:29).

The saints are chosen "according to the foreknowledge of God the Father" (1 Pet 1:2). The death of Jesus also involved a combination of foreknowledge and pre-destination (Acts 2:23). See Rom 11:2; Gal 3:8.

We can understand how God can foreknow those future events that he himself has determined to cause, but the biblical teaching about foreknowledge (includ-ing many predictive prophecies) includes God's knowledge of future contingent choices of free-will beings. How is such foreknowledge possible? The answer lies in the qualitative aspect of God's *eternity*, as described above. The infinite God is not limited by time in that his consciousness transcends the now-moment and embraces the totality of history—past, present, and future—in a single act of knowing.

In a movement known as "openness theology," a growing number of conser-vative theologians have begun to reject the reality of God's foreknowledge.[6] One reason for this is that such foreknowledge seems to rule out free will. If God ac-tually knows what is going to happen before it happens, then it is *certain* to hap-pen (otherwise God would be wrong), and the freedom and contingency of the future appear to be destroyed.

It is true that foreknowledge means that future events are in some sense cer-tain. But the question is, what *makes* them certain? The foreknowledge itself? No, foreknowledge does not *make* things happen or *make* them certain; it only means that they *are* certain. What makes them certain is the acts themselves as freely chosen by their subjects, as viewed by God from his perspective of eternity. Certainty is not the same as necessity.

A final question is how God's foreknowledge can be reconciled with certain OT texts that seem to suggest that God changes his mind or "repents" about cer-tain things he has done or plans to do (see *GRe*, 496-501). For example, "And it repented the LORD that he had made man" (Gen 6:6, KJV); "the LORD changed His mind about this" (Amos 7:3,6, NASB; see Exod 32:14; Jer 26:13,19). How is this consistent with foreknowledge, or even immutability?

At stake here are over 20 OT texts where God is the subject of the Hebrew verb *nacham*. The key is to see that this word has other meanings than "repent" (which the KJV uses every time). The NASB rejects the translation "repent," and uses instead "was sorry," "regretted," "relented," "was moved to pity," "thought better of," and "changed his mind." The NIV omits "changed his mind," and rightly uses "was grieved" in several of the texts. The main point is that *nacham* does not necessarily imply a change of mind based on ignorance. Sometimes it connotes the presence of *strong feelings*, especially grief (Gen 6:6-7; 1 Sam 15:11,35; 2 Sam 24:16; 1 Chr 21:15) and compassion (Judg 2:18).

More often, though, God's "relenting" is based on the fact that his an-nounced intention regarding a certain course of action is *conditional*, depending on the human response to the announcement—a principle clearly stated in Jer 18:7-10. This may be the case even when the condition is not specifically stated, as in Jonah 3:9-10; 4:2. This is the obvious explanation in other passages, too: see Exod 32:14; Ps 106:45; Jer 26:3,13,19; 42:10; Joel 2:13-14; Amos 7:3,6. In such cases God foreknows whether the stated or implied conditions will be met (such as fervent prayers), but he must still announce his (tentative) course of action in order to set the stage for the human response.

Thus we conclude that God's foreknowledge is not compromised by the *nacham* texts, and that his omniscience remains absolute.

G. God Is Omnipresent

To say that God is *omnipresent* is to say that he is infinite with respect to space; he is not limited by space (*GC*, 264-273). Space itself is a product of creation; all created beings are subject to spatial limitations. Even angels exist in their own "spiritual" space or spiritual dimension, and are limited thereby. A major limitation for any creature is that it can be in only one place at any given time. But God the uncreated Creator is not a spatial being. His essence is qualitatively different from space and spatial beings. All the characteristics of space as we know it—extension, location, and distance—do not apply to him.

The main point of God's freedom from spatial limitations is that he is not confined to just one location at any one time. Rather, he is universally present to all of space at all times; he is omnipresent, or everywhere-present. The divine dimension intersects every point of space; it interfaces with the material dimension everywhere. This is not the same as saying that God is present *in* all space. He is present *to* all space, or perhaps we should say that all space is immediately present to him and before him. He can manifest a visible presence (a theophany) in any specific place he chooses, or in a million different places at the same time; but this visible presence should not be equated with the divine essence.

Omnipresence is why God is present to us and can be worshiped by us anywhere or at many earthly places at the same time. He does not actually "dwell" in any one building or on any one mountain (1 Kgs 8:27; John 4:20-24; Acts 7:48-50; 17:24). Also, omnipresence is why it is futile to try to run away from God or hide from God. There is no way to "flee . . . from the presence of the LORD," as Jonah tried to do (Jonah 1:3; see Ps 139:7-10).

Jeremiah 23:23-24 says, "'Am I a God who is near,' declares the LORD, 'and not a God far off? Can a man hide himself in hiding places so I do not see him?' declares the LORD. 'Do I not fill the heavens and the earth?' declares the LORD." No matter where a person may be located, whether in the remotest spot on earth or in a distant galaxy, God is still both very near and also far off. The "far off" is emphasized so that no one may think of escaping God's presence; the "near" is emphasized so that all may know that God may be found if sought. Indeed, God is as near as the nearest point of space, for every point of space is a contact point between us and God (Acts 17:27-28).

H. God Is Immanent

Immanence is that attribute of God that describes his presence and activity *within* the created world (*GC*, 269-273; *GRu*, 295-298). Sometimes immanence is contrasted with transcendence, as if they were opposites. But this is a serious error that is based on the false idea that transcendence is a spatial concept, i.e., that God occupies some kind of space outside the borders of our universe and is thus spatially distant from us. But transcendence is not about distance; it is about difference. It does not mean that God is spatially separated from the world, but that his essence is qualitatively different from it. His transcendence in no way ex-cludes his immanence or presence within the world. In fact, his infinite essence is what makes his omnipresence and his immanence possible.

Immanence is similar to omnipresence; they differ mainly in emphasis. Where-as omnipresence lays stress on the *omni*, or on the universality of God's presence, immanence emphasizes the *presence* itself. Omnipresence means that God is pre-sent everywhere as opposed to just some places; immanence means that God is present in and to his creation as opposed to being outside it or absent from it. This does not mean that God is wholly contained in the world as if he were finite, nor does it mean that he is identified with the world as in some pantheistic views. It simply means that God is present, that he is near or close to his creatures, that they are in his presence at all times. See again Acts 17:27-28; Jer 23:23-24.

The immanence of God is a marvel. Though he is the sovereign King of the universe, yet he is *with us*, in our midst, working among us, by our side, giving his personal, intimate attention to every detail of his creation and of our lives. The whole work of providence (discussed in the next chapter) magnifies the nearness of God. He is present in his general providence as he preserves and oversees all that he has made. He is present in his special providence, stretching forth his hand to curse or to bless. He is present in his miracles, showing forth his mighty power.

God's immanence is especially exemplified in his availability to hear and an-swer our prayers: "The eyes of the LORD are toward the righteous and His ears are open to their cry" (Ps 34:15). "The LORD is near to all who call upon Him, to all who call upon Him in truth" (Ps 145:18). He is near to us in all our wor-ship (Matt 18:20), and his Spirit dwells within the very hearts and bodies of be-lievers (1 Cor 6:19). James 4:8 promises, "Draw near to God and He will draw near to you." This is his immanence.

I. God Is Glorious

The word that best sums up the collective greatness of God is *glory* (*GC*, 446-452). He is the "King of glory," the "God of glory," and the Lord of glory" (Ps 24:7-10; Acts 7:2; 1 Cor 2:8). "Great is the glory of the LORD," says Ps 138:5. "His name alone is exalted; His glory is above earth and heaven" (Ps 148:13).

The principal OT word for glory (*kabod*) in its adjective form literally means "great, heavy, weighty." It is used often in a figurative sense to mean significant, important, noteworthy, or impressive. In this figurative sense it refers to God and is usually translated "glorious" or "glory." The glory of God thus is his infinite significance, the totality of his perfections, the fullness of his deity compressed into a single concept.

But there is another connotation that makes the glory of God something special. God *is* infinitely great and perfect; this remains true whether or not his greatness is ever displayed or manifested in any way. However, he does choose to manifest his greatness, displaying the majesty of his perfections in visible ways. Thus most specifically, the *glory* of God is his greatness as it is manifested and as it shines forth for all to see. "Glory is displayed excellence," says Pentecost (*Glory*, 8).

God's own visible presence manifests his glory; it was "the glory of the LORD" that appeared in the cloud that guided Israel and indwelt the temple (Exod 16:7,10; 40:34-35; 1 Kgs 8:10-11). His glory is declared by the marvelous works of his creation (Ps 19:1). The incarnate Logos, Jesus of Nazareth, manifested his glory (John 1:14). Divine glory is displayed in God's saving grace (Eph 1:6). The glory of God will illumine heaven (Rev 21:23). Wherever God is and wherever God works, there is glory. "Holy, Holy, Holy, is the LORD of hosts, the whole earth is full of His glory" (Isa 6:3).

III. ATTRIBUTES EXPRESSED IN GOD'S RELATIONS WITH FREE-WILL CREATURES

Certain attributes of God are manifested not so much in his relation to the creation as such, but specifically in his relations with human creatures. The two basic attributes in this category are love and holiness, which are expressed in his relationships with human beings as such. These are discussed in this section. Other related attributes are expressed only when sin is introduced into the human scene; these will be discussed in the next section.

A. God Is Holy

One attribute of God that manifests itself in relation to his free-will creatures is *holiness* (*GRe*, 245-275). Earlier we explained that the basic idea of holiness is to be separated or set apart from other things. We explained that God is *ontologically* holy, i.e., set apart from or distinct from all created essence. This is his transcendence. Now we are focusing on his *ethical* holiness, his separation from everything sinful or morally evil. This is how we are using the word "holiness" here.

God's holiness basically is his perfect moral excellence, which has both a positive and a negative aspect. The positive aspect is what God *is*, what he is *for*; the negative aspect is what he is *not*, what he is *against*.

Positively, "God is holy" means that he is absolute moral perfection and purity, that he is unconditionally upright in his essence and his actions. Such divine holiness is clearly affirmed in the Bible: "Thus you are to be holy to Me, for I the

LORD am holy" (Lev 20:26; 1 Pet 1:15-16). "With the blameless You show Yourself blameless; with the pure You show Yourself pure" (Ps 18:25-26). "Good and upright is the LORD" (Ps 25:8; see 92:15). Speaking of the risen Christ, John says "He is pure" (1 John 3:3).

This positive holiness is not just God's own personal moral uprightness, but also his zeal for moral uprightness in his creatures. This leads him both to demand holiness in us and to delight in it (see Ps 24:3-4; 33:5).

Holiness includes a negative side also, which is God's perfect freedom from all sin, his absolute opposition to it, his total hatred of it. There is no hint of moral evil in his nature, will, thoughts, or deeds. As Scripture says, "Far be it from God to do wickedness, and from the Almighty to do wrong. . . . Surely, God will not act wickedly, and the Almighty will not pervert justice" (Job 34:10-12). "You are not a God who takes pleasure in wickedness; no evil dwells with You" (Ps 5:4). "Your eyes are too pure to approve evil, and You can not look on wickedness with favor" (Hab 1:13).

This negative side of God's holiness is not just the absence of sin from his nature, but his strong attitude against it, an attitude of abhorrence and hatred. Just as he has a zeal for the right, so is he zealous in his opposition to all that is wrong. The Psalmist says to the divine Messiah, "You have loved righteousness and hated wickedness" (Ps 45:7). The LORD hates "every abominable act" of sinners (Deut 12:31). Specific sins hated and detested by God include idolatry (Deut 16:22; Jer 44:4); occultism (Deut 18:9-14); haughty eyes, a lying tongue, hands that shed innocent blood, hearts that devise wicked plans, feet that run to do evil (Prov 6:16-18); lying, injustice (Zech 8:17); and divorce (Mal 2:16).

God's holiness in both its aspects is expressed to his free-will creatures in the form of *law*, which refers to any of the precepts and commandments bound upon us as creatures by the Creator. That is, it is the preceptive will of God (Ps 40:8). God gives us his law just because he is a holy God who has an infinite zeal for right and wrong. The commands of the law are for the most part the mirror or the transcript of his own holiness; they are God's holiness in verbalized imperative form. Also, the penalties and curses prescribed by the law reflect God's holy hatred of sin (see Deut 28:15; Gal 3:10). To be holy as God is holy (1 Pet 1:15-16) is to love his law and to hate the sin proscribed by it (Ps 1:2; 119:47,97,126-127).

Holiness as an attribute of God is made known to his creatures even where no sin is present (e.g., Gen 2:15-17). But when sin enters the arena of creation, divine holiness is made manifest in all its majestic glory, especially in the form of jealousy and wrath. These will be discussed in the next main section.

B. God Is Loving

The other side of God's moral nature is *love* (*GRe*, 323-351). This is how the goodness of God expresses itself toward his free-will creatures: "God is love" (1 John 4:8,16). Brunner calls this "the most daring statement . . . in human language" (*Dogmatics I*, 185). Perhaps this is why it is an aspect of God that is specifically enunciated only in the special revelation of the Bible.

The Bible does indeed declare the infinite love of God. "The earth is full of Your lovingkindness, O LORD," says Ps 119:64. His love is directed toward the whole world of human beings (John 3:16; see 1 John 2:2; 4:10). In OT times he loved Israel with a special love (Deut 10:15; Jer 31:3; Micah 7:18-20), and in NT times this special love is directed toward the church (Eph 5:25-30; Col 3:12; 1 John 3:1; 4:19).

To understand the nature of God's love we must note the variety of biblical terms that represent it. The main NT word is *agape* (verb, *agapao*), though *phileo* is used twice (John 5:20; 16:27). The former refers to a genuine concern for another's well-being; the latter refers to the affection one has for a friend. The main OT word is '*ahab* and its cognates; its meaning is similar to *agape*. Other OT words are *chesed*, which means a genuine affection of lovingkindness; *chashaq*, "to desire, to love, to be attached to"; *chapets*, "to favor, to have delight in"; and *ratsah*, "to delight in, to be pleased with."

It is important to see that more than one biblical word is used to represent God's love, because sometimes a limited, distorted definition of it is set forth, based on the meaning of a single word, usually *agape*. *Agape* is rightly understood as selfless caring and concern for the happiness and well-being of another, and this is certainly the heart of God's love. But our overall understanding of God's loving nature must be based on the total biblical picture, not just on one word.

How, then, shall we define the love of God? I offer this definition: God's love is his self-giving affection and selfless concern that lead him to actively seek the happiness and well-being of his image-bearing creatures. This definition includes four basic elements. The first element is indeed the essence of *agape*, which is *concern*. God is genuinely interested in us and cares about us; he is concerned about our well-being. He sincerely and unselfishly wants to bless us. He will not ignore us or be indifferent toward us.

The second element is that he is *self-giving*. He desires to give of himself in whatever way necessary to achieve his creatures' happiness. He shares his power and goodness with us in the bounty of the created world; he shares himself with us in communion and communication. In the ultimate self-giving act he gave us himself in the incarnation of the Logos as Jesus the Christ, who gave himself up to death on our behalf.

The third element of God's love is *action*. Divine love does not remain internal to God; he externalizes it by acting on behalf of those whom he loves. His love is embodied in his providential blessings (Matt 5:43-48), in his chastisement (Prov 3:11-12; Heb 12:5-6), and in the cross (John 3:16; 15:13).

The fourth aspect of divine love is *affection*, an element often omitted by those who exclude all feelings from God or who forget that God's love is broader than *agape*. Several of the words mentioned above include feelings of affection and delight. To describe God's relation to his people, Scripture often uses analogies that embody tender affection: the relationships of father to child (Hos 11:1,4; Rom 8:15), mother to child (Isa 49:15; 66:13), husband to wife (Hos 3:1; Eph 5:25), and shepherd to flock (Ezek 34:11-22; Isa 40:11; John 10:11). Surely these analogies teach us that God's love is warm and tender and deeply personal. See also Isa 30:18; Jer 31:20; Hos 11:8; Matt 23:37.

The love of God is infinitely rich and deep, a fact which is seen in the unlimited bounty of his gifts of creation and providence (Acts 14:17; 1 Tim 6:17; Jas 1:17). Its amazing depth is even more prominent, though, in the way it responds to the presence of sin among his human creatures. When sin enters the picture, his love unfolds in the form of mercy, patience, and grace. These love attributes will be discussed in the next main section.

C. Holiness and Love

It is crucial that we have a proper understanding of the relation between God's love and God's holiness. The temptation is to make one or the other of these the *primary* or inclusive attribute, with the other being just one of the many expressions of it. The more common approach is to take "God is love" as the all-inclusive description of God's nature, with every other attribute, including holiness, being simply one of the ways God's love functions. The same is sometimes done with God's holiness, but less frequently.

Neither approach is correct. God's holiness and God's love are two distinct and equally ultimate attributes of God, with neither being an expression of the other. Love and holiness are two equally fundamental sides of the nature of God, "who is able to save and to destroy" (Jas 4:12). "Behold then the kindness and severity of God" (Rom 11:22). While each side is tempered by the other, each may be expressed independently of the other. Failure to understand this point leads to confusion in the area of ethics, where serious issues such as war, capital punishment, and social justice in general are wrongly decided on the false presupposition of a love-only God. It also leads to confusion in the area of Christology, where the cross is interpreted as a moral influence upon sinners rather than as a propitiatory sacrifice that is necessary to turn away God's wrath.

The fact is that our understanding of the very essence of Christian faith is dependent on a proper understanding of the equal ultimacy of holiness and love. If sin had never been introduced into God's creation, these two attributes would have coexisted side by side within God in perfect harmony. But once sin enters the picture, the holiness and love of God are in a state of tension and opposition. Because God is love, he desires to bestow mercy, grace, and forgiveness upon sinners. But because he is holy, he must pour out his wrath upon them in retributive punishment. Both love and holiness are his nature, and God's righteousness requires him to be true to all aspects of his nature. Thus both grace and wrath are *requirements* of his nature. But how can God fulfill the requirements of both love and holiness toward sinners at the same time? God's solution to this dilemma is the incarnation and crucifixion of Jesus, which are central pillars of the Christian faith.

IV. ATTRIBUTES MANIFESTED IN GOD'S RELATIONS TO SINNERS

The last category of divine attributes includes those known to us especially in the way God relates to his free-will creatures who have sinned. All of these are simply further manifestations of the two basic sides of his moral nature, namely, holiness and love. Because God is holy, he is jealous and wrathful in the presence of sin; because he is love, he is merciful, patient, and gracious toward sinners.

A. God Is Jealous

The holiness of God when provoked by sin sometimes springs forth in the form of *jealousy* (GC, 409-416). In the second commandment Yahweh declares, "For I, the LORD your God, am a jealous God" (Exod 20:5). "You shall not worship any other god, for the LORD, whose name is Jealous, is a jealous God" (Exod 34:14).

Both the OT and the NT words for jealousy refer to an intense feeling of zeal or ardor, a fervor of spirit, a zealousness, a jealousy, even a jealous anger. But we must not think of God's jealousy as a petty spite or envy directed toward some other deity whose legitimate worshipers he covets. Rather, when jealousy is attributed to God, the background always seems to be his relationship with his people understood figuratively as a marriage relationship. Like a husband, God is jealous with a "godly jealousy" (2 Cor 11:2) for both the welfare of his spouse and for the maintenance of her exclusive devotion toward himself. And what is the major threat to both? Idolatry! Thus the biblical references to God as a jealous God most often appear in a context condemning idolatry. This connection is seen in Exod 20:5 and Exod 34:14, cited above. See also Deut 6:14-15, "You shall not follow other gods, any of the gods of the peoples who surround you, for the LORD your God . . . is a jealous God" (see Deut 4:22-24; 29:17-20). In Deut 32:21 the LORD declares, "They have made Me jealous with what is not God; they have provoked Me to anger with their idols." See Josh 24:19-20; Ps 78:58; 1 Cor 10:22.

False gods provoke God to jealousy because they are rivals to his exclusive claim to Godhood and to his exclusive right to the devotion of his creatures. This is where the concept of the marriage relationship enters. Those who are led astray by false gods are being unfaithful to their rightful spouse; idol worshipers are guilty of spiritual adultery or harlotry. See Num 25:1-2; Jer 5:7; Ezek 16:17; 23:25-27. Just as any husband would be hurt and indignant because of his wife's unfaithfulness, the holy God is provoked to jealousy when his people go after other gods. The heart of this attribute is seen in Isa 42:8, "I am the LORD, that is my name; I will not give my glory to another, nor my praise to graven images."

As the only true God, he declares, "I will be jealous for My holy name" (Ezek 39:25).

B. God Is Wrathful

The wrath of God is not a pleasant subject to think about; but it is an essential part of God's nature, and a study of it is crucial for a proper understanding of sin and salvation. In its essence God's wrath is not different from his holiness, but is simply that into which holiness is transformed when confronted by sin (*GRe*, 275-319).

The biblical witness to the wrath of God is overwhelming. God announces his wrath toward rebellious nations: "He will speak to them in His anger and terrify them in His fury" (Ps 2:5). Using the figure of a winepress God declares, "I also trod them in My anger and trampled them in My wrath; and their lifeblood is sprinkled on My garments . . . . For the day of vengeance was in my heart" (Isa 63:3-4). Rebellious Israel did not escape God's wrath: "On this account the anger of the LORD has burned against His people, and He has stretched out His hand against them and struck them down" (Isa 5:25). "For a fire is kindled in My anger, and burns to the lowest part of Sheol, and consumes the earth with its yield, and sets on fire the foundations of the mountains" (Deut 32:22). None of God's enemies will escape: "For the wrath of God is revealed from heaven against all ungodliness and unrighteousness of men" (Rom 1:18).

Leon Morris says that the OT alone has over twenty words expressing this concept in over 580 passages (*Preaching*, 131). Some of these OT words have the connotation of a hot, burning fire. For example, "For I was afraid of the anger and hot displeasure [*chemah*] with which the LORD was wrathful against you" (Deut 9:19). "And when the LORD heard it, His anger was kindled [*charon*], and the fire of the LORD burned among them" (Num 11:1). The most common OT word for God's wrath is *'ap*, which refers to the nose or nostrils; the verb form means "to snort, to be angry." Psalm 18:8 says that when God was angry, "smoke rose from his nostrils; consuming fire came from his mouth, burning coals blazed out of it" (NIV).

The NT uses two basic terms for God's wrath. One is *orge* (John 3:36; Rom 1:18; Rev 6:16-17); the other is *thymos* (Rom 2:8; Rev 14:10,19). If there is a difference between them, the former refers more to a constant and settled state of controlled indignation, like a volcanic fire that is constantly seething beneath the surface; and the latter refers more to a passionate outburst of wrath or a sudden upflowing of rage, like a volcano when it erupts. Thus God's wrath is a constantly burning indignation against all sin, but on specific occasions it bursts forth in acts of consuming judgment. "For our God is a consuming fire" (Heb 12:29).

It is important to see behind the specific outpourings of divine wrath and recognize that the burning fire of wrath is a constant aspect of God's nature, a part of his very essence. Because he is holy, it is impossible for God not to be wrathful in the presence of sin. Wrath is the natural and inevitable and eternal recoil of the all-holy God against all that is unholy. The holiness of God always burns against the very thought of sin, but this is not obvious and not observed until sin actually comes into existence. At that point the holiness of God is unveiled as a "consuming fire" that must by nature engulf and destroy the offending evil, just as a hot stove instantly vaporizes drops of water that fall on it. God's holy nature is like an oven that is constantly maintained at 451 degrees Fahrenheit, and sins are like bits of paper that spontaneously burst into flame when cast into that oven.

To be the object of God's wrath is described in the Bible as a horrible experience: "It is a terrifying thing to fall into the hands of the living God" (Heb 10:31). Those under God's wrath are called his enemies (Rom 5:10; Col 1:21; Jas 4:4). "Behold, I am against you," he says to those under his wrath (Jer 50:31; Ezek 21:3). "The face of the Lord is against those who do evil" (1 Pet 3:12).

Sometimes we hear that God hates the sin but loves the sinner. This is not true; God's hatred is directed against the *person* who sins and not just the sin itself. "You hate all who do iniquity. . . . The LORD abhors the man of bloodshed and deceit" (Ps 5:5-6). "The one who loves violence His soul hates" (Ps 11:5). See also Lev 20:23; Deut 25:16; Ps 78:59; Prov 6:19; 11:20; 16:5; 17:15; Jer 12:8; Hos 9:15; Mal 1:3; Rom 9:13. We cannot ignore the force of these passages.

Basically God's wrath is *retribution,* a deserved punishment for sin. It is a judicial penalty justly inflicted upon the unrepentant sinner by God the righteous Judge. It is the curse prescribed by law; on the day of judgment Christ will say, "Depart from Me, accursed ones" (Matt 25:41). It is divine vengeance that repays the wrongdoer the just wages of his sin: "Vengeance is mine, and retribution," declares the LORD (Deut 32:35; see Heb 10:30). "A jealous and avenging God is the LORD; the LORD is avenging and wrathful. The LORD takes vengeance on His adversaries, and He reserves wrath for His enemies" (Nahum 1:2). The many biblical references to God's wrath as vengeance leave no doubt that it is a form of holy retribution upon those who deserve it.

It is crucial to understand that wrath is an expression of the *holiness* of God, not an expression of his love. The latter is an extremely common idea. The theory is that sin is not what makes God angry; he becomes wrathful only when sinners refuse to respond to his love and grace. Thus wrath is described as "wounded love" (*GRe*, 280). In fact, God's wrath is often represented as nothing more than one of the many forms of God's love. As one influential scholar plainly says, "The wrath of God arises from his love and mercy." When sinners reject God's mercy, "love becomes wrath."[7] The logical conclusion is that eternal punishment in hell itself is an expression of God's love: "In fact, Hell may well be seen as God's final act of love" (Gresham, *Goodness*, 12).

NO! Such a connection between love and wrath must be vigorously repudiated. Wounded love does respond to sin (see the next three attributes), but not in terms of wrath. The overwhelming witness of Scripture is that sin evokes God's wrath because it is a rebellion against his law and therefore against his own holiness (e.g., Isa 5:24-25; see *GRe*, 282-285). In view of everything Scripture says about the wrath of God as involving hatred (of sin *and* the sinner), vengeance, and retribution, I find it simply incredible, even outrageous, that it should be called an expression of his love. *Wrath is not a form of love; it is an expression of holiness.*

C. God Is Merciful

"Behold therefore the goodness and severity of God" (Rom 11:22, KJV). These are the two sides of his moral nature. His severity is expressed toward his free-will creatures as holiness, which is further directed toward sinners as jealousy and wrath. His goodness is expressed toward free-will creatures as love. But now the question is, how does love itself respond to *sinners?* Here we will see that when confronted by sin, love is transformed into three related attributes: mercy, patience, and grace.

First, God is merciful (*GRe*, 351-356). He is "rich in mercy, because of His great love with which He loved us" (Eph 2:4). Mercy must be understood in light of the suffering and misery caused by sin. It is the love of God as directed toward mankind in his sin-caused pain, suffering, need, misery, and distress. It involves a feeling of sympathetic concern that is basically the same as compassion, plus a desire to relieve the sufferer's distress. Sometimes a person brings this distress upon himself because of his personal sin; more often it is the cumulative result of others' sins, including Adam's. But as far as mercy is concerned, it does not matter whether the suffering is deserved or not. In his mercy God wants to remove the suffering regardless of its cause.

At its very core the nature of God is "compassionate and gracious" (Exod 34:6). "For the LORD your God is a compassionate God" (Deut 4:31); "His mercies are great" (2 Sam 24:14). He is "the Father of mercies and the God of all comfort" (2 Cor 1:3). God is moved with compassion in view of our physical needs (Matt 14:14; 15:32; 20:34; Mark 1:41). "He will have compassion on the poor and needy" (Ps 72:13). But more significantly he is filled with mercy in view of our spiritual needs, our lost and sinful state. The sinner's main need is salvation; and because he is merciful, God wants to meet this need, and he has done everything he can to do so. God has saved us not by our works "but according to His mercy" (Titus 3:5). "According to His great mercy" he "caused us to be born again to a living hope" (1 Pet 1:3; see Eph 2:4-6). "Mercy triumphs over judgment" for those who are in Christ (Jas 2:13).

D. God Is Patient

Another specialized form that love takes in the face of sin is *patience* or longsuffering (*GRe*, 357-361), which is of the very inmost nature of God. The OT expression for this means literally "long of nose." As noted above, *'ap*, meaning "nose, nostrils," is a Hebrew word for wrath. Thus the expression "long of nose" means "long of wrath" or "slow to wrath." The NT word *makrothymia* is similar in meaning; its adjective means "long of passion, long-suffering, patient." "The LORD, the LORD God, compassionate and gracious, slow to anger, and abounding in lovingkindness and truth" (Exod 34:6).

God's patience illustrates very well the tension between the two sides of his nature in the face of sin, i.e., the tension between love on the one hand and holiness and wrath on the other hand. This is true because the very essence of divine patience is *delay and restraint in the execution of wrath*. His wrath is real and deserved, but out of his great love (1 Cor 13:4) he withholds it for a time or reduces its intensity or even sets it aside altogether. "For the sake of My name I delay My wrath, and for My praise I restrain it for you," says God of his chosen people (Isa 48:9). If God were to give us what we deserve as soon as we begin to deserve it, we would all have perished long ago. It is his loving patience that puts the punishment "on hold" until it can somehow be set aside or ultimately applied.

Paul explains in Rom 9:22-23 how God "endured with much patience" the idolatrous nation of Israel, though they really deserved his wrath, so that salvation for all nations could be brought about through them. Paul uses himself as a good example of divine patience (1 Tim 1:16). The parable of the unmerciful servant teaches the nature of patience as the delay of wrath. Each debtor asked for patience (Matt 18:26,29), or postponement of the time when the debt must be paid. The lord in the parable (representing God) went a step further and forgave the debt altogether.

What is the purpose for God's patience? Why does he delay the execution of his wrath? Because of his love, he would rather not apply wrath at all; thus he delays it to provide the guilty party time to repent and be forgiven and avoid the wrath altogether. "The Lord is not slow about His promise" regarding the coming of the day of judgment, "but is patient toward you, not wishing for any to perish but for all to come to repentance" (2 Pet 3:9). See Neh 9:30; Rom 2:4-5; 1 Pet 3:20.

God will not, however, delay the execution of his wrath forever. There comes a time when his patience runs out, and the opportunity for repentance is withdrawn (Ps 7:12-13; Jer 44:22; Hos 1:6). One's personal death, or else the second coming of Christ, marks the end of God's patience forever, and the time allotted for repentance will be over. Cries like that of the rich man in Hades—"Have mercy on me!" (Luke 16:24)—will be too late.

E. God Is Gracious

Theologically the term "grace" has three basic connotations. It can refer to the *gift* of salvation, that which is given; it can refer to the *system* of salvation, the manner in which the gift is received; or it can refer to that *attribute* in God's nature that makes it all possible. Here we are discussing this last one, grace in the sense of God's graciousness (*GRe*, 361-399). Grace is the most extreme expression of God's love when it comes face to face with sin. Grace is God's willingness and desire to forgive and accept the sinner in spite of his sin, to give the sinner the very opposite of what he deserves.

To understand this, and to get the full impact of it, we must remember what sin means to the holy God—how it goes against everything that he is, how it violates his good and righteous will, how he hates it with a holy hatred, and how it is his very nature to consume it in wrath. Yet despite all this, in his infinite love he is still willing to receive rebellious sinners back unto himself. He is not just *willing* to receive them, but lovingly *desires* to receive them and *seeks* them. This is his grace.

We cannot base our understanding of God's grace solely on the biblical terms that can be translated "grace." Often, especially in the OT, these terms have the very generic meaning of "gift, favor," and do not refer to salvation as such. For example, the prayer "Be gracious unto me" usually means no more than "Do me this favor; answer this prayer" (2 Sam 12:22; Ps 4:1; 67:1). This is most likely the meaning of God's well-known statement in Exod 33:19, "I will be gracious to whom I will be gracious," i.e., "I will decide what prayers and requests will be answered."

The basic meaning of the NT word for grace, *charis*, is "a gift that brings joy." It can refer to any kind of gift, including God's gifts of creation, his providential blessings, the gifts of the Spirit, and divine aid in general. Sometimes, though, it refers to the gift of salvation, which is our focus here. When the term "grace" refers to *saving* grace, it reflects that aspect of God's nature that causes him to desire the salvation of sinners and to go to whatever lengths are necessary to make this salvation possible. This is displayed most distinctly in God's willingness to forgive sins. See Exod 34:6-7; Num 14:17-20; Neh 9:17; Micah 7:18-20; Rom 3:24-26. As Ps 103:8-12 says,

> The LORD is compassionate and gracious, slow to anger and abounding in lovingkindness. He will not always strive with us, nor will He keep His anger forever. He has not dealt with us according to our sins, nor rewarded us according to our iniquities. For as high as the heavens are above the earth, so great is His lovingkindness toward those who fear Him. As far as the east is from the west, so far has He removed our transgressions from us.

In defining the essence of God's grace we may say that it includes three things. First, grace means *giving*. To say that God is gracious means that it is his nature to give of himself and of his bounty to his creatures. Here is a basic difference between the two sides of God's nature. Grace is a form of love; and whereas holiness *demands*, love *gives*. In the context of sin, love-become-grace gives salvation. "The free gift of God is eternal life in Christ Jesus our Lord" (Rom 6:23;

see Rom 8:32). Because salvation comes to us by grace, it *must* be a gift, because the very essence of graciousness is to give.

Second, grace means *forgiving*. Being forgiven by one whom you have offended is the greatest gift that person can give you. When the one offended is the Holy God, and when the offense is sin against his holy law, then his forgiveness is the greatest imaginable gift. And this is exactly what the God of grace wants to give every sinner. Desiring to forgive those who have sinned against him lies at the heart of God and at the heart of grace: "For you, LORD, are good, and ready to forgive" (Ps 86:5). Wherever the Bible speaks of forgiveness, it is speaking about grace.

Third, grace means "favor bestowed when wrath is owed" (a phrase I owe to Ranny Grady). The definition of saving grace as "unmerited favor" is much too weak, except perhaps in reference to gifts not having to do with salvation. Where salvation is concerned, the gift of eternal life is not simply unmerited or undeserved; it is the very *opposite* of what we deserve. That God is gracious means that he is by nature willing to give us the very opposite of what we deserve, the very opposite of what his own holiness demands. As Packer puts it, "The grace of God is love freely shown towards guilty sinners, contrary to their merit and indeed in defiance of their demerit" (120).

In summary, God's graciousness is his infinite willingness and desire to give sinners the gift of forgiveness, even though they deserve his wrath, and even though it costs him the cross.

NOTES ON CHAPTER THREE

[1]In Paul's writings Jesus is usually the one called "Lord," and the Father is usually the one called "God."

[2]For refutations of modalism in the Oneness movement see Brumback, *God*; and Boyd, *Oneness*. See also *GRe*, 143-145.

[3]No one has completely conformed to the law; thus in an absolute sense "there is none righteous, not even one" (Rom 3:10). But in a relative sense many are called righteous in Scripture. See *GRe*, 201-209.

[4]As Christians we become partakers of the divine nature (2 Pet 1:4) only in an ethical or moral sense, i.e., in our character. We become ethically holy, as God is ethically holy (1 Pet 1:15-16).

[5]E.g., if God creates a rock, he has *already* "moved" it from nothingness to reality. It would thus be a contradiction to say that he *cannot* move it.

[6]See Pinnock et al., *Openness*; Boyd, *God*. For a critique see Geisler, *God*; Ware, *Glory*.

[7]Stälin, 425. When I was doing research for my book on God the Redeemer, I was shocked to see how prevalent this idea is, even among conservatives. See *GRe*, 306-311 for other examples.

CHAPTER FOUR
THE WORKS OF
THE CREATOR-GOD

God's works may be considered under three main headings: the works of *creation*, the works of *providence*, and the works of *redemption*. Here we are discussing the first two; the third will be discussed later in the context of Christology.

Both creation and providence have to do with God's relation to the world in his role as Creator (as distinct from his role as Redeemer). Creation refers to the initial act by which God caused the universe to come into existence. It refers to the origination of the basic material out of which everything is made. Providence refers to God's immanent relationships and involvement with the universe *after* that initial act of creation. It includes the way God upholds all things in their very existence, how he oversees all the events of nature and history, and how he intervenes in both in order to accomplish his purposes.

I. THE WORK OF CREATION

We deal first with creation, which is the primary work of God. It is primary in the sense that it is his first work with respect to his creatures, and also in the sense that it is foundational for everything else that occurs. It is the starting point for our understanding of everything relating to God and man. Gilkey has truly said (4),

> The idea that God is the Creator of all things is the indispensable foundation on which the other beliefs of the Christian faith are based. It affirms what the Christian believes about the status of God in the whole realm of reality: He is the Creator of everything else. On this affirmation logically depends all that Christians say about their God, about the world they live in, and about their own history, destiny, and hope.

"Unless we know God as the Creator of all things, we do not know the true God" (Pohle, 8).

A. The Definition of Creation

Traditional Christian thinking is in general agreement as to how creation should be defined (*GC*, 95-133). The following definition by C.C. Crawford is typical: "By Creation we mean that free act of God by which in the beginning He made, without the use of preexisting materials, the whole visible and invisible universe" (I:47). This definition has three basic ideas: (1) God created the universe out of nothing, or *ex nihilo*; (2) creation was a free act; (3) creation is inclusive of both the spiritual and the material realms.

1. Creation *Ex Nihilo*

Christian theology from the beginning has understood the origin of all things in terms of *ex nihilo* creation. *Nihil* is the Latin word for "nothing, nothingness," and *ex nihilo* means literally "out of nothing." Some have tried to objectify the "nothing" and make it into a "something." They suggest that it was actually a kind of primal chaos of preexisting stuff, and that God simply brought it under his control. Such an idea is completely false. "Out of nothing" means "not out of anything." It means that before creation there was nothing except God, and after creation there was also the universe which was not God but was absolutely distinct from God's own being and existence.

Some pagan philosophers think of the *nihil* as an absolute nothingness, a state where not even God exists. Understanding it thus, they typically deny that such a creation could ever have occurred, on the basis of the dictum, "From nothing, nothing comes." But this also is a false understanding of *nihil*. The "nothing" in creation *ex nihilo* means there was nothing outside of God in existence prior to the act of creation.

Ex nihilo means exactly what the definition says: "without the use of preexisting materials," not out of anything that was already in existence. The alternative would be that God somehow *did* use a preexisting material, such as his own essence. In this scenario God is pictured as the only existing entity prior to creation; but then through some act of emanation or generation he produces the universe out of his own essence. This view is held by some forms of pantheism. But such an idea is completely ruled out by *ex nihilo* creation. Created stuff is in no sense derived from God's own being.

Another scenario identifies the preexisting material as some kind of ontological mass that has eternally coexisted alongside of God. In this case God is pictured as somehow seizing control of this mass and shaping it into the presently existing cosmos. But this theory of origins is likewise ruled out by *ex nihilo* creation. The universe—including both its spiritual and its material content—was neither generated out of God's own essence nor formed out of a mass of eternally existing matter. It was created out of nothing, without the use of preexisting material of any kind.

Much modern "Christian" theology denies *ex nihilo* creation in its true meaning. A common approach is to say that creation as such does not refer to the actual *origin* of the world; whether the universe even had a beginning is considered irrelevant. (This, of course is a tacit acceptance of preexisting materials.) The true meaning of creation, we are told, is that the world stands in a specific *relationship* with God, a relationship of dependence. In Houston's words, "So creation is not principally an account of origins, but of dependence upon God" (163). The idea of creation *ex nihilo*, in this view, simply means that the world and mankind are *absolutely* dependent upon God for everything.

Such an interpretation of creation *ex nihilo* is here rejected as false, and as posing a false choice. Creation *ex nihilo* involves *both* origination and dependence. Surely, the fact of creation entails the absolute dependence of man and the universe upon God. But this is not something contrary to or incompatible with creation as the origination of the universe. In fact, just the opposite is true. It is *just because* creation is the absolute origination of all things that the universe and man are absolutely dependent upon God. The former is what makes the latter true. To affirm dependence without origination is to posit an effect without a cause.

What is the biblical basis for the concept of *ex nihilo* creation? The expression itself is not in the Bible; but the concept is, starting with Gen 1:1-2, which says, "In the beginning God created the heavens and the earth. The earth was formless and void, and darkness was over the surface of the deep, and the Spirit of God was moving over the surface of the waters." Three things should be noted about this. First, the phrase "in the beginning" is unqualified. It refers to *the* beginning—period!—of *all* things.

Second, the Hebrew word translated "created" is *bara'*, and as used in this context it suggests that the creation is *ex nihilo*. *Bara'* does not have this meaning inherently, but it is the Hebrew word closest to it. In the grammatical form (the *qal* form) in which it appears here, it is frequently used for an extraordinary act that initiates something new. When combined with "in the beginning," it can mean only *ex nihilo*.[1]

The third thing to note about Gen 1:1-2 is that verse 2 speaks of bringing order out of "formless and void" matter. If verse 1 does not mean *ex nihilo* origination, then verse 2 is redundant, since formless and void matter would already be in existence prior to the act described in verse 1. It would be saying that God made unformed matter out of unformed matter. It makes much better sense to see verse 1 as referring to the absolute creation ("*exnihilation*") of the universe as a whole, and verse 2 as focusing on the unformed earth specifically, after the initial exnihilation.

Creation *ex nihilo* may also be inferred from John 1:1-3, "In the beginning was the Word, and the Word was with God, and the Word was God. He was in the beginning with God. All things came into being through Him, and apart from Him nothing came into being that has come into being." That John is consciously echoing the language of Gen 1:1 is obvious. Though verse 3 is referring to creation, it does not use *ktizo*, the usual word for "create." It uses instead *ginomai*, which means "come into existence." When used of events it is translated "happen" or "come to pass." As used here of the original creation, it is the most appropriate word to express the idea of *ex nihilo* creation. The translation "came into being" (NASB, NRSV) is right on target; the translation "made" (KJV, NIV) is not strong enough.

A more important point, though, is what is being said here about the divine nature of the Logos (the Word), who became Jesus Christ (John 1:14). John's point is to exalt the Logos by placing him uniquely in the category of deity. One indication of his deity is that he shares eternal preexistence with God: he was in the very beginning alongside of God (vv. 1-2). But if the "coming into being" of "all things" in verse 3 does not refer to *ex nihilo* creation, then "all things" must have been made out of some kind of material that was also eternally preexisting alongside of God and the Logos. But this would negate the whole point of the passage, i.e., the unique preexistence of the Logos as an indication of his deity. Thus *ex nihilo* creation must be the point of verse 3.

Another text affirming creation from nothing is Rom 4:17, which describes God as the one "who gives life to the dead and calls into being that which does not exist." Here the two masterworks in the repertoire of omnipotence are laid side by side: calling life into existence out of its opposite, death; and calling being into existence out of its opposite, nonbeing or nonexistence. The second part of the statement says literally that God calls the not-being-things as being-things. In this context it refers specifically to Abraham's offspring, but it is in fact a general statement that has other legitimate applications as well, especially to the original exnihilation of all things.

In Heb 11:3 we read that "the worlds were prepared by the word of God, so that what is seen was not made out of things which are visible." The point is that the things we see all around us were not made out of other things; they came into being (*ginomai* again) as the result of God's word or God's call (Rom 4:17). See Ps 33:6,9.

The point is that creation was an act of divine origination, an absolute beginning point when God brought into existence without the use of preexisting materials the whole created universe. This is creation *ex nihilo*. It is an absolutely unique concept of beginnings, found only in the Bible. Some pagan myths of creation are sometimes presented as teaching creation from nothing, but a close examination shows that some sort of preexisting material is always involved. The biblical teaching stands alone.

2. Creation as a Free Act

The second element included in most definitions of creation is that it is a *free act* of God. This rules out two extreme views of cosmic origins. The fact of creation in and of itself rules out one extreme, i.e., a chance origin for the universe. The question here is whether there is any sense in which the opposite extreme might be true, namely, whether God created the world out of necessity or constraint or compulsion. The traditional doctrine of creation rightly denies this.

That creation was a free act means that God freely chose to create. He did not have to do it; he did so only because he wanted to.

The idea of creation as a necessary act is sometimes found in pagan cosmologies (though it is not a true creation, of course). But even within Christendom popular theology often describes God as *needing* to create for one reason or another. Sometimes he is pictured as being lonesome and needing companionship, or as needing an outlet for his love and goodness.

Such thinking is false, however; it is totally unsupported by Scripture. God has no lack or internal pressure that requires him to create. Loneliness and love are not problems for God-in-himself because he is tripersonal (i.e., trinitarian). We must not think of God as existing prior to creation as a single, solitary person in splendid isolation. The Father, the Son, and the Holy Spirit (as we now know these persons) existed together in a completely satisfying relationship of mutual love.

Creation was God's freely willed choice. In fact, *whatever* God does he does because he wants to and not because he has to: "Our God is in the heavens; He does whatever He pleases" (Ps 115:3). He "works all things after the counsel of His will" (Eph 1:11). This freedom to choose is specifically applied to creation in Rev 4:11, "Worthy are You, our Lord and our God, to receive glory and honor and power; for You created all things, and because of Your will they existed, and were created."

Because creation is a free-will act of God, it is appropriate to ask concerning the *purpose* for which God decided to create. When God made his decision to create, what did he desire or plan to accomplish by this act? In general there are two approaches to this question. One says that God created for the sake of the creature; the other says he created for his own sake. Actually both are true; creation has a twofold purpose. In short, God created primarily for the sake of his *glory*, and secondarily for the sake of his *goodness*.

Regarding the latter, one obvious reason why God created the world was to bestow the blessings of his goodness and love upon rational creatures who could receive, enjoy, and acknowledge them in loving gratitude. The physical universe as such was created and prepared as a home for mankind, as a domain for him to subdue and rule (Gen 1:28-30). Nature is man's intended servant. Speaking of the bounty of this world, Paul says that God "richly supplies us with all things to enjoy" (1 Tim 6:17). James speaks of the good things and perfect gifts that God bestows upon us (Jas 1:17). God's goodness in nature satisfies our hearts with food and gladness (Acts 14:17).

While we may rightfully consider the treasures of nature to be "presents" God bestows upon us, in the ultimate outpouring of goodness God gives us his own "presence"; that is, he gives us himself in fellowship. This is why he has made creatures in his own image, personal beings who can know him and respond to him in an I-thou relationship. Thus the blessings of nature are not just to be enjoyed as if this enjoyment were an end in itself. We are to enjoy them specifically as gifts of God's love. In other words, we are ultimately intended *to enjoy the Giver himself.* Even apart from or in the absence of things of this world, we are to enjoy God just for himself; we are to rejoice in our knowledge of God and our relationship with him. As the Psalmist says, his one desire is to "dwell in the house of the LORD all the days of my life, to behold the beauty of the LORD" (Ps 27:4). See Hab 3:17-19.

Though the goodness of God's love was a basic motivation for his work of creation, there was an even more basic purpose. Creation was not just for the creature's sake, but also for the sake of the Creator himself. Primarily, God created for the sake of his own glory, that he might both manifest his glory in creation and be glorified by it.

Whatever God does, in the final analysis he does it for the sake of his glory. "For My own sake, for My own sake, I will act; . . . and My glory I will not give to another" (Isa 48:11). "I will set My glory among the nations" (Ezek 39:21). He created Israel for his glory (Isa 43:7), and he finally brings us to redemption "to the praise of His glory" (Eph 1:12,14). Thus it should be no surprise that everything began for the sake of his glory. "Worthy are You, our Lord and our God, to receive glory and honor and power; for You created all things, and because of Your will they existed, and were created" (Rev 4:11). "For from Him and through Him and to Him are all things. To Him be the glory forever. Amen" (Rom 11:36).

The very existence of the universe declares the Creator's glory, along with its massive size and intricate beauty (Ps 19:1-6). But God not only displays his glory through his creatures in general; he also receives glory from the ones that are made in his image when we worship and serve him and acknowledge that he alone is worthy of worship.

The dual purpose of creation is seen in Jesus' teaching that man's *summum bonum* (highest good, primary purpose) is to "seek first His kingdom and His righteousness," with the result being that "all these things [physical blessings] will be added to you" (Matt 6:33). God's "kingdom" in its basic sense is his king*ship*, his dominion, his lordship, his glory. This we are to seek *first*, as our highest goal. Thus our primary purpose for existing is to see that God's kingship and glory are exalted in our righteous deeds and words. When we do this, Jesus promises that we will be able to enjoy all the things that bless our bodies (food, drink, clothing, vv. 25-32). Also, Rom 1:21 suggests that the two duties for which every human being is responsible are to "honor Him as God" (primary purpose) and to "give thanks" (secondary purpose). The first question of the Westminster Catechism asks, "What is the chief end of man?" The answer: "To glorify God and enjoy Him forever."

3. Visible and Invisible Universes

First, creation was from nothing; second, creation was for the purpose of God's goodness and glory; and third, creation includes both the visible and invisible universes. This last point is taken from Col 1:16, "For by Him all things were created, both in the heavens and on earth, visible and invisible, whether thrones or dominions or rulers or authorities—all things have been created through Him and for Him." This is simply affirming the comprehensiveness of creation. Anything that exists besides God belongs to the category of created beings. This includes the visible universe, the physical world of our own existence, and the invisible universe, primarily the spiritual world of angels.

The entire physical universe, organic and inorganic, came into existence by means of God's *ex nihilo* creation. "In the beginning God created the heavens and the earth" (Gen 1:1). "Heavens" refers to "the heavens above" in the sense of the cosmos, or everything that exists in space in addition to the earth itself. The enormity of it all is staggering. That God simply spoke it into existence is beyond our comprehension. "By the word of the LORD the heavens were made, and by the breath of His mouth all their host. . . . Let all the inhabitants of the world stand in awe of Him. For He spoke, and it was done; He commanded, and it stood fast" (Ps 33:6-9).

The invisible universe is the world of spiritual realities as distinguished from physical. This includes the souls or spirits of human beings, which are at home within the physical universe but are not made of the physical stuff of the universe. It mainly includes the whole world of angels, both good and fallen. We must never forget that this invisible universe is part of the creation of God, too. Just because human spirits and angelic spirits are *spirit*, this does not mean that we are metaphysically equivalent to God, who also is spirit. Angels and human spirits are *created, finite* spirits, subject to limitations of space and time. God alone is *infinite, uncreated* spirit, and thus occupies a distinct metaphysical category all by himself. It is important to remember this so that we do not attribute divine characteristics (such as omniscience and omnipresence) to angels, and especially to Satan and the other fallen angels.

B. The Bible's Testimony to Creation

In a work of this size it is impossible to cite all of the biblical references to creation. When I wrote my book on God the Creator, I did collect all the creation passages together; it took more than eight pages of text (*GC*, 134-142). The sheer mass of data clearly shows that the doctrine of creation is not just an incidental aspect of God's teaching; indeed, it is one of the main themes of Scripture. Here I will cite only a few representative texts.

Some passages refer to the act or fact of creation as such, most echoing Gen 1:1. "In six days the LORD made the heavens and the earth" (Exod 20:11; see 31:17). "You alone are the LORD, You have made the heavens, the heaven of heavens with all their host, the earth and all that is on it" (Neh 9:6). "It is I who made the earth, and created man upon it. I stretched out the heavens with My hands and I ordained all their host" (Isa 45:12). "All things originate from God"

(1 Cor 11:12). "By the word of God the heavens existed long ago and the earth was formed out of water and by water" (2 Pet 3:5). Some texts refer specifically to the creation of mankind (e.g., Gen 1:27; 5:1-2; Job 33:4,6; Ps 100:3; Matt 19:4).

Some passages add specific details about the creation in addition to the simple fact that it occurred. First, God created by the word of his command. All things should praise his name, "for He commanded and they were created" (Ps 148:5; see Ps 33:6,9; Heb 11:3; 2 Pet 3:5). Second, God created by his wisdom. "O LORD, how many are Your works! In wisdom You have made them all" (Ps 104:24; see Prov 3:19; 8:22-31). Third, creation is the work of the Father, the Son, and the Holy Spirit. Genesis 1:2 pictures the Spirit as bringing order to the formless mass: "And the Spirit of God was moving over the surface of the waters." The NT ascribes creation to the eternally preexisting Logos, God the Son (John 1:3; 1 Cor 8:6; Col 1:16; Heb 1:2). Fourth, creation is a fact which we accept on faith. We have no eyewitness account; we know it happened only because the Creator has told us so, and we believe him. "By faith we understand that the worlds were prepared by the word of God" (Heb 11:3).

The Bible speaks often not only of the fact of creation; it also speaks many times of God in a way that calls attention to his role as Creator. Sometimes he is simply referred to as the Creator (Eccl 12:1; Rom 1:25; 1 Pet 4:19); often he is called the "Maker" (e.g., Ps 95:6; 115:15; Isa 44:24; Jer 10:16). Sometimes when God speaks or is spoken about, the fact that he is the Creator of heaven and earth is interjected just to emphasize his power or trustworthiness or authority. For example, "My help comes from the LORD, who made heaven and earth" (Ps 121:2). "You have forgotten the LORD your Maker, who stretched out the heavens and laid the foundations of the earth" (Isa 51:13). "I fear the LORD God of heaven who made the sea and the dry land" (Jonah 1:9). "You should turn from these vain things to a living God, who made the heaven and the earth and the sea and all that is in them" (Acts 14:15). "Worship Him who made the heaven and the earth and sea and springs of waters" (Rev 14:7).

C. Implications of Creation

God's work of creation is the fundamental building block of the Christian worldview. Many of the truths we take for granted all our lives depend upon the fact that we live in a God-created world. Here we will point out some of them (*GC*, ch. 4).

1. Creation and Truth

We have already indicated in the introductory chapter that the fact of *ex nihilo* creation is the presupposition for the existence of absolute truth of any kind. All created beings are bound by the egocentric predicament and are thus unable to discover absolute truth on their own. Only the transcendent, omniscient Creator-God has absolute knowledge of all things and can therefore be a source of certain truth. Thus the fact of creation is a death blow to relativism and the foundation of truth and sound doctrine.

2. Creation and Nature

Some monistic world views (e.g., Hinduism) consider the material world and anything made out of physical stuff to be unreal, an illusion; some dualistic cosmologies (e.g., Gnosticism) consider matter as such actually to be evil. Even some Christians down through the centuries have been skeptical of the goodness and value of material stuff. Such notions are all shown to be false by the fact of creation. The fact that God created all things in this natural world and called them "very good" (Gen 1:31) ensures the goodness of matter. Matter is not evil; it is not opposed to God but is part of God's purpose. "Everything created by God is good, and nothing is to be rejected if it is received with gratitude" (1 Tim 4:4).

For example, there is nothing evil about the human body and its natural appetites (see Acts 14:17; 1 Tim 6:17), though like any other material thing, it is subject to evil use and control. The negative elements of bodily existence, such as suffering and death, are the consequences of sin; they are not inherent in human nature as such. Salvation is not the shedding of the body but the redemption of the body (Rom 8:23).

Though creation renders the material world real and good, it also shows that it is not absolute or ultimate; it is not something divine or sacred. Contrary to most pantheism, the forces of nature are natural, not supernatural. Because it is created, the world is finite or limited; it is *contingent*. It is not self-existent; it owes its existence to God and is completely dependent upon him.

One result of regarding the world as created and contingent rather than divine and sacred has been the development of modern science. As long as nature is endowed with an aura of divinity, there is reluctance to probe its mysteries or violate its sacred presence with mundane investigations. Nature is too awesome for science to develop. But the doctrine of creation demythologizes, dedivinizes, desacralizes nature. It brings the world down to an approachable and manageable level where it is seen as finite and contingent and thus appropriate for scientific study. "In historical fact," says Blaikie, "it was only when mediæval Christendom, deeply influenced by Greek thought patterns, was released into the freedom of the Hebrew/Christian distinction between Creator and creation, God and nature, that modern science was born" (52).

3. Creation and Man

Since a full discussion of the biblical doctrine of man will follow shortly, here we will only summarize the importance of creation for our self-understanding.

First, the doctrine of creation means that a human being is *wholly a creature.* Contrary to many pagan concepts, man's entire being—body and spirit—is created and thus good but finite. The human spirit is in no sense divine or inherently immortal; it is not "a little part of God."

Second, the doctrine of creation means that human existence has *meaning and purpose*. Questions such as "Who am I?" and "Why am I here?" do have answers. This is true because creation as such, as a free act of God, has a purpose. As we saw earlier, God created all things for his goodness and glory. Herein lies the purpose of human existence, i.e., to receive God's goodness and to give him glory. But if we are not part of a world that was deliberately created by God, there is no purpose for human existence.

Third, if human beings individually have a purpose, then so does *human history* as a whole. Because of creation there is meaning in the totality of things; the whole of cosmic history is defined in terms of God's creative purpose. History is going somewhere; it was created with a goal. That goal is the universal establishment of God's Kingdom (i.e., kingship). All of history is moving toward the day when God will bring about with finality the universal acknowledgment of his lordship (Isa 45:23; Phil 2:10-11).

4. Creation and Worship

Another implication is that the fact of creation is the very foundation for our worship of God. Creation itself makes God *worthy* of worship. When we consider the awesomeness of creation from nothing, what other response could we possibly make? "By the word of the LORD the heavens were made . . . . Let all the earth fear the LORD; let all the inhabitants of the world stand in awe of Him. For He spoke, and it was done; He commanded, and it stood fast" (Ps 33:6-9). "Come, let us worship and bow down, let us kneel before the LORD Our Maker" (Ps 95:6). "Worthy are You, our Lord and our God, to receive glory and honor and power; for You created all things" (Rev 4:11; see 14:7). Paul says that only fools worship and serve creatures rather than the Creator (Rom 1:22-25).

5. Creation and Ethics

The basic ethical question is, "What ought I to do?" It can be broken down into two more specific problems, the question of ethical *knowledge* (the "what") and the question of ethical *obligation* (the "ought"). The key to answering both of these questions is the reality of the *ex nihilo* creation of all things.

Ethical knowledge is simply the list of the proper commandments or norms by which we ought to live. Do such norms exist? Are there any ethical rules or values that transcend times and cultures and apply to all peoples in all eras? Those who have no room for a transcendent Creator-God in their worldview must answer *No*; without a transcendent Creator all norms are necessarily immanent and relative. In the end each person will have his own personal ethical code, and society will operate according to the principle of "might makes right." But such an approach to ethical knowledge is false, because of the fact of creation. Just as the transcendent Creator-God is the source of absolute truth, so also is he the source of absolute ethical norms.

The other ethical question is the problem of obligation or oughtness. Why is there such a thing as oughtness in the first place? Upon what is obligation based? Does anyone have the authority to require others to obey certain rules? Again, if there is no Creator-God, the answer is no. Without a creator there is no true obligation. The principle of "might makes right" allows only for hypothetical obligation, i.e., "*If* you don't want me to hurt you, *then* you 'ought' to do what I tell you." But in a created universe, the Creator is the rightful Lord and Owner of all things, including human beings. This is what gives him the right or authority to make the rules and enforce obedience to them. Thus creation is the basis of the oughtness assumed by ethics.

A final point about the relation between creation and ethics is the fact that creation rather than redemption is the foundation for ethics. The basic rules for right and wrong are derived from the nature and will of God in his role as Creator, not from his work as Redeemer and the circumstances of redemption. This means that it is a serious error (a part of the "christological fallacy") to think that Jesus Christ in his role as Redeemer is the true basis for ethical obligation and the primary source for ethical norms. Redemption has a profound effect upon ethics, especially in the areas of motivation and ability to obey, but the foundational issues of norm and obligation are based upon creation. (See *GC*, 166-191.)

D. The Primacy of Creation

Sometimes a genuine but misguided piety leads sincere Christians to a christological distortion not only of their ethics, but of their total theology and worldview. In their effort to exalt Jesus Christ they mistakenly try to "make him central" in every aspect of life. We hear that "Jesus is everything," e.g., in doctrine, in ethics, in worship, in church music, in everyday piety. As someone has said, "Jesus is the key to the understanding of the cosmos" (Jenkins, 35-36). Another writer, in an article called "Making Jesus Central," says, "Every spiritual concept, practice, or deed must find its essential meaning and value in Jesus Christ." Also, "every doctrine and ordinance of the faith must be dependent on Him, His nature, character, and deeds, for meaning" (Cook, 35-36).

Again I say, this is a serious error. It tries to make Jesus fill certain roles he was never intended to fill, and it ignores the factors that are meant to be truly central in certain aspects of our lives. It especially ignores the significance of creation and of our relation to God as Creator (*GC*, 171-191).

In answer to the question, "What should be central in our lives?" there are different answers depending on which area of life is being considered. That is, central in what way? If we mean *essentially* central, the answer is that God the Creator, not Jesus, is central. That is, we can explain our essential nature as human beings only in light of creation. At its deepest level the essence of our existence is rooted in the creation, and our primary relationship is to God as Creator. In answer to the question "Who am I?" we must begin with the awareness that we are creatures of God.

The creation-relation is thus the primary reference point for the basic facts of our existence. For instance, the *will* of God (as in ethics) comes to us as the will of the Creator. As we have just seen, ethics is grounded in creation, not redemption. This is why the basic commandments of God (such as those regarding marriage and divorce) apply to all people, not just to Christians. Also, since man's essential relation to God is to God as Creator, this is the universal God-man relationship, the one shared by all human beings. This is the only sense in which we may speak of "the brotherhood of man." All human beings are related to God the Creator in that all know him and his will through general revelation, and all have sinned against him. But not all are related to God as Redeemer; this is an acquired relationship.

The question of centrality must be asked and answered in another way. If we mean what is *epistemologically* central, then the answer is that the Bible, not Jesus, is central. Those who think that such a statement dethrones Jesus and elevates the Bible to the status of an idol just do not understand the role of epistemology and the difference between form and content. The question of epistemology deals with how we get *knowledge* about our subject matter, and it is basic in any field of inquiry. But this is only a formal question and is not in competition with the content learned thereby. When we say that the Bible is epistemologically central we mean that it and it alone is the source of true knowledge about the One who is central in our lives. This is the meaning of the time-honored slogan, "The Bible and the Bible alone is our only **rule** of faith and practice." Faith in the Bible as the source of truth about the Creator and about Christ does not contradict our faith in Christ as the source of our salvation.

This leads to the final way in which the question about centrality must be asked, namely, what is *existentially* central in our lives? When the question is asked this way, the proper answer is Jesus Christ. He is (or should be) the practical reference point around which we organize our lives. In our day-by-day living, Christ is the center of our consciousness. Our strongest *felt* relationship to God is that which we have with Christ our Lord and Savior. He is the One whom we know most about and to whom we feel closest. Since he is the One who has saved us from our sins, we owe him more than we owe anyone else. He is usually central in our worship. We want our lives to be Christ-centered and Christ-honoring. Our very name is *Christ*ian. In short, all our conscious service to God is in the name of Jesus Christ (Col 3:17). This is the way it ought to be.[2]

II. THE WORK OF PROVIDENCE

By "providence" we mean God's continuous activity of preserving and governing the universe by his knowledge, power, wisdom, and goodness, for the fulfillment of his purposes in creation. How does it differ from the work of creation? As explained above, the latter deals with the *origin* of the universe, to that singular activity by which in the beginning God brought the universe into existence. Providence, on the other hand, deals with the ongoing *history* of the universe, and to God's continuing multiformed activity in it.

Certain questions naturally arise about this history. Why do things happen the way they do? Who or what initiates or determines the actions and events that occur day by day? Is there a power other than or greater than man that fixes his destiny and shapes the general or even specific outcome of things? To what extent is God involved, if any?

We may distinguish three possible causes or forces or principles of action which are responsible for whatever happens in the world. Any one of them may be viewed as the sole cause of what happens, or any two or all three may be seen as working together in particular combinations. The first possibility is *God*, whose nature is variously interpreted according to one's religion or worldview. The second is impersonal *law*, another concept with a wide range of interpretations, from the ordinary laws of nature to some mysterious cosmic force. The third is the category of free-will creatures, including both angels and human beings; for the sake of brevity we shall refer to this category as *man*.

A. Three Major Views of God and History

Our first task is to compare and contrast three major approaches to the question of providence. The main issue is how God is related to the ongoing world; thus our three views will be presented from that perspective. They are as follows: (1) God has nothing to do with anything that happens; (2) God has everything to do with everything that happens; and (3) God has something to do with everything that happens but not the same thing.

1. God Has Nothing to Do with Anything

The first explanation of ongoing history may be called the *secular* view, since it omits the transcendent God altogether as one of the causative factors. This is the view of all atheists, who deny the existence of God in the first place, and of all deists, who believe in a Creator but deny his participation in postcreation events. Law and man are all that remain, and both of these forces are completely immanent, i.e., totally contained within the world. In every variation of the secular view law is a factor; the only question is the extent of man's involvement.

Some say the only causative factor is impersonal law alone; some kind of law determines everything, including human thoughts and actions. (This is a secular form of determinism; see *GRu*, 50-66.) For some this is an all-encompassing cosmic metaphysical law such as fate or karma. It is expressed in popular jargon in such platitudes as "Whatever will be, will be" (*"Que sera, sera!"*) and "When your time is up, you're gonna go." For others everything is determined by laws of nature, both psychological and physical. For psychological determinists (behaviorists) all things related to human beings are the product not only of the laws of heredity but also of environmental factors. For others the physical laws of nature alone are sufficient to explain all things. Among these are mechanists, who say that the laws of nature operate like a machine, according to strictly predictable patterns. Even one's thoughts and choices are predetermined by such laws: "The brain secretes thought as the liver secretes bile." Others who attribute everything to the physical laws of nature do not see these laws as locked into a single course of action but rather allow for the possibility of variable results, depending on how two or more independent causal sequences may collide. Thus there is a certain randomness or chance in the way things happen, especially at microlevels such as genetic combinations.

These variations are all similar in that they posit only one major cause for all things, i.e., some form of impersonal law. Not only is God excluded; human input is also ruled out. Thus there is no such thing as free will.

The other main version of the secular view does allow for human input, saying that everything is caused by the two immanent forces working together: law and man. For example, evolutionists often see the law of nature operating alone through the prehuman stages of evolution. But with the development of the human brain, man is now able to take control of the process and add his own decisions to the pattern of ongoing events (e.g., through genetic engineering). Secular Humanism often takes this form. Another combination of law and man posits the existence of cosmic metaphysical energy that can be harnessed and directed by knowing individuals for their own purposes. This is the fundamental cosmology of witchcraft and occultism in general, as illustrated by "the Force" in *Star Wars* mythology, and by the New Age Movement dictum, "Create your own reality."

In general, in these latter forms of the secular view, man in his sinful pride tends to see himself as the one who has the final say as to his own life and destiny: "I am the master of my fate; I am the captain of my soul." (See *GRu*, 40-49.)

What all these views have in common is the exclusion of the personal God as a factor in the events that take place in the history of the world and the life of human beings. God has nothing to do with anything that happens; the world is totally independent of God.

2. God Has Everything to Do with Everything

A second explanation of the ongoing history of the world goes to the other extreme; it says that every detail of every event in every sense is totally dependent upon a personal divine being. God has everything to do with everything that happens; he is the only true causative factor in the universe. "Law" and "free will" are just names we give to certain ways that God works. This is called *theistic determinism* (*GRu*, 66-86). Such a view is found both outside of and within Christendom, the major version of the latter being Calvinism, which will be our main focus here.

For Calvinism the key word is *causation*: God is the ultimate cause of every-thing (*GRu*, 168-187). A distinction is made between primary and secondary causes, or ultimate and proximate causes, or final and immediate causes; but in the end it all comes back to God. As noted above, this omnicausality is central to the Calvinist's concept of divine sovereignty.

The cornerstone of this concept of providence is God's *eternal decree*. This de-cree is the act by which God, in eternity past, for his own purpose and glory and without regard to anything outside himself, foreordained "whatsoever comes to pass." This is the Calvinist doctrine of predestination. The decree is called *eternal* because it was made before the actual creation and existence of anything outside of God. It is thus a detailed blueprint or computer program for everything that would ever happen. By means of the decree everything is predestined; history, or providence, is simply the execution of the decree which was fixed in eternity.

This decree is also *comprehensive*: "whatsoever comes to pass" leaves no excep-tions. All natural events and all human choices are thereby preprogrammed. It is also *efficacious*, which means that everything included in the decree will certainly happen by the unfailing power of the decree as such. To be sure, the world itself includes many causative agents, such as natural laws; but these are only secondary causes or instruments that God is using, and the decree has already ordained the specific effect that will be produced by these causes.

A final characteristic of the decree is that it is *unconditional* or absolute. That is, nothing in the decree has been conditioned by anything outside of God; no part of the decree is a response to or reaction to something outside himself. For example, God does not foreordain anything based on his foreknowledge of crea-tures' free-will acts. What God decrees can in no way be dependent upon or con-ditioned by the creature; else he would not be sovereign. As sovereign, God must always *act* and never *react* (*GRu*, 217-228). This is why the Calvinist must reject the idea of conditional predestination to salvation on the basis of foreseen faith (Rom 8:29). Of course God responds to a penitent's faith just as he responds to or answers prayer. But neither the faith nor the prayer is originated by the crea-ture; both are themselves predetermined by the eternal decree.

One result of such a decree is that no creature has a truly free will in any sig-nificant sense (*GRu*, 175-179). Free will is asserted, but it is redefined so as to be compatible with deterministic sovereignty. Significant freedom is the power to choose between opposites, the ability to choose to do something or not to do it. But Calvinism replaces this concept of freedom with the idea that free will is the ability to choose in accord with one's own inner character, motives, and desires. In other words, a person senses within himself a certain desire or motive or incli-nation to choose a certain way in a given situation, then proceeds to choose in ac-cordance with his own desires. This sounds like true freedom until we realize that God has actually predestined all motives and desires. In the final analysis God predetermines what choices each person will make, simply by predetermining which desires and motives will be present in the person's heart at any given time. Such choices are "free" only in the sense that the person *feels* he is making a voluntary choice, even though everything about the situation has been predetermined and is being caused by God.

According to Calvinism, then, God's providence is simply his ongoing causation of what he has eternally decreed will happen. It is like the production of a gigantic claymation or stop-action movie based on a comprehensive prepared script. Such a view of providence is the origin of the idea that "God has a purpose for everything," an idea that leads some to blame God for every bad circumstance and to agonize over the question, "Why is God doing this to me?"

3. God Has Something to Do with Everything

Neither of the above extreme views of providence is supported by Scripture. The rest of this chapter will present what I believe is the biblical view of why things happen the way they do. The Bible makes it clear that God does indeed have something to do with events in the created world. In fact, he has something to do with everything that takes place. But he does not have *everything* to do with everything, i.e., the nature of his involvement is not the same from event to event. God works in the world in more than one way.

The key question we must ask is, what *kind* of world did God create? Certainly he could have created some other kind if he had so desired, even the kind envisioned by Calvinists. But in fact he did *not* create a world in which he pulls all the puppet strings or punches all the remote control buttons. The world he made is instead governed by a divine providence that has the following characteristics: relative independence, divine self-limitation, sovereign control, and conditionality.

First, God created a world with *relative independence*. That is, creatures are independent from God, but not totally so. God made the world with two distinct forces or self-contained "energy packs" that have an inherent power to initiate action and cause things to happen. One is impersonal, the other personal.

The impersonal causal force is *natural law*, or the physical laws of nature such as gravity, electromagnetism, chemical reactions, animal instincts, and the laws of motion. These natural laws are self-contained forces that are part of the very essence of matter as created by God. Material stuff is designed by the Creator to operate in certain constant, uniform, and predictable ways, without the need for constant input from a divine control panel. These laws work the way they do because of the way atoms were put together by God in the initial creation; they were set in motion by the very act of creation itself.

The personal causal force is *free will*, which is present in human beings and angels. The inherent essence of the spiritual part of our being includes the ability to assess situations where choices must be made, and to initiate specific courses of action in accordance with our own personal and unforced decisions. We are free to act without our acts having been predetermined by God and without constant input from a divine remote control apparatus. We have a truly free will, or the power to choose between options and opposites, with the ability to actualize more than one choice. Being made in God's image, we thus have an ability to create *ex nihilo*, i.e., we have the power to create *events* (not material stuff).

We must remember, though, that the independence of both natural law and free-will beings is not absolute autonomy. It is only a relative, qualified, limited independence. The sovereign, omnipotent Creator maintains *control* over the world and over these two forces, with the ability and option to intervene anytime he chooses and to counteract these forces if that is his will. How he does this will be explained below.

The second characteristic of God's providence is *divine self-limitation*. As a free act, creation was not something God *had* to do. But when he did decide to create, he limited himself in the same way human beings limit themselves when they choose to get a pet, buy a car, buy a house, get married, or have children. When we make such decisions we accept certain responsibilities and commit ourselves to act in certain ways. Such choices are *self*-limiting, however, since we do not *have* to make any of them. The decision to create was such a choice for God; though it was a free act, when he created the universe he brought something into existence he is now responsible for and must relate to.

The divine decision to give relative independence to created natural laws and free-will beings only intensifies the self-limitation. When God made such a world, he committed himself to honor his own decision. In a real sense he made a commitment or a covenant with man to let him be what he was made to be. He must now respect the integrity of his own choice, which means that he must also respect the integrity of the creation as created. He must allow his creatures to operate according to the relative independence he himself bestowed upon them, even if this means that at times man will use his freedom to choose evil.

Some may think that the very suggestion of "divine limitation" is an assault upon the sovereignty of God, but this is not true for two reasons. First, it does not diminish God's sovereignty because it is a freely chosen *self*-limitation. Before God made this particular world, he knew all the other possible options and could have chosen any of them. He knew all the possible things that might happen in this kind of world. But this is the one he made; and he did so voluntarily, freely accepting all the limitations involved. Truly this is not a violation of divine sovereignty but an expression of it.

The second reason why such self-limitation does not violate God's sovereignty is that he reserves the right and has the power to intervene in the course of nature and the processes of human decision-making if his purposes demand it. Most of the time he does not intervene, but sometimes he does. Thus God still has the ultimate word in everything; he is still sovereign.

This ability to intervene or not is the essence of the third characteristic of God's providence, namely, *sovereign control*. Whereas the Calvinist interprets sovereignty in terms of total causation, in biblical perspective the key word is *control*. Some think control is the same as causation, as if it means something akin to sitting at a control panel and pushing all the buttons, and in that way actually causing events to happen. But that is not the sense in which we are using this word. To say that God has sovereign control over his universe means that he is *in control of* everything that happens, even though he does not cause everything.

That God exercises sovereign control in his providence means that his hand is indeed in everything that happens, in one of two ways. That is, whatever happens is either *caused* or *permitted* by God. Of course we do not deny that God directly causes many of the things that happen, in accordance with his purposes. Throughout the history of mankind leading up to Jesus Christ, he caused whatever was necessary to work out his plan of redemption. He causes things to happen to carry out his temporal judgments on his enemies; he causes blessings to fall upon his people, especially in answer to prayer.

The other way that God exercises sovereign control is by permitting whatever he does not cause.[3] In his omniscience God knows everything that has happened, is happening, and is about to happen. In his foreknowledge he sees history unfolding according to the workings of natural law and free will. As he thus monitors the cosmos, he keeps his finger on the "delete" key, as it were, in order either to *permit* a particular thing to happen or to intervene and *prevent* it from happening, as if he were punching "delete." Such intervention in order to prevent something from happening is another example of the way God acts causally in the history of the universe. Thus by saying either "go" or "no go," i.e., either by permitting or preventing, God has the final say about everything.

This is why we say that God has something to do with everything that happens but not the same thing. Some events he causes; the rest he permits. Another way to say this is that "whatever happens is the will of God," but not in the same sense of that term (*GRu*, ch 8). Some things happen according to God's *purposive* will; these are the things that God *causes*. It was his purposive will to create (Rev 4:11); it is his purposive will to accomplish redemption through Jesus Christ (Luke 22:42; Acts 2:23; 4:28; Heb 10:7). God's purposive will is done through his special providential intervention in history (Isa 46:10-11; Jer 23:20; Rom 8:28).

Whatever happens that is not caused by God in terms of his purposive will is nevertheless the will of God in the sense of his *permissive* will. This includes most things that take place via the relative independence of natural law and free will. All such things, even sins, are the will of God in the sense that he allows them to happen. This is the sense of *epitrepo* in 1 Cor 16:7, "I hope to remain with you for some time, if the Lord permits"; and Heb 6:3, "For this we will do, if God permits." The word *eao* has the same sense in Acts 14:16, "In the generations gone by He permitted all the nations to go their own ways"; and in Acts 16:7, "They were trying to go into Bithynia, and the Spirit of Jesus did not permit them." A similar word is *thelo*, as in Acts 18:21, "I will return to you again, if God wills";

and 1 Cor 4:19, "But I will come to you soon, if the Lord wills." The use of *thelo* in the sense of God's permissive will is seen especially in James 4:13-15. Whenever you make a plan, says James, you should not just say, "I will do it." Rather, "you ought to say, 'If the Lord wills, we will live and also do this or that'" (v. 15).

The conditional nature of God's permissive will (the "if" element) simply emphasizes God's sovereign ability to intervene in order to prevent any contingent plan from occurring.

In exercising his sovereign control via causation on the one hand and either permission or prevention on the other, God is manifesting his great attributes of omniscience (especially foreknowledge) and omnipotence. He accomplishes his purposive will in conjunction with his foreknowledge of human decisions (Acts 2:23). Also, through his absolute foreknowledge of every plan of men's hearts and through his absolute prerogative and power to either permit or prevent the carrying out of that plan, God maintains his complete and sovereign control over the universe.

The fourth and final characteristic of God's providence is *conditionality*. The Calvinist idea that everything God does must be unconditioned, i.e., that God cannot react or respond to anything outside himself and be sovereign at the same time, is an unwarranted presupposition. Contrary to this assumption we here affirm that God is constantly responding to and reacting to his creatures, especially man, without the slightest threat to his sovereignty. In fact, most of God's works in this world are his reaction to or response to foreknown human acts. This is the way the Bible pictures it. Virtually every major action of God recorded in the Bible after Gen 3:1 is a response to human sin. The Abrahamic covenant, the establishment of Israel, the incarnation of Jesus, the death and resurrection of Christ, the establishment of the church, the Bible itself—all are part of the divine reaction to man's sin.

An arrangement where God reacts to man's choices would be a violation of sovereignty only if God were forced into it, only if it were a necessity imposed upon God from without. But this is not the case. It was God's sovereign choice to create a universe inhabited by free-will creatures whose decisions would to a great extent determine the course of God's own actions. It is arbitrary and false to say that such a situation negates divine sovereignty when the situation itself is the result of his sovereignty.

Thus in answer to the question, "Why do things happen the way they do?" we can say that there are indeed three causal factors at work in the world: God, free-will beings, and natural law. Thus it is wrong to blame God for every unpleasant or tragic thing that occurs. He may cause some of them, for punishment or chastisement; but most are due to sinful human choices, both our own and those of others (including Adam). It is also wrong to think that everything happens for a purpose, especially a divine purpose. Many things happen because of human sin, carelessness, ignorance, and stupidity. We can learn lessons from them all, but this does not mean that God caused them just to teach us certain lessons. In the same way God can bring good results even out of bad things that he does not cause in the first place (Rom 8:28).

B. Four Kinds of Events

As we now focus specifically upon God's activity in the ongoing world, we will distinguish and discuss four major types of events: events of general providence, events of special providence, miraculous events, and spiritual events.

1. General Providence

General providence (*GRu*, ch. 3) is what we call God's regular, uniform way of acting with respect to nature and human history. This is the rule; the other three kinds of events are exceptions. Even when God is not implementing his causative, purposive will in the course of history to accomplish his special purposes (e.g., redemption, judgment), he is constantly working to bring about his general purposes of sharing his goodness and displaying his glory. As Jesus testified, "My Father is working until now, and I Myself am working" (John 5:17).

As we shall explain below, general providence is primarily the domain of God's permissive will rather than his purposive will. Mere permission, however, is too limited a concept to adequately represent all of God's activity in general providence. On the other hand causation, which applies to God's purposive will, is too strong. Thus I will suggest that God's work of general providence can best be characterized as *participation*. God actively participates in the ordinary events of the ongoing world in three ways: preservation, permission, and presence.

First, God constantly *preserves* in existence all the things that he has created in both the invisible and visible realms. This work began as soon as the creation was completed. "In Him we live and move and exist" (Acts 17:28). Speaking specifically of God the Son, Col 1:17 says that "in Him all things hold together." Also, the Son "upholds all things by the word of His power" (Heb 1:3). This means that God's preserving power does not allow the universe to slip back into nonexistence, the *nihil* or nothingness from which it was created. Whatever has come into being from nothing can revert back to nothing; whatever has been exnihilated can be annihilated. And this is exactly what would happen, if God were not actively holding it all in existence by the constant operation of his preserving power.

In view of this, the key word for all creatures is *dependence*, in contrast with God's aseity or self-existence. We constantly and completely depend upon the power of God for our very existence; we depend upon his faithfulness to his own purposes in creation. God has decreed that his creatures shall continue in existence (Ps 148:5-6), and he will keep that promise. This frees us from the fear of nonexistence; God will not drop us back into the abyss of nothingness.

The second aspect of God's general providential participation in the world is *permission*. This means that all the events that take place by virtue of unaided natural laws and uninfluenced free-will choices are allowed to happen by God's permissive will. True permission of anything presupposes a knowledge of its imminent occurrence. Thus God's permissive will requires that he be continuously monitoring and supervising the cosmos by means of his omniscience, including his foreknowledge. That God has this kind of complete and detailed knowledge is clear from Scripture. The same God who tends the galaxies (Job 38:31-32) and counts and names the stars (Ps 147:4) also knows the number of hairs on our heads (Matt 10:30). "I know every bird of the mountains," he says (Ps 50:11), and he marks the death of every one (Matt 10:29).

This intimate knowledge of all creation is complemented by divine omnipotence, by which God is able to intervene in the normal course of things for his special purposes, e.g., to prevent an imminent event or to redirect natural law through his special providence. But in the absence of such intervention, the course of history proceeds according to God's permission and under his general providence.

The third aspect of general providence is God's *presence* in the world. When we think in general terms of God's universal presence, we call this his omnipresence. When we think of the way he is present to and within every specific point of space, we call this his immanence. The latter concept is more applicable here. Scripture indicates that God is present in the world in such a way that he observes and takes an active interest in the specific events that take place everywhere. In this way he participates in everything that is going on.

This is true of human decisions and events. God is present to us and with us in every situation, not just as the one who will judge our every deed in the end but as the one who is keenly interested in our lives in the here and now. He grieves when sinners reject him (Matt 23:37), and he rejoices when a sinner repents (Luke 15:10[4]). He empathizes when a Christian is tempted (Heb 4:15) and grieves when a Christian sins (Eph 4:30), but it gives him pleasure when we obey him (1 Thess 4:1).

God's presence in the events of the natural world is abundantly noted in the Bible. He is portrayed as being intimately involved in everything that takes place. We get the impression that he loves the world of nature and cares for it with a tenderness and concern that we might observe in a gardener caring for his prize roses. He cares even for territories where no people dwell, sending rain so that its seeds may sprout (Job 38:25-27). He observes the birth of animals (Job 39:1), and not a sparrow dies "apart from your Father" (Matt 10:29; see Ps 104:29). God pictures himself as walking "in the recesses of the deep," as if he enjoys watching the sea creatures he put there (Job 38:16; Ps 104:25-26). Psalm 104 is a marvelous portrayal of God's intimate presence in his world. He makes light his cloak (v. 2). He uses the clouds for chariots and rides on the wings of the wind (v. 3). He feeds and waters his animals, and even waters his trees (vv. 11,14,16,27). Truly, "Let the glory of the LORD endure forever; let the LORD be glad in His works" (v. 31).

God is so close to the events of nature that he is constantly pictured as their primary cause. The movements of the celestial bodies and their relation to the earth are the work of God (Job 38:31-33; Ps 104:19). He controls light and darkness (Job 38:12,19-20; Ps 104:20), and "causes His sun to rise" (Matt 5:45). He generates earthquakes and volcanoes (Ps 104:32). He is the universal shepherd who attends to the needs of ravens, wild donkeys, oxen, ostriches, horses, hawks, and eagles (Job 38:39-41; 39:5-27). He feeds and provides for the animals (Ps 104:10-11,14,21,27-28; Ps 147:8-9; Luke 12:24). In reference to the weather he provides for evaporation (Job 36:27-28; Ps 135:6-7), the formation and movement of clouds (Job 36:29; 37:11-12; Ps 147:8), thunder and lightning (Job 36:30,32; 37:2-5; Ps 29:3-9), rain (Job 38:25-28,34,37; Matt 5:45), and ice and snow (Job 37:6,10; 38:22-23,29-30; Ps 147:15-18). "Fire and hail, snow and clouds; stormy wind, fulfilling His word" (Ps 148:8).

All of these natural events are pictured as the work of God. But how can this be, if they are happening only according to his permissive will? The answer is twofold. First, these are God's works by virtue of creation. God is the one who created the whole realm of nature, designing the basic atomic structure of its matter, arranging it into its present order, and endowing it with its various laws and properties that produce the events described above. When snow and hail fall and the wind blows, they are but fulfilling the mandate of creation (Ps 148:8). When animals act according to their marvelous instincts, they are carrying out the orders laid down for them from the beginning (Job 39–41). Second, the events of nature are God's works by virtue of his intimate providential participation in them as described above in terms of preservation, permission, and presence. The world is his garden. He planted it (creation), and he is lovingly tending it as it grows (providence). He holds it in the hollow of his hand.

2. Special Providence

In the next category of events we move beyond God's permissive will into his purposive will. These are matters of *special providence* (*GRu*, chs. 4, 5), which are things that happen not by unaided natural law and uninterrupted free will, but rather as a result of God's intervention into these processes. They differ from miracles and spiritual events in that they do not involve any kind of violation or overriding of natural law and free will. In special providence God does manipulate natural law and influence free will choices, but he does not suspend or negate them. He thus causes results that would not have occurred without such intervention but which are still within the possibilities of natural law itself and which do not violate the integrity of free will.

This special intervention is necessary so that God can carry out his special purposes, which involve such things as punishing his enemies, blessing and chastising his people, answering prayer, and especially preparing for the coming of the Redeemer through the long and turbulent history of Israel. Much of the history recorded in the OT is a record of God's special providential intervention for this last purpose.

What kinds of events occur as a result of special providence? In the final analysis the purpose of such intervention is to influence human decisions, and the Bible states over and over that many events in human history have been caused by God as the result of such influence. In general terms he is the one who "removes kings and establishes kings" (Dan 2:21), who sets over mankind "whomever He wishes" (Dan 5:21). "The lot is cast into the lap, but its every decision is from the LORD" (Prov 16:33). More specifically God exercised a general control over the nation of Israel and the nations that interacted with it. "For the LORD has driven out great and strong nations from before you" (Josh 23:9). For example, "The LORD has given your enemies the Moabites into your hands" (Judg 3:28); "I will give the Philistines into your hand" (1 Sam 23:4). On the other hand, "the LORD will give over the army of Israel into the hands of the Philistines" (1 Sam 28:19). God used the Assyrian armies like an axe or a club to punish Israel (Isa 10:5,15; see 7:17-20); he did the same with Babylon (Jer 5:15-19; 51:20). "I am raising up the Chaldeans [Babylonians]," he says (Hab 1:6).

How does God control nations? Only by influencing the decisions of individuals. He does this in general terms by controlling life and death: "The LORD kills and makes alive" (1 Sam 2:6; see 2 Sam 12:15,18; Job 34:14-15; Jas 4:15). He establishes kings and influences their decisions (Job 34:24; Ps 75:7). "The king's heart is like channels of water in the hand of the LORD; He turns it wherever He wishes" (Prov 21:1). He stirs up the hearts of kings to punish Israel (1 Chr 5:26; 2 Chr 21:16) and to bless them (Ezra 1:1; 6:22; 7:27). God has even influenced sinful decisions in some, as in the hardening of Pharaoh's heart (Exod 10:1,20), Sihon's heart (Deut 2:30), and the hearts of the Canaanite kings (Josh 11:20). God used the sins of Joseph's brothers to send him to Egypt: "You meant evil against me, but God meant it for good" (Gen 50:20; see 45:5-9). And he used the sins of Judas to deliver Jesus to his redemptive death (Acts 2:23; 4:27-28).

This is only a brief sampling of the many biblical references that speak of God as the one who has caused significant events in the history of redemption involving specific human decisions. The question now is this: *How* does God accomplish this and still maintain the free will of the people actually performing these events? The Calvinist solution is to eliminate significant free will and to make God alone the ultimate cause of all things through his efficacious decree. We must reject this solution as inconsistent with free will, but at the same time we must offer a solution that does justice to the clear teaching that God is in control of human decisions and events. What follows is a brief attempt to do this.[5]

Basically God works through special providence to influence human decisions in two ways. The most obvious way is by the subtle alteration of the processes of nature. Under general providence these processes operate according to fixed patterns (natural laws) without direct interference from God. But the immanent Creator maintains an intimate presence in and control over these processes, and is able to intervene and alter them if he chooses. This is exactly what happens in special providence. Unlike miracles, which violate or bypass natural laws, special providence stays within the boundaries or possibilities of such laws, but nevertheless brings about a result that would not have happened via general providence alone.

For example, God may punish or reward or correct through his manipulation of the weather. For his purposes he may summon a great wind (Jonah 1:4) or call for a drought (Amos 4:7; Hag 1:11). By ordering a heavy snow or rain, "He seals the hand of every man, that all men may know His work" (Job 37:7). A storm cloud "changes direction, turning around by His guidance, that it may do whatever He commands it on the face of the inhabited earth. Whether for correction, or for His world, or for lovingkindness, He causes it to happen" (Job 37:12-13). "This is the way he governs the nations" (Job 36:31, NIV).

Another example is God's control of the natural processes of the body in relation to disease and healing. By manipulating the human immune system and causing certain microorganisms to proliferate, God can cause a plague to strike, leading to sickness and death (2 Chr 21:14-19; Amos 4:10). By inducing a chemical imbalance in the brain God can cause irrational behavior (Dan 4:25). God struck David's son with a sickness that produced death (2 Sam 12:14-18). On the other hand, God can strengthen the body's ability to fight disease and heal itself (Isa 38:1-5; Jas 5:14-16).

Another example of God's subtle alteration of natural processes is his control of muscle movements in the body. By manipulating the impulses of finger and wrist muscles he can determine how the lot falls; thus "the lot is cast into the lap, but its every decision is from the LORD" (Prov 16:33; see Jonah 1:7; Acts 1:26). In the same way God can control the flight of an arrow (1 Kgs 22:34).

A final example of the use of natural law to bring about the purposes of providence is God's control of the animal kingdom. God produced plagues of locusts and caterpillars to chastise his people (Deut 28:38-39; Joel 1–2 [see esp. 2:25]; Amos 4:9). How could God accomplish this within the bounds of natural law? Possibly by granting the species extraordinary reproductive success, or by causing an imbalance in the food chain in their favor. By controlling signals sent by the brain God could arrange for a ram to be caught in a thicket at just the right time (Gen 22:13) or a lion or a bear to appear at just the right moment (1 Kgs 13:26; 2 Kgs 2:24).

The point of such deliberate manipulation of natural processes is to produce certain effects among human beings, sometimes to bless or to punish, and sometimes to influence individuals to make certain decisions desired by God. That such manipulation of natural laws does not violate free will is shown by the biblical teaching that sometimes the desired result was not produced. Amos informed Israel that the Lord sent upon them famine, drought, and various plagues to induce repentance, "'yet you have not returned to Me,' declares the LORD" (Amos 4:6-11). God likewise sent drought and famine upon the postcaptivity Israelites to change their priorities, but they did not respond (Hag 1:1-11).

The second way God works through special providence is by directly planting certain thoughts and mental states into the minds of individuals. For example, God can instill within people's hearts either the attitude of favor toward others (Gen 39:21; Exod 12:36), or the attitude of fear (Exod 23:27; Deut 2:25). Also, I believe that we must grant that God can cause certain memories to arise or certain thoughts to be present in a person's consciousness. We usually think of Satan as doing this very thing as a means of temptation (e.g., John 13:2). If this is possible for Satan, surely it is possible for God. Once these thoughts or memories are present in the mind, they become the occasion for making decisions of one kind or another. These decisions are ours to make, but they may be influenced by the thoughts.

A possible example is Joseph's brothers, when they were planning to kill Joseph. It may be that God pressed upon Reuben's heart the thought of his father's love for Joseph and how much Joseph's death would hurt the old man. In any case something caused him to say, "Let us not take his life" (Gen 37:21). In like manner God may have put into Judah's mind the idea of selling Joseph to the traders who just "happened" to come along at that time (Gen 37:26-27).

It is possible that God hardened Pharaoh's heart in a similar manner. Via divine intervention certain thoughts may have flooded his mind, e.g., what a great loss of free labor it would be to lose these Israelites, or what a laughingstock he would be when other nations heard how a bunch of slaves bested him. God could have made sure that Pharaoh would think of these things at just the appropriate time, i.e., when he was weakening and about to let the people go.

We are suggesting, then, that God accomplishes his purposes in large part by such special providential intervention into the natural order and into human thought processes. Two cautions should be urged, however. First, when God does these things, he is not violating either natural law or free will. Even when inserting thoughts into our consciousness, God is not thereby *causing* anyone to make any particular choice; at most he is seeking to *influence* a decision. As pointed out above, sometimes the desired decision is not made (Amos 4:6-11; Hag 1:1-11). Free will is maintained.

Second, when we read the abundant biblical material about God's intervention to cause certain things to happen in the history of Israel, we must resist the temptation to generalize from these cases and assume that this is the way God works with every decision of every human will. These cases show what God can do and has done when his purposes require it, but we have no reason to think that he governs his world this way as a general rule. For example, God *can* turn the king's heart whenever he wishes (Prov 21:1), but he does not do so for every decision of every king. He does so in order to work out his special purposes; but for most of the world most of the time, general providence prevails.

This discussion of special providence shows how God indeed "rules over the nations" (Ps 22:28), how he is "the LORD Most High over all the earth" (Ps

97:9). "The LORD has established His throne in the heavens, and His sovereignty rules over all" (Ps 103:19).

3. Miraculous Events

The third major mode in which God relates to the ongoing world is *miracle* (*GRu*, ch. 6). In general providence God maintains permissive control over nature and history without intervening into their natural and free-will processes. In special providence he does intervene by redirecting the natural means already available in the world. But miracles are a step beyond special providence in the sense that God thereby overrides or bypasses or even violates natural laws, directly producing certain effects without any natural cause or means.

As an act of God a miracle has three major characteristics. First, it is *visible*; that is, the effect that it produces is observable by our senses, such as a healed body, a floating axe head, or a dozen baskets full of loaves and fishes. This distinguishes miracles from the next category of events, wherein the cause is no less supernatural but the result as such is hidden from our eyes.

Second, miracles are *contrary to natural law*. They supersede, transcend, overrule, or bypass natural law. They set it aside; they interrupt it. In other words, something happens in a miracle that cannot be explained by natural law alone. Even though the result as such is usually quite natural, e.g., a healed body, edible food, fire burning on an altar, the cause of any miraculous result can only be supernatural, as when such a result (e.g., wine) is produced instantaneously instead of by a normally long process.

The third characteristic of a miracle is that it serves as a *sign* (evidence, proof, confirmation) of the revealed truth which it accompanies (e.g., Heb 2:3-4). Indeed, one of the biblical terms for miracles is the word "sign." The reason they are able to function as signs is just because they are visible works of God that are contrary to natural law. As such they create wonder (which is another common term for them), and point beyond the natural world to their supernatural origin. This sign-purpose for miracles is well summed up in the words with which Jesus announced his imminent healing of the paralytic, "So that you may know" (Mark 2:10; see *GRu*, 232-236).

Miraculous events are real, but they are neither arbitrary nor frequent. They occur only in connection with God's redemptive works and the revelation that accompanies such works. Thus unlike general providence they will not be observed by everyone. Like special providence they are the result of God's purposive will, but they are not as abundant as the workings of special providence.

4. Supernatural Spiritual Events

The fourth and last way God works in the world is through *spiritual events*. Like miracles these acts of God are outside the sphere of natural law, but unlike miracles they are invisible and hidden, not detectable by human senses. This is why I am calling them "spiritual" events.

In many ways these are the most important and most powerful of God's works in the world, without which none of the other works matter. This is true because these spiritual events have to do mainly with God's great redemptive works and the salvation of sinners. They include God's saving works accomplished for us through Jesus Christ, especially the incarnation, the atonement, and the defeat of death and Satan through the resurrection. They also include the saving works applied directly to us, especially the forgiveness of our sins, our regeneration through the Holy Spirit, and the Spirit's indwelling to empower us for holy living. We may also include in this category the divine works of revelation and inspiration as worked in the hearts and minds of God's apostles and prophets, as we have already explained. God's saving works are more properly called works of *redemption* than works of providence; they will be discussed in detail in later chapters.

This concludes our discussion of the biblical doctrine of God: his nature, and his works of creation and providence. No wonder we praise him with songs such as "How Great Thou Art," and "What a Mighty God We Serve"!

NOTES ON CHAPTER FOUR

[1]Edward J. Young expressed this judgment in the classroom at Westminster Theological Seminary. See his book, *Studies*, 6-7.

[2]Let us not confuse centrality with exclusivity. Just because Christ is *central* in our daily living, this does not mean that he should be the *exclusive* object of our worship and devotion. For example, we should also sing hymns that praise God as Creator, and we should be consciously aware of the Holy Spirit's role in our lives.

[3]This permission is physical, not moral. In other words, God may allow murder to take place, but he has not given anyone the ethical or moral permission to murder.

[4]This text does not say that the angels rejoice; it says that there is rejoicing *in the presence of* the angels. God himself is in the presence of the angels.

[5]For more detail, see *GRu*, ch. 5; see also Cottrell, "Sovereignty," 97-119.

CHAPTER FIVE

THE INVISIBLE CREATION: ANGELS

We turn now from the nature and works of the Creator to the nature of the creation itself, beginning with a brief look at what the Bible teaches about the invisible creation (Col 1:16), i.e., angels.[1]

Some deny the existence of an invisible (spiritual, supernatural) world altogether. Accepting the philosophy of naturalism, they believe in the reality of this visible (physical, natural) universe only. Considering the history of mankind as a whole, however, this is definitely the minority view; an overwhelming number assume the reality of a spiritual world of some kind. Some believe in God but not in created spirits; an example is the ancient Sadducees, who said that "there is no resurrection, nor an angel, nor a spirit" (Acts 23:8). Others believe in spiritual beings of some kind but not in a Creator-God. Examples are animists and spiritists, as well as many today who have a quasireligious view of the existence of spiritual beings naively called "angels." Those in this last category are more influenced by occult and New Age thinking than by the Bible, however.

According to the Bible there does exist a whole category of beings called (among other things) *angels*, entities that are distinct both from God and from human beings. The purpose of this chapter is to discuss their nature, number, kinds, and work.

I. THE NATURE OF ANGELS

The first thing to note about the nature of angels is that some are unfallen and holy, remaining as they were originally created; and some are fallen and sinful. The latter are the devil and other evil spirits, or demons. The reality, origin, and work of the fallen angels will be discussed in a later chapter; the present chapter focuses mainly on the good angels. However, most of what we say about the *nature* of angels applies to both categories.

A. Angels Are Created Beings

First of all we must emphasize that angels are *creatures*, constituting the main part of the "invisible" creation of Col 1:16.[2] Psalm 148:1-4 exhorts angels and other creatures thus: "Praise Him, all His angels; Praise Him, all His hosts!" Then verse 5 adds, "Let them praise the name of the LORD, for He commanded and they were created."

This is the sense in which angels (even fallen angels) are called "the sons of God" (Job 1:6; 2:1; 38:7) and "sons of the mighty" (Ps 29:1; 89:6). They are sons in the sense that God brought them into existence by the same kind of creative act by which he made the visible universe.[3] Since angels do not reproduce like human beings (Matt 22:30), each individual angel was probably created *ex nihilo*. The time when they were created has not been revealed to us. We may confidently infer that both the creation and the Fall of angels had taken place by Gen 3:1. Some infer that the angels must have been created by the end of the sixth day since God rested from all his work of creation after that day (Gen 2:1-3). Others infer that they must have been created before the work of creating the visible universe began (Gen 1:1), since Job 38:7 says that "all the sons of God shouted for joy" when the foundation of the earth was laid.

Since they are created beings, angels are finite in every way; in no sense do they share God's infinity. They are limited with regard to space, time, knowledge, and power. Their knowledge and power are superior to that of human beings, but they are neither omniscient nor omnipotent. They can be in only one place at any given time, and they do not know the future.

A major implication of the fact that angels are created beings is that under no circumstances are we to put them on the same level as God. It is wrong to worship them in any sense (Rev 19:10; 22:8-9). Also, it is important to remember that Satan, a fallen created angel, is not an evil divine being who is independent from God and God's eternal antagonist in a kind of dualistic universe. Like every other creature, Satan is a finite being and is under the complete sovereign rule of God.

B. Angels Are Spiritual Beings

As part of the invisible universe angels are not composed of physical stuff (see Luke 24:39; Eph 6:12) but are spiritual entities, "ministering spirits" (Heb 1:14).[4] Spiritual substance is real substance, but metaphysically different from physical matter. It has different properties, e.g., it is invisible to human eyes (Col 1:16). But though angels are normally invisible, they can take on a visible human form (Mark 16:5; Luke 1:11,26; 2:8-15; Heb 13:2); and human eyes can be given the ability to see them as they are (Num 22:31; 2 Kgs 6:14-17).

Because they are spirit, angels are personal beings capable of personal interaction with both God (Job 1, 2) and man (Mark 16:5-7; Luke 1:26-38; Rev 22:8-9). As persons they have minds (Eph 3:10; 1 Pet 1:12; Jude 9), and they are moral beings with a knowledge of good and evil and the free will to choose between them. Having the ability to sin, some angels did so (John 8:44; 2 Pet 2:4; 1 John 3:8), but the rest remained holy (Deut 33:2; Ps 89:5-7; Mark 8:30; Rev 14:10). It is usually assumed that fallen angels were given no chance to repent, and that the holy angels are no longer able to sin. Thus each group is confirmed in its blessed or condemned state.

Are angels created in God's image? The Bible does not specifically say so, and some are reluctant to affirm it.[5] In my opinion, however, it seems that angels share the same characteristics with human beings that constitute the image of God in the latter; thus it is reasonable to infer that the former are also in God's image.

C. Angels Are Powerful Beings

Though angels are not omnipotent, they definitely have great power when acting in the physical universe (Matt 28:2 [see Mark 16:3-4]; Acts 5:19; 12:7). They are referred to as dominions, rulers, authorities, and powers (Eph 1:21). They are "mighty in strength" (Ps 103:20) and "greater in might and power" than human beings (2 Pet 2:11). Even the fallen angels are able to perform miracles (2 Thess 2:9; Rev 13:13-14).

D. Angels Are Immortal Beings

As created beings angels had a beginning and do not possess ascity (self-existence) and eternality as God does; they are not inherently immortal. But God has bestowed upon them the gift of immortality; as a result they (like human spirits) are not subject to death (Luke 20:36) and by God's decree will exist forever. Even Satan and his demons will exist forever in eternal fire (Matt 25:41,46).

II. THE NUMBER OF ANGELS

We do not know exactly how many angels God created, but we know that their number is great beyond comprehension. The OT refers to them as God's "hosts" (e.g., Ps 103:20-21; 148:2), a word with a military connotation meaning "armies" (see 2 Kgs 6:14-17). Over 200 times in the OT God is called the "God of hosts" or "Lord of hosts" ("Lord Sabaoth" in Luther's hymn). Jesus' birth was announced by "a multitude of the heavenly host" (Luke 2:13). Another OT term meaning "a great multitude, legion, ten thousand" is used to describe the angels (e.g., Deut 33:2; Ps 68:17). The latter passage says, "The chariots of God are tens of thousands and thousands of thousands" (NIV).

Jesus declared that if he needed them the Father would immediately send him "twelve legions of angels" (Matt 26:53). Lexicons say that a "legion" was about 6,000 foot soldiers plus horsemen. (See Mark 5:9,15.) Several times the number of angels is described as "myriads." This is from the Greek word *myrias*, which as an exact figure means 10,000 but which is often used to indicate a very large number of countless thousands. Hebrews 12:22 says the church exists in the company of "myriads of angels," or "thousands upon thousands of angels" (NIV). In John's vision of the heavenly throne room he saw many angels, numbering "myriads of myriads, and thousands of thousands" (Rev 5:11; see Dan 7:10; Jude 14).

Of these countless numbers, only two angels are given specific names in the Bible. One is Gabriel, a messenger to Daniel (Dan 8:16; 9:21), Zacharias (Luke 1:19), and Mary (Luke 1:26). The other is Michael the archangel, a leader of God's hosts (Dan 10:13,21; 12:1; Jude 9; Rev 12:7).

III. KINDS OF ANGELS

While all angels are powerful spiritual beings, they are not all of the same kind. The most familiar classification is the group called *cherubim*, the plural form for the Hebrew word usually written *cherub*. In popular piety and secular culture a "cherub" is pictured as a chubby, sweet-faced little child with wings. This is nothing like their actual nature as pictured in the OT, where they appear as powerful and majestic beings (with wings, to be sure). After the Fall God appointed cherubim to guard the gate to the Garden of Eden (Gen 3:24). The cherubim were the model for the carved figures placed at each end of the mercy seat in the holy of holies in the OT tabernacle (Exod 25:17-22) and later in Solomon's temple (1 Kgs 6:23-28). When God's visible presence (the cloud of glory, Exod 40:34-35) filled the tabernacle/temple, it rested specifically on the mercy seat between the two cherubim (Exod 25:22; Num 7:89). God is thus often described as the one who is enthroned between or above the cherubim (e.g., 1 Sam 4:4; 2 Kgs 19:15; Ps 80:1; 99:1). He is also pictured poetically as riding a cherub (2 Sam 22:11; Ps 18:10; see Ezek 10:1-22).

Another group of majestic angelic beings are the *seraphim* (plural for *seraph*), a word that means "burning ones." These are mentioned only in Isa 6:1-7 as part of Isaiah's vision of God. God is seated on his throne, and the six-winged seraphim hover above him proclaiming words of worship: "Holy, Holy, Holy, is the LORD of hosts, the whole earth is full of His glory." These may be in the same group as the four four-winged "living creatures" described in more detail in Ezek 1:5-25 and four similar ones (with six wings) described in Rev 4:6-8.

It appears that angels are organized according to rank and levels of power. First Thessalonians 4:16 refers to "the voice of the archangel" that will announce Christ's return. An *archangel* is simply a chief angel, a general in God's angelic armies having power and authority over other angels. Jude 9 calls Michael an archangel, and Rev 12:7 refers to "Michael and his angels waging war" with Satan and his angels. Michael is the only one so named in the Bible, but apparently there are others, since Dan 10:13 calls him "one of the chief princes." (Jewish tradition mentions Raphael, Uriel, and Gabriel as other archangels.) We may speculate that Satan was an archangel before he sinned, based on his apparent equality with Michael in Jude 9 and Rev 12:7.

Whether there are other levels of rank or power among angels is uncertain, but some evidence for it is found in two of Christ's references to fallen angels, i.e., Matt 12:45; Mark 9:29. It is also possible that Paul's references to angels as thrones, dominions, principalities, authorities, powers, and world rulers reflects a hierarchical order within the world of angels, but this also is uncertain. See Rom 8:38; 1 Cor 15:24; Eph 1:21; 3:10; 6:12; Col 1:16; 2:10,15.[6]

The OT frequently refers to someone called "the Angel of the Lord" or "the Angel of Yahweh [Jehovah]" (see also Gen 18:1–19:21). Most likely this is not an angel as such but a manifestation of God (possibly the preexistent Logos) since at times this Angel is identified with God (e.g., Exod 3:2 and 4:5; Judg 13:22). If so the word "angel" is used in these contexts in its generic sense of "messenger."[7]

IV. THE PURPOSE OF ANGELS

Why did God create angels? What are their functions within the created orders? The answer is summed up in Ps 103:20-21, "Bless the LORD, you His angels, mighty in strength, who perform His word, obeying the voice of His word! Bless the LORD, all you His hosts, you who serve Him, doing His will." In other words, they exist to carry out God's orders. The biblical words for angel (OT, *mal'ak;* NT, *angelos*) both mean "messenger" and can be used for anyone bearing a message. In a general sense these terms refer to someone who is representing or performing a task for someone else. In this sense the demons are now Satan's own angels (Matt 25:41), while the good angels are still doing whatever God bids them to do.

We should note that God does not actually *need* angels to carry out his will. Whatever he wants to do he can accomplish himself by simply speaking a word. But sometimes God does things that he does not *have* to do, simply as a matter of choice. For example, he did not *have* to create anything; that he did so was a freely chosen act. In the same way God has chosen at times to carry out his work through angels.

The first and most prominent specific work of angels is to be in the presence of God and offer up praise and worship to him. Micaiah the prophet said, "I saw the LORD sitting on His throne, and all the host of heaven standing by Him on His right and on His left" (1 Kgs 22:19; see Dan 7:9-10). They bow down before him (Neh 9:6) and continually see his face (Matt 18:10). They sing praises of highest worship to him (Isa 6:1-3; Luke 2:14; Rev 4:8-11; 5:8-14; 7:11-12).

In my judgment, when the Bible pictures God seated on his throne surrounded by angels, this should not be understood as the way God actually exists in his "natural habitat," so to speak. God is spirit and angels are spirits, but they are not the same kind of spirit. God is divine, uncreated spirit; angels are created spirits who inhabit their own created spiritual universe or spiritual dimension. *The divine dimension is not the same as the spiritual dimension.* God is not naturally visible either to men or to angels. Thus *even the appearance of God before the angels in heaven is a theophany.* What Moses, Isaiah, and John saw briefly (Exod 24:9-11; Isa 6:1-5; Rev 4, 5), and what angels see continually is not the divine dimension itself, the actual invisible and uncreated essence of God. When God created the angelic beings to attend and serve him, he made himself known to them in their dimension in a permanent theophany (*GC*, 231-233). Here he receives their worship.

The second purpose of angels is to do what their name indicates, i.e., carry God's messages to human beings. In a way not described in Scripture, angels were involved in the giving of the Law of Moses (Acts 7:53; Gal 3:19; Heb 2:2;

see Deut 33:2). An angel was active in the revelation given to John (Rev 1:1). Gabriel carried God's messages to Zacharias (Luke 1:11-20) and to Mary (Luke 1:26-35). Angels spoke to Philip (Acts 8:26), to Cornelius (Acts 10:3-7), and to Paul (Acts 27:23-24). An archangel will announce the second coming of Christ (1 Thess 4:16).

A third main purpose and task of angels is to minister to believers. They are "ministering spirits, sent out to render service for the sake of those who will inherit salvation" (Heb 1:14). Does this mean that each individual has his own personal guardian angel? Possibly, since Ps 34:7 says, "The angel of the LORD encamps around those who fear Him, and rescues them" (see Matt 18:10; Acts 12:15). We cannot be dogmatic about this, however. It may be that angels are dispatched especially on "rescue missions" or whenever protection is especially needed (Ps 91:11-12). Specific cases of such angelic rescue are given in Scripture, e.g., 2 Kgs 6:14-17; Dan 3:28; 6:22; Acts 5:19-20; 12:7-11. Angels ministered to Jesus after his temptation ordeal (Matt 4:11). They are present to and for the church (1 Cor 4:9; 11:10; 1 Tim 5:21; Heb 12:22-23), possibly in visible form at times (Heb 13:2). They convey the souls of believers to Paradise (Luke 16:22).

Fourth, angels are pictured as carrying out God's providential judgments upon the earth. An angel sent a pestilence from the Lord upon Israel (2 Sam 24:15-17), and "the LORD sent an angel" to destroy the Assyrian army (2 Chr 32:21; 2 Kgs 19:35). An angel struck King Herod Agrippa I with a fatal condition (Acts 12:23). See Rev 8:6-7; 16:1.

Fifth, in the spiritual realm angels do battle against Satan and his demons. Michael "disputed with the devil and argued about the body of Moses" (Jude 9). He aided Daniel in a time of intense spiritual warfare (Dan 10:13). He led an army of angels into battle against Satan and his angels (Rev 12:7-9), a clash that probably paralleled the time of Christ's earthly ministry (Luke 10:17-18). Revelation 20:1-3 represents the same event but is given in symbolic language.

A sixth and final way that angels serve God's purposes is that they will accompany Christ at his second coming (Matt 16:27; 25:31; Luke 9:26). Christ leads them forth as an army to wreak vengeance upon his enemies (2 Thess 1:7-8; Rev 19:14,19), and they are dispatched to rapture these enemies away to the judgment and ultimately to hell (Matt 13:40-42). In like manner another group of angels will "gather together His elect from the four winds" and escort them "to meet the Lord in the air" (Matt 24:31; 1 Thess 4:17).

Angels thus have a vital role to play in God's dealings with the human race. A word of caution needs to be voiced, however. Whatever benefits and blessings God may bestow upon us through angels, these beings are simply carrying out God's bidding. Our dependence and gratitude and worship should never be directed toward the angels, but only toward God himself. Focusing and speculating upon the presence and activity of angels must not distract us from our main purpose of glorifying God.

NOTES ON CHAPTER FIVE

[1]See especially C. Fred Dickason, *Angels*.

[2]Most likely the invisible creation also includes a spiritual "space" or universe that serves as the proper habitation for angels. To those of us in the physical world it is a kind of parallel dimension or alternate universe.

[3]Some think the "sons of God" in Gen 6:2,4 are angels, but this is not the best understanding of this text, as we will note in our later discussion of demons. See Erickson, *Theology*, 467.

[4]Fallen angels are often called "spirits" or "evil spirits," e.g., Matt 8:16; 12:45; Luke 7:21.

[5]E.g., Wayne Grudem, *Doctrine*, 170.

[6]See Arnold, *Powers*.

[7]See Dickason, *Angels*, 78-84. See Borland for a full discussion of all the relevant passages.

CHAPTER SIX

THE VISIBLE CREATION: THE NATURE OF MAN

Having surveyed the biblical teaching on the invisible creation, we now turn to the visible creation, with a specific focus on the nature of man.[1] What does it mean to be a human being? How we answer this question is critical for other parts of our worldview. It will determine our approach to many ethical questions, such as abortion and capital punishment. It will also affect how we view sin and salvation. For example, does man have free will? What is the fate of the body? Also, whether we view human nature as including more than a physical body will affect our approach to counseling. For example, are all mental and emotional states purely physical in origin, and all aberrations correctable through drugs? Can "sin" be reduced to genes and chemical imbalance?

In this chapter we are seeking to answer the fundamental question, "What is man?" (Ps 8:4). What is the nature of authentic human existence, the nature of man as first created by God and as God intends for us to be? This is the subject of anthropology, the study of man.

I. THE ESSENCE OF MAN: WHAT ARE HUMAN BEINGS MADE OF?

First we must ask the ontological question: what are human beings "made of"? What is the "stuff" or substance of human existence? Typical modern philosophy regards such metaphysical questions as irrelevant and improper, and some theologians have naively agreed. They say we should define human existence not in terms of essence or substance, but only in terms of relationships. This is an example, though, of that ubiquitous theological demon, the false choice. Biblical teaching does emphasize proper human relationships, but it also presents data about the essence or ontological nature of man. That is the subject of this section.

One way to approach this issue is to ask, *how many kinds of substance is man made of?* Is a human being composed of one, two, or three parts? These three possibilities will now be discussed.

A. Monistic Views: Man Is One

The worldview that says only one kind of substance exists, period, is called cosmological monism. Materialistic monism says that all reality is ultimately material or physical stuff; spiritualistic monism says that everything is ultimately some kind of spiritual, nonmaterial, or divine stuff. A cosmological monist of either type will necessarily hold to *anthropological monism*, the view that man's ontological nature is composed of one and only one kind of metaphysical stuff. Some who are not cosmological monists are anthropological monists, e.g., those who believe in angels and/or God but nevertheless say that man is body only.

That man is composed solely of a physical body is a widespread view. Since cosmological materialists believe that physical matter is the only stuff that exists anywhere, for them it is the only possible stuff of human existence. Examples are the ancient atomist philosophers, Leucippus and Democritus; and modern evolutionists and secular humanists such as Thomas Huxley and Carl Sagan. Sagan, for example, has said that a human being is but "a collection of water, calcium and organic molecules," a "molecular machine" (*Cosmos*, 127), "a superbly constructed, astonishingly compact, self-ambulatory computer" (*Broca's Brain*, 281).[2] Mind or spirit does not exist as a distinct entity; thoughts are purely the result of certain electrical or chemical functions of the brain. As Marvin Minsky has put it, the human mind is no more than "a computer made of meat."[3]

Some of those under the broad umbrella of Christendom are anthropological monists, even though their worldview includes the existence of God and often angels. Included here are groups such as Jehovah's Witnesses and Seventh-day Adventists. Their view that man is body only is an important part of their denial of eternal hell. They argue that the idea of an everlasting punishment arose from a belief in an immortal (indestructible) soul; man does not have an immortal soul; therefore there is no basis for the idea of eternal hell.

Much of modern Christian theology, both liberal and conservative, has espoused materialistic monism. Man is seen as an indivisible unity, having no separable "soul" that survives death. The idea of such a soul, and thus a two-part view of man, is regarded as being the legacy of faulty Greek philosophy and religion. An example within the Restoration Movement is Curtis Dickinson, who says the traditional church teaching is actually "the Greek doctrine, championed by Plato . . . that there is an invisible and mysterious something (called soul) which survives death. From this evolved the belief that the soul is immortal and indestructible," thus neutralizing the gospel of the resurrection and leading to the idea of eternal punishment.[4]

This view that man is body only must be rejected as a serious false doctrine. When espoused by conservative Christians it is usually an overreaction to another false doctrine, the idea that the human soul is "immortal" in the sense of indestructible. It may also be a concession to the materialism and evolutionism of modern Western thought. In any case it is contrary to the biblical doctrine of the soul, as explained below.

Not all monists are materialists. Some believe that physical stuff as it appears to our senses is not real, and that the only kind of substance that actually exists is spiritual. Thus man's physical body is an illusion; our true essence is spirit only. This view is held by what are called the metaphysical cults. For example, the founder of Christian Science, Mary Baker Eddy, wrote, "Man is not matter; he is not made up of brain, blood, bones and other material elements." Man is spirit or mind only. "Matter and Mind are opposites . . . hence both cannot be real." Matter is an illusion. "Spirit and all things spiritual are the real" (270, 289, 475). Another example of this view is the main form of Hinduism, which says that only spirit is real; anything material is an illusion. Man's true nature is his identity with this eternal, divine spirit (see *GC*, 83-84). The New Age Movement, heavily dependent on Hindu metaphysics, says that man's true nature is his participation in the universal, nonmaterial mass of vibrating energy, also known as "god."

The doctrine that man is spirit only and that the body is not real is another false doctrine; it runs contrary to both experience and Scripture. Especially, it is contrary to the fact of creation, through which God gave reality and goodness to the material universe. Thus both forms of anthropological monism are unacceptable.

B. Trichotomy: Man Is Three

Another view of man is called *trichotomy*, which is the idea that a human being is composed of three distinct metaphysical essences. Ancient Greek thought sometimes distinguished three parts in man: a mortal body (*soma*); a mortal, perishable animal soul (*psyche*) that is the seat of passions; and the immortal, rational soul or mind (*nous*) that is the seat of reason. Many Christians have accepted a similar idea, seeing man as composed of body, soul, and spirit.

Christian trichotomists cite four main Bible texts to support this view. One is Gen 2:7, which says in the KJV, "And the LORD God formed man of the dust of the ground, and breathed into his nostrils the breath of life; and man became a living soul." According to Watchman Nee, the dust becomes the body, "the breath of life" becomes the spirit, and the two together produce the soul (I:23). R.B. Thieme says, "Adam was originally created with a body, a human soul, and a human spirit (Gen. 2:7). He began life in what we call a trichotomous condition" (3). A second text is 1 Thess 5:23, which seems to be clearly tripartite: "May your spirit and soul and body [*pneuma, psyche, soma*] be preserved complete." A third text is Heb 4:12, which says the Word of God is like a sword "piercing as far as the division of soul and spirit." This is taken to mean that the soul can be separated from the spirit; thus they must be two distinct entities. Finally trichotomists cite the difference between the "natural [*psychikos*] man" and the "spiritual [*pneumatikos*] man" in 1 Cor 2:14-15 (see 15:44). The former, they say, is ruled by his *psyche* or soul, and the latter is ruled by his *pneuma* or spirit.

A modern example of trichotomy is Alexander Campbell, who based his view of the distinction between soul and spirit almost entirely on Greek thinking. He said that God gives man "a soul or animal life in common with all the animals created; but he infuses into him from himself directly . . . a spirit, a pure intellectual principle." Man's passions come from the soul, but he is intended to be ruled by his "intellect or spirit" ("Man," 463). The soul is mere animal life and perishes with the body; the spirit "can never suffer dissolution. It is the seat of reason, understanding, volition" ("Instinct," 290-291).

More recent examples are Bill Gothard, for whom the threefold distinction is crucial for much of his teaching; and Watchman Nee, who says the body is our point of contact with the world and our spirit is our point of contact with God, while the soul binds the two together and is a buffer between them since "spirit cannot act directly upon the body." Interestingly, Nee says that the soul (not the spirit) is the seat of reason or the intellect (I:21-27).

In my judgment trichotomy, unlike monism, is not a *serious* false doctrine, but is a false view nonetheless. The suggested nature of the distinction between soul and spirit is purely speculative and leads to countless unwarranted applications. More significantly, the biblical texts upon which this view is supposedly based do not require it, as will be explained below.

C. Anthropological Dualism: Man Is Two

The best understanding of biblical teaching is that man is an ontological duality, created by God to be composed of two metaphysically distinct kinds of being: physical and spiritual.[5] This is sometimes called *dichotomy*, the idea that man is divided into two parts (as opposed to trichotomy), and sometimes *dualism* (as opposed to monism). Some call it "substance dualism," and others prefer the term "duality." The terminology is not nearly as important as the concept.

Not all dualistic views of man are biblical, of course. There is an approach to human nature that is generally dualistic, but which is distinctly pagan in origin and antibiblical in content. Pagan dualism agrees that man is composed of a physical body and a spiritual entity, but it says the body is always something negative or evil and not an authentic part of human nature, and the spiritual essence is inherently eternal if not actually divine (the "immortal soul"). The physical and the spiritual are regarded as basically incompatible, with the spirit striving to achieve permanent separation from and freedom from the body. The spirit is thus the only part of man that counts.

This view is expressed in the ancient Greek myth of Dionysus, a son of Zeus. This divine child ran afoul of an earthly race called Titans, and he changed himself into a bull in order to escape them. But the Titans caught him, tore him to pieces, and ate him. The enraged Zeus destroyed them immediately with a lightning bolt, and the human race was created from their ashes. Thus human beings have a gross physical body made from the residue of the Titans; but they have a divine soul derived from the remnants of the unfortunate Dionysus, who was being digested by the Titans at the moment they were zapped. Unfortunately this immortal particle of deity is now trapped within a foul physical body, from which it longs for deliverance. This tragedy is expressed in the Greek phrase, *soma sema*, "the body is a tomb" (Stacey, 62-63).

This view of the soul and its relation to the body was common among Greek thinkers, e.g., Plato and the Stoic Seneca. The latter spoke of the divine soul which must bear "the necessary burden of the body" until death. "When that day comes which shall separate this mixture of human and divine I will leave the body here where I found it and betake myself to the gods" (Seneca, 252-253). Christianity's early antagonists, the Gnostics, had a similar view of the spirit as a divine substance trapped within an evil body and longing for liberation.

This view of man's dual nature has almost no resemblance to the biblical view. However, since Christians sometimes unconsciously import some of this thinking into their theology, it is crucial that we carefully distinguish the anthropological dualism of the Bible from this pagan version. In the rest of this section, over against the views of monism and trichotomy, we will show that the Bible overwhelmingly teaches dualism. In the next section, over against pagan dualism, we will show that man in his entirety is a created being.

1. The Biblical Evidence for Dualism

The Bible teaches that man is a dichotomy, a duality, a twofold creature with a spiritual side and a physical side. This is seen in both the OT and the NT, though the OT vocabulary is not as clearly established as the NT. We should keep in mind that the major terms for the aspects of human nature have other meanings besides their metaphysical uses in view here. Also, English translations do not always reflect the specific meanings of the original terms. The following analysis is based on the original languages.

What should be noted in the following points is that not only is man described as having two parts, contrary to monism; but also these two parts are represented as the totality of human nature, contrary to trichotomy.

a. The *outward man* is distinguished from the *inward man*. "Though our outer man is decaying, yet our inner man is being renewed day by day" (2 Cor 4:16). Paul prays that we may be "strengthened with power through his Spirit in the inner man" (Eph 3:16). See Jer 31:33; Rom 2:14; 7:22; 1 Pet 3:3-4.

b. The *soul* is distinguished from the *body*. "My eye is wasted away from grief, my soul and my body also" (Ps 31:9). Here the word "body" is literally "belly," but in the OT a number of terms are used to represent the body, e.g., flesh, bones, belly, trunk, sheath. "Do not fear those who kill the body but are unable to kill the soul; but rather fear Him who is able to destroy both soul and body in hell" (Matt 10:28). This text is a deathblow to monism; it is also a problem for most trichotomists, who say the soul perishes at death along with the body.

c. The *soul* is distinguished from the *flesh*. "But his flesh upon him shall have pain, and his soul within him shall mourn" (Job 14:22, KJV). "My soul thirsts for You, my flesh yearns for You" (Ps 63:1; see 84:2). "The merciful man doeth good to his own soul: but he that is cruel troubleth his own flesh" (Prov 11:17, KJV). "And He will destroy the glory of his forest and of his fruitful garden, both soul and flesh" (Isa 10:18). "Abstain from fleshly [*sarkikos*] lusts which wage war against the soul" (1 Pet 2:11).

d. The *soul* is mentioned as something separate from the physical nature. "I saw underneath the altar the souls of those who had been slain because of the word of God" (Rev 6:9; see 20:4). In this verse John does not say that he saw the *persons* who had been slain, but the *souls of* those persons. "I pray that in all respects you may prosper and be in good health, just as your soul prospers" (3 John 2).

e. The *spirit* is distinguished from the *body*. "Though the body is dead because of sin, yet the spirit is alive because of righteousness" (Rom 8:10). Paul says he is "absent in body but present in spirit" (1 Cor 5:3). He speaks of those who want to "be holy both in body and spirit" (1 Cor 7:34). "The body without the spirit is dead" (Jas 2:26). "I Daniel was grieved in my spirit in the midst of my body" (Dan 7:15, KJV). Here, as in Dan 4:33; 5:21, the term "sheath" is used to represent the body. "The dust will return to the earth as it was, and the spirit will return to God who gave it" (Eccl 12:7). Here "dust" represents the body. See Eph 4:4.

f. The *spirit* is distinguished from the *flesh*. "The spirit is willing, but the flesh is weak" (Matt 26:41). "Let us cleanse ourselves from all defilement of flesh and spirit" (2 Cor 7:1). "Though they are judged in the flesh as men, they may live in the spirit according to the will of God" (1 Pet 4:6). God is the "God of the spirits of all flesh" (Num 16:22; 27:16). See John 3:6; 1 Cor 5:5.

g. The *spirit* is treated as distinct from and separable from the *body*. God "forms the spirit of man within him" (Zech 12:1). "The Spirit Himself testifies with our spirit that we are children of God" (Rom 8:16). "Who among men knows the thoughts of a man except the spirit of the man which is in him?" (1 Cor 2:11). At his death Jesus "yielded up His spirit" (Matt 27:50). When Stephen died, he cried, "Lord Jesus, receive my spirit!" (Acts 7:59). Referring to saints who have died, Heb 12:23 calls them "the spirits of the righteous made perfect."

h. The *heart* is distinguished from the *body*. "Let us draw near with a sincere heart in full assurance of faith, having our hearts sprinkled clean from an evil conscience and our bodies washed with pure water" (Heb 10:22). To be saved a person must confess with his mouth (a bodily part) that Jesus is Lord, and believe in his heart that God raised him from the dead (Rom 10:9-10).

i. The *heart* is distinguished from the *flesh*. "My heart is glad and my glory rejoices; my flesh also will dwell securely" (Ps 16:9). "My flesh and my heart may fail, but God is the strength of my heart" (Ps 73:26). "My heart and my flesh sing for joy to the living God" (Ps 84:2). "A sound heart is the life of the flesh" (Prov 14:30, KJV). "Therefore remove sorrow from thy heart, and put away evil from thy flesh" (Eccl 11:10, KJV). An unbeliever is "uncircumcised in heart and uncircumcised in flesh" (Ezek 44:7,9; see Deut 10:16; 30:6; Jer 4:4). "Nor is circumcision that which is outward in the flesh," but "circumcision is that which is of the heart, by the Spirit" (Rom 2:28-29).

j. The *mind* is distinguished from our *members* (of the body) and from our *flesh* (Rom 7:23,25).

k. *Death* is a separation of the person from his body. With death as a reference point, until one dies he is still "in the body" or "in the flesh" (see 2 Cor 5:6; 10:3; 12:2-3; Gal 2:20; Phil 1:20-24; Heb 13:3; 1 Pet 4:2). Death then is a *putting off* of the body in the sense of leaving a house or tent (2 Cor 5:1-8; 2 Pet 1:13-14). Cooper's main point in his book *Body, Soul, and Life Everlasting* is that the Bible's teaching about the "intermediate state"—the continuing existence of the soul after death and before the resurrection—is a proof of dualism. See again Rev 6:9; 20:4.

We conclude that the Bible consistently represents man as a duality of material substance and spiritual substance. As Gundry says (154), "Paul along with most Jews and other early Christians habitually thought of man as a duality of two parts, corporeal and incorporeal, meant to function in unity but distinguishable and capable of separation."

2. Dualism or Trichotomy?

Based on a small handful of passages, many Christians have concluded that the *soul* is something distinct from the *spirit* and that man is therefore made of three distinct parts. In my judgment this is false. In most if not all of the passages in the previous section, the two elements (outward/inward, body/soul, flesh/spirit, etc.) seem to be intended to represent man in his entirety. They seem to include the whole of human nature. See, e.g., Matt 10:28; 1 Cor 7:34; 2 Cor 7:1.

Also, where *soul* and *spirit* are referring to a part of man's nature, they are synonymous and interchangeable. For example, both terms are used to refer to that part of man that survives death, i.e., the disembodied element in the intermediate state: soul (Matt 10:28; Rev 6:9; 20:4), spirit (Heb 12:23). Both terms are used for that part of man that departs at the moment of death: soul (Gen 35:18; 1 Kgs 17:21), spirit (Ps 31:5; Luke 8:55; 23:46; Acts 7:59; Jas 2:26).

This interchangeability is also seen in the fact that the highest spiritual activities of man are experienced by both the soul and the spirit (see Murray, *Writings*, II:25-27). This is significant because for most trichotomists, man's *spirit* is supposed to be *the* seat of God-consciousness and spiritual experience (Nee, I:26); the soul is the seat of baser passions. But this distinction is not found in the Bible. For example, religious sorrow or spiritual grief is attributed to Jesus' spirit (Mark 8:12; John 11:33; 13:21) and his soul (Matt 26:38; John 12:27). See Ps 77:2-3. Also, in poetic parallelism Mary expresses spiritual joy and praise to God in both her soul and spirit (Luke 1:46-47). Contrary to the lower position trichotomy usually gives to the soul, the Bible pictures it as the subject of the highest exercises of devotion toward God. "At night my soul longs for You, indeed, my spirit within me seeks You diligently" (Isa 26:9). In Phil 1:27 Paul exhorts us to stand firm in one spirit and strive together with one soul (*psyche*). Love for

God, the highest virtue, comes from the soul (Mark 12:30). Hope is an anchor for the soul (Heb 6:19). We should obey God's will from the soul (*psyche*, Eph 6:6). See Acts 14:22; see the parallel thoughts in 1 Kgs 21:5 and Ps 42:11.

Laidlaw says that such passages as these "render it impossible to hold that 'spirit' can mean exclusively or mainly the Godward side of man's inner nature, and 'soul' the rational or earthward. The terms are parallel, or practically equivalent, expressions for the inner life as contrasted with the outer or bodily life" (90).

But what about the biblical passages that seem to teach trichotomy? These may be readily understood in harmony with dualism. First of all, a close look at Gen 2:7 shows that it gives absolutely no basis for a threefold view of man. In fact this verse contains no direct reference to the spiritual nature of man at all; it refers neither to the spirit nor to the soul. Trichotomists wrongly think it refers to both. How do they arrive at such a conclusion?

First of all, the KJV translation, "and man became a living soul," is the basis for assuming that this verse refers to man's soul. It is falsely assumed that the word "soul" (Hebrew, *nephesh*) in this verse refers to an ontological part of man rather than to the whole being or person. As we shall see shortly, both the Hebrew and the Greek words for "soul" have other meanings, including "being" or "person." This is the meaning in Gen 2:7; the NASB and NIV rightly translate the Hebrew phrase *nephesh chayah* as "a living being." The very same phrase is used of animals in Gen 1:20,21,24; 9:10,15, where the NASB translates it "living creature." The soul as distinct from the body is not mentioned here at all.

The other false assumption is that the word "breath" in the statement that God "breathed into his nostrils the breath of life" is equivalent to the human spirit. This is based on the fact that the usual Hebrew word for spirit, *ruach*, can mean either breath or spirit. Thus it is assumed that we can just substitute the word "spirit" for the word "breath" in Gen 2:7. For example, Saucy says, "God used the matter of the earth and his own breath (i.e., spirit) to create Adam" (39). This is faulty thinking, though, because the word translated "breath" in this verse is not *ruach* but *nshamah*, which usually means the ordinary breath of ordinary physical life, not the metaphysical spirit.

Thus Gen 2:7 refers neither to the soul nor to the spirit. Its main point is the unique manner in which the first human being became a "living creature" endowed with the "breath of life," in contrast with the way the animals became living creatures with the breath of life. The divine inbreathing is probably the point of time when the soul or spirit was created and implanted in Adam's body, but this is an inference and is not specifically stated.

We turn now to 1 Thess 5:23, "Now may the God of peace Himself sanctify you entirely; and may your spirit and soul and body be preserved complete, without blame at the coming of our Lord Jesus Christ." Does this verse not make a distinction between spirit and soul? Not necessarily. The emphasis here is on the wholeness of man rather than on any divisions within him. The point is that the *whole person* should be sanctified. In 1 Cor 7:34 and 2 Cor 7:1 the same point is made by referring only to "body and spirit" and "flesh and spirit."

Why then does 1 Thess 5:23 speak of "spirit *and soul* and body," if spirit and soul are not distinct elements? The answer is that the Bible sometimes lists synonymous terms together to express completeness, without intending to imply that each term refers to a separate, distinct item. An example is Deut 18:10-11, where eight Hebrew expressions are used to prohibit three basic kinds of occult activity. For example, the last three (a medium, a spiritist, one who calls up the dead) all refer to the same thing, spiritism. Another example is Mark 12:30, where Jesus says we must love God with heart, soul, mind, and strength. We do not say that heart, soul, and mind are three distinct entities. Even in Heb 4:12 trichotomists do not try to distinguish the heart from the soul and spirit. This approach is an adequate explanation of 1 Thess 5:23, and it is consistent with the dualism overwhelmingly represented in the texts previously listed.

How, then, can we explain Heb 4:12, "For the word of God is living and active and sharper than any two-edged sword, and piercing as far as the division of soul and spirit, of both joints and marrow, and able to judge the thoughts and intentions of the heart"? The assumption of trichotomy is that this text speaks of a division *between* the soul and the spirit, a dividing or separation of the one from the other. Soul and spirit are seen as distinct but adjacent elements, which the word can disconnect.

We reject this interpretation for three reasons (see Murray, *Writings*, II:29-31). First, the verse does not speak of a division *between* soul and spirit, or a division of soul *from* spirit; it speaks of a division *of soul and of spirit* (which do not have to be two different things, as we have just seen). Second, the word family from which "division" (*merismos*) comes does not refer to a division between two things, but to a division within a single thing (e.g., Matt 12:25-26; Luke 12:13; 1 Cor 1:13). Here it means a division *within* the soul, *within* the spirit. Third, the main point of the verse is the piercing, penetrating power of the Word of God. It penetrates not *between* but *into*—into the most secret, inaccessible recesses of our being, laying them bare (v. 13). Just as a sharp sword can penetrate to the inmost part of the body (to the joints and marrow of a limb, e.g.), so God's Word penetrates to the inner spiritual being (soul, spirit, heart) and lays bare its most secret elements, i.e., its thoughts and intents.

How, then, shall we understand the difference between the *psychikos* (natural) man and the *pneumatikos* (spiritual) man in 1 Cor 2:13-15? The spiritual man is one who is indwelt, directed, and controlled by the *Holy* Spirit; the natural man is one who ignores spiritual things and devotes his life to this natural, material world alone. Thus the contrast is not between man's soul and man's spirit, but between the natural and the supernatural.

We conclude that the few passages sometimes taken to support trichotomy are actually quite consistent with anthropological dualism. The biblical testimony to the dualistic nature of man remains convincing. Man is a physical body plus a spiritual entity sometimes called soul and sometimes called spirit.

Is anything really at stake in this dispute? Does it matter whether we view man as one, two, or three parts? Indeed, it is very important that we understand that man has at least a twofold nature, physical and spiritual, contrary to the false doctrine of monism. Positing a threefold nature by distinguishing between the soul and the spirit is not as serious an issue, but still we should abandon it because it has no true basis in the Bible and because it leads to unwarranted speculation as to the respective functions of the two.

3. Biblical Terminology

Clear thinking on the ontological nature of man requires a clear understanding of the various biblical terms that apply to the physical and spiritual aspects. It is especially important to see that these words have other meanings besides the ones that are relevant here.

One main English word for the physical aspect of man is "body." The OT does not have a clear equivalent for this. The closest is *gviyah*, but it is used only 14 times. More often the physical aspect is represented by *basar* ("flesh") or words referring to part of the body, such as "bones" and "belly." The NT word for "body" is *soma*, and it is used quite often to refer to the physical side of human nature as distinct from the spiritual.

The other main English word for our physical nature is "flesh" (OT, *basar*; NT, *sarx*). Sometimes this term is used in a general sense to refer to human nature as a whole, considered as earthly and weak and limited in comparison with God and with angelic beings (e.g., Jer 17:5; Rom 6:19; 1 Pet 1:24). This meaning is seen especially in the phrase, "flesh and blood" (e.g., Matt 16:17; Eph 6:12; Heb 2:14). More often, though, "flesh" is used in the ontological sense of the physical aspect of human nature, the outer man as distinct from the inner man (e.g., Matt 26:41; Rom 2:28-29; 2 Cor 7:1; Eph 5:28-29).

A common interpretation of the word *sarx*, especially as used by Paul, is that it has an ethical connotation and refers to the whole self (body and soul) as controlled by sin. In a Christian it is thus called the "old self" or "sinful nature" in the sense of the remnants of the sinful side of our nature (e.g., Rom 8:5 and Gal 5:19 in the NIV). In this case the "flesh" would not be the outward man as compared with the inward man, but the old man as contrasted with the new man. After a closer study of the key passages in Romans, however, I have concluded that this view is mistaken. When Paul refers to the flesh, he is referring specifically to the body. (See Cottrell, *Romans*, I:372-377, 426-427.)

The three key words for the spiritual side of our nature are "heart," "spirit," and "soul." The words for "heart" (OT, *leb* and *lebab*; NT, *kardia*) are used hundreds of times, almost always in the spiritual sense equivalent to soul or spirit (see, e.g., Exod 35:21; Ps 73:26; Eccl 11:10; Ezek 44:7; Matt 22:37; Rom 2:28-

29; Heb 10:22; 1 Pet 3:4). The functions of the heart include all those we associate with personhood and the mind, e.g., intellectual activity (thinking, reasoning, understanding), volitional activity (decisions, desires), emotional activity (joy, sorrow, fear), "religious" activity (receiving God's Word, faith, repentance, obedience, worship), as well as sin and unbelief. We should note especially that in the Bible there is a total absence of the common distinction between the *head* as representing reason and the *heart* as representing feelings. What the Bible calls the "heart" includes both. It refers to the inward person as a whole.

Another word for the inner man is "spirit" (OT, *ruach*; NT, *pneuma*). Sometimes this term has the nonmetaphysical connotations of wind (Ps 147:18; John 3:8a), breath (Gen 6:17; Ps 104:29), and attitude or disposition (Rom 12:11; Gal 6:1). When referring to existing entities, this term denotes personal, nonmaterial beings, including God, angels, and human beings. When used of human beings it refers specifically to the nonmaterial aspect of our essence that is distinct from and separable from the body (see, e.g., Deut 2:30; Ezra 1:1,5; Ps 142:3; Ezek 18:31; Luke 23:46; Acts 7:59; Rom 8:16; 1 Cor 2:11; 5:5; 14:32; 1 Pet 3:19; Heb 12:23). In these and many other texts it is completely impossible to regard the *ruach* or *pneuma* as "breath" or as an impersonal "life force," as monists such as Jehovah's Witnesses advocate. Also, the spirit of man should never be equated with the Holy Spirit.

The third main word for man's spiritual nature is "soul" (OT, *nephesh*; NT, *psyche*). Though the KJV translates *nephesh* with over 25 English words, three of the connotations for it and *psyche* are especially relevant. For a true understanding of man's nature it is *absolutely essential* that we understand and distinguish these three meanings, and that we identify which of them is intended in any given text.

First, at times these words do indeed mean the spiritual nature of man and thus are equivalent to heart and spirit (e.g., Ps 63:1; 84:2; Matt 10:28; 3 John 2; Rev 6:9).

Second, at times they mean a creature, a being, an individual, a self, a person as a whole. In this sense they can refer to animals as well as to people (cf. Gen 1:24; 2:7). When applied to people, the basic connotation is "self" or "person" (e.g., Exod 1:5; 12:4; Ps 16:10; Ezek 18:4; Acts 2:41; 7:14; 27:37; Rom 13:1; 1 Pet 3:20).

Third, *nephesh* and *psyche* can mean the *life* of a person (or an animal). In this sense the "soul" is not a distinct metaphysical entity but rather a quality or attribute of an entity (e.g., Lev 17:14; Matt 6:25; 16:26; John 10:11; 15:13; Acts 15:26).

A major and blatant error of materialistic monists is to focus on one or both of the latter two meanings—which are legitimate meanings, and to insist that these are the *only* legitimate meanings; that is, they argue that the fact that *nephesh* and *psyche* mean "person" and/or "life" shows that it does *not* mean "spirit" in the sense of a separable spiritual aspect of man. This, of course, is false logic.

An example of this kind of error is to point to Bible texts that speak of the *nephesh* or *psyche* as dying, and then to say, "Look! These texts say that the 'soul' dies! Thus there is no such thing as an undying spiritual entity that continues to exist after the body dies." It is true that the Bible says a *nephesh* or *psyche* dies (Lev 23:30; Num 23:10; Ezek 18:4; Acts 3:23), but here these terms have the connotation of "person." Also, one may give his *nephesh* or *psyche* unto death (Isa 53:12; John 10:11), but here the terms mean "life." To deny the existence of the separable spiritual nature on the basis of such passages is totally fallacious, since it fails to make the proper distinctions among the three equally legitimate connotations of the terms.

D. What Is Man?

We are now ready to answer the question, "What is man?" What is authentic human existence? Our answer is threefold. First, *man is body*. It is not enough just to say, "Man *has* a body." Part of our very essence, part of our identity as human beings is our bodily nature. The idea that the body is an accidental, alien, degrading aspect of our nature is pagan, not biblical. We should never say things like "Man is not a body, he merely wears one" (Lovett, 58), or "An individual person is a spirit . . . merged temporarily with a shell of flesh"; we are "spirit and immortality trapped in matter" (Yancey, 78), or "This house of flesh is but a prison—bars of bones that hold my soul" (from a song called "The Holy Hills of Heaven").

According to the Bible one's body is part of his nature *as man*, as a human being. It is created by God and is inherently good (Gen 1:31). It makes us intimately related to the rest of the material creation. We are part of the material world; we are at home in it. Human bodies are nevertheless unique, in that they were created never to die. The body's present sinful, disease-ridden, death-bound state is not natural for human beings but is the result of sin. Thus our present bodies are a corruption of the original model and need redemption, just as our souls do (Rom 8:23; Phil 3:21). In the day of resurrection we will receive glorified bodies compatible with our eternal home. The point to be stressed here, though, is that we will still be *bodies*. The redeemed person will have or be a body forever. (The unredeemed will also be bodies forever, but their bodies will not be redeemed and glorified.)

Anthropological dualism thus has a balanced view of the body as it relates to human nature as a whole. Materialistic monism makes the body *everything*. Trichotomy often debases the body and makes it next to nothing. Biblical dualism, though, sees man as a balanced combination of body and soul/spirit.

The second part of the answer to "What is man?" is this: *man is spirit* (soul, heart). Though it is a true substance, the spirit is not made of physical matter and thus is ontologically different from the body. It is constructed not according to atomic physics but according to "spiritual physics," whatever that may be like. It is not visible to our natural sight, nor is it measurable in terms of size or weight, nor do we expect it to be related to space in the same way that the body is.

Though not made of physical stuff, the spirit is integrally interconnected with the material body, especially with the brain.

The spirit is just as much created as is our body, as we shall see in the next main section. Though we can confidently affirm *that* it is created, the Bible does not tell us just *how* this takes place for an individual soul. Some speculate that individual souls exist prior to conception and are implanted in newly conceived infants. There is no biblical basis for this idea, and the notion that such souls have existed for eternity must definitely be rejected. Others speculate that the individual's soul is somehow passed along to the child by his parents (traducianism), or that it somehow emerges from his own bodily nature (emergentism); but no mechanisms for such processes can be identified. It is probably best to think that God simply creates the individual soul or spirit *ex nihilo* for each new person at the time of conception.

Though the spirit is not divine or a part of God, it is the aspect of man that is *most like* God, that is created in his image. It is the seat of personhood and the source of our ability to have communion and fellowship with God. In its present state, though, this potential is not realized, for the spirit no less than the body has been affected by sin and stands in need of redemption. In believers the process of the renewing of the spirit has already begun and will be completed after death (Heb 12:23).

The last part of our answer to the question "What is man?" is this: *man is a unity of body and spirit.* The human body and the human spirit (unlike animal bodies and angelic spirits) are uniquely designed to function together in a psychosomatic unity. Body and spirit are quite compatible; there is no inherent antithesis or antagonism between them, as in pagan dualism. Both are necessary for our whole, authentic existence. This does not mean that they *cannot* be separated, but that they are not *intended* to be separated. Physical death is abnormal because it separates spirit from body and thus divides the whole man. The time between death and resurrection is thus unnatural even for the saved.

We should note that man is just as much body as he is spirit. We should not refer to the spirit as "the real man, the part that counts," as if the body were an alien appendage. Though a governing primacy is assigned to the spirit, both are "the *real* you." (This does not mean that the *present* body is essential to humanness, but that *a* body is essential.)

Sin and salvation involve the whole person, body and spirit. Sin has dire consequences for both soul and body. The soul suffers spiritual death (Eph 2:1,5), and the body suffers corruption and physical death (Rom 8:10,20-22) because of sin. Salvation likewise involves the whole person; "saving souls" means saving *persons*, not just the spiritual part of man. The salvation of the spirit begins with regeneration or spiritual resurrection in Christian baptism and continues in the process of sanctification throughout the Christian life; the full redemption of body and spirit is completed in the day of bodily resurrection.

Man as a unity of body and spirit is unique. Unlike angels, we are bodies; unlike animals, we are spirits. Thus man as a unity of body and spirit is uniquely equipped to occupy a distinctive place in the universe, and to fulfill his responsibilities and tasks in relation to God and to the world. With regard to what is below us (the material world), our bodies make us one with it and thus we can relate to it comfortably and use it for our needs. At the same time our spirits equip us to rule over the world and have dominion over it. On the other hand, regarding what is above us (God), because we are spirit we have a kinship with God and can relate to him as persons in worship and fellowship. At the same time our bodies make it natural and appropriate for us to relate to God by physical means, e.g., water, bread, musical instruments. See 1 Cor 6:19-20; Rom 12:1.

II. MAN IS WHOLLY A CREATURE

We must now address an important truth in some detail, i.e., man is wholly a creature; both body and spirit have been created by God. We have already seen that the doctrine of *ex nihilo* creation is unique to the Bible; therefore the doctrine of man as a created being is unique to Scripture also. In every nonbiblical worldview at least a part of man is eternal. In materialistic monism all matter is eternal; man is simply one stage in the eternal chance evolution of eternal stuff. In spiritualistic monism (e.g., Hinduism) the body is usually not even regarded as real, and the spirit is a part of or is identical with the eternal divine spirit. Pagan dualism usually regards matter—and thus the body—as real but as evil and temporary, but it regards the spirit as eternal and often divine. Over against all such false doctrines the Bible affirms the full creaturehood of man. Only God is eternal, immortal, and uncreated (John 1:3; Rom 1:25; 1 Tim 1:16).

Despite this clear biblical affirmation, it is not uncommon for sincere Christians to naively assume that the soul or spirit is a divine spark or a little piece of God, and somehow inherently eternal and immortal and even divine. Alexander Campbell has said, "Lord, what is man? Thine own offspring, reared out of the dust of earth, inspired with a portion of thine own spirit." Thus man has "something in common with God"; there is "a divinity stirring within him" ("Colleges," 63-64). C.C. Crawford (I:142-143) has said that man's body "was a divine creation; whereas the spirit that was breathed into it was a divine gift." In Gen 2:7 God implants a spirit in the body by "stooping down and placing His lips and nostrils to the inanimate form which he had created, and then expelling an infinitesimal portion of His very own essence into it." Sayers (132) says that in light of Gen 2:7 the soul must survive death because "you cannot destroy the God-part!"

Others within the broad scope of Christendom say that man was not *created* divine but will somehow *become* divine as the climax of the salvation process. This idea is at the heart of Mormon soteriology, and it appears occasionally in more orthodox circles. Texts such as Phil 3:21 and 1 John 3:2, which say that in the resurrection we will be like Christ, are misapplied to his divine nature instead of to his glorified *human* nature. Another text says that we become "partakers of the divine nature" (2 Pet 1:4), but this refers to our ethical oneness with God, not a sharing in the divine essence. That is, we share his *communicable* attributes such as holiness, love, and patience (see 1 Pet 1:15-16).

The very notion that finite creatures could ever acquire the attributes of infinity is illogical and impossible. Only the transcendent Creator-God is and can be infinite. Creatures should neither desire nor expect to "escape" their finitude, as if this were some kind of unnatural prison. Neither death nor salvation causes us to automatically take on some attribute that belongs exclusively to the infinite Creator. When we die we will not "enter eternity" in the sense that we will no longer be limited by time, nor will we "know fully" (see 1 Cor 13:12) by somehow becoming omniscient. We are finite now and will be finite forever.

Divinizing man, either by creation or by salvation, is a most serious false doctrine. It destroys the distinction between God and man, between Creator and creature. It puts man on the same level with God, which is the most basic temptation (Gen 3:5). It is the height of presumption and arrogance, the epitome of sinful pride. It either debases God or overexalts man. It destroys the uniqueness of Christ and his incarnation. Nothing of true Christianity remains (see *GC* 151-154).

To say that the spirit or soul is not divine but nevertheless is inherently immortal is not much better. This idea, too, is pagan, not biblical. It denies the full creaturehood of man and the unique eternality of God. Logically it makes man equal with God, since whatever is eternal is indeed divine: God "alone possesses immortality" (1 Tim 6:16).

The concept of innate immortality has led to false ideas about eternal punishment. Some have said that God created hell not because divine holiness demands it but because the souls of the wicked are indestructible and have to exist *somewhere* for eternity. Others have reacted to this error by teaching an even more serious error. They rightly deny the necessary immortality of the soul, but they then declare that this false idea was what led some in the early church to invent the idea of eternal punishment in the first place, a doctrine which they say is not really taught in the Bible. Thus they deny eternal punishment, believing that their refutation of the "immortal soul" doctrine has removed the basis for it. Examples of this approach are Jehovah's Witnesses and Seventh-day Adventists, who deny not just the immortality of the soul but its very existence; and Restoration Movement writers such as Curtis Dickinson, Russell Boatman, and Edward Fudge.

It is true that because the soul is no less created than the body, the whole being is perishable and destructible. The soul is just as capable of being annihilated and returned to nonexistence as the body, but this does not mean that it *must* do so. The fact is that the soul *does not* pass into nonexistence at death or at some later point, and this is simply God's will and plan. Though capable of perishing, the soul does not perish at physical death but continues to exist in the temporary absence of a physical body, nor is the sinner's soul annihilated along with a resurrected body after a finite period of punishment in hell. After the resurrection the reunited body and soul will exist forever either in heaven or hell, not of necessity but by God's choice.

Accepting either the divinity or the necessary immortality of the soul leads to a false contrast between soul and body, with an undue elevation of the importance of the soul as compared with the body. It leads to the idea that the soul or spirit is the only valuable part of man, the only real and authentic part, the only part that counts. It is true that the soul or spirit is relatively more important than the body, since it is the aspect of man that is in the image of God. It is also true that this present body is under the curse of sin and death and must be redeemed (Rom 8:23). But the idea that the body is *by nature* a temporary, unfortunate expedient, while the soul or spirit is *by nature* uncreated and eternal, is quite false.

III. MAN IS CREATED IN THE IMAGE OF GOD

As human beings we are not just creatures; we are *unique* creatures, i.e., a unique part of the visible creation. We are the only earthly creatures whose essence is more than physical; man alone has a soul or spirit and is thus a combination of matter and spirit. Our spiritual nature makes us like angels, who are wholly spirit; it also makes us like God, who is also spirit, albeit uncreated and divine. Being spirit after the pattern of divine spirit means that we are created *in the image of God*.

This aspect of human nature is emphasized from the first moment of our creation: "Then God said, 'Let Us make man in Our image, according to Our likeness.'. . . God created man in His own image, in the image of God He created him" (Gen 1:26-27). Genesis 5:1 reaffirms this: "In the day when God created man, He made him in the likeness of God." Genesis 9:6 indicates that this is what separates man from animals (v. 3). It also declares that this is the reason why murder warrants the death penalty: "Whoever sheds man's blood, by man his blood shall be shed, for in the image of God He made man." The NT also affirms that man is created in God's image (1 Cor 11:7; Jas 3:9), and describes sanctification as the process of being *recreated* in God's image (Eph 4:24; Col 3:9).

The main words used in these texts are "image" (OT, *tselem*; NT, *eikon*) and "likeness" (OT, *d'muth*; NT, *homoiosis*). The latter refers generally to something that is like something else. The former refers to an image in the sense of a representation of something in one way or another. It may be a portrait, a statue, a reflection in a mirror, or anything that is intended to copy or resemble another thing. The two words do not signify two different things but are used synonymously, after the manner of Hebrew parallelism in Gen 1:26. Together they tell us that human beings are made in the likeness of God in the sense that they embody or model or represent something of the very nature of God.

A. Is Man Unique?

As implied above, what is at stake regarding the image of God is the uniqueness of human beings. This uniqueness is implied in the Genesis account of creation; being made in God's image is what sets man off from the animal kingdom (Gen 1:20-24) and gives man the right and the ability to rule over the animals (Gen 1:26-28). It is implied throughout the Bible in the fact that man alone is the focus of the divine plan of redemption.

The doctrine of the image of God has thus taken on great significance in the last century and a half, since the theory of evolution has had the effect of nullifying the qualitative distinction between animals and mankind. It has taken on even greater importance in the last several decades because the uniqueness of human beings is being challenged by both popular and serious speculations concerning intelligent extraterrestrial life (e.g., the universe of *Star Wars* and *Star Trek*, the movies *ET* and *Close Encounters of the Third Kind*, and Carl Sagan's *Contact*), and by sustained efforts to invent artificial intelligence (AI), after the manner of "HAL" (*2001: A Space Odyssey*) and the *Star Wars* androids, R2D2 and C-3PO. Is man truly any different from animals, possible ETs, and computers?

Probably the most widely known challenge to man's uniqueness comes from the many modern studies of animal behavior. It used to be assumed that only human beings possess such qualities as problem-solving intelligence, tool-making ability, ability to use language, and a sense of morality. But the more we learn about animals of all kinds, the more it seems that their differences from human beings in such matters is one of degree only. For example, primates of various kinds have been taught to communicate with human beings in American Sign Language. In the course of their "conversations" they apparently demonstrate such qualities as humor, a moral sense, guilt, grief, deceit, and creativity. Also, some parrots (especially African Greys) show a remarkable ability to think analytically and converse intelligently. The intelligence and communication skills of dolphins are also widely known.

Do such data about animal intelligence and exploits, along with continuing investigations into ETs and AI, really destroy the uniqueness of man? Is the image of God a myth? No, not at all. What such data and investigations do show is that we must be more careful and precise in our attempts to define what is meant by the image of God. If we define it too broadly, without cognizance of such phenomena as the above, we risk including in it some behavior that we actually share with animals. Then when it is shown that animals exhibit such behavior, this gives unbelievers grounds not only for rejecting the uniqueness of man but also for rejecting the truthfulness of the Bible as such. So in the final analysis, whatever the image of God turns out to be, it must be something that is both *in God* and *not in animals.*

B. Defining the Image of God

With these considerations in mind we shall now try to define the nature of the image of God. Three possible approaches to the question have been suggested. Some say the image is *ontological* (substantive, structural). That is, the image is an inherent quality of man's nature, something built into our very essence and immutably existing within each individual. It is something we possess at all times. This is parallel to the way a statue is the image of a person.

Others say the image is *relational.* That is, it is not something within our nature, but something we possess only when we stand in a certain relation to God. This is parallel to the way a mirror reflects the image of a person only when it is properly positioned in relation to that person. In this view, sometimes the image is in us and sometimes it is not.

A third view is that the image is *functional.* Here it is defined not as something man is, nor as a relationship, but as something man does. Most frequently the function that constitutes the image is identified as subduing the earth and having dominion over it (Gen 1:26-28). In exercising such dominion man is like God, who is the ultimate sovereign over all the earth.

In my judgment the image of God is not limited to just one of these approaches, but involves all three in combination. It is first of all and primarily something built into our very nature. This innate quality then enables or equips us to stand in particular relations to God and to the world, and to perform certain functions related thereto. In other words, the image as a unique quality of our nature is the *cause,* while the unique relationships and functions are the *effect.* The latter depend upon the former and cannot exist without the former.

In defining the image of God specifically, I believe it is necessary to distinguish between its *form* and its *content.* As an illustration, balloons can be manufactured to take on almost any rounded form when inflated (e.g., sphere, tube, spiral, mouse-ears), and they can be filled with almost any gaseous or fluid content (e.g., helium, ordinary air, water, paint). The form will be the same even if the content changes. Likewise the image of God has a form that is the same for all individuals and that remains the same within each individual; this is the image as an innate quality. But the content of the image may change; this has to do with the relationships and functions involved in the image.

C. The Form of the Image

Focusing first on the form of the image, we may define it simply as *personhood.* There is considerable agreement that the basic distinguishing essence of man is his nature as a person. We have already seen that God is personal by virtue of his nature as spirit; by creating human beings as spiritual creatures, he has shared with us his own attribute of personhood. This is why the aspect of human nature that embodies the image of God is not the body but the spirit or soul.

We speak of personhood as the form of the image of God because it involves the *capacity* for the specific abilities and experiences that constitute personhood. The following capacities and abilities are usually included in the concept of human personhood and thus in the image of God. First is a *personal consciousness*, self-consciousness, the consciousness of the self as a person. This includes the awareness of other persons as persons, and the ability to relate to them interpersonally, e.g., in love. This is the capacity for "I-thou" relationships.

Second is an *intellectual* capacity, rational consciousness, the ability to think abstractly, to reason, to plan, to discern, to use logic, to use wisdom.

Third is the capacity to use verbal *language*, something that is very closely related to intellectual capacity. This does not involve any particular language or words, but simply the ability to use them and communicate through them.

Fourth is a *volitional* capacity, the capacity for self-determination, the possession of free will, the ability and freedom to deliberate, to decide, and to choose. This does not refer to any particular decisions, but to the ability to make informed and deliberate choices, as opposed to instinctive reactions.

Fifth is a *moral* or ethical capacity, the sense of right and wrong, the sense of guilt or shame, and the fact of knowing that we are responsible for our choices and deeds. Such things are summed up in what we call the conscience.

Sixth is a *creative* capacity. This includes the ability to invent and to make things to fulfill needs and desires from a utilitarian perspective. It also includes an aesthetic sense, the ability to discern and to appreciate the beautiful, and the ability to create things of beauty whose very existence gives us pleasure. This is the ability to produce what we call "the arts," or such things as painting, sculpture, literature, poetry, and music. This creative capacity clearly reflects the nature of the Creator-God, who made a universe that is filled with beauty, evokes wonder, and is appropriately called "very good" (Gen 1:31).

Seventh is a capacity for *emotions* such as joy and sorrow, grief and elation.

Up to this point one may wonder if we are really making a case for the uniqueness of man. Have we not already pointed out that experiments have shown that some animals have these same abilities and capacities? Yes, we acknowledge that some animals may have self-consciousness and intelligence; they may demonstrate creative and linguistic ability; they may experience emotions and feel guilt. But there is one further capacity included in the form of the image of God, one that is not found in the animal kingdom. We may call this the *religious* or spiritual capacity, the innate capacity for knowledge and consciousness of God, the capacity for worship, the sense of dependence upon the Creator-God. In a real sense this aspect of the form of the image is the truly unique element of personhood and the aspect of man that absolutely sets him apart from animals.

It is significant that this religious capacity is not just uniquely present in human beings in and of itself, but that it also lifts all the other capacities involved in human personhood to a level that is qualitatively different from animals. In other words, the first seven capacities outlined above find their full expression in human beings in that each can be employed spiritually in the course of one's relationship with God. The uniqueness and climactic glory of each of these capacities is its potential for this God-relationship.

This means that our personal consciousness allows us to know the personal God in an interpersonal way, in an I-thou love relationship. Our intellectual capacity is such that we can have true knowledge of God's nature and will. Our linguistic ability can thus be used to receive and understand God's word revelation, and to pray to him and praise him with our own words. Our volitional capacity gives us the free will to voluntarily choose to love and obey God. Our moral capacity allows us to know that right and wrong are grounded in the transcendent God, and that we are responsible to him for our ethical choices. Our creative capacities allow us to make things of wisdom and beauty in imitation of God and to the glory of God. Our emotional capacity is such that we know that our joys and sorrows are experienced in the presence of God.

In summary, the form of the image of God is personhood, every element of which is involved in human beings' unique ability to have a personal relationship with God. Such personhood is not found in any creature whose essence is physical only; the God dimension is the unbridgeable qualitative gap between animals and human beings. Also, personhood as such is not rooted in man's body but rather in his soul or spirit. The human body is uniquely designed to experience and express personhood (see Cosgrove, *Body*), but it does not in itself constitute the image of God.

D. The Content of the Image

We are now ready to discuss the *content* of the image of God. This raises the question of the very purpose and meaning of human existence. *Why* did God make us in his image, with the capacity for a God-relationship? Because he wants us to enter into a very specific kind of relationship with himself. The unchanging form of the image (personhood) means that every mentally mature human being does have some kind of relationship with God, but we do not all have the same relationship. In other words, the content of the image may differ from person to person, and it may change in any individual. Just as a balloon can be filled with either pure helium or poisonous carbon monoxide, so also can our relationship with God be positive or negative; but it will always be one or the other. God's purpose for us is that we have the positive relationship; only then is the image of God complete.

What exactly is our intended relationship with God, the one made possible by the form of the image, i.e., personhood? It is twofold, corresponding to the twofold purpose of creation as such. First, it is the relation of *servant to King*. As Creator, God is the sovereign Lord and King of all things, and our primary purpose is to glorify him as Lord and King. This means that our first and greatest responsibility is to consciously, willingly, and actively acknowledge him as King and ourselves as his servants. All the elements of personhood are intended to be brought to bear upon this duty.

Our relation to God as servant to King is especially expressed through a spirit of total submission in worship and obedience. This is clearly seen in the way the *renewed* image is described in the NT. The new self is "created [anew] in righteousness and holiness of the truth," says Eph 4:24. Positive righteousness and holiness are thus primary elements in the proper content of the image. "The new self . . . is being renewed to a true knowledge according to the image of the One who created him," says Col 3:10. This "true knowledge" is the knowledge of God and his will, which suggests that "the work of the Law written in their hearts" (Rom 2:15), i.e., an innate knowledge of God's moral law, was part of the original image of God.

The second aspect of our intended relationship with God made possible by our personhood is a relationship of *reciprocal love*. This reflects God's secondary purpose for creation, i.e., to share his goodness with us. This means not only that he gives us the total bounty of the created world, but also and primarily that he wants to share *himself* with us, all because of his pure and infinite love for us. Thus God intends that we consciously receive and acknowledge his goodness and love, and that we respond with a reciprocal love—a grateful love—for him.

In summary, man created as a person in the image of God is equipped and intended to be a *servant in fellowship* with the Creator himself. We are to combine worship and obedience to the King with love for and communion with the King. Herein lies the uniqueness of the elements of human personhood—not necessarily in their presence as such, but in the way they enable man and man alone to relate personally to God as servant in fellowship.

The second aspect of the proper content of the image of God is a certain relationship with and function toward the rest of the material universe. Specifically, the secondary purpose of the image is to equip us to exercise *dominion* over the world.

This means that the world was created *for man*. In Genesis 1 man is the climax and crown of creation; he is the creature toward which all other creation points and for which all else is made. This, too, is in accordance with God's secondary purpose of creation in general, i.e., to share his goodness with man. Thus a part of the meaning of human existence is to receive and enjoy the blessings of this physical universe as a gift from God.

The other side of this coin is that man is *over the world*. From the very beginning, creation in God's image is linked with dominion: "Then God said, 'Let Us make man in Our image, according to Our likeness; and let them rule over the fish of the sea and over the birds of the sky and over the cattle and over all the earth'" (Gen 1:26). God's initial command to the human race was this: "Be fruitful and multiply, and fill the earth, and subdue it; and rule over" all living things (Gen 1:28). Part of the Psalmist's answer to the question "What is man?" is this: "You make him to rule over the works of Your hands; You have put all things under his feet" (Ps 8:4,6). This relationship of dominion is part of the proper content of the image of God, made possible by the form of the image as personhood.

If man is the king of the earth, with each man and woman being a monarch sharing in this rule, then the earth and all things in it should be regarded as man's servants. Thus our relationship to the earth is a *king to servant* relationship (see Gen 1:29; 2:19-20; 9:2-3). This is a duplication of the God-to-man relationship in miniature. In other words, man is to the world what God is to man. The human race is not just another product of the earth existing in equality with the rest of the world and with the animal kingdom especially. The animals are not our equals; the earth is neither our sibling nor our mother. This we affirm over against extreme environmentalism (deep ecology), extreme animal rights activists (e.g., PETA), the New Age Movement, and earthism in all forms. Man's dominion over the earth is not "speciesism" or "human chauvinism"; it is a hierarchy based on God's deliberate creation of man in his own image.

The command for mankind to have dominion over the earth is often called the *cultural mandate,* or the divine mandate for humanity to develop to their fullest all the elements of human culture and all the potentialities bound up in the creation in terms of exploration, science, technology, and art. Subduing the earth thus requires the full use of all our creative and rational powers in order to produce and invent such things as wheels, steel, glass, microscopes, telescopes, violins, organs, nuclear reactors, computers, poems, and books.

Man's lordship over the earth is not absolute, however. We may be the crown of creation, but we are still creatures. God alone is the Creator and absolute Lord over all. In our function of dominion we are still God's servants, his stewards. We exercise dominion over the earth not only for our good, but also and primarily for God's glory. Understanding that our lordship is thus a stewardship is essential for a responsible use of earth's resources. The cultural mandate does not give us *carte blanche* to pillage the earth and waste its resources; it requires rather that we manage it wisely for the good of mankind as a whole, both present and future. Thus a proper understanding of our image-dominion helps us to avoid the extremes both of earthism and of selfish exploitation.

In view of our total understanding of the image of God, we may say that the creation order intended by God from the beginning is

GOD

MAN

WORLD

This order is symbolized in man's relation to the trees in the Garden of Eden (Gen 2:16-17). The command not to eat from the tree of knowledge of good and evil was to remind man of his role as servant of God, while permission to eat from all other trees signified his role as king of the earth.

E. Implications of the Image

Being made in the image of God has several important implications. First, authentic humanness can be explained and experienced only in reference to God. At its very core the essence of human nature is spirit, and the essence of spirit is personhood, i.e., being made in the image of God. Thus we can define ourselves only in relation to God, not just in relation to animals, e.g., man is a featherless biped (Aristotle); man is a naked ape (D. Morris, 9).

Second, the concept of the image of God, properly understood, gives us the answer to the question of the purpose or meaning of human existence. That is, we exist for the very purposes of being a servant in fellowship with God and of having dominion in stewardship over the earth.

A third implication is that human beings are truly unique; they are qualitatively different from all other earthly creatures. We stand apart from all other such creatures, and we stand over them, by virtue of the fact that we are made in God's image. This is the basis for a unique respect for human life; this is why the Bible prohibits the unlawful taking of human life (Gen 9:5-6; Exod 20:13) but not necessarily the killing of animals. This is also the primary reason why abortion is wrong. The unborn child is just as much in the image of God as is one who has already been born, in that he or she has the innate capacity for a God-relationship even if that capacity has not yet been developed.

Because human life is unique, it must be *uniquely respected*. The same level of protection and respect the Bible mandates for human beings is not due to animals. Genesis 9:1-6 makes a clear distinction between killing animals and killing human beings. The sixth commandment does not apply to animals. Albert Schweitzer's "reverence for life" philosophy is pagan, not biblical. Most modern approaches to "animal rights" are grounded in monistic worldviews (such as pantheism) and must be rejected.

Fourth, the image of God endows *all* human beings with the same inherent dignity and value. Being made in God's image is our primary identity, and we could ask for nothing greater. Our identity as sinners is secondary and acquired, and it does not negate the primary and inherent identity of the image. Even the worst sinner still has this dignity and worth since the form of the image is found in every person, even in those who have distorted its content through sin. Individuals may be quantitatively different in such things as math skills, musical talent, and basketball ability; but all are ontologically and qualitatively equal. This helps us to understand how God can love even the worst sinners (John 3:16), and how it is possible for us also to love even our enemies (Matt 5:44).

Fifth, being made in God's image is the primary basis for a positive self-image. We do not have to consider ourselves to be divine in order to have self-esteem.

Sixth, the image of God is a basic motivation for evangelism. How can we not be concerned about the eternal destiny of God's image-bearing creatures, no matter how sinful they have become? When a human being dies unsaved, it means that another person made in God's image will spend eternity in hell. It is more important to save one individual made in God's image than to save a whole species that is not.

Finally, the image of God is a presupposition of and creates the very possibility for theology. God communicates truth to us through word revelation. Being made in his image, we have the innate ability to receive and understand this communication; and through studying and analyzing it, we can discern and formulate sound doctrine.

IV. THE REALITY OF HUMAN FREE WILL

The final aspect of human nature to be considered here is the reality of free will. We have seen that the image of God includes a *volitional* capacity, which is the capacity for self-determination, the ability to deliberate, to decide, and to choose between alternatives. Almost everyone grants that there is something in man called the will; the question is whether this will is *free*. Is man, as created, a "free moral agent"?

Determinists of all sorts say that man is not free; the individual's choices are determined by forces outside himself (*GRu*, 49-86, 168-187). This is true of secular determinists such as mechanists and behaviorists, and of religious determinists such as Calvinists. The attempt by some Calvinists to redefine free will as voluntarily acting in accordance with one's inner motives and desires is deceiving, since it is admitted that God sovereignly plants all desires and motives in men's hearts, according to the choices he predetermines them to make. To call this "free will" is misleading double-talk. It is better to simply admit that free will is not compatible with determinism and to declare, as the Calvinist C. Samuel Storms does, "Human free will is a myth" (80-81). The Calvinist Gordon Clark agrees: "It is so obvious that the Bible contradicts the notion of free will that its acceptance by professing Christians can be explained only by the continuing ravages of sin blinding the minds of men" (114).

I and others, however, affirm that human beings do have free will. Whatever effect sin has had on this freedom, man in the beginning was created with a truly free will. This is one result of God's decision to make a world that is relatively independent of himself, as we have already explained. God has created us as persons with the innate power to initiate actions without interference, coercion, or foreordination. This does not imply total autonomy, since the will operates within the boundaries of God's controlling sovereignty and human finitude. It does include, however, the ability to choose between moral opposites, without the choice being fixed or determined (either ahead of time or at the time) by some power outside the person himself. On the one hand this means the absence of force, constraint, or hindrance. On the other hand it means the absence of any condition or manipulating force that limits a person's actual choices to just one.

The reality of free will is a presupposition of the reality of sin and evil in general. One reason why determinist doctrines have been challenged through the ages is that they negate the reality of moral responsibility, thus making the concepts of right and wrong meaningless. Without free will, how can anyone be praised for his good choices, or be held responsible for his wrong choices? Only the concept of a truly free will can do justice to the many passages of Scripture that picture God's blessings and punishments as conditioned upon human choices (e.g., Deut 11:26-28). Only when man is truly free to actualize either right options or wrong options can he be held responsible for his choices and therefore be justly blessed or condemned.

Notes on Chapter Six

[1]Here we are using the English word "man" in its generic sense of "mankind" or human beings in general, including male and female. This applies also to any pronouns relating thereto (he, him, his).

[2]Cited in Robbins, 4-5.

[3]Cited in Johnson, 28.

[4]C. Dickinson, "Theology," 1-2. See his booklet, *What the Bible Teaches about Immortality and Future Punishment,* earlier called *Man and His Destiny.* See also Hayes, "Divorce."

[5]Important works taking this view are Hoekema, *Image;* Cooper, *Body;* R. Gundry, *Soma;* Moreland and Ciocchi, eds., *Perspectives;* and Moreland and Rae, *Body.* The first three are biblical-theological in method; the last two are more scientific and philosophical. The last one is extremely technical. Much of my own material is based on a course taught by John Murray at Westminster Theological Seminary, some of which is included in his *Writings, Volume Two,* Part I.

CHAPTER SEVEN

THE NATURE OF SIN

Outside of Christian circles the concept of sin is practically nonexistent. Secular western man has abandoned the idea. Of course he recognizes that the world is filled with evils, failures, social ills, and conflicts of all kinds; but he just does not want to think of them as *sin*. This is because *sin* connotes a wrongdoing for which one is responsible before God, and modern man does not want to see himself in this light. He will take his evil and his failures to sociologists and psychologists, but not to God. As Karl Menninger points out in his book, *Whatever Became of Sin?* "In all of the laments and reproaches made by our seers and prophets, one misses any mention of 'sin.'" A problem may be "evil, disgraceful, corrupt, prejudicial, harmful," but never sinful (13, 17).

The fact is that philosophies and religions outside the sphere of God's revelation have never had a true concept of sin in the first place. Almost every nonbiblical worldview diagnoses man's basic problem either as ignorance (e.g., Hinduism, Buddhism, Gnosticism), as weakness (e.g., existentialism), or as a combination of the two (e.g., Christian Liberalism, secular Christianity), but not as sin.[1] If sin is mentioned at all, it is usually redefined or even figuratively applied. It may be seen as a residual weakness traceable to man's evolutionary origin, or it may be limited to sins committed against other human beings only. In every case, though, the concept of *sin against a personal God* is missing.

To anyone who has read the Bible, though, it is quite obvious that the reality of sin is a basic and pervasive biblical doctrine. In this chapter we shall summarize this teaching concerning the *nature* or *essence* of sin, and we shall also answer questions about the beginning and the presuppositions of sin.

I. SIN IS LAWLESSNESS

Many different Greek and Hebrew words are used in the Bible to describe sin,[2] but the one that best summarizes the essence of all sin is *anomia*, "lawlessness" (adj. *anomos*, "lawless"). As 1 John 3:4 says, "Everyone who practices sin also practices lawlessness; and sin is lawlessness." Jesus uses this term when he pronounces eternal condemnation upon those "who practice lawlessness" (Matt 7:23; see 13:41). The end-times anti-Christ is called "the man of lawlessness" (2 Thess 2:3; see 2:7-8). Sinners are described as "lawless ones" (Luke 22:37; Acts 2:23; 1 Tim 1:9); sins are "lawless deeds" (2 Pet 2:8).

These Greek words are formed by adding the negating alpha to *nomos*, the word for "law." Just as an atheist (alpha + *theos*, the word for "God") is a "no-God" person, so a sinner is a "no-law" person. Paul says that the knowledge of sin comes through the law (Rom 3:20; see 7:7); this is true because sin by definition is doing the opposite of what the law requires. Every sin is a violation of some law of God.

A. Biblical Terminology for Sin

That the essence of sin is lawlessness is seen in the many other words that are used to represent sinful behavior. In his discussion of terminology Erickson distinguishes fifteen categories of such words. Here we will focus on five of the more common terms.

One NT word for sin is the passive form of *planao*, meaning "to be deceived, to err, to go astray, to wander away." This word, along with its OT counterparts (*shagah, shagag*, and *ta'ah*), is used literally of sheep that wander astray. It is used figuratively of wandering away from the truth, erring, being deceived (Matt 22:29; 1 Cor 6:9; Gal 6:7; Jas 5:19). Like foolish sheep sinners go astray from the paths of righteousness (Ps 119:176; Matt 18:12-13; Heb 5:2; 1 Pet 2:25; 2 Pet 2:15). Sinners "always go astray in their heart" (Heb 3:10).

It is possible, of course, to wander off the path by accident, but the Bible makes it clear that as a rule those who allow themselves to be deceived and led astray are responsible for and thus condemned for their error. As Erickson says, it is "deliberate rather than accidental erring," and "those who fall into error know or ought to know that they are being led astray" (*Theology*, 584-585).

This term clearly demonstrates the essence of sin as lawlessness. One who goes astray, goes astray from a clear, safe path that has been marked out in advance. The path from which sinners stray is the law of God; God rebukes those who wander from his commandments (Ps 119:21,118). We should pray David's prayer: "Make me walk in the path of Your commandments" (Ps 119:35). "How blessed are those whose way is blameless, who walk in the law of the LORD" (Ps 119:1).

A second word for sin is the NT verb *hamartano* (nouns, *hamartia* and *hamartema*), along with its OT counterpart, *chata'* (noun, *chattath*). These are the terms most frequently used for sin, and the basic meaning of both is "to miss the mark." In reference to sin this is not an innocent mistake, an accidental failure to hit the mark, as is usually the case in target shooting; it is rather a deliberate decision and willful failure for which one must bear the blame.

This concept also shows how the essence of sin is lawlessness. The mark that we miss when we sin is the law of God. It is "failure to hit the mark he has set, his standard, of perfect love of God and perfect obedience to him" (Erickson, *Theology*, 587).

A third term for sin is the NT verb *adikeo* (noun, *adikia*; adj., *adikos*). These words combine the negating alpha with the root *dik-*, which is the basis for all the

NT words involving righteousness and justice (e.g., *dikaios*, "righteous"). Thus these words indicate that sin is the opposite of justice or righteousness, i.e., sin is unrighteousness. The verb is often translated "to do wrong" or "to wrong" someone, i.e., to do someone an injustice. The noun is usually rendered as "unrighteousness" or "wickedness" (e.g., Rom 1:18; 3:5; 1 John 5:17, "All unrighteousness is sin").

Referring to sin as unrighteousness also makes it clear that its essence is lawlessness. What is righteousness? It is conformity to the proper norm or law. A righteous person is one whose behavior conforms to the law of God, one whose life is in harmony with the law (*GRe*, 189-201). Thus the unrighteous person is one whose life does not conform to the norm of God's law. In 2 Cor 6:14 and Heb 1:9, righteousness and lawlessness (*anomia*) are opposites (see 1 Tim 1:9).

A fourth term for sin is *apeitheo* (noun, *apeitheia*; adj., *apeithes*), which represents the concept of disobedience. The adjective is used of children who disobey their parents (Rom 1:30; 2 Tim 3:2), but mostly these words refer to disobedience to God (Rom 11:30-32; Eph 2:2; 5:6; Titus 1:16; 3:3). They refer in a general way to any refusal to follow God's will and instructions for our lives. Thus they may have the connotation of lawlessness, or rebellion against and disobedience to the law of God (Eph 2:2; 5:6; Heb 3:18; 4:6,11). They are also used for the act of refusing to accept the gospel, the act of rejecting Christ as Savior and declining to follow the basic instructions for being saved (see John 3:36; Acts 14:2; 19:9; 1 Pet 2:8; 3:1; 4:17).

The last term considered here is *parabaino* (noun, *parabasis*), with the OT counterpart *'abar*. The basic meaning of these words is "to go over, to go aside, to pass beyond." When referring to sin they mean "to transgress," in the sense of "transgressing a command or going beyond an established limit" (Erickson, *Theology*, 589). When used in this sense in the OT, the meaning is almost always that of breaking or transgressing a command of God, or transgressing against the requirements of the covenant (e.g., Num 14:41; Josh 7:11; Isa 24:5; Dan 9:11). The same is true in the NT (see Matt 15:2-3; Rom 2:23; 5:14). That transgression is by definition transgression of law is seen in Rom 4:15, "Where there is no law there is no transgression" (NIV). All these passages clearly show that the essence of sin is the transgression of God's law.

After discussing these and the many other biblical terms for sin, Erickson rightly draws this conclusion: "A common element running through all of these varied ways of characterizing sin is the idea that the sinner has failed to fulfill God's law" (*Theology*, 595). Indeed, "sin is lawlessness" (1 John 3:4).

B. What Is Lawlessness?

The KJV in 1 John 3:4 translates *anomia* as "the transgression of the law." To transgress the law is to break it, to violate it. This occurs most obviously in overt, external actions that are contrary to God's law, such as committing adultery with one's neighbor, breaking the speed limit, or shoplifting from a store. Once we have determined how God's commandments apply to human conduct, both generally and specifically, any behavior that is contrary to the path prescribed by the law is sin.

It is important to understand, though, that not all *anomia* is external. Often God's law is broken in the mind or heart alone, in our thoughts and desires. In fact, any sin that can be committed externally can also be committed internally if the *desire* to perform the sinful act is present. As Jesus says, the law that forbids adultery can be broken by lustful thoughts alone (Matt 5:27-28). John says that "everyone who hates his brother is a murderer" (1 John 3:15); and Jesus says that anger can be the equivalent of murder, thus violating the sixth commandment (Matt 5:21-22). The sins Paul describes as "deeds of the flesh" include the inward attitudes of enmity (hatred), jealousy, and envy (Gal 5:19-21). Though it usually leads to other sins that are external, the tenth commandment— "You shall not covet" (Exod 20:17)—is an attitude of the heart.

At its deepest level, though, *anomia* is more than specific lawless acts and attitudes. It is basically an attitude toward the law of God as such: an inward hatred and hostility toward law, a spirit of opposition to and rebellion against authority, a demonic zeal for autonomy and for freedom from law of all kinds. This lawless spirit is expressed in the words of the kings and rulers who rebel against the Lord and against his appointed King: "Let us tear their fetters apart and cast away their cords from us!" (Ps 2:1-3).

Though some disagree, I agree with Strong (567-573) that the most basic inward essence of all sin is selfishness.[3] However, I disagree with Strong's definition of selfishness as "that choice of self as the supreme end which constitutes the antithesis of supreme love to God" (567). In my judgment this is the wrong contrast. In its most general nature selfishness is more a matter of opposition to law than to love as such. Indeed, love for God is itself a commandment of the law (Matt 22:36-37). When one breaks this or any other law of God, even the least commandment, he is in effect exalting himself over God (Dan 5:23); he is putting his own standard of conduct and his own judgment of what is best ahead of God's law. In a real sense everything that is meant by *anomia*—lawlessness— stems from and is the expression of selfishness.

Whether we grant such a connection between lawlessness and selfishness or not, we must agree that the essence of sin is something internal, something deep within the heart. It is a state of sinfulness, a condition of the heart or the personal center of the self (see Jer 17:9; Matt 15:19-20; Luke 6:45; Heb 3:12).

C. The Universality of Lawlessness

Lawlessness is universal in two ways. First, every sin is, by definition, a violation of the law of God. If an act or attitude is not contrary to the law, then it is not a sin (Rom 4:15; 7:8). Second, every person is a sinner, i.e., every responsible person has broken the law of God. "For all have sinned and fall short of the glory of God" (Rom 3:23). This statement is basically a summary of Rom 1:18–3:20, where Paul has shown that no one can be saved by law-keeping (Rom 3:20) because every individual has in fact broken the law. This is true of Gentiles (1:18-32; 2:14-15) as well as Jews (2:1–3:8). Thus the apostle concludes that "we have already charged that both Jews and Greeks are all under sin" (Rom 3:9).

D. The Seriousness of Lawlessness

The Bible testifies to the fact that the holy God *hates* sin. Since he is infinitely good, God "cannot but abhor unrighteousness, as being most distant from him, and contrary to him." Thus "he doth not hate it out of choice, but from the immutable propension of his nature" (Charnock, 455, 510). "You have loved righteousness and hated wickedness," says the Psalmist to the divine Messiah (Ps 45:7; see Heb 1:9). The Canaanites were destroyed because "every abominable act which the LORD hates they have done for their gods" (Deut 12:31). Specific sins hated and detested by God are idolatry (Deut 7:25; 16:22; Jer 44:4); occultism (Deut 18:9-14); haughty eyes, a lying tongue, hands that shed innocent blood, hearts that devise wicked plans, feet that run to do evil (Prov 6:16-18; see 12:22; 15:26); false weights (Prov 11:1); hypocritical ceremonialism in worship (Amos 5:21; Isa 1:14); arrogance and false trust (Amos 6:8); lying and injustice (Zech 8:17); divorce (Mal 2:16); and "the deeds of the Nicolaitans" (Rev 2:6). Charnock (509) emphasizes God's hatred of sin in a most effective way:

> . . . He cannot look on sin without loathing it, he cannot look on sin but his heart riseth against it. It must needs be most odious to him, as that which is against the glory of his nature, and directly opposite to that which is the lustre and varnish of all his other perfections. It is the "abominable thing which his soul hates," Jer. xliv.4; the vilest terms imaginable are used to signify it. Do you understand the loathsomeness of a miry swine, or the nauseousness of the vomit of a dog? These are emblems of sin, 2 Peter ii.22. Can you endure the steams of putrefied carcasses from an open sepulchre? Rom. iii.13. Is the smell of the stinking sweat or excrements of a body delightful? The word [filthiness] in James i.21 signifies as much. Or is the sight of a body overgrown with scabs and leprosy grateful to you? [See Isa. 1:5-6.] So vile, so odious is sin in the sight of God.

We may now ask, *why* does God hate sin so much? The answer is simple. Sin is a violation of God's law, and his law is a description of his own perfect moral character, a mirror or transcript of divine holiness. We cannot separate God's law from God himself. Thus to commit a sin is not just to break some impersonal, arbitrary rule; rather, it is a rebellion against God personally. To break God's law is an insult to God, a blow against God, a slap in his face, a contradiction of his very nature. Paul says forcefully in Rom 8:7 that not subjecting oneself to the law of God is hostility toward God.

Thus to despise God's law, in the spirit of *anomia*, is to despise God himself. Charnock has well said (509):

> It is no light thing, then, to fly in the face of God, to break his eternal law, to dash both the tables in pieces, to trample the transcript of God's own nature under our feet, to cherish that which is inconsistent with his honour, to lift up our heels against the glory of his nature, to join issue with the devil in stabbing his heart and depriving him of his life. Sin, in every part of it, is an opposition to the holiness of God. . . .

This is why James says, "For whoever keeps the whole law and yet stumbles in one point, he has become guilty of all" (James 2:10). There is a sense in which all laws are one, in that they are all identified with the will or nature of the Lawgiver. No matter which arrows of sin we launch, and whether it be one or many, they all ultimately come to rest in the heart of God. "For He who said, 'Do not commit adultery,' also said, 'Do not commit murder.' Now if you do not commit adultery, but do commit murder, you have become a transgressor of the law" (James 2:11)—and thus a despiser of God's own pure and holy nature. These words from Sproul sum it up well (*Holiness*, 151-152):

> Sin is cosmic treason. Sin is treason against a perfectly pure Sovereign. It is an act of supreme ingratitude toward One to whom we owe everything, to the One who has given us life itself. Have you ever considered the deeper implications of the slightest sin, of the most minute peccadillo? What are we saying to our Creator when we disobey Him at the slightest point? We are saying no to the righteousness of God. We are saying, "God, Your law is not good. My judgment is better than Yours. Your authority does not apply to me. I am above and beyond Your jurisdiction. I have the right to do what I want to do, not what You command me to do."
>
> The slightest sin is an act of defiance against cosmic authority. It is a revolutionary act, a rebellious act where we are setting ourselves in opposition to the One to whom we owe everything. It is an insult to His holiness. . . .

What could be more serious than this?

II. THE BEGINNING OF SIN

How did sin arise within God's good universe? How can we explain its beginning? On the negative side we must stress that sin did not have its beginning with God. The concept of the holiness of God makes it absurd to think that God could be the cause of sin. "Far be it from God to do wickedness, and from the Almighty to do wrong. . . . Surely, God will not act wickedly, and the Almighty will not pervert justice" (Job 34:10,12). "Your eyes are too pure to approve evil, and You can not look on wickedness with favor" (Hab 1:13). "God cannot be tempted by evil, and He Himself does not tempt anyone" (Jas 1:13). Thus when the creation first came into being, it was totally free from sin.

From God's perspective the most that can be said is that he has created a world in which it is *possible* for sin to occur, and that he *permits* sin to occur. He has created free-will beings who have the ability to sin, even though it is not necessary for them to choose to sin. (Free will does not make sin a necessity, but simply a possibility.) Having thus endowed his creatures with free will, God permits them to exercise it even when they use it to rebel against him.

Calvinists have considerable difficulty affirming their basic concept of a universal, efficacious, unconditional decree and at the same time denying that God is responsible for the beginning of sin. Some attempt to do this by including sin within the permissive will of God (e.g., Berkhof, 105, 108, 117). But true permission is not compatible with the concept of an unconditional decree, which is a basic tenet of Calvinism (see *GRu*, 180-182, 219-221). Some Calvinists speak of God's ordaining sin through his *efficacious* permission (Cottrell, "Sovereignty," 105-106), but this is a contradiction of terms. Truly consistent Calvinists simply affirm that God is the origin of sin. John Calvin said, "I thus affirm that God did ordain the Fall of Adam."[4] "Adam fell, not only by the permission of God, but by His very secret counsel and decree" ("Defence," 267). The Calvinist Gordon H. Clark declares "that God determines the choices that men make," and "men often make evil choices." Thus it follows "that God causes evil" (58-59).

Such ideas must be rejected as unbiblical. We must repudiate any concept of divine sovereignty that views God as the ultimate and unconditional cause of everything, even of the beginning of sin.

How, then, may we explain sin's beginning? There is no doubt that it began in the angelic realm before it began among human beings. The Bible speaks of angels who sinned (2 Pet 2:4; Jude 6). John says "the devil has sinned from the beginning" (1 John 3:8); Jesus says he "was a murderer from the beginning" (John 8:44). This does not refer to his own beginning, as if he were created a sinner; it refers to the beginning of this physical universe. The Bible does not give us details about Satan's first sin, but the implication is that the angels were created with free will and thus with the possibility of sinning. Some exercised their free will by choosing to sin, apparently led by Satan. (See the next chapter.)

How may we explain sin's beginning among human beings? This is the question of the Fall of Adam and Eve, as recorded in Genesis 3. In considering the Fall we may speak first of the period of *probation* for the human race. Adam and Eve were created in a state of goodness or positive holiness. In the time immediately after the creation, it was possible for them not to sin. But at the same time, because they were created with free will, it was possible for them to sin by disobeying the commandments given to them by God. Thus they had the power of opposite choice, the ability to choose either good or evil.

After being created in a state of perfect innocence, it appears that Adam and Eve existed in a time of probation. Some think that if they had passed their probationary test, they and the human race with them would have been transformed into a state where it was no longer possible for them to sin, as will be the case for saints in heaven. We cannot know this for sure, though. In any case, God brought this probation to a specific focus in the positive command regarding the tree of knowledge (Gen 2:16-17). This one tree thus became the symbol of Adam's free will and of God's law. Both Adam's conscience and God's law were objectified and brought to focus in one test.

The next step in the Fall was the *temptation* of the first pair. "The tempter" (Matt 4:3) was Satan himself, who is called "the serpent" (Gen 3:1-4,13-15; 2 Cor 11:3). Most likely Satan was working in or through the created animal in some way, though as a result "the serpent" becomes one of his names or titles (Rev 12:9). The temptation itself was threefold: physical, aesthetic, and intellectual (Gen 3:6; see 1 John 2:16). The basic essence of the sin proposed to Adam and Eve was that they should violate the God-given creation order (God over mankind; mankind over the world).

The temptation was followed by the *transgression* itself. Why these good creatures existing in a perfect environment under the love of God should have *wanted* to sin is quite a mystery, but sin they did. The external character of their sin was *anomia*, transgression of the law; its internal character was selfishness, the desire to make the self equal with God and thus independent of God. Like most sins, the transgression that marked the Fall of Adam and Eve began in the heart before the actual deed was done. Before the fruit was touched, the heart had already fallen.

We usually refer to this sin as the *Fall* of mankind, and indeed it was a fall from the state of goodness and a fall from God's favor.[5] We here affirm the Fall as a real event, and as an event that has brought untold misery upon the world. Among those who accept evolution the reality of the Fall is usually denied. For example, John Hick says, "The fall is a mythic conception which does not describe an actual event in man's history. . . . Man has never lived in a pre- or un-fallen state, in however remote an epoch. He has never existed in an ideal relationship with God, and he did not begin his career in paradisal blessedness and then fall out of it into sin and guilt" (*Evil*, 181-182). Those who thus deny the historicity of the Fall usually consider the story in Genesis 3 to be a myth or metaphor for a crucial stage in the evolutionary *advance* of mankind, such as the rise of self-awareness or the beginning of man's moral growth (i.e., man "fell" upward). But here again we accept the transgression recorded in Genesis 3 as a literal event just as Paul does in his theological reflection upon it in Rom 5:12-19.

III. THE PRESUPPOSITIONS OF SIN

The reality of sin is grounded in certain other realities which we may call the *presuppositions* of sin. These are the factors that must exist in order for sin to be real as such and real in the life of an individual.

A. The Existence of Law

Since sin is by definition lawlessness, there can be no such thing as sin without a valid body of law. Paul says the law gives us our knowledge of sin (Rom 3:20). He says, "I would not have come to know sin except through the Law; for I would not have known about coveting if the Law had not said, 'You shall not covet'" (Rom 7:7).

Scripture gives abundant attestation to the existence of law, using many terms to describe it. Eight of these appear in Ps 119 alone: "law," "commandments," "statutes," "testimonies," "word," "judgments," "precepts," and "ordinances."

The two most general kinds of law have been called *moral laws* and *positive laws*. The former are commandments that generally reflect the holy nature of God and thus are absolute and unchanging. They are meant to apply equally to all people in all times and places. Examples are the commandments that forbid murder, adultery, stealing, lying, and coveting (Exod 20:13-17). Positive laws are commandments that express God's will for specific persons or peoples in specific times and places. Examples are the requirement of circumcision for the OT people of God, and the requirement of the Lord's Supper for his NT people. Disobedience to either kind of law constitutes sin.

While the moral law applies universally, the existence of positive laws designed for limited application means that more than one law code may be identified. A law code is the totality of the body of commandments that apply to an individual and for which that individual is responsible.

We may distinguish at least three such codes. One consists of the *moral law only*. This applies to those who have access to this law only as known in their hearts (Rom 2:15) and in the creation (Rom 1:18-21), and who have no access to any form of special revelation of positive laws. Thus even pagans with no knowledge of the Bible have a law code and commit sin when they disobey it (Rom 1:18-32).

The second main law code is the *Law of Moses*, including Israel's Old Covenant responsibilities. This code included both the moral law and many positive laws (e.g., circumcision, the Sabbath, animal sacrifices). In its Mosaic form it was intended only for the Jews and for OT times only; disobedience thereto is what constituted sin for OT Israel.

The third law code is the totality of NT commandments as they apply in the New Covenant age. These include the moral law as well as various New Covenant ordinances, all of which are intended to apply to everyone living in this New Covenant age. Today all those who have access to the NT yet disobey its commandments are guilty of sin.

B. The Existence of the Creator-God

For sin to exist there must be law, and the existence of law depends on the existence of the transcendent Creator-God of the Bible. Why should any rule or set of rules be regarded as law? What gives it the force of law? All human opinions and all man-made rules are finite and relative; they can function as law only by mutual agreement or by unilateral power, not by inherent authority. But the commandments of the Creator come to us from outside the boundaries and relativities of creation; they come from the one who is absolute in knowledge and power and whose authority is absolute.

The fact that God is the *ex nihilo* Creator of all things is crucial for the reality of law and thus the reality of sin. Because God is the Creator of all things, including human beings, he thereby owns all things and has the sovereign right to do whatever he chooses with his creatures. In reference to human beings he thus has the inherent right to tell us what to do, i.e., to lay down laws for us. He is our Lawgiver, Judge, and King (Isa 33:22; Jas 4:12). Because he is the Creator, his commandments are an absolute norm for conduct, and our obligation to obey them is absolute (*GC*, 163-166).

The basic reason why our modern Western culture has lost the concept of sin is that the reality of the true Creator-God has been abandoned. The basic reason why all nonbiblical philosophies and religions lack a true concept of sin is that none includes the concept of a Creator-God whose will is *law*. The doctrine of *ex nihilo* creation and the doctrine of sin are thus inseparable; sin is a meaningful concept only in the light of the fact of creation.

C. The Knowledge of Law

A third presupposition of sin in the life of the individual is the *knowledge* of God's law, or at least the possibility of knowing his law. Knowledge of sin comes through knowledge of law (Rom 3:20; 7:7). The first three chapters of Romans make it clear that because of general revelation, in one form or another law is in fact everywhere (Rom 1:18-21,32; 2:14-15). This means that the knowledge of law is available to everyone.

But in Rom 4:15 Paul notes that "where there is no law, there also is no violation." In view of Rom 1–3 (especially 2:15), how can there be any situation "where there is no law"? In the final analysis this must refer to an individual's unavoidable ignorance of the law, as in the case of children who have not reached the age of accountability and in the case of the mentally handicapped, i.e., anyone who is unable to understand the origin and nature of law as commandments of God bearing the penalty of eternal wrath (Rom 7:9). *Willful* ignorance of the law, however, is no excuse (Rom 1:18; Eph 4:18).

D. Free Will

The last presupposition of sin is the reality of free will among both angels and human beings. The angels who sinned (2 Pet 2:4) must have had free will at least at that time; all human beings must also have free will in order to be counted guilty for their sin. Only if a person breaks God's law of his own free choice can he be held responsible for his transgression and blamed for it; only then can it truly be regarded as sin. All forms of determinism, which by definition deny the existence of truly free will, are inconsistent with the reality of sin. Without the ability to choose, one can neither be praised for good choices nor held responsible for wrong choices.

NOTES ON CHAPTER SEVEN

[1] See *GRe*, ch. 2, "Alternatives to Redemption."

[2] See Erickson, *Theology*, 583-595.

[3] Those who disagree include Berkhof, 229-230; and Erickson, *Theology*, 597-598.

[4] John Calvin, "Treatise," 126. After saying this Calvin waffles and adds that he is not thereby conceding "that God was therein properly and really the *author* of that Fall," since he was only the *ultimate* cause of the Fall and not its *proximate* (secondary) cause (126-128). For a critique of the whole concept of "second causes," see *GRu*, 221-223.

[5] It was perhaps more of a *leap* or *jump*, since it was a deliberate choice and not an accident, and since a "fall" is usually accidental. It is not likely, though, that we will be able to convince the world to speak of "the Jump of mankind" rather than "the Fall of mankind."

CHAPTER EIGHT
ANGELIC SIN:
SATAN AND HIS DEMONS

We have already noted that the overall product of God's work of creation includes both a visible and an invisible universe. The latter encompasses the realm of created spirits, especially angels. Some of the inhabitants of this sphere are *evil* spirits: Satan and his demons. These were not created evil but became so through the exercise of their God-given free will. The corruption of the old creation began with the introduction of sin into the spiritual universe by these powerful spiritual beings, who then became actively involved in the initial and ongoing corruption of the visible universe. These evil spirits are thus a contributing factor in the proliferation of sin and evil among human beings. Thus a full understanding of the fallenness of our world requires us to understand the reality, nature, and work of these spirits.

I. THE REALITY OF EVIL SPIRITS

Many of those influenced by materialistic, secular culture deny the existence of spiritual reality altogether, including evil spirits. Others accept the existence of good angels but not the devil and his demons. For example, J.B. Russell has several books on the devil but does not grant his actual existence. He says, "I assert the reality of the Devil, but by this I do not intend a judgment as to the metaphysical reality of such a being." Rather, "the Devil is the personification of whatever is perceived in society as evil" (43, 46). Some attribute the biblical teaching about demons to the superstitions of unsophisticated people. The ones from whom Jesus "cast out demons" were suffering from various kinds of mental derangement; our Lord was merely accommodating himself to their superstitions.

We reject all such attempts to demythologize or explain away the reality of evil spirits. The Bible clearly testifies to the literal existence of both Satan as the ruling evil spirit and the demons as his messengers (angels).

A. Satan, the Prince of Demons

The usual name for the ruler or prince of demons (Matt 12:24; Luke 11:15) is *Satan*. This name is a transliteration of a generic Hebrew word meaning "adversary, opponent, one who tries to block your way" (Num 22:22; 1 Kgs 11:23,25), or "accuser" (Ps 109:6). Of its 52 OT uses, the word refers to Satan in 1 Chr 21:1; Zech 3:1-2; and Job 1-2 (13 times). The corresponding Greek word is *satanas*; all 33 of its NT uses refer to the devil. This name represents his basic nature as an opponent or enemy of both God and mankind.

Another NT word for Satan is *diabolos*, taken from the verb *diaballo*, meaning "to accuse, to slander." It is used 30 times for Satan in the NT and is translated "the devil," who is thereby identified as a slanderer or accuser and thus again as the adversary of both God and man.[1] He is also specifically called our adversary (*antidikos*, 1 Pet 5:8), our enemy (*echthros*, Matt 13:25,28,39; Luke 10:19), and our accuser (*kategor*, Rev 12:10).

Other names applied less frequently to Satan are Abaddon and Apollyon, meaning "destruction" and "destroyer" (Rev 9:11);[2] Belial or Beliar, a name applied to a powerful evil spirit in the Qumran literature and having the connotation of worthlessness (2 Cor 6:15); and Beelzebul or Beelzebub (Matt 12:24,27; 10:25; Mark 3:22; Luke 11:15,18,19). This name may be taken either from the pagan deity Baal-zebub (2 Kgs 1:2-6,16), meaning "lord of the flies," or from a similar deity named Baal-zibbul, meaning "lord of the dung-heap" (Bietenhard, 3:469).

Some think the reference to Lucifer in Isa 14:12 applies only to the king of Babylon; others think it refers to Satan or to both Satan and the king. The name itself is based on Latin terms meaning "light-bearer." The KJV used it to translate the Hebrew term *helel* ("radiant or shining star") in Isa 14:12, and it has been applied to Satan ever since. (Later versions translate this as "star of the morning," NASB; "morning star," NIV; and "Day Star," NRSV.) As a reference to Satan it would call to mind 2 Cor 11:14, which says that "Satan disguises himself as an angel of light."

Satan is also described as a serpent (Gen 3:1-4,13-15 [see Rom 16:20]; 2 Cor 11:3; Rev 12:9,14-15; 20:2) and a dragon (Rev 12:3-17; 13:2,4,11; 16:13; 20:2), indicating his sly and sinister nature. In a similar vein he is called the tempter (Matt 4:3; 1 Thess 3:5), a deceiver (Rev 12:9; 20:3), and "a liar and the father of lies" (John 8:44).

Satan's power and position are indicated when he is called "the ruler of this world" (John 12:31; 14:30; 16:11), "the ruler of the demons" (Matt 9:34; 12:24; Luke 11:15), "the god of this world [age]" (2 Cor 4:4), and "the prince of the power of the air" (Eph 2:2). The essence of his fallen nature is summed up in his description as "the evil one" (e.g., Matt 13:19,38; Eph 6:16; 2 Thess 3:3; 1 John 5:18-19).

B. The Demons, Satan's Angels

In addition to the devil, the Bible speaks of a whole host of evil spiritual beings commonly known as *demons*. This term comes from the Greek word *diamonion*, used 63 times in the NT.[3] Used by Greeks to refer to their lesser deities, its origin is uncertain. Some trace it to a root word suggesting "knowing ones," others to a word suggesting "disrupting or rending ones."

Demons are called "evil" spirits (*poneros*, Luke 7:21; 8:2; 11:26; Acts 19:12, 15-16) and "unclean" or impure spirits (*akathartos*, e.g., Matt 10:1; 12:43; Acts 5:16; Rev 16:13).[4] That the demons are called *spirits* as such indicates their basic metaphysical nature as a part of the invisible universe. That they are called *evil* and *unclean* indicates their basic moral nature.

In the OT demons are called *shedim* (cf. the English word "shades"); see Deut 32:17; Ps 106:37. The *shedim* represented pagan deities to which sacrifices were made; the term shows a close connection between demons and idolatry (see 1 Cor 10:19-21). They are also called *se'irim*, a term used for wild goats (Isa 13:21; 34:14) but which came to apply to goatlike idols, goat-demons, or demon-satyrs (Lev 17:7; 2 Chr 11:15). The portrayal of Satan and demons as having goat features has persisted until today (cf. satyrs, the god Pan, the Baphomet figure). The "deceiving spirit" in 1 Kgs 22:19-23 was probably a demon.

Paul's references to spiritual beings as thrones, dominions, authorities, powers, rulers [principalities], and world forces[5] no doubt includes demons. Such terms emphasize their power, their hierarchical organization, and their usurped authority over "this present evil age."

What is the relation between demons and Satan? Satan is their leader and ruler; the Pharisees knew him as "the ruler of the demons" (Matt 12:24). Matthew 25:41 refers to "the devil and his angels." Since the term "angel" means messenger, we conclude that the demons are under the authority of Satan and carry out his plans and instructions.

II. THE NATURE OF EVIL SPIRITS

Our understanding of the nature of Satan and other evil spirits depends on our understanding of their origin. Four major views have been defended by Bible-believers (see Unger, *Demonology*, 42-55). One is that demons are the spirits of wicked men who have died. The Jewish historian Josephus said that demons are "the spirits of the wicked, that enter into men that are alive and kill them" (*Wars*, 844). This was Alexander Campbell's view: "The demons of Paganism, Judaism, and Christianity were the ghosts of dead men" ("Demonology," 384). Some modern Restoration writers have agreed with Campbell.[6] However, this view is unacceptable for two reasons. One, demons exhibit a supernatural knowledge and power that is far beyond the capacity of human spirits. Two, such a view is without any biblical foundation whatsoever.

A second view of the origins of evil spirits is that they are the disembodied spirits of a superior but rebellious race of creatures who inhabited the earth prior to Adam. This presupposes that the original earth (Gen 1:1) included this superior earthly race. However, these creatures rebelled against God, and in the ensuing conflict they were destroyed and the earth itself was reduced to chaos (Gen 1:2). Then God began all over and brought this present world into existence (Gen

1:3ff.). The disembodied spirits of the original race continue to roam the earth and plague its present inhabitants (mankind), though.

This view must also be rejected as pure speculation. It has no biblical basis, and the whole idea of a "gap" between Gen 1:1 and Gen 1:2 is based on faulty exegesis (see Whitcomb, 115-134).

A third view is that demons are the offspring of a perverse mating between angels and human women. This is based on the idea that the "sons of God" in Gen 6:2 were angels, and that the "Nephilim" in verse 4 were their demon-offspring. This view must also be rejected because of its very unlikely assumptions, i.e., that the "sons of God" were angels rather than the godly descendants of Seth; that angels can literally mate with human beings and produce monstrous hybrid offspring (see Matt 22:30; Mark 12:25; Luke 20:35-36); and even if this were possible, that such offspring would be spiritual, nonphysical beings only.

The fourth and best view is that Satan and other evil spirits are *fallen angels*, the "angels that sinned" (2 Pet 2:4, KJV). The Bible does not explicitly identify demons with the fallen angels, but it is reasonable to draw this conclusion based on the similarities between demons ("the devil and his angels") and good angels. For example, both groups are powerful spiritual beings, and the two groups are depicted as being involved in head-to-head combat (Rev 12:7-9). In Rev 12:7-9 as well as Jude 9 Satan is portrayed as the evil equivalent of Michael the archangel, which suggests that he may have been an archangel himself before he fell. Also, if the "angels that sinned" are not Satan and his demons, then we have absolutely no clue as to the nature and fate of these fallen angels.

When did the angelic sin occur? It must have preceded the fall of man, since Satan had already become evil by then (Gen 3:1ff.). Possibly it occurred before the physical universe was even created. John 8:44 says Satan "was a murderer from the beginning," and 1 John 3:8 says "the devil has sinned from the beginning." What is this "beginning"? Probably the beginning of this universe. Thus the sinful angels were already in their fallen state when this physical universe was created.

If evil spirits are the fallen angels, then their metaphysical nature is basically the same as that of all angels, as described in chapter 5. That is, they are *created* beings and thus finite (limited) in every way and subject to the sovereign rule of the Creator. They are *spiritual* beings, created out of spiritual and not physical substance. They are *powerful* beings, not omnipotent but certainly more powerful than human beings. They are *immortal* beings, destined to exist forever in eternal punishment (Matt 25:41-42). Finally they are a *hierarchical order* of beings, with some having authority over others and Satan having authority over them all.

Concerning the actual fall of Satan and his demons, the Bible tells us very little. The main passages usually connected with it are probably referring to other events. Isaiah 14:12-17 and Ezek 28:12-19 most likely are poetically extravagant descriptions of God's judgments upon arrogant and presumptuous pagan kings ("the king of Babylon," Isa 14:4; "the king of Tyre," Ezek 28:12). Luke 10:18

and Rev 12:7-9 almost certainly refer to Christ's confrontation with and defeat of Satan at the time of his first coming.

This leaves only 2 Pet 2:4 and Jude 6 as probable references to the beginning of angelic sin, and they do not say much. Peter simply says that "God did not spare angels when they sinned, but cast them into hell [Tartarus] and committed them to pits of darkness, reserved for judgment." Jude says these angels "did not keep their own domain, but abandoned their proper abode." Therefore God has kept them "in eternal bonds under darkness for the judgment of the great day."

These verses say that before the angels sinned they existed in "their proper abode," literally "their own habitation"; and in "their own domain." "Domain" translates the Greek word *arche*, which can mean "rule, domain, sphere of influence"; but it can also mean "beginning," and I believe this is the better sense here. Jude thus says that these angels did not retain their original status as angels but forfeited their own proper and intended abode in the spiritual realm by rebelling against God. As an act of judgment God expelled them into the nether regions of the spiritual universe. Jude characterizes this as an existence "in eternal bonds" and in darkness. Peter concurs that they were banished to "pits of darkness" and "cast . . . into hell." The latter is not a good translation because the English word "hell" usually connotes the place of final judgment, which this is not. The word is actually a verb meaning "send to Tartarus," indicating a state or place of divine (but not final) punishment. Their final condemnation is certain, however, since they are "reserved for judgment," "the judgment of the great day" (see Matt 25:41).

Exactly where do Satan and his demons exist, then? As spiritual beings they still exist in the spiritual universe, but not in the heavenly throne room of God with the good angels (Rev 5:11-12). We infer that God must have designated a certain part of spiritual realm as a new and exclusive habitation for Satan and his demons, turning it into a punitive place of hopelessness and gloom. This is what Peter calls Tartarus, with its "pits of darkness."

This state of intermediate condemnation does not mean that the fallen angels are in absolute confinement. The "pits" and "bonds" indicate their degraded status and their certain doom, not a complete restraint of activity. After his fall Satan still has had access to God's throne (Job 1:6-12; 2:1-7; see 1 Kgs 22:19-22), and he and his demons are still able to interact with the physical universe. Indeed, they are hard at work, engaged in spiritual warfare against God and against mankind.

III. THE WORK OF EVIL SPIRITS

Exactly what is the work of Satan and his demons? In general, their overall goal is to defeat God's plan and purpose by all possible means. In the beginning (Gen 3:1ff.) Satan tried to do this by corrupting mankind at its fountainhead; but foreknowing this, God had already prepared his plan of redemption through

Christ. Then when Christ came, Satan tried to achieve his goal by attacking the Redeemer himself. Working through Herod, he tried but failed to kill him in his infancy (Matt 2:1-15; Rev 12:1-5). He then tried and failed to tempt Jesus to abandon his mission (Matt 4:1-11). Finally, working through Judas, he sought Jesus' death (John 13:2; 1 Cor 2:8), not knowing this would be the means of his own defeat (Heb 2:14).

Having failed to prevent God from carrying out his plan of salvation, Satan now focuses on specific individuals, seeking to cut them off from God's saving grace (1 Pet 5:8). As a finite creature he cannot do this alone (he is not omnipresent), but must enlist the help of the lesser evil spirits, the demons, who are his "angels" or representatives. Working together they assault individuals in three ways: on the levels of the mind, the will, and the body.

Satan's main strategy is to attack our minds through false teaching. Above all else he is a liar and a deceiver (John 8:44; Rev 12:9; 20:3,7-10). Since the beginning he has been lying about God and attacking his Word (Gen 3:4-5; Luke 8:12). He disguises himself as an angel of light (2 Cor 11:13-15) and blinds the minds of the unbelieving (2 Cor 4:4). His strategy depends upon deceitful schemes and snares (2 Cor 2:11; Eph 6:11; 2 Tim 2:26). We are constantly bombarded by "deceitful spirits and doctrines of demons" (1 Tim 4:1), as they work through false prophets (1 John 4:1 3). Demons inhabit the false religions of the world and are the reality behind all idolatry (1 Cor 10:14-22; Deut 32:17; Ps 106:36-38). Satan can even empower people to work miracles to give pseudosupport to his lies (Matt 7:21-23; 2 Thess 2:9; Rev 16:14).

The second strategy is to attack our wills through temptation. Satan is evil, and he wants to make us like himself. He wants us to share his sin so we will share his condemnation (Matt 25:41). By putting pressure on our wills he leads us to act in sinful ways. The mechanics of temptation are not clearly explained to us, but we can discern some of them. Often the acceptance of a lie in itself creates a path that the will gladly follows. Demons may manipulate our subconscious through subliminal suggestions (e.g., John 13:2). They may influence our thoughts by bringing certain ideas and images into our consciousness. They stoke the fires of our sinful desires and exploit our spiritual weaknesses. They work indirectly upon our wills through other people.

Satan's third strategy is to attack our bodies through demonic presence and control. This is commonly called demon possession, but a better term is demonization. The Bible shows us that Satan and his demons can manipulate aspects of the physical world (Job 1:12,16,19; 2 Thess 2:9). They can cause some physical illnesses (Job 2:7), often by their very presence within the body (Matt 9:32-33; 12:22; Mark 9:17-27; Luke 13:11,16; Acts 10:38). When they control the body, they control the nervous system. Thus if a demon has entered a person's body, it can bypass that person's own mind and will and can directly produce thoughts, words, and actions through the commandeered brain and body.

Are Satan and his demons still working today? Yes, on all three levels. Few Christians doubt that he still employs the first two strategies; thus they are on guard against temptation and false doctrine. The controversial issue is whether demons are able to invade the bodies of individuals in our time. Again, the answer is yes. Westernized, secularized skeptics need only to hear the testimony of anyone who has done mission work in an animistic culture to know this is the case.[7]

Some believe that demonization was a phenomenon in the first century but ceased to exist after the apostolic era. A common argument is that God would not permit demonization and then leave us with no means of deliverance; but deliverance requires miraculous power, and miraculous gifts ceased after the apostolic age; thus God does not permit demonization today. The flaw in this argument, though, is the idea that deliverance requires miraculous power. In NT times some deliverance, like some healing, was definitely miraculous. But just as God can and does heal through his special providence in answer to prayer, so he can and does deliver people from demons through providential intervention in answer to prayer. This is truly a supernatural event, but supernatural events are not necessarily miraculous.

Another common argument against demonization today is based on the view that Satan was bound by Jesus at his first coming through his death and resurrection (Matt 12:22-29; Rev 20:1-3), which precludes any further demonization. This argument is also flawed. We agree that Satan has been bound since Christ's first coming (see the later discussion of eschatology), but we reject the notion that this rules out subsequent demonic activity. Obviously the binding of Satan has not curtailed his other two strategies; why should it end all demonization? This is an arbitrary inference from the fact of his binding. In fact, Rev 20:3 actually specifies the purpose and result of this binding, i.e., "so that he would not deceive the nations any longer." This places certain limitations on his work, but does not produce the absolute cessation of any of it.

We judge that these and other arguments against demonization in our day are not valid. The devil is still a roaring lion, looking for victims (1 Pet 5:8).

IV. CHRISTIANS AND SPIRITUAL WARFARE

A question to be asked at this point is whether Christians are susceptible to Satan's attacks. The answer is yes, and this is seen in the fact that the NT frequently directs Christians to be on guard against the devil and his wiles. Satan is "your adversary," says 1 Pet 5:8; therefore "be on the alert." James 4:7 warns us to "resist the devil." "Do not give the devil an opportunity," says Eph 4:27. We are in a struggle with these spiritual forces, says Paul, and thus must be sure we are clothed with the full armor of God (Eph 6:10-17). Those who are not on guard against deceitful spirits may fall away, says 1 Tim 4:1 (see 2 Cor 11:3).

Though Satan and his demons are doing their best to take control of our minds, wills, and bodies, we must remember that they are created beings and do not have infinite powers; they are under God's control. Also, we must remember that Jesus Christ has already met them in battle and decisively defeated them, and we are on his side and share his victory over them. One of the reasons Jesus came was to meet and defeat the devil (1 John 3:8). Through his death and resurrection he has rendered Satan powerless (Heb 2:14) and disarmed the demons (Col 2:15). He has defeated and bound the devil, limiting his power (Rev 12:7-9; 20:1-3). The Holy Spirit within us is greater than evil spirits (1 John 4:4).

Nevertheless we will share in this victory and power only if we heed the warnings noted above. We are under attack, but we have been given sufficient resources to repel these attacks—*if* we avail ourselves of these resources. How can we do this?

First, we can prevent Satan from taking control of our minds by *knowing the truth*. The first item in the armor of God is truth: "having girded your loins with truth" (Eph 6:14). This is our most basic form of defense against the devil; knowing the truth set forth in God's Word is crucial to freedom from deception (John 8:32). Just knowing what the Bible teaches is not enough, however; we must also *believe* the truth and *love* the truth (2 Thess 2:10-12). We must take it into our hearts and delight in it, and wield it boldly and proudly in our personal lives and in our church activities.

Second, we can resist Satan's temptations by submitting our wills to the sanctifying power of the indwelling Holy Spirit (Eph 6:14-18). Through his power we can put sin to death in our lives (Rom 8:13). He gives us an inner strength to walk in paths of righteousness, a strength that is greater than Satan's alluring temptations (Rom 8:14; 1 John 4:4). The more we actually walk in and practice righteousness, the stronger we will be. Righteousness is, in fact, the second item of the armor of God: "having put on the breastplate of righteousness" (Eph 6:14).

Third, we can prevent demons from entering into our bodies by avoiding activities that give them an opportunity to enter (Eph 4:27) and by consciously trusting in the protecting name and blood of Jesus Christ ("the shield of faith," Eph 6:16). Activities that open one up to demonic intrusion include idol worship, gross immorality, occult practices, seeking supernatural knowledge or powers, and mysticism or mystical trance states. When one walks in paths of righteousness and wears the armor of God, he need not fear being invaded by evil spirits.

A common idea is that demons cannot inhabit the bodies of Christians at all; thus we need not be concerned about this. The main argument is that a demonic spirit and the Holy Spirit cannot be present in a person's body at the same time: "Demons cannot occupy the same place as the Holy Spirit" (Ben Alexander, *Exposing Satan's Power*, Nov./Dec. 1994, p. 1). Such a view is never taught in Scripture, however; it is an inference based on false assumptions. It assumes that the Holy Spirit and evil spirits are present in a person's body in the same way, as if somehow they would be competing for space. This is not true. The Holy Spirit and evil spirits are two completely different kinds of spirits, existing on two vastly different metaphysical levels. The Holy Spirit is divine, infinite, uncreated Spirit; demons are finite, created spirits. They may both indwell the same body because they do not do so in the same sense. Those involved in deliverance ministries are practically unanimous in affirming that Christians may be demonized.[8]

Nonmiraculous deliverance from evil spirits ("casting out demons") is sometimes necessary and always possible today for oppressed persons who are nonetheless surrendered to the Lordship of Christ. "Release to the captives" is part of the gospel (Luke 4:18). In general the works of Neil Anderson may be used for this purpose, especially the steps he outlines in *The Bondage Breaker*. See also the works by Ed Murphy and by Ensign and Howe (footnote 8).

In short, Satan and his demons are real, active, powerful, and dangerous; but they are no match for our divine and almighty Redeemer, Jesus Christ. Jesus has already crushed the serpent's head (Gen 3:15) in his victorious death and resurrection, and he will soon crush Satan under our feet (Rom 16:20).

NOTES ON CHAPTER EIGHT

[1]"There is no difference in the meaning between *diabolos* and *satanas*," says Böcher, I:297).

[2]See John 8:44, "He was a murderer from the beginning."

[3]A similar word, *daimon*, is used only once, in Matt 8:31, except for the Textus Receptus, which has it also in Matt 5:12; Luke 8:29; Rev 16:14; 18:2. The KJV regularly translates these words as "devils," but this is misleading. The word for "devil" (*diabolos*) is used only for Satan.

[4]That demons and evil spirits are the same is seen by comparing Matt 8:16; Mark 7:25-26; Luke 8:27-38; 10:17-20.

[5]Rom 8:38; 1 Cor 2:6,8; 15:24; Eph 1:21; 3:10; 6:12; Col 1:16; 2:10,15.

[6]E.g., Knowles, 201-209; Beam, 86.

[7]See especially Van Rheenen, *Christ*; and Peterson, *Roaring Lion* [previously *Are Demons for Real?*].

[8]See Ensign and Howe, *Counseling*; Dickason, *Possession*; Murphy, *Handbook*, 429-430; Arnold, *Questions*, 88; Anderson, *Bondage Breaker*. Anderson says, "Nothing has done greater damage to diagnosing spiritual problems than this untruth," i.e., "that Christians cannot be severely oppressed by demons" (21; see 99, 107). See also Unger, *Saints*, 55, 60, 69-70.

CHAPTER NINE

ORIGINAL SIN—
OR ORIGINAL GRACE?

The term *original sin* refers not to the first or original sinful act, but to the state of being or the condition in which every natural descendant of Adam is born. The corresponding concept is *personal sin*, or the sins actually committed by an individual, as distinct from the sinful state in which he was born.

The basic question is this: what is the relation between the first sin of Adam and the condition in which all his offspring are born? What are its consequences, both physical and spiritual, for the human race as a whole? Most Bible-believers agree that Adam's sin had physical effects on all his progeny, i.e., laborious toil, pain in childbirth, physical death (Gen 3:16-19), though a few have denied that physical death is an Adamic legacy. The big question, though, is whether Adam's sin has affected mankind *spiritually*. Is a child born guilty as a result of Adam's sin? Is he born depraved or sinful in any sense, because of what Adam did?

The earliest reflections on such questions began in the late second century with Irenaeus, who concluded that infants do indeed inherit from Adam a sinful state or spiritual sickness, but not a state of guilt and not total depravity. Irenaeus declared that all are "born in sinfulness" (103). Tertullian (early third century) declared that "every soul . . . by reason of its birth, has its nature in Adam" and is therefore unclean and actually evil "until it is born again in Christ." Nevertheless, he says, infancy is "the innocent period of life."[1] "No one is free from defilement, not even the day-old child," said Origen in the early third century (cited in Rondet, 82).

This view of partial depravity prevailed until the late fourth and early fifth centuries, when the controversy between Pelagius and Augustine polarized Christendom. Pelagius declared that Adam's sin had no hereditary consequences for his offspring, not even partial depravity. On the other hand, Augustine went in the other direction and constructed the first full-fledged doctrine of original sin, including inherited guilt and total (not partial) depravity. At the time of the Reformation both Martin Luther and John Calvin adopted Augustine's view.

I. COMPARISON OF VIEWS

In answering the question of original sin one must consider two variables: guilt and depravity. Disagreement over these points has led to a spectrum of differing views within Christendom. Four of the major ones will be explained here, moving from the least to the most severe.

The mildest approach is the *Pelagian* view, obviously named for Pelagius and agreeing with him that Adam's sin had no hereditary spiritual effects upon the human race. Every baby is born in a state of spiritual purity, without any depravity or corruption and with free will intact. Also, every infant comes into the world in a state of natural innocence, without bearing any guilt from the sin of Adam. Adam's sin affects us only indirectly, in that our sin-filled environment influences us to imitate his sin. Thus there really is no such thing as "original sin."

An example of the Pelagian view is the Restoration writer Moses Lard. He says there is no proof "that Adam's sin ever touched or in any way affected the spirit of one of his posterity." In fact, "the spirit is as free from its influence as though the sin had never been committed" (177-178).

The next approach in the spectrum is *semi-Pelagianism*, which is still too mild to be called "original sin" in any complete sense. This view says that the only hereditary spiritual effect of Adam's sin is a state of partial depravity. Every baby is born partially depraved, having a soul that is corrupted with spiritual sickness or weakness, i.e., with a "bent" or inclination toward sinning. Still, it is not a *total* depravity; free will is not lost. Also, as in the previous view, a child is born innocent, and thus free from guilt and condemnation.

This is the view that prevailed in the early church from Irenaeus to Augustine, though of course it was not then called semi-Pelagianism. This name arose only in the aftermath of the Pelagius-Augustine conflict, and was applied to those who continued on this middle road between these two antagonists. In the Reformation era the Anabaptists held to a version of this view, and later so did John Wesley and most of his followers. Also, this view was espoused by Alexander Campbell, who declared that "our nature was corrupted by the fall of Adam before it was transmitted to us; and hence that hereditary imbecility to do good, and that proneness to do evil, so universally apparent in all human beings." We are all "greatly fallen and depraved in our whole moral constitution . . . in consequence of the sin of Adam." This does not involve, however, "an invincible necessity to sin"; thus there is still freedom of the will. Nor does anyone suffer guilt and everlasting punishment as the result of Adam's sin (*System*, 15-16).

The third approach is that officially adopted by the Roman Catholic Church in the wake of the Reformation. This view agrees with semi-Pelagianism in that it accepts only a partial depravity and thus freedom of the will. It differs from the previous views, however, in that it says all inherit a state of guilt and condemnation from Adam. An infant dying in this condemned state is excluded from heaven, but he is not consigned to hell either. His fate is to be eternally in limbo, conscious of neither pain nor bliss.

The last approach is the classical doctrine of original sin, the view proposed by Augustine and carried over into Protestantism by Luther and Calvin. This view says that Adam's sin had two devastating spiritual consequences for the entire human race. First, every baby is born in a state of total depravity or bondage of the will. In other words, his spiritual nature is so corrupted that his free will is gone, and he grows up with a total inability to come to faith and repentance in response to the gospel call. Second, every child is born guilty and condemned to hell, to which he will go unless the grace of God sovereignly intervenes.

This last view is held today principally by Bible-believing Lutherans, Presbyterians, Reformed church groups, and some Baptists. It is part of the essence of what is called Calvinism. As J.O. Buswell Jr. (a Calvinist) says, "All men naturally descending from Adam, without exception, are guilty sinners, lost, judicially under the wrath and curse of God." He declares, "I became a wicked guilty sinner in the Garden of Eden" (I:294-295).

II. ALLEGED BIBLICAL BASIS FOR ORIGINAL SIN

Some feel justified in holding to some version of original sin based on human experience alone. How else, they ask, can we account for the universality and intensity of sinfulness in the world? But we must be careful here not to substitute experience for the inspired Word of God as the norm for our theology. The key question is, what does the Bible say?

Proponents of original sin usually cite several key biblical texts as the alleged foundation for this doctrine. One is Ps 51:5, "Behold, I was brought forth in iniquity, and in sin my mother conceived me." Is David here affirming that he was sinful as soon as he was conceived and born?

Several comments are in order. First, there are other ways to understand the grammar of this verse. Strictly speaking, David does not apply the sin and iniquity to himself, contrary to the NIV, which says, "Surely I was sinful at birth, sinful from the time my mother conceived me." But he does not actually say, "I was sinful." The prepositional phrases "in iniquity" and "in sin" are used to modify the *act* of being conceived and the *act* of being born. It is possible that the sin belongs to the mother. It has been pointed out that "in sin my mother conceived me" is grammatically parallel to "in drunkenness my husband beat me." Another possibility is that the phrases "in iniquity" and "in sin" are meant to describe the pervasiveness of sin in the world into which David was born.

It must be granted, though, that the major theme of the Psalm is David's repentance for his own sins, specifically the sins connected with his lust for Bathsheba. But if the focus is on David's *personal* sins (vv. 1-4) and not on some kind of inherited sin, why does he refer to iniquity connected with his birth (v. 5)? Basically he does so in order to express and confess his awareness of the depth of sin in his heart and the seriousness of his sin with Bathsheba. He is humbling himself before God in figurative language, in the same way that biblical writers sometimes refer to man as a worm (Ps 22:6; Job 17:14; 25:6; Isa 41:14). This is hyperbole, or exaggeration for emphasis. The same device is used in Ps 58:3, "The wicked are estranged from the womb; these who speak lies go astray from birth." This is not an affirmation of original sin since it is not applied to all human beings; it is an exaggeration intended to insult the wicked and emphasize the depth of their perversity. So with Ps 51:5, which is meant to apply to the repentant David alone.

Even if we should grant that Ps 51:5 is meant to teach some form of universal original sin, it could not be used to support the Augustinian and Catholic versions of this doctrine. The most that could be drawn from it is partial depravity, as in semi-Pelagianism; it neither affirms nor implies total depravity and inherited guilt.

A second passage used to teach the doctrine of original sin is Eph 2:3, where Paul says that "we too . . . were by nature children of wrath, even as the rest." This is used especially to infer inborn ("by nature") guilt and condemnation ("wrath"). How may we evaluate this claim?

First we must clarify what is meant by "children of wrath." The word for "children" is *teknon*, which refers to someone's offspring in either a literal or figurative sense. Literally it refers to someone's child, whether young or adult in age (for the latter see Matt 21:28; Luke 15:31). When used figuratively it often denotes membership in a family group having a certain spiritual parentage. (As such it implies nothing about the age of infancy or childhood.) The word is used, e.g., to refer to children of God (John 1:12; Rom 8:16,21; 1 John 3:1,10), children of the devil (1 John 3:10), children of Sarah (1 Pet 3:6), and children of light (Eph 5:8). In Eph 2:3 *teknon* is used in this latter sense, for those who belong to a figurative family group who share the characteristic of being under the wrath and condemnation of God.

Paul is referring, of course, to the pre-Christian state. In Eph 2:1-2 he has addressed the Gentile Christians ("you") and described their pre-Christian life in very harsh terms. But in verse 3 he admits that the Jews themselves ("we"), before they came to faith in Christ, were also slaves of sin and "were by nature children of wrath" (i.e., lost and on their way to hell), "even as the rest" (i.e., the Gentiles). His main point is that unbelieving Gentiles and unbelieving Jews are thus part of the same spiritual family, the family of the damned.

Our question, though, is this: how did they get that way? How did they become members of that family? By birth, or by choice? As implied above, the term *teknon* (as in "children of wrath") has no connotation here of infancy and therefore birth. But what about the expression "by nature"? Does this imply that every person is born into the family of wrath, i.e., in the lost state of original sin?

The key word here is the Greek *physis*, used in the dative form and translated "by nature." It refers to the nature or essence of something, or that which belongs to the very nature or identity of something, e.g., God (2 Pet 1:4) or idols (Gal 4:8). When used of man it refers to the natural order of things as created by God in the beginning, e.g., sexuality (Rom 1:26), gender differences (1 Cor 11:14), and moral intuition (Rom 2:14). It is also used of the fact that some are Jews and some are Gentiles "by nature" or by physical birth (Rom 2:27; 11:21,24; Gal 2:15).

After the pattern of such passages, many have concluded that Paul is saying in Eph 2:3 that everyone is actually born under the wrath of God in the Augustinian sense. I would suggest, however, that in its most general sense *physis* refers to the actual identity or to an inward characteristic of something, however that identity or characteristic was acquired. The *physis* of God (2 Pet 1:4) is his own eternal essence; it is who he is by nature. Sexual and gender characteristics (Rom 1:26; 1 Cor 11:14) are ours "by nature" in the sense that they are a part of the divinely intended creation order. They are built into the universe as part of the proper nature of things. Jewishness is a characteristic that belongs to some people and Gentileness to others by physical birth; but these respective identities are not the result of creation per se but of divine appointment related to the history of redemption.

When Paul says in Eph 2:3 that we were "by nature children of wrath," he is simply saying that in our pre-Christian state the characteristic of lostness—membership in the family of the damned—was *who we were*. Sinfulness was our nature, our identity. Our main point here, though, is that this language implies nothing about *how we got that way*. None of the other New Testament uses of *physis*, summed up in the previous paragraph, can appropriately lend its meaning to Eph 2:3. It is not our *eternal* nature to be children of wrath; it is not our *created* nature to be children of wrath; nor are we children of wrath by *divine appointment*.

How then did we become children of wrath? This very text shows that we entered this state not via original sin but as the result of our own personal sins. Ephesians 2:1 refers to this spiritual state as being "dead in your trespasses and sins." It is significant that Paul makes no reference to the one sin of Adam as the cause of this spiritual state of death, but instead relates it to "your [not Adam's] trespasses and sins [plural]." Verse 5 likewise attributes the death to multiple "transgressions."[2] In other words, by abandoning yourselves to sin you made sin to be your very nature; you joined the family of the lost. Thus the state of lostness is acquired by our own choice, not born in us as a result of Adam's sin.

It is interesting and supportive that Ignatius of Antioch, one of the first post-New Testament writers, uses the word *physis* when speaking of the true inward nature of Christians. In "To the Trallians" (I:1) he says, "I know that you have a disposition that is blameless and unwavering in patient endurance, not from habit but by nature."[3] It is obvious that for Ignatius what the Christian is "by nature" is an identity that is acquired. We conclude that there is nothing in Eph 2:3 that requires us to think of our pre-Christian identity as "children of wrath" in any other way.

The third and most significant biblical text that is used to support the doctrine of original sin is Rom 5:12-19. In this passage Paul is contrasting the consequences of Adam's sin with the consequences of Christ's atoning death. Focusing on the former, those who teach original sin stress Adam's role as a representative for the entire human race. When Adam the representative sinned, all men sinned in him at the same time ("because all sinned," v. 12b). As a result God counted all human beings guilty and condemned them all to death (vv. 12-15,17). This death is not limited to physical death, but also includes spiritual death (total depravity) and eternal death (condemnation to hell). This conclusion is based on Paul's further characterizations of these consequences as "condemnation" (vv. 16,18) and "made sinners" (v. 19). It is based also on the gravity and scope of the saving remedies which Paul says offset the Adamic legacy: "grace" (vv. 15,17), "justification" (vv. 16,18), and "made righteous" (v. 19).

III. THE MEANING OF ROMANS 5:12-19

Romans 5:12-19 is of critical importance in reference to the doctrine of original sin for two reasons. First, at least since the time of Augustine it has served as the fundamental proof text for original sin. Second, this text is in fact the clearest and best *refutation* of this doctrine, actually teaching its opposite: all human beings are born not in original sin but in *original grace*. Thus it is imperative that we here explain the teaching of this passage in detail. We will do this by answering four questions (from Cottrell, *Romans*, I:330-339).

The first question is this: *What is the purpose of this passage in relation to the epistle as a whole?* It is best understood as continuing the theme of assurance that began with 5:1. In 5:1-11 Paul assures us that we can put all our hope and confidence in *one saving act* (the cross) of *one man* (Jesus Christ). In those eleven verses the apostle makes ten references to the saving efficacy of Christ and his cross. In light of this someone might begin to wonder, "Isn't this expecting an awful lot from just one man?" This is indeed what the gospel asks us to believe—that essentially one act of just one man has the power to save the whole world from all its sins. It calls upon us to "put all our eggs in one basket," so to speak. But how can this be possible?

In order to show that this is not as far-fetched as we might at first think, Paul calls attention to another man whose one act has already been demonstrated to have a universal effect upon the human race, namely, Adam. Then he uses this by way of comparison and contrast to show that the "one righteous act" of the one man, Jesus, will surely be just as efficacious and universal as the "one sinful act" of the one man, Adam—and even "much more" (5:15,17). His argument moves from the lesser to the greater. If we can accept the fact that the one sin of a mere man has brought sin and death upon the whole world, then we can surely believe that the atoning death of the Son of God has brought salvation upon the whole world. The purpose of the passage, then, is to increase our confidence in the all-sufficiency of the death of Christ.

The second question is this: *Does this paragraph teach the doctrine of original sin?* Do Paul's references to the consequences of Adam's sin mean that every child is conceived and born sinful, and born condemned to death and eternal punishment? Is this the main doctrine Paul wants to establish in this passage? Without doubt Paul is here affirming that Adam's sin did bring serious consequences upon all his offspring. Our understanding of the exact nature of these consequences depends upon how we interpret the terms "death," "judgment," "condemnation," and "made sinners" as used in the text. Many have tried to limit them all to physical death only, thus denying that 5:12-19 teaches any sort of original sin. Others believe that these terms, both in themselves and as compared with the blessings received from Christ, must refer to something much more serious than physical death by itself. Thus they conclude that this text does indeed teach original sin.

The biggest problem with this whole approach is that it implicitly assumes that Paul's main subject here is Adam's sin and its consequences, which is not the case. Paul did not write this passage just to teach a doctrine of original sin. Yes, he does declare that Adam's sin brought all these terrible things upon the human race, but that is not his main point. His main subject is *Jesus and his cross*, and the universal, all-sufficient consequences of that saving event. His purpose is not to emphasize what happened to the race as the result of Adam's sin, but to emphasize what has happened to it as the result of Christ's saving work.

The fact is that it really does not matter which view of "original sin" one holds. Did Adam's sin bring only physical death upon us? Or did it also bring spiritual depravity—partial or total? Did it also make us guilty sinners, condemned to eternal punishment in hell? In the final analysis it does not matter what content anyone feels compelled to pour into the concept of "original sin," because Paul's main point is this: *whatever the whole human race got (or would have gotten) from Adam has been completely canceled out for the whole human race by the gracious atoning work of Jesus Christ*. Make the Adamic legacy as dire as you want: physical death, total depravity, genuine guilt, and condemnation to hell. The whole point of the passage is that Christ's "one act of righteousness" (5:18) has completely intercepted, nullified, negated, canceled, and counteracted *whatever* was destined to be ours because of Adam. All the potential spiritual consequences of Adam's sin are intercepted even before they can be applied. The only consequence that actually takes effect is physical death, and it is countered with the promise of resurrection to eternal life.

This understanding of 5:12-19 has been clearly understood at least since the Reformation, when it was taught by Anabaptist writers. Those within the Wesleyan tradition also generally hold this understanding.[4] This principle has been most clearly stated in earlier Restoration Movement writings. As A.I. Hobbs (269) succinctly puts it,

> It should be emphasized that, under the reign of grace, whatever death was brought upon our race through Adamic sin by reason of his federal headship was annulled by reason of the federal headship of the second Adam. . . . What, without our will or consent, we lost in the first Adam, we have regained or shall regain in the second Adam, without our will or consent.

Moses Lard (174) agrees: "Whatever evils Adam's sin brought upon the world, without our agency, are all countervailed and remedied by the single act of Christ without our agency." Commenting on Romans 5:15 J.W. McGarvey says, "We are here informed that the result of the sacrificial act of Christ fully reversed and nullified the effects of the act of Adam, and that it did even much more. . . . Christ's act equaled and nullified Adam's act"; it "completely counteracted Adam's act" (*Romans*, 336-337). Robert Milligan (60) repeats this principle and concludes that "no man need, therefore, feel any concern or anxiety about the sin of Adam and its effects on his posterity."

What does this mean? It means that there is no doctrine of original sin taught in 5:12-19. No child is actually conceived and born under the curse of Adam's sin. If anything, this passage teaches a doctrine of *original grace*: every child is born under the grace of God, born saved, "born free" from all spiritual effects of Adam's sin, and born with the guarantee of ultimate freedom from all physical effects of that sin by means of the resurrection unto glory. God began to apply this "original grace" (sometimes called "prevenient grace") to the first generation of Adam's own children, in the same way that the results of the cross were applied retrospectively to believing adults in the pre-Christian era (3:25).

We are now ready for the third question: *What is the scope of the words* many *and* all *as they are used in 5:12-19?* These terms appear at crucial points in the text. "Death came to all men" (5:12). By Adam's trespass "many died," but Christ's grace overflowed "to the many" (5:15). Through Adam came "condemnation for all men," but through Christ came justification of life "for all men" (5:18). In Adam "the many were made sinners," but in Christ "the many will be made righteous" (5:19). Exactly who are meant to be included in these terms?

What is at stake here is this: if the answer given to the second question above is correct, as it so obviously seems to be, why do so many still believe and teach a doctrine of original sin? The answer lies in how they interpret "many" and "all" in the verses just cited.

Most interpreters, even those who hold to original sin, generally agree that there is no difference in scope between the two terms themselves. That is, "many" and "all" refer to the same group of people. The term "many" is not intended to be set in contrast with "all," but rather in contrast with "one." Even though Adam is just one man, his one sin had consequences that extend to *the many* (i.e., more than one). Even though Christ is just one man, his one act likewise applies to *the many*. The term "all" is then used to convey the connotation of totality, but is not meant to be broader in scope than "the many." I am in total agreement with this.

Wherein lies the problem, then? It lies in the way the advocates of original sin apply these two terms to Adam on the one hand and to Christ on the other hand. The common approach is that, when these terms are used in relation to Adam's sin, they are completely universal in scope; but when they are used in relation to the work of Christ, they are more limited and restricted in scope and do not really mean "all." In John Stott's words, "The 'all men' who are affected by the work of Christ cannot refer to absolutely everybody," as it does for Adam (159). Adam did indeed inflict the entire race with the consequences of his sin, but the atoning work of Christ canceled out these consequences only for the smaller group of those who are actually saved. "Original sin," however understood, thus remains intact for the rest of mankind.

One way of saying this is that Christ's one righteous act is *able* to cancel original sin for everyone, that it has the power or potential to do so; but in fact it does so only for those who consciously receive the gift of grace through faith (5:17). For example, John MacArthur says the passage teaches that "all *can* be made righteous in Christ," that "Christ's one sacrifice made salvation *available* to all mankind" (297, 302; italics added).

More often, however, especially for those who hold to the classical Augustinian doctrine of original sin, the distinction between Adam's "all" and Christ's "all" is stated thus: the consequences of Adam's act extended to all who were in him or belonged to him when he sinned—which includes the whole race; but the consequences of Christ's act extended only to "all" who were in him or belonged to him when he died—which includes only the elect. "Both Adam and Christ would then be viewed as 'inclusive' representatives whose actions can be considered as the actions also of *those who belong to them*" (Moo, 328, fn. 61; italics added). In verse 18, says Mounce, the contrast is between "all who are *in Adam*" and "all who are *in Christ*" (145; italics added).

It must be emphasized, though, that all such approaches to 5:12-19 are false; all attempts to reduce the "many" and "all" when used of Christ to anything less than their scope when used of Adam must be rejected. The reason should be obvious: such a discrepancy in the numbers would negate the whole purpose of the Adam-Christ comparison! The question of assurance is this: Can I have confidence that Christ's work is sufficient for taking away all my sins—and those of the whole world as well? Paul's answer is "Yes! You *can* have such assurance! Look at what has already been done as the result of his work: his one righteous act has *already* counteracted *everything* brought upon *everyone* by Adam. This is the stepping-stone for our confidence that his work is capable of 'much more' (5:15,17), i.e., it is capable of taking away all the consequences of our personal sins as well."

Thus to maintain the basic theme of assurance, we must insist that the terms "many" and "all" when used of Christ are at least as broad in scope as when used of Adam. Adam's sin brought sin, death, judgment, and condemnation upon *every* member of the human race; likewise Christ's atoning act brought righteousness, justification, and life upon *every* member of the human race. The failure to acknowledge this is the greatest hindrance to a proper understanding of this passage; it is also the single most influential reason why many still believe this passage teaches a doctrine of original sin.

This leads to the fourth question: *Does this passage teach universal salvation, then?* Some believe that Paul's use of "all" and the inclusive "many" do indeed suggest universalism. Reflecting on 5:18 James Dunn opines that we should not "exclude the possibility that Paul . . . cherished the hope of such a universal salvation. . . . How, after all, can grace be 'so much more' in its effect if it is less universal than the effect of death?" (I:297). Many of those who limit the "all" to whom Christ's work applies in 5:12-19 do so because they think that to do otherwise would require such universalism. For example, Stott (159) very clearly implies that taking "all" to mean "everybody without exception" is "to believe in universal salvation." Many have uncritically assumed this to be so.

The answer to the question, however, is *no*! Romans 5:12-19 does not teach universal salvation, and taking the "all" and "many" who receive Christ's grace to refer to the whole human race does *not* entail such universalism. Why not? Because the primary focus of the passage as a whole and of these words specifically is how the work of Christ counteracts and cancels in their entirety the consequences of *the one sin of Adam* for every single individual. This is not a matter of possibility or potentiality; it is not just something Christ is able to do, or something that is offered to all and accepted by some. No, this is a reality; it is an accomplished fact; it has been done and will be done for the entire race; it is a sure thing.

However, Paul here absolutely does *not* say the same thing about the consequences for all *our own personal sins.* This is another matter altogether. As Scripture makes perfectly clear, the guilt and penalty for our personal sins are removed only through personal faith. The language of possibility and potentiality applies to our personal sins, and 5:12-19 certainly implies that Christ's sacrifice is sufficient to take care of these also; indeed, this is the ultimate conclusion to which Paul's argument leads. But the universal language in the text applies only to what we have all received from *Adam's* sin.

In other words, from a practical point of view, this passage addresses the question of the spiritual state of infants when they are conceived and born. Do infants "inherit" anything from Adam, or is anything imposed upon them as the result of Adam's sin alone? Quite obviously so, particularly physical death. Paul affirms in 5:12 that death comes to all men as the result of sin, but this cannot mean personal sins since even infants sometimes die. Therefore death must come upon all because of Adam's sin. This is Paul's point in 5:13-14, where "those who did not sin by breaking a commandment" must refer to infants. (This is the force of the word *kai*, "even," in v. 14.) It is likely that the language used in other verses (judgment, condemnation, made sinners) means that Adam's sin brought serious spiritual consequences upon infants as well.

The point of the passage, though, is that Christ's one atoning act cancels out *all* of these consequences for *all* infants. Because of Jesus Christ no infant is born sinful, depraved, or condemned. All do face the inevitability of physical death, but insofar as such death derives from Adam's sin, it too will one day be canceled out in the final resurrection from the dead. Every baby is thus conceived and born in a redeemed or saved state: original grace! The gifts of righteousness and justification and life are received universally and automatically by every infant as the means of salvation from Adam's sin. This is the only "universalism" in 5:12-19.

At the same time in this passage Paul alludes to the fact that babies grow up and reach the age of accountability and commit personal sins ("many trespasses," v. 17). Commenting on the "much more" in 5:15 McGarvey (*Romans*, 336-337) says,

> If we had only Adam's sin to answer for, then the teaching of this passage would establish the doctrine of universal salvation, for Christ's act completely counteracted Adam's act. But there are other sins beside that first one committed by Adam, and other punishments beside natural death. It is in its dealings with those that the range of Christ's act exceeds that of Adam, and it is here also that salvation becomes limited.

When a child reaches the age of accountability and begins to become responsible for his personal sins, he forfeits the original grace under which he has been living since conception. He comes under the wrath of God and bears the full consequences of the sins that he is now committing by his own choice. He has even forfeited the redemptive resurrection gained through the cancellation of the death derived from Adam. If he dies in his own sins, he will be raised from the dead, but not redemptively in a glorified body like that of Christ.

The only way to escape the consequences of one's personal sins is by conscious choice and personal faith. Since everyone does not so choose and believe, there is no universal salvation.

Thus the spiritual odyssey of the individual has four possible stages: (1) *Original sin*, even if this is understood to involve only the penalty of physical death as the result of Adam's sin. Many understand it to include much more, of course. The main point about this stage is that (except for physical death) it is theoretical or potential only; it is never actually experienced because it is intercepted and canceled for everyone by the all-sufficient work of Christ. Thus no one ever actually passes through this stage, and children are certainly not born in it.

(2) *Original grace*, which is the stage we enter when we first come into existence and under which we stay until we reach the age of accountability, thanks to the work of the Second Adam. All infants and young children are here, as are those whose mental abilities never develop beyond those of young children. This is a state of salvation and it is universal; thus the concept of "universal salvation" applies here.

(3) *Personal sin*, the stage all enter when they reach the age of accountability and lose the original grace under which they were born. Those in this stage are the lost, the unsaved. If they die here they will be condemned forever to hell.

(4) *Personal grace*, a term we might use for the position occupied by all believers, or those who have personally repented and believed God's gracious

promises. This is a state of salvation, but it is not universal. It is available to all, but is entered only through personal choice.

Our conclusion is that the doctrine of original sin as usually understood is based on false exegesis of crucial biblical texts and thus must be rejected. All children are born in a state of original grace, not original sin.

NOTES ON CHAPTER NINE

[1]"Treatise," 40, *ANF* 3:220; and "Baptism," 18, *ANF* 3:678.

[2]There is no Greek word for "our" in v. 5.

[3]In *Apostolic Fathers*, 97. See also Ignatius, "To the Ephesians" (I:1), ibid., 86.

[4]Within these traditions it is generally held that babies still are born with partial depravity (i.e., semi-Pelagianism), which in my opinion makes the application of Christ's work to Adam's sin incomplete.

CHAPTER TEN
PERSONAL SIN

In Christian theology a distinction is usually made between original sin and personal sin. This distinction can be seen in Rom 5:14, which says that "death reigned from Adam until Moses, even over those who had not sinned in the likeness of the offense of Adam." The sin committed by Adam is here called a *parabasis*, which means "stepping over a boundary, a deviation from the prescribed path or norm, a trespass, a transgression." What Adam transgressed was the law of God (Gen 2:17; 1 John 3:4). His transgression was a voluntary, conscious, deliberate decision to disobey a divine command. This is the essence of *personal* sin.

But, says Paul, there is another way of sinning that is not like the transgression of Adam, i.e., not a voluntary, deliberate, personal sin. This is the sin that everyone committed representatively in Adam in the Garden of Eden ("because all sinned," Rom 5:12), which along with its consequences is called *original* sin. In the previous chapter we discussed the effects (potential and actual) of Adam's representative sin upon the entire human race. We saw that these effects, though devastating, are nullified and canceled by the atonement of Jesus Christ. Indeed, if we apply Paul's teaching in Rom 5:12-19 consistently, we must conclude that *whatever* would have come upon us as a result of that sin is automatically removed in advance by the work of Christ. Thus the Pelagians are right in teaching that a child is born into this world with a spiritual nature that is pure, free, and innocent.

Our main focus now, though, is personal sins, and especially the effects they bring upon the one who commits them. Even though no one is born condemned and depraved by original sin, in fact everyone who reaches the age of accountability commits personal sins; and these sins in themselves bring condemnation and depravity upon the sinning individual. The nature of these effects will be explained here.

I. THE AGE OF ACCOUNTABILITY

A definite implication of Rom 5:14 is that there is a period of life during which one has not yet committed personal sins, or at least during which one is not held *accountable* for them. This is the age of infancy and young childhood. The point is not that young children never do anything wrong as measured by God's law, but simply that they are not accountable to God for such wrongdoing. Thus we do not say a child reaches "the age of sin," but rather "the age of *accountability*" for sin.

What is the age of accountability? How can we tell when a child has reached that stage in his life? It is not determined by calendar years (e.g., his tenth or twelfth birthday), but by spiritual development. In an earlier chapter we noted four presuppositions of sin: the existence of law, the existence of a Creator-God as the source of law, a knowledge of that law, and free will (pp. 166-169). Crucial for discerning the age of accountability is the third one, knowledge of the law. We must remember that law includes two elements: commands to be obeyed and a prescribed penalty for disobedience. Until a child understands that certain things he is doing are a violation of commands of God and will ultimately be punished by God, he is not accountable to God for these things. Once he does reach this understanding, he is then accountable to God in the sense that he is liable for the eternal penalty deserved by his sins.

The basis for this understanding of the age of accountability is Paul's teaching in Rom 4:15 and 7:9. The former text says that "where there is no law, there also is no violation." Some law actually exists everywhere, even in each individual's heart (Rom 1:18-32; 2:15). Thus Paul must mean "where there is no consciousness of law," in the sense of unavoidable ignorance. This refers to children (and the mentally handicapped) who do not yet perceive moral rules as coming from God (rather than from parents and teachers), and are not conscious of the eternal penalty attached to them. See Rom 7:8b, "Apart from the Law sin is dead."

Romans 7:9 says, "I was once alive apart from the Law; but when the commandment came, sin became alive and I died." Paul here seems to be referring to his own "coming of age," or the time when he reached the age of accountability. Thus he gives us insight as to when this occurs for everyone. "I was once alive apart from the Law" refers to the age of childhood innocence when one is living under original grace (Rom 5:12-19), before he comes to understand the significance of living in a world subject to the laws of the Creator. "Apart from the Law" does not mean that a child has no knowledge of the laws as such, since children can learn the ten commandments at a very young age and can know it is wrong to break them. It refers rather to that age before a child connects the law to God and connects disobedience with eternal penalty. Before that time the child is "alive" in that his soul is not yet dead in his trespasses and sins (Eph 2:1) and he is not yet under the penalty of the second death (Rev 21:8).

But, says Paul, "when the commandment came," i.e., when it came into his consciousness as a command of God having eternal condemnation for disobedience, "sin became alive" in his heart and life as a full-blown reality. At this point, he says, "I died." Thus the beginning of the age of accountability is the death of innocence, the time when a child becomes dead in his sins and subject to the penalty attached thereto.

Discerning when a child reaches this point requires a careful and prayerful monitoring of his spiritual development.

II. THE SINNER IS GUILTY

We now turn to the question that lies at the heart of this chapter, namely, what effects do personal sins have on the sinner? What happens to the person who sins against God? What problems does the sinner face as the result of his own sins?

As a seminary student in the early 1960s I was one day preparing a particular homiletics assignment and suddenly became aware of the implications of the words at the end of the first verse of the old hymn "Rock of Ages." This hymn calls upon the blood of Christ to "be of sin the *double cure*; save me from its guilt and power" (or "save from wrath and make me pure"). I saw for the first time the twofold nature of salvation, which makes it a "double cure." It was also obvious, though the song does not use these words, that God saves us from a "double trouble." Since that time I have been using this terminology to explain sin and salvation.

In the hymn the "double trouble" is called the *guilt* and *power* of sin, or in its other version *wrath* and *impurity*. In other words, our sins make us guilty; they put us in a wrong relationship with God and his law, and bring us under his wrath. This is a *legal* problem. At the same time our sins corrupt our natures and make us spiritually sick and depraved. This is a problem with our spiritual *health*. The former is being discussed in this section; the latter will be addressed in the next section.

The reality of personal guilt is one of the most difficult things for sinful man to admit. The unredeemed sinner has the constant tendency to deny his guilt and his personal responsibility for his sins. The ancient excuse "the devil made me do it," whether invoked seriously (Gen 3:13) or flippantly, is an example of the continuing desire to blame someone else for our evil deeds (Gen 3:12). Another common excuse is "I'm only human," as if finitude and/or free will makes sin inevitable rather than simply possible.

Why is the denial of personal guilt such a widespread phenomenon today? As we have noted, the very idea of sin presupposes the existence of law, which presupposes the existence of a transcendent Creator-God; it also presupposes the reality of human free will. But these are among the very things that are most frequently attacked and denied in our modern world. The Creator-God is replaced by chance evolution, and various forms of secular determinism are constantly used to cancel man's responsibility for his antisocial behavior. For example, some say that such behavior is due to childhood trauma and other forms of negative environmental conditioning. People are not sinners; they are victims. Others attribute it all to quirks in one's genes or chromosomes or brain structure; thus we have "natural-born" killers, alcoholics, homosexuals, and adulterers.

If we accept the biblical worldview, however, we cannot avoid the concept and reality of personal guilt with respect to sin. The Bible clearly teaches the existence of a Creator-God who has given his human creatures laws to obey and the free will to do so or not. Given these truths, we must affirm that sin makes us *guilty*.

Guilt is a concept that has meaning only in the context of law. It is a state that is brought about by a conscious violation of the law and that results in liability to punishment. When one breaks a law of God (which is the essence of sin, 1 John 3:4), he becomes guilty in the sense that he now stands in a wrong relationship with that law and is liable to the penalty prescribed by it. Because such breaking of the law is a matter of the sinner's personal, free-will choice, he is fully responsible for his deeds and justly subject to the punishment they deserve. As Colin Brown says, "Guilt is a legal and judicial term which implies criminal responsibility in the eyes of a court of law, whether that court is human or divine" ("Guilt," 137).

As a wrong relationship to the law of God, guilt is not an inward, subjective condition. Rather, it is an external, objective state. In other words we must not confuse guilt with guilt feelings. A hardened sinner may have no guilt feelings whatsoever, and at the same time be burdened with intense guilt before the divine Lawgiver and Judge.

Scripture clearly teaches the concept of guilt. James 2:10 says, "For whoever keeps the whole law and yet stumbles in one point, he has become guilty of all." The word used here is *enochos*, which is a technical legal term meaning "guilty, subject to or liable to penalty." This term is used four times in Matt 5:21-22, e.g., "Everyone who is angry with his brother shall be guilty before the court."

Romans 3:19 declares that the whole sinful world is "guilty before God" (KJV). The Greek word is *hypodikos*, which means "liable to judgment or punishment, worthy of punishment, answerable, accountable." The NASB and NIV have "accountable to God" in this verse; but this translation is too weak to capture the full meaning of the term, since some connotations of "accountable" do not specify whether a person is guilty or not, but simply imply that he must give account for his actions, good or bad. But *hypodikos* refers to someone who *has* done something wrong and has been brought before the court to answer for it. The picture, says C.E.B. Cranfield (I:197), is "of men standing at God's bar, their guilt proven beyond all possibility of doubt, awaiting God's sentence of condemnation" (see also Maurer, 557-558).

Another term denoting the sinner's guilt is *opheilo*, meaning "to owe, to be in debt, to be under obligation." One noun form of this word, *opheilema*, is used in Matt 6:12 as a synonym for sin: "Forgive us our debts." Another noun form, *opheiletes* ("debtor") is used in Luke 13:4 to describe those who are guilty of sin and deserving of punishment (see v. 2); the NIV translates it as "guilty." These words are used throughout the parable of the unmerciful servant (Matt 18:23-35), which uses the image of a debtor's prison to convey the idea that sin puts us into debt to God. Specifically, we owe to God the debt of eternal punishment in hell.

Related biblical concepts are wrath, judgment, penalty, punishment, and condemnation. These are legal or judicial terms expressing that which the law requires of those who are guilty of breaking it.

Now that Christ's original grace has nullified for everyone any possible guilt deriving from Adam's sin, each person is counted guilty because of his own sin and no one else's. This idea of personal responsibility for personal sins is taught, e.g., in Jer 17:10; Ezek 18:4,20; Rom 14:12; 2 Cor 5:10; and Rev 2:23.

III. THE SINNER HAS A SINFUL NATURE

The second part of the "double trouble" caused by sin is that it gives the sinner a sinful nature. That is, sin affects not only our objective relationship with God and his law; it also affects us subjectively and personally, in our very being. It brings about a weakness of the soul, making it harder to resist temptation. The sinner's spirit is corrupted, diseased, and depraved. The sinner is spiritually sick and evil in his inner nature; he has a sinful heart.

Many have denied the reality of spiritual depravity for various reasons. Some simply declare that sinfulness applies only to actions and not to persons as such. This view is usually associated with Pelagius, though it is not necessarily connected with the Pelagian approach to the question of original sin. Such a view must be rejected because it is contrary to biblical testimony, as will be shown below. Buswell has rightly said, "One of the most difficult lessons for us to learn is that sin is not only what we do, but also what we are. Sin, in the form of corruption, is in our very nature" (I:286).

Others deny the reality of spiritual depravity because they think of it only as something that would be derived from Adam as part of an original-sin package (as in semi-Pelagianism or Augustinianism). It is not necessary, however, to think of the sinful nature as an inborn result of Adam's sin. I do not personally regard it as such, in view of the biblical teaching that original grace has negated all such potential consequences of Adam's sin (see the previous chapter). Since this is the case, and since the Bible affirms that sinners *are* evil and sinful, we must thus infer that this inward depravity is something we *acquire* as the result of our own sin. In this I agree with Lard (177-178), who declares, "I hence deny that Adam's sin ever touched or in any way affected the spirit of one of his posterity." Adam's sin causes our bodily death, but "our own sin corrupts our spirits." Concerning Adam's descendants, "spiritually they die for their own sins, and by these only are they spiritually depraved."

Still others deny the reality of spiritual depravity because they fail to understand the difference between partial depravity and total depravity (which will be discussed below). They assume that any view of spiritual corruption is equivalent to *total* corruption. This is not the case, however. I am here affirming that the sinner's spiritual nature is depraved as a result of his own sins, but that this depravity is only partial and not total.

A. The Biblical View of Depravity

The biblical teaching to this effect is abundant and clear. The sinner is pictured as not just guilty in relation to God's law, but as being sinful in his very nature or being. Sin is the soul's fatal disease. It does not alter our essence into something other than human, of course. Rather, it affects our spirits in a way analogous to the way physical disease affects our bodies.

Jesus makes this point when he compares people to trees, and their deeds to fruit produced by trees: "So every good tree bears good fruit, but the bad tree bears bad fruit" (Matt 7:17). Here he speaks not just of bad *fruit*, i.e., actions, but also of a bad *tree*, i.e., the person himself. He says the tree—the person—is bad or rotten, using the word *sapros*, which means "rotten, putrid, corrupted, worn out, bad, unfit for use."

Jesus says something similar in Matt 12:33, then adds in 12:34-35, "You brood of vipers, how can you, being evil, speak what is good? For the mouth speaks out of that which fills the heart. The good man brings out of his good treasure what is good; and the evil man brings out of his evil treasure what is evil" (see Luke 6:45). Here Jesus specifically speaks of persons who *are evil* and who have *evil hearts*, using the word *poneros* ("wicked, evil, bad, base, degenerate") four times.

Jesus uses the same word on other occasions to describe people (e.g., Matt 5:39,45; 7:11). Paul likewise uses it not just for evil deeds but also for the people who perform them. In 2 Thess 3:2 he asks for prayer, "that we will be rescued from perverse and evil men." In 2 Tim 3:13 he says that "evil men and impostors will proceed from bad to worse." See also Acts 17:5; 1 Cor 5:13. In numerous places this word is used to describe demons or evil spirits, and also the devil himself ("the evil one," e.g., Matt 5:37; 13:19,38; John 17:15; Eph 6:16).

We simply cannot deny that the Bible describes sinners as being evil in their very natures.

For further biblical evidence, some texts affirm the reality of spiritual depravity by using the analogy of physical sickness. In Isa 1:5-6 the prophet describes the collective body of Israel thus: "The whole head is sick and the whole heart is faint. From the sole of the foot even to the head there is nothing sound in it, only bruises, welts and raw wounds, not pressed out or bandaged, nor softened with oil." This represents the spiritual nature of the people of Israel. In other passages blindness is used to represent hearts that are closed to the truth of God (Matt 15:14; 23:16-26; 2 Cor 4:4; 2 Pet 1:19; Rev 3:17).

The Bible also describes sinners as being feebleminded in a spiritual sense: they are "darkened in their understanding" (Eph 4:18), "men of depraved mind" (2 Tim 3:8). The heart (equivalent in Scripture to the soul or spirit and including all parts of man's spiritual nature) is pictured as being in a state of corruption. "You are each one walking according to the stubbornness of his own evil heart" (Jer 16:12). "The heart is more deceitful than all else and is desperately sick" (Jer 17:9). Ezekiel 36:26 speaks of the sinner's "heart of stone," and Paul refers to "the hardness of their heart" (Eph 4:18; see Rom 1:21). Sinners are "uncircumcised in heart" (Acts 7:51). See Matt 12:34; 15:17-18; Luke 6:45.

Sinners are in a state of weakness or helplessness (Rom 5:6), a state of captivity to the devil (Col 1:13; 2 Tim 2:26), a state of slavery to sin (Rom 6:6,16-20).

Their condition is so bad that it is described as a kind of *death*: sinners are "dead in your trespasses and sins, . . . dead in our transgressions" (Eph 2:1,5; see Col 2:13). Paul says a woman "who gives herself to wanton pleasure is dead even while she lives" (1 Tim 5:6; see Luke 15:24,32). Jude 12 describes sinners as "doubly dead." Such spiritual death refers to the soul's separation from God and its loss of all sensitivity to godly things.

Thus far in examining what the Bible says about the sinner's sinful nature we have focused upon the depravity of the soul or spirit. But the Bible also pictures the *body* of the sinner as being spiritually corrupted. In addition to the Adamic curse of physical death, the body has become invaded by sin and has become the seat of sinful lusts and passions. This "law of sin and of death" (Rom 8:2) pervades the body and exerts a drawing power upon the soul, pulling it toward sin and bondage.

In my study of the book of Romans, especially chapters 6–8, I have concluded that the conventional understanding of Paul's use of the term "flesh" (*sarx*) is wrong. The usual view is that "flesh" means the whole man, body and spirit, as controlled by sin. The better view, however, is that the sinful "flesh" is just the physical body, not the whole person. This negative state is not inherent, however, but is acquired through personal sin and will be removed when (but not before) the body is redeemed through resurrection (Rom 8:23). (See Cottrell, *Romans*, I:372-377, 393-395, 401-402, 426-428, 445-454.)

Paul says that sin actually "dwells in" the flesh (Rom 7:17-20). It commandeers the body and uses it as a headquarters. As permeated by the power of sin, the body is called the "body of sin" (Rom 6:6). That is, as infected and controlled by sin it is a beachhead or staging point for temptations and lusts of all kinds. A sinner is "in the flesh" (Rom 7:5), i.e., governed by his bodily desires in such a way that they become the center of his life and are promiscuously indulged without regard for moral boundaries. Thus the physical body is "the body of death" (Rom 7:24, NIV) not just in a physical sense but in a spiritual sense also.

Is man basically good, then, or basically evil? The answer is that the human race was *created* good (Gen 1:31), and thanks to original grace every individual is *born* good. However, as a result of our yielding to temptation and committing sinful deeds, as individuals we *become* evil. This in turn creates a vicious cycle, since the sinful nature then gives rise to more and more sinful acts (Matt 7:17; 12:33-35; 15:18-19; Luke 6:45).

B. The Question of Total Depravity

We have just seen that the Bible teaches that sinners have a sinful, corrupted, depraved nature. This sinful nature is something we acquire through our personal participation in sin, since neither guilt nor depravity is derived from Adam, thanks to original grace (see the previous chapter).

One question must still be addressed, namely, is our acquired depravity partial or total? Many believe that it is total, though they usually see this total depravity as an aspect of the Augustinian version of original sin. Our view, though, is this: not only is sin's depravity always acquired; it is also always partial and never total. Our purpose in this section is to explain and refute the doctrine of *total depravity*.

According to Augustinians (including Calvinists), total depravity does not mean that a sinner is 100% corrupt, or as depraved as he can possibly be. Nor does it mean that every act of the sinner is both internally and externally evil. Even a totally depraved person can do things that are outwardly good.

What total depravity does mean is that the total person is corrupted by sin; every aspect of human nature is depraved, including the intellect and the will. Because the intellect has been corrupted, a sinner cannot truly understand the things of God, including the Bible. Because the will is sinful, a sinner cannot do anything that is inwardly good and acceptable to God. The latter is the key element of total depravity. It is called *the bondage of the will*.

The most significant implication of this bondage is that sinners are totally unable to respond to the gospel and turn to God in faith and repentance. As Berkhof says, the sinner "cannot change his fundamental preference for sin and self to love for God, nor even make an approach to such a change" (247). This *total inability* is thus the heart of total depravity. Because the sinner is unable to believe the gospel by his own choice, *regeneration must precede faith*, with both regeneration and faith being the unilateral and unconditional gifts of God, and with God himself unconditionally choosing those to whom he will give them.

In other words, the doctrine of total depravity is the foundation for the "five points" of Calvinism, designated as TULIP. The T in TULIP is total depravity, with the entire human race being totally depraved as a result of Adam's sin. This means that God must decide whom he will save, and he does this prior to the creation itself. This is the U in TULIP, unconditional election or unconditional predestination. Then, knowing the exact number of those who would be saved, God determined to limit the suffering of the Savior to the exact amount needed by the chosen ones. This is the L in TULIP, limited atonement. The I in TULIP is irresistible grace. It follows logically from the T and the U. If sinners are totally unable to believe on their own, then God must bestow the gift of faith upon those prechosen to receive it, in an act that cannot be resisted. The P in TULIP is perseverance (or preservation) of the saints, in which God guarantees that those who receive the gift of faith will never lose it. This "once saved, always saved" status is thus the final necessary result of total depravity.

It is obvious, then, that total depravity is a pivotal doctrine. If it is true, it necessitates the entire Calvinist system. If it is false, it negates the entire system. In my judgment it is false. The Bible does not teach that sinners are totally depraved, either at birth or by their own sin. In particular, it does not teach that a sinner is totally unable to believe the gospel and turn to God for salvation.

Those who accept total depravity point out that many biblical texts teach that man has a depraved heart and is spiritually dead (e.g., Jer 17:9; Eph 2:1,5). In the preceding section we have already examined such passages and have agreed that sinners are depraved, but we must remember that depravity as such is not the same as *total* depravity. Also, we cannot simply assume that spiritual death is equivalent to total depravity. We must not be guilty of defining spiritual death *a priori*, before examining what the Bible itself says a spiritually dead person can actually do. As we will see below, Col 2:12-13 says such a person can believe the gospel.

Those who accept total depravity claim that Scripture teaches that sinners are unable to do anything good. Matthew 7:18 is quoted: "Nor can a bad tree produce good fruit." This is true, but in Matt 12:33 Jesus says, "Either make the tree good and its fruit good, or make the tree bad and its fruit bad." Since this is an exhortation addressed to men, it implies that the decision to be either a good tree or a bad tree lies within the sinner's power. Even though he cannot change himself, the sinner can submit himself to God, who then transforms him from a bad tree into a good tree.

But does not Rom 8:7-8 say that the unbelieving mind "does not subject itself to the law of God, for it is not even able to do so, and those who are in the flesh cannot please God"? Is this not a "total inability" to believe the gospel? Absolutely not! The context clearly shows that the inability here is related to the *law*, not to the *gospel*. As long as a person is controlled by the flesh, he is unable to obey any command of the law as God wants it done and as the law requires. In the unbelieving state he cannot please God with respect to the law. But this text says nothing about a sinner being unable to respond to the gospel, or through the power of the gospel being unable to redirect the set of his mind from flesh to Spirit. In other passages it is clear that sinners are able and expected to respond to the gospel in faith and repentance (Matt 23:37; John 3:16; Rom 1:17; Rev 22:17).

But does not Jesus say, "No one can come to Me unless the Father who sent Me draws him" (John 6:44)? This is certainly true, but contrary to Calvinism this drawing is not selective and irresistible; it is universal and resistible. All are drawn to Jesus by the power of the gospel (Rom 1:16; 10:17; 2 Thess 2:14; Heb 4:12), but only some respond (Matt 23:37). On the universality of the call, Jesus said, "And I, if I am lifted up from the earth [on the cross, v. 33], will draw all men to Myself" (John 12:32). Denying that the Word of God has the power to draw all sinners to Christ disregards the very purpose and character of the written word as being addressed to sinners. The gospel is the good news of salvation to sinners and is clear to sinners. John says his accounts of Jesus' life and miracles "have been written so that you may believe that Jesus is the Christ, the Son of God" (John 20:31). This writing has not been in vain.

But does not the New Testament teach that faith and repentance are the gifts of God? Does this not imply the sinner's inability to believe and repent? It is true that some passages use this language, but they are not referring to the irresistible gift of saving grace to totally depraved sinners. Acts 5:31 and 11:18 say that God granted repentance to Israel and to the Gentiles, but this means only that he is granting these *groups* (not individuals) the *opportunity* and *means* to believe and repent by taking the gospel to them. This is how Phil 1:29 and 2 Tim 2:25 should be understood also, though the latter is not referring to initial conversion repentance.

Some passages cited as proof that faith is a gift are not actually speaking of saving faith at all. Romans 12:3 means that God has measured out (distributed) to each Christian a spiritual gift that is appropriate to his own faith (Cottrell, *Romans*, 2:319-321). First Corinthians 12:9 refers to miracle-working faith as a gift of the Spirit (see 1 Cor 13:2), and Gal 5:22 refers to faithfulness in Christian living.

Some mistakenly conclude that Eph 2:8 says faith is a gift: "For by grace you have been saved through faith; and that not of yourselves, it is the gift of God." This is disproved, though, by the rules of Greek grammar. The Greek word for "faith" (*pistis*) is feminine in gender; the pronoun referring to the gift ("that," *touto*) is neuter. If it were referring back to faith, it too would be feminine in form. (There is no word in the Greek corresponding to the pronoun "it.") This verse actually shows that faith is *not* a gift since grace and faith are carefully distinguished. We are saved *by* grace, as God's part; but *through* faith, as our part, as distinct from the grace given. Faith is not a gift of grace and the result of regeneration; it is a response to grace and a prerequisite to regeneration.

That faith precedes regeneration and is a prerequisite for it is specifically affirmed in Col 2:12, "Having been buried with Him in baptism, in which you were also raised up with Him through faith in the working of God." Here "raised up with Him" refers to regeneration (see v. 13, "He made you alive together with Him"), and faith is the *means* by which the regeneration is received: we are "raised . . . through faith." The spiritually dead unbeliever makes his decision to believe of his own free choice, moved by the power of the gospel, before being "raised up" in regeneration. See Eph 1:13-14, where "hearing" and "believing" are aorist participles, suggesting that these acts precede the action of the main verb, the sealing with the Spirit (see also Acts 5:32; 15:7-9; 16:30; 1 Peter 1:22).

In conclusion, we see that there is no biblical basis for the doctrine of total depravity. Augustinianism begins at the wrong end of the process of salvation. It begins with a definition and description of sin and spiritual death in the abstract, including an *a priori* conception of what a sinner can and cannot do; then it makes the process of conversion fit this preconception. It is much better to take the biblical description of conversion itself, and use this to help us to understand the limits of man's sinful condition. We must not decide what a sinner can and cannot do before seeing what the Bible says that he can and does do in relation to conversion.

IV. THE SINNER HAS A CORRUPTED IMAGE

A final point is that sin has corrupted the image of God within us. To what extent is this true? Contrary to any view that sin has totally destroyed the image, the Bible pictures sinners (i.e., human beings in general) as still being in the image of God in some sense (see Gen 5:1-3; 9:6; Acts 17:28; 1 Cor 11:7; Jas

3:9). But at the same time it describes salvation as in some sense restoring or renewing the image (Eph 4:22-24; Col 3:9-10). How may we explain this?

Earlier we saw that the image of God consists of both *form* and *content*. The form of the image is personhood, which consists especially of the capacity for a relationship with God. Sin does not change this aspect of the image. Even sinners are still persons with all the capacities of personhood, including the capacity for an interpersonal relationship with God.

The content of the image, though, is significantly affected by sin. In its uncorrupted state the image includes true knowledge of God and a holy character in imitation of God's own holiness. But when sin takes control, the knowledge is replaced with ignorance and falsehood, and the holy character is replaced with wickedness.

Once the image of God has been damaged, the relationships for which it equips us are broken and corrupted. What this means is that sinners still have a relationship with God, but it is a negative rather than a positive one. Once sin enters a person's life, he is no longer a willing servant in loving fellowship with God, but a rebel living in fear of the wrath of his Sovereign. Just as Adam and Eve as sinners sought to hide from their Maker in the Garden of Eden (Gen 3:8-10), so do all rebels desire to hide from God in one way or another.

The corrupted image also means that man's original relationship with the world has changed. In the unfallen state mankind had dominion over the earth with the intention that the earth and everything in it should be our servants. But when we come under the power of sin, we are no longer masters of the creation, but are *slaves* to created things and to the conditions of this world. Sinners become enslaved to worldly elements such as alcohol, drugs, money, sex, and time. Things which are supposed to be our servants and friends become our enemies instead.

The result is that man loses his favored place in the creation order, which originally was thus:

GOD

MAN

WORLD.

When we sin against God, we are basically trying to move up a notch in this hierarchy by elevating ourselves to God's own level, thus denying his lordship over us. But sin has an opposite effect. Instead of raising us to a higher level, it causes us to sink to a lower one. As sinners we not only are still under the sovereign rule of God, but are also under slavery or bondage to the world itself, thus:

GOD

WORLD

MAN.

CHAPTER ELEVEN
HUMAN DEATH

Pierre Maury has said that Christian anthropology, or the Christian study of man, "is essentially a consideration of death and the reasons for it" (250). We should not only agree with this observation, but should also broaden its scope thus, that the whole Christian study of sin and salvation is a consideration of death and its remedy.

In this chapter we are focusing especially on the fact and meaning of human death. What is the biblical view of the place of death in the world? Just how and why do human beings die? How are God and Satan connected with this seemingly inevitable event? Is death a foe or a friend?

I. THE ESSENCE OF DEATH

Literal death can be defined only in negative terms in relation to life. A dictionary defines "dead" as "no longer living, deprived of life, not endowed with life." "To die" is "to cease to live"; "death" is "the end of life, the absence of life." Some materials (e.g., plastic, minerals, stones) lack life; but this is irrelevant because they were never alive in the first place and were never intended to be, thus we usually do not refer to them as "dead."

The very essence of death thus implies that the normal state is *life*, i.e., the normal and original state for any dead thing is its former state of life. In nature nothing proceeds from death to life; dead things always start out as living things, not vice versa. Life comes from other life, and living things die. Thus life is the norm; and death is the absence of life, the removal of the principle of life, separation from the source of life.

It is clear that man is intended to be alive. The living God made man as a "living being" (Gen 2:7) with the intention that he should live forever in fellowship with his Maker. But when sin entered, so did death (Gen 2:17; Rom 5:12), and man the living creature became man the dying creature. This happens because sin separates the sinner from God (Isa 59:2a). This separation occurs because sin by its very nature is the opposite of God, the very contradiction of his own morally pure and holy essence (Ps 5:4-6; Isa 6:3-5; Hab 1:12-13; 1 Pet 1:15-16). Thus sin by its very nature involves and even requires separation from God. The sinner turns his back upon God, and God turns his face away from the sinner (Isa 59:2b; 64:7). Thus the sinner becomes dead since he is separated from the only true source of life, the only one who "has life in Himself" (John 5:26). The sinner is "excluded from the life of God" (Eph 4:18).

II. THE ASPECTS OF DEATH

The terminology for death is used in several senses in the Bible. Sometimes the event to which it refers is a positive aspect of our salvation, e.g., dying with Christ (Rom 6:4,7-8; Col 2:20; 3:3) and dying to sin (Rom 6:2,11; see 8:13). More often, though, the relevant terms refer to the curse of death which we bring upon ourselves by our sins. This curse of death takes three forms: spiritual, physical, and eternal.

Spiritual death is called "spiritual" because it affects primarily the soul or spirit of a sinner. It is actually the same as the second part of the "double trouble" discussed in the previous chapter. It is the state of sinfulness or depravity that permeates a sinner's nature like a sickness. The sinner is "dead" in his trespasses and sins (Eph 2:1,5; Col 2:13). The prodigal son in the fallen stage of his life is described as dead (Luke 15:24,32); a hedonistic widow "is dead even while she lives" (1 Tim 5:6; see Rev 3:1). When Paul entered the age of accountability, he says, "sin became alive and I died" (Rom 7:9). "The mind set on the flesh is death," he says (Rom 8:6). Conversion is passing from a state of death into a state of life (1 John 3:14).

This spiritual depravity is truly a state of death because a sinner becomes separated from the source of life, which is God himself (Isa 59:2; Eph 4:18). The sinner's spiritual life is gone; he has lost his spiritual energy and power; spiritual decay has set in. He is alienated from God and is unresponsive toward God, having a scarred conscience that lacks feeling and sensitivity (1 Tim 4:2). Leon Morris points out that Rom 8:6 does not merely say that the flesh-oriented mind is headed for death or deserves death; rather, it *is* death. And in the next verse (8:7) this is equated with enmity or hostility against God, "which seems to give the essence of death as enmity with God," which is "the real horror of death" (*Wages*, 17).

The second form of death is the one with which everyone is familiar, namely, physical death. Man is intended to be a unity of spirit and body. As long as the two are united, the body is alive. The presence of the spirit is in some way linked to the life of the body; Jas 2:26 says that "the body without the spirit is dead." Physical death occurs when the spirit leaves the body (see John 19:30).

There is a sense, though, in which the body is already dead even before its decisive separation from the spirit. "The body is dead because of sin" (present tense), says Paul (Rom 8:10). This may refer to the spiritual death that permeates the body as the result of the sin that indwells it (Rom 7:17-18,23). That is, the body is so much in the grip of sin's power that it can be called a "body of death" (Rom 7:24, NIV) in a spiritual sense of the word. Most obviously, though, Rom 8:10

refers to the physical death to which the body is already a prisoner. Even though it is presently alive, it is already subject to death, smitten with death, under the curse of death, doomed to die. It is already experiencing the harbingers of death in the form of a multitude of diseases, deformities, infirmities, aches, and attacks.

The third aspect of death's curse follows the final judgment. It is called eternal death because it takes the form of eternal punishment in hell. Being thrown into "the lake that burns with fire and brimstone" is "the second death" (Rev 20:14-15; 21:8). L. Morris (*Wages*, 18-19) includes this eternal second death in the expression "twice dead" or "doubly dead" in Jude 12, since Jude 13 seems to equate it with "the blackness of darkness" that has been forever reserved for the wicked (KJV). Those who are eternally lost will experience this death both in their sinful spirits and in their reconstituted sinful, unredeemed bodies (Matt 10:28).

In the final state the wicked will experience the true essence of death in its full intensity, i.e., an eternal, irreversible separation from God and therefore an absolute absence of life and hope. "Depart from Me" will be among the final words they hear from the Judge (Matt 7:23; 25:41). They will spend eternity "away from the presence of the Lord and from the glory of His power" (2 Thess 1:9). They will have no part in "the holy city, new Jerusalem," where God himself will dwell among the redeemed (Rev 21:1-3,27).

When the full scope of death—spiritual, physical, and eternal—is thus understood, we can easily see, as L. Morris says (*Wages*, 20), that "death is not simply an event, it is a state, it is the sphere in which evil has its sway, and sinners are, and must be, within this sphere with all that that means, until they are redeemed from it." Of course, "if a man continues in sin he continues in death"—forever.

Since spiritual death was discussed more fully in the previous chapter, and since eternal death will be discussed later in the section on eschatology, the rest of this chapter will deal only with physical death, with the exception of a few references in the following section.

III. THE SOURCE OF DEATH

"Why do people die?"

This is really two separate questions. One is about death as such: why is there such a thing as physical death in the first place? That is, why does *anyone* die? The other question is about the death of specific individuals: why did this person die in this particular manner at this particular time? It is important to see that these two questions cannot be answered in the same way.

In answering these questions we must proceed through two stages. First, we must decide whether death is a natural phenomenon, or whether it is somehow the unnatural product of sin. Second, if the latter, we must then decide whether death is a natural consequence of sin, or whether it is a deliberate judicial penalty pronounced upon sinners by God.

A. Death Is the Result of Sin

One view of the source of death—probably the most common one—is that mankind is a part of the natural order in the same way that everything else is; therefore death must be just as natural for human beings as it is for all other living creatures. This is part of the Trojan-horse legacy of naturalistic evolutionary theory: human life evolved by the same process as all other life; therefore human death is as normal as insect death or elephant death. As Kübler-Ross puts it, "Death always has been and always will be with us. It is an integral part of human existence" (*Growth*, 1).

Many people within the Christian community, sometimes influenced by evolutionary theory, have also spoken of death as if it were the natural, normal end to human life. The liberal Christian theologian Paul Tillich says that "man is naturally mortal." He "comes from dust and returns to dust" in his "natural finitude." "Sin does not produce death," but gives us an unnatural anxiety about it.[1] The Restoration writer J.S. Lamar declared that man was originally created mortal (i.e., intended to die), and that the only death resulting from sin was spiritual death (100-101). A well-known modern preacher, commenting on death as the wages of sin (Rom 6:23), declared that this must refer to spiritual death and not to physical death, since "even the finest saints of God die." A speaker at the 1976 North American Christian Convention said, "Mortal death is not related to sin but is a part of the created order from the beginning." An article in *Christian Standard* declares that "death belongs to us as a natural part of existence. Death is as natural as birth" (Howden, 11).

To say that death is "a natural part of existence" does apply to plants and animals; there is no biblical basis for the idea that even animal death is the result of Adam's sin. But to apply this to human beings is a grievous error; it ignores the clear biblical teaching that human death, including physical death, is the result of sin.

The connection between sin and death is asserted in many places in Scripture, beginning with Gen 2:17 when Adam was warned that if he disobeyed God's command, he would surely die (see Gen 3:19). "The person who sins will die," says Ezek 18:20 (see v. 26).[2] In Rom 1:32 Paul says that those who practice sin are "worthy of death." He also declares that death is the wages of sin, and that "the body is dead because of sin" (Rom 6:23; 8:10). James 1:15 lists the genealogy of death thus: "When lust has conceived, it gives birth to sin; and when sin is accomplished, it brings forth death." Romans 5:12 explains that death entered into the world and spread to all men through one man, Adam. That is, individuals do not die necessarily because of their own sin; it is a curse upon the whole race. So even when infants and saints die, it is the result of sin.

It is obvious, then, that human death is not a natural phenomenon but is the result of sin. In the final analysis, there is no such thing as death "from natural causes." But how do we know that the passages that link death to sin are talking (at least) about *physical* death? We grant that the other aspects of death are probably in view in some of them, but it is impossible to say that these texts do not intend to include physical death also. For example, in Gen 2:17 the penalty for disobedience is death; and when this penalty is imposed in 3:19, the only kind of death mentioned is physical death (returning to dust).

One difficulty with this understanding of Gen 2:17 is the qualification that "in the day that you eat from it you will surely die." How can this be physical death, since Adam did *not* die physically on that day, but actually lived for 930 years (Gen 5:5)? Our response to this question is twofold. First, we should not *limit* the death imposed on Adam to physical death. Based on what we know from NT teaching, it also involved spiritual death, which *did* occur on that very day. Second, even Adam's physical death *began* on that same day, in the sense that God canceled his immunity to this death, and his body began the process of dying. On that day Adam the living creature (Gen 2:7) became Adam the dying creature. Genesis 3:19 includes this death as part of the curse for sin (3:14-19), not as a parenthetical "By the way, remember that you will die some day."

That physical death is included in Adam's legacy in Rom 5:12 is quite clear from the total context of the passage. In Rom 5:6-10 the physical death of Christ is in view (see 6:9), and in Rom 5:14 the physical death of infants. Romans 8:10 specifically relates sin to the death of the body. Also, that Adam's sin brought physical death is clearly shown in the parallel text, 1 Cor 15:22, "For as in Adam all die, so also in Christ all will be made alive." That this refers to physical death is clear from the ensuing discussion of the resurrection of the body.

Some considerations related to salvation also make the same point. For instance, the fact that the resurrection of the body is an act of redemption (Rom 8:23) shows that the death of the body is the result of sin. Also, if physical death is natural, in what sense can Christ's death on the cross be a curse and be a part of the penalty he paid for our sins? (See Gal 3:13; Heb 2:14-15.)

It is quite plain, then, that all forms of human death, including physical death, are the wages of sin. Without sin, human beings would not have died. Man was not created with the intention or assumption that he would just naturally die like everything else. We can say that human beings were created mortal in the sense that they were *able* to die, or that death was a *possibility* for them; but it was not necessary or inevitable. Erickson refers to Adam's original state as "conditional immortality." That is, "he was not inherently able to live forever, but he need not have died" (*Theology*, 630).

The bottom line is that people die because of sin. That the two are unrelated is one of the devil's lies (Gen 3:4). This does not mean, though, that every person dies as the result of his own personal sin, or even as the result of some other contemporary person's sin. This may happen sometimes, but the basic point is that death as such has been brought upon the entire human race as the result of *Adam's* sin. "In Adam all die" (1 Cor 15:22).

B. Death Is the Penalty for Sin

One issue regarding death is, "Why do people die at all?" The answer is, "Because of sin." The other issue is whether the connection between sin and death is a *natural* one or a *judicial* one. That is, is death just a natural and inevitable consequence of sin, or is it a judicially imposed penalty upon sin?

The answer to this question depends upon which aspect of death is in view. In my judgment *spiritual* death is primarily an inevitable consequence of sin; by its very nature sin separates us from the holy God. Also, it seems clear that *eternal* death, the second death in the lake of fire, is a penalty imposed upon sinners by the Righteous Judge. But what about *physical* death? Sometimes it is suggested that it is only a natural result of sin. For example, in discussing God's warning to Adam in Gen 2:17, Owen Crouch says, "We should note that death was not judicial execution; it would come as a consequence involved in the nature of the choice," similar to the way death follows the drinking of poison (12). This view, however, must be rejected. The death of the body must be regarded as a part of sin's penalty. Even if there is some natural connection between sin and death, says L. Morris (*Wages*, 15), there is more; "death and sin are connected by divine appointment, so that we are to discern the hand of God in the death which is visited upon the sinner."

The Bible clearly points us to this conclusion. Sin by its very nature is the transgression of the law of the righteous and holy God. Divine holiness demands that sin be punished and erupts against sin in the form of divine wrath. As Berkhof says of sin (255),

> It is not only a transgression of the law of God, but an attack on the great Lawgiver Himself, a revolt against God. It is an infringement on the inviolable righteousness of God, which is the very foundation of His throne (Ps. 97:2), and an affront to the spotless holiness of God, which requires of us that we be holy in all manner of living (I Pet. 1:16). In view of this it is but natural that God should visit sin with punishment.

Berkhof continues (257), "Justice requires the punishment of the transgressor. Back of the law stands God, and therefore it may also be said that punishment aims at the vindication of the righteousness and holiness of the great Lawgiver. The holiness of God necessarily reacts against sin, and this reaction manifests itself in the punishment of sin." God is "righteous and upright" (Deut 32:4). "He pays a man according to his work" (Job 34:11). In Gen 3:19 death is included in the curse. Romans 6:23 says death is the *wages* of sin. The word for wages "denotes that which is due, and the expression gives us the thought that sin not only results in death, but that it deserves to result in death" (L. Morris, *Wages*, 15). Those who indulge in the catalogue of sins named in Rom 1:28-31 not only die, but are "worthy of death," says Paul (Rom 1:32). No wonder "it is appointed for men to die once and after this comes judgment" (Heb 9:27).

At this point it is important to distinguish between God's holy judgment as the ultimate cause of death as such, and the immediate cause of the death of specific individuals. God imposed death as such upon the human race as the judicial penalty upon Adam and upon all his offspring, who sinned representatively in him (Rom 5:12). Also, God may be the immediate cause of certain specific deaths (Luke 12:5), sometimes as a penalty for personal sin (Acts 5:1-11; 12:21-23) and sometimes for other reasons (2 Sam 12:15-18).[3] In fact, sometimes it may be an act of mercy, as in the cases where we pray for God to take the lives of saints who are facing great suffering.

We must understand, though, that God's direct causation of individual deaths is the exception rather than the rule. Most occur under the sovereign control of God's permissive will, either as God permits individual free-will choices that lead to death, or as he permits the cumulative effect of the original curse to take its toll via accidents, disease, or aging. It is very important to remember this, especially when unexpected, untimely, or suffering-filled deaths occur. Those who wrongly assume that God deliberately causes every specific death agonize over questions such as "Why did God take my wife, the mother of my three young children?" or "Why did God take my baby?" The confusion is compounded for those who think this way and yet rightly understand that death is the punishment for sin: "What did my teenager do wrong that God should punish him with death?" or "Why is God punishing me with this fatal cancer?" Such questions miss the point. Most individual deaths are not deliberate acts of God, judicial or not; they are the result of the imposition of the death penalty on the human race as such as a consequence of Adam's sin.

Confusion over God's role in the imposition of death sometimes leads to a similar confusion over Satan's role. In response to the question, "Why do people die?" One writer correctly insists that individual deaths are usually not the result of some tailor-made purpose of God, and that people do not die because God is "calling them home." But then the writer commits the error of attributing all death to the devil, reasoning that death is caused by sin and sin is caused by the devil's temptations. "So then, death strikes us all, not by the hand of God or His Son, Jesus, or through His 'call,' or by the will of God, but because the devil is at work in this world and tempts all men to sin." Thus the devil himself is "the true author of death" (Fowler, 9-10).

It is true that Satan has an indirect connection with death in that he tempts us to sin, and death is the penalty for sin. This is one reason why Satan is called the one "who had the power of death" (Heb 2:14). As the tempter in the Garden of Eden Satan was indirectly involved in the universal death-curse placed on Adam's sin; he is also the tempter and deceiver that leads us into personal sins. He may even be the immediate cause of some specific deaths (Job 1:12-19). But there is no valid sense in which we can say that the devil is "the true author of death." This is so for two reasons. One, even if Satan is the one who tempted Adam and Eve to sin, and who tempts us to sin, we are all free-will creatures who bear the responsibility for our own sins. So if we say that the one who causes the sin is the cause of the death which is its penalty, then we ourselves would be the author of death. Two, and more significantly, even though Satan is the tempter, and even though we ourselves make the actual decision to sin, God is still the one who decided from the beginning that the wages of sin would be death. Thus even if the death of any given individual is not God's immediate will or desire, it *is* the judicial will of God that every human being should die because of sin. In this sense God is indeed the true author of death.

IV. THE CHARACTER OF DEATH

In view of the above data it is difficult to view death in anything but a negative way. But for reasons that will be explained below, the fact is that many want to portray death in a most positive light. This temptation must be resisted, and death must be unmasked for what it truly is: the enemy of mankind. When a person dies, he is not just "doing what comes naturally." He has been overtaken and overwhelmed by an alien attacker that has pursued him since his conception in the role of a relentless enemy.

Death is specifically called an enemy in 1 Cor 15:25-26, "For He must reign until He has put all His enemies under His feet. The last enemy that will be abolished is death." It is the enemy of God, the enemy of Christ, and the enemy of mankind.

A. Death Is a Reigning Enemy

We have pointed out above [p. 31] that the key word, the dominant theme for the old creation in its original state, was *life*. That is still true in many ways; the world of nature still teems with living things. But from the standpoint of man this has changed. Regarding mankind's place in the universe, the ruling concept is no longer life but *death*. Death is not just our enemy, but a *reigning* enemy. What once was man's servant is now his master—a usurper to be sure, but his master nonetheless.

The language of death as a ruling monarch is used in Romans 5. Because of Adam's sin death not only spread to all men (v. 12) but "reigned" over all (vv. 14, 17). Here death is personified as a tyrant having everyone under its power. Depicting it as a reigning monarch emphasizes its universal scope, its oppressive domination, and its inescapable certainty.

Death reigns as king because it controls how we approach life as such. Life becomes just the absence of death or the delay of death. The dominant purpose in life is simply to avoid death, a preoccupation which is seen in the way health care and safety concerns are always on our minds. As part of the curse (Gen 3:17-19), work itself has become "earning a living"; it is how we "keep death away from the door." One suggested definition of life is "the totality of all those functions that resist death."

Death reigns as king because its forerunners spread like tentacles through all of life long before we reach that final event itself. As Wolff says (46),

> Weakness, sickness, even imprisonment and oppression, are but forerunners of death, part of its accoutrements. Every shadow, even darkness itself, is a messenger of the king of terrors. The power of death casts a shadow over all of life. The medieval saying, "in the midst of life we are surrounded by death," is a fit description. . . .

Death reigns as king because it places absolute limits upon life. No matter how we may fight it, we know we will die at some point. Not many of us can plan more than a few decades ahead. No one can plan a thousand years ahead, or even a hundred. In the face of inevitable death, life itself becomes absurd and meaningless, which is a major theme of the philosophy of existentialism.[4] On a practical level this generates a "Who cares?" attitude toward life with a tendency toward hedonism: "Eat, drink, and be merry, for tomorrow we die!"

Death reigns as king finally because it fills all of life with a deep and persistent fear of our own personal death, both the upcoming event of dying and the state of death that will follow it. This fear keeps death on the throne and keeps us in a state of slavery all our lives, says Heb 2:15.

B. Death Is a Feared Enemy

The fear of death is real. "Psychologists and psychiatrists assert that fear of death is universal," and some believe it is "the instinctual root of all other fears" ("Thanatology," 92). Kübler-Ross says, "Death is still a fearful, frightening happening, and the fear of death is a universal fear even if we think we have mastered it on many levels" ("Death," 5). In his later years, as he got closer to death, the prominent humanist Corliss Lamont, having rejected the reality of God and the soul, uttered these chilling words: "Today, more than ever, I feel the haunting sense of transiency. If only time would for a while come to a stop! . . . I sympathize with everyone who has ever longed for immortality and I wish that the enchanting dream of eternal life could indeed come true" (19).

What causes men to fear death? For those like Lamont who deny any afterlife, there is certainly the fear of extinction, the dread of their consciousness being forever snuffed out like a candle flame. Others may say it is the fear of the unknown. More likely, though, it is the fear of the *known*, since general revelation makes every person aware of the existence of God as Creator and Lawgiver (Rom 1:18-32; 2:14-15). As sinners we all know we are worthy of death (Rom 1:32), and in our hearts we know that Heb 9:27 is true: "It is appointed for men to die once and after this comes judgment." This is why death is terrible; we do not fear the moment of death so much as what we know follows it. Death is the threshold to the courtroom of the righteous Judge, the one "to whom we must give account" (Heb 4:13, NIV). "The sting of death is sin" (1 Cor 15:56), and thus for sinners "it is a terrifying thing to fall into the hands of the living God" (Heb 10:31).

C. Death Is a Deceiving Enemy

Because men fear death, they seek to abolish this fear in many futile ways. One sense in which Satan has the power of death (Heb 2:14) is that he exploits the universal fear of dying and prompts men to manufacture false solutions to this problem. This is a real sense in which sinners are slaves to the fear of death (Heb 2:15), i.e., they become slaves to a myriad of lies and false approaches to death. They create ways to think of the enemy as beautiful and friendly, or at least as a normal and harmless part of life. Like the residents of Jerusalem in Isaiah's day, they try to convince themselves that these lies are a safe haven from death: "'We have made a covenant with death, and with Sheol we have made a pact. The overwhelming scourge will not reach us when it passes by, for we have made falsehood our refuge and we have concealed ourselves with deception'" (Isa 28:15).

What are some of the false bargains people have made with death? From a secular perspective Darwinism takes the sting out of death by making it an evolutionary necessity. Others have found false hope in cryogenics, having their bodies frozen and trusting that science will someday discover a cure for what was killing them and then will be able to thaw them out and apply it. Sigmund Freud "believed that the fear of death is usually the result of guilt feelings" ("Freud," 33), which of course is very close to the truth. But, agreeing with Freud, modern unbelieving psychotherapy tries to erase this fear by destroying the concepts of sin and guilt themselves.

Still others attempt to focus only on the "bright side" of death. Kübler-Ross says, "For those who seek to understand it, death is a highly creative force. The highest spiritual values of life can originate from the thought and study of death" (*Growth*, 1). Picturing death as the great inspirer of philosophy, literature, art, and music, she champions the one important message "that death does not have to be a catastrophic, destructive thing; indeed, it can be viewed as one of the most constructive, positive, and creative elements of culture and life" (ibid., 2).

Similar deceptions are even more abundant in religious or spiritual contexts. Belief in reincarnation is popular in the Western world because here it is viewed as a way to nullify death. In some occult circles death is regarded as simply a welcome transition to a higher stage of existence. This is the main message of spiritism: there is no death; it's nothing; it's just a door you pass through.[5] The widely reported "near-death" or "life-after-life" experiences are either caused by or exploited by demonic spirits to depict death as a gateway to glory for nearly everyone, whatever their concept of or relationship with God. Such experiences serve to "anesthetize the mind against the piercing reality of death as curse and judgment" (Albrecht and Alexander, 10).

As Wolff says, "All false glorification of death is alien to Christianity" (45), and all such covenants are false and futile. God pronounces the following doom upon those who try to hide behind these falsehoods: "Then hail will sweep away the refuge of lies and the waters will overflow the secret place. Your covenant with death will be canceled, and your pact with Sheol will not stand; when the overwhelming scourge passes through, then you become its trampling place" (Isa 28:17-18).

In its basic nature death is nothing but a curse, an enemy, a foe. Even for Christians both the event of dying and the disembodied state of death are unnatural. But Christians do know one thing no one else does: though death is an enemy, it is a *defeated* enemy.

D. Death Is a Defeated Enemy

Death reigns as king in the old creation, but it is a pretender, a usurper. It has no right to be on the throne. It has disrupted the normal state of things; it has turned the world upside down.

The good news is that this usurper is already in the process of being overthrown and dethroned. Jesus Christ came into the world for the very purpose of meeting this enemy in battle and defeating it. This is specifically declared in Heb 2:14-15: "Therefore, since the children share in flesh and blood, He Himself likewise also partook of the same, that through death He might render powerless him who had the power of death, that is, the devil, and might free those who through fear of death were subject to slavery all their lives."

When Jesus died and rose again, he struck a deathblow to death; and in this sense the enemy is already defeated. The risen Christ has brought death under his control, and is able to release its captives (Luke 4:18). He cries out, "Do not be afraid; I am the first and the last, and the living One; and I was dead, and behold, I am alive forevermore, and I have the keys of death and of Hades" (Rev 1:17-18).

Through his death and resurrection Jesus established a refuge from this mortally wounded enemy, death. That refuge is his church. After Peter confessed him as "the Christ, the Son of the living God," Jesus declared, "Upon this rock I will build My church; and the gates of Hades will not overpower it" (Matt 16:16-18). The rock is Jesus himself, and the gates of Hades are the forces of death. Jesus is alluding to the divine promise in Isa 28:16, "Therefore thus says the Lord God, 'Behold, I am laying in Zion a stone, a tested stone, a costly cornerstone for the foundation, firmly placed. He who believes in it will not be disturbed.'" This stone, the Rock on which the church is built, is God's alternative to the lies and deceptions behind which desperate people try to hide from the overwhelming scourge of death (Isa 28:14-15), as discussed above. The forces of death will sweep away all these lies and those deceived by them (Isa 28:17-19), but those who take refuge in the Church built upon the Rock "will not be disturbed." They have already begun to share in Christ's victory over the enemy.

It is true that Christians still must go through the experience of death and endure the disembodied state of death (unless they are alive at the time of the second coming), but we face this not with fear but with confidence in the promise of redemptive resurrection when Christ returns. In this glorious event the enemy death will be completely abolished (1 Cor 15:25-26), being itself cast into the lake of eternal fire (Rev 20:14).

Thus when individuals respond to the preaching of the gospel and accept Christ as their Lord and Savior, they are set free from the curse and the fear of death. In Acts 17:6 (KJV) unbelieving Jews at Thessalonica accused the Christians of turning the world upside down through their preaching. They were right in a sense, but they did not understand the whole picture. The world had already been turned upside down when sin entered and death ascended to the throne. The preaching of the gospel is simply turning the world right-side up again, one convert at a time.

This is why Christians can have an attitude toward death that is different from the rest of the world, which is still in slavery to fears and lies. We know that death is an enemy, but we know it is a *defeated* enemy. Thus we know we need not fear it, and in one sense can view it positively. In 2 Cor 5:1-8 Paul shows that for believers the negative aspects of death are offset by the positive. He expresses dread (v. 4) at the thought of being unnaturally "unclothed," i.e., without a body, in the interim between death and resurrection. But he knows that believers will ultimately be reclothed in new bodies (vv. 1-3), and that in the unclothed interim our spirits will actually be in the presence of the Lord Jesus (vv. 6-8). In view of the latter prospect we can actually welcome death and "prefer to be away from the body and at home with the Lord" (v. 8, NIV). This is why Paul says that "to die is gain" (Phil 1:21), and that he himself had "the desire to depart and be with Christ, for that is very much better" (Phil 1:23). This is the reason Ps 116:15 can say, "Precious in the sight of the LORD is the death of His godly ones." Indeed, "blessed are the dead who die in the Lord" (Rev 14:13).

It is important, though, to remember that only Christians can have this positive perspective upon death. We do a terrible disservice to unbelievers when we endorse in any way the idea that death is normal, natural, and friendly. Those outside Christ's saving grace should stand in terror before death and the judgment that follows it. We want them to be free from this terror, of course, but we must make it clear that the only true escape from it is by accepting the Christian gospel and being a part of the church that is built on the Rock.

The whole story of redemption is God's solution to the problem of death—spiritual, physical, and eternal. Christ's saving work delivers us from the penalty, power, and fear of death. This is what Christianity is all about. This is the glory of the gospel. We must not rob the gospel of its glory by mistaking a defeated enemy for an old friend.

The content of this chapter is well summed up in the following quote from Leon Morris (*Wages*, 28):

What emerges clearly from our study of the New Testament documents is the fact that death characteristically is regarded as something completely unnatural, an alien, a horror, an enemy. It is not simply an event, but a state, and it is connected very closely with sin. But the important teaching of the New Testament is not that death is an evil, or that man cannot overcome it, but that death has been decisively defeated in the atoning death of the Saviour, who "abolished death, and brought life and incorruption to light through the gospel" (2 Tim. i.10). On this we rest our hope.

NOTES ON CHAPTER ELEVEN

[1]Tillich, II:66-67. Emil Brunner expressed basically the same view in *Dogmatics II*, 129.

[2]Both Ezek 18:4 and 18:20 are often translated, "The soul who sins will die," which may lead some to think that the prophet is talking about the death of the soul and not the death of the body. But the word used in both verses is *nephesh*, which is often used for the person as a whole, including the body as well as the soul. That is its meaning here; thus physical death is included in this pronouncement.

[3]God caused the death of David's child as the penalty for David's sin, but not for any sin in the child.

[4]See Jean-Paul Sartre's short story, "The Wall," 223-240.

[5]See the book by former spiritist Raphael Gasson, *The Challenging Counterfeit*, 34-37, 64, 115.

CHAPTER TWELVE
THE COSMIC CURSE

The corruption and condemnation resulting from sin are experienced not only by human beings but also by the entire universe. Man as the image of God is designed to stand in a particular relationship with both God and the world. When sin corrupts the image, these relationships are also distorted. Thus when the human race fell into sin, in a real sense the physical creation as a whole experienced a *fall*. The penal consequences of sin apply not only to human beings, but also to the whole of creation. Thus in addition to human death there is a kind of cosmic death, a cosmic curse.

The cosmic curse affects the world in two ways. One is the distorted relationship with mankind, which was intended by God to be the world's ruler (Gen 1:28) but has ended up being its slave. The other is an actual state of disorder, disruption, and decay into which the universe as such has fallen.

I. "THIS PRESENT EVIL AGE"

Galatians 1:4 says that Christ "gave Himself for our sins so that He might rescue us from this present evil age" or this present evil *aion*. Paul refers to Satan himself as the "god of this world," this *aion* (2 Cor 4:4), and says that we must not conform our minds and lives to it (Rom 12:2). The term *aion* as used in these texts does not refer to the physical universe as such, but to the age in which we live, the era of the old creation. Nor does the word mean just a bare period of history. It refers to a period of history as marked by a certain ethical or spiritual character, a certain worldview or value system. "This present evil age," the age to which we must not be conformed, is the world as fallen and corrupted, the world as it exists under the power of Satan, sin, and death.

The alien character of this fallen age is also reflected in Col 3:2, "Set your mind on the things above, not on the things that are on earth [*ges*]." First John 2:15 is similar: "Do not love the world [*kosmos*] nor the things in the world." That John is not referring to the cosmos as created but as fallen is seen in his following explanation: "For all that is in the world, the lust of the flesh and the lust of the eyes and the boastful pride of life, is not from the Father, but is from the world. The world is passing away, and also its lusts" (1 John 2:16-17).

Thus does the Bible describe this world or this age as *evil*, or as alien to man's best interests. This does not mean that the physical world is inherently evil; it means that it has become evil because it shares in the corruption that has been caused by human sin and in the condemnation that God has poured out upon it.

II. THE FUTILITY OF THE CREATION

The text that most clearly and forcefully describes the cosmic curse is Rom 8:18-22.[1]

> For I consider that the sufferings of this present time are not worthy to be compared with the glory that is to be revealed to us. For the anxious longing of the creation waits eagerly for the revealing of the sons of God. For the creation was subjected to futility, not willingly, but because of Him who subjected it, in hope that the creation itself also will be set free from its slavery to corruption into the freedom of the glory of the children of God. For we know that the whole creation groans and suffers the pains of childbirth together until now.

Here Paul speaks of "the creation," the physical or natural world; and he personifies it as experiencing an "anxious longing" for, or "eager expectation" (NIV) of, the day when the sons of God will be revealed. This is the day when God's family of believers will be raised from the dead (v. 23). Why is the universe earnestly, breathlessly awaiting this day? Because it is not just the human race that is under the curse of death and in need of redemption; the whole cosmos likewise has been plunged into a state of corruption and stands in need of healing.

This text presents the status of this condemned world in three vivid pictures. First, it has been "subjected to futility" (v. 20), or "subjected to frustration" (NIV). This takes us back to Genesis 1–3. When God placed the human race in charge of the rest of the material creation (Gen 1:26-28), from that point on the fate of the latter was tied to that of the former. When Adam sinned, God declared, "Cursed is the ground because of you" (Gen 3:17). Instead of being man's servant, the earth became his antagonist. Instead of perpetuating man's life indefinitely, it is forced to engorge man's dead body into its dusty maw (Gen 3:18-19).

Through this curse the creation was subjected to futility. "Subjected" (*hypotasso*) means "placed under the power or authority of." Figuratively the creation was placed under the power of "futility." This word is *mataiotes*, which conveys the idea of vanity, emptiness, purposelessness, and meaninglessness. The main idea is that the physical universe was originally created to play the role of servant under the lordship of man (Gen 1:28). Under this benevolent dictatorship it was intended to serve man's needs and in so doing to glorify God. Man's first sin, however, included an attempt to manipulate the creation and to misuse it for vainglorious purposes. As a result of this sin and its subsequent curse, man became the servant's slave instead of its master. Thus the creation itself was wrested from its original role in the intended order of things and can no longer fulfill its intended function or purpose. That is, it is subjected to futility or purposelessness.

This is why it is eagerly awaiting the revelation of the sons of God. When man's redemption fully comes, the creation will then be able to fulfill its own original purpose.

The second phrase that describes this present evil age is "slavery to corruption" (v. 21), or "bondage to decay" (NIV). "Decay" (*phthora*) can mean moral corruption (2 Pet 1:4; 2:19); or, as here, it can mean breakdown and decay in the physical world (2 Pet 2:12). Some decay is natural and was no doubt a part of the good creation from the beginning. The growth and seasonal cycles of plants and trees, and their production of edible fruit, vegetables, seeds, and leaves, will necessarily leave a residue that is reabsorbed by the earth through the process of decay.

The cosmic fall, however, resulted in a *bondage* to decay. This means that death and decay overran their intended boundaries and engulfed what was never meant to die and dissolve, especially the bodies of human beings (Gen 3:19; 1 Cor 15:42). It also means that the entire universe is undergoing an inexorable process of cosmic decay, which is sometimes called the law of entropy. This is "the constant and irreversible degradation of matter and energy in the universe to increasing disorder," says MacArthur. Indeed, "the natural bent of the universe—whether of humans, animals, plants, or inanimate elements of the earth and heavens—is obviously and demonstrably downward, not upward" (I:455-456).This is not really a "natural" bent, though. Rather, it is quite unnatural, being the result of God's curse and the source of the frustration noted in verse 20.

The third sorrowful picture of cosmic fallenness is that "the whole creation groans and suffers the pains of childbirth" (v. 22). The frustration resulting from being in bondage to decay expresses itself in groaning and suffering as if in pain. These parallel verbs have a prefix that means "with," i.e., "to groan *with*" and "to suffer *with*." This signifies that all parts of the creation are jointly participating in the pain of purposelessness.

Without the prefix the former of these two verbs means to sigh or groan or even complain because of undesirable circumstances from which one longs to be free (see v. 23). The second verb means especially to be in travail or to suffer the pains of childbirth. This is appropriate in view of the fact that pain in childbirth is part of the very curse which is the source of the creation's pain (Gen 3:16). The main point in referring to "the pains of childbirth" is to emphasize the seriousness of the curse under which the creation groans.

It is important to notice what Paul says about the *cause* of this state of cosmic meaninglessness, bondage, and pain. In verse 20 he says that the creation "was subjected" to all of this, "not by its own choice, but by the will of the one who subjected it" (NIV). In other words, its state of meaninglessness is not its own fault; it did not choose to rebel against its Maker and abandon its intended role. Its present state is the result of someone else's choice. Indirectly it came from Adam and Eve's decision to sin. Thus some say "the one who subjected it" is Adam. It is better, however, to see this as a reference to God. "Subjected" is an authoritative action, a judicial decision, and thus something only God could rightfully have done (Cranfield, I:414). Man committed the sin, but God pronounced the curse and brought it about.

Just as there is hope for fallen man, so there is hope for the fallen universe. When God subjected the cosmos to this curse, he did so "in hope" (v. 20). This refers to his plan one day to redeem the fallen creation itself, via the construction of "new heavens and a new earth" (2 Pet 3:13). Even at the very beginning of this age of the curse and of suffering and frustration, God saw fit to include the promise of redemption through the seed of the woman (Gen 3:15). This provided a basis for hope, and this hope in turn became the basis for the creation's eager anticipation (v. 19).

In verse 21 Paul says this old creation "will be set free from its slavery to corruption," i.e., from all the consequences brought upon it by sin. It will participate in the "glory of the children of God." This final glory of God's children will include not just new and glorified bodies (v. 23), but also a completely renewed and restored universe to serve as our eternal home. Thus the second coming of Christ will be the time of "the renewal of all things" (Matt 19:28, NIV), or "the period of restoration of all things" (Acts 3:21). Out of the cleansing cosmic fire will come new heavens and a new earth, completely purged of sin's effects and fully indwelt by righteousness (2 Pet 3:10-13; Isa 65:17; 66:22; Rev 21:1). In that day the meek will inherit the new earth (Matt 5:5), in which there will no longer be any curse (Rev 22:3).

III. THE PROBLEM OF EVIL[2]

The fact that both mankind and the cosmos as a whole lie under the corruption and condemnation of sin gives rise to what is commonly known as "the problem of evil." Even to the casual observer it is obvious that the world as it presently exists cannot be consistently called "very good" (Gen 1:31). There is still much beauty and wonder in it, but it is also permeated with pain, ugliness, and disaster—collectively called "evil."

Two kinds of evil are usually distinguished: moral and natural. Moral evil is the sin or wickedness which originates in the hearts of free moral creatures (human beings and fallen angels) and which expresses itself in their sinful actions. Examples include greed, hatred, selfishness, deceit, stealing, lust, and envy. Natural evil (sometimes called physical evil) is that which originates from natural processes or the perversion thereof. Examples are genetic defects, diseases, insanity, famine, suffering, and death; also any natural event—flood, lightning, earthquake, tornado, hurricane—that results in suffering or death. Sometimes moral evil and natural evil may be combined into a single event. For example, an act of murder is a moral evil on the part of the murderer which results in a natural evil (i.e., death) for the victim. Other examples are torture; rape; spouse and child abuse; and drug or alcohol abuse that results in birth defects, injury, or death.

The presence of such elements in the universe can be understood by those who accept the biblical teaching concerning sin, death, and the cosmic curse. But for those who do not view the world with this understanding, it is easy to see how evil can be a problem. Actually there are two separate problems. One has to do with the cause of particular instances of evil, e.g., "Why did my baby die?" or "Why did lightning strike my neighbor?" The other has to do with the origin of evil as such, e.g., "Why is there such a thing as human death in the first place?" "Why are there such things as birth defects at all?" "Why does any sort of weather disaster occur?" The latter are the more basic kinds of questions that constitute "the problem of evil."

What makes the existence of such phenomena a *problem*? Of course, there is always the practical problem of how to deal with or cope with pain and suffering. But the basic problem of evil is more theoretical than practical. That is, it is problematic to think that evil could exist alongside a particular view of God, specifically, the view found in traditional Christianity and presented in this book. It is the view that God is all-wise, all-good, and all-powerful. The problem is this: how is the existence of such a God consistent with the existence of evil? It seems impossible that the following three assertions could all be true at the same time: "God is all-good." "God is omnipotent." "Evil exists." David Hume notes that Epicurus's old questions are still unanswered: "Is [God] willing to prevent evil, but not able? then is he impotent. Is he able, but not willing? then is he malevolent. Is he both able and willing? whence then is evil?" (198). What kind of God really exists, then? How can we reconcile the existence of an all-good, omnipotent God with the existence of evil?

Many inadequate answers to this problem have been suggested. Some are unacceptable because they deny the biblical God. On the one hand, some have rejected an all-powerful God. He is good and does not want evil to exist, they say, but he is not able to prevent it or remove it. This approach to evil has considerable popular appeal, as illustrated by the fact that in the early 1980s one of the general best-selling books was Harold Kushner's *When Bad Things Happen to Good People*. His basic thesis is that although God is good, he simply is not omnipotent. Thus the world sometimes gets out of his control. Evil runs wild, and he cannot do anything about it.

The fact that this book was a best-seller shows that people are open to this explanation of the problem. However, in view of the Bible's teaching concerning the omnipotence of God and his sovereign control over all of nature and history, this is simply not an option open to the Bible believer. It is an inadequate solution.

A few others have dared to present the opposite option, that God is all-powerful but not all-good. Frederick Sontag, for example, says that in view of events such as the Jewish holocaust we must simply rethink our view of God. This means that "all easy and sweet views of God disappear," and "our notions of love must be rethought" (148-149). Such a view as this, of course, is completely ruled out by the Bible's teaching that God is good and all-loving.

Other inadequate answers to the problem of evil have been suggested by Bible believers who accept an omnipotent and all-good God, but who say that this God has actually planned for evil to exist in his world for good and necessary purposes. One view is the idea that God had to include evil in the world as a necessary *contrast* to all the good in his creation, so that we may be able to *appreciate* the good. How could we appreciate beauty if we never saw anything ugly? Would we really enjoy pleasure if we never experienced pain? So goes the argument.

This view has several weaknesses. In the first place it is only speculation since no one since the pre-Fall Adam and Eve has had the opportunity to try to appreciate a world with only good in it. Second, even if this argument could apply to natural evil, it would not account for moral evil. Third and most significantly, there seems to be no biblical support for this idea. Nowhere in Scripture is there any suggestion that God thought we needed this kind of contrast in order to appreciate his good creation. Such an idea is simply inadequate philosophical speculation.

Another quite common but inadequate view is that God deliberately caused evil to be present in the world because it is necessary for man's spiritual growth. This view rightly assumes that God desires to make creatures who will be mature persons of fully developed moral character. But according to this view, moral perfection cannot be created *ex nihilo*; it must be developed. But the development of such virtues as patience and forgiveness is impossible apart from the experience of evil. Thus it was necessary for God to include evil in the world by his own deliberate decision and purpose. In defending this view Norman Geisler says, "The presence of evil is in fact a necessary condition for the maximization of moral perfection for free creatures" (*Philosophy*, 365).

Such a view must be rejected. Moral growth does not depend upon the necessity of evil, but only on the possibility of it as an element inherent in free will. This possibility makes temptation real and the conquest of it a character-building experience. This view has many other weaknesses that cannot be explored here (see *GRu*, 394-397).

The best answer to the problem of evil is what is called the free-will defense. It says in essence that God created the world with neither moral evil nor natural evil existing in it; everything was originally "very good" (Gen 1:31). But he did create free-will beings for whom moral evil was a possibility. Why did God do this? The Bible does not give an explicit answer to this question; but we infer from other teaching in Scripture that God's chief purpose and desire were to have creatures who would love, serve, and glorify him of their free choice and not by coercion or manipulation. We infer this, for example, from the fact that the first and greatest commandment is that we should love God with all our hearts and minds (Matt 22:37). That this is the most important thing we can do suggests this freely chosen love is what God desires from his creation more than anything else. Giving his creatures free will was a necessary means to this end.

The capacity to freely love God, though, also requires the capacity to choose to hate and reject God. Thus in a sense the creation of free-will beings entailed a risk. But God was willing to risk the free choice of evil in order to have freely chosen love and worship. Here is the extent of God's responsibility for evil: he is responsible for its possibility, but not its actuality. He made the free creatures who had the potential for choosing evil.

Sadly, God's creatures have chosen to use their free will to commit sin. And as a consequence of this free choice, all the evil that exists in the world has come into existence, the physical as well as the moral. It is not difficult to see how moral evil is the result of free will. Angels and men were created with the capacity to sin; some of the angels and the first human beings exercised that capacity under the permissive will of God, and moral evil became a reality.

But what about physical evil? Free will can explain the presence of moral evil in the world, but how do we explain evils such as birth defects, disease, and death? The answer is that free will is the ultimate origin of physical evils, too. Physical evils are present in the world because of sin, and sin is present because of free will. This point must be explained very carefully. Even though it is a very important truth, it is easily misunderstood. Here is the best way to say it: all physical evils are ultimately the consequence of sin, but they do not all derive from sin in the same way.

What are the ways in which physical evils derive from moral evil (sin)? First and most important, as explained earlier in this chapter, the very introduction of sin into the pristine world by the first couple instilled an element of corruption into the entire cosmos that will remain until the second coming of Jesus. Bodily disease and death, as well as a breakdown in the intended harmony between man and the physical world, are all a part of the cosmic curse (Gen 3:16-19; Rom 5:12-19; 8:18-22). Evil has been unnaturally incorporated into the very fabric of the universe. This is the explanation for most of the individual instances of suffering that occur around us, including birth defects, disease, death, and even natural disasters. They happen because sin has distorted nature, and the sin happened through the free-will decision of our first parents.

Some instances of physical evil have a more immediate connection with moral evil. Sometimes a person's own sins cause him to suffer pain and untimely death. For example, one may contract a sexually transmitted disease through promiscuity, or he may injure or kill himself through reckless violation of traffic laws. But sometimes a person's pain and suffering may be caused by someone else's moral evil. Child abuse, rape, and murder are examples. On rare occasions physical suffering may be caused by satanic or demonic evil (e.g., Job 2:7; Matt 9:32-33; Luke 13:11-16). Finally we should note that God himself may use natural evils as a means of chastising or punishing some people for their sins. The ten plagues upon Egypt are an example, as are the drought and famine God occasionally sent upon his own people (Amos 4:6-8; Hag 1:7-11; see Job 37:13). These occasions for suffering were not just the normal product of God's creation; they were deliberate divine responses to human sin.

Thus we see that evil in both its forms (moral and physical) is the consequence of the free-will choices of men and some angels to commit sin against God. It is not a necessary element of God's creation. But given the existence of free-will beings, it was from the beginning a possibility. As it happened, it was a possibility that became a reality.

It is safe to say that most of the individual instances of evil in the world are not caused by God but are allowed to happen according to his permissive will. This is in keeping with his commitment to the relative independence of his creation, including the relative independence of the natural processes and creaturely free will. This applies to all moral evil, including the first sins in the Garden of Eden. God allows man the integrity of free choice. When evil is chosen, he allows the evil consequences that flow from it to pour out their cup of suffering upon mankind, and does not choose to intervene and prevent it.

Thus in the face of personal calamity and suffering it is probably improper to ask, "Why is God doing this to me?" In all likelihood God himself is not doing it; it is probably the result of somebody's free-will choice, either directly or indirectly. A baby born with a birth defect, for example, may be suffering the direct consequence of his mother's drinking alcohol during her pregnancy. Or the genetic flaw may go back much further, perhaps even to the garbling of nature that occurred with Adam's sin.

In view of the sovereignty of God's permissive will, it is proper to ask, "Why did God *allow* this to happen?" This is so because nothing happens without God's foreknowing it and deciding not to prevent it. To say that God permits something to happen means that he *could* have prevented it if he had chosen to do so, if he had had a good reason for doing so. It is true, then, that God could have prevented this birth defect or that accident or that disease. When a saint of God in the throes of undeserved suffering cries out, "Why is God allowing this to happen?" this is indeed one of the most difficult questions to answer.

Two considerations are relevant. First, we must remember that the possibility of evil is the price of free will. Now that creaturely freedom has made evil a reality, there is no turning back. God cannot overrule every evil choice of man and every evil consequence therefrom without contradicting his own purposes in creating beings with free will. This is part of the price we pay for freedom, and which God himself pays for creating us thus. When a child lies suffering from an incurable illness and his parents stand beside him in grief, do we think that God suffers any less than the child or his parents? Yet God has decided that having creatures with free will is worth the price of suffering, even the suffering of sacrificing his own Son on the cross. If we cannot penetrate the mystery of a particular experience of suffering, at least we can appreciate the fact that God is suffering with us and in his wisdom and goodness has judged the final result to be worth it.

The second thing to remember is that God has promised that all things will work together for good to those who love him and are called in accordance with his purpose (Rom 8:28). Thus even the suffering which he permits can be used for the benefit of those who experience it or for the benefit of those whose lives are touched by it. See Rom 5:3-4; 2 Cor 1:3-6; Jas 1:2-4.

This may be one reason why God does not always answer our prayers for protection and deliverance from evil. Sometimes he does protect and deliver us, of course; so we should never fail to pray for God's special providence in these matters. But sometimes he does not intervene; rather he allows the affliction to occur or to continue. In these cases we must trust that the wisdom of God has discerned a higher good that will come from the affliction. Perhaps we ourselves will observe or experience this higher good; perhaps it will take place without our ever being aware of it. After all, God sees the whole pattern of providence while we see only small parts of it, often just the darker parts. In such cases there is no alternative to trusting the goodness and wisdom of the Sovereign Ruler of the universe.

NOTES ON CHAPTER TWELVE

[1]See Cottrell, *Romans*, I:486-491.

[2]This material is presented in more detail in *GRu*, ch. 11.

CHAPTER THIRTEEN
THE PERSON OF CHRIST

Just who *is* Jesus, exactly? And what exactly has he done in order to save us from our sins? These are the two most basic questions about Jesus, and they refer to the two subjects of the *person* of Christ and the *work* of Christ.

We must understand that these two subjects are intimately related. What is ultimately important to us, of course, is Christ's work. What did he have to accomplish in order to bring us salvation? What does the Bible say he actually did in order to redeem us? These questions are crucial, but they cannot be properly answered without a consideration of the nature of the Redeemer himself. This is true because the scope and the power of the Redeemer's work either will be limited by or will be made possible by who he is. If he is merely a human being, then his saving work will be severely limited to such things as leadership, teaching, example, and persuasion. But if he is also divine, then his saving work can include whatever the infinite power of God is able to accomplish.

In this chapter we shall present the doctrine of the person of Christ, and we shall see that the Bible does indeed teach that Jesus is not only human but divine as well. He is one person with two natures. Then in the next chapter the biblical teaching about the work of Christ will be set forth. The content of these two chapters together constitute the core of Christianity.

I. THE HUMAN NATURE OF JESUS

To anyone who knew him personally during his life on earth, Jesus' most obvious identity would have been that of a human being. He lived as a human male in human society and did most of the things that ordinary human beings do. Indeed, he was "like His brethren in all things" (Heb 2:17).

A. The Biblical Picture of the Man Jesus

The Bible pictures Jesus as having a full and complete human nature. This includes first of all a real, flesh-and-blood human body. Since all of God's earthly children "share in flesh and blood, He Himself likewise also partook of the same" (Heb 2:14). He "was revealed in the flesh" (1 Tim 3:16); "the Word became flesh" (John 1:14; see Heb 10:5). Thus the human Jesus was subject to all the physical needs and infirmities of his human family.

Between his conception and birth Jesus inhabited his mother's womb as any other baby did (Matt 1:18; Luke 2:5). When the time came, he was "born of a woman" (Gal 4:4; see Luke 2:7), being the seed or offspring of Eve the first woman (Gen 3:15), the seed or offspring of Abraham (Gal 3:16), and "a descendant of David according to the flesh" (Rom 1:3; see Matt 1:1). After his birth he had to be cared for as an infant (Luke 2:7,12) and protected from harm (Matt 2:13-15).

As a young child and youth Jesus "continued to grow and become strong" (Luke 2:40) and mature in age and physical stature (Luke 2:52). He was "brought up" (reared and nourished) in Nazareth (Luke 4:16), and was observed by his neighbors as part of the family of Mary and Joseph (Matt 13:54-56). He was known as a young man who earned his living as a carpenter (Mark 6:3).

During the rigors of his earthly ministry Jesus experienced the bodily limitations of any other human being. He got physically tired and weary (John 4:6), and he needed sleep (Matt 8:24; Luke 8:23). His body needed food and drink, and he experienced hunger (Matt 4:2; 21:18) and thirst (John 19:28).

Whether Jesus suffered from any kind of physical diseases we do not know. We do know that his body was subject to pain and death like that of any other human being, and indeed this ability to suffer and die was a vital prerequisite for his saving work (Heb 2:14-15).

Jesus' human nature included not only a body, but also a human soul with all the sinless human feelings and emotions experienced by Adam's race.[1] One of the emotions most frequently attributed to Christ is compassion, which he felt when confronted with the needs and sufferings of others, e.g., hunger (Matt 15:32), sickness (Matt 14:14; 20:34; Mark 1:41), bereavement (Luke 7:13), and helplessness (Mark 6:34).

Jesus also felt love for those around him, including the rich young ruler (Mark 10:21); Mary, Martha, and Lazarus (John 11:5); and the disciple "whom Jesus loved" (John 13:23; 19:26; 21:7,20). He also loved his disciples as a group (John 13:1,34; 15:9-13), and he loves all who love and follow him (John 14:21). His love included not only the objective concern for and desire for others' well-being that is characteristic of *agape* (as in all of the above texts), but also the tender affection and friendship represented by the verb *phileo* (John 11:3,36; 20:2).

At the opposite end of the spectrum of emotions Jesus sometimes felt anger toward circumstances and people that displeased him. Some religious leaders were opposed to his healing a man on the Sabbath day. "After looking around at them with anger [*orge*]," Jesus healed the man anyway (Mark 3:5; see Rev 6:16-17). He was indignant toward those who tried to keep the children from him (Mark 10:14). John reports that at Lazarus' tomb Jesus was "deeply moved" (John 11:33,38). The word used here is *embrimaomai*, which has the sense of snorting with anger and displeasure (AG). Warfield makes a good case that Jesus was here feeling rage and fury against the enemy death that had caused so much sorrow and suffering for his friends ("Emotional Life," 110-117).

Jesus also felt joy (John 15:11; 17:13; Heb 12:2); indeed, "He rejoiced greatly in the Holy Spirit" (Luke 10:21). On the other hand he experienced deep grief and distress. Isaiah 53:3 foretold that he would be "a man of sorrows and acquainted with grief." He was grieved with the sins and infirmities of men (Mark 3:5; 7:34), even to the point of weeping (Luke 19:41 [see 13:34]; John 11:35). His grief was especially strong in the Garden of Gethsemane, where he said, "My soul is deeply grieved, to the point of death" (Matt 26:37-38; Mark 14:34).

No doubt the most intense human feeling Jesus experienced was the anguish and suffering that overwhelmed his soul in the face of the death he was to undergo because of our sins. As he was preparing for this ordeal, in Gethsemane he was "in agony" and "was praying very fervently; and His sweat became like drops of blood, falling down upon the ground" (Luke 22:44; see Heb 5:7). This is included in what Scripture calls his *passion* or sufferings (Luke 22:15; Heb 2:9-10; 5:8; and often).

All of the above emotions are indeed human, and Jesus no doubt felt them in his human soul. But these emotions may also be experienced by God himself, and thus are not absolute indicators of Jesus' humanity. There are two other emotions, though, that would seem to be below the level of divine experience and which are thus true evidence of Jesus' human nature. The first of these is *astonishment*. Jesus "was astonished" at the faith of the centurion who asked him to heal a servant (Matt 8:10, NIV), and he "was amazed" at the unbelief of his old neighbors (Mark 6:6, NIV). The same word (*ekthambeo*) is used in Mark 14:33 to describe the feeling that overwhelmed Jesus at the beginning of his Gethsemane experience: "And he . . . began to be greatly amazed" (ASV). The word is used of men in this sense in Mark 9:15; 16:5-6 (see Acts 3:11).

The other emotion felt by Jesus which can hardly be attributed to God is *dread*. The key word is *tarasso*, which has a gamut of meanings including "to trouble, disturb, terrify, startle, frighten." It is used of Herod (Matt 2:3), Zecharias (Luke 1:12), and the apostles (Matt 14:26; Luke 24:38). It is used in Christ's exhortation, "Do not let your heart be troubled" (John 14:1; see 14:27). Spicq says that when the word is used of individuals it "usually expresses simple uneasiness mixed with fear" (3:374). Three times it is used for Jesus: when he was "troubled" at Lazarus' tomb (John 11:33), when he contemplated his destiny of the cross (John 12:27, "Now My soul has become troubled"), and when he spoke of his betrayal (John 13:21, "He became troubled in spirit"). Spicq says that in these three texts "trembling and dread are envisioned: Jesus was upset" (3:375). This experience of dread, he says, "emphasizes the real humanity of the innocent Christ" (3:376). We should note that this was not a fear of the unknown, but simply a dread of what he knew he had to endure for our sakes. This is the human emotion that led him to cry out in Gethsemane, "My Father, if it is possible, let this cup pass from Me" (Matt 26:39).

Our conclusion is that the Bible pictures Jesus as possessing a human nature in every sense. He had a physical human body and a human soul or spirit just as other human beings do.

B. Jesus and Gender

The NT pictures Jesus not only as a human being, but as a *male* human being. This may seem too obvious to mention, but in view of the claims of many feminists it must be asserted and demonstrated. Feminists in general are distressed at the idea that the Savior of the world would become incarnate as a male, thereby apparently supporting the notion of male headship. Thus they offer numerous ways of counteracting such an argument, including the assertion that Jesus was not actually male but was simply a generic human being. For example, Mollenkott (48) has claimed, "When New Testament writers refer to the incarnation of Jesus, they do not speak of his becoming *aner*, 'male,' but rather of his becoming *anthropos*, 'human'" (see also Spencer, 22). Others declare that Jesus was actually both male *and* female in some significant way, especially in his psychological characteristics. His female side was manifested in such attitudes as compassion, suffering, nurture, tenderness, meekness, patience, humility, delight in children, and weeping (Torjesen, 17; Atkins, 67).

Such claims have no basis in Scripture, however.[2] First of all, the implication that Greek terms for "male" are never used of Jesus in the NT is simply false. He is described as *aner*, "male," in Luke 24:19; John 1:30; Acts 2:22; 17:31; 2 Cor 11:2; and Rev 21:2. The parallel word *arsen*, "male," is used in Luke 2:23 and Rev 12:5,13. A second point is that *anthropos* itself does not always have the generic meaning of "human being." Sometimes it is used to refer to the human race in general (e.g., Mark 10:27; Acts 5:29), but in the NT, when it is used for specific individuals, it *always* refers to males. There are no exceptions. This is why it is sometimes used interchangeably with *aner* (e.g., compare Matt 7:24,26 with Luke 6:48; compare Matt 17:14 with Luke 9:38; compare Acts 15:25 with Acts 15:26). This is also why *anthropos* is sometimes used for males as contrasted with females, as in Matt 10:35; 19:5,10; Luke 22:57-60; 1 Cor 7:1; and Eph 5:31. In the third place, it is completely arbitrary to declare that such characteristics as compassion, patience, humility, weeping, and love for children are "feminine" and are not natural to men as well as women.

The fact that Jesus was a male is affirmed from the beginning of the Bible to its end, from the masculine seed of woman in Gen 3:15 to the bridegroom in Revelation 21. From prophecy to promise to reality, Mary's child was called a *son*, not a daughter (Isa 7:14; Matt 1:21,25; Rev 12:5). He is the *Son* of God (Ps 2:7; Matt 3:17; 17:5; Acts 13:33; Heb 1:5) and the *Son* of Man. He accomplished his messianic work in specifically male roles: Prince (Isa 9:6; Acts 3:15), King (Matt 21:5; John 18:37), high priest (Heb 2:17), and sacrificial lamb (Exod 12:5; 1 Cor 5:7; Lev 16:3,5; Heb 10:1-10). He is the bridegroom to whom we are betrothed

(2 Cor 11:2; Rev 19:7; 21:2,9), the "Son over His house—whose house we are" (Heb 3:6). He reigns from heaven now as "King of kings and Lord of lords" (1 Tim 6:15; Rev 19:11-16).

It is true that Jesus was and is a human being in the very same sense that every man and every woman is a human being; he shares the humanity that we all share together. But this does not nullify the fact that he was a *male* human being. The biblical data show that it was God's intentional plan to redeem the world not just through a human being but through a human being who is male. The Messiah's maleness is not arbitrary or accidental (see Cottrell, *Gender Roles*, 166-169).

C. The Sinlessness of Jesus

Scripture testifies that Christ "has been tempted in all things as we are, yet without sin" (Heb 4:15). This means that he never willed to do anything sinful; he never did or thought anything contrary to divine law. He "committed no sin, nor was any deceit found in His mouth" (1 Pet 2:22). To his enemies he cried out, "Which one of you convicts Me of sin?" (John 8:46; see John 8:29; 15:29). He "knew no sin" (2 Cor 5:21); "in Him there is no sin" (1 John 3:5). He came in real flesh, but only in the "likeness" of *sinful* flesh (Rom 8:3). The phrase "sinful flesh" alludes to the fact that the human body has come under the power of sin, but this did not apply to Christ's body. His body was fully human in the truest sense, but it did not have any of the corruption caused by sin.

Someone may think that the absence of sin somehow means that Christ was less than human, since in fact all human beings do sin (Rom 3:10,23). Indeed, we often use our humanness as an excuse for sin ("I'm only human"; "To err is human"), as if sin were natural and expected from anyone truly human. The implication is that if Jesus were really human, he would have sinned! But this reasoning is seriously flawed. Sin is *not natural* for human beings; God made us as free-will creatures who are *able* to sin, but who are also able *not* to sin and indeed are commanded and expected not to sin. Rather than being a mark of true humanity, sin is a gap in or deviation from true humanness. The fact is that Jesus, just because he is the only one who never participated in sin either in body or spirit, is the only one who has a truly perfect human nature.

A question that often arises concerning Jesus' sinlessness is whether or not it was *possible* for him to sin. This question cannot be answered with certainty. Many assume that he could have sinned since he was truly human; others (including myself) reason that he could not sin since he was truly God. What complicates the issue is that, although he had two natures (human and divine), Jesus was just one person with one center of consciousness and one will. His sinlessness therefore was just as much an accomplishment of his human nature as his divine nature.

Those who aver that Jesus could have sinned use two basic arguments. One, Heb 4:15 says that he was "tempted in all things as we are." If he was not able to sin, then the temptation would not have been real and similar to ours. Two, if he was unable to sin, then his value as an example for our own holy living is negated. What is the use of trying to follow "in his steps" (1 Pet 2:21-22) if his sinless steps were the result of a divine nature that we do not share?

In my judgment, even if Jesus could have sinned, this cannot be established by these two arguments, since they are not conclusive. That Jesus was truly tempted cannot be denied (Matt 4:1-11; Heb 2:18; 4:15), and he surely felt the force of the temptations whether he could have succumbed to them or not. As Joseph Stump says,[3] we can subject pure gold to the most extreme test, all the while knowing it will stand the test because we know it is pure gold. The test is no less real, even if the result is not in doubt.

Likewise, that Jesus' sinless life was in some sense an example for us cannot be denied (Matt 11:29; 16:24; John 13:15; Eph 4:20; Phil 2:5; 1 Pet 2:21-22). But this does not imply that Jesus lived a sinless life just for the purpose of providing us with an example, i.e., just to show us that it could be done. This is in fact a false notion, and is an aspect of the christological fallacy. Jesus did not come for the purpose of showing us how to live a sinless life but to be the sacrifice for our sins. Some aspects of his life, e.g., his attitude of unselfishness (Phil 2:5), do provide us with an example; but the crucial aspects of his life are those things that are unique about him and that we *cannot* imitate, e.g., the incarnation itself (Phil 2:6-7), his atoning death (Phil 2:8), and his efficacious resurrection and victorious enthronement (Phil 2:9-11).

The fact that Jesus' life was an example for us at all is actually incidental to the main purpose of both his incarnation and his sinlessness. In particular, the sinlessness of Jesus' life was necessary so that he could be an acceptable sacrifice for our sins. He was "a lamb unblemished and spotless" (1 Pet 1:19) who "offered Himself without blemish to God" (Heb 9:14). If he had committed even the least sin, he would have been a guilty sinner (Jas 2:10). In such a case he could not *be* our Savior, but would himself *need* a savior.

D. Heretical Views of Jesus' Humanity

That Jesus had a fully human nature has always been the accepted belief of Christendom; any other view has been regarded as heretical. One such heresy is known as *docetism*, which is the teaching that Jesus did not have a real human body. The name itself comes from the Greek word *dokeo*, which means "to seem, to appear to be." Those who taught this view said that Jesus only *appeared* to have a physical body; what others saw as a body was actually a phantom or apparition.

This view was first developed under the influence of the Gnostics, who held to a dualistic view of the universe and declared that all physical matter is evil and can have nothing to do with spirit or with the true God. Thus if Jesus is truly God and truly good, and if he is truly our Savior, he cannot have a physical body, since such a body is inherently evil. This view was already appearing at the end of the first century and seems to be the very falsehood John is condemning in 1 John 4:1-3, where he says that only the spirit of antichrist would deny that "Jesus Christ has come in the flesh." See John 1:14; 1 John 1:1; see also Luke 24:38-39.

Another heretical view of Jesus' humanity is known as Apollinarianism, named for its advocate Apollinaris, a church leader in the mid-fourth century A.D. This is the view that Jesus had a body, to be sure, but he did not have a human soul or mind. Instead, the divine Logos took the place of a human spiritual nature in the person of Jesus. His human nature was limited to the fleshly body; all his psychological, intellectual, volitional, and spiritual activities were experiences of his divine nature alone. In fact, the Logos was so closely joined with Jesus' flesh that it was the source even of the biological life of his body. The Logos and the flesh were so conjoined or fused that the flesh itself became glorified or divinized (see Kelly, 292-294).

The early church as a whole rejected Apollinaris's view, and any view that denied the full humanness of Jesus. They rejected the idea that Jesus' flesh was made divine since this would mean that not even his body was truly human, thus making Apollinarianism little different from docetism. But most significantly they declared that without a complete and genuine human nature, Jesus could not be a true Savior. They properly reasoned that whatever aspect of humanity was not *possessed* by Jesus could not be *redeemed* by Jesus (Kelly, 296-297). As Heb 2:17 says, "He had to be made like His brethren in all things, so that He might become a merciful and faithful high priest in things pertaining to God."

E. The Necessity for Jesus' Full Humanity

This leads us to our final point concerning the human nature of Jesus, namely, the necessary connection between his full humanity and the efficacy of his saving work. If Jesus were not fully human, he could not perform the work necessary to save us from our sins.

One thing that is at stake is the reality of his saving death and resurrection. Only a person with a real human body could sacrifice his life and suffer death (Heb 2:14; 9:22), and then be raised bodily from the dead (see 1 Cor 15:12-19). "For since by a man came death, by a man also came the resurrection of the dead" (1 Cor 15:21).

A second thing that is at stake is the totality of our salvation. As mentioned above, the early Christians rightly perceived that, regarding any aspect of human nature, if Jesus did not assume it, then he did not save it. This applies to the soul or spirit as well as to the body. Our entire being is involved in sin and is corrupted by sin; therefore our entire being is the object of God's salvation. If Jesus saves us by identifying himself with us as sinners, and by taking our place and suffering the consequences of sin for us (2 Cor 5:21), then he must be like us in all respects.

The final reason for the necessity of Christ's full humanity is that his availability as our Mediator depends upon it. The one who stands between us as sinners and the holy God is "the man Christ Jesus" (1 Tim 2:5). His work as high priest, including both his offering himself as the perfect sacrifice (Heb 2:17) and his present mediatorial work (Heb 4:14-16), depends on his having experienced human life on our level (Heb 2:10-18).

II. THE DIVINE NATURE OF JESUS

Jesus was a man with a fully human nature, but he was more. He was also *God* with a fully divine nature. We find this clearly taught in the NT, and we find it also in the OT when we understand the latter in the light of the later revelation of the former.

A. Christ's Deity in the Old Testament

Even before the NT revelation was available, it was still clear from the OT itself that God was promising to send a Messiah or Redeemer, and that the promised Messiah would be divine. When OT prophecy is examined, two distinct yet interrelated strands are found. First, it was foretold that "a Redeemer will come to Zion" (Isa 59:20), i.e., that God will send a Savior to deliver his people. A child will be born to reign from David's throne and restore righteousness to the kingdom (Isa 9:6-7; 11:1-5). One anointed by God will arise to bring freedom, peace, renewal, and prosperity to his people (Isa 61:1-9). From Bethlehem "One will go forth for Me to be ruler in Israel. . . . He will arise and shepherd His flock in the strength of the LORD" (Micah 5:2-4).

Second, the OT foretold that God himself will personally come to save his people. "'Comfort, O comfort My people,' says your God. . . . A voice is calling, 'Clear the way for the LORD in the wilderness; make smooth in the desert a highway for our God'" (Isa 40:1,3; see Isa 60:1-2). "Behold, I am going to send My messenger, and he will clear the way before Me. And the Lord, whom you seek, will suddenly come to His temple . . . ,' says the LORD of hosts" (Mal 3:1). "Let the rivers clap their hands, let the mountains sing together for joy before the LORD, for He is coming to judge the earth; He will judge the world with righteousness and the peoples with equity" (Ps 98:8-9; see Ps 96:10-13).

Even in the OT these two strands are harmonized in the many passages that speak of the coming Messiah in the language of divinity. Psalm 45 pictures the mighty and victorious King who in majesty and splendor rides forth as a bridegroom to receive his bride, and in verse 6 he is specifically addressed as God: "Your throne, O God, is forever and ever" (see Heb 1:8). In addition to addressing him as God, the psalmist indicates that his kingdom or reign is eternal.

Psalm 110 in its entirety describes the Messiah in terms of deity. David, the human author of the Psalm, calls him "my Lord" (v. 1). "The LORD"—Yahweh himself—invites David's Lord to be seated at his own right hand (v. 1). That he is seated at God's right hand means that he fully participates in the majesty and power of God, and that he reigns with God over all his enemies (v. 2). In verse 4 the Messiah-King is also installed for eternity in the office of a priest. In Matt 22:42-45 Jesus uses Ps 110:1 to show that the Messiah's sonship would be divine.

The deity of the coming Messiah is most clearly affirmed in Isa 9:6, "For a child will be born to us, a son will be given to us; and the government will rest on His shoulders; and His name will be called Wonderful Counselor, Mighty God, Eternal Father, Prince of Peace." The name "Wonderful Counselor" underscores the child's divine wisdom: as a counselor, he is a wonder. The Hebrew term for "wonder" in the OT often has divine or supernatural overtones, usually referring to divine miracles or wonders. See Exod 3:20; 15:11; 34:10; Judg 13:18-19; Ps 72:18; 77:11; 78:12. Isaiah 28:29 declares that it is the LORD (Yahweh) who "has made His counsel wonderful and His wisdom great."

Isaiah 9:6 also calls the messianic child "Eternal Father," or "father of eternity," thus ascribing to him both paternity and eternity. To be eternal is in itself a characteristic of deity; to be the *father* of eternity only magnifies this reality.

Most dramatically, Isaiah 9:6 says that the Messiah shall be called "Mighty God." The shortened name for God, *'el*, is here combined with the word *gibbor*, which means "a mighty one, a hero." The latter term is also applied to the Messiah-King in Ps 45:3 ("O Mighty One"). The exact same phrase (*'el gibbor*) is applied to Yahweh in Isa 10:21.[4] Thus the divine nature of the coming Messiah could not be more unambiguously affirmed.

Two texts from Micah should also be noted. In Micah 2:12-13 the Messiah is pictured as a Shepherd and King who will deliver his people from bondage: "So their king goes on before them, and the LORD at their head." The King is thus identified with Yahweh. Also, in Micah 5:1-4 this same Shepherd-King is pictured as coming forth from Bethlehem, but as also having preexisted for eternity before that: "But as for you, Bethlehem Ephrathah, too little to be among the clans of Judah, from you One will go forth for Me to be ruler in Jerusalem. His goings forth are from long ago, from the days of eternity." The concept of eternal preexistence applies only to God.

A final OT prophecy indicating the deity of the Messiah is Mal 3:1. Here Yahweh says first, "'Behold, I am going to send My messenger, and he will clear the way before Me.'" The messenger is identified in the NT as John the Baptist (Matt 11:10; Mark 1:2; Luke 1:76); that his task is to "clear the way *before Me*" indicates that Yahweh himself will come. But then Yahweh's declaration shifts grammatically to the third person: "'And the Lord, whom you seek, will suddenly come to His temple; and the messenger of the covenant, in whom you delight, behold, He is coming,' says the LORD of hosts." In the first sentence the coming one is the speaker (first person, "Me"), who is the "LORD [Yahweh] of hosts." In the second sentence the coming one is "the Lord," *ha-'adon*. The name *'adon* (compare *'ªdonai*) is a common word for "master, lord"; but in the OT when it has the definite article, it refers to God. Thus the coming Lord in the second sentence is God. This conclusion is reinforced by the fact that the temple belongs to him: it is "His temple." This is clear: the Lord who is coming to his temple is Yahweh of hosts.

Thus even without viewing the OT through the interpretative lenses of the NT, we can see that the prophets identified the coming Messiah as God himself.

B. Christ's Deity in the New Testament

The NT does not hesitate to identify Jesus of Nazareth as the prophesied Messiah and to apply to him these and other OT indications of his deity. As B.B. Warfield correctly observes ("Messiah," 104),

> The New Testament proceeds throughout its whole extent on the unchanging supposition that in the coming of Jesus Christ there is fulfilled the repeated Old Testament promise, made in Psalm and Prophet alike, that God is to visit His people, in his own good time, to save them. It is therefore, indeed, so we are told, that He is called Jesus,—precisely because "it is He that shall save His people from their sins."

The NT also adds much testimony of its own to the divine nature of Jesus. This will be summarized below.

1. Jesus Is Given Titles of Deity

First of all, several of the titles ascribed to Jesus in the New Testament imply his deity. Perhaps the most significant of these is the title "Lord" (*kyrios* in Greek), which is used for Jesus almost five hundred times. In its most basic meaning, *kyrios* refers to the owner or possessor of something, to the one who has the rights of ownership and thus who is master of or who exercises control over his property. This meaning also applies to the English word "lord," as in the common term "landlord." This is the sense in which God is "Lord of heaven and earth" (Matt 11:25), and in which it is declared of Jesus: "He is Lord of all" (Acts 10:36). In the ancient Greek and Roman worlds *kyrios* was also used to show respect ("sir"), and was a title of honor as used for royalty ("my lord, your majesty"). In pagan religions it was a title of worship applied to the gods (1 Cor 8:5), and came to be used in a quasireligious sense of the Roman emperors.

Most relevant and most significant, though, is the way the title *kyrios* was used among the Jews. In most extant manuscripts of the Septuagint (the Greek translation of the OT), *kyrios* is the Greek word used around 8,000 times to refer to the God of Israel. Sometimes it translates the Hebrew term *'ᵃdonai* ("Lord" in a literal sense) and *'ᵉlohim* ("God"), but mostly—over 6,000 times—it appears in the place of "Yahweh," the divine name itself.[5] Nearly a thousand times *kyrios* appears in combination with *theos*, "God," in the common expression "the LORD God." It is never used for pagan deities and idols.

The bottom line is this: any Jew who knew his OT in its Septuagint form would have associated this title immediately with the one true God. This is certainly the case with the Apostle Paul and other NT writers, who frequently quote from the Septuagint version of the OT.

It is significant, then, that the NT writers use this title so frequently—in Paul's case, almost exclusively—for Jesus. There is no way that they could have applied this title to Christ in its religious sense without in their minds identifying him with Yahweh. As Wainwright (89) says, "There are indications that Christians consciously transferred the title from God to Christ in such a way as to suggest that Christ was almost identical with God." This is especially true after his resurrection from the dead, as a result of which Thomas addressed him as "my Lord and my God" (John 20:28), God the Father declared him to be "both Lord and Christ" (Acts 2:36), and the whole world will ultimately "confess that Jesus Christ is Lord" (Phil 2:11), indeed, the "Lord of lords" (Rev 17:14; 19:16). The latter is a title used for God (Deut 10:17; 1 Tim 6:15), and surely there can be only one "Lord of lords." Thus when the early Christians confessed "Jesus is Lord" (Rom 10:9; 1 Cor 12:3), they were confessing belief in his deity.

Another title with divine implications is "Son of Man." Though many throughout Christian history have used this title to represent the human nature of Jesus (in tandem with "Son of God" to represent his divine nature), in all probability it points to Jesus' deity. This is said in view of the content usually given to this title in NT times. The apocryphal Book of Enoch applies it to a supernatural, heavenly figure who judges men and angels on the day of judgment. Daniel 7:13-14 depicts the Son of Man as a heavenly figure appearing before the throne of the Ancient of Days. It is probably a prophecy of the risen and glorified Lord Jesus ascending into heaven and about to be seated at the Father's right hand. His deity is suggested by the fact that he receives an eternal kingdom and universal worship. Thus "Son of Man" is a title associated with transcendent, divine glory.

In NT times it would have been difficult for Jews to apply this title to anyone without being aware of this exalted meaning in Dan 7:13-14. Thus it is significant that this is the title Jesus applies most often to himself. When he does so, as Stauffer (108-109) says, he "claims for himself all the heavenly majesty of this Son of Man," since this "is just about the most pretentious piece of self-description that any man in the ancient East could possibly have used!" Vos (*Jesus*, 254) calls this the "greatest and most celestial of all titles." Cullmann (*Christology*, 177) agrees that "the statement 'Jesus is the Son of Man' is primarily an exalted declaration of majesty, not a title of humiliation."

One other title with divine content is "Son of God." In pagan circles this was a common title for deities (Wainwright, 173), but in the OT it was used in a variety of ways. Israel collectively was God's son (Exod 4:22-23; Hos 11:1); angels were "sons of God" (Job 1:6; 2:1), as were Israel's kings (2 Sam 7:14; Ps 89:26-27). The promised Messiah would be the Son of God: "'You are My Son, today I have begotten You'" (Ps 2:7).

In the NT this title is frequently applied to Jesus. At his baptism the Father declared, "'This is My beloved Son, in whom I am well-pleased'" (Matt 3:17; see 17:5). He is the Father's "only begotten Son" (John 3:16; see 1 John 4:8). Peter's famous confession names him as "the Son of the living God" (Matt 16:16). The demons acknowledge him as such: "When the unclean spirits saw Him, they would fall down before Him and shout, 'You are the Son of God!'" (Mark 3:11; see 5:6-7). Jesus was "declared the Son of God with power by the resurrection from the dead" (Rom 1:4).

How, then, shall we understand this title when it is applied to Jesus? Probably the most significant and decisive interpretative factor is the way the Jews themselves in NT times understood this claim. On two occasions when Jesus referred to God as his Father, the Jews accused him of blasphemy and wanted to kill him because he "was calling God His own Father, making Himself equal with God" (John 5:18; see John 10:33,36).

The first incident occurred when Jesus healed a sick man at the pool of Bethesda on a Sabbath day. When the Jewish leaders objected to Jesus' healing on the Sabbath, he responded, "'My Father is working until now, and I Myself am working'" (John 5:17). This is when the leaders decided to kill him because in their minds, when he "was calling God His own Father," he was "making Himself equal with God" (John 5:18). What is most important about this encounter is that in his long response to this charge (John 5:19-47), Jesus never denies it. He never says, "Oh, no! You have misinterpreted me!" In fact, everything he says in his reply actually expands upon and confirms the implication that his claim to divine sonship was a claim to deity itself. This is especially true of John 5:23, where he asserts that the Son deserves equal worship with the Father: ". . . so that all will honor the Son even as they honor the Father. He who does not honor the Son does not honor the Father who sent Him."

The other incident that shows clearly that the Jews in Jesus' time understood the title "Son of God" as a claim to deity is recorded in John 10. In a dispute with the Jewish leaders about his identity, Jesus affirmed his close relationship with "My Father" (John 10:25,29), concluding with the remarkable claim, "I and the Father are one" (John 10:30). This caused the Jews to attempt to stone him to death because, they said, by making such claims Jesus was blaspheming and making himself out to be God (John 10:33). Their key concern again was Jesus' claim to divine sonship. This is seen in Jesus' own summary of their charge against him: you say of me, "'You are blaspheming,' because I said, 'I am the Son of God'" (John 10:36).

Again the crucial point, as in John 5, is that Jesus never denied claiming to be the Son of God; and he never denied that by claiming to be such, he was affirming his own deity. Later, at his trial he was asked, "Are You the Son of God, then?" and his answer was affirmative (Luke 22:70; see Mark 14:61-64; John 19:6-8). Again he was accused of blasphemy and thought worthy of death, as the Jews said to Pilate, "We have a law, and by that law He ought to die because He made Himself out to be the Son of God" (John 19:7). It is apparent from incidents such as these that Jesus' reference to himself as the Son of God was taken to be a claim to deity. Such was the content of this title. As Wainwright (172) says, "Of all the titles which describe Jesus' interaction with God, 'Son of God' is best fitted to express the idea of Jesus' divinity."

Jesus is Lord; Jesus is the Son of Man; Jesus is the Son of God. Each of these titles in its own way testifies to the divine nature of Jesus Christ.

2. Jesus Performed Divine Works

In the NT Jesus is described as performing works that only God has the power or prerogative to do. He is seen first of all as Creator of the universe. Colossians 1:16 says, "For by Him all things were created . . . all things have been created by Him and for Him." John 1:3 says of the Logos who became incarnate in Jesus of Nazareth, "All things came into being by Him; and apart from Him nothing came into being that has come into being." First Corinthians 8:6 and Heb 1:2 tell us the same thing. What is the point of these passages? Nothing less than to identify Jesus as the Creator, as God himself. (See *GC*, 138-139, 184.)

Scripture also attributes the work of providence to Jesus. Colossians 1:17 says that "in Him all things hold together." Hebrews 1:3 says he "upholds all things by the word of His power." Such a work as this, i.e., preserving in existence all that has been created from nothing, is a work of which only the Sovereign Creator is capable. Jesus is thus identified as divine.

Salvation, too, is a divine work; and this work is attributed to Jesus. He is called "Savior" sixteen times in the NT. Of special significance is his authority to forgive sins (Mark 2:10), a claim the Jews equated with blasphemy, for "who can forgive sins but God alone?" (Mark 2:7). Jesus never denied that this was something that only God has the authority to do; he just performed a miracle to show that he had such divine authority.

The works of creation, providence, and salvation are truly the works of God, but they are works in which Jesus shares. This can only mean that he himself is God.

3. Jesus Is Called God

A third line of evidence concerning the deity of Christ is the fact that he is specifically called God in several NT passages. All of these are disputed in one way or another by those who deny Christ's deity, of course, but the best exegesis shows that they refer to Jesus and testify to his divine nature. The first is John 1:1, "In the beginning was the Word [the *Logos*], and the Word was with God, and the Word was God." Each of these clauses affirms the divine nature of the Logos. The first asserts his eternity, since he was already there when everything else had its beginning (see vv. 2-3). The second asserts his eternal coordination with God. He is distinguished from God, yet placed alongside God. The third clause declares his identity or equality with God. Who is this Logos? In verse 14 he is identified with Jesus, thus establishing Jesus' divine nature. Efforts to limit the last clause in John 1:1 to something less than full deity destroy themselves against the requirements of Greek grammar, especially Colwell's Rule.[6]

Another passage is John 20:28, where Thomas, upon seeing the risen Christ for the first time, "said to Him, 'My Lord and my God!'" This would be the most blatant blasphemy if Jesus were not indeed God, and Jesus himself would be guilty of it for not immediately rejecting such ascriptions. But Jesus does not rebuke Thomas; instead he commends all those who would come to share this conviction.

Another passage in the Johannine literature is 1 John 5:20, "And we know that the Son of God has come, and has given us understanding, in order that we might know Him who is true, and we are in Him who is true, in His Son Jesus Christ. This is the true God and eternal life." Who is here being called "true God"? The nearest antecedent to the demonstrative pronoun ("this," *houtos*) is "His Son Jesus Christ," who is also identified as "eternal life" here and in 1 John 1:2. Jesus is the true God.

In Rom 9:5 the Apostle Paul concludes a list of the privileges accorded the Jews with a doxological blessing: "Whose are the fathers, and from whom is the Christ according to the flesh, who is over all, God blessed forever. Amen." Some try to place a period either after "flesh" or after "over all," thus making the doxology a separate statement referring to God the Father rather than to Christ. For example, the TEV translates the verse, "They are descended from the famous Hebrew ancestors; and Christ, as a human being, belongs to their race. May God, who rules over all, be praised forever! Amen." Bruce Metzger (95-112) has shown, however, that such efforts are not justified.

The evidence in fact shows that the last part of Rom 9:5—"who is over all, God blessed forever"—refers back to "the Christ." The word "Christ" is the immediate antecedent that matches the form of the relative pronoun "who." Also, Paul's doxologies of praise in other places never stand alone but are attached to a word in the preceding context (Rom 1:25; 11:36; 2 Cor 11:31; Gal 1:5; 2 Tim 4:18). Also, the reference to Christ's human nature in the first part of the verse calls for a complementary reference to his divine nature. Finally, taking verse 5b as affirming Christ's deity is appropriate in view of the climactic nature of this last and highest privilege bestowed upon Israel (Rom 9:4-5). Thus the translation that appears in most versions (e.g., NASB, NIV, NRSV) is true to the original intention of Paul. Jesus Christ himself is the one who is "God blessed forever."

Other passages referring directly to Jesus as God include Titus 2:13, "Looking for the blessed hope and the appearing of the glory of our great God and Savior, Christ Jesus." That "our great God" and our "Savior, Christ Jesus" are the same is shown by the fact that the possessive pronoun "our" occurs only once. Another such passage is Heb 1:8, "But of the Son He says, 'Your throne, O God, is forever and ever.'" Here Ps 45:6 is being quoted and directly applied to Jesus. Finally, 2 Pet 1:1 refers to "the righteousness of our God and Savior, Jesus Christ."

4. Jesus Is Equal with God

Many other passages do not specifically refer to Jesus as God, but in just as forceful a way ascribe to him full equality with God. In our earlier discussion of the Trinitarian nature of God we pointed out that a number of NT texts link all three persons of the Trinity together in a way that emphasizes their essential equality. These texts include the familiar baptismal instruction in Matt 28:19, "Go therefore and make disciples of all nations, baptizing them in the name of the Father and the Son and the Holy Spirit." It is significant that Jesus does *not* say "in the *names* of," or "in the name of the Father, and in the name of the Son, and in the name of the Holy Spirit." He says rather that we should baptize in the *one name* of Father, Son, and Spirit. In the biblical world a person's name was not just an arbitrary means of identification but was considered to be intrinsically related to the person himself, representing his qualities and his character and his very nature. Thus when Jesus speaks of the *one name* of Father, Son, and Spirit, he is saying that they share the same qualities, the same nature, and the same authority. Other trinitarian texts reinforce this equality among the persons of the Trinity (see p. 72).

Other passages likewise establish Jesus' equality with God. As already noted, John 5:23 is such a passage. Here Jesus himself says that the Father has given all judgment to the Son, "so that all will honor the Son even as they honor the Father." The key phrase is "even as" (*kathos*), which indicates that the Son is to receive equal honor with the Father.

Another passage that should be noted is Gal 1:1, "Paul, an apostle (not sent from men, nor through the agency of man, but through Jesus Christ, and God the Father, who raised Him from the dead)." Here Paul clearly distinguishes Jesus from the category of men and at the same time coordinates him with God the Father as the source of his apostleship. The fact that there is only one preposition makes the coordination even closer.

One of the strongest testimonies to the deity of Christ is Phil 2:6, which says that "although He existed in the form of God," he "did not regard equality with God a thing to be grasped." Speaking of his preincarnate state, Paul says Christ was "in the form of God" (*en morphe theou*). The term *morphe*, translated "form," refers to the sum of those characteristics which make a thing precisely what it is. So here it means the sum of those characteristics which make God *God*. That Christ existed "in the form of God" means that he possessed all the qualities and attributes of deity. This fact is reinforced by the expression "equality with God." This was something Christ did not have to grasp after because it was inalienably his by nature; it was something he did not have to jealously cling to because he could never lose it. (This passage will be discussed more fully below.)

Colossians 2:9 states simply, "For in Him all the fullness of Deity dwells in bodily form." We could not ask for a more clear and straightforward affirmation of Christ's deity. Our Savior in his human nature ("bodily form") has the totality of Godhood dwelling within him as its permanent abode; it is impossible for him to be more divine than he is. Warfield says it means that "everything that enters into Godhead and constitutes it Godhead, dwells in Him" ("Trinity," 47).

Another passage indicating equality between Christ and God the Father is Heb 1:3, which says that "He [the Son] is the radiance of His [the Father's] glory and the exact representation of His nature." David Wells says that these expressions "make an unmistakable assertion of divinity." The latter one especially "has the idea . . . of conveying the exact reality of God." It "does not have the connotation of a pale representation, but such a precise replica that it conveyed the essential nature of the thing."[7] Thus are Father and Son set forth as being fully equal.

Finally we should note how the book of Revelation coordinates the work of the Father and the work of the Lamb in their heavenly glory. The day of judgment is the great day of "their wrath" (6:17). The saved have both the Lamb's name and the Father's name on their foreheads (14:1). God and the Lamb have one throne (22:1,3), and together they are the temple and the light of heaven (21:22-23). Also, eternity is ascribed to each. In 1:8 God the Father says, "I am the Alpha and the Omega, . . . who is and who was and who is to come" (see 1:4; 4:8; 10:6; 15:7; 21:6). But the very same language is also used to describe Jesus. In 22:13 Jesus says, "I am the Alpha and the Omega, the first and the last, the beginning and the end" (see 1:17; 2:8). That the speaker here is Jesus is seen by comparing verse 12 with verse 20; the "Lord Jesus" is the one who is "coming quickly." (See Rev 3:3,11; 16:15; 21:7.) Thus the Father and the Son share the same eternal nature which in the OT is ascribed to God alone (Isa 40:10; 62:11).

5. Jesus Is Worshiped

In view of the abundant data concerning Christ's deity already noted, we should not be surprised to see that he is worshiped along with the Father. Neither men (Acts 10:25-26) nor angels (Rev 19:10; 22:8-9) rightly receive worship. The angel exhorts John to "worship God" (Rev 22:9). When Satan tempted Jesus to worship him, Jesus replied, "You shall worship the Lord your God, and serve Him only" (Matt 4:9-10). Yet we have already seen how Jesus asks us to honor him even as we honor the Father (John 5:23), and how he received the sincere worship of the Apostle Thomas (John 20:28). Philippians 2:10-11 says that those who worship the Son bring glory to the Father. Some believe that 1 Tim 3:16 and Phil 2:6-11 were early Christian hymns honoring Christ. Romans 9:5; 2 Tim 4:18; and 2 Pet 3:18 are doxologies of praise to him.

The book of Revelation pictures the heavenly hosts giving explicit worship to the Lamb (5:8-11). They say, "Worthy is the Lamb that was slain to receive power and riches and wisdom and might and honor and glory and blessing" (5:12). Then follows perhaps the most irrefutable evidence of the deity of Christ in all of Scripture, as "every created thing" (a category in which Christ is *not* included) offers worship to the Father *and the Lamb* identically: "To Him who sits on the throne, and to the Lamb, be blessing and honor and glory and dominion forever and ever" (5:13).

It is significant that this text makes a clear distinction between Jesus and "every created thing." The Bible soundly condemns those who have "worshiped and served the creature rather than the Creator" (Rom 1:25). Yet all created things worship Jesus Christ the Lamb of God. Indeed, when the Father brought the Logos into the world as his firstborn Son, he commanded the angels, "And let all the angels of God worship Him" (Heb 1:6). This shows that Jesus Christ himself cannot be a created being and must be the Creator.

This means that we must be very careful not to interpret Rev 3:14 incorrectly. Here Jesus identifies himself as the "*arche* of God's creation." The word *arche* can mean "beginning" (see NASB), and some who deny Christ's divine nature insist upon this meaning here and interpret it to mean that Jesus was the first being created by God. This is completely false, however. If indeed the word does mean "beginning," it is referring to the *risen* Christ as the beginning or firstborn of the *new* creation, the firstborn from the dead (Rev 1:5; see Rom 8:29; Col 1:18). It could also meaning "beginning" in the sense of "origin" or "first cause."

However, we must note that the Greek word *arche* also means "ruler," i.e., the one who is first in terms of *rank* (see Luke 12:11; Titus 3:1) rather than first in time. As such it is equivalent to *archon* in Rev 1:5, which calls Jesus the "*ruler* of the kings of the earth*.*" Any of these last three interpretations is appropriate, but it is totally inconsistent with the rest of the Bible to interpret *arche* in any way that includes Jesus in the category of creatures.

6. Jesus Is Identified with Yahweh

We have already seen how the title "Lord" relates Jesus with Yahweh of the OT. There are other connections that are even more direct. In a number of instances NT writers apply to Jesus Christ specific OT passages that speak unequivocally of Yahweh. For example, Matt 3:3 says that Isa 40:3 is talking of John the Baptist's ministry as the forerunner of the Messiah: "Make ready the way of the LORD, make His paths straight!" But Isa 40:3 speaks specifically of Yahweh: "Clear the way for the LORD in the wilderness; make smooth in the desert a highway for our God."[8] The same is true of Mal 3:1, where Yahweh says, "Behold, I am going to send My messenger, and he will clear the way before Me." In Matt 11:10, however, the Holy Spirit sees fit to change *Me* to *You*, thus showing that the specific reference is to Jesus: "Behold, I send My messenger ahead of You, who will prepare Your way before You."

Other passages are equally insistent that OT references to Yahweh are speaking of Jesus Christ. Hebrews 1:10-12 quotes Ps 102:25-27 and applies it to our Savior, thus ascribing to him Yahweh's work of creation and attribute of eternality. Joel 2:32 is especially significant: "And it will come about that whoever calls on the name of the LORD will be delivered." The NT quotes this passage on two occasions and refers it to Christ (Acts 2:21,36; Rom 10:9,13). In Isa 8:13-15 Yahweh describes himself as a stumbling stone, and in Isa 28:16 he declares that he will lay in Zion a firmly placed cornerstone. In Rom 8:32-33 Paul quotes from and combines these two texts, and implies that the stumbling stone is Jesus Christ (see also 1 Pet 2:6-8). Similar comparisons can be made between Ps 68:18 and Eph 4:6-8; between Isa 45:23 and Phil 2:10-11 (see Rom 14:11); between Deut 10:17 and Rev 17:14, 19:16; between Ps 34:8 and 1 Pet 2:3; between Isa 8:14 and 1 Pet 2:5-8; and between Ps 24:7-10 and 1 Cor 2:8.

After surveying passages such as these and many others, Kaiser says, "We conclude that Jesus is identified with Yahweh, the God of Israel, in virtually all the strata of the New Testament, early as well as late" (35). This does not mean that Jesus *alone* is Yahweh, but that Yahweh of the OT *includes* Jesus, along with the Father and the Spirit.

This survey has shown that the NT testimony to the divine nature of Jesus is both abundant and varied.

C. Heretical Views of Christ's Deity

From the very beginning of the Christian era it was readily understood that Jesus was more than just an ordinary human being, but it took a couple of centuries for the early Christians to identify the unacceptable ways of explaining his divine nature. Some of these unacceptable ways were declared to be heretical, i.e., they are not just false but false in such a way that they constitute a denial of the true nature of Christ's deity. Those who promote such heresies usually do not deny that Jesus is "divine" in some sense, but they deny that he is divine in the same sense as the Father. Only the Father is considered to be inherently, eternally divine; the Son is divine in some inferior or acquired sense.

1. Adoptionism

The earliest example of such a heresy is adoptionist Christology, also known as dynamic monarchianism. The forerunners of this approach were the Ebionites of the early or mid-second century. They emphasized the human nature of Christ but denied his true divinity. Because of his perfect life, God gave to Jesus a special anointing at his baptism, raising him above ordinary men. Thus "the Christ of the Ebionites may be said to be a religious superman, more glorious . . . than the prophets, perhaps even a kind of angelic being, but no 'metaphysical' eminence in the Biblical sense" (Skard, 37). Christ may have been superior to other men, but he was inferior to the true God.

Those specifically called adoptionists date from near the end of the second century and reached their peak in Paul of Samosata, who died around A.D. 275. Their basic view was that Jesus began as merely a man; but again because of his exemplary life God honored him by adopting him as his own Son, thus bestowing a special measure of power and "divinity" upon him. Since Jesus' baptism was accompanied by some special acts of God, many adoptionists held that this is where he was promoted to sonship. Others placed the event at Christ's resurrection. In either case his deity was not his own by nature but was more or less honorary. In such a system there can never be any equality of essence between the Father and the Son; the Son remains inferior in every way to the Father.

2. Arianism

Another heretical view of the deity of Christ is Arianism, named after its most famous proponent, Arius, who flourished in the early fourth century. The difference between adoptionism and Arianism is that the former has Jesus beginning on a purely human level, while the latter has him beginning as an exalted heavenly being, usually the first being created by the Father.

According to Arius God is so transcendent and so separate from everything else that he needs a mediator or go-between for every relation he has with the world, even to accomplish its creation. Thus he created the Son or Logos as a kind of semidivine being to act as his agent in creating the physical universe. Following his exalted beginning as the very first creature and his exalted work of creating the world, the Logos became incarnate as Jesus of Nazareth and lived such a perfect life that he was honored further by being given the title of Son of God. (This is an adoptionist element in the system.) In fact, it is even proper to call him "God," but not in the same sense as the Father is God, of course.

Thus Jesus is not eternal as God is; he is a creature who had a beginning. The Arians had a slogan: "There was a time when the Son was not." Nor is Jesus equal with the Father in his nature; his essence was created *ex nihilo* (out of nothing) and thus is finite. To be sure, he is second only to God on the scale of being, having a truly supernatural nature far above any other creature. Nevertheless he *is* a *creature*, and his essence can never be the same as that of the Father. In comparing the Father and the Son most Arians used the term *homoiousios*, i.e., having a "similar essence." In this they opposed the orthodox view that Father and Son are *homoousios*, i.e., having the "same essence." In other words, the essential equality of Father and Son is denied. As Skard (117, 119) says, for Arians the Son is merely "an under-god of a lower metaphysical order." The fact is that "this *Logos*-souled super-man of Arianism is neither one thing nor the other. He is not God, nor is He man."

In view of the Bible's teaching concerning the full deity of Christ, it is clear that Arianism is an heretical approach to Christology. This was the decision of the early church, which in the early fourth century took a decisive stand against Arius's *homoiousios* view. The council of Nicaea in A.D. 325 pronounced it heretical, and declared the *homoousios* view, that Christ is of the *same* essence as the Father, to be orthodox or correct. The decision of this council, as given here (from Bettenson, 35), was a major milestone in Christology:

> We believe in one God the Father All-sovereign, maker of all things visible and invisible.
> And in one Lord Jesus Christ, the Son of God, begotten of the Father, only-begotten, that is, of the substance of the Father, God of God, Light of

Light, true God of true God, begotten not made, of one substance [*homoousion*] with the Father, through whom all things were made, things in heaven and things on the earth; who for us men and for our salvation came down and was made flesh, and became man, suffered, and rose on the third day, ascended into the heavens, is coming to judge living and dead.

And in the Holy Spirit.

It should be noted that the Arian heresy is still being taught in modern times, notably by the Jehovah's Witnesses cult. This group teaches that neither the human Jesus nor the preexisting, prehuman Logos was coeternal with God and coequal with God in his essence. The Logos was in fact brought into existence as the very first created being. Prior to becoming Jesus of Nazareth he existed as the archangel Michael, and was "a god," even a "mighty god," but was not equal in any sense with Jehovah God.

3. Liberalism

One other heretical view of the deity of Christ is that held by most modern Liberal theologians. It does not have a name as such, but consists of reducing the divinity of Christ to his *ethical* oneness with the Father's will. All thought of Jesus' metaphysical oneness or oneness of essence with the Father is abandoned. In reality Jesus was a human being who was qualitatively equal with all other human beings in every way; but he was quantitatively different from anyone who had ever lived, in that his understanding of God and his ethical oneness with the character of God were complete. As such he was not only the complete revelation of God, but also what every human being ought to be and theoretically can be, i.e., a perfect human being. His complete revelation of God and his uniquely perfect humanity were what constituted his deity.

A typical example is Henry P. Van Dusen. According to Van Dusen (214), in defining Jesus' oneness with God we must avoid such metaphysical terms as "essence" and "substance" (as in "Christ has the same essence as the Father"). His oneness with God is rather a matter of his thought, will, purpose, goodness, and love. This is the only way God can be incarnate in any human being. And in fact, "God is in some measure incarnate in the life of every man" (215). What makes Jesus different is that God was present in him more completely than in anyone else. In fact, in Jesus God was as fully present as it is possible for him to be present in a human life. But this was not a matter of essence or substance. "The identity of Jesus with God was of outlook, of purpose, of will, of compassion" (216-217).

In and through Jesus' words and acts and attitudes and inmost spirit, the Life of God spoke and acted as fully as the Sovereign of Reality could find expression through a man of Nazareth in the days of the Caesars. His life was the full meeting point of divinity and humanity—an individual soul altogether responsive to and possessed by the Divine Intention for him, God indwelling that soul as fully as is possible in a genuinely human life. That is the meaning of "a perfect human life," the meaning of "the Divinity of Christ." . . . The Divinity of Christ affirms that God was as fully present in Jesus of Nazareth as it is possible for him to be in a genuine human being. (218)

None of these approaches to the deity of Jesus—adoptionism, Arianism, Liberalism—is acceptable. None of them does justice to the biblical teaching that Jesus Christ is God, that he is equal with God, that he is indeed identified with Yahweh, the God of Israel.

D. The Importance of Jesus' Deity

It is crucially important that we understand and accept the biblical teaching about the deity of Jesus Christ. This doctrine is indeed an essential doctrine of Christianity. It is not just an arbitrary fact presented to us to test our faith. It is absolutely necessary for the whole work of redemption.

Periodically we find those among us who suggest that one may have a true saving faith in Jesus without accepting him as being equal with God. As long as someone believes Jesus is the Messiah, they say, why should anything more be required? Do we really have to agree with the Nicene Creed, that Jesus is of the same essence or substance as the Father?

The answer is *yes*, for two reasons. First, Jesus' equality with God is not just a fourth-century interpretation of the New Testament, but is the specific teaching of the Bible itself. Second, one cannot accept Jesus as the Messiah or Christ without also accepting his divine nature. This is seen in Peter's inspired confession that Jesus is both the *Christ* and the *Son of God* (Matt 16:16-17).

Jesus' saviorhood and deity are inseparable. The latter is essential to his being able to do what the New Testament says he has done, both in his atonement and in his resurrection.

1. Deity and Atonement

As we shall see in the following chapter, the essence of the atonement is that Jesus gave himself as a substitute to suffer the penalty for sin in our place. Some challenge this idea on the grounds that it is immoral to punish an innocent person in the place of the guilty one who actually deserves it, even if the former is willing.

This could well be true if the innocent substitute were just an indifferent third party picked at random to suffer the divine Lawgiver's wrath on behalf of the guilty lawbreaker. But this is not the case. Because the Substitute is himself the divine Logos in human form, he is not just an innocent bystander in the matter. He is the eternal Lawgiver and Judge himself, suffering the penalty of his own law.

The point is, as Guillebaud (148) says, that substitutionary atonement "is not defensible apart from a full recognition of the Bible teaching of the Divinity of Christ. For if the Victim is not truly identical with the Judge, then the sacrifice is of a third party, and becomes unjust." Thus Christ's deity is a prerequisite of the saving efficacy of the cross.

Another challenge to the substitutionary atonement is that it is logically impossible for just one person to pay the penalty for all the sins of the whole world. Since the penalty involves physical and eternal death, and since any one person has only *one* life to give, *one* individual could be a substitute for only one other.

We grant this to be true, *if* the substitute is *only* an ordinary human being not qualitatively different from those whose penalty he is bearing. One finite person could not possibly pay the penalty for more than one other finite person.

But here is the essentiality of the *divine* nature of Jesus. He is not just a finite creature. In his divine nature he is the infinite God. When he suffered for our sins, he suffered not just in his physical human body but in this divine nature as well. Such suffering was *infinite* and thus sufficient for all the sins of the whole world. The infinite nature of the divine Savior's suffering was more than equivalent to eternal punishment in hell for every member of the human race.

One other requirement for the atonement was that the substitute had to be sinless. If Jesus had committed even one sin, he himself would have deserved to die and thus would not have qualified as a substitute for us. But he was sinless (2 Cor 5:21; Heb 4:15) and thus was an acceptable substitute. The only way this sinlessness could be guaranteed from the beginning is if he were divine. Since Jesus was God, he could not sin. (Though not everyone agrees with this point, I affirm it without hesitation.)

2. Deity and Resurrection

Others besides Jesus have been raised from the dead. By God's miraculous power any dead person can be renewed to physical life. Jesus did not have to be divine in order to experience resurrection. But his resurrection was much more than this. When he arose from the dead, Jesus was not merely the *recipient* of God's life-giving power; he was its very *source*. The resurrection of Jesus was the unleashing of universal, infinite power.

This power defeated our enemy death, and the one who wielded it against us like a sword, namely, Satan. No mere man could have won this victory, and even Michael the archangel had to call upon God in order to overcome Satan's opposition (Jude 9). But Jesus is more than a man, and more than an angel. He is God enfleshed, the embodiment of all power and authority (Matt 28:18). Thus his victory over Satan and death was never in doubt.

The infinite power that flows from the risen Christ is able to redeem the universe itself, including our own mortal bodies (Rom 8:18-23). This is not merely a restoration of the old, original order of things, but an advance to a new and eternal and glorified state. Such an act of redemption is a combination of resurrection and creation—the two masterworks in the repertoire of divine omnipotence (Rom 4:17). It is the work of deity, the work of God's Son, Jesus.

In conclusion, we agree with Robert Gromacki: "Only if Jesus was God could He rightfully be called the object of saving faith" (31). Without his deity, there is no gospel of salvation, and there is no such thing as Christianity in its original and true sense.

III. THE INCARNATION

The Bible portrays Jesus as fully human and fully divine. How is this possible? How did such a being come into existence? This happened when the eternally preexisting Logos, the second person of the Trinity, entered into or was united with the human person Jesus of Nazareth in connection with the latter's miraculous conception in Mary's womb. This event is called the *incarnation* (the enfleshment, the embodiment).

A. The Eternal Preexistence of Jesus' Divine Nature

On the one hand, the human nature of Jesus—in fact, the very person known as Jesus of Nazareth—had a beginning. Strictly speaking, Jesus the Christ did not exist prior to his virginal conception. But on the other hand, the divine nature of Jesus did not have a beginning; it is in fact eternal. As the Logos or second person of the Trinity, he has existed forever. This is usually called the *preexistence of Jesus Christ*, even though the quality of preexistence applies only to the divine being who *became* Jesus Christ.

On many occasions Jesus declared or implied that he existed before he came into this world. He said that he "came down out of heaven" (John 6:41; see 3:31; 6:38) or "descended from heaven" (John 3:13), and he spoke of being sent by the Father (John 8:16; see Matt 15:24; John 3:34). "I came forth from the Father and have come into the world" (John 16:28). John the Baptist, who in fact was conceived about six months prior to Jesus' miraculous conception (Luke 1:24-36), declared that Jesus existed before him (John 1:15,30).

Not only did Jesus exist prior to his birth; he existed prior to the creation of the world. Jesus speaks of existing in glory with the Father "before the world was" (John 17:5; see v. 24). Jesus is described as having existed "from the beginning" (1 John 1:1; Heb. 1:10). Indeed, Jesus himself (specifically, the Logos) was active in the very creation of the world (John 1:3; 1 Cor 8:6; Col 1:16; Heb 1:2,10).

To say that Jesus Christ was preexistent does not in itself imply that he was divine. Even the Arians' Jesus existed prior to his incarnation and prior to the world since he was the first being created by the Father. The only kind of preexistence that is consistent with true deity is *eternal* preexistence, and Scripture does in fact attribute eternal preexistence to Jesus (as the Logos).

In John 1:1-2 the Logos who became Jesus Christ is described as having been "in the beginning with God." In whatever sense God was "in the beginning," so also was the Logos. Then John 1:3 says, "All things came into being through Him, and apart from Him nothing came into being that has come into being." Here the Logos not only is named as the Creator of all things, but is carefully distinguished from the category of things that have themselves been created or have "come into being" (see also Rev 5:13). The Logos himself is uncreated, beginningless, eternal. Similarly Col 1:17 says that God the Son "is before all things," i.e., he exists (present tense) prior to all created things. George Lawlor (39) says,

> The One through whom everything was called into existence necessarily existed before all else was created. Prior to this creative work, Christ filled all the unmeasured periods of an unbeginning eternity. He preexisted all matter and material things. Everything is posterior to Him. All created things celebrate a point of origin. Christ does not, in terms of His divine existence.

In a remarkable testimony to his eternal preexistence Jesus said, "Before Abraham was born, I am" (John 8:58). Jesus is obviously claiming that he existed *before* Abraham was born, but the language he uses implies more. The word used for Abraham (*ginomai*) refers to his coming into existence as a past event; but the word Jesus used for himself was the simple word "to be" in an emphatic present tense, *ego eimi*, "I am." Such a use of the present tense implies that even prior to Abraham he was existing in an eternal, continuing existence. In other words, Abraham had a beginning, but Jesus did not. Also, the use of the present tense where we would have expected the past tense seems to be a deliberate echo of the divine name in Exod 3:14.

Other texts basically affirm the eternality of Jesus. Micah 5:2 prophesies of the Messiah, "His goings forth are from long ago, from the days of eternity." He is "Eternal Father" (Isa 9:6). Hebrews 1:10-12 applies Ps 102:25-27 to Jesus, and thus attributes eternal immutability to him: "You are the same" (Heb 1:12). "Jesus Christ is the same yesterday and today and forever" (Heb 13:8). Jesus declares, "I am the Alpha and the Omega, the first and the last, the beginning and the end" (Rev 22:13).

The eternal preexistence of Jesus Christ in the person of the divine Logos is consistent with the OT "angel of Yahweh" phenomena (Lawlor, 42-44), and with the NT's application of OT statements about Yahweh to Jesus.

B. "The Word Became Flesh"

According to the divine plan of salvation, in the fullness of time "God sent forth His Son," the second person of the Trinity, to be "born of a woman" (Gal 4:4). The eternally preexistent Logos entered into this spatial, material universe by becoming united with the newly conceived male infant miraculously formed in Mary's womb. In other words, "The Word became flesh" (John 1:14). This does not mean that he became something different and thus was no longer the same divine essence that he had been for eternity. His divine essence did not undergo a process of transformation in any way. He *became* flesh by being in some mysterious way identified with a human being made of flesh and blood (Heb 2:14).

The passage that gives us the most information about this incarnation event is Phil 2:5-8:

> Have this attitude in yourselves which was also in Christ Jesus, who, although He existed in the form of God, did not regard equality with God a thing to be grasped, but emptied Himself, taking the form of a bond-servant, and being made in the likeness of men. Being found in appearance as a man, He humbled Himself by becoming obedient to the point of death, even death on a cross.

This text affirms the preexistence of Christ, declaring that he was already existing before he became a man. It also forcefully affirms that in this preexistent, prehuman state he was fully divine.

In Phil 2:6 two phrases are applied to the preexistent Christ: "in the form of God" and "equality with God." The word for "form" is *morphe*. Sometimes in English we use the word "form" to represent the outward, nonessential, changeable aspects of something, as opposed to its essence or content. But that is definitely not the connotation of *morphe*. This Greek word actually refers to the intrinsic, essential nature of a thing, its unchanging essence. It refers to the sum of those characteristics that make a thing precisely what it is. Thus that Jesus existed in the *morphe* of God means that in his prehuman state he possessed all the attributes of deity, all the intrinsic characteristics that make God *God*. The other expression is parallel to this: he existed in a state of "equality with God." This phrase "expresses the God-equal existence of our Lord Jesus Christ in His prehuman state, and He has this condition of existence because He is very God from all eternity" (Lawlor, 61). His deity is complete.

Paul's main point in this text has to do with the Logos's preincarnate state of mind or attitude toward his equality with God, an attitude we are exhorted to emulate (v. 5). Exactly what was this attitude? He "did not regard equality with God a thing to be grasped." "A thing to be grasped" translates *harpagmos*, which occurs only here in the NT. It is from the verb *harpadzo*, meaning "to steal, to seize, to snatch up, to take away forcefully." This is why the KJV says he "thought it not robbery to be equal with God." But robbery is not the point. Here the noun refers to an act of grasping or clutching. Thus it could mean that the Logos did not consider his equality with God a thing to be grasped after, since it was already his by nature. The contextual emphasis on the attitude of the Logos suggests another meaning, though. That is, he did not consider his status of equality with God as something to be selfishly guarded or clutched or clung to, but he was willing to set it aside in some sense in order to accomplish salvation for lost mankind. Herein lies his exemplary unselfishness.

As a result of his unselfish attitude, the Logos "emptied Himself" (v. 7). The verb here is *kenoo*, which means "to empty, to make void." This is related to the noun *kenosis*, which, though not found in the NT, is usually used in discussion of this verse. What does it mean to say that the Logos "emptied Himself"? One major approach, represented especially by 19th-century kenosis theology or kenotic theology, is that in the incarnation the Logos emptied himself of some or all of his divine attributes. He "laid aside his deity," or at least divested himself of certain metaphysical attributes such as omniscience, omnipresence, and omnipotence. As the TEV translates it, "He gave up all he had."[9] The result is that the incarnate Logos is less than fully God. Such a view is, of course, impossible because it requires the rejection of certain basic attributes of God, especially his unity of simplicity and his immutability (see *GC* 35-37). It also contradicts Heb 13:8, as well as Col 2:9. The latter says that in Christ Jesus "all the fullness of Deity dwells in bodily form." Lawlor rightly says (89),

> Thus it is impossible for Christ to cease to be God, to divest Himself of any or all of His attributes, to empty out of Himself His essential nature, or even to exchange it for another, at any time. The self-emptying must conform with this fact; hence, it does not, cannot, teach that our Lord surrendered, laid aside, exchanged, emptied out, or divested Himself of His deity or of any part of it.

What, then, does it mean to say that the Logos "emptied Himself"? Basically it has to do with function, not essence. Though the Logos continued to be equal with God in his nature, as the incarnate Son of God he voluntarily laid aside the prerogatives, privileges, and advantages of deity and chose instead to experience the limitations of human life, even in the role of a servant. He did not selfishly insist on his "rights" as a divine being. He did not cling to the glories and luxuries of his divine status. Instead the unselfish Prince volunteered to live as a pauper (2 Cor 8:9). As Lawlor puts it, he did not give up "the possession of the divine attributes, nor entirely their use, but rather the independent exercise of those attributes" (85). As the KJV says, he "made himself of no reputation." He "made himself nothing" (NIV).

How did he do this? Not by *subtracting* something from his divine nature, but by *adding* something to it, i.e., by "taking the form of a bond-servant, and being made in the likeness of men" (v. 7). He added to it not just the full human nature of Jesus of Nazareth, but also the subordinate role of a servant who was unselfishly willing to go to his death on the cross for our salvation (v. 8). As Lawlor says, "Our Lord Jesus Christ, in becoming man, entered into the experience of human limitation, human weakness and impoverishment, human dependence, and human subjection. This was in singular contrast with the glory and plenitude He possessed in the form of God" (82). But through all of this, "He did not thrust aside and renounce his Godhead"; "He never ceased to be God" (80, 82).

What sort of being, then, resulted from the incarnation? The orthodox way of summing it up is this: Jesus of Nazareth was *one person* with *two natures* (compare the Trinity, which is *three persons* with *one nature*); i.e., he has two complete natures: a complete human nature and a complete divine nature. At the same time he has only one center of consciousness, one unified center of thinking, willing, and emotional experience.

It is important that we not think of Christ as somehow being two persons with two wills and two centers of consciousness, one human and one divine, with one or the other dominating as the circumstances may require. This view is called *Nestorianism* and was condemned as a heresy in the fifth century A.D. It is equally important that we not merge or mingle the divine and human natures of Christ into one composite nature. When this is attempted, one or both natures are usually diminished. An example is the heresy called *Eutychianism*, in which Christ's humanity is so absorbed into his deity that the former is nearly lost. Another example is Lutheran Christology, in which all the attributes of deity are said to apply to Christ's human nature as well.

Christians struggled with these issues for centuries before they came to a consensus about the person of Christ. It was summed up in the conclusions of the Council of Chalcedon in 451 A.D.:[10]

> Following, then, the holy fathers, we unite in teaching all men to confess the one and only Son, our Lord Jesus Christ. This selfsame one is perfect [*teleion*] both in deity [*theoteti*] and also in humanness [*anthropoteti*]; this selfsame one is also actually [*alethos*] God and actually man, with a rational soul [*psyches logikes*] and a body. He is of the same reality as God [*homoousion to patri*] as far as his deity is concerned and of the same reality as we are ourselves [*homoousion hemin*] as far as his humanness is concerned; thus like us in all respects, sin only excepted. Before time began [*pro aionon*] he was begotten of the Father, in respect of his deity, and now in these "last days," for us and on behalf of our salvation, this selfsame one was born of Mary the virgin, who is God-bearer [*theotokos*] in respect of his humanness [*anthropoteta*].
>
> [We also teach] that we apprehend [*gnoridzomenon*] this one and only Christ—Son, Lord, only-begotten—in two natures [*duo physesin*]; [and we do this] without confusing the two natures [*asynkytos*], without transmuting one nature into the other [*atreptos*], without dividing them into two separate categories [*adiairetos*], without contrasting them according to area or function [*achoristos*]. The distinctiveness of each nature is not nullified by the union. Instead, the "properties" [*idiotetos*] of each nature are conserved and both natures concur [*syntrechouses*] in one "person" [*prosopon*] and in one *hypostasis*. They are not divided or cut into two *prosopa*, but are together the one and only and only-begotten Logos of God, the Lord Jesus Christ. Thus have the prophets of old testified; thus the Lord Jesus Christ himself taught us; thus the Symbol of the Fathers [N] has handed down [*paradedoke*] to us.

C. The Virgin Birth of Christ

We have presented the preexistence and the incarnation of Christ. We are now ready to discuss the miraculous event during which the preexistent Logos became flesh in Jesus of Nazareth, namely, the event called the "virgin birth." This event is closely related to the deity of Christ and cannot be understood apart from it.

The title of Gromacki's book correctly reflects this connection: *The Virgin Birth: Doctrine of Deity*. Gromacki says, "If the Biblical presentation of the person of Jesus Christ is correct, then He must have been God. Once this is accepted, it is only logical to assert that His entrance into the world must have been supernatural. There was only one means that could properly provide the channel for His incarnation: THE VIRGIN BIRTH" (68). Thus "to confess the virgin birth is to confess the deity of Christ; to confess the deity of Christ is to confess the virgin birth" (189).

Other births recorded in the Bible were supernaturally caused in the sense that one or both parents were barren or beyond the age of natural childbearing. This includes Isaac (Gen 18:9-14), Samuel (1 Sam 1:1-20), and John the Baptist (Luke 1:5-25). But these births were all different from the birth of Jesus in that they involved two human parents and produced ordinary human children. The virgin birth of Jesus was unique in that it involved only one human parent and produced an offspring who was both fully human and fully divine.

The virgin birth of Jesus was foretold in Isa 7:14: "Behold, a virgin will be with child and bear a son, and she will call His name Immanuel." Matthew records the virgin birth of Jesus from Joseph's perspective, declaring that it is the fulfillment of Isa 7:14 (Matt 1:18-25). Luke records it from Mary's perspective (Luke 1:26-35). Paul does not specifically mention the virgin birth; but whenever he refers to the birth of Jesus (Rom 1:3; Gal 4:4; Phil 2:7), he uses the Greek word *ginomai* ("become, come into being") and avoids the word *gennao*, the common term for "be born" which has the connotation of paternal begetting.

1. Explanation of the Virgin Birth

The virgin birth is a unique event that will always be shrouded in mystery. While we cannot explain the mechanics of this miracle, we can understand some general facets of it in light of biblical teaching.

First, it was not a natural event and has no resemblance to any kind of natural birth, human or animal. In some lower species of animals, unfertilized female eggs normally develop into males or females of the species. This is called "parthenogenesis": virgin birth. Through artificial stimulation eggs from some other species, including mammalian, have been induced to develop into normal animals. In mammals, however, because of chromosomal distribution, the offspring are always female. There simply are no natural parallels to and no natural explanations for the virgin birth of Christ.

Second, the conception of Jesus was not the result of some corporal sexual coupling between Mary and a bodily Deity. Greek mythology sometimes portrays Olympian deities mating with human beings in this fashion. Mormon theology, which portrays God as having a humanlike body, explains Jesus' conception thus.[11] Contrary to all such notions, the virgin birth of Jesus was not a sexual event in any sense in reference to its cause.

Third, the virgin birth was not just the *ex nihilo* creation of the person Jesus, who was simply housed within and nourished by Mary's womb. The human nature of Jesus began as an ovum produced by Mary. He was literally Mary's offspring or "seed." Otherwise he would not really be a part of the human race and would not be physically descended from Eve (Gen 3:15), from Abraham (Gen 22:18; Gal 3:16), and from David (2 Sam 7:12; Rom 1:3).

Fourth, the supernatural act of God that brought Jesus into the world was not at his birth as such but at his conception. Thus we could more precisely speak of his "virgin conception." This was the point of time when the new and specific person known as Jesus first came into being, and Mary's ovum began to grow.

This is comparable in a way to the beginning of other human persons. Each of us began our new existence as the result of the union of two preexisting entities: our father's sperm and our mother's ovum. But in the case of Jesus there was no paternal sperm. The two preexisting entities that came together to initiate his existence were Mary's ovum and the eternal, personal, divine Logos (John 1:1-3). At the appointed time the preexisting Logos entered into some unexplainable union with the ovum. At this point, through the power of the Holy Spirit (Matt 1:20; Luke 1:35), a new and unique individual came into existence, as the divine person of the Logos was incorporated into the fully human personhood of the nanoseconds-old Jesus.

Fifth, from the point of conception onward, the unique person Jesus continued to develop in Mary's womb in a natural way until the time of birth, under the providential protection of the Father. The birth itself occurred in a natural way, except of course that Mary was still a virgin when the birth occurred.

Sixth, it is obvious that Jesus had only one earthly parent: his mother, Mary. Joseph was his father only in a legal sense (see Luke 2:27,41; 4:22) and was his official guardian. Matthew's genealogy of Jesus (1:1-17) is probably that of Joseph, while Luke's (3:23-38) is probably Mary's. (See Gromacki, ch. 17.)

2. Significance of the Virgin Birth

What is the rationale for the virgin birth of Christ? Why did the Savior come into the world in this fashion? Why was it necessary?

It should be obvious that the doctrine of the virgin birth is not a doctrine about Mary but about Jesus. Mary's submissive obedience is highly commendable and her privilege unmatched, but she is not the focal point of this event.

It should be stressed, too, that the virgin birth was not essential as a mechanism for preserving Jesus from "original sin," though many have tried to give it this significance. As James Taylor (282) put it, because of his miraculous conception, "this Child of Mary's womb does not stand in the fallen sequence of Adam, sharing mankind's guilt and sin," or "man's foul taint."

There is no basis for this idea, however. Some (including myself) reject it because they see no biblical evidence for a concept of original sin in the first place.

But even if there were some sort of inherited "taint," God could have miraculously preserved Jesus from it without the necessity of a virgin conception as such.

The only real significance of the virgin birth lies in its necessary relation to the deity of Jesus. To perform the great saving works of atonement and resurrection, the Redeemer must be a sinless human being who is also God. The virgin birth is the means by which such a person has come into being.

The virgin birth is a means, not an end. Its main point is not the birth itself, but the divine nature of the one born thereby. As the angel announced to Mary, "The holy Child shall be called the Son of God" (Luke 1:35). Because he is virgin born through the power of the Holy Spirit, his name is Immanuel: "God with us" (Isa. 7:14; Matt 1:23). The virgin birth is thus the means by which the divine Savior was born, and it is the guarantee to us of his deity.

IV. CHRIST'S RELATION TO THE FATHER

Our final topic for the biblical doctrine of the person of Christ is the relation between Jesus Christ and God the Father. Some of these points were touched on briefly in the section on the Trinity in a previous chapter, but here we present them a bit more fully and from the christological perspective. There are three main points: Christ is equal to the Father in essence, he is distinct from the Father as a person, and he is subordinate to the Father in his incarnate state.

A. Christ Is Equal to the Father

That Christ is equal to the Father in essence and power and glory has been fully established in our earlier discussion of his divine nature. He participates in the same divine works as the Father (creation, providence, redemption); he is worshiped alongside the Father and in the same way as the Father is worshiped; and NT writers identify him with Yahweh of the OT. In several Trinitarian passages he is given equal prominence with the Father and the Holy Spirit.

How can a man—Jesus of Nazareth—possibly be considered equal with God, on an equal par with the Creator, Sustainer, and Redeemer of the universe? Because he is not only a man, but also the eternal, divine Logos incarnate.

B. Christ Is Distinct from the Father

Jesus Christ is not only equal with the Father; he is also distinct from the Father in that he is a separate, distinct person, i.e., a separate center of consciousness with his own distinct thoughts, emotions, and actions. This point seems more than obvious to most Christians; but occasionally, in a misguided effort to explain the Trinity, some have embraced a seriously false view called modalism.[12] From its earliest known forms in the late second century, modalism seems to have been a serious attempt to account for God's threeness while emphasizing his oneness. Thus it may be called a particular view of the Trinity, albeit an heretical one.

H.O.J. Brown (99) says that this is "the most common theological error among people who think themselves orthodox," mainly because "it is the simplest way to explain the Trinity while preserving the oneness of God." But, as Brown says, "unfortunately, it is incorrect."

Modalism is basically the view that in his inner nature there are no distinctions within God, threefold or otherwise. However, in his external relationships with his creatures, God assumes different modes in which to make himself known and accomplish his purposes among men. In its original form the contention was that in the Old Testament era God revealed himself as Father; then he became incarnate as the Son; finally, after Jesus' ascension, God relates to his creatures as the Holy Spirit. Thus these modes of relationship are successive, not simultaneous. It should be noted that viewing the Trinity this way allows one to say that Jesus as God the Son was fully divine, and that the Holy Spirit is also divine. The problem is that the Father, Son, and Spirit are not really distinguished from one another. In their true being they are one and the same person, a person who assumes different modes in his outward relationships to his creatures. God the Father *is* God the Son, who also *is* God the Holy Spirit.

The best known early modalist was Sabellius in the early third century; thus the view is sometimes called Sabellianism. In more recent times varying versions of this view are found mainly in modernistic religion, but also in certain conservative circles such as Oneness Pentecostalism (see *GRe*, 141-142). Modalism also appears from time to time within the Restoration Movement (see *GRe*, 143).

All forms of modalism must be rejected as seriously false doctrine. This view simply cannot do hermeneutical justice to the many, many passages of Scripture which speak of Father, Son, and Spirit together, not only alongside each other but interacting with one another. Sometimes all three persons are described together, and sometimes just two of them, but the implication is the same: the relationship or interaction is real and not just a charade. Luke 1:35 is an example: "The angel answered and said to her, 'The Holy Spirit will come upon you, and the power of the Most High will overshadow you; and for that reason the holy Child shall be called the Son of God.'" The most natural explanation is that both the Father (Most High) and the Spirit were involved in the incarnation of the Son. Another example is the baptism of Christ, where Father, Son, and Spirit are described as simultaneously being involved in different ways: "And the Holy Spirit descended upon Him in bodily form like a dove, and a voice came out of heaven, 'You are My beloved Son, in You I am well-pleased'" (Luke 3:22). Here the Father speaks to the Son in direct address. If this is not one person speaking to another, then the narrative or even the act itself is deceptive. The same applies to the many occasions when Jesus addressed the Father in prayer (e.g., Luke 22:42; 23:34; John 11:41-42; 17:1-26). Jesus' teaching concerning the coming of the Holy Spirit in John 14–16 is a welter of double-talk if Father, Son, and Spirit are not distinct. For example, Jesus said, "I will ask the Father, and He will give you another Helper" (John 14:16; see also John 14:26; 15:26). The same applies to the record of the fulfillment of this promise in Acts 2; see especially 2:33.

Many other passages are robbed of their natural meaning by modalistic presuppositions. The following examples will suffice: "Therefore, when He comes into the world, He says, . . . 'Behold, I have come . . . to do Your will, O God'" (Heb 10:5,7). "I will surely tell of the decree of the LORD: He said to Me, 'You are My Son, today I have begotten You'" (Ps 2:7). "The LORD says to my Lord: 'Sit at My right hand, until I make Your enemies a footstool for Your feet'" (Ps 110:1). "But of that day or hour no one knows, not even the angels in heaven, nor the Son, but the Father alone" (Mark 13:32). "And the Word was with God" (John 1:1). "For God so loved the world, that He gave His only begotten Son" (John 3:16). "God has sent forth the Spirit of His Son into our hearts" (Gal 4:6). "I also overcame and sat down with My Father on His throne" (Rev 3:21). "Salvation to our God who sits on the throne, and to the Lamb" (Rev 7:10).

Many other passages could be cited, but these are enough to show that Father, Son, and Spirit are distinct persons who exist simultaneously and interact with one another.

H.O.J. Brown points out that modalism not only leaves us with hermeneutical chaos, but also raises serious doubts about the reality of the works of redemption themselves. "Logically," he says, "modalism makes the events of redemptive history a kind of charade. Not being a distinct person, the Son cannot really represent us to the Father" (99). He is thinking of the reality of the substitutionary atonement, where the Father "made Him who knew no sin to be sin on our behalf" (2 Cor 5:21), where God set Jesus forth publicly "as a propitiation" (Rom. 3:24-25; see also Isa 53:6,10). He is thinking of the reality of Christ's role as a mediator between us and the Father (1 Tim 2:5-6), as our intercessor with the Father (Heb 7:25; see 1 John 2:1). Brown is surely correct: these vital works of redemption lose all their meaning in a modalistic view of Christ's relation to the Father.

C. Christ Is Subordinate to the Father

The key to understanding Christ's subordination to the Father is to distinguish his prehuman existence as the divine Logos from his incarnate state as the God-man.[13] There has been confusion on this issue almost from the beginning of Christian history.

An early assumption was that the basic clue for understanding how the Father and the Son are eternally related lies in these very names themselves, *Father* and *Son*. The natural relationship between a father and a son is that of begetting, i.e., "His only begotten Son" (John 3:16). It has been asserted since Origen that the eternal, intratrinitarian relationship between Father and Son is that of *begetting*. Even though no one understands the content of this term when applied to the Trinity, its use has been considered vital as a way of refuting the Arian contention that the Son was created or made by the Father. If the Son is created (as Arius said), then his essence is inferior to that of the Father. But something that is begotten is of the same essence (*homoousios*) as the begetter. Hence the creed says, specifically in opposition to Arius, "begotten not made." Thus the unique property of the Father, in eternal distinction from the Son and Spirit, is that he is the one who begets or generates but is not himself begotten. And the unique property of the Son, in eternal distinction from the Father and the Spirit, is that he is generate or begotten.[14]

Though this has been the accepted way of explaining the Father-Son relationship since the fourth century, we must seriously ask whether it is justified by Scripture. In my judgment it is altogether doubtful whether the Bible ever intended the concept of begetting to apply to the eternal relationship between the Father and the Son. For example, the NT applies Ps 2:7 ("You are My Son, today I have begotten You") to the resurrection (Acts 13:33), when Jesus became the firstborn from the dead (Col 1:18). The term might well apply to the incarnation (Luke 1:35), as might the term *monogenes* ("only begotten"). It is almost certain that the "proceeding" of the Spirit in John 15:26 refers to Pentecost and not some supposed eternal relationship. Thus I would agree with Buswell, who proposes that we "completely drop the doctrine of the eternal generation of the Son" as well as the idea of the eternal procession of the Spirit (I:110-112, 119-120). This idea is all the more attractive in view of the fact that these terms were never understood in their ordinary senses; in fact, they were never given any content whatsoever. They have served as empty code words which we do not need as a support for the concept of the ontological Trinity and the reality of Christ's full deity.

What, then, of the very concept of the *eternal sonship* of Christ? Is the Father-Son relationship ontological and eternal, even if the concept of generation is not? The eternal sonship of Jesus has long been a traditional Christian doctrine, and some are convinced that it is essential to orthodoxy. This is not really the case, however. Not everyone otherwise orthodox in his theism has accepted it. Alexander Campbell, for example, taught that Christ was preexistent as the Logos, but his sonship began with the incarnation. "While, then, the phrase 'Son of God' denotes a temporal relation, the phrase 'the Word of God' denotes an eternal, unoriginated relation. There was *a word of God* from eternity, but the Son of God began to be in the days of Augustus Caesar." The entire "*relation* of Father, Son, and Holy Spirit began to be" when the Christian system began (*System*, 9-10).

I support this view; and I do not see any issue of orthodoxy at stake here, since nothing seems to be lost by limiting the Father-Son relationship to Christ's incarnate state nor gained by extending it into eternity past. Especially I would argue that Christ's deity and equality with God do not depend upon an eternal sonship relation. Extracting deity from eternal sonship is an inference anyway, and there are surely enough explicit references to Christ's deity in the Bible to make this truth independent of this doubtful doctrine.

This leads to the issue of the *subordination* of the Son to the Father. Without doubt the Bible speaks of such subordinationism. "The Father is greater than I," says Jesus (John 14:28). Christ is the Father's servant (Isa 52:13; 53:11; Matt 20:28; Phil 2:7); he came to do the Father's will: "Yet not as I will, but as You will" (Matt 26:39; see 26:42). "I do not seek my own will, but the will of Him who sent Me" (John 5:30; see 4:34; 6:38). "Behold, I have come . . . to do Your will, O God" (Heb 10:7). "God is the head of Christ," says Paul (1 Cor 11:3). "Christ belongs to God," says 1 Cor 3:23. How shall we explain such passages? The question is whether they imply an *eternal* subordination of the Son to the Father, or whether they apply only to the relation between the incarnate Logos and the Father.

Many Christians from the earliest times have applied this relationship of subordination to the persons of the Trinity in their eternal nature. That is, even before the Logos became incarnate as Jesus of Nazareth, he was subordinate to God the Father even though the two were equal in essence. Thus a relationship of authority and submission, a chain of command, is present within the Trinity by nature. This conclusion is drawn not only from the passages just listed, but also from the concepts of eternal generation and eternal sonship as discussed above. If the Son is eternally begotten by the Father, then his very existence in some way depends on the Father. The concept of subordination seems to be a natural corollary.

In my judgment, though, this is not correct. The very concepts of eternal generation and eternal sonship are very questionable, as already shown. But what of the many passages just cited that actually affirm the subordination of Christ to the Father? These are best understood as referring to the role of servant which the Logos voluntarily assumed as a result of the incarnation. There was no relationship of subordination among the three persons of the Trinity before this. The subordination of the Son to the Father is functional, not ontological. It has to do with the Son's office and work, not his person. Jesus Christ the God-man is the Father's servant, and he does the will of the Father; but this is an aspect of the humiliation that he freely chose to endure for the sake of our salvation.

NOTES ON CHAPTER THIRTEEN

[1] See B.B. Warfield, "Emotional Life," 93-145.

[2] See my book *Gender Roles*, ch. 4: "Feminism and Jesus Christ," especially 156-160. The same material is presented in my article "Gender of Jesus," 171-194.

[3] Joseph Stump, *The Christian Faith*, 148, cited in Loraine Boettner, *Studies*, 211.

[4] This refutes any attempt to distinguish the Messiah as only a "*mighty* god" from Yahweh, who is obviously the *All-mighty* God.

[5] In many English versions of the OT the English word "Lord" is used to translate both *ªdonai* and the divine name *Yahweh*, and when it translates the latter, it appears in small capital letters, LORD.

[6]E.C. Colwell, 13. Those who deny the Logos's deity plead the fact that "God" (*theos*) in the last clause does not have the definite article "the"; thus they say it should be translated "a god." But Colwell's rule of Greek grammar states, "A definite predicate nominative has the article when it follows the verb; it does not have the article when it precedes the verb." In John 1:1 the latter applies. *Theos* as a predicate nominative does not have an article, even though it is definite, because it precedes the verb. See Gruss, *Apostles*, 115-119.

[7]Wells, *Christ*, 54, 188 (n. 55).

[8]We should remember that in many versions of the Bible, when the word LORD appears in small capital letters in the Old Testament, it stands for *Yahweh* (*YHWH*) in the original.

[9]See Stephen M. Smith, "Kenosis," 600-602.

[10]Translation by Albert C. Outler, in Leith, 35-36.

[11]For shocking quotations on this point see J. and S. Tanner, 179-182.

[12]This was discussed briefly in our consideration of God as Trinity, above.

[13]This was briefly discussed earlier under the distinction between the ontological Trinity and the economic Trinity. See p. 72.

[14]The *procession* of the Holy Spirit, based on the word "proceeds" in John 15:26, is treated in a similar fashion.

CHAPTER FOURTEEN
THE WORK OF CHRIST

The medieval theologian Anselm wrote a famous treatise called *Cur Deus Homo?* or "Why Did God Become Man?" After our discussion of the person of Christ this question is certainly on our minds. That God would become incarnate in a human person must be the least expected and most radical of all imaginable events. Surely God would never have done this unless it were absolutely necessary. What made it necessary? Why did Jesus come into the world?

In a word, Jesus came to reverse the effects of sin on God's good creation. "Christ Jesus came into the world to save sinners," says Paul (1 Tim 1:15). The Son of Man came "to give His life a ransom for many," said Jesus (Matt 20:28). This had been God's plan from the beginning of the world (Rev 13:8, NIV), from the time he foreknew that sin would enter into his planned creation. Because God's original purpose for creation was interrupted by the Fall, Jesus came to restore fallen mankind and the fallen universe to eternal righteousness and fellowship with God.

The incarnate Christ fulfilled this purpose mainly through his death and resurrection. Exactly what was Jesus accomplishing through these redemptive deeds? How we explain this depends on how we understand sinful man's basic need. If man's main problem is ignorance, then we would expect Christ's main work to be the revelation of saving knowledge. If our problem is some form of spiritual weakness, then Christ's main work must be to provide us with a corresponding spiritual power. Almost all the world's religions and philosophies do indeed interpret man's predicament in one of these two ways (see *GRe*, ch. 2).

Ignorance and weakness are certainly involved in man's plight, but neither of these is the main problem. We have seen that the essence of sin is the transgression of the law of the personal, holy God, which results in the double trouble of guilt and depravity. Because of our guilt, our harmonious relationship with God has been broken; we are under the wrath of God and are the objects of his just condemnation to hell. Because of our depravity, we are indeed spiritually weak and thus are easy prey for temptation.

Jesus came to resolve our problems of guilt and depravity through his death and resurrection. In general terms his death on the cross provides the basis for the removal of our guilt and condemnation, and his resurrection from the dead lays the foundation for the healing of our sin-ravaged natures.

I. THE ATONEMENT

Reconciling God and man, or bringing them into a relationship of at-one-ment, is the chief task Jesus came to accomplish. In an indirect sense the whole of Jesus' life and work could be called atonement, but in the most direct and specific sense the atonement was the work of the cross. Exactly how the cross accomplishes atonement has been a point of strong disagreement throughout Christian history. Many of the so-called "theories of atonement" are not true to Scripture. These need to be identified because they dishonor God and rob him of his glory by distorting the true nature of Christ's work. Thus in this section we will first survey some false views of the atonement, then we will examine the biblical data about the meaning of the cross.

A. False Concepts of the Atonement

B.B. Warfield rightly says we can best categorize most views of the atonement by arranging them "according to the conception each entertains of the person or persons on whom the work of Christ terminates" ("Atonement," 356). The question is, who is the specific object of Christ's work? The cross is intended to do something very specific, but to whom? for whom? Within whom lies the problem that only the cross can solve? Within whom lies the obstacle to salvation that can be removed only by the cross? Though some combinations may be found, there are really just three main answers to this kind of question. The work of the cross will terminate either on Satan, or on man, or on God.

1. Satan as the Object of the Cross

A rather unlikely view of the cross is that it was directed primarily toward the devil (ibid., 356-357; see Aulen, 47-55). This view was held by a number of the early church fathers into the fifth century (including Augustine), and appears even later in modified form in such men as Bernard and Luther.[1] The basic idea seems to be based on Christ's statement that he came "to give His life a ransom for many" (Matt 20:28). The reasoning was that a ransom must be paid to somebody, and the most likely such person is Satan. Sinful man is seen as being in Satan's control, with some even acknowledging the control to be legal and just since man has sold himself into Satan's grip by his sin. In any case man can be saved only by being rescued from this bondage to the devil. According to this view, this was the main purpose of the cross (though not necessarily its only purpose). In one way or another the cross was an integral part of a plot to wrest man away from Satan. For some it was a simple power play; for others it was the payment of a demanded ransom; for still others it was part of a plot by which God deceived or outwitted the devil.

The deception involved putting Christ on display as a miracle worker, thus leading the devil to regard him as such a prize that he would be willing to accept Jesus in trade for everyone else. What the devil did not realize was that through the incarnation the divine Logos was concealed within the human nature of Jesus of Nazareth and would implement his own escape from Satan via resurrection once the captives had been released. As Gregory of Nyssa (fourth century A.D.) put it,[2] "Hence it was that God, in order to make himself easily accessible to him who sought the ransom for us, veiled himself in our nature. In that way, as it is with greedy fish, he might swallow the Godhead like a fishhook along with the flesh, which was the bait." Augustine used the simile of baiting a mouse trap.

It seems quite out of character for the holy and omnipotent God to resort to deception, however. There is certainly an element of truth in the idea that Christ's work was in part directed against Satan (Heb 2:14-15; I John 3:8), but it is a matter of overcoming him through sheer power and not by deception nor by ransom. Also, it is accomplished more directly by the resurrection than the cross. The main object of the cross is not Satan, but someone else.

2. Man as the Object of the Cross

Others have said that the main object of the cross was man, not Satan. The idea here is that the only real obstacle to salvation is in man himself; thus the main purpose of the cross is to have some kind of effect upon the heart and life of man. Most examples of this view stem from other errors. For example, most of them assume that man's basic problem is ignorance or weakness rather than sin against a holy God. Thus the cross is designed to provide knowledge and/or power; it is God's way of *revealing* something to us, which in turn *influences* us to act in a certain way. Other errors include a weak view of the wrath of God, a weak view of the deity of Christ, and a weak view of the supernatural as such.

Among those who see the atoning work of Christ as terminating on man, there are two main approaches: the moral influence theory and the governmental theory. The essence of the classical moral influence theory is that God himself is ready, willing, and able to forgive man; the only thing man must do to receive the gift of forgiveness is to accept it in repentance and faith. Nothing else is needed: no cross, no resurrection, no incarnation. The problem, however, is that man in his stubbornness refuses to accept the gift. Therefore as a demonstration of his infinite love God goes to the extreme of sending his Son into the world, even to die on the cross if necessary, in order to break down man's resistance and convince him to believe and repent. This is the "moral influence," i.e., the power to persuade and to motivate the will of man to do what is necessary for him to receive salvation. When we thus perceive just how much we are loved, this "breaks down our opposition to God, melts our hearts, and brings us as prodigals home to the Father's arms" (Warfield, "Atonement," 362).

The first major example of this view is Peter Abelard (1079–1142), who was quite a free-thinking liberal for his day. He taught that God's giving up his Son to suffering and death reveals his amazing love for us, and thereby enkindles in us a responsive love and repentance, on the basis of which God forgives our sins. Christ's great example of love evokes a similar love in us.

This view is standard in modern Liberal theology. For example, W.A. Brown (365) says of Christ's atonement that "its saving efficacy consists in its moral influence in arousing repentance and faith." Another example is L.H. DeWolf (268), who says that the cross reconciles us to God by revealing the awfulness of sin and the love of God, which in turn move us to repent and return to God.

Of course, there is truth contained in this view. Jesus' death *is* a revelation or demonstration of God's infinite love and of the terrible nature of sin. It certainly is a power that softens and moves the hardened wills of sinners (John 12:32; Rom 1:16). The serious error of this view, however, is to say that this is the only purpose of the cross, or even its main purpose. That which gives the cross its revelatory and influencing power is the deeper and more significant fact that it is a propitiation for man's sins. Unless it is primarily this, its inner logic is lost; and explaining just *how* the cross is a revelation of God's love and just *why* it should move the soul will always be a challenge and an opportunity for the enterprising theologian.

Under the general heading of views that see the atonement as terminating on man as such, we also include what is called the governmental theory. With regard to its form it is practically identical with the moral influence theory. It sees no obstacle to forgiveness within the nature of God, who is ready, willing, and able to forgive as far as he himself is concerned. The only problem is a particular attitude in man which can be corrected by the cross. Thus God gave his Son to be crucified in order to demonstrate something to man, and to persuade man to engage in a certain course of action. As a result God is able to dispense his forgiveness freely.

Though similar in form, the governmental theory is quite the opposite of the moral influence theory. Basically it sees the cross as a demonstration of God's *wrath* against sin, the purpose of which is to instill *fear* into the hearts of men in order to deter them from the wholesale sinning that would probably break out once forgiveness is known to be freely available. In reality God could simply forgive sin without requiring any punishment for it. But in order to prevent moral chaos he sends Jesus to the cross as an object lesson to show us the heinousness of sin and the wrath it actually deserves. It acts as a deterrent to sin, allowing God to forgive us and at the same time maintain order and respect for his moral government.

This view was formulated first by Hugo Grotius (1583–1645), a Dutch lawyer and theologian, in his *Defence of the Catholic Faith*. His explanation of the atonement was influential in some circles, notably New England Puritanism and Wesleyan Arminianism. A major theologian from the latter group is Richard Watson, whose teaching on this subject in his *Theological Institutes* is excerpted by Alexander Campbell in a lengthy quotation in *The Christian System* (27-30).

We may mention just two problems with the governmental theory. One is the idea that the holy God is free either to punish sin or not to punish sin as he chooses. This does not seem to be consistent with the Bible's teaching concerning the holiness and wrath of God. The other problem is that this view is almost totally speculative and has practically no biblical basis. The texts that describe the death of Christ present a different picture altogether.

3. Other False Views of the Cross

Some false or inadequate views of the atonement do not fit neatly into either of these two categories. One is the covenantal theory.[3] It interprets the death of Jesus purely in terms of God's covenant relationship with man. A common version of this is to begin with God's covenant with Israel as God's definitive relationship with mankind as a whole. The terms of this covenant relationship are that God will bless and save Israel (mankind) if Israel (mankind) will obey God's commands. As the history of Israel shows, God remains faithful to his side of the covenant, but the human partner constantly fails and thus threatens the whole relationship. What is needed, then, is a representative covenant-keeper who can take the place of sinful man and render acceptable obedience to God and thus preserve the covenant. This is how the work of Jesus is understood.

The covenantal interpretation of the atonement is erroneous. For one thing, it is undergirded by a faulty view of God's righteousness and thus an unwarranted exclusion of the penal or propitiatory aspect of the cross. Also, there is little or no biblical warrant for imposing the covenant framework on the meaning of the work of Jesus. Christ's death is the means of establishing the new covenant to be sure (Luke 22:20; Heb 9:16; 10:29); but the idea of Christ's death as the culmination of a life of representative covenant-keeping is completely speculative and ignores the teaching of the passages that do speak about the meaning of the cross. More seriously, it reverses the biblical relationship between the covenant with Israel and the death of Christ. In Scripture the covenant is a means and Christ's death is its purpose or goal (Rom 9:3-5). But in the covenantal view the cross (along with Jesus' life as a whole) is just a means to preserving the covenant relationship established at Sinai. This view is thus seriously flawed and fails to do justice to the scriptural teaching on the work of redemption through Christ.

Another inadequate view of the atonement is the interpersonal theory set forth by Virgil Warren in his book, *What the Bible Says about Salvation*. Warren's basic (and arbitrary) presupposition is that salvation must be understood *only* in *interpersonal* terms such as love, friendship, forgiveness, repentance, and reconciliation. The language of ransom, sacrifice, substitution, sin-bearing, and especially imputation is merely legal imagery based on the OT; it is figurative only and is not definitive for understanding the cross (Warren, 5, 68-69, 79-80). Man's basic problem is broken fellowship with God and the need for reconciliation. This can be accomplished through repentance, confession, and commitment to future righteousness on our part, and forgiveness on God's part. How does the atoning work of Christ fit into this picture? First, the cross provides sinners with the *motivation* to repent. Second, Christ's sinless life provides us with a model of righteousness with which we can identify and which we can commit ourselves to imitate (Warren, 56-58, 70-78).

This view of the atonement is seriously flawed. First, the setting aside of legal concepts and the exclusive focus on interpersonal concepts (as far as what *really* happened is concerned) is completely arbitrary and has no basis in Scripture. It is acknowledged that the NT uses such legal terminology extensively. It should also be noted that there is no suggestion in Scripture itself that such language should be taken as merely figurative. The fact is that the very distinction between personal and legal is quite arbitrary since the legal and the personal are not necessarily exclusive. This is especially true in the Bible, where the law of God cannot be separated from God himself, and where our relation to his law is the same as our relation to him. Also, Warren's outright rejection of the whole concept of imputation does violence not only to the atonement but to other major doctrines of Scripture as well, especially justification.

Most seriously, in the final analysis according to the interpersonal theory the death of Christ is not strictly necessary and has no inherent connection with the forgiveness of sins. In fact, the real atoning power of Christ comes from his sinless life and example, of which his willingness to die even a violent death is simply a fitting climax. As Warren says, "That incarnate obedience unto violent death qualified him in the Father's mind for appointment as the Sinless One with whom men are called to identify as a condition for forgiveness. Atonement derives from Christ's obedience to the extent of bloodshed, not from the blood shed" (83-84). The following comments (84-85) show that, according to this theory, in the final analysis the death of Christ is superfluous for reconciliation and atonement:

> . . . It is at least conceivable that Jesus of Nazareth would not have had to die even though it is *most* appropriate that his obedience be demonstrated to this extent in order to become a complete opposite of what it antithesized and in order to demonstrate in the basis for atonement the extent of obedience his followers are called upon to perform. . . . The reason for the Father's will that he die came, we infer, from the added appropriateness of appointing Jesus as Messiah; it also set the stage for resurrection in proof of his claims.
>
> . . . His death would certainly happen, but it did not have to happen of necessity. Had the Jews accepted him, the program of world-wide reconciliation to God could have gone forward without his death. Had the Jews accepted their Messiah, the preceding prophecy would have been worded otherwise and the system of animal sacrifice would not have been divinely instituted in anticipation of his death.

We must not hesitate to reject such a view that makes the death of Jesus of such little import. Paul's summary of the gospel in 1 Cor 15:3-4 says nothing of Christ's sinless life but includes "as of first importance . . . that Christ died for our sins according to the Scriptures, and that He was buried, and that He was raised on the third day according to the Scriptures." This view must be rejected, along with the others.

B. The Biblical Concept of Atonement

We have said that some views of the atonement picture either Satan or man as the primary object of Christ's atoning death. In my judgment neither of these approaches gets to the heart of the Bible's teaching on the work of Jesus Christ. Only the third option can be defended biblically, namely, that the primary object of the cross is God himself. The cross is necessary, not because of something in Satan or something in man, but because of something in God. The only obstacle to forgiveness that requires the cross is God's own holy wrath. That this is the case can be seen by examining two of the main terms used in the NT to describe the meaning of Christ's death, namely, propitiation and redemption.

1. Christ's Death as a Propitiation

The concept that best summarizes and explains the meaning of Christ's death is "propitiation," the basic meaning of which is "an offering that turns away wrath." It comes from a family of Greek words, three of which are used in the NT: *hilaskomai*, "to propitiate, to turn away wrath by an offering" (Luke 18:13; Heb 2:17); *hilasmos*, "a propitiation, a propitiatory offering" (1 John 2:2; 4:10); and *hilasterion*, "a propitiation, a propitiatory offering, that which propitiates God" (Rom 3:25), and sometimes "mercy seat" (Heb 9:5). In pagan circles these terms had the connotation of appeasing or placating angry deities. This crude pagan connotation must not be carried over into the biblical usage, however, not because the terms mean something different in the Bible, but because the God of the Bible is different from the false heathen deities. He is not merely a God of wrath but is also a God of love and grace who takes the initiative in providing the offering that turns away his own wrath. He does not wait in an angry pout until the anxious sinner brings him an offering that he deems suitable, nor does the kindhearted Son "win over" the hard-hearted, angry Father through his death on the cross. We must not think that the term "propitiation" carries only such primitive connotations. The terms are used often in the Septuagint, where they do not have "the usual pagan sense of a crude propitiation of an angry deity," something which "is not possible with the God of Israel."[4]

In the Septuagint *hilasterion* is used to represent the mercy-seat (the lid that covered the ark of the covenant), and it seems to have that meaning in Heb 9:5. This is a unique connotation, however; it does not have this specialized meaning in its other NT use in Rom 3:25 where the context shows that it has the more general meaning of propitiation.

The key element in the concept of propitiation is the wrath of God. It is "an offering that turns away *wrath*." If God were not a God of wrath, then the concept of propitiation would not apply at all. Of course there are many who deny God's wrath or who compromise its integrity by making it an aspect of his love. This is why many prefer the translation "expiation" in such passages as Rom 3:25 since it does not necessarily include the connotation of wrath. But the reality of

God's wrath is a theme that pervades the Bible. Also, in the context leading up to Rom 3:25 especially, Paul's main point is that all sinners are under the wrath of God (Rom 1:18; 2:5-9; 3:9-20). His main point in this section, in agreement with the Bible as a whole, is that no one can be saved by law-keeping because everyone has broken whatever law applies to him and thus is under the condemnation of the law and the wrath of God. This is man's basic problem. Thus when this section of Romans ends at 3:20, we would expect the next section (3:21ff.), which deals with the solution to this problem, to say something about how we may escape God's wrath. Thus as Leon Morris says (*Preaching*, 69), the context not only makes the reference to propitiation in 3:25 natural, but even demands such a reference.

Since man's basic problem is that his sin has made him the object of divine wrath, we would expect the solution to the problem of wrath to be at the very heart of Christ's redemptive work. Thus when we speak of the purpose of the incarnation or the mission of Christ, we must bring to mind above all else the words of 1 John 4:10, that God loved us and "sent His Son to be the propitiation for our sins." And exactly what is there about the mission of Christ that accomplishes propitiation? It is not his life as such, including his ministry, his sinlessness, or his example. It is not his prophetic work of teaching and of revealing the Father. Rather, it is his death on the cross. On Calvary he offered himself up as an offering to turn God's wrath away from us. There can be no mistake about this. First John 2:2 says Christ "is the propitiation for our sins." John has just made the remark in 1 John 1:7 that "the blood of Jesus His Son cleanses us from all sin." It is his blood poured out in death that is the propitiation; Christ on the cross is the propitiation for our sins. This is made explicit in Rom 3:25, which says God displayed Jesus publicly as a propitiation. How was he displayed? On the cross. This is clear from the reference to "in His blood." Though I prefer the translation "a propitiation through faith in His blood" (KJV), some translations reverse the latter two phrases and make it "a propitiation in His blood through faith" (NASB). But either way, the propitiation is accomplished only through his blood.

This brings us to the crucial question, exactly how is the death of Jesus a propitiation, or how does it turn the wrath of God away from us? In the most simple terms, Jesus turns God's wrath away from us by taking it on himself. Our sin makes us guilty and places us under the penalty of wrath. When we say that Jesus "died for our sins" or "bore our sins upon Calvary," we mean that he put himself in our place and let our sins be counted as his own. Thus he bore the *guilt* of our sins and the consequent *penalty* which they deserve; he bore the wrath of God in our place. Herein lies the concept of *imputation*: our sins, along with their guilt and penalty, are imputed to Christ. This means that they are reckoned or charged to his account so that they are treated as his own. Herein also is the idea of *satisfaction*: Jesus satisfied the requirements of God's law for us; he satisfied the retributive justice and the wrath of God in our place. As Packer says, "Jesus Christ has shielded us from the nightmare prospect of retributive justice by becoming our representative substitute, in obedience to His Father's will, and receiving the wages of sin in our place" (170). And herein also is *substitution*: Jesus not only did all these things for us or on our behalf; he actually did them in our place and instead of us.

This is the consistent and uncontradicted testimony of Scripture. The great prophecy of Isaiah 53 stresses the Messiah's role as sin-bearer: "Surely our griefs He Himself bore, and our sorrows He carried. . . . He was pierced through for our transgressions, He was crushed for our iniquities; the chastening for our well-being fell upon Him, and by His scourging we are healed" (vv. 4-5). "The LORD has caused the iniquity of us all to fall on Him" (v. 6). "For the transgression of my people he was stricken. . . . By his knowledge my righteous servant will justify many, and he will bear their iniquities. . . . For he bore the sin of many, and made intercession for the transgressors" (vv. 8,11-12; NIV). Alluding to this prophecy 1 Pet 2:24 says, "He Himself bore our sins in His body on the cross, so that we might die to sin and live to righteousness; for by His wounds you were healed." Galatians 3:13 shows that his death was both substitutionary and forensic: "Christ redeemed us from the curse of the Law, having become a curse for us— for it is written, 'Cursed is everyone who hangs on a tree.'" Both substitution and imputation are found in 2 Cor 5:21, "He made Him who knew no sin to be sin on our behalf, so that we might become the righteousness of God in Him." Christ's work as sin-bearer made it natural for him to be compared with the OT sacrificial lamb: "Behold, the Lamb of God who takes away the sin of the world!" (John 1:29). "For Christ our Passover also has been sacrificed" (1 Cor 5:7); as a lamb he was slain so that his blood could deflect the wrath of God from us. To these passages should be added those which specifically call Christ our propitiation (Rom 3:25; 1 John 2:2; 4:10).

If Christ actually took our place in bearing the wrath of God, this means that he bore the full force of God's wrath; he suffered the equivalent of eternity in hell for every sinner. Some do not understand how this can be possible because they do not understand the nature of Christ's suffering. It included not just the moment of death, but all the torture and anguish he began to suffer at least as early as the Garden of Gethsemane. Also, it included both physical and spiritual dimensions. The physical agony of scourging and crucifixion has been well documented, so we have some idea of the bodily pain Jesus suffered in the hours before his death.[5] But even as intense as this was, if this were all that Jesus suffered, we still might wonder how that could be the equivalent of the eternal punishment of the whole human race. After all, there were others who went through this kind of torture both before and after Christ, and many Christian martyrs endured untold cruelties at the hands of sadistic pagans and "Christians" alike. So what was different about Jesus' suffering? The difference lies mainly in the spiritual agony he bore.

Spiritual (mental, emotional, psychological) suffering is quite common, and many have testified that it is by far worse than its physical counterpart. As someone put it, "Soul suffering is more grievous than physical pain." When applied to

Jesus Christ, this spiritual agony takes on infinite, unimaginable proportions. This is so for two reasons. First, he was *sinless*, yet he was facing the penalty for sin. His soul was not toughened and scarred by numerous trespasses; thus the searing, piercing wrath of God must have penetrated to its infinite depths with unbelievable intensity. Second, he was *God*, the living God, yet he was facing the very antithesis of both life and deity—death itself. What kind of feelings must have crowded his consciousness as he came face to face with that enemy and that curse that God himself had imposed upon mankind as the penalty for sin? How can we measure the agony permeating his whole being as the divine nature itself experienced what it was like to die?

We must keep in mind that both the physical and the spiritual suffering of Christ was experienced by one who was by nature divine and thus infinite in his being. Thus, even though he suffered for only a finite period of time, the suffering itself was infinite; it cannot be quantified. This helps to answer two questions. First, how can the suffering of Christ, which lasted only a few hours, be the equivalent of eternity in hell for the whole human race? *Because he was God.* The finite suffering of an infinite being would seem to be equivalent to the infinite suffering of finite beings. This is one of the main reasons why the atonement could be accomplished only by God himself and not by any creature, man or angel. Second, did Christ suffer only for the "elect" or those who will be ultimately saved? No, his suffering was infinite and has no limit. Thus it is improper to try to quantify the atonement in any sense or to think that it could be limited to a certain number of people. His suffering was infinite and thus satisfied the wrath of God for every human being.

The death of Jesus as a propitiation of the wrath of God is the basis of the justification of those who put their trust in Christ and what he has done for them. Because of the cross God is able to forgive sins without violating his own holy nature. It makes forgiveness possible. This is how God can be both *just* and *justifier* (Rom 3:26). This is how he is able to resolve the sin-caused tension within his own nature between his holiness and his love, with his holiness demanding that sin be punished and his love desiring to forgive the sinner. Christ as a propitiatory sacrifice enables him to do both; this is why we can only be "justified by His blood" (Rom 5:9).

It should be noted that although the wrath of God has been satisfied with reference to "the sin of the world" (John 1:29), this does not mean that everyone is actually forgiven; it does not lead to universal salvation. Justification is not only "by His blood," but also "by faith" (Rom 3:28; 5:1). The pardon purchased by Christ on Calvary is offered to all, but it is actually given only to those who accept it through a faith commitment to Christ as Savior and Lord. Some of those bought by his blood will be lost (2 Pet 2:1).

The modern attack on propitiation, while expected, is unjustified. Much of it comes from those who deny divine wrath in the first place, but such denials are inconsistent with clear biblical teaching. Others argue that propitiation is a concept unworthy of God, but they usually present only a caricature of the biblical teaching patterned after pagan ideas of appeasement. God is pictured as an angry deity who is persuaded to love and forgive man only after Christ offers himself on Calvary. As noted above, this ignores the Bible's own teaching that it was God's prior love that provided the propitiation in the first place (1 John 4:10). Others take the position that propitiation is an immoral concept; it is immoral for one person to suffer the punishment for another's sins. The problem here, says Guillebaud, is trying to understand the atonement in terms of human analogies, especially the analogy of human justice. Perhaps it would be wrong for a human judge to punish an innocent third party for a crime someone else has committed against the law of the land. But this does not apply to God, because he himself is not only the Judge but also the Law sinned against as well as the innocent Substitute. Guillebaud says that "God was not administering someone else's law, but His Own, and the sin was not committed against someone else but against Him: and above all He did not take someone else and accept him as substitute for the condemned sinner . . . , but He came Himself, took upon Him the nature of the guilty ones, and bore the penalty of His own Law" (147). This is another reason why only God himself could make atonement for our sins, and thus why Jesus the Redeemer must be divine. "We may freely admit that the Bible doctrine of vicarious punishment is not defensible apart from a full recognition of the Bible teaching of the Divinity of Christ" (148).

Still others attack propitiation by trying to show that the Greek words do not actually mean propitiation but rather mean only a covering or a canceling of sin. C.H. Dodd takes this position, arguing from the way the words are used in the Septuagint (82-95). Packer (164) responds to Dodd by claiming that at best he has shown only that the word-group does not always *have* to mean propitiation, "*but* he has not shown that the word-group cannot mean 'propitiation' in contexts where this meaning is called for." And the context of Rom 3:25 especially *does* call for this meaning.

Those who reject the concept of propitiation usually prefer expiation instead. Whereas propitiation is aimed toward God and denotes the removal of his wrath, expiation is aimed toward the sin itself and denotes its removal or covering. Since this latter concept is included within propitiation also, Packer (163) keenly notes that "expiation only means half of what propitiation means." Propitiation not only speaks of the covering of sin, but shows *how* it is covered, i.e., through the blood of Christ which absorbs the wrath that would otherwise be poured out upon it. Expiation speaks of the covering of sin, but there is no coherent explanation of how the blood of Christ accomplishes this.

The doctrine of propitiation is crucial. I agree with Packer (161-163) that it is "the heart of the gospel." He says, "A gospel without propitiation at its heart is another gospel than that which Paul preached. The implications of this must not be evaded."

2. Christ's Death as Redemption

The other key concept for understanding the atonement is redemption as such. The significant OT words for this concept are the verb *ga'al*, "to set free, to liberate, to redeem," and its noun form *go'el*, sometimes translated "kinsman-redeemer" (Ruth 2:20, NIV).[6] The NT words are derived from *lyo*, which means "to loose, to set free, to ransom"; and from *agora*, which means "a marketplace." The simple noun form derived from *lyo* is *lytron*, which has the unambiguous meaning of "a ransom, a ransom price." It is used by Jesus to describe his mission (Matt 20:28; Mark 10:45). The word *antilytron* is similar in meaning and is used of Christ in 1 Tim 2:6. The verb *lytroo* is derived directly from *lytron* and thus has the specific connotation of ransoming. In the active voice it means "to hold for ransom"; in the middle voice it means "to pay a ransom." The latter form occurs in key New Testament passages (Luke 24:21; Titus 2:14; 1 Pet 1:18). Another noun form is *apolytrosis*, which means "redemption" (Rom 3:24; 8:23; Heb 9:15).[7] Two other key words are derived from *agora*. They are *agorazo*, "to buy, to purchase" (1 Cor 6:20; 7:23; 2 Pet 2:1; Rev 5:9); and *exagorazo*, "to buy, to purchase" (Gal 3:13; 4:5). The former has the connotation of a simple purchase: "to buy in the marketplace," while the addition of the preposition *ek* to the latter word gives it the connotation "to buy *out of* the marketplace."

The fundamental idea in all these words is the same, namely, the payment of a price in order to release someone or set him free. This is the essence of redemption. The Old Testament practice providing the sharpest background for understanding Christ's redeeming work is the redemption of firstborn males from their status of special consecration to God (see Exod 13:11-13; Num 18:15-17). God decreed that every firstborn male, man or beast, belonged to him. From those animals classified as clean, the firstborn was to be sacrificed as an offering to God. With unclean animals such as a donkey, there was a choice. One could either break its neck, thus destroying it; or he could redeem it—buy it back—by paying the price of a lamb to be sacrificed in its place (Exod 13:13).[8] It was expected that everyone would choose the second option (Num 18:15). With regard to human beings there was no choice. Every firstborn male had to be redeemed—bought back from God—by paying the "money of the redemption," five shekels of silver (about two and one-half ounces). See Num 18:16.

This practice demonstrates the basic meaning of redemption, i.e., the payment of a price to set someone or something free. The term *lytron* is literally the ransom price paid to set someone free from some kind of bondage or captivity. Thus when this concept is used with reference to the atonement, there can be no mistake: when Jesus died on the cross, he was giving his life or his blood to set us free from the consequences of our sins. He declared that he came "to give His life a ransom for many" (Matt 20:28). His own life was the price paid. This does not mean his life simply as he *lived* it, but his life as he gave it up unto *death*. This is clear from the references to his blood as the price of our redemption: "You were not redeemed with perishable things like silver or gold . . . but with precious blood, as of a lamb unblemished and spotless, the blood of Christ" (1 Pet 1:18-19). "In Him we have redemption through His blood" (Eph 1:7). The church was "purchased with His own blood" (Acts 20:28; cf. Rev 5:9). For other references to Christ as the ransom price, see 1 Tim 2:6 and Titus 2:14. See also Heb 9:15.

Exactly how is Christ's death a ransom price? From what does he set us free? The terms for redemption were commonly used with reference to slavery. Someone could be redeemed from slavery through the payment of the proper price (see Exod 21:8; Lev 25:47-55). This would certainly apply to our redemption in Christ: we are redeemed from slavery to Satan and to sin (Rom 6:16-18; 2 Tim 2:26). The main point of redemption, however, seems to lie elsewhere. Precisely speaking, through his death on the cross Jesus redeemed us from the *penalty* of sin. We have seen how sin involves us in debt to God; as a result of it we owe to God the debt of eternal punishment. No greater debt could be imagined. In NT times the debtor's prison must have been a reality; in his parable of the unforgiving servant Jesus pictures him as having his fellow servant cast into prison until he paid what was owed (Matt 18:30). Because of his own debt, his lord "handed him over to the torturers until he should repay all that was owed him" (Matt 18:34). This well describes our own condition and our prospect for eternity, and it is exactly that from which Christ has redeemed us. He redeemed us from the debt of eternal punishment by paying the debt for us in his own infinite suffering on the cross. "Christ redeemed us from the curse of the Law, having become a curse for us" (Gal 3:13). Barclay (*Words*, 190) describes a *lytron* or ransom as "a payment which releases a man from an obligation which otherwise he was bound to fulfil." We are no longer obligated to pay the penalty for sin, because Christ has paid it for us. This answers the question of *to whom* Christ gave himself as a ransom (Matt 20:28): the ransom was paid to God himself. God is the one who demands that the penalty be paid; Jesus pays it for us. In this way redemption is seen to be practically identical with propitiation, as we would expect from the way they are paralleled in Rom 3:24-25. Likewise, since it is the removal of the penalty of sin, redemption is equated with pardon or forgiveness when it is applied to the sinner (Eph 1:7; Col 1:14).

The nature of atonement as summed up in the words *propitiation* and *redemption* makes Christianity's doctrine of salvation absolutely unique. Of all the religious systems of the world, Christianity alone provides the only thing that can save man from his lost state, namely, a sin-bearer. Of all the alleged redeemers in the world, Jesus alone can and does bear the sins of mankind in such a way that their consequences may be escaped. Other religions honor prophets, heroic figures, and even alleged saviors; but none has a sin-bearer, a propitiator, a true redeemer. Christ and Christ alone "bore our sins in His body on the cross" (1 Pet 2:24). He alone was able to do so, because he alone was God incarnate in the person of a sinless man. This shows the supreme importance of a right doctrine of both the person and the work of Christ. Those who compromise the deity of Christ and the propitiatory nature of his death are not simply arguing abstract theology; they are removing the very foundation of the doctrine of salvation itself.

II. THE RESURRECTION

In the broader sense of the term, the work of redemption was not completed when Jesus died on the cross. When he cried, "It is finished!" (John 19:30), he was not referring to his work as such but only to that aspect of his work that involved humiliation and suffering. The triumphant phase of his work was yet to come, and was begun just three days later when he arose from the dead. Thus the resurrection of Jesus is a vital and integral part of the redemptive process. How this is so is the subject of this section.

To understand the significance of the resurrection of Jesus, we must understand the nature of the penalty imposed upon sinners and upon the sinful world by God's holy judgment. It can be summarized in the word *death*: "the wages of sin is death" (Rom 6:23). This judgment includes physical death; all human beings die physically as the result of Adam's sin (Rom 5:12; 8:10). It also includes spiritual death; all sinners are spiritually dead before God even while they live in this world (Eph 2:1,5; 1 Tim 5:6). Finally the judgment culminates in eternal death in the lake of fire (Rev 20:14-15). Now, the penal aspect of death in all its forms is removed for the redeemed by the blood of Jesus Christ; but death as a condition still remains. Here is where "the power of His resurrection" (Phil 3:10) does its redemptive work. Through his resurrection from the dead Jesus makes available to us a power that is able to reverse the condition of death and restore us to life.

Concerning the nature of Christ's resurrection, two things must be stressed. One is that the resurrection was a literal, historical, bodily event. This is an essential part of the gospel (1 Cor 15:4) and must be believed in order for anyone to be saved (Rom 10:9). By no means can it be equated with the subjective "rise of faith" in the hearts of his disciples, nor can it be explained in terms of a nonmaterial apparition that did not involve his actual body. What happened in the resurrection happened to the dead body of Jesus; it was brought back to life so that Jesus was able to walk about and meet people face to face in his body just as he did before his death. The change or transformation that we call "resurrection" occurred in the physical aspect of his human nature. It is crucial to maintain this truth because the consequences of his resurrection are to be felt ultimately by the whole of God's physical creation, including the bodies of the redeemed. Attempts to redefine the resurrection of Jesus as anything less than the resuscitation and transformation of his original body have the effect of diluting the fullness of our redemption.

A second point to be stressed is that the event we call the resurrection of Jesus really includes two separate but related events, namely, his actual rising from the dead *and* the later transformation of his body into the glorified human nature that it now is. Contrary to the common assumption, Jesus' body was not glorified in the tomb at the moment of his resurrection. When he came out of the tomb, he had the same recognizable, wound-bearing body that he had when he was buried. We cannot relegate the resurrection to some special level of history or reality outside the sphere of our everyday experiences. The unusual events related to his resurrection appearances are easily explainable by "ordinary" miracle and have parallels in other miraculous events unconnected with the resurrection.[9] The Apostle John, who certainly saw Jesus after he arose from the dead, testifies that the present glorified nature of our Lord is not known to us: "It has not appeared as yet what we shall be. We know that when He appears, we will be like Him, because we will see Him just as He is" (1 John 3:2). It may be that the Apostle Paul saw the glorified Christ (Acts 9:1-9; 1 Cor 9:1; 15:8), but what he saw was surely more than the other apostles had seen prior to the ascension.

It seems best to conclude that Jesus arose in his not-yet-glorified body so that there could be no mistake on the part of those who knew him that he was the same Jesus who had died on the cross and that he was now truly alive again. Also, the best inference is that he received his transformed and glorified body at the time of his ascension. Thus what is often called "the resurrection body of Jesus" was not actually received at the resurrection but upon his reentry into the spiritual or heavenly dimension when he ascended into "the glory of the LORD" (Exod 40:34-38). He was "taken up in glory" (1 Tim 3:16). However, for theological purposes it is proper to think of these two events (the rising from the dead and the ascension) as simply two stages of a single event which may appropriately be called "the resurrection."[10] Thus our conclusions concerning the nature and theological meaning of the resurrection of Jesus must *not* be based on the phenomena of his resurrection appearances, but on the apostolic teaching. The meaning and implications of the resurrection are known only by revelation; they are not perceivable from the postresurrection (i.e., postresuscitation) appearances or actions of Jesus.

Our main question here is this: what is the theological meaning of the bodily resurrection of Jesus? What is its saving significance? Here we will present seven ways in which Christ's resurrection is related to our salvation.

A. Christ's Resurrection Demonstrates His Lordship

First, Christ's resurrection demonstrates his Lordship. During his earthly ministry Jesus made many claims that seem outrageous coming from a mere carpenter of Nazareth. He claimed to be the Christ, the Son of God (Matt 16:16-20); to be sent by God (John 8:42); to be one with the Father (John 10:30); to deserve honor equal with that given to the Father (John 5:23); to have authority to forgive sins (Matt 9:2-6); to be King (John 18:37) and Lord (Luke 6:46); to be Lord of the temple (John 2:14-22), Lord of the Sabbath (Matt 12:8), and Lord of angels (Matt 24:31).

All these claims were put on the line when Jesus was put to death. But when God raised him from the dead, they were shown to be true. Jesus was indeed who he claimed to be. He was "declared the Son of God with power by the resurrection from the dead" (Rom 1:4). The risen Christ declared that he had been given all authority in heaven and on earth (Matt 28:18). By raising him from the dead and inviting him to sit at his own right hand, the Father demonstrated Jesus' Lordship to the whole world (Acts 2:32-36).

To say that the historical event of the resurrection demonstrates Christ's Lordship is to recognize its importance for Christian apologetics. From the very beginning of the church, those who were eyewitnesses of the risen Christ cited the fact of his resurrection as proof that he is indeed who he claimed to be (see Acts 1:3). Testimony to the evidential significance of the resurrection was a vital part of Peter's Pentecost sermon (Acts 2:22-36) and of the apostles' continuing presentation of the gospel (Acts 3:15; 4:10,33; 5:30; 10:40-41). Following his own life-changing encounter with the risen Christ, the apostle Paul continued to bear witness to the resurrection (Acts 13:30-37; 17:3,18,31; 26:23).

B. Christ's Resurrection Devastates His Enemies

Second, the resurrection devastates Christ's enemies. Through the fall of Satan and the Fall of mankind, vicious enemies were empowered to strive against God and against his plan for the creation. These enemies include Satan himself, his demonic hosts, sin, the forces of death, and Hades (the place of death). One major purpose for the incarnation of the divine Logos as Jesus of Nazareth was to set up a confrontation between God and Satan in order to bring Satan and his confederates to a crushing defeat. "The Son of God appeared for this purpose, to destroy the works of the devil" (1 John 3:8). He became a human being so "that through death he might render powerless him who had the power of death, that is, the devil" (Heb 2:14).

Throughout his earthly ministry Christ engaged in preliminary skirmishes with the devil. These encounters began with Herod's attempt on his life (compare Matt 2 and Rev 12:1-6) and later included the temptations (Matt 4:1-11) and many instances of deliverance from demons (e.g., Matt 8:28-32). In these events Jesus was already beginning the process of evicting Satan from his usurped throne (Luke 10:17; Rev 12:7-9) and binding him and limiting his power (Matt 10:22-29; Rev 20:1-3). Shortly before the cross Jesus warned his disciples that a final battle with "the ruler of the world" was approaching (John 12:31; 14:30; 16:11).

The decisive battle between Christ and his enemies began with the cross, where Satan indeed bruised Jesus' heel (Gen 3:15; John 13:2) and probably thought he had gained the victory over him (1 Cor 2:8) by bringing him under the power of death (Acts 2:24; Heb 2:14). We can imagine Satan's short-lived glee as he gloated over the crucified Christ. What he did not know was that in this presumed victory he had already lost his war against God, because the cross itself was already pulling the penal sting of sin and death (1 Cor 15:55-57) and thereby rendering the devil's main weapon powerless (Heb 2:14-15). By taking on himself the penalty and condemnation for the sins of the whole human race (1 John 2:2), Jesus "disarmed the powers and authorities" and "made a public spectacle of them, triumphing over them by the cross" (Col 2:15).

What Satan also did not know, or apparently did not believe, was that Jesus would actually rise from the dead. The eruption of divine power that brought Jesus back to life and set him free from the tomb absolutely devastated all his foes. He was indeed put to death, "but God raised Him up again, putting an end to the agony of death, since it was impossible for Him to be held in its power" (Acts 2:24). He broke death's power (Heb 2:14-15) and crushed the Serpent's head (Gen 3:15). The risen Christ declares, "I am . . . the living One; and I was dead, and behold, I am alive forevermore, and I have the keys of death and of Hades" (Rev 1:17-18). This shows his complete power over death, since "Christ, having been raised from the dead, is never to die again; death no longer is master over Him" (Rom 6:9). He has "abolished death and brought life and immortality to life" (2 Tim 1:10).

Christ's life, death, and resurrection are symbolically described in Rev 12:7-9 as a "war in heaven," in which Satan as "the great dragon" and all his angels (the demons) were soundly defeated. Paul declares that when the risen Christ "ascended on high, He led captive a host of captives" (Eph 4:8). These captives are his enemies for whom the final devastation was Christ's glorious resurrection.

Christ's enemies are our enemies, too; but we do not fear them because Christ shares with us his own victory over them. "Release to [Satan's] captives" is part of the gospel (Luke 4:18). Jesus not only binds the devil; he also enters into his stronghold and carries off his property (Matt 12:29). He delivers us "from the dominion of Satan" (Acts 26:18) and gives us a power that is greater than Satan's (1 John 4:4). He helps us to crush Satan under our feet (Rom 16:20). Thus he enables us to experience in our present lives "the power of His resurrection" (Phil 3:10).

C. Christ's Resurrection Inaugurates His Kingdom

Third, the resurrection inaugurates the kingdom of Christ. The OT foretold that the great King would come and establish his eternal kingdom (Dan 2:44; 7:13-14). Jesus was that King, and his very presence on earth made the kingdom near (Matt 3:2; 12:28). By defeating his enemies through his cross and resurrection, he formally and literally established his kingship over all things. After his resurrection he declared, "All authority has been given to Me in heaven and on earth" (Matt 28:18). By virtue of his resurrection he has "been exalted to the right hand of God" (Acts 2:32-33), i.e., enthroned as King at God's own right hand.

From a theological perspective the resurrection, ascension, and enthronement of Jesus are one grand, interlocking event that can be designated as his *exaltation*. Philippians 2:9 sums up this package, simply saying that after his crucifixion, "God highly exalted Him." The forty days Jesus spent on earth between his resurrection and ascension were for apological purposes, to give us "many convincing proofs" that he had truly risen (Acts 1:3; see 10:40-42). But for all practical purposes, after the resurrection occurred, the next logical step was to return to the heavenly throne room and begin his messianic reign over his kingdom.

When Jesus "ascended on high" (Eph 4:8) or was "taken up in glory" (1 Tim 3:16), Acts 1:9 says he was received into a cloud. This was not an ordinary vapor cloud, but the cloud of God's glory, made visible for this very purpose (see Exod 40:34-37; Matt 17:5). When Jesus ascended, he went up only as far as the cloud; when he entered into it, he received his glorified human body and passed through the dimensional barrier into the throne room of heaven (Ps 24:7-10). Here he was triumphantly ushered into the presence of the Father (the "Ancient of Days"); "and to Him was given dominion, glory, and a kingdom, that all the peoples, nations, and men of every language might serve Him. His dominion is an everlasting dominion which will not pass away; and His kingdom is one which will not be destroyed" (Dan 7:13-14). He was seated at God's right hand, given the scepter of power, and told to "rule in the midst of Your enemies" (Ps 110:1-2; see 1 Pet 3:22). Being thus risen from the dead and enthroned at God's right hand, and declared to be "both Lord and Christ" (Acts 2:32-36), Jesus reigns now from heaven as King of kings and Lord of lords (Rev 19:16).

We cannot avoid the conclusion that the promised kingdom of the Messiah has already begun. It is so closely connected with his resurrection that the one follows naturally upon the other. The risen/ascended Christ cannot help but reign as King over all things. The power of his resurrection goes forth over all, subduing his enemies and blessing his saints. Paul speaks of "his incomparably great power for us who believe." This power is according to

> . . . the working of his mighty strength, which he exerted in Christ when he raised him from the dead and seated him at his right hand in the heavenly realms, far above all rule and authority, power and dominion, and every title that can be given, not only in the present age but also in the one to come. And God placed all things under his feet and appointed him to be head over everything for the church, which is his body, the fullness of him who fills everything in every way (Eph 1:19-23, NIV).

It is clear from this that Christ's resurrection power has inaugurated the kingdom, since he rules over all things "in the present age" (v. 21). It is also clear that he wields this power "for the church" (v. 22), on behalf of his people.

D. Christ's Resurrection Validates His Cross

Fourth, Christ's resurrection validates the cross. His death was itself a defeat for his enemies (Heb 2:14-15; Col 2:15), but this did not become obvious until the resurrection. His enemies thought they had beaten him through the cross (1 Cor 2:8), but when he arose, they realized it was the other way around. Satan cannot automatically drag us down with him to eternal death merely by luring us into sin. The cross has paid that penalty of eternal death for us, and the risen Christ is enthroned at God's right hand as the constant reminder that the price for our sins has been paid (Heb 4:14-16; 7:25; 8:1). "Christ Jesus is He who died, yes, rather who was raised, who is at the right hand of God, who also intercedes for us" (Rom 8:34).

In Rom 8:34 the relationship between Christ's resurrection and his present intercessory work as our great high priest is made clear. If Christ had not risen from the dead and ascended to the right hand of the Father, the atoning work of the cross would have been nullified. The resurrection/ascension is thus in a real sense the completion of Christ's work of atonement, the continuation of his priestly work.

That Christ's session at the Father's right hand would involve not only his kingship but also his priesthood is prophesied in Ps 110:1-4. Verse 4 says, "The LORD has sworn and will not change His mind, 'You are a priest forever according to the order of Melchizedek'" (see Heb 5:10; 6:20; 7:1-25). Christ began his work as priest by offering himself as the perfect sacrifice for our sins, and he continues his work as priest by presenting himself before the Father as our perpetual intercessor.

Scripture makes clear that Christ's humanity and sinlessness are prerequisites for his work as priest (1 Tim 2:5; Heb 2:14-18; 4:14-16; 7:26-28). But it also teaches that his resurrection from the dead is what enables him to be our heavenly high priest who can make eternal intercession between us and the Father. What qualifies Jesus to be our high priest is not physical descent from the line of Levi and Aaron, but "the power of an indestructible life" (Heb 7:16). This is how he can be "a priest forever" (Ps 110:4; Heb 7:21). All OT priests were only temporary "because they were prevented by death from continuing, but Jesus, on the other hand, because He continues forever, holds His priesthood permanently" (Heb 7:23-24). This is why "He is able also to save forever those who draw near to God through Him, since He always lives to make intercession for them" (Heb 7:25).

E. Christ's Resurrection Originates the New Creation

Fifth, Christ's resurrection is the origin of the new creation. The first or "old" creation in its entirety has suffered the effects of sin, particularly in the presence of disease, decay, and death. But the promise of salvation is the promise of a new creation: "Behold, I am making all things new" (Rev 21:5). This promise and this reality are grounded in the resurrection of Jesus unto glory.

1. The Beginning of the New Creation

The resurrection of Jesus (including especially his ascension in his glorified nature) was the actual beginning of God's new creation. Colossians 1:18 calls Jesus "the firstborn from the dead," which in this case means not only preeminence but also first in time. His resurrection was the first event of its kind, ever.

It was something entirely new, unlike any previous miracle or even any previous resurrection. Jesus alone was "raised from the dead . . . never to die again" (Rom 6:9; see Acts 13:34). By virtue of the glorification of his body he was raised into a new kind of existence, a new dimension of physical creation. This was a stupendous event comparable only to the original creation of Gen 1:1 (see the paralleling of creation and resurrection in Rom 4:17). Karl Heim has said,[11]

> . . . The Resurrection of Christ is in no way an event belonging to the present order of time as a link in the chain of events. Neither is it one of those miraculous events which do happen from time to time in our order of time, like the miracles of healing or the raising of dead as we find them in the apostolic age. The Resurrection of Christ is something fundamentally distinguished from all events which take place on the level of the present time. It is the beginning of the perfecting of the world. . . . The Resurrection of Christ therefore is the beginning of the new creation of the world which has been interrupted for a certain time by the "creative interval" in which we are still living at the moment, before it is entirely completed.

Thus we may think of Jesus' resurrection as inaugurating a whole new order of existence, the "new heavens and a new earth" of the eschaton itself (2 Pet 3:13). It is the prelude to the eschatological age, the most significant feature of which is that it will be cleansed of all the effects of sin and death, and will never again be touched by their alien power. "There will no longer be any death," nor any of the things related to it: no "mourning, or crying, or pain" (Rev 21:4). The glorified body of Jesus was the first instance of the new order from which death is forever excluded. This is why Jesus' resurrection is often called an "eschatological event." The new and eternal eschatological age has actually already begun; it began with his resurrection!

2. The Foundation of the New Creation

Jesus' resurrection is not only the beginning point of the new creation; it is also the very foundation of it. In other words, there is a cause-and-effect relationship between what happened to Jesus and what will happen to the rest of creation. We may compare the original creation with a magnificent building that has fallen into ruins. When it first came from the hand of its builder, it was beautiful indeed. But now it lies collapsed, its once-glorious wood and stone reduced to a pile of splinters and chips. Then in the fullness of time the original builder comes to the very site of the ruins in order to begin anew. When his work is finished, there appears amidst the heap of rubble a new and firm foundation laid upon solid rock. This unshakable foundation is our risen Lord himself.

As the foundation of the new creation, Jesus' resurrection is the event upon which all eschatological resurrections rest; his is the life upon which all life now depends. It is his "power of an indestructible life" (Heb 7:16) that infuses new life into our souls and bodies, sustains the living church in the midst of a dying world, and offers hope for the new creation to come. This is what Paul calls "the power of His resurrection" (Phil 3:10).

Paul's designation of Jesus as the second and last Adam (1 Cor 15:45,47) emphasizes the foundational nature of his resurrection. The image is introduced into the midst of the description of the nature of the resurrection body. Because of his resurrection Jesus has established a new family that will be like him rather than like the first Adam. When we are raised, we will bear his likeness, "so that He would be the firstborn among many brethren" (Rom 8:29).

3. The Guarantee of the New Creation

Finally, the resurrection of Jesus is not only the beginning and the foundation of the new creation, but it is also the *guarantee* that such a new creation will occur and will continue. The risen Christ is described as the "first fruits" (1 Cor 15:20,23). The first fruits are a promise of further harvest. If Jesus is the *first*, this in itself implies a second, and a third, and so on. The same is implied in his description as the "firstborn" (Rom 8:29; Col 1:18; Rev 1:5). Heim (*Jesus*, 166) makes this comment on the concept of first fruits:

> . . . According to Paul the Risen One is the first fruits . . . of the approaching harvest of the world. "For as by one man came death, by one man has come also the resurrection of the dead. For as in Adam all die, so also in Christ shall all be made alive" [I Cor. 15:21-22]. That is to say, as the process of death, once the stone has started rolling, can no longer be stopped but changes the whole of world history into one great dance of death, so also can the resurrection of the world once it has started no longer be stopped. It is like the awakening of the spring of the world. The movement cannot cease until the whole creation has become new. . . .

As the guarantee of the new creation, the resurrection of Jesus is the basis of our faith in the promises of salvation, which require us to believe in God's power to raise the dead to life again. Why should we believe the promises of spiritual and bodily resurrection? Why should we believe that it will happen to us? Because God raised *Jesus* from the dead, thereby demonstrating his sovereignty over death and the validity of the facts and promises revealed in his name. This is an aspect of the apologetical value of the resurrection of Christ. It is the very reason for our hope (1 Pet 3:15); we are "born again to a living hope through the resurrection of Jesus Christ from the dead" (1 Pet 1:3).

By way of contrast, we should also note that the resurrection of Jesus is the guarantee of judgment upon those who reject him, for God "has fixed a day in which He will judge the world in righteousness through a Man whom He has appointed, having furnished proof to all men by raising Him from the dead" (Acts 17:31).

F. Christ's Resurrection Reanimates the Dead

Sixth, Christ's resurrection reanimates the dead. When he personally burst the bonds of death, he unleashed renewing, life-giving power that will ultimately envelop the universe (2 Pet 3:13). As the first fruits of the new creation, he is the source and guarantee of a more abundant harvest. As believers we are a part of that harvest, and the power of his resurrection (Eph 1:18-20; Phil 3:10) saves us from death in two ways. (These will be discussed in more detail in later chapters.)

1. The Resurrection of Our Dead Spirits

The first phase of the new creation following the resurrection of Jesus began on the day of Pentecost when the risen Christ poured forth the Holy Spirit upon his waiting disciples (Acts 2:24-33). The purpose of this outpouring was to bestow a new gift upon the people of God, one not present in OT times (John 7:37-39). This was the gift of the indwelling of the Holy Spirit in the very life and body of believers (Acts 2:38; 1 Cor 6:19). Certain OT saints were given the Holy Spirit as an equipping power; but the Spirit's indwelling, life-giving presence was a gift from the risen Christ.

The immediate result of the Spirit's presence goes by many names in the New Testament, such as new birth (John 3:5), "regeneration and renewing" (Titus 3:5), and new creation itself (2 Cor 5:17; Eph 2:10). But the most significant description of the result of the Spirit's redemptive presence within us is *resurrection* or *making alive*. Through "the power of His resurrection" (Phil 3:10) brought into our souls in the person of the life-giving Spirit (John 6:63), our condition of inner spiritual death is replaced by spiritual life: "Even when we were dead in our transgressions, [God] made us alive together with Christ (by grace you have been saved), and raised us up with Him" (Eph 2:5-6). We have "passed out of death into life" (John 5:24; 1 John 3:14). Romans 6:3-4 says that, when a sinner is buried in the waters of baptism, he encounters the saving power of Jesus' death; and when he arises from the waters of baptism, he has within him the power of Jesus' resurrection, enabling him to "walk in newness of life."

This connection between baptism, Christ's resurrection, and our own spiritual resurrection is seen also in Col 2:12-13, which says we have "been buried with Him in baptism, in which you were also raised up with Him through faith in the working of God, who raised Him from the dead. When you were dead in your transgressions and the uncircumcision of your flesh, He made you alive together with Him, having forgiven us all our transgressions." This passage tells us what in part is going on during the act of baptism: nothing less than a resurrection from the dead, a work of new creation. This redemptive work of God takes place "through faith in the working of God," i.e., through faith that God is doing something here to save us from our sins as he has promised (Mark 16:16; Acts 2:38). We do not trust the water or the one baptizing us; our trust is completely in the power of God. We believe that just as surely as we are being buried into and raised up out of the water, so also is God raising our soul up out of that grave of spiritual death. Why should we believe that God can and will do this for us? Because he is the same God "who raised Him from the dead." The resurrection of Christ is thus the foundation of our faith that God can give life to our dead souls. The power which he displayed in raising Christ is the measure of the power he exerts upon us (Eph 1:19-20). This is why Peter can say that "baptism now saves you . . . through the resurrection of Jesus Christ" (1 Pet 3:21).

Those who have experienced this spiritual resurrection constitute the collective body called the church, which is built only from "living stones" (1 Pet 2:5). The church itself is the form in which the new creation exists in this present age. It has already begun to overcome the reign of death (Rom 5:14) and thus forms an island of life in the midst of a sea of death. Because it is built upon the risen Christ, the "gates of Hades," i.e., the "forces of death" (NEB) will never overpower it (Matt 16:18).

2. The Resurrection of Our Dead Bodies

The second phase of the new creation will be the day of the second coming of Jesus, when all the redeemed will receive new, glorified bodies.[12] Most will receive them at the moment of resurrection itself, but living believers will receive them in an instantaneous change: "In a moment, in the twinkling of an eye, at the last trumpet . . . the dead will be raised imperishable, and we will be changed" (1 Cor 15:52). This event is called "the redemption of our body," and Paul says this is what we are "waiting eagerly for" (Rom 8:23). See 2 Cor 5:1-5.

The glorified resurrection body of Jesus is the prototype or model after which our own glorified bodies will be patterned. Jesus "will transform the body of our humble state into conformity with the body of His glory, by the exertion of the power that He has even to subject all things to Himself" (Phil 3:21). This is what Paul means when he says that foreknown believers are "predestined to become conformed to the image of His Son" (Rom 8:29). That is, our own new bodies will be of the same nature as the glorified human body of Jesus. "We will be like Him, because we will see Him just as He is" (1 John 3:2); i.e., we shall be like him in his human bodily nature, not in his divine nature.

Again, the guarantee of the redemption of our bodies is the resurrection of Jesus from the dead. We know that we will be raised from the dead because Jesus himself has already been raised. "We know that the one who raised the Lord Jesus from the dead will also raise us with Jesus and present us with you in his presence" (2 Cor 4:14, NIV). Our bodily resurrection is just as certain as that of Jesus (1 Cor 15:12ff.). This again shows why it is so important that we maintain a firm faith in the literal, historical, bodily resurrection of Christ, and why Paul says that believing "that God raised Him from the dead" is a condition of salvation (Rom 10:9). Salvation in a very large measure *is* resurrection, and it flows from the redemptive fountain of the resurrection of Jesus Christ.

G. Christ's Resurrection Renovates the Universe

Finally, Christ's resurrection renovates the entire universe. The final phase of the new creation is the making of a new heavens and a new earth (2 Pet 3:13; Rev 21:1). In this expression "heavens" refers to the "starry heavens" above, or the farthest reaches of space. The expression as a whole thus refers to the totality of this physical universe, or "the creation." The renewal of the whole of this material creation is the ultimate result of the work of Jesus' resurrection.

When God first created this universe, it was "very good" (Gen 1:31); but the entrance of sin brought everything under the pall of corruption and death (Rom 8:20). Exactly how this has affected the nature of matter itself is not spelled out; we only know that it now exists in a kind of "slavery to corruption" (Rom 8:21) that makes it unfit or unsuitable for eternal existence. For this reason the whole material universe is included within the scope of redemption. Paul promises "that the creation itself also will be set free from its slavery to corruption into the freedom of the glory of the children of God" (Rom 8:21). How this will be done is described in 2 Pet 3:10-13, where the apostle pictures a great conflagration "in which the heavens will pass away with a roar and the elements will be destroyed with intense heat, and the earth and its works will be burned up." This will happen in the final day, "the day of God," in which "the heavens will be destroyed by burning, and the elements will melt with intense heat." But out of this cosmic holocaust will come "new heavens and a new earth, in which righteousness dwells." Whether we take the judgment on the old creation to be annihilation or just purification, the result is the same: a new creation that includes a new earth that will be a suitable eternal home for creatures with glorified bodies (Rom 8:22-23). See Rev 21:1–22:5.

Romans 5:10 well sums up the work of Christ: "For if while we were enemies we were reconciled to God through the death of His Son, much more, having been reconciled, we shall be saved by His life." Both his death and his risen life are absolutely essential for our salvation. Apart from the cross, there is no other sacrifice for sins (Heb 10:26). And if Christ did not rise from the dead, our faith is vain and we are still in our sins (1 Cor 15:14,17). But to the eternal praise of God's grace and to our everlasting gratitude, Christ's propitiatory atonement and his bodily resurrection are both real!

NOTES ON CHAPTER FOURTEEN

[1]On Luther's occasional use of the imagery, see Aulen, 103ff.

[2]Gregory of Nyssa, "Address," 22-26, *Christology of the Later Fathers*, 299-303.

[3]See my discussion of three examples of this view—Hendrikus Berkhof, P.J. Achtemeier, and Robert Brinsmead—in *GRe*, 420-423.

[4]L. Morris, *Preaching*, 155. Morris's treatment of propitiation in this volume is unsurpassed.

[5]See Don Clark, 3-4; Bishop, 302-303, 320-326.

[6]See *GRe*, 15-18. Also significant is the Hebrew word *padah*, "to redeem, ransom, rescue." See ibid., 20.

[7]For a meticulously detailed study of this word group, see B.B. Warfield, "'Redemption,'" 429ff.

[8]This presents an interesting image of the atoning work of Christ: "a Lamb for a donkey."

[9]E.g., walking on water (Matt 14:22-33); the multiplication of the loaves and fishes (John 6:1-13); the dematerializing and rematerializing of Philip (Acts 8:39-40).

[10]For a more complete presentation of this view, see Jack Cottrell, "Faith," 143-160.

[11]Karl Heim, *Jesus*, 166. Heim accepts the common but questionable view that Jesus received his new body as soon as he was revived from the dead. His comments are quite pertinent, however, when taken as referring to the ascended, glorified Christ.

[12]Only the redeemed will receive glorified bodies. The nature of the eschatological bodies of the lost is not described in the Bible, but we can safely conclude that it will not be the same as that of the bodies of the saved. The lost do experience a resurrection (Dan 12:2; John 5:29), but it is not redemptive in nature. In no sense do the lost share in the results of the redemptive work of God.

CHAPTER FIFTEEN

THE PERSON AND WORK OF THE HOLY SPIRIT

This chapter deals with the biblical doctrine of the Holy Spirit, both his person (who he is) and his work (what he does). First we shall see that the Holy Spirit is a *divine person*, one of the three persons of the Trinity. Then we shall see that the Spirit's main work is twofold: he gives us *knowledge* and he gives us *power*. We shall also see how the Spirit's work is crucial to the beginning of the New Creation. As is true of the Logos, although he was active in the OT era, his principal and unique work is related to the New Creation, to the lives of Christians.

The principal words for "spirit" are *ruach* in the OT and *pneuma* in the NT. In addition to "spirit," these terms can also mean "breath" and "wind," as determined by the context. The terms are used of created spirits, i.e., angels (fallen and unfallen) and the spiritual aspect of human beings, as well as of divine, uncreated spirit. In our earlier discussion of the nature of God we pointed out that every spiritual being is living, personal, nonmaterial, and invisible. All these characteristics apply to the Holy Spirit.

Why is the Holy Spirit called the *Holy* Spirit? Two reasons may be given. First, the term "holy" means "to be separate, distinct, set apart." The Holy Spirit is holy in this sense because he is set apart from all finite, created spirits. Second, he is called the *Holy* Spirit because, in comparison with the Father and Son, his main work is to make us *holy* in the ethical sense. Holiness is his distinctive work.

Many different biblical expressions are used to refer to the Holy Spirit. For example, in the OT he is called the Spirit of God, the Spirit of Yahweh, and the Holy Spirit (Ps 51:11; Isa 63:10-11). In the NT he is called (e.g.) the Spirit, the Holy Spirit, the Spirit of holiness, the Spirit of God, the Spirit of the Lord, the Spirit of Christ, the Spirit of truth, and the Spirit of life. Sometimes the definite article is used ("*the* Spirit"), but often it is not. No conclusions can be drawn from the presence or absence of the article, or from the presence or absence of the adjective "holy." The context will determine whether the term "spirit" is being used of the Holy Spirit or of some other kind of spirit.

I. THE PERSON OF THE HOLY SPIRIT

Who or what is the Holy Spirit? In answering this question there are two main issues. First, is the Spirit a *person* who is distinct from the Father and the Son? Second, if he is a person, is he a *divine* person?

Many aberrant versions of Christianity deny the divine personhood of the Spirit. Unitarianism and modern liberal theology usually deny the existence of the Spirit as a person separate from the Father. This is true of several cults also. For example, Jehovah's Witnesses equate the "holy spirit" (never capitalized) with God's impersonal, invisible active force or power. The same is true of Victor Paul Wierwille's group, The Way International.

In the early Christian centuries the trinitarian formula (especially Matt 28:19) was used faithfully but with little theological reflection. Up to A.D. 325 most of the church's theological attention was given to Jesus, as is shown in the original Nicene Creed, which spelled out the meaning of his divine nature in some detail. But of the Spirit this creed simply stated, "We believe . . . in the Holy Spirit." In the next half-century, though, more attention was focused on the person of the Spirit. At the Council of Constantinople in A.D. 381 a revised Nicene Creed was produced, with a slightly more complete statement on the Spirit: "We believe . . . in the Holy Spirit, the Lord and the Life-giver, that proceedeth from the Father, who with Father and Son is worshiped together and glorified together, who spoke through the prophets" (Bettenson, 37).

A. The Holy Spirit Is a Person

What do the biblical data show about the nature of the Spirit? First of all, the Bible portrays the Spirit as a *person* in every sense of the word. This is seen in several ways. For one thing, in the Bible a spiritual being is by nature a personal being; there is no such thing as an impersonal spirit.

For another thing, Jesus' designation of the Spirit as *allos parakletos* ("another Helper") in John 14:16 is a twofold demonstration of his personhood. A *parakletos* is a "counselor for the defense," equivalent to an attorney, which is in itself a personal concept. Also, the word *allos* means "another of the same kind" (in contrast with *heteros*, "another of a different kind"). In other words, the Spirit would be another Helper of the same kind as Jesus himself. Thus the Spirit must be personal, like Jesus.

Another way the Bible portrays the Spirit as a person is that it puts him in lists parallel with other persons, e.g., Matt 28:19 and Acts 15:28.

For another thing, in the Bible the Holy Spirit is pictured as doing the kinds of things persons do. For example, he exhibits intellectual activity (Rom 8:26-27; 1 Cor 2:10-11); he exhibits volitional activity such as choosing or making decisions (Acts 13:2; 15:28; 16:6-7; 20:28; 1 Cor 12:11); he speaks (John 16:13-14; Acts 8:29; 13:2; 1 Tim 4:1; Rev 2:7); he teaches (John 14:26; 1 Cor 2:13); and he experiences emotions or feelings such as love (Rom 15:30) and grief (Eph 4:30; Isa 63:10).

Finally, the Spirit is treated like a person. He may be lied to (Acts 5:3), tempted (Acts 5:9), blasphemed (Matt 12:31), and insulted (Heb 10:29).

Some mistakenly think that because the Greek noun for "spirit" is neuter in gender (*to pneuma*), rather than masculine or feminine, therefore the Spirit must be a *thing* rather than a person. Such an idea simply shows an ignorance of Greek grammar. Actually the gender of a noun (along with any adjectives and pronouns referring to it) is not necessarily related to the gender of the reality for which it stands. *Things* are often represented by nouns that are masculine or feminine (e.g., *ho artos* [masc.], "bread"), and persons are often described with nouns that are neuter (e.g., *to paidion*, "infant, child"). Thus the fact that *pneuma* is neuter is completely irrelevant. What is more significant is the fact that, when using this neuter noun to refer to the Holy Spirit, Scripture sometimes uses *masculine* pronouns when grammatically they should be neuter (e.g., John 14:26; 15:26; 16:13-14; Eph 1:14). This is a testimony to the Spirit's personal nature.

Since the Holy Spirit is a person, we should never refer to him as an object. We should never refer to him as "it," but should always use the personal pronouns "he," "his," and "him."

B. The Holy Spirit Is a Divine Person

The Bible portrays the Holy Spirit not only as a person, but also as a *divine* person. We have already noted several trinitarian references that treat the Father, Son, and Spirit as equal or parallel in majesty and achievement (Matt 28:19; 1 Cor 12:4-6; 2 Cor 1:21-22; 13:14; Eph 4:4-6; 1 Pet 1:2). Also, divine characteristics are applied to the Spirit: he is eternal (Heb 9:14; see 1 Tim 6:16), he is omniscient (1 Cor 2:10-11; see Isa 40:13-14), he is omnipresent (Ps 139:7-10), and he is omnipotent (Gen 1:2; Ps 104:30; Zech 4:6). Also, Jesus says that blasphemy against the Holy Spirit is the worst of all sins, even unforgivable (Matt 12:31-32; Mark 3:28-29). This is incomprehensible unless he is divine.

A final indicator of the Spirit's deity is the fact that in Acts 5:1-4 he is specifically referred to as God. When Ananias lied about the selling price of his property, Peter informed him that he was lying not just to the apostles but to the Holy Spirit (v. 3). Then he says, "You have not lied to men but to God" (v. 4), thus identifying the Holy Spirit as God.

Also, we must stress that the divine Spirit is not just the person of God the Father manifesting himself in a different mode. There are passages that make it clear that Father, Son, and Holy Spirit are persons who are distinct from one another (see Luke 3:21-22; John 14:26; 16:7; Acts 2:32-33; Rom 8:11,26-27; Eph 2:18; Isa 48:16). See the discussion of modalism above (pp. 73, 253-255).

Since the Holy Spirit is divine, is it proper to worship him? Yes, in fact, it is wrong *not* to worship him. As the song says, "Praise Father, Son, and Holy Ghost." We should point out, though, that there are no biblical examples or precedents for addressing the Holy Spirit directly in praise or in prayer. The biblical pattern for prayer seems to be that we should pray to the Father (Matt 6:9), in the name of Jesus as mediator (John 14:13-14; 1 Tim 2:5), through the power of the Holy Spirit (Rom 8:26-27).

II. THE WORK OF THE HOLY SPIRIT: HE GIVES US KNOWLEDGE

We turn now to the *work* of the Spirit, which can be divided into two main categories: he gives us *knowledge* and he gives us *power*. Here we are discussing the former. The main point is that the Spirit gives us knowledge through the teaching of the Bible, which he inspired.

A. The Holy Spirit and the Bible

How the Holy Spirit relates to the Bible is a matter of both strong agreement and strong disagreement among Christians. The one thing that all conservative believers agree on is that the Spirit is the ultimate *author* of the Bible. We are far from unanimous, though, as to whether or how the Spirit helps us to *understand* the Bible.

1. The Holy Spirit and the Origin of the Bible

Throughout our discussion of biblical revelation and inspiration (see pp. 44-57), it was clear that the Bible portrays the Holy Spirit as the person of the Trinity who was the principal agent in transmitting God's own words to the biblical writers and in guaranteeing that everything they wrote was accurate and complete. In this sense we may speak of the Holy Spirit as the ultimate source or origin of the Bible.

In both the OT[1] and the NT[2] the Holy Spirit is presented as the source of oral or *spoken* prophecy, and he is likewise cited as the source of the *written* Word, the Bible. The Psalmist David is probably referring to the latter when he says, "The Spirit of the LORD spoke by me, and His word was on my tongue" (2 Sam 23:2; see Isa 59:21; Ezek 2:2). New Testament testimony to the Spirit as the source of the written Word is abundant. He is cited as the source of OT Scripture. A typical passage is Acts 1:16, where the apostle Peter says that "the Scripture had to be fulfilled, which the Holy Spirit foretold by the mouth of David." In 2 Pet 1:21 the apostle says the OT Scriptures were produced when "men moved by the Holy Spirit spoke from God."[3] The NT also specifies the Spirit as the source of its own content. Jesus promised that the Spirit of truth would guide the apostles into all the truth (John 16:13; see 14:26; 15:26). The apostle Paul says that NT prophets and apostles have spoken to us "not in words taught by human wisdom, but in those taught by the Spirit" (1 Cor 2:13).[4]

We do not have to understand the mechanics of how the Spirit accomplished this; what is important is simply the *result* of the Spirit's work of revelation and inspiration, i.e., a permanent, errorless record of God's works and will for us and his message of hope for our salvation and eternal life. When we consider the deep questions of life that are answered for us in the Bible, e.g., questions about origins, ethics, and eternal life, and when we consider the futile and ever-changing efforts to answer such questions by those who reject the Bible, then we can appreciate the truth of this statement: *the most important thing the Holy Spirit ever did for us was to give us the Bible.* As believers we are so familiar with the role of the Scriptures as the answer-book for tough questions that we take it for granted, and we forget what a blessed gift of knowledge the Spirit has given us therein.

2. The Holy Spirit and the Understanding of the Bible

Many Christians believe that the Holy Spirit not only has given us the Bible as such, but also gives us definitive, subjective help in understanding it. This is called the doctrine of illumination, which is the idea that the Spirit speaks directly to our minds, directly stimulating our intellects to perceive the true meaning of Scripture. The following texts are said to promise this gift of knowledge to every believer: Matt 10:19-20; John 14:26; 16:13; 1 Cor 2:10-13; Heb 8:10-11 (Jer 31:31-34); 1 John 2:20,27. Some take this to be the main purpose of the Spirit's indwelling, and they pray, "Open my eyes, illumine me, Spirit divine."

The doctrine of illumination as commonly taught is not a biblical doctrine. This is true for four reasons. One, Christian people who claim to be illumined by the Spirit often have different and even opposing understandings of the same passages of Scripture, e.g., texts about gender roles or the millennium.

Two, In the final analysis it is a useless idea, for even those who believe in illumination recognize that individual Christians grow in their understanding and sometimes change their interpretations of Scripture. When this happens, one always assumes that he is changing from a mistaken view to the correct view, or from a nonillumined view to an illumined view. But does this not mean that what he once thought was an illumined view was actually a mistaken view? So how can he be sure that his present views are illumined rather than mistaken, and that no further changes will occur?

Three, the doctrine of illumination is actually the product of the doctrine of universal total depravity. Illumination is necessary because the totally depraved person is completely blind in his intellect and *cannot* understand the Bible unless illumined by the Spirit (see Palmer, 54-57). But as we have already seen above, the doctrine of total depravity is itself not biblical. The sinner's blindness is partial and willful, not total and inborn (Rom 1:18; Eph 4:18).

The fourth reason for rejecting the doctrine of illumination is that it has no exegetical basis in Scripture. Ironically, the passages cited as proof-texts for this doctrine are themselves misinterpreted and misapplied. For example, Matt 10:19-20; John 14:26; 16:13; and 1 Cor 2:10-13 apply only to the *apostles*, and refer to revelation and inspiration. They are not general promises to all Christians; to apply them thus is a serious error.

Hebrews 8:10-11 (citing Jeremiah 31:31-34) is talking about the nature of the New Covenant as opposed to the Old Covenant. Individuals were under the Old Covenant as soon as they were born physically, without having any internal commitment to or understanding of the covenant itself as written externally on tablets of stone. But a person enters the New Covenant through the *new* birth only *after* he has understood and committed himself to its terms, i.e., only after he has internalized it in his heart. *How* it is internalized is not the point.

In 1 John 2:20,27 the "anointing" does not refer to the Holy Spirit received from God, but to apostolic revelation itself as received from the Holy Spirit. In verse 20 the Holy One is the Holy Spirit, the anointing is the apostolic revelation (for Christians today, the Bible), and "you all know" refers to the knowledge received through the apostolic revelation (the Bible). That which "abides in you" (v. 27) is the apostolic revelation "which you heard from the beginning" (vv. 14,24). John here is warning against the false teachings of the antichrist (vv. 18,26). His point is this: the original truth, which you heard from the beginning (v. 7), is still true; it is the standard of truth. Go back to it and you can see that these false teachers are lying.

Even though the doctrine of illumination is false, this does not mean that we receive no help from God in our effort to understand Scripture. What it means is that such help is not a distinctive work of the Spirit. It is rather something God promises to us as a part of his special providential answer to prayer. See Ps 119:18; Eph 1:17-18; Phil 1:9-10; Col 1:9. All these Scriptures are prayers; and answers to prayer may be the work of the Father, the Son, or the Spirit. God will not answer such prayers by directly feeding knowledge into our minds, but by providing us with the means to achieve this knowledge through personal study. He will sharpen our mental processes, clear our preoccupied minds, prevent distractions, help us to concentrate, and help us to recall ideas or put ideas together. Also, James 1:5 instructs us to pray for wisdom. This is not a prayer for new knowledge, but for discernment in how to use and apply what is already known.

B. The Holy Spirit and Special Gifts of Knowledge

Does the Spirit give us knowledge in any way besides the pages of Scripture? Some Christians assume that the "gift of the Holy Spirit" received in Christian baptism (Acts 2:38) is for the very purpose of supplementing our knowledge by providing us with subjective guidance that helps us know the will of God for our lives. This is a mistaken view of the purpose of the Spirit's indwelling. We receive the gift of the Spirit not to add knowledge to our minds but to stimulate and strengthen our *wills* for obedience and service. To be "led by the Spirit" (Rom 8:14) is not to receive subjective intellectual enlightenment but to receive inward empowerment to overcome moral weakness and put sin to death in our bodies (Rom 8:13).

It is true that some of the Spirit's special gifts to the early Christians were gifts of supernatural knowledge, i.e., prophecy, the word of knowledge, the word of wisdom, and the gift of tongues when accompanied by the gift of interpretation (1 Cor 12:8-10). In such ways the Spirit gave knowledge to the churches, providing them with authoritative teaching in the period between Pentecost and the writing of the NT. Many Christians believe that the Spirit is still giving such gifts of supernatural knowledge to the church. Others believe these gifts ceased when the NT writings came into existence. I take the latter view. The Holy Spirit does not give knowledge to us in these ways today, as will be discussed below.

We conclude, then, that the Holy Spirit's gift of knowledge is mediated to Christians today through the Bible and in no other way.

III. THE WORK OF THE HOLY SPIRIT: HE GIVES US POWER

The second main work of the Spirit is to bestow power upon God's people. He does this in two ways. First, he equips certain individuals with abilities that enable them to meet the needs of the group, i.e., he empowers them for service. Second, he enters into the hearts and lives of all believers to give them the ability to fight the power of sin in their lives, i.e., he indwells them for sanctification. It is especially important to understand how these two works of the Spirit are related to the OT era and the NT era respectively.

A. The Holy Spirit's Work in the Old Testament Age

The OT pictures the Spirit as acting upon the world in general, first of all in reference to creation. He was active in the initial creation (Gen 1:2) and in the creation of mankind (Gen 1:26). Though Gen 2:7 may imply that he acted in the creation of Adam, the Spirit is not actually mentioned in this verse; and attempts to equate him with the "breath [*n'shamah*] of life" are totally erroneous. The Spirit was also active in God's providential control of the world (Gen 6:3), and especially in the history of Israel (Neh 9:20,30; Isa 30:1; 63:10-11,14; Zech 4:6).

In Israel the Spirit's main work was of the first kind mentioned above, i.e., he gave various abilities to individuals in order to enable them to perform special tasks and ministries in the service of the nation as a whole. The most prominent of these abilities was the gift of prophecy, which was given to a large number of men from Moses to Malachi. This enabled them to speak inspired messages from God.[5] The Spirit equipped various men to be great leaders of the people, e.g., Moses (Num 11:17,25), Joshua (Num 27:18; Deut 34:9), Saul (1 Sam 10:1-13; 16:14), and David (1 Sam 16:13; Ps 51:11). He also equipped the various judges of Israel to lead the people.[6] Also, the Spirit equipped a large number of Israelites with gifts of craftsmanship, to enable them to build the tabernacle according to God's instructions (Exod 31:2-6; 35:30-35; 36:1-2). In these texts the language suggests that the Spirit sharpened and intensified natural skills that may already have been present.

This is also true of the seventy elders of Israel who were chosen to be Moses' special assistants in Num 11:16-30. They were already in positions of leadership among the people, but the Spirit came upon them in order to enhance their skills. The unique thing about this event is that the occasion of their reception of these nonmiraculous leadership skills was at that moment accompanied by miraculous manifestations called prophesying (v. 25; see 1 Sam 10:6,10; 19:20-24). This was not just ordinary praise to God (contrary to the opinion of Wood, 110-111), but consisted of miraculous ecstatic utterances that were not repeated.[7] The prophesying was such a unique occurrence that it was considered abnormal and worth reporting (vv. 26-27). The purpose of this miraculous prophesying was to provide evidence that the equipping gifts of the Spirit had indeed been bestowed upon these seventy men.

It is clear that the Spirit bestowed ministering power in OT times, but what about moral power? Was the Spirit given to individual Israelites as a source of moral or spiritual power? The answer seems to be no; the saving, sanctifying work of the Spirit was probably not a part of his work prior to the New Covenant. The Spirit was an external influence, equipping individuals physically and mentally, and using them instrumentally. But there was no indwelling presence, no inner influence upon the heart. He worked *upon* rather than *within*. When David implored God, "Do not take Your Holy Spirit from me" (Ps 51:11), he was referring to the equipping presence of the Spirit given to him when he was anointed by Samuel (1 Sam 16:13).

The fact that Israelites did not have the indwelling, sanctifying presence of the Spirit may be why it was important for them to be geographically and culturally isolated from the pagan nations surrounding them (unlike Christians, who are told to "go into all the world," Mark 16:15). It may also be why Moses' law had to take account of the Jews' "hardness of heart" (Matt 19:8). In OT times God's plan was holiness through separation; in NT times it is separation through holiness.

We may sum up the Spirit's work in OT times in the following seven statements: 1) The Spirit's gifts were not given to all God's people, even among the saved within Israel. 2) The Spirit's gifts were bestowed to equip for service, not to sanctify inwardly. 3) The Spirit's gifts were not given to individuals for personal benefit, but for the good of the whole body of Israel. 4) Such gifts were temporary and lasted only as long as the need for the person's services remained (cf. 1 Sam 10:10 and 16:14; cf. 1 Sam 16:13 and Ps 51:11). 5) Miraculous signs accompanied such gifts at least once for evidential purposes, but these signs were temporary (Num 11:25). 6) One did not have to be a believer to receive this kind of empowering from the Spirit (e.g., Balaam, Num 24:2; Saul, 1 Sam 19:20-24). 7) Sometimes the gifts were given through human agency such as anointing or laying on of hands (Deut 34:9 [see Num 27:18-20]; 1 Sam 16:13; 2 Kgs 2:9-15), and sometimes were given directly without human agents (Num 11:25-26).

B. From Old Creation to New Creation

As Christians we know that world history is divided into two major periods: the Old Covenant era and the New Covenant era, and on a deeper level, the Old

Creation and the New Creation. We also know that the dividing line is Jesus Christ; even the world in general marks dates in terms of B.C. and A.D., in reference to the birth of Christ.

It is certainly true that the coming of Jesus Christ was the turning point in history, and that the present age is the Messianic age. But this is not the whole truth. Another crucial factor in the bisection of history was the coming of the Holy Spirit to be present within his people in a new and unprecedented way. This new work of the Spirit began on the Day of Pentecost, which in a real sense was as much a turning point in history as was the day Christ was born.[8] History from that point onward could well be called the age of the Holy Spirit, because the Holy Spirit is truly the dynamic power at work in this new era.

Just as the OT prophesied the coming of the Messiah, so did it prophesy the coming of the Spirit: "For I will pour out water on the thirsty land and streams on the dry ground; I will pour out My Spirit on your offspring and My blessing on your descendants" (Isa 44:3; see 32:15; 43:19-20). Ezekiel 36:27 promises, "I will put my Spirit within you and cause you to walk in My statutes" (see 39:29). A crucial prophecy, quoted in Acts 2:16-21 as being fulfilled on Pentecost, is Joel 2:28-32. God says through Joel, "It will come about after this that I will pour out My Spirit on all mankind; and your sons and daughters will prophesy, your old men will dream dreams, your young men will see visions. Even on the male and female servants I will pour out My Spirit in those days" (vv. 28-29). See Zech 12:10.

All these texts point forward to a new age with important differences regarding the role of the Spirit. Joel says the Spirit will be a *universal* gift, given to all God's people and not just to a few. Ezekiel says the Spirit will be an *inward* gift, working within the heart to empower for holy living. The event of the Spirit's coming is couched in the imagery of *water*, of a great outpouring of life-giving water.

The water imagery is continued in the Gospels, as both John the Baptist and Jesus continued to point forward to a new age marked by a new kind of work of the Holy Spirit. In a figure suggested by his work of baptizing in the waters of the Jordan River, John declared that the Messiah himself would offer a baptism in the Spirit (Matt 3:11; Mark 1:8; Luke 3:16; John 1:33; Acts 1:5). In another water image suggested by different circumstances, Jesus promised to provide "living water" for thirsty people to drink: "If anyone is thirsty, let him come to Me and drink. He who believes in Me, as the Scripture said, 'From his innermost being will flow rivers of living water'" (John 7:37-38; see 4:10-14). John 7:39 explains: "But this He spoke of the Spirit, whom those who believed in Him were to receive; for the Spirit was not yet given, because Jesus was not yet glorified." In other words, this living water, the Holy Spirit, would not be poured out until after Jesus' ascension and enthronement, i.e., until Pentecost (Acts 2:32-36).

What is the nature of this new-creation work of the Spirit? What is he doing today (since Pentecost) that he was not doing in the OT era? It is a work of salvation performed directly upon the hearts of individual believers, and it has to do with the second part of the double cure. It is best explained in terms of conversion, as the next section will show.

C. The Holy Spirit's Work in the New Testament Age

In examining the Spirit's work in the present era we are using an individual's conversion as the reference point. We shall see that the Spirit works in a specific way prior to conversion, in a different way during conversion, and in still other ways after conversion. I am using the term "conversion" not in the sense of the entire process by which an unbeliever becomes a member of the body of Christ, but in the narrow sense of the *precise moment* when an unsaved person becomes saved.

1. Before Conversion

Prior to conversion the Spirit's work is focused upon causing faith and repentance to arise in the heart of an unbeliever. The Spirit exerts an influence upon unbelievers' hearts, to "convict the world concerning sin and righteousness and judgment" (John 16:8). The word for "convict" (*elencho*) refers to the act of making one's sins known to him in order to prompt him to feel a sense of personal guilt and then to correct his behavior. This is done by the presentation of truth or proof to the intellect and not simply by emotional manipulation. The Spirit may accomplish this in two ways, i.e., through the power of the written Word of God and through providential intervention in a person's life. The first is always involved; the second may or may not be.

The main way the Spirit works on the heart of an unbeliever is through the inspired message of the Bible. The power of the Word of God is always the principal agent that leads to faith and repentance. John says of his Gospel that these things "have been written so that you may believe" (John 20:31). The gospel is "the power of God for salvation" (Rom 1:16). "Faith comes from hearing, and hearing by the word of Christ" (Rom 10:17). See also Luke 8:11-15; John 6:44-45; 1 Cor 4:15; Heb 4:12; Jas 1:18; 1 Pet 1:23. The influence of the Word upon the hearts of sinners can be called the work of the Holy Spirit, since the Holy Spirit is the one who inspired its writing in the first place. What the Word accomplishes, the Spirit accomplishes.

The second way the Spirit may work to bring a sinner to faith and repentance is through providential means, similar to what was discussed earlier in the section on how the Spirit may help us to understand the Bible. As in that case, this is not an exclusive work of the Spirit but may also be performed by the Father and the Son. The idea is that, in addition to the influence of the Word (which will always be present), God may work on the heart in providential ways to bring about a confrontation with the truth and an encouragement to believe and repent. For example, he may lead a person to cross paths with someone who can witness to him; he may raise certain thoughts or memories to consciousness; he may soften the heart through natural disasters, sickness, family tragedy, or an overheard remark or song. The possibility of such providential activity makes it appropriate for us to pray for the conversion of the lost.

We must be careful to avoid two extremes in our understanding of how the Spirit works prior to conversion. First, we must reject the idea that the *only* way that God the Spirit works in this context is through the Bible. We must not forget the possibility of providential activity. Second, we must reject the Calvinist idea that the Holy Spirit directly plants faith and repentance into an unbeliever's heart through an act of selective, irresistible grace. Whatever the Spirit does prior to conversion, his work is *universal* and *resistible*. The gospel of the Savior's death exerts a drawing power upon all who hear it (John 12:32), but this power can be resisted (Acts 7:51).

Although it is true that the Spirit works prior to conversion in the ways indicated, this aspect of his work is not really the new kind of work associated exclusively with the New Covenant era. Even in OT times the Spirit worked through the power of the prophetic word and through providential means to bring sinners to repentance and faith. The Spirit's new work is performed in the event of conversion itself, and in his work following conversion.

2. During Conversion

As noted above, I am using the term "conversion" to denote the exact moment when a lost person becomes saved, i.e., the moment when justification, regeneration, and initial sanctification occur. The question is, what is the Holy Spirit himself doing at this moment? What work is he performing upon the sinner's heart in order to make salvation a reality? The answer is that at the moment of conversion, at the same time that justification occurs, the Spirit performs the work of regeneration upon the sinner's heart.

A great deal of confusion has arisen over this subject, especially in the Restoration Movement, because of a failure to properly distinguish between what God promises to do for us in order to save us (e.g., justification and regeneration), and what God requires of us as preconditions for doing his work (e.g., faith and repentance). This has led many in effect to equate the change of heart that takes place in faith and repentance with regeneration itself. That is, they say that the only change that takes place in the heart is the change the sinner himself brings about when he makes his decision to believe and repent. When faith and repentance occur, regeneration occurs. They do not mean that faith and repentance *lead to* regeneration, but that faith and repentance *are* regeneration. Because of this equation, the heart-change known as regeneration is in reality the sinner's own work; he regenerates himself. The Holy Spirit is involved only insofar as he was the ultimate author of the Word of God which motivates the sinner to believe and repent.

This is seriously false doctrine. The regeneration that takes place at the moment of conversion is the work of the Holy Spirit, not the work of the sinner.

Later we will discuss the nature of regeneration as such; at this point we simply want to stress the biblical testimony that it is something accomplished by the Holy Spirit as he works directly upon the believing soul. It is not accomplished directly by the power of the Word, or even through faith in the Word. It is accomplished by the Spirit alone on the precondition of faith in the gospel as motivated by the Word.

As we shall see later, the essence of regeneration is resurrection from spiritual death (John 5:24-25; Rom 6:4-11; Eph 2:5; Col 2:11-13; 1 John 3:14). The Holy Spirit is the source and giver of life (see John 6:63; Rom 8:2,6,11,13; 1 Cor 15:45; 2 Cor 3:6; Gal 6:8). He is the "living water" (John 4:10; 7:38), i.e., the water that gives life. When he enters the sinner's heart, he brings new life. The sinner is born again into new life through the Spirit's power (John 3:5). The regeneration and renewing that occur in the heart are from the Spirit (Titus 3:5). The gift of the Holy Spirit promised in Acts 2:38 is the same as the "times of refreshing" in Acts 3:19.

It is very important that we understand this inner regeneration as a work of the Holy Spirit himself, and that we regard it as part of the new work of the Spirit in the age of the new creation. This is one of the blessings God reserved for his NT saints. Whatever else the Spirit did for sinners in the OT era, he did not regenerate them as he has now been doing since Pentecost. This inward presence of the living water did not begin until after the ascension and enthronement (John 7:37-39).

Precisely when does the Spirit accomplish regeneration? We have said that faith and repentance are preconditions for it, but that does not mean that regeneration occurs *as soon as* faith and repentance are present. In fact (as we shall discuss later) regeneration takes place during the act of Christian baptism. This does not happen as the result of any inherent power in the water of baptism or in the act itself, but only through the power of the Holy Spirit working during this event in accordance with God's promises.[9] That regeneration occurs at this point is taught in Rom 6:3-4 and Col 2:12; that it is the work of the Spirit in this event is seen in Titus 3:5 and John 3:5, and implied in Acts 2:38-39.[10]

What about those cases in the book of Acts where the Holy Spirit seems to be given apart from baptism, i.e., Acts 2:1-4; 8:14-18; 10:44-48; 19:1-7? The main point is that the giving of the Spirit in these contexts is not the Spirit's internal presence for the purpose of salvation as in Acts 2:38, but the bestowing of miraculous manifestations that functioned as signs that proved the truth of the accompanying revelation.

This regenerating work of the Spirit during water baptism is what the Bible calls being baptized in the Holy Spirit, something it was promised that Jesus would do (Matt 3:11; Mark 1:8; Luke 3:16; John 1:33; Acts 1:4-5; 11:16). It is a serious error to connect the baptism of the Spirit with the miraculous manifestations that sometimes accompanied it as signs (Acts 2, Acts 10), whether this be regarded as something available to all Christians (as in Pentecostalism and the

Charismatic movement) or as something intentionally limited to Pentecost and Cornelius (as often in the Restoration Movement). In 1 Cor 12:13 Paul affirms that we were *all* baptized by the one Spirit into the body of Christ.[11] This is not some special event or experience limited to a few. It is the general experience of all Christians and is equivalent to the Spirit's work of regeneration and the beginning of his indwelling. There is no necessary connection between baptism in the Spirit and miraculous gifts of the Spirit.

3. After Conversion

The Spirit works in two main ways in the lives of individual Christians after conversion. First, he continues to indwell the bodies and lives of Christians in order to give us moral power to live a holy life. This is his work of sanctification, which is a continuation of what was begun in regeneration and which is also part of the Spirit's new work in the age of the new creation.

The fact of the Spirit's indwelling is clearly taught in the Bible. It was prophesied in Ezek 36:27, "I will put My Spirit within you." Jesus said the Spirit would be like "rivers of living water" flowing up from the believer's innermost being (John 7:38). "Your body is a temple of the Holy Spirit who is in you," says Paul (1 Cor 6:19). "The Spirit of God dwells in you," he says (Rom 8:9-11; see 2 Tim 1:14); he is "in our hearts" (2 Cor 1:22; see Gal 4:6).

This indwelling should not be equated with simple divine omnipresence, nor should we limit it to the fact that the Word of God dwells in our hearts (Col 3:16). The Holy Spirit himself actually, personally, and uniquely dwells within the hearts and bodies of NT saints. We do not know *how* this occurs, but we do know *why*. It is not for the purpose of knowledge, but for power. The Spirit continues to dwell within us to give us the *moral power* to overcome sin and to live according to God's holy will (Rom 8:13; 1 Cor 12:3; Gal 5:22-23; Eph 3:16: Phil 2:13). This is how he leads us (Rom 8:4,14; Gal 5:16,18,25); this is how he fills us (Eph 5:18). He produces the fruit of holiness in our lives (Gal 5:22-23). When we spurn his sanctifying power and continue in sin, we quench him (1 Thess 5:19) and grieve him (Eph 4:30). (Sanctification itself will be discussed in more detail in chapter 18.)

The second way the Spirit works after conversion is that he equips Christians for service by bestowing "spiritual gifts" upon them. Spiritual gifts are gifts or abilities given to individuals by the Spirit (1 Cor 12:11), whereas in the work of sanctification the Spirit himself is the gift given to believers. Also, the purpose of spiritual gifts is to equip individual Christians to meet the needs of the church as a whole (Rom 12:4-5; 1 Cor 12:7; 14:12; Eph 4:12-16; 1 Pet 4:10-11), whereas the Spirit's sanctifying presence is for the spiritual benefit of the individual himself. Such NT spiritual gifts are in continuity with the way the Spirit equipped saints in the OT and are not part of his prophesied and promised new work.

The NT has four lists of spiritual gifts: Rom 12:3-8; Eph 4:11; 1 Cor 12:8-10; 1 Cor 12:28-30. Some of these gifts involve miraculous powers (e.g., apostles, prophecy, supernatural knowledge, tongues, healing, miracles). Most of the gifts do not involve miraculous powers, though, but consist of the ability to lead or to rule, the ability to teach and preach the Word, and the ability to assist or to serve in various specific ways.

These lists are not necessarily exhaustive. The Spirit may give abilities such as the ones specifically named or others such as counseling and computer expertise. He may give abilities where none existed before, or he may enhance natural talents and direct them toward service to the body of Christ as a whole. Just as gifts of craftsmanship were given in the OT to enable the Israelites to build the tabernacle of the Lord, so today the necessary gifts are given to enable us all together to build up the Lord's spiritual temple (Eph 2:19-22; 4:11-16; 1 Pet 2:5).

IV. DOES THE HOLY SPIRIT GIVE MIRACULOUS GIFTS TODAY?

A subject of major disagreement among Christians is whether the Spirit gives miraculous gifts to individuals today. This category refers to gifts that equip individuals to perform deeds that are supernatural or miraculous in character. This includes miraculous powers: miracle-working faith (1 Cor 12:9; 13:2), healing (1 Cor 12:9,28,30), miracles as such (1 Cor 12:10,28-29), and the ability to speak in tongues (1 Cor 12:10,28,30). It also includes supernaturally revealed knowledge: prophecy, or speaking a divinely inspired message from God (Rom 12:6; Eph 4:11; 1 Cor 12:10,28); supernatural knowledge, or receiving information directly from God (1 Cor 12:8; 13:2,8); the word of wisdom (1 Cor 12:8); discerning of spirits, or the supernatural ability to detect false doctrine (1 Cor 12:10; see 1 Tim 4:1; 1 John 4:1); and tongues plus interpretation (1 Cor 12:10,30).

Many today, including Pentecostals and Charismatics, believe that the Spirit is still giving all these gifts to Christians. As a rule they believe that the Spirit performs a postconversion work upon some or all true Christians, a work called the baptism of the Holy Spirit. This work is performed for the specific purpose of bestowing these miraculous gifts, especially the gift of tongues. Those who hold this view believe that such gifts, especially tongues, were the promised blessing for Pentecost and the new era. They claim that the Bible itself makes no distinction between miraculous and nonmiraculous gifts. They also point to the actual presence of such gifts within Christian circles today.

My judgment is that the Holy Spirit is not giving miraculous gifts to Christians today. This is called the cessationist view, i.e., miraculous gifts ceased at the end of the apostolic era. This conclusion is based on several lines of reasoning.

A. The Purpose of Miracles in General

First, the purpose of miracles as such would seem to rule out modern-day miracles. Hebrews 2:3-4 (NIV) suggests that miracles are part of a package of three things that usually occur together. These are *redemptive events*, or acts of God which save his people ("such a great salvation"). These are accompanied by *revelation*, or words of God to promise and explain the redemptive events ("announced by the Lord"). Revelation is accompanied by *miracles*, or signs from God to confirm the revelation ("confirmed to us . . . by signs, wonders and various miracles, and gifts of the Holy Spirit"). This passage itself declares that the purpose of miracles is to confirm the accompanying revelation (see *GRu*, 232ff.). This can be seen also in Mark 2:10; John 10:38; 20:30-31; Acts 2:22; 4:16; 8:6; 1 Cor 14:22; 2 Cor 12:12. We must also notice that Heb 2:3-4 includes "gifts of the Holy Spirit" in the category of confirming miracles.

If these three things are interconnected—redemptive events, explanatory revelation, and confirming miracles—then we should expect miracles today only if God is working new redemptive events and giving new revelation to explain them.

B. The Purpose of Pentecost

The usual pentecostal and charismatic interpretation of Pentecost is that this was the day God began to bestow miraculous powers (especially the gift of tongues) on God's people as a universal, permanent blessing. But this is a false understanding of Pentecost. The unique thing about that day was not the miraculous *gifts*, but the divine *gift* of the Spirit to indwell and empower for holy living. The OT prophecies and gospel promises point to something *new* and *marvelous* in the history of redemption: the permanent gift of the Spirit for regeneration and sanctification. Certainly there were miraculous manifestations on Pentecost; but miracles were nothing new in the history of redemption. Moses, Elijah, Elisha, and the apostles themselves prior to Pentecost had worked miracles. *So why should the miraculous manifestations on the Day of Pentecost be considered the purpose and essence of the new-creation outpouring of the Spirit? These things were nothing new!*

Certainly Joel's prophecy (2:28-32) included a prediction of miraculous speaking, and this occurred on Pentecost (Acts 2:16-21). But what was the purpose of this miraculous speaking? It was the same as the purpose for any miracle: to provide confirmation of the truth of Peter's claim that a new redemptive event was about to take place: the outpouring of the promised living water, the Holy Spirit. But the miracles themselves are not the purpose of this outpouring of the Spirit; they are just the initial sign that the promised Spirit is now present and will continue to be present and available, even after the tongues cease.[12] Contrary to a widely held view, the purpose of tongues on Pentecost was *not* to enable the apostles to proclaim the gospel in the languages of the many nationalities present. There was no evangelistic need for this; Greek was the common language shared by all the Jews present. The content of the tongues-speaking is described simply as "the mighty deeds of God" (Acts 2:11), and the result was exactly what God intended: not faith in Jesus, but wonder and amazement (Acts 2:6-7,12) that would cause them to believe and heed Peter's sermon. To use an analogy, the

Holy Spirit himself was the *gift* of Pentecost; the tongues were the *wrappings* for the gift. Having served their purpose, these wrappings may be reverently discarded.

Peter's explanation of Pentecost (Acts 2:14-39) may be summed up thus: "This is the day God is beginning to fulfill his promises to give you the Holy Spirit. These tongues are the prophesying mentioned by Joel, and they are given as proof that God is now giving you the promised Spirit to renew you and indwell you. You have seen the Spirit's presence miraculously manifested by the apostles, so you know that he is here. Now, if you repent and are baptized for the remission of your sins, this same Holy Spirit will be given to you also, in a much more wonderful way. For the promised Spirit is for you, and you can believe this because the miracle of tongues proves it."

C. The Purpose of Holy Spirit Baptism

Many see a connection between the baptism of the Spirit and miraculous gifts, especially tongues. Thus they believe that every Christian should be able to speak in tongues or do something comparable since all Christians have been baptized in the Spirit. But this is a serious misunderstanding of the purpose of this event called the baptism of the Spirit, as we have seen above. Baptism in or of the Spirit is another name for regeneration, and there is no necessary connection between it and miraculous spiritual gifts.

But what about the apostles on Pentecost (Acts 2) and Cornelius (Acts 10)? It is true that these events involved both the baptism of the Spirit (Acts 1:5; 11:16) and speaking in tongues (Acts 1:1-4; 10:44-46), but the miraculous tongues were not the *purpose* of baptism in the Spirit. On both occasions the tongues accompanied the gift of the Spirit, as a preliminary demonstration that the indwelling Spirit was indeed being given on these occasions. The very nature of these events shows that the use of tongues on those occasions was not a pattern for all times in the church. They were signs related to the *uniqueness* of these events. On Pentecost the tongues were evidence that the Spirit was on that day poured out from heaven for salvation purposes for the very first time, as promised by God. With Cornelius the tongues were evidence that the indwelling Spirit was intended for Gentiles as well as for Jews. It was a kind of "Gentile Pentecost," and the way the Holy Spirit fell upon these Gentiles was parallel only to the Pentecost of Acts 2 (Acts 11:15).

If miraculous gifts were the purpose of Pentecost, we should expect to read more about them in the descriptions of early church life in the chapters following Acts 2. Indeed, the same Holy Spirit who came upon the apostles was promised to anyone who would receive him (Acts 2:38-39), and thousands did. Yet the only ones specifically portrayed as working miracles in these early days of the church were the apostles: Acts 2:43; 3:6; 4:33; 5:12-16. Only when the apostles began laying their hands on others do we find anyone besides apostles performing miracles (e.g., Acts 6:6-8; 8:6).

D. The Purpose of Spiritual Gifts as Such

Some conclude that since miraculous powers are included in the lists of spiritual gifts, it must be the Spirit's purpose to bestow all these gifts throughout the entire church age. But this fails to take into account the very purpose for spiritual gifts. As in OT times, the equipping gifts are given to Christians to meet the specific needs of God's people as a whole. But the fact is that some of these gifts were meant to be temporary, simply because some of the early church's *needs* were temporary and have not existed since those first few decades. These temporary needs arose basically from the unique historical situation of the early church. God's people were living under a totally new covenant, with a new kingdom administration and new responsibilities. Yet they lacked an authoritative written revelation explaining God's will for those under these new conditions. That is, they did not yet have a written *New* Testament, comparable to the written *Old* Testament. Thus temporary gifts were provided to fill this temporary need.

The primary temporary spiritual gift was the gift of apostleship (1 Cor 12:28-29; Eph 4:11). There is no question that this gift was temporary, since this office could be filled only by someone who had been in the company of Jesus during his ministry and could give eyewitness testimony to his resurrection (Acts 1:15-26). This is why Paul refers to the work of apostles as belonging to the foundation-era of the church (Eph 2:20). The fact that this gift was obviously temporary shows that it is proper to make the distinction between temporary gifts and permanent gifts.

The apostles' main function was to provide authoritative teaching for the new-covenant era (John 16:13) as confirmed by their ability to work miracles (2 Cor 12:12). As long as they lived, they could provide this teaching in person; but they also committed their inspired revelation to writing, thus bringing into existence the New Testament. Once their authoritative teaching was widely available in written form, the gift of apostleship would no longer be needed.

In these early days, though, even apostles could not be present in every local congregation. This meant that other temporary gifts, providing access to the mind and will of God, would also be necessary. These included gifts of revealed knowledge, especially the gift of prophecy. Prophets basically did what the apostles did, except they did not possess the apostles' general authority over the church; i.e., they received and delivered inspired messages from God. This was mostly on the local-church level, but also some New Covenant writings were probably produced by some who had the gift of prophecy. Thus their teachings also had foundational significance for the church (Eph 2:20). Other gifts of revealed knowledge included the word of knowledge, the word of wisdom, discerning of spirits, and tongues (when interpreted).

Another category of temporary gifts is gifts of miraculous power, whose function was to confirm the divine authority of those who had the gifts of revealed knowledge (Heb 2:3-4). As mentioned earlier, these included miracle-working faith, the power to heal the sick, the power to work miracles in general, and tongues (1 Cor 14:22).

The point is that these gifts were temporary because in the beginning they were filling a vacuum created by the lack of an authoritative canon of divinely given instructions for the church age—what we call the New Testament. Once the NT was present, these gifts ceased.

E. The Apostolic Laying-on-of-Hands

Another reason for believing miraculous gifts have ceased is that in the book of Acts there seems to have been a necessary connection between such gifts and being touched by an apostle's hands. As noted above, in the earliest days of the church, though thousands were baptized and thus were receiving the Holy Spirit as promised (Acts 2:38-41; 4:4; 5:14,32), only the apostles are specifically said to be performing miracles (Acts 2:43; 3:6; 4:33; 5:12-16). But when the apostles began laying their hands on others, some of them too were able to work miracles (e.g., Acts 6:6-8; 8:6).

The church in Samaria is a prime example. Philip, one of the seven upon whom the apostles had earlier laid their hands (Acts 6:5-6), went to Samaria as an evangelist. He preached the gospel and confirmed its truth by working miracles (Acts 8:5-6,13). Converts were baptized, but the Holy Spirit was not "falling upon" any of these new Christians (Acts 8:16). This means that even though they were receiving the indwelling of the Spirit (Acts 2:38-39; 5:32), none of them were automatically receiving any miracle-working powers from the Spirit. This is why the apostles Peter and John came to Samaria, so that these new Christians might "receive the Holy Spirit" (Acts 8:14-15). To accomplish this, the apostles "began laying their hands on them, and they were receiving the Holy Spirit" (Acts 8:17). That this apostolic laying-on-of-hands had nothing to do with the receiving of the indwelling Spirit for the purpose of regeneration is evident from the fact that nowhere else in the NT is such an act related to conversion as such. That its purpose and result were to impart miraculous spiritual gifts is evident from the reaction of Simon the former sorcerer: "Now when Simon saw that the Spirit was bestowed through the laying on of the apostles' hands, he offered them money, saying, 'Give this authority to me as well, so that everyone on whom I lay my hands may receive the Holy Spirit'" (Acts 8:18-19). This reaction proves that the laying on of apostles' hands produced some amazing visible results, no doubt miraculous physical manifestations such as speaking in tongues.

Acts 19:1-7 reports a parallel event. The apostle Paul met a dozen disciples who had been baptized with John's baptism, but had not been baptized with New Covenant baptism in order to receive the gift of the Spirit. After teaching them, Paul baptized them in the name of the Lord Jesus, and we may assume that they then received the gift of the indwelling Spirit as promised (Acts 2:38-39; 5:32). But after he baptized them, he laid his hands on them. As a result "the Holy Spirit came upon them, and they began speaking with tongues and prophesying" (v. 6).

These incidents suggest that there was a firm connection between the laying on of an apostle's hands and the reception of miraculous spiritual gifts. Pentecost and Cornelius stand out as exceptions to this rule, and their uniqueness was duly noted by the apostle Peter (Acts 11:15).

F. 1 Corinthians 13:8-13

The final argument for cessationism is the specific statement in 1 Cor 13:10 that certain primary miraculous gifts were meant to cease: "But when the perfect comes, the partial will be done away." This paragraph as a whole (13:8-13) presents two contrasts. The main contrast is between things that are temporary (tongues, prophecy, miraculous knowledge), verse 8, and things that are permanent (faith, hope, love), verse 13. All of these things were already present when Paul wrote, but he declares that only the latter group will abide throughout the church age. Things in the former group will cease.

But there is also an important secondary contrast, designed to show *why* the gifts mentioned in verse 8 are only temporary. This contrast is in verses 9-12, which form a parenthesis between verse 8 and verse 13. The irony is that the very things the Corinthians prized most highly were only temporary. But why? Because they were only *partial*, i.e., composed of bits and pieces. These partial things were never meant to be permanent, but were intended to be replaced by something that is *complete*. In verse 10 the key Greek word is the neuter adjective *teleion*, which can mean "perfect" or "mature," but which can also mean "complete." That it definitely means "complete" here is shown by the contrast with "partial." Thus verse 10 should read, "When the complete thing comes, the partial will be done away." The fact that *teleion* is neuter shows it is referring not to a person, such as Jesus, but to a thing.

What is this complete thing? It must be something that was not yet present when Paul wrote since he is pointing to the future. This rules out anything in verse 13, including love. Also, it must be something that will appear *before* the second coming of Christ, since verse 13 shows that the partial things will cease while faith, hope, and love continue to abide in the church. But at the second coming there will no longer be any reason for *hope* to exist, since the things for which we now hope will then be a present reality (Rom 8:24-25). This rules out all eschatological interpretations of the *teleion*.

What could possibly appear on the scene between the writing of 1 Corinthians and the time of the second coming that fits the description of "the complete thing"? A clue is the nature of the things that it is intended to replace: prophecy, knowledge, and tongues. These are all in the category of *revealed knowledge*, but they are only partial. Whatever replaces them must also be in the category of revealed knowledge, but it must be complete. The only thing that satisfies this requirement is *the completed New Testament*. Christians would expect such a completed NT, similar to the OT for those under the Old Covenant.

Some think that verse 12 requires an eschatological interpretation of the *teleion* since it says that when the *teleion* appears we shall see "face to face" and shall "know fully." It is assumed that such things will be true only in heaven.

This is not the case, however. The "face-to-face" reference has nothing to do with seeing Jesus (which *will* happen, 1 John 3:2). "For now we see in a mirror dimly, but then face to face" is a contrast between two kinds of mirrors, one cloudy and one clear. This represents two kinds of revelation: one partial and enigmatic, and one clear and complete. The key to understanding this is the obvious parallel with the language of the Septuagint version of Num 12:8, where two kinds of revelation are being compared, the less clear and the more clear.[13] Also, in 2 Cor 3:7-18 and Jas 1:23-25, "looking in a mirror" and seeing clearly refer to looking into the Word of God in the form of the NT. We may paraphrase 1 Cor 13:12a thus: "For now, while we depend on occasional revelations through prophecy or interpreted tongues, it is like trying to see yourself in a scratched and cloudy mirror. But then, when the completed NT has been given, it will be like seeing a sharp, clear image of yourself in a bright new mirror."

But what about verse 12b, "Now I know in part, but then I will know fully just as I also have been fully known"? Does not "know fully" refer only to our heavenly state? In the first place, there is no justification for the translation "know fully." The word is *epiginosko*, which in the NT is used interchangeably with *ginosko* and means simply "to know." Second, finite beings will never have "full knowledge," not even in heaven. Only God is omniscient. Third, the object of the knowledge is not given. Perhaps it means only that when the completed NT comes, we shall know *ourselves* even as God knows us, because it will show us who we really are and who we ought to be (Heb 4:13; Jas 1:23-25).

The conclusion is that 1 Cor 13:12 is not speaking of knowledge that will be ours only when we get to heaven. The statements are quite consistent with the interpretation of *teleion* in verse 10 as the completed NT, which gives us a body of knowledge that is relatively clear and complete when compared with the fragments of knowledge given in the earliest days of the church through sporadic miraculous gifts. By far, the best understanding of 1 Cor 13:10 is that it refers to the completed NT, thus confirming the view that miraculous gifts ceased being passed along after the death of the apostles.

G. An Explanation of Miraculous Phenomena Today

If the Holy Spirit is not giving miraculous gifts today, how can we explain the phenomena that occur in pentecostal, charismatic and third-wave contexts? A detailed answer to this question is not possible here, but I will summarize my convictions.

Obviously some of the phenomena are not truly miraculous. Sometimes they are staged, and sometimes they are psychological in origin. But in my judgment a good number of the phenomena are definitely miraculous, manifesting supernatural powers and requiring a supernatural origin. It is my conviction that their origin is demonic, paralleling similar phenomena in occult circles. They are the result of satanic deception. One evidence of this is the procedure known as the "testing of tongues," wherein the source of the tongue is shown to be demonic. (See Ensign and Howe, Appendix J, "Speaking in Tongues and the Testing of Tongues.")

Is such satanic activity possible in the life of a God-fearing person? Yes. We have already seen that it is a fallacy to think that demons cannot work through Christians. But why would Satan want to empower Christians to do miraculous things that often have good and beneficial results, such as healing the sick? Because this helps him all the more to deceive those who have not received "the love of the truth" (2 Thess 2:9-12; 2 Cor 11:13-14). Where miraculous powers are present, dependence upon and fascination with such experiences can easily replace a commitment to truth and sound doctrine. This opens the way for a new kind of ecumenical movement, where unity is based on experience.

I must stress that those who are wielding such miraculous powers are not deliberately cooperating with Satan. Usually they truly believe that their powers are from the Holy Spirit. Thus they are victims, not villains; but they are in danger of losing a spiritual battle they do not even know they are fighting.

NOTES ON CHAPTER FIFTEEN

[1]Num 11:25; 24:2; 1 Sam 10:6-13; 19:20-24; 1 Chr 12:18; 2 Chr 15:1; 20:14; 24:20; Neh 9:30; Zech 7:12.

[2]Mark 13:11; Luke 2:26; Acts 2:4; 4:8; 8:29; 10:19,44-46; 11:12; 13:2; 16:6; 19:6; 20:23; 21:10-11; 1 Cor 12:8-11; 1 Pet 1:12.

[3]See also Matt 22:43; Mark 12:36; Acts 4:25; 28:25; Heb 3:7; 9:8; 10:15; 1 Pet 1:10-11.

[4]See also 1 Cor 7:40; Eph 3:5; 1 Tim 4:1; Rev 1:10; 2:7; 4:2; 19:10.

[5]This included such men as Balaam (Num 24:2), David (2 Sam 23:2), Amasai (1 Chr 12:18), Azariah (2 Chr 15:1), Zechariah (2 Chr 24:20), Isaiah (Isa 59:21), and Ezekiel (Ezek 2:2).

[6]These include Othniel (Judg 3:10), Gideon (Judg 6:34), Jephthah (Judg 11:29), and Samson (Judg 13:25; 14:6,19; 15:14).

[7]"But they did not do it again" (v. 25). The KJV ("and did not cease") follows a faulty textual tradition.

[8]In fact, one might argue that the coming of the Spirit was *the* decisive break in history, and that the advent and work of Jesus Christ, from his virginal conception up through his ascension and enthronement at the Father's right hand, was done simply to prepare for this new era and to make it possible.

[9]This view should never be described as "water regeneration" or "baptismal regeneration," terms which have always implied that there is something about the water or act itself that changes the heart.

[10]See the chapters on each of these texts in my book, *Baptism*.

[11]See Cottrell, *Baptism*, ch. 8; see Robertson, "Holy Spirit."

[12]The event in Num 11:16-30 is an exact parallel to Pentecost, i.e., a onetime gift of miraculous speaking was used to confirm the continuing presence of the Spirit for another purpose.

[13]Anyone who wants to understand this passage *must* read Gerhard Kittel's article on *ainigma* ["riddle"] in *TDNT*, I:178-180.

CHAPTER SIXTEEN

SALVATION: BY LAW OR BY GRACE?

The death and resurrection of Jesus Christ, along with the Pentecostal outpouring of the Holy Spirit, may be summarized as *redemption accomplished*. These works constitute the beginning of the new creation. They lay the foundation for the subsequent and ongoing process of new creation, which may be described as *redemption applied*. We will cover this subject from the perspectives of both individual salvation and corporate salvation (i.e., the church).

In discussing personal salvation the first point to be covered is the meaning of grace. What is at stake here is a proper understanding of *how* salvation is applied to the individual. This does not refer to the mechanics or procedure by which salvation is offered and received, but rather refers to the underlying principle that governs and shapes the procedure. That is, "by grace you have been saved" (Eph 2:8) means that we are saved by a specific method or system of salvation, the system of grace.

The best way to understand grace as a way of salvation is to explain it in contrast with its only alternative, which is law. Thus this chapter looks at both law and grace as possible ways to get to heaven, with an emphasis on Paul's joyful words to all Christians, "You are not under law but under grace" (Rom 6:14).

I. THE TERMINOLOGY OF GRACE

Several biblical words help us to understand the concept of grace. In the OT the terms are all taken from the same root or stem. They are *chen*, a noun often translated "grace"; *chanan*, the verb "to be gracious"; and *channun*, the adjective "gracious" (*GRe*, 361-365). These words are only mildly helpful in understanding God's saving grace, because most of the time they do not refer to salvation, even when used of God. Most often the noun means "favor," as in "do me a favor" or "finding favor" in someone's eyes (e.g., Gen 6:8; Exod 33:13,17; 1 Sam 16:22; Esth 2:15). The verb usually means "to act favorably toward someone, to bless, to come to someone's aid." Even when translated "be gracious," this is usually what is meant (e.g., Gen 43:29; 2 Sam 12:22; 2 Kgs 13:23; Ps 4:1; Isa 33:2). When we read such language from the perspective of the NT, we are tempted to think that "be gracious unto me" means "forgive my sins and save me for eternity," when it will most often mean something like "do me this favor" or "please answer my prayer." To say that God is "gracious" means that he is kind and loving, and willing to aid us and answer our prayers.[1]

The NT terminology is more relevant and more directly helps us to understand God's saving grace (*GRe*, 365-367). The basic word is the noun *charis*, most often translated "grace." Its general meaning is "a gift that brings joy," and it is used for many kinds of gifts, even divine gifts, that have nothing to do with salvation as such.[2] It may refer to material blessings (2 Cor 8:19; 9:8), spiritual strength or divine aid in general (2 Cor 12:9; Heb 4:10), and equipping gifts of the spirit (e.g., 1 Pet 4:10; Rom 15:15). The point is that we must be aware of other meanings of the term and must guard against interpreting every occurrence of the word *charis*, as well as the English translation "grace," as a reference to *saving* grace.

What is at issue here is the *scope* of the concept of grace. In reference to the working of God, some have tried to make grace include *everything* God does, with no part of divine activity falling outside its scope (as does Ditmanson, 62, 66, 73). This is seriously contrary to Scripture, however. If grace includes everything God does, then divine wrath and hell either must be seen as strange expressions of grace or must be denied altogether. Neither conclusion is acceptable.

A more common approach is to regard all of God's good and positive acts toward man as works of grace. Thus grace would include the blessings of creation and providence as well as redemption. The first two categories are called common grace in Reformed circles and natural grace in Roman Catholic theology, in contrast with the saving or supernatural grace of redemption. From the standpoints of terminology and biblical usage, the concept of grace as "a gift that brings joy" can legitimately be used in this qualified inclusive sense. As Donald Nash says, "Grace, then, stands for all God has done for us, His children," including creation, revelation, incarnation, crucifixion, and resurrection ("God," 10).

While acknowledging the legitimacy of the above approach, I and others prefer to limit the English terminology of grace to God's works of salvation, to the manner in which his love and good will respond to man *as sinner*, not just as creature. God's saving grace is a unique, special grace that comes through Jesus Christ alone, a grace that counteracts the effects of sin. "We are saved through the grace of the Lord Jesus" (Acts 15:11; see John 1:17). "For the grace of God has appeared, bringing salvation to all men" (Titus 2:11). The ultimate grace-gift comes "through the redemption which is in Christ Jesus" (Rom 3:24; see 5:15). Thus it is my judgment that unless otherwise qualified, in contemporary usage the English word "grace" should have the connotation of *saving* grace.

As thus applied to salvation the term "grace" has three basic connotations. It refers to the *source* of salvation, i.e., to grace as the attribute of God's nature that desires our salvation and impels him to accomplish it through the incarnate Christ. It also refers to the *content* of our salvation, i.e., to the actual gift we receive from God when he saves us. In this sense grace is the double cure of salvation, justification on the one hand and regeneration-sanctification on the other. Finally it refers to the *way* in which God saves us, i.e., the method or system God uses to bestow salvation upon us. This last usage is the focus of this chapter.

II. TWO COMPETING SYSTEMS

In the non-Christian world there is a universal misunderstanding of the way of salvation (see *GRe*, ch. 2), and considerable confusion exists even among Christians. To a great extent this misunderstanding and this confusion are the result of a failure to see that there are two separate and distinct ways of relating to God, and thus two ways of seeking salvation or eternal happiness. Sometimes these two ways are called the egocentric and the theocentric ways of approaching God. In the former "fellowship with God depends ultimately on man's achievement and is sought ultimately for man's own ends" (Watson, 35). In the latter fellowship with God is initiated by God, accomplished by God, and sought ultimately for God's own glory. The Protestant Reformation is sometimes attributed to Martin Luther's discovery of the difference between the two, as he underwent a "Copernican revolution" or paradigm shift from egocentric to theocentric thinking (Nygren, 681-691).

Some describe the same contrast as the difference between *religion* and *Christianity*. This may hark back to Karl Barth's distinction between revelation and religion, in a section of his *Dogmatics* called "The Revelation of God as the Abolition of Religion" (*CD* I/2, 280). This is the distinction intended by Fritz Ridenour in the title of his book, *How to Be a Christian Without Being Religious*. In the introduction to this book Ridenour says that

> . . . every religion has one basic characteristic. Its followers are trying to reach God, find God, please God through their own efforts. Religions reach up toward God. Christianity is God reaching down to man. Christianity claims that men have not found God, but that *God has found them*. . . . Christianity . . . is not religious striving. To practice Christianity is to *respond* to what God has done for you.

This distinction between two systems of relating to God is real, but the preferable terms for it are *law* and *grace*, as in "You are not under law but under grace" (Rom 6:14). These are the only two choices. As Christians we are relating to God in terms of grace, while everyone else is still under law. The difference between the two is summed up in Rom 6:23, "For the wages of sin is death, but the free gift of God is eternal life in Christ Jesus our Lord." The key words here are *wages* and *gift*. Those relating to God in terms of wages will eventually get what they have earned or deserved by their works during this earthly life. This is the law system, and it operates according to the strict dictates of the *holiness* of God. Those who choose the alternative way of relating to God will receive their eternal reward as a free gift; in fact, their reward will actually be contrary to what they deserve. This is the grace system, and it operates according to the impulses of God's *love*.

In Rom 3:27 Paul calls these two competing systems *the law of works* and *the law of faith*. In this verse the word "law" (*nomos*) is used in an unusual, very general sense. The NIV acceptably translates it as "principle." Other possibilities are "method, arrangement, order, system, set of rules." Also in this verse the term "works" (*ton ergon*)—inexcusably obscured by the NIV translation "observing the law"—sums up the essence of the law system, i.e., it operates on the principle of works. Also in this verse the term "faith" sums up the essence of the grace system; it operates according to the principle of faith. "Works" and "faith" here are thus parallel to "wages" and "gift" in Rom 6:23 and parallel to "law" and "grace" in Rom 6:14.

In reference to salvation, those who are confronted with the gospel must make a choice. As sinners they may choose to continue to relate to God as the holy and just lawgiver, and expect to receive the wages they deserve on the day of judgment; or they may accept the gospel offer and begin relating to God as the good and loving giftgiver, and expect to receive eternal life as a free gift on that day. This is the choice between law and grace.

III. LAW AS A WAY TO HEAVEN

Just as there are two ways of relating to God, so also are there two (possible) ways of salvation or of being accepted by God. That is, there are two distinct principles of judgment, two (possible) ways of getting into heaven. For illustrative purposes we may picture heaven as a walled city with two gates, the law-gate and the grace-gate. Theoretically it is possible to enter heaven through either gate, even the law-gate. Here we will explain how this is so.

A. The Nature of the Law System

How does the law system work? What are the rules that determine how law operates? According to Rom 3:27 it has to do with works, or obedience to the Creator's commandments. This is because the law system is governed solely by the holiness of God. The holy God will treat us in terms of strict justice by giving us what we deserve, or the wages we have earned by our works of obedience to his commands. As Paul says in Rom 10:5, "The man who practices righteousness which is based on law shall live by that righteousness." In other words, "Do this and live!" (see Matt 19:17). Thus getting to heaven under law depends on how one responds to the commandments or law code for which he is responsible.

At this point I want to stress that it is *absolutely crucial* that we distinguish between law as a *code* or list of commands, and law as a *system* or way of entering heaven. On the one hand, a *law code* is any set of rules and commandments one is obligated to obey by the decree of the Creator. It is not always the same for all people. For those who have no access to special revelation, their law code is "the requirements of the law . . . written on their hearts" (Rom 2:15, NIV). For Jews living in OT times, the applicable code was the Law of Moses. For everyone living in the NT era, the applicable law code is the ethical and religious teaching of the Bible as seen in and through the New Covenant Scriptures.

On the other hand, the *law system* has to do with the way one tries to *use* the law code he happens to be living under. It has to do with the *function* of one's relevant law code. It is common to distinguish among four uses of a law code: (1) the didactic use, in which law functions as a teacher; (2) the governmental use, in which law functions as a restrainer of evil; (3) the normative use, in which law functions as a normative standard for living; and (4) the soteric use, in which law functions as a way of entering heaven (see *GRe*, 271-274). The first three are generally regarded as valid uses of law at all times in this fallen world. The fourth, the soteric use, is at issue here; it is, in effect, the *law system*. It has to do with trying to enter heaven by means of obedience to one's law code, i.e., by works.

Failure to distinguish between law as a code and law as a system usually leads to a misunderstanding of grace itself. This is true because grace as a system of salvation can be understood only if it is contrasted with law as a system of salvation (e.g., in Rom 6:14). The problem is that there is an almost universal tendency to contrast grace with the Law of Moses, which is a law *code*. The gospel of grace is then presented as "the principle that Christians and the church are free from the bondage of the Mosaic law" (D. Nash, "Law," 15). It is true of course that Christians *are* set free from bondage to the Law of Moses, but this is not really the point of the law-grace distinction. The point is that grace sets us free from the necessity of trying to enter heaven by *any* law code. Jews in OT times who accepted God's grace were themselves set free from bondage to the Law of Moses as a way of entering heaven, just as Christians today are set free from the New Covenant law code as a way of entering heaven. However, when grace is seen merely as an alternative to the Mosaic Law code, the tendency is to view grace itself as nothing more than a Christianized law code. When this happens the true nature of grace is lost, and even many Christians still struggle with an egocentric concept of salvation. Even though in reality they are under grace, they still think of themselves as facing judgment in terms of the law system.

What, then, is the nature of the law system? How does it work? If getting to heaven were like a game, what would be the rules of the game under law? How do you know if you are winning? We may sum up the ground rules of the system of law in the following succinct formula: "Keep the commandments; escape the penalty. Break the commandments, suffer the penalty." (The commandments are one's applicable law code; the penalty is eternal hell.) This formula is a summary of Rom 2:7-10, a passage that should be understood *only* as a description of how one may get to heaven under the law system (Cottrell, *Romans*, 190-194). Verses 7 and 10 state the first part of the law formula; verses 8-9 state the second part.

The point is that under law, getting to heaven depends on how one responds to his applicable law code.

B. The Universality of the Law System

In God's original creation the dominant factor was law, including natural or physical laws to rule the material universe and moral laws to rule the hearts of free-will beings. Law was simply the natural framework of existence, and the original and natural way of relating to God was through law. Acceptance by God and fellowship with God were contingent upon proper obedience to his commandments. Since no sin was present, there was no need for saving grace.

Even after sin entered the creation, thanks to God's plan to send Christ Jesus to pay sin's penalty, every child is born under what I have called *original grace* (pp. 184-190). Original grace functions as a kind of protective cocoon in which a child safely dwells though surrounded by law and its penalty. But when the child reaches the age of accountability, the cocoon dissolves, and he finds himself immersed in law and living under a law code. He cannot escape the necessity of responding to the commands of the law code, either in obedience or disobedience. *How* he responds determines whether he will ultimately be saved or lost. In other words, every individual comes to moral consciousness under the law system, and he remains there unless he is confronted by the gospel and chooses to come under the grace system instead.

C. The Impotence of the Law System

I have said that it is theoretically possible for one to enter heaven under the principles of the law system, i.e., by law-keeping. The ground rules specify, "Keep the commandments; escape the penalty." Thus to enter the law-gate into heaven, all one has to do is keep the commandments of his applicable law code. But here is an important qualification: to enter heaven under the law system, one must keep *all* the commands *all* his life, and keep them *perfectly*. Only perfect obedience—absolute righteousness—will earn heaven. There will be no balance-scale judgment, with 51% obedience being sufficient for entering heaven; it must be 100%. This is dictated by Jas 2:10, "For whoever keeps the whole law and yet stumbles in one point, he has become guilty of all" (see Gal 3:10).

Herein lies the impotence of the law system. Though it is theoretically possible for anyone to enter the law-gate into heaven, in reality *no one* will do so, because no one has kept all the commandments. The law system provides that "the doers of the law will be justified" (Rom 2:13), but that applies only if one is a *perfect* doer of the entire law. Since "all have sinned and fall short of the glory of God" (Rom 3:23), the fact is that "by the works of the Law no flesh will be justified in His sight" (Rom 3:20). Rather, under the law system where everyone gets the wages he deserves, everyone is destined for eternal death in the lake of fire. This is actually the one main point of the entire first main section of Romans,

1:18–3:20, as summed up in 3:20. Because of the universality of sin, no one will be saved by the system of law or law-keeping, the system of works, the system of "being good enough." The law-gate into heaven is closed and sealed shut by the sins of mankind.

IV. GRACE AS THE ONLY WAY TO HEAVEN

In view of the nature of the law system and its requirement of perfect obedience, the bad news is that "all have sinned." But the good news is that God's love has provided another way, another gate into heaven as an alternative to law. After sadly shutting and sealing the unused law-gate, God has constructed a new and different gate through which even *sinners* may enter heaven. This is the way of grace. The main point of Rom 3:21–5:21 is to explain how the grace system of salvation works, and that is my purpose here.

A. The Nature of the Grace System

In our attempt to understand grace it is extremely important to see that it is not just a revised or amended version of the law system. Whether they realize it or not, this is exactly how many Christians look at grace. They see it as a sleeker and more efficient law code that replaces the Mosaic law, with one set of commandments being substituted for another. But this approach to grace is seriously wrong. Grace does not get us into heaven by forcing open the law-gate and enabling us to squeeze through the crack. It is a totally new gate with a totally different set of rules governing entry into heaven. In fact, the rules of grace are the exact opposite of those in the law system.

As noted above the ground rules for law are these: "Keep the commandments; escape the penalty. Break the commandments; suffer the penalty." This sounds perfectly reasonable. But here are the rules according to which grace operates: "Keep the commandments, but suffer the penalty. Break the commandments, but escape the penalty." Upon seeing this our first reaction is to think that there must be a misprint here. This is such a radical approach to salvation that we almost instinctively feel that something must be wrong. Something just does not "sound right" about it.

What appears to ring false about these rules of grace is really quite simple: they lack the quality of *fairness*. It simply is not *fair* for an innocent person to be punished, and for a commandment-breaker to escape the penalty deserved by his sin. All our lives and in many contexts we have been conditioned to stand up for justice and fairness. We have been taught that anyone charged with a crime should get a fair trial and be judged with absolute fairness. It is only natural, then, to think that this quality of fairness will surely apply on the day of final judgment and will surely determine whether we get to heaven or not. But here is a question that everyone should seriously ask himself: "Do I really want God to be *fair* with me on the day of judgment?" Before answering we should remind ourselves that the only fair (just, deserved) treatment for sinners of any kind is hell!

Does this mean that grace is *not fair*? Of course it does! That is the very point of grace, i.e., that under grace God does *not* treat us in terms of fairness or justice; he does *not* pay us the wages our works have earned and deserved. For those who break the commandments, hell is fair. But grace is entirely different; it has nothing to do with fairness: "Break the commandments, but escape the penalty." Is this fair? No! It is in fact the exact opposite of fairness; it is antifair. It's *grace*! Such grace is not just "unmerited favor"; it is "favor bestowed when wrath is owed."[3]

As sinners whose only fair treatment is hell, we should welcome the second half of the grace formula, "Break the commandments, but escape the penalty." Someone might agree with this but nevertheless object to the first half of the formula, "Keep the commandments, but suffer the penalty." This too is surely the very opposite of fairness, and it appears to be quite unappealing and even ominous and offensive. Also it seems to be irrelevant, since no one has acceptably kept the commandments anyway (Rom 3:23). Why not just discard this part of the grace formula, since it does not seem to apply to anyone anyway?

It is not true, of course, that no one has kept the commandments perfectly. One person has indeed lived a perfect, sinless life; and that same person has also suffered sin's penalty on behalf of sinners: *Jesus Christ*! The fact is that this part of the grace system was never intended to apply to anyone but Jesus. Also, if we remove this first part of the system, there will be no basis for the second part. The fact that the sinless Christ has suffered eternal condemnation in our place is the only reason God can say to sinners, "Even though you have broken my commandments, you may still escape the penalty you deserve."

The essence of the grace system as explained here is summed up in 2 Cor 5:21, "He made Him who knew no sin to be sin on our behalf"—Jesus kept the commandments but suffered the penalty, "so that we [sinners] might become the righteousness of God in Him"—we have broken the commandments but still can escape the penalty. This verse shows the antifair nature of grace. Under grace we trade places with Jesus. He takes our sin upon himself and is treated as we deserve to be treated, so that we might take his righteousness upon ourselves and be treated as he deserves. Under grace we also in a sense "trade faces" with Jesus. When the Father looked at Jesus on the cross, he saw our faces; and he poured out upon him the wrath we deserve. Now for those who are "in Him," under grace, when God looks at us he does not see our sinful faces but sees the pure face of Jesus; he does not see our sin but Jesus' righteousness.

If this sounds "too good to be true," it is—as long as we are confined within the sphere of law and our brains are locked into a law mentality. But this is not law; it's grace. And grace is a different way of salvation that should produce a different way of thinking—a grace mentality that focuses upon God's wonderful *gift* that brings *joy*, peace, and assurance. The task facing many Christians is not just being able to explain what grace is for others, but coming to a full understanding of it for themselves. Many Christians under grace still think and act as if they are under law. Their mentality does not match their reality. To solve this problem we must be open to a Lutherlike Copernican revolution or paradigm shift, and be ready to accept the radical nature of the grace system of salvation.

B. The Uniqueness of the Grace System

Grace as a specific doctrine of salvation is unique to Christianity. There is no true doctrine of grace outside the Bible. In every non-Christian religion and philosophy, the way of salvation (however salvation is understood) is always by human works, human merit, human achievement. Leon Morris has well said,

> Salvation by grace is a characteristically Christian idea. It is a truth of revelation, not an idea common to mankind at large. In fact men at large almost invariably tend to think of salvation in terms of merit. All kinds of religions from the most primitive to the most cultural can be found to agree on this one point, that however salvation is understood, it is brought about as the result of man's striving. ("Grace," 14).

In my book *God the Redeemer* a lengthy chapter (ch. 2, "Alternatives to Redemption," 45-116) illustrates this point. For example, in Hinduism salvation is achieved by human knowledge and works. There is no system more antagonistic to the grace of Jesus Christ than the Hindu doctrines of karma and reincarnation (*GRe*, 49-56). Classical Buddhism is very similar. What is regarded as lostness can be escaped by following the Buddhist "eightfold path" of knowledge and self-effort (*GRe*, 56-62). Ancient Gnosticism was very similar; as the name indicates, salvation was by knowledge (*gnosis* means "knowledge"). In the Gnostic system attaining saving knowledge in itself is not easy, but when found this knowledge turns out to be nothing more than an explanation of how the lost person may save himself (*GRe*, 68-72).

Although traditional Hinduism and traditional Buddhism are unequivocally religions of law proclaiming salvation by works, sometimes we hear that a particular form of Hinduism known as Bhakti and a particular form of Buddhism known as True Pure-Land Buddhism are religions that teach salvation by grace in a near-Christian sense (*GRe*, 55-56, 62-64). These cannot be regarded as true parallels, though, for several reasons (see *GRe*, 406, 441). For one thing. those who make such claims usually operate with a weak or limited definition of grace. For example, Ditmanson says, "In the most general sense, the Christian testimony to the grace of God means that life is worth trusting despite the threat of chaos and inevitable death" (24). In Bhakti Hinduism what passes for grace is little more than divine aid. Second, one must consider the possibility of Christian influence regarding the origins of Bhakti Hinduism and True Pure-Land Buddhism. The former arose in the ninth or tenth century A.D., and the latter in the thirteenth century A.D. Finally, even if any non-Christian religion desires and claims to offer salvation purely by the grace of a savior-figure (such as Amida Buddha in True Pure-Land Buddhism), in reality the offer is hollow because no religion outside Christianity has what is absolutely necessary for salvation from sin, i.e., a divine, sinless Sin-bearer. Such a Savior is found only in Christianity. Thus it is and ever will be true that salvation is possible only through grace, and grace is found only in Christianity.

C. The Perversion of the Grace System

As we have noted above, even within Christianity there is much confusion about the nature of grace. Many who know the word and can quote its dictionary definition still do not understand how it affects their lives. One reason this is the case is that even within Christendom grace is not always taught in its pure biblical form. Often the proper distinction between law and grace is missed; and instead of teaching a doctrine of salvation by pure grace many actually are teaching a hybrid of grace and law, or salvation by a combination of grace and works.

The most prevalent of such perversions of grace is known as Galatianism. This name is derived from the false doctrine Paul addresses in his letter to the Galatians, i.e., the Judaizers' claim that one can be saved by Jesus Christ only if he keeps the commandments of the Law of Moses. Perversions of grace that follow this pattern are usually summarized thus: the sinner is *initially saved* by the grace of Jesus Christ, then he is *kept saved* by obedience to the commandments of some law. Thus Galatianism divides grace into two stages. In the first step, which is true grace, a *sinner* is justified at conversion by faith in the blood of Christ, thereby receiving forgiveness for his past sins. In the second stage, the *Christian* is empowered by grace to obey God's law and develop a Christlike character. On the basis of this personal righteousness he will be judged and saved.

The most obvious example of such Galatianism is Roman Catholic theology, which teaches that one receives initial salvation in Christian baptism through the application of the blood of Christ. This is called "sanctifying grace," even though it is equivalent to what Protestants call justification. This aspect of grace includes the forgiveness of all prebaptismal sins, original and actual. Then, through the divine aid of what is called "actual grace," the saved person is enabled to do meritorious good works that help to cancel out part of the penalty for sins committed after baptism. This is accomplished especially through the sacrament of penance (now called the sacrament of reconciliation) and the practice of indulgences.

Another example is traditional Seventh Day Adventism, which teaches a Galatianism similar to that of Catholicism. According to Adventism at conversion one receives true grace for the remission of preconversion sins plus an indwelling grace that provides inner power to obey God's commands. This much is true doctrine; the perversion lies in making this grace-enabled obedience the basis for our acceptance by God on the judgment day. As Geoffrey Paxton (97-98) sums it up, in traditional Adventist thinking salvation by grace and by Christ's righteousness

. . . has generally meant having Christ's *indwelling grace* in order to keep the law well enough to meet the judgment's scrutiny, and having Christ's *indwelling righteousness* (i.e., sanctification). Justification has been seen as only the initial step taken by the novice Christian. Justification merely makes one a candidate for the "seal," but this supreme attainment depends upon becoming sanctified enough to qualify at God's awful tribunal.[4]

In the final analysis one will be saved if he is good enough.

Such a perverted view of grace is frequently found in the Restoration Movement also. A major example is Alexander Campbell himself, who at least early in his reforming career taught a full-blown Galatianism. In a letter "To 'Paulinus'" in the May 7, 1827, edition of *The Christian Baptist*, Campbell wrote, "Sinners are justified by faith, and christians by works." In other words, after baptism the continued enjoyment of God's favor rests completely on our behavior. "In the final judgment when men's actions and not their states will be examined, faith is not then accounted to any man for righteousness." To say "that no man is justified by works is a general truth. But general as it is, it must, from its context, be restricted to unbelievers, for it is just as true and just as general that every christian will be justified by his works. Nothing else comes in review on the day of judgment." See also Campbell's treatise on "The Three Kingdoms" from *The Christian Baptist* of June 1, 1829.

The mixing of merit and mercy is not uncommon in present-day Restoration circles. I heard the following statements in Bible college chapel sermons: "God will give to those who merit it, the blessings of eternal life." "We are saved only by the grace of Christ and our obedience to him." A minister wrote in his church paper that "working out our own salvation" (Phil 2:12) is like athletes who sign with professional sports teams.

> For certain services performed, they receive specified wages and benefits. In like manner, if we obey the Lord's commands and live our lives according to His Will, we will be paid handsomely in the wages of Eternal Life. Hence, we have worked out our salvation. It is *not a matter* of ever making ourselves deserving on our own merits or rights—we must first accept Christ as Lord and obey His Gospel—then fulfill our end of the "contract." . . . We have an agreement with God—for our love, devotion, dedication, obedience and service in this life, He will reward us with Eternal Life.

One reason for the perversion of grace and the prevalence of Galatianism within Christendom is the widespread acceptance of a balance-scale concept of judgment, i.e., that judgment is a matter of weighing all our deeds in a balance scale, with good deeds on one side and sins on the other. Thus we must strive to be at least 51% good, so that our good works will outweigh our sins. This assumes that if I do something wrong, I can then do something right to make up for it. By an act of righteousness I can cancel out a sin or part of the punishment that is owed on account of that sin.

Underlying this false idea is the even more prevalent concept of *extra merit*. This is the notion that we are actually obligated to obey only a limited number of divine commands, and that we can in fact go beyond what is required of us and produce righteousness that exceeds our obligations. This is our "extra merit," or credits that we have earned that can be used to cancel our sin-debts. This idea is presupposed by the Catholic doctrine of indulgences as it relates to the forgiveness of postbaptismal sins.

Jesus' teaching in Luke 17:7-10 completely rules out the concept of a balance-scale judgment and the concept of extra merit. In this parable of the "unprofitable servant" (KJV), Jesus pictures a slave who labors in the fields all day, then must come home and prepare his master's evening meal before he is allowed to eat his own. For doing this he receives no reward and no thanks since he is simply rendering the obedience that a slave owes his master. No matter how hard he works, he earns no extra merit. Jesus makes this application: "So you too, when you do all the things which are commanded you, say, 'We are unworthy [unprofitable] slaves; we have done only that which we ought to have done'" (v. 10). In other words, starting today, even if we could render perfect obedience to God, we would have no merits left over to make up for our past sins. This is because every good work we perform is already owed to God since we are commanded to "be perfect" (Matt 5:48) and to be as holy as the holy God himself (1 Pet 1:15-16).

This is why there is no such thing as extra merit, and no such thing as a balance-scale judgment. We cannot use our good works to pay even the slightest sin-debt owed to God, since any good work that we as creatures can do is itself already owed to God. We cannot pay both our debts of obedience and our sin-debts with the same currency. This helps to explain why no one will ever be saved under the law system. Even one sin creates a debt of punishment that we ourselves can never pay with our deeds. This is why we must rely on the grace of Jesus Christ alone, unmixed with our works, as our only way into heaven.

NOTES ON CHAPTER SIXTEEN

[1] In light of this survey of the meaning of the OT words for grace see especially my discussion of Exod 33:19 (*GRe*, 364).

[2] Compare the related words *charizomai*, "to give freely, as a favor"; *charisma*, "gift"; *charitoo*, "to bestow favor upon, to bless"; *chara*, "joy"; *chairo*, "to rejoice, to be glad."

[3] My thanks again to Ranny Grady for this phrase.

[4] I have examined this teaching of traditional Adventism in some detail and have shown that this evaluation is warranted by Adventist writings and is shared by most Evangelicals. (See my "Adventist" articles.) We should note that a reformation of sorts has occurred within Adventism, so that many Adventists no longer hold to this traditional view but have come to a more Evangelical understanding. See Samples, "Truth."

CHAPTER SEVENTEEN
JUSTIFICATION

Earlier we saw that personal sin takes two basic forms; it burdens the sinner with a "double trouble." On the one hand sin makes us guilty. Guilt is a wrong relationship with the law of God, involving a liability to punishment. On the other hand, sin gives us a sinful or depraved nature. It infects the soul (and the body) with spiritual weakness and corruption.

Because the sinner's problem is twofold, grace as the content of salvation must also be twofold—a "double cure." The first aspect of salvation received by the believing, penitent sinner is the gift of *justification*, which solves the problem of guilt and removes all punishment. God as Judge declares that the penalty for sin no longer applies to us. The second aspect of salvation, resulting from the gift of the indwelling Spirit, consists of the divine works of regeneration and sanctification. God as Physician cures the disease of sin that afflicts our natures, thus resolving the problem of spiritual corruption and restoring us to spiritual wholeness.[1]

This chapter deals with the first part of the double cure, as we seek to explain the concept, the basis, and the means of justification.

I. THE CONCEPT OF JUSTIFICATION

We may think of justification both as a specific act of God upon the sinner by virtue of which the sinner passes from the lost state to the saved state, and as the continuing state in which the saved person exists. The Christian may say both "I have been justified" (the act), and "I am justified" (the state). Our main concern here is the act.

Robert Horn (18-19) has rightly said, "Justification means something God does. Indeed, it means a very specific thing God does." It is true that God also regenerates, sanctifies, and glorifies; but these are not the same as justification. "Justification has a distinct meaning." What is this meaning? A brief look at some Greek terminology will put us on the proper track. The noun usually translated "justification" is *dikaiosis*; the verb "to justify" is *dikaioo*. These terms are from the same word family as "righteous" (*dikaios*) and "righteousness" (*dikaiosyne*), which suggests that justification has something to do with righteousness. The problem is to identify the proper connection between them.

In Christian theology since the Reformation there have been two main competing views of the meaning of justification as it relates to righteousness. One is that justification means that God *declares* us righteous by *imputing* righteousness to us; the other is that justification means that God *makes* us righteous by *imparting* righteousness to us. Most Protestants believe that God actually does both of these things; the issue is, which is the proper definition of justification?

In the latter view "imparted righteousness" is the personal obedience and good works God enables us to perform by the power of his grace working in us; it is the right moral character we are enabled to attain by this power. Justification as God's act is thus his ongoing process of making us more and more righteous or holy. To Protestants this process is actually sanctification, not justification; but in classic Roman Catholic theology this is how justification itself is understood. As Buchanan put it, in Catholic doctrine "faith justifies, not by uniting the sinner to Christ, and making him a partaker of Christ's righteousness,—but by 'working' in him, and 'sanctifying' him." In this view faith justifies by producing within the believer "a real inherent righteousness, which is, on its own account, acceptable to God, and which constitutes the immediate ground of his acceptance;—in short, by *making him righteous*, subjectively" (132-133).

The official conclusion of the Catholic Church's authoritative Council of Trent (1545–1563) was that justification "is not only a remission of sins but also the sanctification and renewal of the inward man through the voluntary reception of grace and gifts whereby the unjust man becomes just" ("Decrees concerning Justification," ch. 7, in Leith, 411). The formal cause of this justification "is the justice of God . . . by which he makes us just [i.e., righteous], . . . and not only are we reputed but we are truly called and are just, receiving justice within us" (ibid., 412). Buchanan summarizes Trent's decree thus, "that the righteousness, by which we are justified, is a righteousness infused and inherent; that it is called our own righteousness, because it is inherent in us,—and that it is also called the righteousness of God, because it is infused by Him" (142).

According to this view justification is a subjective process that takes place within the individual, an inward change in one's moral character. This means that justification is tied to one's works in a direct way, and because it is a process, one can never be certain that he has reached a level of works that makes him acceptable to God.

Herein lies one of the major differences between classic Roman Catholicism and Reformation Protestantism. To most Protestants this view of justification is seriously wrong and is a major stumbling block to a proper overall understanding of salvation and to a Christian life of peace and assurance. They understand God's act of justification to be not the impartation of righteousness, but the *imputation*[2] of righteousness. "To justify" means not to make righteous, but to *declare* righteous, to *count* or *accept* as righteous. The state of justification is not an ever-increasing holiness of character, but a complete *right legal standing* before the law of God and a freedom from the law's penalty. This is generally the Reformation (Protestant) understanding, and I am presenting it here as the biblical view.

That justification means to declare righteous rather than to make righteous is seen in the use of the verb *dikaioo* in Luke 7:29, which says literally that the people who heard Jesus' teaching about John the Baptist "justified God" (KJV). Obviously this cannot mean that the people *made* God righteous; they were simply declaring or acknowledging him to be righteous. Thus the NASB translates this as "They acknowledged God's justice," and the NIV says they "acknowledged that God's way was right." Likewise when God justifies us he is not making us righteous but is declaring us so.

That this is the proper meaning of the concept is also seen in the fact that in Scripture justification is basically a legal (judicial, forensic) concept. That is, in the Bible it is a judge's verdict or finding after he has considered the evidence and found a person to be innocent. "To justify" is always the opposite of "to condemn." For example, Deut 25:1 says that when men go to court, "the judges decide their case, and they justify the righteous and condemn the wicked." Likewise Prov 17:15 condemns a corrupt judge "who justifies the wicked" and "condemns the righteous" (see Isa 5:23). This same contrast between justification and condemnation is seen in God's own judicial verdict: "Who will bring a charge against God's elect? God is the one who justifies; who is the one who condemns?" (Rom 8:33-34; see Matt 12:37). Obviously when a judge condemns someone he does not thereby *make* that person guilty; he only discovers and declares him to be so. Likewise when a judge justifies someone he does not thereby make that person innocent or righteous; he simply declares him to be so.

There is a major difference between justification as an act of a human judge and justification as a saving act of God. Human judges, unless they are corrupt (Prov 17:15), justify only the innocent; they declare someone righteous only if he is indeed already righteous or innocent. This is what the law requires. But in the act of salvation God justifies *guilty sinners* (Rom 4:5); he declares the unrighteous to be righteous! How can God go against the standards of his own law (Deut 25:1) and do the very thing that he himself has forbidden in Prov 17:15? When God justifies us, he is declaring that, even though we are sinners, we are now "square" with the law. How can this be since we as sinners have broken the commands of the law?

First we must remember that the way of salvation is *grace*, not law; and the principles by which grace operates are the very opposite of law, as we saw in the previous chapter. But this is not the whole story. In order to understand precisely what is happening in justification, we must remember that law consists not only of commands but also of penalties. There is no longer any way that a sinner can be right with the law (i.e., justified) in reference to its commands, since we are guilty of breaking them. When God justifies us, he is not declaring that we are innocent and have never broken the law's commands. Rather, justification is God's declaration that we are right with the law in reference to its *penalty*. It means that God treats us not as if we are innocent, because we are not; rather, it means that he treats us as if our penalty has already been paid—which it has!

The best way for a Christian to understand what it means to be justified is to picture himself as a defendant standing in a courtroom before God as the presiding Judge, and to hear God pronounce his verdict: "*No penalty for you!*" Many will say that God's judicial declaration is "Not guilty!" but I do not accept this. Justification does not *remove* our guilt, but it deals with it by removing the *condemnation* that goes with it (Rom 8:1). Thus the Judge's precise declaration is "No penalty for you!" To be **justified** thus does not mean that God treats me *just* as *if I'd* never sinned, but rather *just* as *if I'd* already paid my penalty.

Basically justification is the same as forgiveness of sins, remission of sins, and the washing away of sins (in the sense that God removes them from the books and does not hold them against us). This becomes clear as we follow Paul's line of thought from Rom 3:27 through Rom 4:8 (see Cottrell, *Romans*, I:287-288). After asserting the fact of and using the language of justification throughout this passage, Paul proves his point by citing Ps 32:1-2, "Blessed are those whose lawless deeds have been forgiven, and whose sins have been covered. Blessed is the man whose sin the LORD will not take into account." This shows that justification and forgiveness are one and the same. God justifies sinners by forgiving them, by not holding their sins against them.

It is important to see that justification is thus not a change in our character or in our inner nature; it is a change in our relationship to God and especially to God's law. The change is objective, not subjective. It solves the problem of guilt, not the problem of corruption. It is also important to see that this change is not a gradual process, but is an immediate and complete change in our status before God. By God's pronouncement, at a specific, instantaneous moment we are changed from being 0% forgiven to being 100% forgiven before God. The abiding state of justification begins in that instant and continues in its fullness (100%) for as long as we remain in union with Christ. Justification is not just the forgiveness of individual sins, but the forgiveness of the entire person.

II. THE BASIS OF JUSTIFICATION

We have defined justification as a divine declaration. It means that God as Judge declares us to be righteous with respect to his law. We are now asking the question, on what *basis* does God make this declaration? Because God himself is righteous, he cannot say or do anything that violates his own holy nature or that ignores the requirements of his holy law. Thus if God justifies us or declares us righteous, there must be a basis or rationale for that declaration. What is it?

One possible basis for justification would be the individual's own personal righteousness, his own works or accomplishments. This would be the case if the person were completely righteous with respect to the law's commandments, i.e., if he were 100% innocent. In this case the Judge would be required to say, "No penalty for you," since the person is literally not guilty of any sin and does not deserve any punishment. Such would be a true justification by works. This possibility will never become a reality, though, since all have sinned and no one is 100% innocent (Rom 3:20,23).

There is another possible way for a person to be justified (declared righteous) by his own personal righteousness. This would happen if one did indeed break the law but then himself actually took the full punishment for doing so. In this case the person would be righteous with respect to the law's penalty rather than its commands. Once the penalty was paid, the Judge could declare, "No *further* penalty for you." This happens on a human level when a criminal serves his full sentence, thus "paying his debt to society," and is released from prison. The reason this will never happen in the divine Judge's courtroom, though, is that the penalty for sins is eternal suffering in hell. Because the penalty is eternal, condemned sinners will never reach the point when they have completely satisfied the law's penal requirement. They will forever be paying their debt of punishment.

Thus because of the fact of universal sinfulness, and because of the nature of the punishment deserved by sin, no one will ever be justified on the basis of any type of human righteousness.

What is the alternative? The only alternative, and the only true basis for justifying sinners, is *God's own righteousness imputed or credited to the sinner's account.* If we attempt to stand before God on the judgment day dressed only in our own righteousness—a "filthy garment" (Isa 64:6)—we will be condemned, not justified. That is why God offers to clothe us with "a robe of righteousness" that he himself has prepared (Isa 61:10). This leads Paul to say that on that day he wants to "be found in Him, not having a righteousness of my own derived from the Law, but that which is through faith in Christ, the righteousness which comes from God on the basis of faith" (Phil 3:9). The gospel is the power of God for salvation because "in it the righteousness of God is revealed," to take the place of our own futile human righteousness (Rom 1:16-17). Anyone who rejects God's righteousness and seeks to establish his own righteousness as a basis for acceptance by God is doomed to be rejected (Rom 10:3).

The righteousness of God that serves as the basis for justification is not the divine *attribute* of righteousness or justice as such, especially if this is understood as God's own perfect moral character and his perfect legal justice that requires sin to be punished. The righteousness of God that justifies is rather a *gift* given to sinners, like a robe woven by God then offered to and accepted by the sinner, who wears it as if it were his own (Isa 61:10). It is a righteousness that is outside of God and "comes from God" (Phil 3:9) and is applied to us. When God sees this righteousness in our possession, he declares, "No penalty for you!"

Specifically, this righteousness of God is the righteousness of God the Son in the person of Jesus Christ. In fact the main purpose of the incarnation was to establish a divine righteousness that could be used as the basis for justifying sinners. An image frequently used to represent this transfer of righteousness is *imputation*, which is based on the Greek verb *logizomai*. When used in the context of justification, this word derives its meaning from the way it was used by Greeks in the field of business or commerce. It was a technical term that described the procedure of entering a credit or a debit to someone's account. It is properly translated "to credit, to set down to one's account, to impute, to reckon, to count as, to regard as." An illustration of the concept is Paul's exhortation to Philemon (v. 18, NKJV) regarding any debt owed to him by his runaway slave Onesimus: "Put that on my account." This concept explains what was happening on the cross, when our sins were imputed to Christ; and it explains what is happening in justification, when Christ's righteousness is imputed or credited to us.

Exactly what is the righteousness of Christ that is imputed to our account? We will remember that strictly speaking righteousness means "conformity to a norm." Where salvation from sin is concerned, the relevant norm is the law of God, and justification can happen only when the requirements of the law have been satisfied as mandated by God's own holy nature. This is what Jesus came to accomplish. In essence the righteousness of God and the basis for our justification is the fact that Jesus satisfied the requirements of the law in our place, and in justification his satisfaction of these requirements is imputed to our account.

Most Protestants are in agreement up to this point, but here a serious error is usually made. It is almost universally assumed that the righteousness of Christ that is imputed to us includes his active righteousness, i.e., his satisfaction of or obedience to the commandments of the law. With Christ's perfect obedience put down on our account, God can look at us and declare us "not guilty," thus treating us just as if we had never sinned. But this is not correct. Christ did indeed obey the law perfectly, but he did so because as a human being this was his own personal responsibility and duty. It was necessary for his own sake; it was what he ought to have done, even apart from his saving purposes. Thus in terms of his active righteousness, even the sinless Christ is an "unprofitable servant" (Luke 17:10, KJV). He has no extra merits left over, so to speak, to share with anyone else. (This does not mean, of course, that his perfect obedience is irrelevant to our salvation. His perfect life was a prerequisite for his perfect sacrifice. Without the former, he could not have been the latter.)

What, then, is imputed to our account as the basis for our justification? Not Christ's active righteousness—his *doing*, but his passive righteousness—his *dying*. Jesus not only satisfied the commandments of the law; he also satisfied the law's requirements for penalty. He took its punishment in our place through his substitutionary and propitiatory death on the cross. This is the "one act of righteousness" that constitutes the righteousness of God: "Even so through one act of righteousness there resulted justification of life to all men" (Rom 5:18). Thus the righteousness of God revealed in the gospel and imputed to our account is *Christ's satisfaction, on our behalf, of the law's requirement for penalty.* In essence the righteousness of God is the blood of Christ.

This is why I have said that to be **justified** (declared righteous) does not mean that I am treated *just as if I'd* never sinned, but *just as if I'd* already paid the penalty of eternal hell. As sinners justified by the blood of Christ we do not have to worry about hell because (as far as God is concerned) we have already been there, have paid our eternal debt, and have been released (Rom 8:1).

III. THE MEANS OF JUSTIFICATION

To be justified means to be declared righteous with respect to God's law, based on the fact that Jesus has suffered in our stead the full penalty the law imposes upon sinners. But this gift of justification is not bestowed automatically upon everyone for their personal sins. Rather, it is given only to those who possess the proper and necessary means of receiving it. What is this God-appointed means for receiving justification?

One of the main issues at stake here is the relation between faith and works and the relation of each to justification. Are we justified by faith apart from works (Rom 3:28), or are we justified by works and not by faith alone (Jas 2:24)? How to answer this question correctly is a point of serious disagreement among Christians, and it must be addressed here.

A. Works, Conditions, and Means

We must first clarify what is meant by the concept of *means*. To do so we must explain how it is related to *works* and to *conditions*. In the broadest sense a person's works may be defined as anything one does as the subject or author of the act. This includes internal, mental acts as well as external, physical acts. In this sense even faith itself is a work, according to John 6:28-29: "Therefore they said to Him, 'What shall we do, so that we may work the works of God?' Jesus answered and said to them, 'This is the work of God, that you believe in Him whom He has sent.'" The people are asking Jesus to name something *they can do* that will qualify as a *work* desired by God and pleasing to God. In his reply Jesus specifies the work God desires of them, namely, that they believe in him as their Messiah. Thus in this broad sense of "something we do," even faith is a work.

This is not the connotation that applies to the term "works" in the rest of the NT, however, especially in the writings of Paul and James. This is evident from the fact that both of these writers separate faith from the category of works (e.g., Rom 3:28; Eph 2:8-9; Jas 2:18-26). Thus "works" in these other contexts must have a different meaning. I suggest that the key passage that helps us understand this meaning is Rom 3:28, "For we maintain that a man is justified by faith apart from works of the Law." The latter part of this verse says literally, "apart from works of law." The NASB errs in capitalizing the word "law" and in adding the definite article "the," implying that Paul is referring to the Law of Moses. This is not the case. Here, as in many other places in this context (e.g., 3:19-21a), "law" (*nomos*) refers to any and all law codes imposed upon mankind as creatures by the sovereign Creator. "*Works* of law" then refers to any response by the creature to the Creator's laws. Rom 3:20 uses the same expression in the same sense, literally, "By works of law no flesh will be justified in His sight."

To be more precise, a "work" (i.e., a work of *law*) in terms of Rom 3:28 refers to *any* response to the Creator's laws, whether good or bad, whether in obedience or disobedience. In fact, in this context the main emphasis seems to be upon sinful works, a fact that becomes clear when we see that 4:6-8 is just an elaboration of 3:28 (Cottrell, *Romans*, I:269-270). Paul's statement in 3:28 thus means that a person is justified apart from a direct consideration of how he is responding to his relevant law code, whether in obedience or disobedience.

How then is faith different from works in this Pauline sense? Whereas works are the *creature's* response to the *Creator's* law, faith is the *sinner's* response to the *Redeemer's* instructions on how to receive the gift of salvation. That is, faith in Jesus is not something God as Creator requires in the law that applies to mankind simply as creatures; it is not a "work of law." It is rather our response to God in his role as Redeemer. This is true, of course, only of justifying faith, which is specifically faith in the death and resurrection of Jesus Christ (Rom 3:25 [NIV]; 10:9); it does not apply to the creature's generic faith in the existence of the good Creator (Heb 11:6).

Are we to assume, then, that everything we do must be placed in one of these two categories, either faith or works? No, that is incorrect. We are justified by faith as a response to the Redeemer's instructions on how to receive salvation, and not by any response to the Creator's law. But there are other "things we do" that are in the former category and not the latter, namely, the other conditions of salvation. This leads us to a consideration of the difference between *means* and *conditions*.

As we will see in chapter 19, there are several conditions for salvation (none of which is a work of law), and faith is just one of them. Nevertheless faith is unique in that it is the only *means* by which the sinner may receive the gift of salvation, and justification in particular. In other words the means of justification is a particular kind of condition for salvation, and does not exclude other kinds of conditions.

Specifically what is meant by the *means* of justification? An unabridged dictionary defines "means" as "an agency, instrument, or method used to attain an end." The means of justification is the specific instrument by which the gift of justification via Christ's blood can be received. It is the receptacle into which that gift must be placed; it is the specific condition that makes direct contact with the blood of Christ.

B. Faith, Not Works

What is the one means by which the sinner is justified? It is *faith* in the saving work of Jesus. Faith is the receptacle for justification; it is the one thing that we do that directly touches the cross. As an illustration, the power of electricity is available through numerous outlets to run various appliances in our homes, but this power can be accessed only when a specifically designed plug is inserted into the outlet. Likewise, direct access to the justifying power of Christ's blood is possible only through faith as the one compatible means.

Almost everyone agrees that faith is at least the primary means by which justification is received; but some attempt to add works to faith, and some even make faith and works equal means of justification. Those who take this last approach usually do so out of a sincere desire to do justice to James 2:24, "You see that a man is justified by works and not by faith alone." Thus they imply the equivalence of faith and works by comparing them to the two oars that row a boat, the two wings of an airplane, the two ends of a seesaw, or the two blades of a pair of scissors. One writer points out that Scripture tells us that we are saved by repentance, confession, baptism, fruit bearing, and steadfast endurance in the faith. He concludes, "So the doctrine of justification by both faith and complete obedience can be harmonized on the simple ground that both are taught in the Bible" (Blakely, I:96).

Another approach which in effect makes faith and works equivalent means for justification is the view that faith by definition includes obedience (i.e., works, in the sense of "good works," as in Eph 2:10). This view is widely accepted in the Restoration Movement, particularly under the influence of Gareth Reese's essay, "The Faith That Saves" (*Acts*, 598-610). John Corson has summarized this view in an article entitled "Faith Alone Involves Obedience, Too!" Corson says that "*faith alone* can bring us to a saving relationship with God," but this "saving faith must include *obedience*" (5, 6). Whether or not the concept of faith actually includes obedience will be examined in chapter 19.

In my judgment views such as these contradict the strong biblical teaching that faith, not works, is the means of justification. Many texts suggest that there is a unique relation between faith and salvation in general,[3] while others specifically connect faith with justification. Romans 3:22 speaks of "the righteousness of God through faith in Jesus Christ for all those who believe"; Rom 3:26 says God is "the justifier of the one who has faith in Jesus." He justifies both Jews and Greeks by faith (Rom 3:30). Throughout Romans 4 Paul explains the implications of the fact that Abraham was justified by faith: "Then he believed in the LORD, and He reckoned it to him as righteousness" (Gen 15:6). Then Paul concludes, "Therefore, having been justified by faith, we have peace with God" (Rom 5:1). The Gentiles "attained . . . the righteousness that is by faith" (Rom 9:30; see 10:10). The Law of Moses leads to Christ, "so that we may be justified by faith" (Gal 3:24). Paul desired only the righteousness "which is through faith in Christ, the righteousness which comes from God on the basis of faith" (Phil 3:9).

But Paul is actually even more specific than this. Over and over he declares that we are justified by faith, and *not by works*. "A man is justified by faith apart from works of the Law" (Rom 3:28). Abraham was justified by faith, not by works (Rom 4:2-3). If it comes through works, then salvation is wages and not a gift; "but to the one who does not work, but believes in Him who justifies the ungodly, his faith is credited as righteousness" (Rom 4:4-5). God rejected the Jews because they pursued righteousness by works rather than by faith (Rom 9:31-32; 10:3). "Nevertheless knowing that a man is not justified by works of the Law but through faith in Christ Jesus, even we have believed in Christ Jesus, so that we may be justified by faith in Christ and not by the works of the Law" (Gal 2:16; see 3:1-15). Paul sums up this contrast between faith and works regarding salvation in general in Eph 2:8-9, "For by grace you have been saved through faith; and that not of yourselves, it is the gift of God; not as a result of works, so that no one may boast." He also says, "But if it is by grace, it is no longer on the basis of works, otherwise grace is no longer grace" (Rom 11:6).

All of this points us to the fact that God's designation of faith, not works, as the means of justification is not an arbitrary decision on his part but is determined by the very nature of the situation. Since justification is by grace, i.e., since it is a gift, the means of receiving it must be consistent with that fact and cannot in any sense be regarded as earning or deserving it. Works as a means are thus ruled out (Rom 4:4-5; 11:6), but faith as a means is perfectly consistent with grace: "For this reason it is by faith, in order that it may be in accordance with grace" (Rom 4:16).

There is another factor that makes faith apart from works the only compatible means of justification. This is the fact that someone else's work—the work of Christ on the cross—is totally responsible for the gift: we are "justified by His blood" (Rom 5:9). This means that the very nature of salvation through Christ determines that faith is the means by which it is received. As an illustration, if a doctor treats me for a sore throat, there are many things he can tell me to do that will directly bring about a cure, e.g., gargle, take pills, avoid certain foods. But if the doctor must perform open heart surgery on me, the only means by which I can receive his lifesaving treatment is to passively surrender myself to him and trust him to do what he has promised. In a similar way, the very nature of justification through Christ's blood suggests that faith in his life-giving work is the only consistent means for receiving its benefits. My own works can no more be the means of justification than a surgeon could require me to cut open my own chest and hold my split rib cage apart while he operated on my heart. Such would be contrary to the very nature of the procedure. Just as I can only trust the skill of my surgeon, so the only consistent means of justification is faith in the blood of Christ (Rom 3:25, NIV).

Thus we may conclude that the sole means of justification is faith in Christ's saving work. It is this faith that initially receives justification (in baptism, Col 2:12); and it is this faith that keeps us in a justified state. In other words, the Christian continues to be justified—fully forgiven for all sins—as long as he continues to believe in Christ's saving blood. We have entered "by faith into this grace in which we stand" (Rom 5:2), and "you stand by your faith" (Rom 11:20); "in your faith you are standing firm" (2 Cor 1:24). The Spirit strengthens you with inward power "so that Christ may dwell in your hearts through faith" (Eph 3:16-17). Thus we "are protected by the power of God through faith" (1 Pet 1:5).

C. A Faith That Works

We cannot close our discussion of the means of justification without explaining James's statement that "a man is justified by works and not by faith alone" (2:24). How is this consistent with Paul's teaching? Since we believe that all Scripture is God-breathed (2 Tim 3:16) and that James is a legitimate part of Scripture, we cannot simply declare that they contradict each other. Nor can we be satisfied with clever, brief summaries of the difference between the two, e.g., "Paul opposes dead (false) works, while James opposes dead (false) faith"; "Paul opposes faithless works, while James opposes workless faith"; or "Paul *opposes* works produced *for* righteousness, while James *advocates* works produced *by* righteousness." Such statements may be true, but they do not fully explain the stark contrast between the language of the two writers.

Several attempts to explain the difference must be rejected. One such view is that Paul and James are talking about two different groups of people. That is, Paul is talking about *unsaved sinners* and how they *become* justified, namely, by faith apart from any works; James is talking about *Christians* and how they *remain* justified, namely, by faith *and* works. This cannot be the point, though, since it seems to be the very view Paul is condemning in the book of Galatians: saved initially by faith, and kept saved by works (i.e., Galatianism). Also, if this were true, then none of Paul's great teaching on justification by faith would be applicable to Christians. This would seem to contradict the very purpose for Paul's writing the book of Romans (Cottrell, *Romans*, I:44-48).

Another inadequate view is the idea that Paul and James are talking about two different kinds of justification. Paul is said to be referring to *absolute* justification in the sight of *God*, with such a limitation being suggested by Rom 3:20 ("in His sight") and Rom 4:2 ("but not before God"). On the other hand, James is said to be referring to *relative* justification in the sight of *men*, for which works are necessary as the proof of the presence of faith, as in Jas 2:18, "I will show you my faith by my works." This view, though held by many, seems to be weak exegetically. It is unlikely that Paul has such a distinction in mind in Rom 3:20, and in Rom 4:2 he speaks of works not as giving evidence of faith but as something to boast about for their own sake. Also, James's main example of justification by works is Abraham's offering of Isaac (2:21-24), a deed that was done to demonstrate his faith not to other men but to God (Gen 22:12).

The most common explanation of the difference between Paul and James is that they are talking about two different kinds of works. For example, some say Paul speaks of works of the OT law and excludes them from justification, while James speaks of works of the NT law and makes them conditions for justification. This view contradicts Paul's treatment of law in Romans, however, where his exclusion of works of law includes not only the Law of Moses but also all other law codes, such as the Gentiles' heart-law (Rom 2:15). Another version of this view is McGarvey's suggestion that the works of which Paul speaks "are clearly works of perfect obedience to moral law," which are not necessary for justification; while James refers to "works of obedience to positive law, as distinguished from moral law"—which *are* necessary for justification. For sinners the justifying obedience is to the positive command of baptism; for Christians the justifying obedience is the positive command of confession, as in 1 John 1:9 ("Justification," 120, 122-129). This view, however, is inconsistent with the contents of the entire second chapter of James, where the moral law is certainly in view (vv. 8-11,14-17).

The most common version of the two-kinds-of-works view is the idea that Paul and James are referring to works done from different *motives*. Paul excludes "works of law," which are works done with wrong motives; James requires "works of faith," or works done with right motives. In fact, the works as such may be the same for both, with only their motives being different. What is this difference? The usual explanation is that Paul's "works of law" are any works that we do specifically to earn or deserve our salvation. Such works are called "meritorious works" or "works of merit." But works done for such a legalistic purpose cannot justify. Only works done purely from faith, without any thought that they are being done for salvation, can justify—which is James's point.

This view is impossible to sustain for a number of reasons. First, there is no reference in either Paul or James to motivation of any kind. Second, we have already seen that Paul's use of the expression "works of law" (as in Rom 3:28) means something totally different from "meritorious works." It refers to any response of the creature to his Creator's laws, whether that response be good (obedience) or bad (sins), and thus whether the motives be good or bad. Third, the main reason works of law cannot justify, even if rightly motivated, is that such justification requires perfect obedience, which does not exist. Thus for anyone who has sinned, it is impossible to be justified even by works that are rightly motivated. In fact, the impossibility of a sinner's being justified by works is what makes certain motives false. Finally, there seems to be a contradiction, or a "catch-22," in saying, "If you want to be justified, you must do good works; but you must not do them because you want to be justified." Or, "I am justified only by works done *not* to be justified; therefore to be justified I must do good works, but not in order to be justified." In other words this view first says, "Works done with the motive of receiving salvation thereby are legalistic and nonjustifying." It then says, "Only works done in faith are justifying works." This leads to the impossible situation of having to do good works *only* from faith *in order to be justified.*

Thus we conclude that Paul and James are not talking about two different kinds of works. In the final analysis, acceptable works are the same for both.

What, then, is a reasonable explanation of the difference between Paul and James? In my judgment the best understanding is that both faith and works are related to justification, but in different ways. Faith has an *immediate and direct* relation to justification, since it is the only means that is compatible with justification as a free gift made available solely through the work of Jesus Christ. Thus says Paul. James's point, though, is that there is also a necessary indirect relation between works and justification, since true saving faith by its very nature will produce works, i.e., it will desire to obey and will seek to obey God's laws. Thus James can say that justification is by works, but only in a *secondary and indirect* sense insofar as works are the necessary expression of and evidence of faith. In summary, Paul's concern is to deny that justification is equally related to both faith and works, while James reminds us that works cannot be excluded from the picture since they are the inevitable result of faith—a point Paul himself makes in Rom 6:1ff. The contrast may be depicted as follows:

PAUL DENIES: JAMES AFFIRMS:

Justification   Justification

Faith   Works   Faith ⟶ Works

What, then, actually justifies us? Faith *without* works? No, says James. Faith *plus* works? No, says Paul. A *faith that works?* Yes, say Paul and James.

This understanding of Paul and James helps us to understand how a Christian can be both justified by faith and judged by works. That we will be judged by works is a truth taught throughout Scripture. For example, Jer 17:10 says, "I, the LORD, search the heart, I test the mind, even to give to each man according to his ways, according to the results of his deeds." Jesus says in Matt 16:27, "For the Son of Man is going to come in the glory of His Father and with His angels, and will then repay every man according to his deeds." He declares in Rev 22:12, "Behold, I am coming quickly, and My reward is with Me, to render to every man according to what he has done." That this includes the saved and the unsaved alike is clear from 2 Cor 5:10, "For we must all appear before the judgment seat of Christ, so that each one may be recompensed for his deeds in the body, according to what he has done, whether good or bad."[4]

Surely one reason why Christians will be judged according to their works, both good and bad, is to determine the degree of reward to be received by each (Grudem, *Doctrine*, 456-457). But another reason for exposing all our works on the day of judgment will be to demonstrate the presence or absence of the faith which justifies. Such an examination is not necessary for God's own sake, but it will be done in order to demonstrate that God's judgment is impartial or without favoritism, that he is no "respecter of persons" (Acts 10:34-35; Rom 2:6,11; Eph 6:8-9; Col 3:25; 1 Pet 1:17).

NOTES ON CHAPTER SEVENTEEN

[1] Traditional hymns refer often to this double cure: "Be of sin the double cure; save me from its guilt and power" (or, "Save from wrath, and make me pure," from "Rock of Ages"); "Born of His Spirit, washed in His blood" ("Blessed Assurance"); "It was on that old cross Jesus suffered and died, to pardon and sanctify me" ("The Old Rugged Cross"); "Grace to cleanse, and power

to free" ("Savior, Like a Shepherd Lead Us"); "He breaks the power of canceled sin" ("O, for a Thousand Tongues To Sing"); "Sin pardoned, man restored" ("Thy Hand, O God, Has Guided"); "Grace that will pardon and cleanse within" ("Marvelous Grace of Our Loving Lord").

[2] This term will be discussed in the next section.

[3] E.g., John 1:12; 3:16,18,36; 5:24; Acts 13:39; 16:31; Rom 1:17; Gal 3:26; Eph 2:8; 1 John 5:1.

[4] See also 2 Chr 6:30; Job 34:11; Ps 62:12; Prov 24:12; Eccl 12:13-14; Isa 59:18; Jer 32:19; Ezek 33:20; Matt 12:36-37; 25:31ff.; Acts 10:34-35; Rom 2:6; 14:12; 1 Cor 3:13; Eph 6:8; Col 3:25; 1 Pet 1:17; Rev 2:23; 20:12-13.

CHAPTER EIGHTEEN
REGENERATION AND SANCTIFICATION

Salvation is more than forgiveness of sins! As we have seen, sin causes two basic problems for sinners: it makes us guilty; and it produces an inward sickness, weakness, or corruption of the soul. But God's gracious salvation includes a remedy for each of these problems. In the first part of this "double cure," justification or forgiveness solves the problem of our guilt. But if that were all there is to salvation, we would still be weak and helpless and held down by the chains of sin. We would be unable to make much headway in conquering our sinful habits, tendencies, and desires.

But maybe that does not matter. After all, if we are justified by grace through faith, are works even necessary? Do we still *have* to obey God's commands? Does it really matter whether we keep on sinning or not (Rom 6:1)? We can understand how some may be prompted to ask such questions, since the gospel of grace is so amazing, even radical, when compared with ordinary concepts.

But of course sin still matters! How could anyone even think otherwise (Rom 6:2)? This is why God has made provision not only to remove our guilt, but also to restore our sin-weakened natures to a state of spiritual life and health. This is the second part of the "double cure" in which God destroys sin's power over us and makes us pure.

The remedy by which God accomplishes this begins with an event usually called *regeneration*, and continues with a process usually called *sanctification*. This aspect of salvation is very different from justification. Whereas justification is an objective, legal change in our relationship to God's law, regeneration and sanctification are inward, subjective changes in our nature, character, and behavior. The differences may be summed up thus:

JUSTIFICATION	*REGENERATION/ SANCTIFICATION*
a. deals with our legal problem	a. deals with our condition
b. solves the problem of law-breaking	b. solves the problem of law-keeping
c. removes guilt	c. removes corruption
d. God acts as Judge	d. God acts as Physician
e. outward and objective	e. inward and personal
f. declared righteous by decree	f. made righteous by degrees
g. an act completed from the beginning	g. a process continuing until we die

h. Christ died for us	h. we die with Christ
i. imputed righteousness	i. imparted righteousness
j. the sinner's great need	j. the Christian's great need

I. REGENERATION

A. The Nature of Regeneration

Regeneration is an instantaneous, onetime event that happens in the moment of conversion, the moment when a sinner passes from his lost state into the saved state. Viewed as to its cause, regeneration is a divine act, a work that God the Holy Spirit performs upon the sinful soul. Viewed as to its effect, regeneration is an inward change in the sinner's very nature.

This is not a legal change, though such a change (justification) does occur at the same moment as regeneration. Nor is it simply a moral change, i.e., a voluntary change of mind and heart that the sinner himself accomplishes through an act of his own will as motivated by the gospel. Such a moral change (faith and repentance) occurs prior to regeneration and is a prerequisite for it, but it is not the same as regeneration and cannot of its own power produce regeneration. Rather, regeneration is a metaphysical change, a change that takes place within the very essence of the soul.

This does not mean, of course, that the soul's essence is transformed into a different kind of stuff. It means simply that the damage sin inflicts upon the soul is repaired; it means that the sin-sickness that infects the soul is healed. Or rather, it means that the long process of healing and repair has begun. By way of analogy, a bodily sickness is healed first of all by an initial treatment, e.g., an injection or an operation, which is then followed by a period of recuperation and recovery. On the spiritual level the initial operation is the act of regeneration, and the period of recovery is sanctification.

To follow this analogy, in the act of regeneration God assumes the role of the Great Physician, rather than the role of Judge as in justification. Ezekiel 36:26 prophetically describes this work in terms of a heart-transplant operation: "Moreover, I will give you a new heart and put a new spirit within you; and I will remove the heart of stone from your flesh and give you a heart of flesh." Here the "heart of stone" is the soul hardened and calcified by sin. It is removed and replaced by "a heart of flesh," i.e., one that is soft and yielding to the will of God.

This event of regeneration is described in Rom 6:1-14 in terms of *death* and *resurrection*. Here Paul says that in the moment of baptism the sinner's "old self," i.e., the "heart of stone," was crucified or put to death with Jesus (v. 6); in this moment we "died to sin" (v. 2). But this death-event is immediately followed by the experience of resurrection and the infusion of new life (vv. 4-5), by virtue of which the sinner is now "alive from the dead" (v. 13) and able to "walk in newness of life" (v. 4). As the result of regeneration one is thus "dead to sin, but alive to God in Christ Jesus" (v. 11).

In Col 2:11-13 Paul describes the regeneration event in almost the same way, except the image of death is replaced with the image of spiritual circumcision: "In Him you were also circumcised with a circumcision made without hands, in the removal of the body of the flesh by the circumcision of Christ" (v. 11). This is equivalent to the "old self" dying with Christ or being crucified with Christ in Rom 6:6. (See Col 2:13, where spiritual death and spiritual uncircumcision are equivalent concepts.) It takes place as a result of "having been buried with Him in baptism,"[1] and is followed by an act of resurrection: "In which [baptism] you were also raised up with Him" and in which "He made you alive together with Him" (vv. 12-13). See also Col 3:1.

In view of the centrality of Christ's death and resurrection in the scheme of redemption, it is no accident that this specific act of salvation (i.e., regeneration) should itself have the character of death and resurrection. As we have seen already [pp. 280-281], Christ's resurrection unleashes the power of life that destroys the curse of death in all its forms. This includes the power to give new life to souls that are dead in their trespasses and sins. Thus the language of resurrection—being made alive—is used in Scripture for the act of regeneration more than any other imagery. Besides Rom 6:1-14 and Col 2:11-13, we may cite Eph 2:5-6, which says that God "made us alive together with Christ . . . and raised us up with Him." John also speaks of the Christian as having "passed out of death into life" (John 5:24; 1 John 3:14).

Other language and images are used that convey the same general concept of the beginning of new life. In John 3:3-8 Jesus speaks of regeneration as a new birth—being "born again" (v. 3); Peter says that God "has caused us to be born again to a living hope through the resurrection of Jesus Christ from the dead" (1 Pet 1:3; see v. 23). An equally strong image depicting the new-life nature of regeneration is that of creation. Paul says that those who have been saved by grace are "God's workmanship, created in Christ Jesus" (Eph 2:10). This refers not to the original creation of Genesis 1, but to the new creation of regeneration (2 Cor 5:17; Gal 6:15). To describe it as an act of creation marks regeneration not only as a time of new beginnings but also as an act that can be accomplished only by God. As applied to this event the term "regeneration" itself appears only in Titus 3:5, where it is used synonymously with "renewing." In its basic meaning it is the practical equivalent of rebirth.

B. The Cause of Regeneration

It is extremely important to understand that the act of regeneration is a saving act worked upon our hearts by God himself and not by our own effort or power. It is part of "the gift of God" (Eph 2:9) that constitutes salvation.

In the chapter on the Holy Spirit it was pointed out that a common Restoration Movement approach to regeneration is to regard it as a moral change of heart accomplished by the sinner himself. This is the essence of Alexander Campbell's view that regeneration (which he also called conversion and sanctification) is a moral or spiritual change accomplished by the Holy Spirit, but only indirectly through the Word of God. "A moral change," he said, "is effected only by motives, and motives are arguments; and all the arguments ever used by the Holy Spirit, are found written in the book called the Word of Truth." Thus there is no difference "between what the Word, *per se*, or the Spirit, *per se*, severally does; as though they were two independent, and wholly distinct powers, or influences" (*Debate*, 613-614). In another place he says, "And when we think of the power of the Spirit of God exerted upon minds or human spirits, it is impossible to imagine that that power can consist of any thing else but words or arguments" ("Holy Spirit," 294-295). If this is true, then regeneration occurs only when the hearer decides to respond to the Spirit-inspired Word in faith and repentance, with that decision in itself being the event of regeneration.

This same approach to regeneration is taken by other Restoration Movement authors who equate the sinner's dying to sin and rising to new life with his pre baptismal decision to believe and repent. For example, Moses Lard declared that "we die to sin when we believe in Christ and repent of our sins"; thus "we died to sin before our baptism" (195-196). Following Lard, Don DeWelt says that the sinner's death to sin "was brought about by our belief and repentance preceding our baptism"; that is, "the method of attaining the crucifixion of self and thus being released from the bondage of the flesh is by way of faith and repentance before baptism" (90-91). K.C. Moser says the same: "In repentance one dies and is raised to righteousness." In our repentance, which is a human act, "two changes take place. First, like Christ and with him, we die unto sin. Second, like Christ and with him, we are raised to live unto God" (89-90). As we have already seen, this death and this resurrection are the same as regeneration; thus according to this approach a sinner regenerates himself when he believes and repents.

We strongly reject such a view. In the Bible regeneration is a work of God, not a work of man. We are spiritually reborn into God's family "not of blood nor of the will of the flesh nor of the will of man, but of God" (John 1:13). Our death with Christ and resurrection with him are "the working of God" (Col 2:12); thus in our new natures "we are His workmanship" (Eph 2:10). The biblical images chosen to represent this mighty act—resurrection, new creation, rebirth—in themselves point to divine activity; they are hardly feats we are capable of accomplishing by our own puny strength.

In several places it is clearly attributed to the Holy Spirit, but in fact the ultimate power that accomplishes this regeneration—this spiritual death and resurrection—flows from the saving work of Jesus in his own death and resurrection. This is Paul's clear teaching in Rom 6:1-14, as reinforced by his references to our being buried *with Christ* and raised up *with Christ* (Eph 2:5-6; Col 2:12-13; see 1 Pet 1:3; 3:21).

In Rom 6:4 Paul says that "we have been buried with Him through baptism into death." The death into which we are buried is without doubt our own death to sin (v. 2), but this is accomplished only because we are at this time being buried into Christ's death (v. 3). The implication is that in some true and significant sense, the death of Jesus has a death-dealing power in reference to sin. When we become united with Christ's death in baptism, our old sinful self is put to death—not by our own will power, but by the power of his holy cross. By God's design and God's power, in some manner the death of Jesus with all its saving benefits is literally present to us as believing sinners and actually touches us in the act of baptism, and this union produces not only justification but also our death to sin. It is as if, in his death, Jesus became a flame that is capable of extinguishing everything having to do with sin and death. When we are baptized into his death (buried with him in baptism), we touch this flame; and it consumes the "old man" of sin and sets us ablaze with a holy fire that continues to purge the residual sin from our lives.

Paul states this idea in Rom 6:6 when he affirms "that our old self was crucified with Him." Here the "old self" refers specifically to the unregenerated soul or inner man. Thus in the event of regeneration the power of the cross is applied to our fallen soul, putting it to death as to its sin-ridden existence.

In like manner the resurrection aspect of regeneration is accomplished by our union with the resurrection of Jesus. Christ's resurrection has generated infinite life-giving power (Eph 1:18-23; Heb 7:16), a power that produces in us the ability to walk in newness of life (Rom 6:4-5).

The main point of Paul's teaching in Rom 6:1-14 is the significance of *Christ's death* as the source of the death of our sins via our union with him in his death, and *Christ's resurrection* as the source of our resurrection to new life via our union with him in his resurrection. Christ died to sin; and when we are united with him in his death, we too die to sin *by virtue of his death*. Christ also rose from the dead, and when we are united with him in his resurrection, we too pass from spiritual death to spiritual life *by virtue of his resurrection*. This does not happen by virtue of some inner strength of our own.

Why do we say, then, that the *Holy Spirit* is the one who works regeneration in the believing sinner's heart? Because the specific saving work of the Spirit is to *apply* the saving benefits of Christ's death and resurrection to the sinner. He is the person of the Trinity who brings the power of Christ's death and resurrection to bear upon us. As such he is the very embodiment of the death-dealing and life-giving power that changes us in the moment of regeneration.

Even before that moment, the Holy Spirit has been indirectly instrumental in our regeneration by working upon our hearts through the Word of the Gospel, thus leading us to faith and repentance as necessary prerequisites of regeneration. In this indirect sense "He brought us forth by the word of truth" (Jas 1:18), and we were "born again . . . through the living and enduring word of God" (1 Pet 1:23). Since the Spirit is the ultimate author of the Word, any impact the Word of God has upon our hearts is indirectly the work of the Spirit.

But we must not confuse the way the Spirit works to bring about faith and repentance with the way he works in regeneration itself. His main work in regeneration is to act directly upon the heart to initiate the healing process within the sin-deadened soul. As the Living Water (John 4:10-14; 7:37-39), the Holy Spirit is the one who imparts and implants new life into our spiritual natures. "It is the Spirit who gives life" (John 6:63), because he is "the Spirit of life" (Rom 8:2). The regeneration and renewing that take place in baptism are specifically attributed to the Holy Spirit in Titus 3:5.

A main reason why many in the Restoration Movement reject the idea of regeneration as a direct work of the Spirit upon the sinner's heart is that they think it is an implicit form of Calvinism, similar to the Calvinist doctrine of irresistible grace. As we have seen, Calvinism's doctrine of total depravity includes the belief that all unsaved people are totally unable to respond to the gospel or to the influence of the Word, and thus are totally unable to make the decision to believe and repent. Therefore, if anyone at all is going to be saved, God himself must decide who that will be (via unconditional election); and then he must act directly upon the chosen ones' hearts to enable them to believe. This direct, effectual, and irresistible act, performed by the Holy Spirit, is a main element of the total package called irresistible grace, and is the Calvinist version of regeneration. As a consequence of this act, the sinner immediately begins to believe in Jesus Christ. Thus regeneration precedes and bestows faith as an irresistible gift.

Thus it is true that in Calvinism regeneration is a direct work of the Holy Spirit upon the sinner's heart, but this is completely different from the view of regeneration explained here as the biblical view. In the latter view the Spirit does work upon sinners' hearts to influence them to believe and repent, but this work is indirect (through the Word) and resistible. Some choose to believe and repent, and some choose not to do so. Only after one has chosen to believe and repent does he submit himself to the Great Physician's healing touch, and only then does the Holy Spirit work directly upon his heart to effect regeneration. Such an understanding is quite the opposite of Calvinism.

C. The Result of Regeneration

Regeneration is a change in the sinner's nature, but it is not a complete change or a complete healing of the soul's sin-sickness. It is rather the reversal of the general direction of one's life. It is the beginning of a process of further change, the beginning of a lifelong healing process known as sanctification. It is similar to an event often depicted in old Western movies where a principal in the story would be wounded and develop an infection and a fever. With no antibiotics the local doctor could only monitor the sick man's condition until either he died or "the fever broke," as they would say. The time when "the fever broke" was the turning point, the beginning of the wounded man's recovery. Likewise, regeneration is the time when the sin-fever breaks and the life-giving power of the Holy Spirit sets the sinner on the road to spiritual wholeness.

The result of regeneration, then, is that the saved person can now say, "I *can* obey God's will; I *am able* to obey the law's commands"—which the unregenerated person was unable to do (Rom 8:7-8). We died and rose with Christ, "so that we would no longer be slaves to sin" (Rom 6:6). A bad tree cannot produce good fruit (Matt 7:18); but the regenerated person is no longer a bad tree. He is a good tree who is now able to bear good fruit (Matt 7:17). The spiritual heart transplant of which Ezekiel speaks (36:26-27) enables one to walk in God's statutes and observe his ordinances. "For we are His workmanship, created in Christ Jesus for good works" (Eph 2:10). That is, the ability to do good works is the very purpose and result of regeneration.

Now that we as Christians have this ability, we cannot be content to continue in sin and disobedience. This is Paul's point in Rom 6:1-14. He has just completed the section in Romans where he explains that we are *justified*—freed from sin's guilt and condemnation—through faith in the blood of Christ. But he knows that some will be tempted to conclude that sin is no longer a big deal, since we are living in a state of grace and justification. Why not just continue in sin, so that grace may increase (Rom 6:1)? Paul responds to this erroneous conclusion by reminding us that salvation is *more* than forgiveness of sins. It includes *regeneration*—the gift of a new nature which is now free and able to live apart from sin.

Thus "how shall we who died to sin still live in it?" (Rom 6:2). This would be like a man, after his fever has broken or his heart transplant has been successful, being content to lie in bed for the rest of his life. It would be like someone who has a new Mercedes in his garage continuing to ride a broken-down bicycle everywhere he goes. "May it never be!" says Paul (Rom 6:2). You have been *changed*! "Therefore do not let sin reign in your mortal body so that you obey its lusts, and do not go on presenting the members of your body to sin as instruments of unrighteousness; but present yourselves to God as those alive from the dead" (Rom 6:12-13)!

II. SANCTIFICATION

Regeneration is an event that happens in a single moment, but its effects are meant to be eternal. It is the beginning point for a process that lasts throughout this life and reaches perfection in heaven. This process is usually called *sanctification*.

The term "sanctification" is part of the word family having to do with holiness. Though some disagree, I believe the root idea in this word family is *separation*. The OT word for "holy" (*qadosh*) most likely comes from a word that means "to cut, to divide, to separate." Thus a holy person or thing is one that is separated or set apart from others.

We have seen that God is holy in two senses. First is his ontological holiness, or transcendence. This means that God as eternal and uncreated is set apart from or distinct from all created beings in his very essence. Second is his ethical holiness, or perfect moral purity. This means that he is separate in every way from sin and everything sinful.

In the NT the main adjective for "holy" is *hagios*. Variations are the verb *hagiazo*, "to make holy, to set apart or consecrate, to sanctify"; and the noun *hagiasmos*, "holiness, sanctification, consecration." Thus sanctification is basically the same concept as holiness. We should also note that the adjective *hagios* is often used as a noun, i.e., "holy one." When used thus of Christians, it is usually translated "saint."

A. Aspects of Sanctification

For Christians there are two main aspects of sanctification, corresponding to the two senses in which God is holy. The first aspect may be called *initial* sanctification, which refers to the onetime event in which the unsaved person joins the ranks of the saved, the moment in which he is set apart from the world as such, from his old way of life, and from "this present evil age" (Gal 1:4). It is a change of status or change of position in relation to God and in relation to the world. It transfers the sinner from the domain of darkness into the Kingdom of Christ (Col 1:13). Just as God in his ontological holiness is ever set apart from and distinct from the creation as such, so does the sinner in his conversion transcend the old (sinful and condemned) creation and become identified with the new creation (2 Cor 5:17; Eph 2:10).

This act of initial sanctification is mentioned in 1 Cor 6:11, "Such were some of you; but you were washed, but you were sanctified, but you were justified in the name of the Lord Jesus Christ and in the Spirit of our God." That it is a onetime event is shown by the aorist tense for the three main verbs in this verse, representing completed past action. It is not equivalent to regeneration, but it is the *result* of regeneration and of the justification mentioned here. Being justified and regenerated is the very thing that sets the Christian apart from the world of unsaved sinners. That this initial sanctification is not due to our own efforts is also clear from this verse; it occurs only through the power of Jesus' name and through the power of the Spirit. Indeed, it may correspond to the concept of being *sealed* with the Spirit (Eph 1:13; 2 Cor 1:22). A seal is a mark of ownership; thus the Spirit's presence marks Christians as being set apart from the rest of the world and as belonging to God. See 1 Pet 1:1-2.

Also, 1 Cor 6:11 shows that this initial sanctification occurs in connection with baptism ("you were washed"). This is consistent with the biblical teaching that we have been sanctified by the blood of Jesus Christ (Heb 10:10,29; 13:12), which is applied to us when we are baptized into his death (Rom 6:3).

Everyone who has been thus washed, sanctified, and justified is a saint, a holy one, a separated one. Saints are not an elite group of especially righteous Christians; every member of the body of Christ is a saint, a set-apart one (Acts 9:13,32; Rom 1:7; 15:25-26; 1 Cor 1:2; Phil 1:1), sanctified in this initial sense.

The second aspect of sanctification may be called *progressive* sanctification, because it is the ongoing process in which the Christian becomes more and more separated from sin itself. This aspect of sanctification is not a change in status or relationships, but a continuing transformation of our inward character and mental attitudes, as well as our outward behavior and conduct. This is how we "grow in the grace and knowledge of our Lord and Savior Jesus Christ" (2 Pet 3:18), and "work out [our] own salvation with fear and trembling" (Phil 2:12). In this aspect of sanctification we become more and more like God in righteousness and holiness of truth (Eph 4:22-24). Our pattern and goal are God's own ethical holiness, as we are commanded to imitate his perfect moral character: "But like the Holy One who called you, be holy yourselves also in all your behavior; because it is written, 'You shall be holy, for I am holy'" (1 Pet 1:15-16). As Jesus says it, "Therefore you are to be perfect, as your heavenly Father is perfect" (Matt 5:48). Our goal is to "share His holiness" (Heb 12:10) or to "become partakers of the divine nature" (2 Pet 1:4) in this moral sense. We are to purify ourselves, even as he is pure (1 John 3:3). See Luke 1:75; Rom 6:19,22; 2 Cor 6:14–7:1; 1 Thess 3:13; 4:7.

The fact that most of the passages just cited are exhortations to Christians (who have already been initially sanctified or set apart) shows that this aspect of sanctification is indeed a process and warrants calling it "progressive." This is also seen in Paul's prayer for God to complete the process in 1 Thess 5:23, "Now may the God of peace sanctify you entirely." It is reflected too in the present participle form of *hagiazo* in Heb 10:14, "Because by one sacrifice he has made perfect forever those who are being made holy" (NIV).

When does this process come to its intended end? In other words, when do we as Christians attain complete sanctification? When do we indeed become perfect as our heavenly Father is perfect (Matt 5:48), holy as he is holy (1 Pet 1:16), and pure as he is pure (1 John 3:3)? Some conclude from the very fact that we are commanded to be perfect (holy, pure) that we can and must achieve such a state in this lifetime. We agree that such complete sanctification is our obligation and goal and that we should never be satisfied with anything short of it. Whether it will in reality happen before we die is very doubtful, however. It is true that "ought implies can," but it does not follow from this that "can implies will."

A major factor in reaching a decision on this issue is whether Paul in Rom 7:14-25 is speaking of his past or pre-Christian life, or of his present Christian life. Many argue for the former, especially on the basis of Paul's seriously negative self-descriptions: "sold into bondage to sin" (7:14), "nothing good dwells in me" (7:18), "evil is present in me" (7:21), "prisoner of the law of sin" (7:23), and "wretched man" (7:24). When Paul wrote these things, he was a chosen apostle of Jesus Christ and a man not ashamed to present his Christian character as a model to others: "I exhort you, be imitators of me" (1 Cor 4:16; 11:1; see Phil 3:17; 4:9; 1 Thess 1:6; 2 Thess 3:9). Could such things still apply to Paul the Christian? Perhaps so. Such confessions are no worse than Paul's present-tense declaration that "I am the worst" of sinners (1 Tim 1:15, NIV). Also, even Christians must be exhorted and warned about sin (e.g., Rom 6:1-2,12-13,19; 8:12-13).

Actually there are many solid reasons for taking Paul's testimony in Rom 7:14-25 as referring to his Christian life (see Cottrell, *Romans*, 1:443-444). First, the major theme of this section of Romans (chs. 6–8) has to do with the Christian life. Second, Paul does use the present tense throughout. Third, Paul's strongly positive statements about the law and about his desire to obey it, plus his sorrowful confession of sin and his hatred of it, are incompatible with a non-Christian's state of mind. Fourth, the spiritual struggle pictured here exists only in a Christian's heart and life. Fifth, the longing for deliverance (7:24) suggests the tender heart of a Christian. Sixth, the assurance of triumph (7:25) belongs only to a Christian. Last, the order of the sentences in verse 25 is incompatible with a non-Christian's experience; i.e., even after resting his soul on Christ's salvation, Paul once again laments his conflict with sin.

But how can we account for such an intense conflict within the life of a believer? How can a person who experiences such hatred for sin still be a slave to it? The answer lies in the fact that our nature is twofold, i.e., in the distinction between the flesh (outer man, body) and the spirit (inner man, soul). Our redemption comes in two stages. First, at conversion the sinful soul (spirit) is crucified with Christ and raised up into a state of spiritual life (Rom 6:1-6; see Cottrell, *Romans*, 369-396). Then, at the second coming the body will be redeemed through resurrection (Rom 8:23) or transformation (1 Cor 15:51-54). But in between these two events, at least while we are still living in this body on earth, we exist as an awkward combination of redeemed soul and sin-infested, as-yet-unredeemed body. *This* is the source of the Christian's continuing conflict with sin, as Rom 7:14-25 itself shows.[2]

This suggests in all probability that the process of sanctification will not be completed—that we will not be perfectly holy and pure—until our spirits have been set free from this old, sin-ridden body at death.[3] In Heb 12:23 the phrase "the spirits of the righteous made perfect" probably refers to Christians who have died and who are presently existing only as spirits who are still awaiting the resurrection of their new bodies. These are the ones, says Hebrews, who have been "made perfect."

B. The Norm for Sanctification[4]

If the Christian's obligation is to be holy as God is holy, then the norm for sanctification is no less than the very nature of God. The more we know about the moral nature of God, the more we will know what we, as creatures made in his image, are supposed to be like.

Our most precise and complete knowledge of God's moral nature comes from the law he has revealed to us. The commandments of the law, i.e., the law code that constitutes the moral law of God, are basically God's holiness or his perfect moral character put into verbal form. The moral law is thus the mirror or the transcript of divine holiness. This is why the moral law is the primary source of our knowledge of his holiness and therefore the most basic norm for our own holiness or sanctification. In order to imitate God's holiness, we must look to his law and obey his law. (See *GRe*, 263-264.)

To a degree the content of this law is written on every heart (Rom 2:15), but our clearest knowledge of it comes through the Spirit-inspired Word of God. Thus the written Word provides us with the knowledge we need as to the kind of life God wants us to live. Indeed, this is one of the very purposes for which God has given us the Bible. As Paul says, Scripture is "profitable for teaching, for reproof, for correction, for training in righteousness" (2 Tim 3:16). As David said, "Your word is a lamp to my feet and a light to my path" (Ps 119:105). Thus on a practical level the Bible is our norm for sanctification, our "only rule of faith and practice."

C. The Power for Sanctification

God's word exhorts Christians to "be holy" (1 Pet 1:15), to "be perfect" (Matt 5:48), to grow in grace (2 Pet 3:18), and to work out our salvation (Phil 2:12). Such exhortations are abundant, e.g., "Do not let sin reign in your mortal body" (Rom 6:12). "Abstain from every form of evil" (1 Thess 5:22). "Submit therefore to God. Resist the devil . . . . Cleanse your hands, you sinners" (Jas 4:7-8). "Abhor what is evil; cling to what is good" (Rom 12:9). "Be imitators of God" (Eph 5:1). "Glorify God in your body" (1 Cor 6:20). "Seek first His kingdom and His righteousness" (Matt 6:33). The very fact that such exhortations are addressed to us shows not only that we have an *obligation* to obey them, but also that we have the free-will *ability* to obey them. Sanctification is thus our responsibility, and it will happen only as a result of our own decision and effort.

But this is not the whole story. Though God lays the responsibility for sanctification upon us, he does not leave us to accomplish it through our sin-weakened ability alone. The whole point of the second part of the double cure is to give us power from outside ourselves to conquer sin and be holy as God is holy. The power for sanctification thus comes from God, in particular God the Holy Spirit.

The Spirit's role in our sanctification begins with the saving event of regeneration. As explained earlier in this chapter, this Spirit-caused change within our hearts sets us free from slavery to sin and enables our wills to operate as God intended, i.e., to freely choose to love him and obey his laws. In the moment of regeneration we are "created in Christ Jesus for good works" (Eph 2:10); we are restored to a proper working order for the very purpose of making sanctification possible.

The Spirit's role does not end here, though. As we saw in an earlier chapter, at conversion the Spirit not only regenerates us but at that moment actually enters into our lives and becomes an indwelling presence. He is thus constantly present within our hearts and bodies as a source of a moral and spiritual power that enables us to live a holy, sanctified life. He dwells within us not to give us knowledge but to give us power, not to address and supplement our intellects but to empower and strengthen our wills. He provides us with the moral power and spiritual strength to do what we already know is right on the basis of the Bible's teaching.

Described in negative terms, sanctification means that we must be "putting to death the deeds of the body" (Rom 8:13). These are the sinful deeds that result from the law of sin that continues to reside in our flesh, in our as-yet-unredeemed bodies (Rom 6:6; 7:18,23-25). These sins must be put to death, killed, destroyed, overcome, driven from our lives. This eradication of sin is the Christian's personal responsibility: "If . . . *you* are putting to death the deeds of the body." It is not automatic and inevitable; we must personally will and do it. Paul's main point, though, is that we will not accomplish this alone but only "by the Spirit." The indwelling Spirit is the key to our victory over sin. On our conscious level we are aggressively putting sin to death, but below the level of our consciousness the Spirit's energizing power is making it possible.

Described in positive terms, sanctification means that we must obey God's commands and work out our salvation in fear and trembling (Phil 2:12). In other words, the overwhelming responsibility to be holy as God is holy predictably fills us with awe and trepidation. What a daunting task! But this is why we must not stop reading this text at verse 12 but must also read verse 13, "For it is God who is at work in you, both to will and to work for His good pleasure." God has indeed commanded us to pursue sanctification (Heb 12:14), but he has not left us to do this from our own resources alone. He himself, in the person of the Holy Spirit, is at work in us, to help us both to *want* to do what is right ("to will") and to help us actually to *do* it ("to work").

The sanctifying power of the indwelling Spirit is the substance of Paul's prayer for us in Eph 3:16, where he prays that God "would grant you, according to the riches of His glory, to be strengthened with power through His Spirit in the inner man." This is how we are "led by the Spirit of God" (Rom 8:14), i.e., we use his power to slay the sins in our lives (v. 13). When strengthened with power from the Spirit, we produce the fruit of holiness (Gal 5:22-23). Being "filled with the Spirit" (Eph 5:18)—a command and therefore our responsibility and choice— means that we must be more completely submitted to the Spirit's already present sanctifying power. When we spurn or ignore this power by continuing in sin, we grieve the Holy Spirit (Eph 4:30).

On a practical level, we may personally appropriate the Spirit's power and allow him to work within us by following the Christian's "eightfold path" to sanctification. The eight steps are as follows: (1) *Information*. Know from Scripture the ideal Christian life, what constitutes sin, and where your own life stands. (2) *Awareness*. Know from Scripture *that* the Spirit is in you, and *why* he is in you. (3) *Prayer*. Make each of these steps a matter of earnest prayer. Pray especially for the Spirit's aid in developing a hatred of sin (Prov 8:13), in growing as a Christian, in resisting temptation, and in doing good works. (4) *Desire*. Have a sincere desire to be rid of sin and to be holy. Make such desire itself a matter of prayer, and realize that the Spirit is within you to help you develop such desires (Phil 2:13). (5) *Surrender*. Yield to the Spirit's power, acknowledging personal weakness. Abandon an exclusive dependence on will power and self-help. (6) *Trust*. Have faith that the Spirit will really provide the needed and promised power for sanctification (see Acts 26:18). (7) *Action*. Being fully informed and filled with the Spirit, exercise your will to do what is right. (8) *Thanksgiving*. Thank God for this wonderful gift of spiritual power, and give him the praise and credit for every victory over sin.

D. The Motive for Sanctification

Why should Christians seek to do good works? Why should we make every effort to obey God's commands? Why should we be serious about sanctification? What motivates us?

Those who do not understand grace, i.e., those who are still under law or are bound by the law mentality, usually are motivated to obey by the desire to escape hell and gain eternal life. Assuming that the sinner is saved *by* good works, they do good deeds for the purpose of deserving eternal life or being good enough to go to heaven. But those who understand grace and know what it means to be justified by faith have rightfully repudiated such egocentric motives.

On the other hand, sometimes those who have an incomplete understanding of grace go to the opposite extreme and conclude that, since we are under grace and not under law (Rom 6:14-15), we are actually saved *from* good works. That is, they assume that grace sets us free from all legal obligation to obey the Creator's laws. Sanctification thus is optional, and continuing in sin and thus allowing God to multiply grace might even be construed as bringing more glory to him (Rom 6:1).

To such a perverse conclusion Paul shouts an emphatic "NO!"—*me genoito*, "May it never be!" (Rom 6:2). In the sixth chapter of Romans he presents two reasons why such an idea is false. First, as Christians we cannot repudiate the necessity for good works because God has given us *new life*, via regeneration, for the very purpose of enabling us to obey the Creator's commands (Rom 6:1-14). That is, we are saved neither *by* works nor *from* works, but *for* good works (Eph 2:10).

Second, we cannot eschew law-keeping because acceptance of salvation through Jesus Christ gives us a *new master*. As non-Christians we were indeed slaves—slaves to sin and death (Rom 6:16-17). As Christians we have been delivered from such slavery, of course. But even as Christians we are still slaves; we have simply switched masters. Then we were slaves of sin; now we are slaves of God and his righteousness (Rom 6:18-22). "So now present yourselves as slaves to righteousness, resulting in sanctification" (Rom 6:19). Salvation by grace frees us from the law *system* as a way of salvation (Rom 6:14), but it does not free us from the obligation to obey the law *code* that applies to us. Such obligation is grounded in the fact of creation (Ps 24:1-2); it is absolute and irrevocable. Good works are still necessary, not as a means of salvation but simply because God has commanded them.[5] We should obey God simply because it is the right thing to do.

Coming under the grace of God thus does not change our obligation to obey him, but it does (or should) change our *motivation*.[6] We are set free from the self-ish motives of fear of punishment and desire for reward. When we understand that Christ's death has paid our penalty of eternal hell, and that "there is now no condemnation for those who are in Christ Jesus" (Rom 8:1), we are no longer motivated to avoid sin simply to avoid hell. Such a motive is in fact a rejection of the efficacy and sufficiency of Christ's atonement. Also, when we understand that salvation is a free gift (Rom 6:23; Eph 2:8-9) and that we cannot work to deserve a gift (Rom 4:4; 11:6), we are no longer motivated to do good works in an attempt to be good enough to go to heaven. Such a motive is inconsistent with the fact that salvation is a gift.

Why, then, do we obey God's laws? Why do we pursue sanctification? The primary motive is simply *love*, grateful love. Love and fear are at opposite ends of the spectrum of motives. "There is no fear in love; but perfect love casts out fear" (1 John 4:18). Such love is kindled and nurtured by our gratitude for Christ's loving sacrifice on our behalf (1 John 4:19). Such love is moved to do whatever the Loved One requires: "If you love Me, you will keep My commandments" (John 14:15). Saving faith works through love (Gal 5:6); its fruit is a "labor of love" (1 Thess 1:3). We obey the Creator's commands not in order to be saved, but because we are saved (Eph 2:8-10). Good works are the result, not the cause of our salvation. God does not save us because we are good; we are good because God is saving us. We need no greater motive for sanctification.

Notes on Chapter Eighteen

[1] "Having been buried" is an aorist participle in the Greek, indicating action that precedes the action of the main verb, "You were also circumcised." See Deut 30:6 for a prophecy of this spiritual circumcision.

[2] See Cottrell, *Romans*, 445-454. To understand this point it is crucial to see that human beings are a dualism of body and spirit, and that when Paul speaks of "the flesh" he is referring to the body. See the discussion of depravity, above p. 197.

[3] We will ultimately have a new body, of course—one that itself is completely free from sin and all its consequences. See Rom 8:10-11,23.

[4] From this point on our discussion will focus on progressive sanctification.

[5] As some put it, good works have the *necessity of precept*, but not the *necessity of means*.

[6] Obligation is why we *ought* to obey; motivation is why we actually *do* obey.

CHAPTER NINETEEN
CONDITIONS OF SALVATION

The last two chapters have explained the essential content of salvation. The question now is, how does God initially apply this salvation to sinners? How does one receive it? What decides whether a person receives it or not? Does God make the choice, or does the sinner?

The basic issue is whether the sinner has free will. If there is no truly free will, then not only must God himself choose how he will bestow his salvation; he must also choose the specific sinners upon whom he will bestow it. But if there is such a thing as free will, then God chooses *how* he will apply salvation, i.e., he sovereignly decides according to what conditions he will bestow it, and then he offers it to all who meet those conditions. Whether any particular sinner meets the conditions is his own decision.

In this book we have argued for the reality of human free will; thus we must also defend the view that salvation is conditional. In this chapter we will first affirm conditionality itself; then we will explain the basic conditions for receiving and retaining salvation; finally we will discuss the nature of these conditions.

I. SALVATION IS CONDITIONAL[1]

Those who say that salvation is unconditional are those who deny that sinners have a significantly free will. This especially includes Calvinists, along with other Augustinians. Such unconditionality is affirmed for several reasons. First, the sinner's totally depraved nature destroys his ability to make any positive response to the gospel. Even if God were to lay down certain conditions for receiving salvation, no sinner would be able to meet them. Thus we must not consider any act that Scripture associates with the reception of salvation (such as faith and repentance) as conditions which the sinner must choose to meet before he can be saved.

Second, the very nature of divine sovereignty as understood by Calvinists rules out the whole concept of conditions, including conditions for salvation. As noted earlier (p. 114), Calvinists understand sovereignty as meaning that God must be the *initiating cause* of *everything* that happens. A sovereign God always acts; he never reacts or responds. This means that nothing that happens can originate from any source or power outside of God, and nothing he does can be conditioned upon anything outside himself.

Thus no human choices of any kind can be truly free, especially those connected with receiving salvation. If God were to set forth conditions which sinners must meet before he saves them, then he would have to wait to see who will meet those conditions, and the bestowing of salvation would be a response to human decisions. Thus God would become dependent upon man, and would no longer be sovereign. But this is unthinkable; thus Calvinists speak of *sovereign* grace, which means *unconditional* grace. Sovereignty *per se* is thus incompatible with conditions.

A third reason why salvation must be unconditional, according to Calvinists, is that salvation is *by grace*, and grace is by definition a free gift. Thus the very essence of grace as a free gift requires that salvation be unconditional.

It is true, of course, that Calvinists sometimes speak as if salvation were conditional. They affirm justification by faith, with faith being regarded as a necessary means for receiving justification. Does this not imply that faith is a condition for salvation? On the surface it may seem so, but this is just an illusion. Though faith is a necessary precondition for justification, the limitations imposed by total depravity and divine sovereignty require that God himself *unconditionally* implant this prerequisite faith in the hearts of the sinners whom he *unconditionally* chooses to save. In the words of the Calvinist R.C. Sproul, "Faith itself is a gift given to the elect. God himself creates the faith in the believer's heart. God fulfills the necessary condition for salvation, and he does so without condition" (*Grace*, 156).

For Calvinists the divine act that creates faith is regeneration. This is the point of a dogma that is part of the very essence of Calvinism, namely, that regeneration must precede faith. As Sproul says, "Faith is a result of the Spirit's sovereign work of regeneration. . . . Regeneration must occur first before there can be any positive response of faith. . . . When speaking of the order of salvation (*ordo salutis*), Reformed theology always and everywhere insists that regeneration precedes faith" (ibid., 156, 186, 195). A sinner thus responds to the gospel call only because he is unconditionally enabled to do so by a secret inward call that is selective and irresistible (effectual).

A straightforward explanation of this idea is given by W.E. Best in his book, *Justification before God (Not by Faith)*. He says, "Most religionists . . . believe justification before God is on the basis of their faith. [But] neither faith nor works justify one before God. Exhorting a person to make a decision for Jesus Christ and be saved is erroneous. The decision is God's not man's" (2). "Saving faith is a new disposition implanted by the Holy Spirit of regeneration which enables the recipient of grace to believe and embrace Jesus Christ as Savior and Lord. . . . Saving faith is the gift of God which is the fruit of election and regeneration" (3-4). "We believe through grace (Acts 18:27). One does not believe and then get God's grace. Out of God's unmerited favor one is enabled to believe. . . . Faith is God's gift to us in our being made alive with Christ . . . . Being born of God precedes faith" (62).

This is the essence of the doctrine that salvation (grace) is unconditional. Over against it we affirm the opposite view, that salvation is conditional.

We must be precise in how we speak of this point. Certainly we agree that God's *love* is unconditional as well as universal, in that he loves every sinner without waiting for any to meet any condition. We can even agree that *grace* itself is unconditional in the sense that God freely gave his Son to die for the sins of all (1 John 2:2) and unconditionally desires that all be saved (1 Tim 2:4; 2 Pet 3:9). The conditions apply only to the actual bestowing of that salvation, that grace, upon specific individuals.

Basically we affirm that salvation is conditional because we accept the reality of a truly free will both in man as originally created and even in man in his state of sinful depravity. As we have seen, the main theological reason for the denial of free will and the resultant unconditionality of salvation is the avowal of an innate total depravity in every sinner. But as we saw in the chapter on personal sin, the Bible does not teach the doctrine of total depravity with its bondage of the will. It teaches a partial depravity with a limited inability to do certain things, but the sinner's basic ability to respond to the gospel is not destroyed. Sinners have the ability to believe and repent of their own free will.

This does not mean that sinners will necessarily seek salvation on their own initiative. Their sinfulness still requires the Spirit to enable them to respond to saving grace by convicting them and by prompting and influencing them toward faith, through original grace, through the power of the Word, and sometimes through special providence. Contrary to Calvinism, however, such enablement is universal and resistible. Having free will, sinners may resist this divine influence and refuse to respond to the gospel. But likewise they may choose to respond by meeting God's stated conditions. As H.O. Wiley says, "Without the grace or power to believe no man ever did or can believe; but with that power the act of faith is a man's own" (270). Only when the conditions are met does the Holy Spirit regenerate them.

Even apart from the issue of depravity and its effects upon the will, Calvinists declare that divine sovereignty precludes a truly free response to the gospel and thus genuine conditions for salvation. We cannot agree with this, however, since the very concept of sovereignty with which Calvinists operate is unbiblical and false.[2] True sovereignty does not rule out a truly free will in God's human creatures since the very presence of such free will is the result of God's own free and sovereign choice. The presence of free will within God's creation does indeed mean that God is constantly responding to and reacting to human choices, and he is doing so without the slightest threat to his sovereignty. This is the way the Bible pictures it. Virtually every major action of God recorded in the Bible after Gen 3:1 is a response to human sin, e.g., the Abrahamic covenant; the establishment of Israel; the incarnation, death, and resurrection of Christ; and the establishment of the church.

Such an arrangement, i.e., where God reacts to man's choices, would be a violation of sovereignty only if God were forced into it, only if it were a necessity imposed upon him from without. But this is not the case. It was God's sovereign choice to bring into existence a universe inhabited by free-will creatures who could freely respond to him and to whom he could respond. Thus the sinner's use of his free will to respond to the gospel is not a negation of God's sovereignty; it is an expression of it.

God offers the free gift of salvation to all people, and he graciously tells us what we must do to receive the gift. (A gift offered is not necessarily a gift received.) God sincerely calls all sinners to return to him, but the sinner himself must answer the call. The essence of such conditionality is clearly seen in God's lament over Israel in Isaiah 65, "I permitted Myself to be sought by those who did not ask for Me; I permitted Myself to be found by those who did not seek Me. I said, 'Here am I, here am I,' to a nation which did not call on My name. I have spread out My hands all day long to a rebellious people" (vv. 1-2). In other words, God is so eager to welcome his sinners back that he in effect jumps into their path, waves his arms, and yells "Here I am!" But the people ignore him; thus he declares, "I will destine you for the sword, and all of you will bow down to the slaughter. *Because I called, but you did not answer; I spoke, but you did not hear*" (v. 12, emphasis added).

II. THE CONDITIONS FOR SALVATION

By its very nature salvation is conditional, but the conditions have not always been the same. To be specific, with the transition from the Old to the New Covenant, from the Day of Pentecost forward, the conditions have been changed. This has nothing to do with an alleged dispensational shift from an age of law to an age of grace. Rather, the changes are the result of the new historical realities and doctrinal knowledge arising from the incarnation and saving activity of God in and through Jesus Christ. New conditions have been added and even old ones have been modified, all for the purpose of acknowledging and glorifying Jesus Christ as the source of salvation.

Here and in the next chapter we shall present the following acts as conditions for salvation in the New Covenant (post-Pentecostal) age: faith, repentance, confession, and baptism.

A. Faith

The primary condition for receiving (and retaining) God's saving grace always has been and continues to be *faith*. This was clearly stated as early as Abraham: "Then he believed in the LORD; and He reckoned it to him as righteousness" (Gen 15:6). It is also affirmed in other OT texts (2 Chr 20:20; Jonah 3:5; Hab 2:4). That salvation is still conditioned upon faith is stressed in the NT especially by John (1:12; 3:15-18,36; 6:47; 20:31) and by Paul. When the jailer at Philippi asked Paul and Silas, "'Sirs, what must I do to be saved?'" they replied, "'Believe in the Lord Jesus, and you will be saved'" (Acts 16:30-31). The very theme of

Romans is that "a man is justified by faith apart from works of law" (3:28; see also 1:16-17; 3:22,25; 5:1-2; 10:9-10). Abraham (as in Gen 15:6) is cited as the continuing paradigm of justification by faith (Rom 4:1-25; see Gal 3:1-14). See also 1 Cor 1:21; Gal 2:16; 3:26; Eph 2:8; 3:17; Phil 3:9.

The basic NT words for faith are the noun *pistos* and the verb *pisteuo*. When these words are used to represent faith as a condition for salvation, they have two main connotations, each of which is a necessary aspect of the total concept of saving faith.

The first aspect of saving faith is usually called *assent* (sometimes, *belief*). Assent is an act of the mind, a judgment of the intellect that a particular idea or statement is true. Not all statements accepted as true are matters of faith; some we *know* to be true by personal experience or by logical reasoning. Technically speaking, the ideas that we accept by faith (assent) are those that enter our consciousness via the testimony of other people. This applies to all ideas accepted on the authority of someone else's testimony, whether religious or secular. It is a frequent element of everyday life, from newspapers to casual conversation ("How was your day?" "It was fine.") As an aspect of saving faith it means assenting to the truth of Christ's own testimony concerning himself as recorded in Scripture, as well as to the truth of the testimony of the apostles and prophets who bear witness to Christ through the biblical writings (Eph 2:20). We believe the testimony is true, even in the absence of firsthand experience (2 Cor 5:7; Heb. 11:1).

Though we call ideas accepted via testimony *faith* (i.e., assent) and ideas received via experience or reason *knowledge*, this does not mean that ideas accepted through faith have no solid, rational foundation. Some have the seriously mistaken notion that faith comes into the picture only when we have run out of any rational evidence for accepting something as true, as in the following assertions: "Faith takes over where reason leaves off." Christian faith requires "rational self-immolation." "Faith is an illogical belief in the improbable." One must make a "leap of faith" or have "blind faith." "Faith is believing what you know ain't true." "Faith is belief in something without adequate evidence or proof." "When you have faith in something, you are not using reason."

Such ideas are completely false. In reality, in matters of faith, the subjective conviction that a particular testimony is true is based on the sufficiency of objective evidence. We accept another's testimony about something only if we have good reason to do so. Where *Christian* faith is concerned, we accept others' testimony concerning our Savior and our salvation because this testimony is verified as true by corroborating evidence, as analyzed and presented by Christian apologetics.

In biblical terminology the assent aspect of faith is represented by the phrase "believe that" (*pisteuo hoti*), i.e., believing with the mind *that* various statements and claims are true. Hebrews 11:6 says that we must *believe that* God exists and that He rewards those who seek him. Jesus said those who do not *believe that* he is who he claims to be will die in their sins (John 8:24). Jesus exhorts Philip to *believe that* he is in the Father, and the Father is in him (John 14:10-11). John wrote his Gospel so that we may *believe that* Jesus is the Christ, the Son of God (John 20:31; see 11:27). Those who *believe that* God raised Jesus from the dead will be saved (Rom 10:9). This assent aspect is also represented in such concepts as believing Jesus' words (John 5:47), believing all things written in the law and prophets (Acts 24:14), believing the gospel (Mark 1:15), and believing the truth (2 Thess 2:12-13).

The fact that faith includes this aspect of assent accounts for the NT use of the word *faith* in the sense of the body of doctrine which is believed or accepted as true, i.e., "the faith." In this sense one can be "obedient to the faith" (Acts 6:7), be "sound in the faith" (Titus 1:13), "contend earnestly for the faith" (Jude 3; see Phil 1:27), have "unity of the faith" (Eph 4:13), and go "astray from the faith" (1 Tim 6:21).

The second aspect of saving faith is usually called *trust*. Whereas assent is a judgment of the mind regarding the truth of a statement, trust is a decision of the will to act upon the truth assented to. It is a personal surrender to the implications and consequences of this truth. Such trust is most often directed toward persons. To trust a person is to surrender ourselves or something in our power to that person, as when we place our health and life in the hands of a doctor, or our children into the care of a baby-sitter, or our country into the hands of a particular presidential candidate.

The faith that is a condition for salvation includes such trust, specifically, a decision of the will to surrender everything about ourselves—our time, our possessions, our abilities, our life itself, and our eternal destiny—into the hands of Jesus Christ. Trust is the decision to rest our hope of eternal life upon the saving power of Christ's cross and resurrection. It is the decision to say, with Paul, "I know whom I have believed and I am convinced that He is able to guard what I have entrusted to Him until that day" (2 Tim 1:12).

The biblical concept of trust is represented by the same Greek words as assent (*pistis, pisteuo*), but by a different kind of phrasing. Assent is believing "that" (*hoti*) the gospel facts are true; trust is believing "in" (*eis*) or believing "on" (*epi*) the person and work of Jesus Christ himself. "Whoever believes in [*eis*] Him shall not perish, but have eternal life" (John 3:16). "Everyone who believes in [*eis*] Him receives forgiveness of sins" (Acts 10:43). "'Believe in [*epi*] the Lord Jesus, and you will be saved'" (Acts 16:31). We "believe in [*epi*] Him for eternal life" (1 Tim 1:16).

In the OT era the faith that saved included both assent and trust, i.e., believing that God is truly a gracious God and that his promise to forgive sins is sincere, and believing in or on him as one's personal Savior. In the NT era saving faith must be directed specifically to Jesus Christ, as we both assent to and trust in the saving power of his death and resurrection (Rom 3:25; 10:9). Assent alone does not meet this condition for salvation. Even demons believe that the God of the Bible is the true God (Jas 2:19) and that Jesus is his Son (Mark 1:24; 5:7). Thus it is incorrect to define faith simply as "belief in testimony," or even "belief that Jesus died for your sins." Such assent is necessary, but by itself it is incomplete and insufficient. It is a necessary first step, but it must be followed by a decision of the will to surrender oneself to the mercy and lordship of Jesus Christ.

Some believe that faith by definition includes more than assent and trust. Sometimes the element of *knowledge* or understanding is added (Grudem, *Doctrine*, 305). It is argued that one cannot intelligently assent to the truth of a statement that he does not understand. I agree with this, but this does not mean that understanding is a *part* of faith. It means rather that it is a *prerequisite* of faith.

Others declare that the element of *obedience* must be included in the definition of faith (Bultmann, 175-178, 197-199, 205-206). This would mean that one does not truly believe unless and until he obeys. This view is popular in the Restoration Movement because it allows one to profess both that salvation is by "faith alone," and that baptism is necessary for salvation since as an act of obedience it is part of the very essence of faith.[3]

In my judgment this view of faith is seriously false and ultimately leads to a negation of grace. It is true that faith is a work or an act of obedience in the sense that we are commanded to believe in Jesus Christ (John 6:28-29; Acts 16:31; see Acts 6:7). This means that faith is indeed the opposite of disobedience (John 3:36), and unbelief is the same as disobedience (Heb 3:18-19). This does not mean that faith includes obedience, however; it merely shows that *obedience includes faith*. This is a crucial difference.

Also, certain NT references make a clear distinction between faith and obedient works (e.g., Rom 3:28; 4:4-8; Eph 2:8-10). This makes it impossible to include obedience in the definition of faith. This applies especially to baptism, which is clearly distinguished from faith in Mark 16:16; Gal 3:26-27; Eph 4:5; and Col 2:12.

The most serious problem with this view, though, is that, if we say that obedience is part of the definition of faith, there is no way to limit that obedience just to a few acts (e.g., confession and baptism). It must also include one's lifelong obedience ("faithfulness forever") to every relevant commandment. Thus salvation by "faith alone" becomes salvation by the whole range of Christian good works, a position that seriously compromises grace.

While we cannot say that faith *includes* obedience, we must indeed say that it *produces* or results in obedience. The faith that saves is a faith that obeys. Just as surely as the double cure of salvation includes justification, which is by faith, so also does it include regeneration and sanctification, which are the possibility and essence of obedience (see Rom 6; Jas 2). Thus just as understanding is the prerequisite for faith, obedience is its assured result. Faith itself, though, is assent (believing *that*) and trust (believing *in/on*).

Why is faith a condition for salvation? Is it simply God's arbitrary choice that makes it so? Not at all. In fact, given the nature of salvation, it is a *necessary* condition. This is because the actual source of our salvation lies in a work that has been done by someone else—Jesus. We can be saved only by accepting and relying on what he has done as being sufficient for us. This act of relying on him and his work (instead of ourselves and our works) is the very essence of faith.

Another reason why faith is a necessary condition is that salvation comes to us not through God's law but through his promises (Rom 4:13-21; Gal 3:14-29). God offers salvation through his promise; the only way to respond to a promise is by *believing* it.

To say that salvation is by God's promise and Christ's work is just another way of saying it is by grace, and faith is the natural and proper response to grace. Since salvation "is by grace, it is no longer on the basis of works, otherwise grace is no longer grace" (Rom 11:6). Grace-salvation is not wages paid; it is a gift freely given (Rom 4:4-5). "For this reason it is by faith, in order that it may be in accordance with grace" (Rom 4:16). Faith is not a work accomplished in response to the Creator's law. It is a submissive and receptive disposition of the heart in response to the Redeemer's promise of grace, and thus is a natural condition for receiving it.

Some may wonder how something that appears to be so frail—i.e., faith—can be so powerful as to appropriate salvation. But the power is not in the faith itself. It lies rather in the object of faith, the almighty God and his almighty works through Jesus Christ. We should not have faith in our faith any more than in our works. Our faith is in God and his promises and in Christ and the power of his saving works. Again this is why salvation by grace can only be through faith, since faith is just our acknowledgment that it is "all of God."

Faith as a condition for salvation is the *means* by which grace is received; it is not a part of the grace itself. We must be careful not to destroy the free-will character of faith by making it one of the gifts of grace. Paul clearly distinguishes God's gift of grace from man's response of faith ("By grace . . . through faith," Eph 2:8).

B. Repentance

The second condition for receiving (and retaining) salvation is *repentance*. Jesus says that "unless you repent, you will all likewise perish" (Luke 13:3,5). Our only choices are "to perish" or "to come to repentance" (2 Pet 3:9). Sinners in need of salvation are called to repentance (Matt 3:2; Luke 5:32; Acts 8:22; 17:30; 26:20), and repentance is specifically linked to forgiveness of sins (Mark 1:4; Luke 3:3; 24:47; Acts 2:38; 3:19; 5:31; 8:22). Repentance leads to life (Acts 11:18) and to salvation (2 Cor 7:10).

What is repentance? In the NT the noun is *metanoia* and the verb *metanoeo*, from a combination of the Greek words *meta*, meaning "after," and *noeo*, meaning "to perceive, know, understand, think" (cf. *nous*, "mind"). Thus the basic meaning is to "know after" in the sense of reconsidering or rethinking a past act or opinion (Spicq, 2:472). In essence, then, repentance is a *change of mind*, a *turning* from one attitude or viewpoint to another. Specifically, it is a change of mind or attitude toward *sin*, one's own sin in particular.

This changed mind is first of all a *hatred* of sin. This is the heart and core of repentance: instead of loving sin, we hate it. Some hate the punishment that comes from sin, but not the sin itself. This is not repentance. Thus even though they may outwardly avoid sin, they are still lost, because they continue to love and treasure the thought of sin in their hearts. But the repentant (saved) person has come to despise sin because the holy God himself despises it, because it is counter to and destructive of true human nature, and because this is what sent the Savior to the cross.

The mind that has changed toward sin also includes *remorse* (sorrow, grief) for having committed sins against God. When David repented of his sin with Bathsheba, he spoke of his "broken spirit," his broken and contrite heart (Ps 51:17). Paul relates repentance to godly sorrow (2 Cor 7:9-10).

Repentance as a change of mind toward sin also includes a sincere *desire* to be rid of it (the kind of desire David expresses in Psalm 51), as well as a *determination* to forsake it. This determination is what Grudem calls "a sincere commitment to forsake [sin] and walk in obedience to Christ" (*Doctrine*, 309).

The biblical concept of repentance is sometimes expressed as a *turning* from sin. In the OT the Hebrew word *shub* is used often to refer to the sinner's turning *from* his transgressions (Isa 59:20; Ezek 14:6; 18:21,30) and his turning *to* the God of salvation (Isa 55:7; Jer 3:12,22; Hos 6:1; 12:6). In the NT the gospel call is likewise a plea to turn. The Gentiles are exhorted to "turn from these vain things [idols] to a living God" (Acts 14:15). Christ commanded Saul (Paul) to preach to the Gentiles "that they may turn from darkness to light and from the dominion of Satan to God" (Acts 26:18). Through Peter's ministry many "turned to the Lord" (Acts 9:35). In Antioch "a large number who believed turned to the Lord" (Acts 11:21). "Repent and turn to God," is the call (Acts 3:19; 26:20; see Ezek 14:6; 18:30).

To speak of repentance as a turning from sin does not mean that repentance itself includes the actual change of lifestyle or reformation of life that flows from regeneration and constitutes sanctification. Faith does not include obedience, and neither does repentance. Repentance is a change of *mind* about sin, a new mental or spiritual attitude toward sin: hatred, remorse, desire and determination to be rid of it. The turning that constitutes repentance takes place in the heart, and it *leads to* a change of life, as we "bear fruit in keeping with repentance" (Matt 3:8), "performing deeds appropriate to repentance" (Acts 26:20). To equate repentance as a condition for salvation with the change that results from it compromises grace and is equivalent to salvation by works.

Why is repentance a condition for salvation? First of all, the very nature of salvation requires it. Salvation is salvation from *sin*, and we cannot be saved from our sin while we are still holding on to it in our hearts. When confronted with the gospel, one must make a choice between sin and salvation: he must choose one and repudiate the other. To choose sin one must repudiate salvation; to accept salvation one must repudiate sin. The repudiation of sin is the essence of repentance.

Second, the very nature of saving faith requires that it be accompanied by repentance. On the one hand, faith includes a belief that Jesus died for our sins (assent), and a personal commitment to rely upon his death for salvation (trust). The point is that we cannot sincerely accept what Jesus did for us on the cross without hating the sin that put him there. Every sin is like another nail in the hands or feet of our Savior. If we have the right attitude toward Jesus and his cross (i.e., faith), we cannot help but have the right attitude toward our sin (i.e., repentance).

On the other hand, faith includes believing that Jesus is who he claims to be: not just our Savior, but also our *Lord*, as accomplished and demonstrated by his resurrection (Acts 2:24-36; Phil 2:9-11). This is part of our assent. But faith also includes the personal surrender of our very lives and bodies to Christ as Lord; this is part of our trust. Accepting him as our Lord requires the repudiation of sin, because we cannot be slaves of sin and slaves of Christ at the same time (Rom 6:15-22). "No one can serve two masters" (Matt 6:24).

Thus we conclude that if faith is a condition for salvation, so also must repentance be a condition.

This raises a serious question: if repentance is also a condition for salvation, how do we explain all the biblical texts that mention faith *alone* as a condition?[4] One approach is to say that faith *includes* repentance, that repentance is a part of faith or the core of faith or in some sense the "flip side" of faith. This approach must be rejected; the integrity of both faith and repentance as distinct mental states must be preserved, as in Mark 1:15 and Acts 20:21.

Another approach is to focus all attention on the "faith alone" texts, making faith the sole condition for salvation and eliminating repentance as a condition except as redefined as a simple change of mind as to who Jesus is (Ryrie, *Salvation*, 94-95, 99). Repentance, as a change of mind and heart about sin and as a commitment to live under the lordship of Christ, is rejected as a condition. Those who take this view call themselves the "free grace" movement. Zane Hodges, a representative, says, "Faith alone (not repentance *and* faith) is the sole condition for justification and eternal life" (144).

This view must be vigorously rejected. We cannot ignore or explain away the repentance texts so easily. The fact is that there are many biblical texts which mention repentance alone or without faith as a condition for salvation.[5] It is true that faith is often mentioned by itself, but this is because faith is the one act that is the specific *means* (instrument, vehicle, channel) through which God's saving grace is received. "An instrumental cause is the 'means by which' something takes place. . . . In our justification, faith is the means by which we are linked to Christ and receive the benefits of his saving work" (Sproul, *Grace*, 66). Faith is thus singled out as the sole *means*, but not as the sole *condition* for receiving salvation. All means are conditions, but not all conditions are means.

This is very significant for understanding the conditions of salvation. That many texts *mention* only faith as a condition for salvation does not mean that faith *is* the only condition, any more than the texts that mention only repentance mean that it is the only condition. Since faith is mentioned in some texts and repentance in others, good hermeneutics requires us to put all the texts together to get the total picture. Thus we can assume that where one is specifically mentioned, the other is implicit or assumed (Erickson, *Mind*, 120).

C. Confession of Faith

The third condition for salvation is *confession*, specifically, a confession before the world of one's faith in Jesus as Savior and Lord. In Matt 10:32-33 Jesus says, "Therefore everyone who confesses Me before men, I will also confess him before My Father who is in heaven. But whoever denies Me before men, I will also deny him before My Father who is in heaven." The apostle Paul teaches "that if you confess with your mouth Jesus as Lord, and believe in your heart that God raised Him from the dead, you will be saved; for with the heart a person believes, resulting in righteousness, and with the mouth he confesses, resulting in salvation" (Rom 10:9-10). The apostle John adds, "Whoever denies the Son does not have the Father; the one who confesses the Son has the Father also. . . . Whoever confesses that Jesus is the Son of God, God abides in him, and he in God" (1 John 2:23; 4:15).

The Greek for the verb "to confess" is usually *homologeo*,[6] which means literally "to say the same thing, to agree," and thus to acknowledge the truth about something. In this context it is a confession that one believes in Jesus Christ; the confession that saves is a confession about Jesus, as shown in the passages cited above. It is a "confession of the gospel of Christ" (2 Cor 9:13); Jesus is "the Apostle and High Priest of our confession" (Heb 3:1). See Phil 2:11; 1 John 4:2-3; 2 John 7.

Often the specific content of our confession, modeled after Peter's confession in Matt 16:16, is that Jesus is "the Christ, the Son of the living God." What does it mean to confess Jesus as *the Christ* (see Cottrell, *Fundamentals*, 46-56)? Our English word *Christ* comes directly from the Greek term *christos*, which is a translation of the Hebrew term *mashiach* (from which we get the word *Messiah*). Both the Greek and the Hebrew words mean "the anointed one." So when we confess Jesus is the Christ, we are confessing him to be the anointed one (see John 9:22).

But what is the significance of this? In the OT, kings (1 Sam 16:3,12,13), priests (Exod 29:7,29), and prophets (1 Kgs 19:16) were anointed, thereby being set apart for their specific work. In prophecy God promised to send a great King and High Priest (Ps 110:1-7) who would be the universal Ruler and Savior of the world. He would be the "Messiah" (Ps 2:2), the *Christ*, the one anointed to work this work of salvation. So when Peter said, "You are the Christ" (Matt 16:16), he was confessing Jesus to be the long-awaited, divinely sent Savior. Likewise, when we confess "Jesus is the Christ," we are acknowledging him as our only Savior by virtue of the efficacy of his saving death (Rom 3:25, NIV) and his victorious resurrection (Rom 10:9).

The other part of Peter's confession is that Jesus is "the Son of the living God" (Matt 16:16; see 1 John 4:15). What did this mean for Peter and for other Jews living at that time? Several incidents in the life of Jesus[7] show that they understood this title to be a designation of deity. Thus when we confess Jesus to be the Son of God, we are professing our faith that he is divine, that he is God the Son incarnate in the human person, Jesus of Nazareth. The apostle Thomas confessed the risen Christ as "my God" (John 20:28). In John's letters we see that it is important to confess the true humanness of Jesus as well (1 John 4:2; 2 John 7).

Though we usually call Peter's confession "the good confession," the Bible actually uses this phrase only for the confessions of Timothy and of Jesus himself (1 Tim 6:12-13). The content of Timothy's confession is not given: "You made the good confession in the presence of many witnesses" (v. 12). Jesus is said to have "testified the good confession before Pontius Pilate" (v. 13). In John 18:33-37 we learn specifically what his "good confession" was: he acknowledged his *kingship* before Pilate's court.

That Jesus confessed his kingship is significant in light of the fact that in the NT, following his death and resurrection, the principal confession is Christ's *lordship*: "Jesus is Lord."[8] Thomas's full confession before the risen Christ was "My Lord and my God!" (John 20:28). In Rom 10:9 the saving confession is that "Jesus is Lord" (NIV). The confession that distinguished Christians from pagans was "Jesus is Lord" (1 Cor 12:3). The confession every tongue will ultimately make is "Jesus is Lord" (Phil 2:11). See Acts 2:36; 10:36; 2 Cor 4:5.

What are we actually saying when we confess Jesus as Lord? We are ascribing to him two things: *ownership* and *deity*. The basic generic connotation of the word is that of the owner or master of something (as in "landlord"). To confess Jesus to be our Lord is thus to confess that he is our owner and we are his slaves. It is the external expression of an internal spirit of complete submission to every aspect of his word and will.

The religious significance attached to the title "Lord" (Greek, *kyrios*) in NT times shows also that confessing Jesus as Lord is to confess that he is fully divine, that he is God the Son, equal with God the Father and God the Spirit in essence, power, and honor. "Lord" is the name above every name (Phil 2:9-11); it is Paul's trinitarian title for Jesus (1 Cor 8:6; 12:4-6; Eph 4:4-6). It is also the Greek word used to represent the holy name of God—Yahweh—in the Greek OT. Thus when first-century Jews (such as Paul) confessed Jesus as *Lord*, they were identifying him with Yahweh himself. It is equivalent to confessing him to be the Son of God—God the Son.

It is important to note that this confession of Jesus as one's personal, divine Savior and Lord must be oral and public. Paul says this confession is "with your mouth" (Rom 10:9-10). Jesus says our confession must be "before men" (Matt 10:32). Timothy's good confession was "in the presence of many witnesses" (1 Tim 6:12). Christ's was "before Pontius Pilate" (1 Tim 6:13).

The confession of one's faith in Jesus is quite clearly described as a condition for salvation. Jesus says if we do not confess him before men, he will not confess us before the Father (Matt 10:32-33). In Rom 10:9 Paul expresses its character as a condition for salvation with the word "if," i.e., "If you confess with your mouth Jesus as Lord, . . . you will be saved." In verse 10 this conditionality is made even more clear: "With the mouth he confesses, resulting in salvation." "Resulting in" translates the Greek preposition *eis*, which expresses purpose and thus result. The sinner thus confesses for the purpose of receiving salvation, and that is indeed the result of his confession.

When is this confession made? Since it is a confession of *faith*, it is appropriate for it to be made at the very outset of faith, as a prelude to baptism. In Rom 10:9 the verbs "confess" and "believe" are both aorist tense, suggesting that Paul had in mind a specific past act associated with the sinner's initial and decisive confession of faith. In Rom 10:13 confessing Jesus as Lord is equated with "calling on the name of the LORD," which is the sinner's initial baptismal prayer for salvation.[9] Thus it is appropriate for a new convert to announce his faith upon his acceptance of Christ and as a preparation for baptism.

But this is by no means the only occasion for confessing one's faith. It must be done throughout the Christian life, especially as a witness to the unbelieving world. In fact, most NT references to confession have to do with situations where mature believers are called upon to confess their faith under adverse circumstances in the face of great risk, where the only alternative is to deny him (see John 9:22; 12:42). Jesus' warning in Matt 10:32-33 is addressed to his apostles as he sends them out on a preaching mission to hostile audiences (Matt 10:1-5,16-31). Paul makes his confession as a prisoner before Felix (Acts 24:14, ESV). First Corinthians 12:2-3 seems to refer to situations where Christians were arrested and told to renounce Christ or die. In such a dire situation, those who relied on the strength of the indwelling Spirit could still confess "Jesus is Lord." Jesus' own "good confession" was made in a context where his life was at stake (1 Tim 6:13; John 18:33–19:16). Whether we face circumstances like these or not, confession of faith is our responsibility for as long as faith itself exists in our hearts.

Again the question must be raised, if we are justified by faith alone, how can *confession* also be a condition for salvation? As noted in our discussion of repentance, it is incorrect to use only the passages that name faith as a condition and take them in isolation from texts that name other conditions. The fallacy of such a practice is clearly shown in Rom 10:9-10, where the references to confession and faith are grammatically parallel. The two verbs are identical in form and are related to "if" in exactly the same way, i.e., as equal conditions for salvation. If faith is a condition, then so must confession be.

This is not to say that these two acts are related to salvation in the same way. Both are conditions, but they do not play the same role in bringing the sinner to salvation. Faith is still the primary condition because it is the sole *means* by which salvation is received, but this does not rule out the addition of other conditions that serve other purposes. What purpose does confession serve as a condition for salvation? We must remember that it is a confession of *faith*, a faith that is directed specifically toward Jesus Christ as Savior and Lord. It is a confession of the full and sole efficacy of Christ's death and resurrection as the way to heaven. The very essence of such a confession is thus a renunciation of any attempt to save oneself through one's own futile works, and an open acknowledgment that salvation is *all of Jesus, all of grace.*

D. Baptism

The fourth condition for salvation in the NT age is baptism. This will be discussed in the following chapter.

NOTES ON CHAPTER NINETEEN

[1]See Cottrell, *GRe*, 389-399.

[2]See *GRu*, ch. 5, "Special Providence and Free Will." Also, see Cottrell, "Sovereignty."

[3]See Reese, "Faith"; Corson, "Faith." Corson declares, "Saving faith must include *obedience*." Thus "one who does not submit to baptism does not have 'faith.'" Faith, repentance, confession, baptism, and faithfulness forever are "essentially one" (6).

[4]E.g., John 3:16; Acts 16:31; Rom 3:28; Eph 2:8-9; and many more.

[5]See Matt 3:2; Mark 1:4; Luke 5:32; 13:3,5; 24:47; Acts 2:38; 3:19; 5:31; 11:18; 17:30; Rom 2:4; 2 Cor 7:10; 2 Pet 3:9.

[6]Sometimes the form *exhomologeo* is used. The noun is *homologia*.

[7]Matt 26:63-66; John 5:17-23; 10:22-39; 19:7.

[8]On the equivalence of kingship and lordship see 1 Tim 6:15; Rev 17:14; 19:16.

[9]Acts 22:16; see Joel 2:32; Acts 2:21. See Cottrell, *Baptism*, 74-76.

CHAPTER TWENTY
BAPTISM

Acomprehensive explanation of baptism must answer three main questions. First, what is the purpose of baptism? Second, who should be baptized? And third, how should baptism be performed? These are the questions of the *meaning*, the *subjects*, and the *mode* of baptism. This chapter will attempt to answer them in this order.

I. THE MEANING OF BAPTISM

Most important is the *meaning* of baptism, since the answer to this question helps us to determine the answers to the other two. It is important also because it has been a source of serious controversy ever since the Reformation of the sixteenth century. The heart of the issue is whether baptism has a crucial role in the reception of salvation. More specifically, is baptism something a sinner does in order to receive salvation and *become* a Christian, or is it simply a good work (an act of obedience) done for some other purpose by someone who is *already* a Christian?

The Bible is very clear about this. In every NT passage that says anything at all about the meaning of baptism, the only purpose with which it is connected is the salvation of sinners.[1] The various aspects of salvation are described as being bestowed upon the believing, repentant sinner in the act of baptism. This is the consistent and exclusive NT witness; no other purpose for baptism is mentioned or even hinted at. This is why I choose to discuss baptism here in the general theological context of personal salvation, rather than in the context of the church. This is also why we may speak of baptism (along with faith, repentance, and confession) as a *condition* for salvation.

A. Baptism and the Double Cure

We have seen that the contents of salvation may be summarized as a "double cure." Sin creates two problems for the sinner, both of which are addressed by God's saving grace. First, sin brings the legal problem of *guilt*, resulting in the sinner's liability to the penalty of eternity in hell. Also, sin makes a person *sinful*. That is, it affects the person's very nature; it makes him depraved or spiritually sick. This corrupts the sinner's inner being, sapping his spiritual strength and trapping him in the grip of sin.

God's gracious salvation addresses both sides of this predicament. On the one hand, God's solution to guilt is justification, also called the forgiveness or remission of sins. This is accomplished only by the redeeming blood of Christ by which he paid the penalty deserved by those who have broken God's divine law. When the blood of Christ is applied to the penitent sinner, his guilt and condemnation are washed completely away. On the other hand, God's cure for the sinner's depraved nature is the gift of the Holy Spirit, whose life-giving presence renews and regenerates the sin-sick heart and breaks the death-grip of sin upon the soul. Biblical terms for this work of the Holy Spirit include new birth, new creation, being made alive, resurrection, regeneration, renewal, and circumcision without hands. Following this initial act of spiritual resurrection, the Holy Spirit dwells within the saved person as a source of spiritual strength and continuing sanctification.

In summary, in the double cure of salvation God takes away the sinner's guilt through the blood of Christ and renews his heart through the life-giving power of the Holy Spirit. Only divine power can accomplish these things. The question being addressed here, though, is *when* does God choose to work these powerful works in the heart of the sinner?

Almost everyone would agree that the Bible relates salvation to baptism in some sense. All would acknowledge, for example, that baptism and salvation are connected at least *symbolically*. That is, the act of baptism is a physical symbol of the reality of spiritual salvation. It is "an outward sign of an inward grace"; the application of water to the body depicts the cleansing of the soul.

Some would go further and discern a *psychological* connection between baptism and salvation. They see the act of baptism as affecting the mental state of the person being baptized, as confirming or sealing upon his heart a deeper assurance of the salvation that God has already bestowed upon him. The baptized person can say to himself, "Just as surely as I am experiencing the baptismal water upon my body, I can be sure that God has applied his grace to my soul."

Some have gone to the extreme of affirming a *causal* connection between baptism and salvation. They have attributed to the baptismal water or to the baptismal act the power to cleanse the soul from sin, or at least the power to convey that divine cleansing to the soul. Thus anyone who submits to the physical act of baptism will surely be saved, even in the absence of a proper knowledge of Christ and a positive faith in him. This is the doctrine of "baptismal regeneration," and is usually held in connection with certain forms of infant baptism.

How shall we evaluate these views in the light of Scripture? Actually, none of them adequately expresses the NT teaching about the relation between baptism and salvation. The causal view described in the previous paragraph must be rejected altogether. There is no basis for ascribing any saving power to the baptismal water or to the act of baptism itself. God's power and God's action alone can save; the sinner is saved when God applies the blood of Christ to his heart and gives him the gift of the Holy Spirit.

Also, the symbolical and psychological views must be rejected, not because they are off the mark but because in themselves they do not go far enough. That is, they do not give us the whole picture of the relation between baptism and salvation. It is true that water baptism symbolizes the reality of inward salvation, and that it strengthens faith in Christ and increases assurance of salvation. The problem is that those who emphasize these points often limit the meaning of baptism to these effects alone, while denying that baptism is also the *specific time* when God bestows his gifts of salvation. They claim that as a rule a person is already saved before he is baptized. Baptism is a *subsequent* outward sign of a *previously given* inward grace, they say; thus it only strengthens one's faith in a salvation already possessed. Such a limited view, however, is much too weak. It does not do justice to the NT teaching about what really happens during baptism.

In summary, we reject any causal relation between baptism and salvation. Also, we agree that baptism is symbolically and psychologically related to salvation, even though this is never actually stated in Scripture and is only inferred from what *is* taught therein. Most important, we affirm that the clear and specific teaching of the NT is that baptism is the *time during which* God graciously bestows upon the sinner the double cure of salvation. As such it is a divinely appointed condition for salvation during this New Covenant era.

Our purpose now is to set forth the biblical evidence for this temporal relation between baptism and salvation. First, we will look at the passages which connect both aspects of the double cure with baptism, beginning with Acts 2:38: "Peter said to them, 'Repent, and each of you be baptized in the name of Jesus Christ for the forgiveness of your sins; and you will receive the gift of the Holy Spirit.'" This is Peter's response to an audience of Jews whose rejection of their Messiah had put them into a lost state and who thus needed salvation. Their question to Peter (v. 37) was, "What shall we do?" That is, what shall we do to be saved? Peter names two things they must do: repent, and be baptized. He also names two things they would receive as a result: forgiveness of sins, and the gift of the Holy Spirit—the double cure.

This verse specifically says that baptism is "for the forgiveness of sins." Forgiveness (or remission) is equivalent to justification; it is the cancellation of all guilt by the power of the blood of Christ. This is the first part of the double cure. A key word in this statement is the word *for*, which translates the Greek preposition *eis*. Physically this term represents motion toward something; conceptually it signifies purpose or intention or result. In other words, Peter says to be baptized *for the purpose of bringing about* the forgiveness of sins. It is used in exactly the same way in Matt 26:28, where Jesus spoke of his blood as being "poured out for many for [*eis*] forgiveness of sins," i.e., for the purpose of bringing about the forgiveness of sins. Early editions of the NIV translated the sense of Acts 2:38 quite accurately: "Repent and be baptized . . . so that your sins may be forgiven."[2]

This verse also says that those who are baptized "will receive the gift of the

Holy Spirit." This refers to the indwelling presence of the Spirit as promised by Jesus in John 7:37-39; the specific immediate result of this indwelling is the new birth promised in John 3:3-5. The Spirit's presence raises the spiritually dead sinner to a state of spiritual life, which is the second aspect of the double cure. This gift of the indwelling Spirit is specifically stated to be a consequence or result of baptism.

Thus Acts 2:38 makes the meaning of baptism clear. It is the time God has appointed for removing the sinner's guilt and for bestowing upon him the regenerating presence of the Holy Spirit.

Another passage that expressly states that baptism is the time when God works the double cure is Col 2:12. It speaks of being "buried with Him in baptism, in which you were also raised up with Him through faith in the working of God, who raised Him from the dead." Here two things are said to happen in baptism. First, we are "buried with Him," i.e., with Christ. According to Rom 6:3-4 this means we are buried into the death of Christ. To be buried with Christ into his death means to receive all the saving benefits of his atoning death; it means to come into contact with his justifying blood and thus to receive the forgiveness of sins.

The second thing that happens in baptism is that we are "raised up with Him." This refers to the initial act of the indwelling Holy Spirit. As soon as God gives us his Spirit (as promised in Acts 2:38), the Spirit infuses new life into our dead souls. Our spirits are raised from the dead by the same life-giving Spirit that raised Jesus' body from the tomb (Rom 8:10-11; see Col 2:13).

Colossians 2:12 is important because it clearly and expressly says that these things happen "in baptism." This does not mean before baptism, nor does it mean after baptism. It means exactly what it says: *in* baptism, in the act of baptism, at the time of baptism. We could not ask God to be more specific than this. *In baptism* God works the twofold work of salvation upon our hearts. This same relation between baptism and salvation is specified in Rom 6:3-5. In the baptismal act we are united with the death and resurrection of Christ, the result being justification and regeneration (see Cottrell, *Romans*, I:383-390).

Other NT passages relate baptism to the two aspects of the double cure individually. For example, Acts 22:16 connects it with the washing away of sins, which is equivalent to forgiveness. Thus when Ananias said to Saul, "Get up and be baptized, and wash away your sins, calling on His name," he was saying exactly what Peter said in Acts 2:38: "Be baptized, for the purpose of bringing about the forgiveness of your sins." The fact that baptism is the time of salvation is seen in the addition of the phrase, "calling on His name." According to Joel 2:32 and Acts 2:21, the purpose of calling on His name is to be saved.

Passages which individually relate baptism to the second part of the double cure are John 3:5 and Titus 3:5. In John 3:5 Jesus says, "Unless one is born of water and the Spirit he cannot enter into the kingdom of God." This is a reference to being "born again" (John 3:3), which is the same as the spiritual resurrection that Col 2:12 says takes place in baptism. That this new birth is somehow the result of both water and the Spirit brings to mind Acts 2:38, which connects water baptism with the gift of the Spirit. For this and other reasons we may rightly conclude that Jesus' reference to water in John 3:5 speaks of baptism and makes it a condition for being born again.

Titus 3:5 in a similar way refers to baptism ("the washing") as the time when the Holy Spirit regenerates and renews us. It says that God "saved us . . . by the washing of regeneration and renewing," which are accomplished in that moment "by the Holy Spirit."

The passages discussed above clearly set forth the meaning of baptism as the time when God bestows salvation's double cure. Other NT passages relate baptism to salvation in the same way, only in more general terms. For example, Matt 28:18-20 says we are baptized into union with the Trinity; Gal 3:27 says we are baptized into union with Christ; and 1 Cor 12:13 says we are baptized into the body of Christ. Two other verses state simply that the result of baptism is salvation: "He who has believed and has been baptized shall be saved" (Mark 16:16); and, "Baptism now saves you" (1 Pet 3:21).

B. Why "Baptism Now Saves"

Many do not understand why God would add a new condition for salvation not required in OT times. If faith in God's gracious promises and a repentant heart were sufficient for salvation then, why not now? In reply we can identify at least two good reasons why God has connected salvation with baptism.

First, this new condition has been added because the salvation process under the New Covenant includes new elements not present under the Old Covenant. Baptism brings these new elements into focus and assures that the sinner is coming to God in full cognizance of them and not in terms of a framework that is obsolete and no longer adequate.

What are these new elements that raise New Covenant salvation to a higher level? First, there is a more complete revelation of the nature of God and thus an advanced understanding of the very object of our faith. We now know unequivocally that God's nature is triune, i.e., that the Lord God of the OT is a Trinity of Father, Son, and Holy Spirit. Baptism was established to ensure that this new understanding of God would not be lost. This is why Jesus commanded that baptism be "in the name of the Father and the Son and the Holy Spirit" (Matt 28:19).

Another new element in New Covenant salvation is the historical reality and the living presence of the Redeemer himself, Jesus of Nazareth. The fact that Jesus is the incarnation of God the Son gives concrete reality to the doctrine of the Trinity. His death on the cross and his resurrection from the dead—prophesied in the OT but for all practical purposes unknown in that era—are the literal source of our salvation. Baptism was established to ensure that we would never separate our salvation from the divine Redeemer Jesus nor from his saving death and resurrection. Thus baptism is not just in the name of "the Son" (Matt 28:19) but "in the name of Jesus Christ" (Acts 2:38), who we must never forget is God the Son. Also, baptism is intended to draw our attention unmistakably to his death and resurrection as the works that bring us salvation (Rom 6:3-11; Col 2:12).

Still another new element is the specific saving work of the third person of the Trinity, the Holy Spirit. In OT times the Spirit worked to empower some of God's people for roles of service, but he did not enter a sinner's heart to work salvation therein. The latter was something God reserved for his New Covenant saints, as promised by Jesus (John 7:37-39) and as begun on the day of Pentecost (Acts 2:38-39). Baptism was established as the time when the penitent sinner receives this gift of the Spirit, thus highlighting the newness and uniqueness of this blessing for this Messianic age.

All of these new elements in the New Covenant salvation process necessarily lead to one more, namely, a newness of the very faith that is required for salvation. Though not different in form, the faith that is necessary for salvation in this age is very different in content from that of the Old Covenant. A general faith in the general promises of the God of Israel no longer qualifies a person to receive salvation. When confronted with the new revelation of God as Trinity and especially with the identification of Jesus as the divine Savior, even Jews who once enjoyed a saving relationship with the God of Israel had to adjust their faith accordingly or be lost (Rom 11:17-23). To accept baptism as the concrete embodiment of all this new faith-content is a humble confession that one does indeed believe these things; thus Christian baptism is inseparably linked with *Christian* faith.[3]

This is one reason why "baptism now saves," namely, because the newness of salvation in this age requires a new and distinguishing element in the process of receiving it.

The second reason why God has connected salvation with baptism in the NT age has to do with our need for a personal assurance that God has indeed saved us. Sometimes it is easy to be plagued by doubts and uncertainties as to whether we have truly met the God of our salvation and have truly received his gifts of saving grace. We know what God has promised, but has it really happened to *us*?

As a concession to our human frailty in this respect, God has tied his promises to baptism as a concrete, objective event that will always stand out in our memories. It is an unforgettable reference point to which we can always return when we begin to doubt that we have received God's grace. It is the "stake" that God himself has provided for our comfort and assurance. We do not have to torture ourselves, wondering at what point our faith was strong enough or our repentance sincere enough to be saved. The sufficiency for our salvation lies in the power of God and the truth of his promises. He has promised to save us in baptism. Just as surely as we can remember our baptism, so can we be sure that God has kept his promises to us.

This is the sense in which there is a psychological connection between baptism and salvation. Knowing that we have been baptized has a definite effect on our state of mind, in the sense that it undergirds our assurance of salvation. This psychological effect is possible, though, only because baptism is in itself the time when salvation is given.

II. THE SUBJECTS OF BAPTISM

Who should be baptized? Everyone agrees that adults and young people who have reached the age of accountability are proper subjects for baptism. The main issue here is whether infants and young children ought to be baptized.

Today many denominations practice infant baptism. Some, such as Roman Catholics and Lutherans, baptize babies for salvation. They do this because they believe that babies in a sense "inherit" the double trouble of guilt and sinfulness from Adam and Eve, and because they rightly understand the NT's teaching that baptism is the time when God gives sinners the double cure of forgiveness and new birth. Thus infants are baptized so that they may be saved.

Others, such as Presbyterians and Methodists, baptize babies because they believe that the children of Christian parents are automatically members of the covenant community (the church), and because they equate baptism with OT circumcision and take it to be an outward sign that such infants do indeed belong to the church. They assume a continuity of the covenants and thus of the covenant people and the covenant signs. Since babies were members of the covenant people by physical birth under the first covenant, so are they today. And since the sign of membership, i.e., circumcision, was applied to (male) babies then, so should baptism be applied to babies today as the sign of their membership in the church.

There are several good and decisive reasons, however, why infants should not be baptized. First and foremost, the very meaning of baptism rules out infants as proper subjects of baptism. Baptism is indeed for salvation; therefore it is meaningful and necessary only for those who are lost sinners. Babies, however, are not in this category. They should not be regarded as sinners in need of salvation. Whatever sin and condemnation all children may have potentially inherited from Adam has already been nullified and canceled for every member of the human race by the atoning work and original grace of Christ (Rom 5:12-19). As a result babies are not born guilty or sinful; thus they do not need baptism. Only when children become old enough to understand the meaning of God's law and the significance of breaking that law are they considered accountable for it and thus in need of baptism (Rom 4:15; 7:7-11).

Another reason why infants should not be baptized is that Christians are under a New Covenant, which does not imitate the conditions for membership which existed under the Old Covenant. The Old Covenant, even the provisions that began as far back as Abraham, was completely fulfilled in the first coming of Jesus (cf. Acts 13:32-33). Jeremiah 31:31-34 prophesies the coming of a new and different covenant, and Jesus declared that this New Covenant was established with his own blood (Luke 22:20). Therefore it could not have been in existence prior to his death (Heb 9:17).

One of the main differences between the covenants is the basis or means of membership. A baby born to Jewish parents was a member of the Old Covenant community simply by means of physical birth. As the child grew, he had to be taught to know the Lord, even though he was already under the covenant. But it is quite different today. One becomes a member of the New Covenant community not by physical birth but by the new birth or spiritual birth, which is possible only for those who are old enough to make a conscious decision for God and "believe in His name" (John 1:12-13). We are children of God "through faith in Christ Jesus" (Gal 3:26). For this reason a distinctive characteristic of the New Covenant is that those who are under it do not have to be taught again to know the Lord, "'for they will all know Me, from the least of them to the greatest of them,' declares the Lord" (Jer 31:34).

Male children born under the Old Covenant indeed were circumcised as infants, but this has no parallel whatsoever under the New Covenant and is not in any sense a pattern for the practice of baptism today. Nowhere in the NT is baptism described or depicted as a sign of belonging to the church. The only connection the NT makes between circumcision and baptism is in Col 2:11-12, and the relationship given there is not substantive but figurative. That is, the physical removal of a bit of skin by human hands is a figure or a type of the spiritual removal of the old sinful nature "without hands," which is equivalent to the regeneration or spiritual resurrection that takes place during baptism. Imposing the meaning and use of circumcision upon Christian baptism is completely without biblical warrant, and it leads ultimately to a denial of everything the NT does teach about the meaning and subjects of baptism.

A third reason why infants should not be baptized is that there is absolutely *no mention* of infant baptism anywhere in the NT. Some maintain that infants must have been baptized because the NT refers several times to the baptism of households (Acts 11:14; 16:15,33; 18:8; 1 Cor 1:16), and it is assumed that such households would have included infants. This is only an inference, however, and an unwarranted one at that. Such references most likely include only those old enough to make a conscious response to the gospel. This seems obvious from the fact that the members of these households are also said to have *feared God* (Acts 10:2), *heard* (Acts 10:44; 16:32), *believed* (Acts 16:34; 18:8), and *rejoiced* (Acts 16:34). Thus the NT's silence concerning infant baptism remains complete.

A final reason why infants should not be baptized is that in the NT baptism is preceded by other actions which by their very nature can be performed only by those old enough to have a conscious understanding of what is taking place. Before being baptized a person should be able to hear the gospel (Acts 18:8), believe its promises (Mark 16:16; Acts 2:41; 8:12-13; 16:14,31,34; 18:8; Col

2:12), repent of his sins (Acts 2:38), and call upon the Lord (Acts 22:16). Since infants cannot do such things, baptism has no relevance for them.

Because of these reasons we must conclude that infants need not be baptized, nor should they be baptized, indeed they *cannot* be baptized. They can of course be dipped in water, but such a dipping would have no spiritual significance. Infants cannot be baptized any more than they can vote or get married. It is simply not something that applies to them. Baptism applies only to adults and to young people who are old enough to know what they are doing.

III. THE MODE OF BAPTISM

The last main question in reference to baptism is its mode: *how* is it applied to the penitent, believing sinner? The specific issue here is whether immersion in water is the only valid way to baptize. While accepting immersion as true baptism, many in Christendom believe it is proper to apply the baptismal water in other ways also, especially by daubing it or sprinkling it or pouring a small amount of it on the head. Others believe that immersion is the only valid form of baptism. The latter view is the one presented and defended here.

We may state unequivocally that, in its physical form, baptism is by definition the momentary immersion of the body into a pool of water.[4] Nothing else really counts as baptism. To say that one can *baptize* in some way other than immersion is like saying one can *drink* from the cup of the Lord's Supper (Matt 26:27) in some way other than swallowing, e.g., by pouring the juice out on the floor, or rubbing a bit of it on one's forehead. Such actions as sprinkling and pouring have no more relation to baptizing than these actions do to drinking.

In defense of this view we may cite the two main arguments Martin Luther used for it when he said, "I would have those who are to be baptized completely immersed in the water, as the word says and as the mystery indicates" ("Captivity," 191). That is, the Greek words for baptism *mean* immersion, and the symbolism of the act requires it.

First, the word "baptize" in the Greek language literally means "to dip, to immerse." As Luther says, the act of baptism "is that immersion in water from which it derives its name, for the Greek *baptizo* means 'I immerse,' and *baptisma* means, 'immersion'" (ibid., 186). In explaining the meaning of these words, Greek lexicons consistently use such terms as "dip," "plunge," "immerse," "submerge," "sink," "go under," and "drown." When the emphasis is on the result of the action rather than the action itself, other terms may be used, e.g., "dye," "drench," "soak," and "overwhelm." In any case the only action inherent in baptism is immersion.

Second, the symbolism of baptism requires immersion. Earlier we pointed out that some people see only a symbolic relation between baptism and salvation. While this is completely inadequate as the *sole* meaning of baptism, it is certainly true as far as it goes. The action of immersion in water is by design intended to symbolize the saving events of death, burial, and resurrection, as Rom 6:3-11 and Col 2:12 clearly show. This is true in two ways. On the one hand, immersion symbolizes the death, burial, and resurrection of Jesus; on the other hand, it symbolizes the sinner's own spiritual death, burial, and resurrection that are taking place simultaneously with the act of baptism itself.

Romans 6:4 says that "we have been buried with Him through baptism into death, so that as Christ was raised from the dead through the glory of the Father, so we too might walk in newness of life." Colossians 2:12 says we were "buried with Him in baptism," in which we were also "raised up with Him." Can anyone honestly say that sprinkling or pouring a small amount of water on a person in any way even comes close to the events that are supposed to be symbolized in baptism? This is why Luther says that nothing except immersion can "bring out the full significance of baptism," because it is "a symbol of death and resurrection" (ibid., 191).

Thus we conclude that the literal meaning of the word and the figurative significance of the act both require that baptism always be done by immersion.

IV. CONCLUDING QUESTIONS

The preceding discussion has raised several questions that must be briefly addressed. First, if the Bible truly teaches that baptism is the point of time when God bestows the double cure of salvation, why is this view not more widely held in Christendom? Most Protestants (with Lutherans being a major exception) acknowledge only a symbolical and perhaps a psychological connection between baptism and salvation; they deny that baptism is in any way a condition for salvation. How did the latter view—that baptism *is* a condition for salvation—arise?

A study of the history of this aspect of baptism is very enlightening. The fact is that baptism was viewed as the time when God bestows the double cure of salvation from the beginning of Christian history, and this remained the practically unanimous consensus for nearly 1,500 years—up to and including Martin Luther (see Cottrell, "Consensus," 17-38). For example, in the mid-second century Justin Martyr said that "we have learned from the apostles this reason" for baptism, i.e., "in order that we . . . may obtain in the water the remission of sins." Quoting John 3:5 he said that converts "are brought by us where there is water, and are regenerated" (Justin Martyr, "Apology," *ANF* I:183). Augustine (d. A.D. 430) declared that "the salvation of man is effected in baptism" ("Letters," III:5, p. 301). Except for martyrs, he said, the apostolic tradition taught "that without baptism . . . it is impossible for any man to attain to salvation and everlasting life" ("Merits," I:34, p. 35).

Martin Luther's teaching on this subject was most forceful (see Cottrell, "Consensus," 31-34). He declared that "both the forgiveness and the driving out of sins [the double cure] are the work of baptism" ("Sacrament," 15, p. 38). "What Baptism promises and brings," he said, is "victory over death and the devil, forgiveness of sin, God's grace, the entire Christ, and the Holy Spirit with his gifts" ("Large Catechism," IV:41-42, pp. 441-442). "To put it most simply, the power, effect, benefit, fruit, and purpose of Baptism is to save" (ibid., IV:23-24, p. 439). One is baptized so that he "may receive in the water the promised salvation" (ibid., IV:36, p. 441).

This consensus view of the meaning of baptism reigned for 1,500 years, until it was challenged and changed by one man, a contemporary of Luther, the Swiss reformer Huldreich Zwingli. "In this matter of baptism," he decided," all the doctors have been in error from the time of the apostles" (Zwingli, 130). And so in the years 1523 to 1525 he completely repudiated any connection between salvation and the time of baptism, and replaced this view with an explanation of baptism hitherto unknown.[5] In essence he transferred the exact meaning of OT circumcision to baptism, and explained it as a covenant sign, i.e., as a public testimony and witness that the recipient of baptism is (already) saved and is a member of God's covenant people. This newly minted understanding was accepted by John Calvin and became what is commonly called the Reformed view of baptism. As an explanation of baptism's meaning and purpose, this Reformed view has been adopted by almost all non-Lutheran Protestants.

The bottom line is that the view of baptism that I have presented in this chapter, that baptism is the point of time when God bestows the double cure of salvation, is *not* the new view but was the consensus view of all Christendom until Zwingli changed it in the sixteenth century. The nonsalvation view held by most Protestants is actually the new view. Those of us who agree with the original consensus do not have to feel at all uncomfortable or apologetic about it.

This does, however, raise a second question, namely, *on what basis* do Zwinglians reject the original consensus view?[6] Zwingli himself argued that the older view attributed to water a power that belongs only to the blood of Christ. This argument is off the mark, though, since the blood of Christ was always regarded as the only source of forgiving power; baptism was merely the time during which (or for some, the instrument by which) this saving power is applied to the sinner. It was never regarded as a substitute for the blood of Christ.

Another version of this objection is that a physical event such as baptism can have no connection with the spiritual effect of cleansing the soul. In this connection Zwingli's favorite verse was John 6:63, "It is the Spirit who gives life; the flesh profits nothing."[7] But this objection also overlooks the fact that the baptismal waters effect no cleansing; this event is simply the *occasion* for the Spirit's work. Also, those who think a physical event can have no connection with a spiritual result should consider the crucifixion of Christ and its connection with their own salvation.

Another reason Zwingli rejected a conditional connection between baptism and salvation was that he regarded this as a negation of the sovereignty of God. God sovereignly chooses to save *whomever* he wishes (in unconditional election), and he sovereignly bestows his salvation *whenever* he wishes. To say that he must save a person in baptism makes God's saving work dependent upon an act of man. However, this objection overlooks the fact that a truly sovereign God has the prerogative to limit himself and to establish conditions for salvation if he so chooses. To do so is simply an expression of his sovereignty. Besides, Augustine and Luther had views of divine sovereignty similar to that of Zwingli, and they had no problem seeing baptism as conditional for salvation.

Another objection to the consensus view is that it confuses *water* baptism with *Spirit* baptism. It is likely that Zwingli was the first to separate the "one baptism" (Eph 4:5) into two separate events, and most Protestants have subsequently accepted this bifurcation. They say that a sinner receives *spiritual* baptism from the Holy Spirit, which is the baptism that actually saves, as soon as faith begins. Then usually at some later time he is baptized *in water* as a witness to the salvation already received. Zwinglians then declare that any NT text that appears to connect baptism with salvation (e.g., Rom 6:3-5, Gal 3:27; Col 2:12) must be talking about *spiritual* baptism, not water baptism.

In response to this idea we need only go back to Eph 4:5, which affirms that just as there is "one Lord" and "one faith," so there is but "one baptism." A sinner is baptized once, period. This one event has an external side, which is immersion in water; it also has an internal side, which is the saving work of God. We may call the latter "spiritual baptism," but it is not separated in time from the former. Thus unless we want to deny this cardinal truth of Scripture—that there is but one baptism—we must understand the NT passages about baptism and salvation as referring to our baptism in water.

Probably the most common reason for rejecting the original consensus view (that baptism is the time when salvation is received) is based on the relation between grace and works. How can baptism be for salvation, if "by grace you have been saved through faith; and . . . not as a result of works" (Eph 2:8-9)? Martin Luther tells us that his Zwinglian opponents challenged his view of baptism with this very argument. They claimed that Luther was teaching works-salvation, since baptism must surely be regarded as a work. Luther absolutely denied that his view constituted works-salvation, however. "Yes," he said, "it is true that our works are of no use for salvation. Baptism, however, is not our work but God's" ("Large Catechism," IV:35, p. 441). Luther is exactly right on this point.

The problem with this whole objection is that it is based on a faulty view of works. In view of texts such as Eph 2:8-9, Rom 3:28, and Gal 2:16, where works and faith are contrasted, Zwinglians assume that everything besides faith must be placed in the category of works, with works being understood as "things we do." Since baptism is a "thing we do," it must be a work and therefore cannot be for salvation.

This view of works is seriously false, however. For one thing, faith itself is a work in the generic sense of "things we do," according to Jesus in John 6:28-29.

Thus whatever "works" means in Pauline texts such as Rom 3:28 and Eph 2:8-9, it must mean something besides "things we do."

I agree that there are just two categories of "things we do," one of which consists of conditions for salvation that are consistent with grace, the other of which consists of human acts that cannot be conditions for receiving grace (Rom 11:6). We may label these categories "faith" and "works," but these terms must be regarded as *shorthand* or abbreviated labels for the categories and not the exclusive contents of each. That faith cannot be the only "thing we do" in the category of grace conditions has already been established by the inclusion of both repentance and confession therein. When these are accepted as belonging in the same category as faith, there can be no grace-based objection to adding baptism to the list.

What, then, is the nature of the category labeled "works"? The key to a proper understanding of this term, especially as used by Paul, is in Rom 3:28 (see Cottrell, *Romans*, I:267-271). Here Paul says "that a man is justified by faith apart from works of the Law." The exact translation of the latter prepositional phrase (*choris ergon nomou*) is "apart from works of law." There are no definite articles, and the word "law" should not be capitalized. Paul is referring not to the Law of Moses exclusively, but to all forms in which the law of God is available to his creatures, including the internally inscribed laws which are known even by pagans (Rom 2:15).

The category labeled "works," then, is really "works *of law.*" In this expression "law" includes any and all commands given by God *as Creator* to human beings as his *creatures*, and "works" includes any response of man as creature to the law commands of the Creator.[8] Nothing in this category can be a condition for salvation under the grace system.

What, then, is the nature of the category labeled "faith"? This category includes anything that human beings as *sinners* must do in obedience to God *the Redeemer's* instructions on how to receive salvation. God issues these instructions not in his role as Creator but in his role as Redeemer. We respond to them not as a creature responds out of duty to the law commands of his Creator, but as a sinner responds out of hope to the gospel commands of the Redeemer. This is what is called "becoming obedient to the faith" (Acts 6:7), or obeying *the gospel* (Rom 10:16 [ESV]; 2 Thess 1:8; 1 Pet 4:17). Faith is the *representative* act of obedience to gospel commands; but this category also includes repentance, confession, and baptism. Why? Because these are all acts of obedience to the Redeemer's instructions *to sinners* for receiving salvation. None of these can be called a "work of law," since none is required of us merely as creatures.

We conclude that baptism as a condition for salvation is consistent with grace. It is not in the category of human works in the sense of passages such as Rom 3:20,28; 4:4-5; 11:6; Eph 2:8-9; Gal 2:16. The primary sense in which baptism is a work is that it is a *work of God.* The only saving work accomplished in baptism is being done by God himself. The sinner enters the baptismal waters with "faith in the working of God" in his heart (Col 2:12), trusting that God will at that moment keep his promises to bestow forgiveness and the gift of the Holy Spirit.

This leads to a final question, namely, what is the spiritual status of the millions of people who have mistakenly followed the false views of baptism, whether in regard to meaning, subjects, or mode? This is a very difficult question and cannot be thoroughly answered in the brief space available here. In general, though, we may answer it in two steps.

First, in view of the clear teaching of Scripture on the subject, we must say that only those who have consciously received immersion as a saving work of God can be confident of their *present* status as Christians and as members of the body of Christ. It is, of course, possible that in some cases God has made exceptions and has acted outside his stated plan of bestowing salvation upon believers in immersion, but we have no right to presume upon God in this respect. If someone who has not been biblically baptized is convinced that God has saved him, we may follow this procedure. One, while granting that God may have made an exception, we must insist that no one can know this for sure. Experience can be deceiving (Matt 7:21-23). Two, we must make sure that the biblical teaching on baptism is clearly understood and accepted. Three, we must invite the person of unsure status to receive baptism properly, while calling upon God to work upon him whatever works of salvation he has not already worked. Only then can a person be sure of his present status before God.

Second, with regard to the *future*, in the final judgment we can expect God to judge all persons who have received baptism improperly in the same way that he will judge everyone else, namely, in accordance with their *conscientious response to available light*. No one will be condemned for failing to meet some particular requirement as long as he is conscientiously responding to whatever light is available to him (see Rom 4:15). It is obvious that human traditions have seriously distorted and limited the light of Scripture concerning baptism, and many sincere people have responded in good conscience to what light they have. For this reason we may hope to see such people in heaven.

This last point does not permit us to give anyone false assurance about his present state of salvation, however; nor does it give us the right to change the clear teaching of Scripture on believers' immersion for salvation. The "available light" principle applies only to future judgment, and it can be applied only by the omniscient God. For us today, as individuals and as the church of Jesus Christ, we must continue to believe and proclaim the clear biblical teaching about baptism without cowardice and without compromise.

NOTES ON CHAPTER TWENTY

[1]See Cottrell, *Baptism*. This book is a detailed analysis of twelve NT texts: Matt 28:19-20; Mark 16:15-16; John 3:3-5; Acts 2:38-39; Acts 22:16; Rom 6:3-4; 1 Cor 12:13; Gal 3:26-27; Eph 5:25-27; Col 2:11-13; Titus 3:5; 1 Pet 3:21.

[2]Later editions, at least since 1984, have changed this to "for the forgiveness of your sins."

[3]At this point it should be clear that we are talking about *Christian* baptism only, and not John's baptism. Some have wrongly equated the latter with the former and have assumed that the two have the same meaning. It is obvious, though, that John's baptism could have no relation to any of the new elements of salvation (trinitarian knowledge, death and resurrection of Christ, the gift of the Spirit), since they were not yet known or had not yet happened when John began baptizing. Baptism for salvation began only on the Day of Pentecost.

[4]The nature or location of the pool is irrelevant as long as it provides a quantity of water sufficient for the act of immersion. Anything from the ocean to a bathtub may suffice.

[5]See my doctoral dissertation on Zwingli's new view of baptism, "Covenant and Baptism," and my summary of it, "Reformed Tradition."

[6]For a fuller discussion of all the following points see Cottrell, "Reformed Tradition," 42-48, 62-68.

[7]For Zwingli this objection actually grew out of his incipient metaphysical dualism, i.e., his view of a strong antithesis and incompatibility between matter and spirit as such. His idea of the inherent negativity of the physical world, including the body, was close to paganism. See Cottrell, "Reformed Tradition," 64-68.

[8]Even sins are "works of law," since they are the creature's negative response to the Creator's law commands. The flow of Paul's argument from Rom 3:28 to 4:8 shows that this is true. See Cottrell, *Romans,* 1:269-270.

CHAPTER TWENTY-ONE

ASSURANCE OF SALVATION

"**I**f the final judgment were held at this very moment, would you be saved?" Assurance of salvation is the ability to answer "Yes!" to this question, rather than to respond with an ambiguous "Maybe"; "I hope so, but I'm not really sure"; "I don't know." How we answer this question obviously makes a world of difference concerning our happiness and peace of mind during this life. Our greatest conscious need is for a feeling of confidence regarding our present acceptance with God and our future participation in glory. We need "blessed assurance," assurance of salvation.

The good news is that such assurance is possible. Indeed, it is the natural result of a proper understanding of grace, especially of the key concept of justification by faith. Every Christian should have this assurance. The bad news is twofold. On the one hand, many of those who are actually in a saved state are confused about their relationship with God and lack assurance, peace, and joy in their Christian life. On the other hand, many believers who do have confidence in their possession of eternal life also have a distorted concept of it and a false basis for it.

Our purpose here is to explain the proper nature of assurance, as well as the proper basis for it. First we will examine the two extreme and unacceptable approaches to assurance, namely, "once saved, always saved," and "always trying, never sure."

I. "ONCE SAVED, ALWAYS SAVED"

A widespread belief in Christendom is that once a person has become saved, he not only can be sure of his present status of salvation but also has God's guarantee that he will never lose it in the future. Once he is saved, he will remain saved forever; once the gift of salvation has been received, it is irrevocable. This is the "once saved, always saved" view, also described as "once in grace, always in grace," "final perseverance," and "eternal security."

A. The Origin and Basis of This Doctrine

This doctrine has its origins in the theology of Augustine, who by introducing the concept of total depravity seriously compromised the reality of free will. Unconditional predestination to salvation and the gift of assured perseverance became inseparably linked.[1] As Augustine put it, "But now to the saints predestinated to the kingdom of God by God's grace, . . . perseverance itself is bestowed, . . . so that by means of this gift they cannot help persevering" ("Rebuke," 103). The doctrine was later taught by John Calvin and is commonly known as the fifth point (P) in the five points of Calvinism (TULIP), i.e., the *Perseverance* (or Preservation) of the saints. It is the logical conclusion of the earlier points, especially *Total* depravity, *Unconditional* election, and *Irresistible* grace. Taken together these points mean that God determines every step in the process of salvation from beginning to end. Free will is not a factor. In this system one can neither *accept* salvation nor *cast it aside* of his own free choice.

Those who seek to support this view from the Bible usually concentrate on two kinds of data. On the one hand they cite passages that stress the Christian's assurance, e.g., the Christian's "full assurance of understanding" (Col 2:2), his "full assurance of hope" (Heb 6:11), his "full assurance of faith" (Heb 10:22), his assured status as an adopted son and heir (Rom 8:15-17; Gal 4:6), and the ability to "know that you have eternal life" (1 John 5:13). On the other hand they cite those texts that emphasize God's own faithfulness in keeping his promises to believers and protecting them from their enemies: "No one is able to snatch them out of the Father's hand" (John 10:27-29); "He who began a good work in you will perfect it until the day of Christ Jesus" (Phil 1:6); "The gifts and the calling of God are irrevocable" (Rom 11:29); "I am convinced that He is able to guard what I have entrusted to Him until that day" (2 Tim 1:12); we are "protected by the power of God" (1 Pet 1:5); and nothing "will be able to separate us from the love of God" (Rom 8:31-39).

These texts certainly teach important truths about assurance. They show that assurance of salvation is something that every Christian should have. They show that it is God's desire and God's plan to maintain us in the state and process of salvation until the end. They show that God can and will protect us from all outside forces that seek to draw us away from him. But none of these texts specifically affirms that every saved child of God will unconditionally and infallibly remain in his saved state until he dies. All such texts allow for the possibility that the believer himself may exercise his free will and voluntarily give up his salvation. God himself will never leave us and will never initiate the severing of our saved relationship with him, but he will not prevent us from leaving him if that is our choice.

In other words the texts that support the doctrine of assurance of salvation do not teach unconditional perseverance. They teach assurance, but an assurance that is consistent with our continuing to meet the conditions upon which salvation was given to us in the first place. In fact, the overwhelming testimony of the NT is that *staying* saved is just as conditional as *becoming* saved. These are gracious conditions, of course, and not legalistic ones. As Christians we remain justified by faith, not by works of law (Rom 3:28).

B. The Biblical Teaching That Staying Saved Is Conditional

The conditionality of staying saved is clearly affirmed in numerous passages. John 8:31 says, "So Jesus was saying to those Jews who had believed Him, 'If you continue in My word, then you are truly disciples of Mine.'" The key word here, and in the following texts, is *IF*: "if you continue." Here Jesus speaks to those who were already believers, and declares that *continuing* in his word—continuing to believe his teaching—is a condition for true discipleship. This clearly implies that it is possible for believers to stop believing and to cease being disciples.

The conditional nature of staying saved and the possibility of a believer becoming lost are clearly taught in John 15:1-6. Here Jesus is discussing those who are already truly in a saved state; they are branches that are "in Me" (v. 2), fully attached to the life-giving vine. But Jesus exhorts these branches to "abide in Me" (v. 4), clearly implying that whether we abide or remain in the vine is our own responsibility. Verse 6 clearly shows that it is possible for one to choose *not* to abide in Christ: "If anyone does not abide in Me . . . ." If anyone makes this choice, two things follow. First, the one who does not abide in Christ (i.e., ceases to believe) "is thrown away as a branch and dries up." The expression "thrown away" is *eblethe exo*, literally, "thrown outside." He was at one time *inside*—inside the church, inside the love of God, inside the circle of grace; but now he is *outside*, excluded from grace, as the result of his own initiative, not God's. Second, those who choose to stop believing and who are thus excluded from grace are finally condemned to hell: "They gather them, and cast them into the fire and they are burned" (see Matt 13:40-42). This is not equivalent to 1 Cor 3:15, where one's *works* are subjected to the test of fire, thus affecting only the believer's reward. Here the excluded branches themselves—the fallen ones—are burned.

A similar text that clearly shows the conditional nature of staying saved is Rom 11:17-22 (Cottrell, *Romans*, 2:248-262). Here the original olive tree represents OT Israel, with the natural branches standing for the Jews; and the present version of the olive tree represents the church, with the combination of natural and engrafted branches standing for Jews and Gentiles who have become believers in Christ. In explaining this analogy Paul makes two points that totally disprove the "once saved, always saved" doctrine. First, when the natural branches (the Jews) were confronted with the gospel and then refused to accept Jesus as their Messiah and Lord, "they were broken off for their unbelief" (v. 20). Even if they were true believers in Yahweh and in a saved state prior to hearing the gospel, by virtue of rejecting Christ they became unbelievers—they "fell" (v. 22)—and thus were rejected by God and lost their salvation. Second, for the Gentiles who became believers and were grafted into the olive tree, Paul warns them to remain faithful, "for if God did not spare the natural branches, He will not spare you, either. Behold then the kindness and severity of God; to those who fell, severity, but to you, God's kindness, if you continue in His kindness; otherwise you also will be cut off" (vv. 21-22). The final responsibility for staying saved clearly belongs to the believer: "*if you continue* in His kindness." The result of not continuing is made very clear; "otherwise you also," like the unbelieving Jews, "will be cut off."

Another such passage is 1 Cor 15:1-2, "Now I make known to you, brethren, the gospel which I preached to you, which also you received, in which also you stand, by which also you are saved, if you hold fast the word which I preached to you, unless you believed in vain." Here Paul speaks to those who have known the gospel facts concerning Jesus (vv. 3-4), who have received them (past tense), who are standing in them (present tense), and who are saved by them (present tense). Surely he is speaking of those who have truly "believed" (v. 2). But Paul clearly says that continuing in this saved state is conditioned on continuing to hold fast to these facts, or continuing to trust in the saving work of Jesus for salvation: "if you hold fast." If you do not hold fast, your past faith and your present faith will mean nothing; that faith will be "in vain."

A similar text is Col 1:21-23. Verse 21 describes the Colossians' (and every Christian's) former state: "formerly alienated and hostile in mind, engaged in evil deeds." Verse 22 then relates our present and future states. We are "now reconciled," i.e., no longer aliens and enemies, but in a saved state because of our faith in the gospel (v. 23). Our future is the full sanctification and deliverance from sin that characterizes heaven: "in order to present you before Him holy and blameless and beyond reproach." But whether we reach that final salvation is clearly conditioned upon whether we continue to believe in Jesus Christ. Verse 23 states this condition unequivocally: "if indeed you continue in the faith firmly established and steadfast, and not moved away from the hope of the gospel." The unavoidable implication is that we may choose *not* to "continue in the faith," and may allow ourselves to be "moved away from the hope of the gospel." Such a contingency would not be the result of a lapse in God's protection, nor the triumph of an enemy power; it would simply be the individual's exercise of his God-given free will.

The passages just discussed uniformly emphasize the conditionality of staying in a saved state: "if you continue . . . if anyone does not abide in me . . . if you continue . . . if you hold fast . . . if indeed you continue." Even though now you are truly saved, if you do not continue to hold on to Jesus with true faith, you will be truly lost.

This understanding is greatly reinforced by a number of texts that specifically affirm the reality—either potential or actual—of falling away from the saved state into a state of lostness. In Rom 11:22 Paul speaks of the Jews who became unbelievers as "those who fell," and he says that any Christian who does not continue to trust in the provisions of God's grace "will be cut off." In the former case the lostness is actual, and in the latter case it is potential; but in both cases it is real.

In 1 Cor 9:24-27 the Apostle Paul says that it is possible to run in a race and still lose and not receive the prize (v. 24). Some think this means that undisciplined believers (vv. 25-26) will simply lose their rewards, but not their salvation as such. Verse 27, however, shows this is not the case: "But I discipline my body and make it my slave, so that, after I have preached to others, I myself will not be disqualified." The alternative to finishing the race is to be "disqualified" (*adokimos*). In every other NT use of this word, it refers to the state of lostness, not to a loss of rewards.[2] Paul is indeed saying that he himself could lose his salvation if he does not persevere in the race unto the end.

In addressing the Judaizers in Gal 5:4, Paul specifically affirms that they "have been severed from Christ" and "have fallen from grace." This is clearly a state of lostness, which was preceded by a state of salvation. They could not have been severed from Christ unless they at one time were joined to him; they could not have fallen from grace unless they at one time had been standing in it (Rom 5:2).

In 2 Pet 2:4 we are told that angels who sinned are "reserved for judgment," i.e., lost and destined for hell. We must assume that all angels were originally created holy and in a right relationship with God, also that all were created with the free will to remain holy or to rebel against God and become lost. In this chapter Peter uses the "angels who sinned" as an analogy for Christian teachers who stray into heresy and wickedness, and thus lose their salvation (vv. 1-3,9-19). That these teachers at one time were true believers is seen in verse 15, which says they have *forsaken* the right way and "have gone astray." This is especially seen in verses 20-22, where these false teachers are described as earlier having "escaped the defilements of the world by the knowledge of the Lord and Savior Jesus Christ" (v. 20), and as having "known the way of righteousness" (v. 21). Thus they have experienced three states: lost, saved, and lost again, just as "a sow, after washing, returns to wallowing in the mire" (v. 22). The bad news is that "the last [lost again] state has become worse for them than the first" [original] lost state (v. 20). Without doubt this passage refers to specific individuals who actually fell from grace and lost their salvation. They are "twice dead," as Jude 12 (NIV) says.

An even clearer teaching on the reality of falling from grace is Heb 6:4-8. Actually the entire letter to the Hebrews is based on the fact that such a fall is possible. The letter is apparently being written to Jews (i.e., Hebrews) who had become Christians, but who are now thinking they had made a mistake and are seriously considering abandoning their Christian faith and reconverting to Judaism. The theme of the entire letter is the danger and the foolishness of such a decision. If this decision is not possible, then the whole book of Hebrews is a sham. It is filled with warnings against turning away from Jesus Christ, the only source of salvation (2:1-3; 3:12-14; 4:1,11; 10:26-39; 12:25).

The clearest such warning is Heb 6:4-8. On the one hand, here the writer is without doubt speaking of those who are *truly saved*, since they possess five characteristics of the saved state. 1) They are "enlightened," i.e., they possess true knowledge and understanding of the gospel. 2) They "have tasted of the heavenly gift," the gift of salvation in general (Eph 2:8-9). 3) They "have been made partakers of the Holy Spirit," having drunk the living water (John 7:37-39; 1 Cor 12:13).[3] 4) They "have tasted the good word of God," having believed and received its promises. 5) They have tasted "the powers of the age to come," referring to the already experienced resurrection from spiritual death (Eph 2:5; Col 2:12-13), in anticipation of the future redemptive resurrection of the body.

The use of the word "taste" (*geuomai*) in these verses does not imply a tentative, aborted sampling of salvation in contrast with actual eating or consuming. (See Heb 2:9, where the same word is used for Christ's *tasting death* on the cross.) It is used rather to contrast the real but incomplete salvation experienced in this life with the *fullness* of salvation to be received in glory, in the same sense that the present gift of the indwelling Holy Spirit is but a pledge or down payment of the full inheritance that is to come (2 Cor 1:22; Eph 1:13-14).

The fact that those to whom this passage speaks are true Christians is also shown in the statement that, if they fall away, "it is impossible to renew them again to repentance" (v. 6). To speak of *renewing* them *again* to repentance indicates that they were once in a state of repentance, indicative of salvation.

On the other hand, it is also clear that this passage warns against the reality of becoming *truly lost*, as opposed to simply losing one's rewards. Verse 6 warns against becoming "fallen away," a state devoid of repentance and hostile to Christ. The fallen one's life yields "thorns and thistles"; it is "worthless [*adokimos*] and close to being cursed, and it ends up being burned" (v. 8; see John 15:6).

Passages such as these are completely contrary to the "once saved, always saved" idea. They cannot be explained away as referring only to people who were never saved in the first place, nor can they be reduced to the loss of rewards rather than of salvation as such. Nor can we say that they are merely *hypothetical* warnings, by which God motivates us to remain faithful by threatening us with a scenario that in actuality could never occur. Such a ploy would be deceitful and cruel, and is unworthy of our gracious and loving Savior.

C. How Does One "Fall from Grace"?

We conclude, then, that it is possible for a believer to fall from grace and lose his salvation. The next question is, what constitutes "falling from grace" or "falling away"? To answer this question we must remember the central doctrine of grace, that a sinner is justified by faith apart from works of law (Rom 3:28). We not only initially become justified by faith; we also *remain* justified by faith in the atoning death of Jesus Christ. Falling from grace occurs, then, when faith in the blood of Jesus dies. Thus the Christian must be on constant guard concerning his faith, using every opportunity to strengthen it and being constantly aware of ways by which it may die.

What are the ways in which faith may die? I will suggest three. First, faith may be put to death through an act of *sudden suicide* (spiritual, not physical), i.e., by a deliberate decision to stop believing in Christ and his saving work, thus renouncing the Christian faith. This is apparently the choice being contemplated by the converts from Judaism to which the letter to the Hebrews was originally written.

They seem to be wondering if they had made a mistake by becoming Christians, and were considering renouncing Christ and returning to their OT faith and practice. A similar decision may be and sometimes is made by Christians from other backgrounds, e.g., by someone who has begun to have intellectual doubts' about the historicity of Christ and his works, or who allows a personal tragedy (such as the death of a loved one) to destroy his belief in an all-powerful, all-loving Creator.

A second way faith may die is through *slow starvation* (spiritual, not physical). Faith does not come into existence full-grown but begins with a stage of infancy, often tender and fragile and definitely in need of maturing and strengthening. Thus faith must constantly be nurtured and nourished and exercised. To this end God has provided us with spiritual disciplines such as those in Acts 2:42: "the apostles' teaching," or in postapostolic times, Bible study; "fellowship," which includes an active church life; "breaking of bread," or consistent and faithful participation in the Lord's Supper; and "prayer." These are the means by which faith is nourished; to neglect them allows faith to weaken or even to die. This is a true sense in which "faith without works is dead" (James 2:26).

In his parable of the sower Jesus warns us of this danger. Sometimes, he says, the seeds of the Word fall "on the rocky places, where they did not have much soil; and immediately they sprang up, because they had no depth of soil. But when the sun had risen, they were scorched; and because they had no root, they withered away" (Matt 13:5-6). This represents "the man who hears the word and immediately receives it with joy; yet he has no firm root in himself, but is only temporary, and when affliction or persecution arises because of the word, immediately he falls away" (13:20-21). Faithful participation in the spiritual disciplines mentioned above is a necessary means of extending the roots of faith beyond and around and beneath the rocky places of life, enabling them to anchor and nourish the Christian life. If we are not careful to extend these roots, spiritual starvation is the result.

The third way that faith may die is through *strangulation by sin*. After conversion, if a Christian allows sins to continue and to flourish without fighting against them, they will sooner or later choke the life out of his faith. Again in the parable of the sower Jesus speaks of seeds that "fell among the thorns, and the thorns came up and choked them out" (Matt 13:7). Jesus explains, "And the one on whom seed was sown among the thorns, this is the man who hears the word, and the worry of the world and the deceitfulness of wealth choke the word, and it becomes unfruitful" (13:22).

Some are tempted to think that because God's grace forgives all sins and salvation is assured, it does not matter if we keep on sinning (Rom 6:1). In response Paul points out that becoming a Christian involves not just forgiveness but also regeneration, in which we are raised up from a state of spiritual death (Eph 2:1,5) to walk in a new spiritual life where sin does not belong (Rom 6:2-14). But if one continues to live a life controlled by the sins of the flesh, he will surely go back into that state of spiritual death: "For if you live according to the flesh you will die, but if by the Spirit you put to death the deeds of the body, you will live" (Rom 8:13, ESV). Peter warns those who have "escaped the defilements of the world" of the danger of again becoming "entangled in them" and being "overcome" (2 Pet 2:20). Continuing to sin after becoming a Christian is like opening the gates of the fort and inviting the enemy inside.

The conclusion is that the presence of faith is not an absolute guarantee that one's salvation is eternally secure. God will indeed protect us (1 Pet 1:5), but we must make a deliberate effort to keep our faith alive and strong. We cannot relax our guard, tranquilized by the false assurance generated by the false teaching of "once saved, always saved."

D. Restoring the Fallen

The fact that the NT teaches the possibility (and in some cases the actuality) of falling from grace raises another question: is it possible for one who loses his salvation ever to be restored thereto? Many say this is not possible. If a saved person abandons or loses his salvation, for whatever reason, it is impossible for that person ever to be saved again. This conclusion is usually based on Heb 6:6, which says of fallen ones that "it is impossible to renew them again to repentance, since they again crucify to themselves the Son of God and put Him to open shame." This seems to be an unequivocal locking of the door to salvation to anyone who voluntarily forsakes Christ.

In my judgment, however, this is a seriously false conclusion, based on a false interpretation and translation of Heb 6:6. This verse, rightly understood, does *not* teach that it is impossible for a fallen person ever to return. The main affirmation in the verse is indeed "it is impossible to renew them." The key to understanding this, however, is the two modifying participles, "crucifying again" and "putting to open shame." How a participle is related to the main verb is always a matter of interpretation, since there is no connecting word (such as "since") in the Greek text. Sometimes a participle states the *cause* of the action of the main verb. That is how most translators interpret the two participles in Heb 6:6; hence they add the word "since." In other words, it is impossible—period—to renew fallen ones to repentance, and that is because they have crucified Christ to themselves again and put him to an open shame.

This interpretation of the participles must be vigorously rejected, however. Their relation to the main verb is not causal but *temporal*, i.e., they state a time frame in which the action of the main verb is true. This is true for two reasons. First, they are *present* participles, not *aorist* (past) participles. Since present participles generally refer to action that is contemporaneous with (rather than action that precedes) the main verb, it is much better to connect them with the main verb with words such as "while" or "as long as" (as the NASB and NIV footnotes allow). Thus the meaning of the verse is something *very different* from what appears in most translations. It is saying that the impossibility is conditional, i.e., it is impossible to renew the fallen *as long as* they continue to crucify Christ to themselves again and put him to an open shame.

The second reason why these participles should be interpreted in this temporal sense ("while, as long as") is that other Scripture supports the possibility that the fallen may be restored. The clearest such text is the one that addresses the fate of those Jewish branches on the olive tree that were broken off because of their unbelief (Rom 11:20). It cannot be doubted that at least some of these were Jews who once had a sincere faith in Yahweh as he was known from OT revelation and who were thus in a saved state, but who, when confronted with the gospel of Christ, chose to reject him and thus became unbelievers and were broken off from the tree. Of these Paul says, "And they also, if they do not continue in their unbelief, will be grafted in, for God is able to graft them in again" (Rom 11:23). If they will restore their own faith, God will restore them to his grace.

Another text that gives support to the possibility of restoring the fallen is the parable of the prodigal son (Luke 15:11-32). The story of the prodigal is often taken as having at least a secondary application to the work of evangelism. That is, the prodigal is pictured as a lost sinner who experiences conversion. When interpreted on this level, however, it is much more reasonable to regard it as parallel to a believer who falls away and is then restored. In the parable the son is first pictured as being *alive in his father's house*. This represents the believer in the state of grace. Then the son is pictured as being *dead in a far country*, representing a believer's free choice to allow his faith to die. Finally the son is shown to be *alive again in his father's arms*, indicating that a fallen believer can be restored to grace again. Verse 24 says the son "has come to life *again*," showing he was once alive, then dead, then alive again.

In view of these considerations it is tragic that most Bible versions mistranslate Heb 6:6 and thus close the door of hope to the fallen.

How does the restoration of a fallen believer take place? Romans 11:23 shows that he must not remain in unbelief but must again begin to believe in the saving work of Jesus. Also, Acts 8:9-24 may properly be regarded as an actual instance of a believer, Simon the former sorcerer, who fell from grace and is then instructed by Peter to *repent* and *pray* in order to be received into grace again (v. 22).

II. "ALWAYS TRYING, NEVER SURE"

The second extreme and unacceptable approach to assurance may be called "always trying, never sure." This is in truth a denial of the reality of assurance altogether. Those who hold this view may live as good a Christian life as they can, fighting against sin and immersing themselves in good works of all kinds; yet they never experience the assurance, peace, and joy that come from knowing they are saved. As mentioned earlier, in response to the question, "If the judgment day were to be held this very moment, would you be saved?" their answer would be something like this: "Maybe. It's possible, but I'm not really sure. I don't know."

Some go to this extreme when they reject the eternal security idea. They mistakenly equate the unconditional assurance of "once saved, always saved" with assurance as such. Thus when they reject the former, they cast aside all assurance along with it.

What is the reason for this uncertainty, this lack of assurance of personal salvation? Basically it stems from a failure to understand the nature and implications of salvation by grace, and justification by faith in particular. Those who struggle with assurance are still laboring under the false idea that, in one way or another, a sinner is saved (justified) by works, i.e., by being good enough. Those who think this way most often are very conscious of their sins and their unworthiness of heaven, and thus are filled with fear and anxiety about death and the final judgment. The best they can hope for is to die in church or while praying their 1 John 1:9 prayer for forgiveness.

Such a lack of assurance does not mean these Christians are lost, but it does mean that they are missing out on the joy and peace that assurance brings.

This "always trying, never sure" approach to assurance has as little biblical support as "once saved, always saved." Both extremes must be rejected. What does the Bible say, then?

III. "SIMPLY TRUSTING, FULLY FORGIVEN"

The best approach to assurance is summed up in the phrase, "simply trusting, fully forgiven." This simple formula acknowledges the fact that the believer is completely, 100% forgiven (justified) by the blood of Christ; i.e., he is completely free from the condemnation for sin (Rom 8:1) even if he is not completely free from the sin itself. This means that assurance of salvation is based on the first part of the double cure (justification) rather than on the second part (sanctification). The Christian is a *forgiven* person, even though he is not a *perfect* person.

The biblical approach to assurance is well summed up in the words of 1 Pet 1:5: we are "protected by the power of God through faith." This text emphasizes both God's faithfulness and the Christian's faith as essential elements in assurance.

A. "Protected by the Power of God"

"Protected by the power of God" stresses God's faithfulness. We can be sure that He will never forsake us or cast us aside (Heb 10:23). We can be sure that he will provide all the resources we need to protect us from our enemies.[4] These resources include the indwelling Holy Spirit, the Bible, prayer, and the church with its supporting fellowship and shepherds.

The greatest resource of all is God's own faithful and unfailing love. This love is a firm basis for assurance, according to Paul in Rom 5:1-11. Our hope (assurance) will not be disappointed, he says, because God's love with all its effects has been poured out within our hearts (5:5). This is the love that God demonstrated toward us "in that while we were yet sinners, Christ died for us" (5:8).

God's love gave us the cross, and our faith in his cross brings justification; and because we are justified, we are in a state of objective peace with God (5:1), i.e., we are no longer his enemies but have been reconciled to him and are now his friends (5:10). Having been justified by faith, we are actually standing in—are positioned in—the saving grace of God (5:2). The result is that we have "hope of the glory of God," a hope that causes us to "exult" or rejoice (5:2). Our lives are full of joy, and we are "happy on our way to heaven," as Brother Don DeWelt liked to express it.

A key word in this text is *hope* (Greek, *elpis*). Biblical hope has three characteristics. First, it is an attitude of *confident expectation*, and thus is quite unlike the wishful thinking or futile desire for the unexpected that we often describe as hope (e.g., "I hope I win the *Reader's Digest* sweepstakes this year!"). Biblical hope is a feeling of certainty, not uncertainty, and thus itself is equivalent to assurance. Second, hope is a confident expectation of *something good*. One may confidently expect something bad, such as the pain of a surgical procedure; but this is dread, not hope. As Christians we have "hope of the glory of God," the confident expectation of experiencing all the blessings of eternal life in the presence of God's glory. That's as good as it gets! Third, biblical hope is the confident expectation of something good that lies *in the future*. The object of hope is not already present but is always yet to come (Rom 8:24-25). Thus even though we do not yet possess the fullness of salvation, we have assurance it will be ours on the day of judgment.

The interlocking "eight steps to glory" in Rom 5:1-11 are thus:

The eternal, infinite love of God, which provides —

The saving work of Jesus Christ, which is the object of —

Our faith, through which we have access to —

The grace of God, which includes —

Justification (forgiveness), which gives us —

Peace with God (reconciliation), which results in —

Hope (assurance of salvation), which results in —

Joy, in anticipation of the glory of God!

Paul's point in the latter part of this text (5:6-11) is to show us *why* it is possible to have such assurance. Specifically he says that justification by faith is a firm ground for confident hope, because the love of God that made reconciliation possible *while we were still his enemies* will not fail us *now that we are his friends*. This point is made by comparing the two basic transitions made by those who are saved. The first transition, from our past to our present state, is from *wrath to grace*; the second transition, from our present to our future state, is from *grace to glory*. The first transition is by far the most difficult, the most extreme, and the most unlikely. But the love of God found a way to make it possible. How can we doubt, then, that his love will take us through the next transition, which is so much less radical by comparison?

It is vital that we see the progression of Paul's thought in this passage. What did God's love do for us while we were his unreconciled, sinful, helpless enemies? No less than give his own Son to suffer in our place (5:5-8). But if God's love would do that for us while we were his enemies, we can have every assurance that he will do even more for us now that we are justified and reconciled to him (5:9-10). Will not God save those at peace with him, if he went to the extremity of dying for his enemies? Will not his love suffice to make the less radical change that remains? Can God's love for his friends be less than his love for those who hate him? If the love of God and the cross of Christ can span the vast chasm between wrath and grace, how "much more" (5:9-10) can the same love and the same cross span the lesser chasm between grace and glory! This "much more" of God's love is a firm basis for assurance.

B. "Through Faith"

First Peter 1:5 says we are protected by God's power "through faith." This simple phrase tells us two things about assurance. First, it shows that assurance is not absolute but conditional. Certainly God's love is unconditional, but whether we allow ourselves to continue receiving the saving benefit of his love is conditioned upon our continuing trust in Jesus Christ. This means that as free-will creatures we have a part in maintaining our saving relationship with Christ. As long as we continue to keep our faith alive, God will keep us in his grace. If we cease to trust him, then by our own decision we cut ourselves off from him.

That God's power protects us "through faith" leads to a second conclusion, namely, that our assurance of salvation is not conditioned upon works. From our side it is indeed *faith* that keeps us safely within the sphere of grace, that holds us under the justifying blood of Jesus Christ. We do not have to ask ourselves whether we have "done enough" or are "good enough" to be saved. It is *Christ alone* who has done enough to save us; we are simply asked to believe that this is so.

When we were baptized into Christ, we were baptized not just for the forgiveness of *sins past* (contrary to a common error), but for the forgiveness of *sins period*. That is, we were baptized into a continuing relationship with Jesus Christ (Gal 3:26-27), and we stay in this relationship—and in the state of forgiveness (justification)—as long as we continue to trust in the forgiving power of his blood.

The bottom line is this: *knowing that we are justified by faith is the real key to assurance.* To be *justified* means to be at peace with God (Rom 5:1), to be free from condemnation (Rom 8:1). To be justified *by faith* means that this peace and freedom are not conditioned on how good we are (i.e., works), but on our continuing trust in the all-sufficient blood of Christ. Returning for a moment to Paul's discussion of the two transitions in Rom 5:1-11, we see that our part in the first transition is summed up in the word *faith*. We have been justified and have crossed the chasm from wrath to grace by faith, not by works (5:1-2). And just as surely as we did not span this first and forbidding chasm by any works of our own, neither will the second chasm be spanned by our works. God spans them both by his grace, and we cling to his grace by our faith.

To put it another way, our sense of assurance derives from knowing we are *justified* by the blood of Christ, not from our having achieved a certain level of *sanctification*. The question is not "How *good* am I?" but "How *forgiven* am I?" Does this mean that we have no need or obligation to pursue holiness? Of course not. Paul deals with this false conclusion in Romans 6, and so does the Apostle John in this statement: "And everyone who has this hope fixed on Him purifies himself, just as He is pure" (1 John 3:3).

NOTES ON CHAPTER TWENTY-ONE

[1] Portalie, 58-59. See especially Augustine's treatises, "Perseverance" and "Rebuke."

[2] Rom 1:28, referring to the "depraved" or reprobate mind of pagans; 2 Cor 13:5-7, referring to "failing the test," in contrast with being in the faith and being united with Christ; 2 Tim 3:8, "rejected" in regard to the faith; Titus 1:16, "worthless" or unfit for anything good; and Heb 6:8, "worthless" and ending up being burned.

[3] "Partaking" refers to the real possession of something; see Heb 2:14; 3:1,14.

[4] See John 10:28-29; Rom 8:31-39; 1 Cor 10:13; 2 Thess 3:3; 1 John 4:4.

CHAPTER TWENTY-TWO
PREDESTINATION

The last several chapters have dealt with the subject of personal (individual) salvation, i.e., the *way* of salvation: grace; the *content* of salvation: justification, regeneration, and sanctification; the *conditions* for salvation: faith, repentance, confession, and baptism; and *assurance* of salvation. This chapter deals with a final topic related to personal salvation, namely, predestination.[1] The term "predestination" refers to God's prior decision to perform a particular act or fulfill a certain purpose, or his prior determination to cause something to come to pass.

God's predetermining activity is not limited to matters of salvation; it also includes other aspects of his eternal purposes.[2] As applied to persons God has not only predestined some to *salvation*; but has also predestined some to roles of *service* whereby he uses them as instruments to carry out his purposes as related to salvation. Discerning the difference between the two is crucial for a proper understanding of what it means to say that God has predestined some to salvation.

Concerning terminology, the Greek verb "to predestine" occurs six times in the NT (Acts 4:28; Rom 8:29,30; 1 Cor 2:7; Eph 1:5,11). The word is *proorizo*, a combination of *horizo*, "to determine," and *pro*, "before." The literal meaning thus is "to determine beforehand, to predetermine, to foreordain." The English word "predestine" suggests the nuance "to predetermine the destiny of." In reference to salvation the prefix *pro* indicates that the determination in view took place before the world was created (see Eph 1:4; Rev 17:8).

When used of persons with reference to salvation, the concept of predestination is closely related to that of election. *Eklegomai*, the common word meaning "to choose," sometimes refers to God's predestining activity (e.g., Mark 13:20; Luke 9:35; Eph 1:4). Related words are the noun *ekloge*, meaning "election, the elect, the chosen" (e.g., Rom 9:11; 11:5,7,28), and the adjective *eklektos*, meaning "elect, chosen" (e.g., Matt 24:22,24,31; Rom 8:33; 1 Pet 1:1). In reference to persons there is no significant difference between predestination and election (*GRu*, 331).

I. THE GOAL OF PREDESTINATION

To understand predestination we must first inquire as to its purpose or goal, i.e., predestined *to what*? What specific *destiny* are some people predetermined to fulfill? While our main concern is to see how predestination relates to salvation, it is necessary first to see that God has predestined some to specific roles of service.

A. Predestination to Service

Among those predestined to fill specific roles in the accomplishment of redemption, the primary character is the Redeemer himself, Jesus of Nazareth. The election of Jesus is the central and primary act of predestination. In Isa 42:1 the LORD speaks of Jesus as the elect one: "Behold, My Servant, whom I uphold; My chosen one in whom My soul delights." Matthew 12:18 quotes this passage and refers it to Jesus. At the transfiguration God announced the election of Jesus in these words: "This is My Son, My Chosen One; listen to Him!" (Luke 9:35). See 1 Pet 2:4,6.

The election of Jesus was part of the divine plan even in eternity, before the worlds were created. Foreknowing both the obedience of the Redeemer and the disobedience of his enemies, God predetermined the accomplishment of redemption through Jesus of Nazareth (Acts 2:23; 1 Pet 1:20). Jesus was foreordained to die for the sins of the world (Acts 4:28).

At times other individuals were chosen for special roles in order to facilitate God's purposes. To create the nation of Israel God chose Abraham, Isaac, and Jacob (Neh 9:7; Rom 9:7-13; see Cottrell, *Romans*, 2:73-97). He chose Moses (Ps 106:23) and David (Ps 78:70; 139:16) among others. He even chose certain Gentile rulers to help carry out his purpose for Israel, e.g., Pharaoh (Rom 9:17; see Cottrell, *Romans*, 2:97-106) and Cyrus (Isa 45:1).

As instruments for establishing the church another group of individuals were chosen, namely, the apostles. From among his disciples Jesus "chose twelve of them, whom He also named as apostles" (Luke 6:13). Later he asked them, "Did I Myself not choose you, the twelve?" (John 6:70). Christ says to the apostles, "You did not choose Me, but I chose you, and appointed you, that you would go and bear fruit" (John 15:16; see 13:18; 15:19). Likewise was the Apostle Paul chosen for special service (Gal 1:15-16).

That such election was for service and not salvation is seen from the fact that even Judas is among the chosen twelve (Luke 6:13; John 6:70), though his predetermined role was that of the betrayer of Jesus (John 6:71). God did not *cause* Judas to fulfill this role, but rather *foreknew* what he would do as an apostle (Acts 2:23). In other words, Judas did not betray Jesus because he was chosen to do so; he was chosen because God foreknew that he would betray Jesus.

One of the most important of God's acts of predestination for service applies not to an individual but to a group, namely, the nation of Israel: "For you are a holy people to the LORD your God; the LORD your God has chosen you to be a people for His own possession out of all the peoples who are on the face of the earth" (Deut 7:6; see Deut 14:2; 1 Chr 16:13; Acts 13:17). This election of Israel was the election of the nation in general, not the election of individuals as such. The nation was chosen specifically to prepare the way for the coming Messiah.

This purpose was served through God's dealings with the nation as a whole, not necessarily through every individual member of the nation. Also, this corporate election for service had no necessary connection with the salvation of any particular Israelite. The nation could serve its purpose of preparing for the Messiah even if the majority of individual Jews were lost.

The Bible's main teaching on Israel's election for service is Romans 9. Some wrongly teach that this difficult chapter deals with "the predestination of individuals to their respective eternal destinies" (Piper, 218). Unfortunately this misses the entire point of the chapter, which in regard to predestination is to defend God's sovereign right to unconditionally choose either individuals or groups for roles of service without being bound to guarantee their salvation. By establishing this point Paul thus defends the faithfulness of God in his dealings with Israel. That is, he shows how God could elect them for service and reject them for salvation at the same time (see Cottrell, *Romans*, 2:23-141).

Since Israel was chosen specifically to prepare the way for the Messiah's appearance, her purpose was accomplished and her destiny fulfilled in the incarnation, death, and resurrection of Jesus (Acts 13:32-33; Rom 9:3-5). Thus the nation of Israel is no longer God's elect people. In the New Covenant age God has a new elect body, a new Israel, the church. While not strictly parallel to OT Israel, in this age the church as a body is now God's chosen people (1 Pet 2:9); and this election is in part an election to service. When Peter describes the church as a "chosen race," he adds this purpose for the choosing: "that you may proclaim the excellencies of Him who has called you out of darkness into His marvelous light" (1 Pet 2:9). Thus in terms of service, whereas Israel was elected for preparation, the church is elected for proclamation.

B. Predestination to Salvation

When most people hear the word "predestination," they think not of service but of salvation. The question is, are certain individuals predestined to be saved, and others to be lost? If so, in what way? Such questions as these have long been the center of confusion and controversy. Since the Reformation era no biblical doctrine has been more misrepresented and more maligned than the doctrine of predestination (or election). Many people do not consider the idea to be biblical at all. This is because they have equated it in their minds with a particular interpretation of predestination, namely, the determinist view developed by Augustine and popularized by John Calvin. Recognizing Calvinist predestination as alien to the Bible, they dismiss the doctrine or explain it away altogether.

This is extremely unfortunate since the doctrine of predestination is definitely scriptural; and when rightly understood it is one of the most significant and rewarding teachings of the Bible. It enhances the majesty, wisdom, love, and faithfulness of God; and it strengthens the heart of the believer. The whole counsel of God is not proclaimed when this doctrine is ignored.

It is important to understand exactly what followers of Augustine and Calvin mean when they say that some are predestined to salvation. According to Calvinists, before the world was ever created, God not only predestined certain specific individuals to be in heaven for eternity; he also predestined that these individuals, and these alone, would at a specific appointed time in their lives become believers in God's saving promises through Jesus Christ. In other words, they are predestined not just to salvation, but to faith itself; not just to heaven as the *end* or goal of salvation, but also to faith and repentance as the *means* of salvation.[3] That is, God predestines some sinners to become believers and to remain believers forever. The chosen sinners themselves have no say in their own election.

Some non-Calvinists respond to this view by denying that predestination to salvation applies to individuals as such; they say instead that it applies only to a certain class or group without reference to any particular individuals that may be in that group. Whether one is actually a part of this predestined group is a matter of his own choice. Thus predestination to salvation is corporate, and the body of people who are thus predestined is the church. An example of this view is Robert Shank. Election, he says, is primarily corporate and only secondarily particular (45, 122). Individuals become elect only when they identify with or associate themselves with the elect body (50, 55). As some put it, "God predestines the plan, not the man."

It is true that the NT church as a group is God's "chosen race" (1 Pet 2:9; see Col 3:12), and that when one is added to the church he becomes one of "the elect." But this does not mean that predestination to salvation in no way applies to individuals. Such a view is an overreaction to Calvinism and a distortion of biblical teaching. The fact is that predestination is very much individual or personal.

When the Bible speaks of predestination to salvation, it usually refers to specific persons who are predestined and not to an abstract group or an impersonal plan. In Rom 8:29-30 Paul speaks of *persons* who are not only predestined, but also called, justified, and glorified. In 2 Thess 2:13 he says that "God has chosen you," the Christians of Thessalonica, "for salvation." In Rom 16:13 Rufus is identified as an elect person. In 1 Pet 1:1-2 the apostle greets the elect Christians in several specific geographical areas. Revelation 17:8 implies that specific names have been written in the book of life from the foundation of the world. Who can these be except those whom God has predestined individually to salvation? Their very *names* have been known to God from the beginning. What can this be but individual predestination? "Rejoice that your names are recorded in heaven" (Luke 10:20).

How is it possible that God could determine even before the creation which individuals would be saved, and could even write their names in the book of life? The answer is found in the fact and nature of God's foreknowledge, which according to Scripture is the very basis for predestination (Rom 8:29; 1 Pet 1:1-2)—a point that will be discussed in detail in the next section. That God has foreknowledge means that he sees the future; and he sees it not as a nearsighted man might see vague outlines at a blurry distance, but as someone with perfect vision sees every far-off detail through a powerful telescope. One cannot believe in predestination according to foreknowledge and at the same time deny individual predestination.

We must say, then, that God predestines specific individuals to salvation. Is this the same as Calvinism? Far from it. As mentioned above, Calvinism teaches not just a predestination to salvation, but a predestination to faith itself: God determines which unbelievers will become believers. The biblical teaching is that certain individuals are predestined to *salvation as such*. Which individuals? The ones whom God *foreknows* (Rom 8:29) will become believers of their own free choice. These are the ones whose names he records in the Lamb's book of life and who are predestined to glory. In short, rather than certain God-selected unbelievers being predestined to become believers, all foreknown believers are predestined to enjoy the benefits of salvation.

This is seen in 2 Thess 2:13, where Paul says that "God has chosen you [Thessalonian believers] from the beginning for salvation." In 1 Pet 1:1-2 this salvation is seen to include the double cure: a life of good works and justification by the blood of Jesus ("chosen . . . to obey Jesus Christ and be sprinkled with His blood"). Romans 8:29 states clearly that those whom he foreknew were "predestined to become conformed to the image of His Son, so that He would be the first-born among many brethren." Some mistakenly take this to be a reference to the sinner's spiritual re-creation in the moral image of Jesus, but the context shows it is a reference to our final inheritance, the redeemed and glorified body we will receive at the final resurrection (Rom 8:11,23). "The image of His Son" refers to the fact that our resurrection bodies will be like that of Christ (Phil 3:21; 1 Cor 15:29; 2 Cor 3:18). Thus we as believers are chosen to become God's glorified children (Rom 8:30) with Christ being the "first-born among many brethren" because he was "the first-born from the dead" (Col 1:18; Rev 1:5), i.e., the first to be raised in a gloried body (Acts 13:34; 26:13; Rom 6:9; 1 Cor 15:20).

This is the only sense in which some are predestined to be saved. That is, God predestines believers to go to heaven, just as he predestines unbelievers to go to hell. But he does not predestine anyone to become and remain a believer, or to remain an unbeliever. This is a choice made by each individual, a choice that is foreknown by God.

II. THE BASIS OF PREDESTINATION

That God does predestine some to go to heaven raises a serious question: how does he decide which individuals to save and which not to save? *On what basis* does God predestine or elect certain ones to eternal life? How this question is answered is the real difference between Calvinists and non-Calvinists on this issue. In a word, Calvinists declare that predestination or election is completely *unconditional*, while non-Calvinists say it is *conditional*.

A. Calvinism and Unconditional Election

"Unconditional election" is the second main point (the U) in Calvinism's TULIP system; it follows logically upon the T point, total depravity. Calvinists affirm that every human being since Adam and Eve (except Jesus) is born in a state of original sin, which includes a totally depraved nature. This is a universal bondage of the will, which means that every person is totally unable to respond to the gospel and become a believer by his own unaided choice. The only way anyone will ever be saved is if God himself supernaturally and unilaterally enables sinners to believe, which he does in the act called irresistible grace (the I in TULIP).

According to Calvinism this whole process begins prior to creation when God in one all-encompassing, efficacious decree predestines in detail everything that will ever take place within the created universe. From this vantage point of eternity past, God in his foreknowledge looks out upon the entire future human race in its state of total depravity. Then from among this total mass of sinful humanity, even before it is created, he chooses which individuals he wants to become believers and thus be part of his heavenly family. These "elect" ones he determines to irresistibly and eternally save; the rest (the "reprobate") he determines to leave in their sin and exclude from heaven.

Now comes the crucial question: *on what basis* does God choose whom he will save? What criteria does he use for selecting one rather than another? The answer is: we have no idea. The reasons for his choices (if there are any) are known only to God himself, and he has determined not to reveal them to us (Berkouwer, *Election*, 60). Thus from the standpoint of human knowledge, the election is totally unconditional. God's decision is not contingent upon whether or not anyone will meet certain announced conditions, such as faith and repentance.

John Calvin put it this way, that in his predestining decree "God was moved by no external cause—by no cause out of Himself—in the choice of us; but that He Himself, in Himself, was the cause and the author of choosing His people" ("Treatise," 46). Here is how it is spelled out in the Westminster Confession of Faith III:5 (Schaff, III:609):

> Those of mankind that are predestined unto life, God, before the foundation of the world was laid, according to his eternal and immutable purpose, and the secret counsel and good pleasure of his will, hath chosen in Christ, unto everlasting glory, out of his mere free grace and love, without any foresight of faith or good works, or perseverance in either of them, or any other thing in the creature, as conditions, or causes moving him thereunto; and all to the praise of his glorious grace.

Thus the predestination of individuals to salvation is unconditional.

B. The Bible and Conditional Election

As pointed out in chapter 19, one of the major differences between Calvinism and non-Calvinism as such is that Calvinists say all of God's works, including the bestowing of salvation, are unconditional. This is mandated by the very concept of sovereignty as Calvinists understand it; a sovereign God cannot act in response to anything outside himself. Thus because of both this and total depravity, God cannot predestine anyone to be saved based on whether or not that person is seen as meeting certain conditions, even divinely imposed ones.

But we have already seen that this reasoning is false, since neither this concept of sovereignty nor total depravity is a biblical teaching. Also, we have seen that salvation is indeed conditional: God has promised that he will bestow salvation upon whoever meets certain specific gracious conditions by their own free-will choice. The doctrine of predestination is simply an extension of this point; election too is conditional. The reason God predestines some to go to heaven is that from the vantage point of eternity past God knew in advance who would meet the conditions and who would not. In other words, predestination to eternal life is based on God's foreknowledge of who would and who would not meet the conditions that constitute a proper response to his grace.

Here we come to the crucial point, i.e., the relation between foreknowledge and predestination. "For those whom He foreknew, He also predestined to become conformed to the image of His Son" (Rom 8:29). In his first epistle Peter writes to those "who are chosen according to the foreknowledge of God the Father" (1 Pet 1:1-2). These verses say only that God foreknew certain *persons*; they do not say specifically what he foreknew about them. In view of the Bible's teaching about salvation in general, many assume that God foreknew those who would meet the conditions for salvation.

Actually Rom 8:28 identifies the objects of the foreknowledge mentioned in verse 29. We must not overlook the connection between these two verses, as if verse 29 exists apart from any context. Verse 29 begins (after the conjunction) with the relative pronoun "whom" (or "those"). The antecedent for this pronoun is in verse 28, namely, "those who love God." God foreknew those who would love him, i.e., he foreknew that at some point in their lives they would come to love him and would continue to love him unto the end. See the parallel in 1 Cor 8:3, "But if anyone loves God, he is known by him." This is exactly the same idea as Rom 8:29, the former referring to knowledge and the latter to foreknowledge.

We should also note that Rom 8:29 begins with the causative conjunction *hoti*, "for, because." This most likely goes with "we know" in verse 28. Thus the thought is quite simple: We know that God works all things for the good of those who love him and are called into his eternal family according to his purpose. How do we know this? Because, having foreknown from eternity that they would love him, he has already predestined them to this state of eternal glory! Thus we can be sure that the temporary trials of this life are not able to nullify what the

Almighty God himself has already predestined will occur! Rather, he uses them in ways that prepare us to enjoy eternity even more.

Calvinists reject this simple explanation, of course. At issue, they say, is the meaning of the word "foreknow" (*proginosko*). Since *ginosko* means "to know," and *pro* means "before," it would seem obvious that *proginosko* means "to know beforehand" in the sense of prior cognitive or mental awareness. God certainly has such precognition. Because of his unique relation to time, his knowledge is not limited to the now; he knows the past and the future as well as he knows the present (*GC*, 255-259, 279-289). The verb "foreknow" is used here and in four other places in the NT: Acts 26:5; Rom 11:2; 1 Pet 1:20; 2 Pet 3:17. (The noun is used twice: Acts 2:23; 1 Pet 1:2.) Everyone agrees that in Acts 26:5 and 2 Pet 3:17, where it refers to human foreknowledge, it has this simple meaning of precognition or prescience.

But Calvinists argue that in the passages in which God is the subject, both the verb and the noun have another connotation altogether, namely, *distinguishing love*.[4] Included here are two concepts: loving and choosing. Since the word "know" itself at times is "practically synonymous with 'love,' to set regard upon, to know with peculiar interest, delight, affection, and action," foreknowledge in Rom 8:29 (and 1 Pet 1:1-2) must mean "whom he knew from eternity with distinguishing affection and delight," or "whom he foreloved" (Murray, *Romans*, I:317).

The key word, though, is "distinguishing." For Calvinists God's foreknowledge is an act by which he (unconditionally) *chooses* some people out of the mass of future mankind to be the sole recipients of his saving grace; i.e., foreknowledge is the same as election. As Moo sums it up, "The difference between 'know or love beforehand' and 'choose beforehand' virtually ceases to exist" (533). For Rom 8:29 Arndt and Gingrich (710) give the definition of "choose beforehand." It has the "connotation of electing grace," says Bruce (177).

On what do Calvinists base this peculiar definition of foreknowledge? Mainly upon a few selected biblical uses of the verbs for "to know," in which they find the connotations of "choose" and/or "love." These include the places where "know" is a euphemism for sexual intercourse, plus a few other OT uses of *yada'* (Hebrew for "know"), usually Gen 18:19; Exod 2:25; Jer 1:5; Hos 13:5; and Amos 3:2. Also cited are these NT texts: Matt 7:23; John 10:14; 1 Cor 8:3; 13:12; Gal 4:9; and 2 Tim 2:19. Since "know" in all these passages allegedly means much more than simple cognition, we may conclude that "*fore*know" in Rom 8:29 and elsewhere also means much more, namely, "distinguishing love bestowed beforehand." Thus, "whom He *chose* beforehand, he also predestined."

How may we respond to this? By a thorough study of the way the Bible uses the words for "know" and "foreknow." The details of such a project are outside the scope of this volume, but we may offer a summary analysis.

First, noncognitive connotations for *ginosko* are virtually nonexistent in secular Greek. Moo admits that the Calvinist definition of foreknowledge sounds "somewhat strange against the background of broad Greek usage" (532).

Second, the use of "know" as a euphemism for sexual relations contributes nothing toward this Calvinist view, since it refers specifically to the sexual act and not to any love that might be associated with it. Also, the act of sexual "knowing" in no way includes the connotation of choosing, but rather presupposes that a distinguishing choice has already been made (via marriage). Finally, the use of "know" for this act is much closer to cognition than either loving or choosing; it connotes cognitive knowing at the most intimate level.

Third, biblical texts where "know" and "foreknow" seem to have a connotation of love or affection (e.g., Exod 2:25; Hos 13:5) prove nothing, because they usually do not specify the *reason* for God's love-knowledge, and they certainly do not suggest that it was unconditional. In fact, 1 Cor 8:3 seems to say it is conditional: "The man who loves God is known by God."

Fourth, an analysis of the NT texts where the words for "know" have persons as their objects, i.e., where the action of knowing is specifically directed toward persons and not facts as such, shows that in such cases these words never have the connotation of "choosing" or "imposing a distinction." This applies to *ginosko* (used c. 52 times in this way), *epiginosko* (c. 15 times), and *oida* (c. 43 times).

Such an analysis yields very helpful insights into the meaning of God's foreknowledge. In order of increasing specificity, the three basic connotations of "know a person" are as follows. (1) *Recognition.* In this case "to know" means to recognize someone, to know who he is, to know his identity or his true identity, to be able to identify him for who he is, to be acquainted with him, to be familiar with him, to understand him, to know his true nature. This is by far the most common connotation.[5] It is a purely cognitive act. It does not impose an identity upon someone, but perceives that identity. This includes the idea of recognizing someone as belonging to a particular group, as distinct from those who do not. This is the sense in which Jesus "knows" his sheep (John 10:14,27), even as his sheep know him (John 10:14; see 2 Tim 2:19). This is the connotation of "know" that applies to "foreknow" in Rom 8:29 and 1 Pet 1:1-2.

(2) *Acknowledgment.* Here "to know" means not only to have a cognitive knowledge of someone's identity, but also to admit or acknowledge that identity. As such it is an act of will, though it presupposes an act of cognition. The most important thing is that this acknowledging does not impose a particular identity upon anyone, but simply confesses it.[6]

(3) *Experience.* The third and most intense connotation of "to know" when a person or persons are its object is to know experientially, to experience a relationship with someone. Again, it presupposes cognition but goes beyond it. Most significantly, such knowing is not an act that initiates a relationship but simply experiences it. This connotation is found especially in 1 John.[7] Matthew 7:23; 1 Cor 8:3; and Heb 8:11 could be either (1) or (3).

In each case the act of knowing does not create a person's identity or his distinction from other people. It rather presupposes an already existing identity or distinction; the act of knowing perceives and in some cases acknowledges that identity or distinction. These connotations for knowing fit the term "foreknowledge" very well as it is used in Rom 8:29 and elsewhere. Those whom God from the beginning recognized and acknowledged as his own, he predestined to be members of his glorified family in heaven. (The connotation of experiencing a relationship does not transfer well to the concept of *fore*knowledge, since foreknowledge as such precedes the existence of its object, precluding an experienced relationship.)

In any case, an analysis of *all* the uses of "know" with persons as the object undermines the notion that it means "choose" and thus does not support the Calvinist idea that foreknowledge is the same as election or choosing beforehand.

Fifth, the various NT uses of "foreknow" and the two uses of "foreknowledge" do not comfortably bear the connotations of "forelove" and "choose beforehand." Acts 26:5 and 2 Pet 3:17 do not refer to God's foreknowledge, but they clearly refer to precognition. Romans 11:2 refers to God's foreknowledge of Israel as a nation and not to any individuals within it. The context suggests that Paul is referring to God's precognition of Israel's rebellion and idolatry. Despite the fact that he foreknew all of this (see Rom 9:22,27-29; 10:16-21), it was never his plan to reject his people altogether.

In 1 Pet 1:20 Christ is the one foreknown from the foundation of the world; and in the context precognition, not choosing, is the preferred meaning. The contrast is between the hidden and the revealed. Even though the Father knew from the foundation of the world that Christ the Son would be our Redeemer, he did not reveal it until the last days.

The use of the noun "foreknowledge" in 1 Pet 1:1-2 is consistent with the non-Calvinist understanding of "foreknow." This text says that the chosen (are chosen) according to the foreknowledge of God the Father. Thus a clear distinction is made between foreknowledge and choosing, and there is no reason to see in foreknowledge anything other than its basic meaning of precognition. Thus the relationship between foreknowledge and election here is exactly the same as that between foreknowledge and predestination in Rom 8:29.

Acts 2:23 also refers to the foreknowledge of God the Father; its object is Jesus Christ and the circumstances of his death. Jesus was delivered up "by the predetermined plan and foreknowledge of God." "Predetermined plan" is equivalent to predestination; i.e., God had already determined from eternity that Christ would die for our sins. That he was delivered up "by foreknowledge" means that God foreknew all the human acts of participation in Christ's betrayal and death, such as those of Judas and Herod. God did not predetermine these acts, but he knew them in advance and therefore could work his plan along with them and through them.

Sometimes Calvinist exegetes try to equate the foreknowledge and predetermined plan in Acts 2:23 by invoking a rule of Greek grammar. Here is how MacArthur (I:496) argues:

According to what Greek scholars refer to as Granville Sharp's rule, if two nouns of the same case (in this instance, "plan" and "foreknowledge") are connected by *kai* ("and") and have the definite article (the) before the first noun but not before the second, the nouns refer to the same thing . . . . In other words, Peter equates God's predetermined plan, or foreordination, and his foreknowledge.

Wuest (143-144) puts it almost exactly the same way, that in such a case the second noun "refers to the same thing" as the first; therefore Acts 2:23 shows that predestination and foreknowledge "refer to the same thing."

This argument, however, is seriously flawed. Both MacArthur and Wuest misquote Sharp's rule. The rule does not say that the two nouns in the construction described above "refer to the same thing." It says only that in such a case the second noun "always relates to the same person that is expressed or described in the first noun." There is a huge difference between *relating* to the same person (or thing) and *referring* to the same person (or thing). Carson says it is an exegetical fallacy to assume that the latter or strict form of Sharp's rule has universal validity. He says, "If one article governs two substantives joined by *kai*, it does not necessarily follow that the two substantives refer to the same thing, but only that the two substantives are grouped together to function in some respects as a single entity" (84-85). Also, Sharp states his rule as applying only to persons, not to things. As one Greek scholar says, "Non-personal nouns disqualify the construction"; he cites Acts 2:23 as a specific example of this (R. Young, *Greek*, 62).

In conclusion, the preponderance of evidence shows that "foreknowledge" is not equivalent to election or choosing, and that in Rom 8:29 and 1 Pet 1:1-2 it refers to nothing more than the cognitive act by which God knew or identified the members of his family (as distinct from all others) even before the foundation of the world. He identified them by the fact that they were (would be) the ones who met (would meet) the required conditions for salvation. Knowing through his divine omniscience who these individuals would be, even at that point he predestined them to be part of his glorified heavenly family through resurrection from the dead after the pattern established by the firstborn brother, Jesus Christ.

In summary, the Bible teaches that God predestines or chooses by name certain individuals to eternal salvation, but he does so only on the basis of his foreknowledge or precognition that these individuals will meet the conditions for salvation as set forth in his Word.

NOTES ON CHAPTER TWENTY-TWO

[1]For more on this subject see *GRu*, ch. 9, "Predestination" (pp. 331-352); and my *Romans*, 1:502-514; 2:23-141.

[2]While God's purposive will deals mainly with matters of salvation (*GRu*, 304-310), it also includes a predetermination (based on foreknowledge) to answer specific prayers in specific ways (*GRu*, 367-371).

[3]Some also believe that the rest are predestined to remain unbelieving sinners all their lives and thus to be condemned to eternal hell. This is the doctrine of reprobation.

[4]*Proginosko* "is not the foresight of difference but the foreknowledge that makes difference exist . . . . It is sovereign distinguishing love" (Murray, *Romans*, I:318).

[5]"Know" with a person or persons as its object occurs in this sense at least 80 times. A few examples are Matt 11:27; 14:30; 17:12; 26:72,74; Luke 7:39; 10:22; 13:25,27; 24:16,31; John 1:10,26,31,33,48; 7:27-28; 14:7,9,17; Acts 7:18; Rom 1:21; 1 Cor 13:12; Heb 10:30; 1 John 4:2,6.

[6]A few examples of this connotation are Mark 1:24,34; Acts 19:15; 1 Cor 1:21; 16:12; 1 Thess 5:12. (This is almost all of them.)

[7]Examples are John 17:3; Phil 3:10; 2 Tim 1:12; Titus 1:16; 1 John 2:3,4,13,14.

CHAPTER TWENTY-THREE
THE CHURCH: ITS NATURE

The last several chapters have dealt with the doctrine of salvation from the perspective of the individual. But salvation is not a solitary experience; it is a shared experience, a shared reality. Whoever makes the transition from the lost to the saved condition immediately enters a state of union not only with Christ but also with all others who are already united with him. This corporate or collective aspect of salvation is what *the church* is all about. It is true that each sinner who receives the double cure of God's saving grace becomes "a new creature" (2 Cor 5:17); but in the broader perspective the church as a whole is God's new creation: "The Church's one Foundation is Jesus Christ her Lord; she is His new creation, by water and the word."

In this chapter our task is to set forth the *nature* of the church. We will see how the Bible pictures the church as a holy nation, the people of God, the body of Christ, and the new Israel.

I. THE CHURCH IS A HOLY NATION

The first thing to understand about the church's nature is that it is a group of people who are qualitatively different from and distinct from everyone else on earth. It is composed of those who have been separated from the mass of fallen mankind and who constitute the new creation as it presently exists in the very midst of the old creation. Thus the human race is divided into two groups: the church, and the not-church.

This aspect of the church's nature is emphasized in the image of the church as a *holy nation* (1 Pet 2:9). This concept was applied first to the literal nation of Israel when God called them out of Egypt and entered into a special covenant relationship with them. At Mount Sinai he told them, "You shall be to Me . . . a holy nation" (Exod 19:6). We have already seen that the biblical words for "holy" most likely have to do with *separation*. The verbs mean "to cut, to separate, to divide"; the adjectives mean "separated, set apart." This is exactly what God was doing with Israel at Sinai by making them holy: he was separating them from every other nation on earth and putting them in a category by themselves.

The root of this principle of separation is found in the Edenic distinction between the serpent's seed and the woman's seed (Gen 3:15) and in the post-Adamic distinction between "the sons of God" and "the daughters of men" (Gen 6:2).

This culminated in the separation of Noah and his family from the rest of the human race (Gen 6:7-8). The prelude to Israel's isolation from all other nations was the special relationship into which God entered with Abraham and his descendants through Isaac and Jacob (Gen 12:1-3; 26:23-24; 28:13-15; Rom 9:6-13). Even before Sinai God had made a division between Jacob's descendants and the people of Egypt, protecting the former from the plagues (Exod 8:22-23). Then at Sinai he formalized this separation through the distinguishing words, "You shall be My own possession among all the peoples, for all the earth is Mine; and you shall be to Me a kingdom of priests and a holy nation" (Exod 19:5-6). By virtue of this unique relationship with God, Israel was "distinguished from all other people who are upon the face of the earth" (Exod 33:16; see Lev 20:24-26; Num 23:9).

In a similar but by no means identical way, in the NT era the *church* is God's "holy nation" (1 Pet 2:9), the "people who dwells apart" (Num 23:9). The church is not a literal nation in the sense that Israel was, i.e., a political entity occupying a specific geographical locality. Nor does one enter its roll of citizens by physical birth. Rather, the church is a spiritual nation entered by spiritual rebirth, its citizens coexisting in this world side-by-side with noncitizens and being distinguished by their lifestyle rather than their location. Whereas OT Israel sought purity through (geographical) separation, the church seeks separation through purity.

The nature of the church as a holy, separated nation is seen in two Greek words that are used to describe it. One is *ekklesia*, the word most often (nearly 110 times) translated "church" (hence "ecclesiology," the doctrine of the church). Its basic meaning is "assembly," an assembly of people as such (as in Acts 19:32,39,41). In the LXX (Greek OT) it is used around 80 times for the community of Israel as a whole, which explains why it is used twice in the NT for Israel (Acts 7:38; Heb 2:12). The word is a combination of *kaleo*, "to call," and *ek*, "out of, from." Thus its literal meaning is "the called-out ones."

In the NT Christians are frequently identified as those who have been "called."[1] Called—by whom? By God himself (Rom 8:30; 9:24; 1 Cor 1:9; 1 Thess 2:12; 2 Thess 2:14; 1 Pet 1:15; 2:9; 5:10; 2 Pet 1:3). Called out—from where? From the old creation, the world as it exists under the curse of sin and darkness (Col 1:13; 1 Pet 2:9), from the mass of unbelieving Jews and Gentiles alike (Rom 9:24). Called—by what? Not by some secret, selective, irresistible call heard only by "the elect," but through the gospel of grace (Gal 1:6; 2 Thess 2:14), which is the power of God unto salvation (Rom 1:16). The *ekklesia*, the church, is the collective group of people who have answered this gospel call.

What exactly does the gospel call invite us to do? It invites us to "come out" from the world in general and to live a holy, pure, and separated life (1 Thess 4:7; 2 Tim 1:9; 1 Pet 1:15; see Eph 4:1). As Paul puts it, we are "called to be saints" (Rom 1:7, NIV; see 1 Cor 1:2). We are "the camp of the saints" (Rev 20:9). Here is the second Greek word that characterizes the nature of the church as a holy, separated nation: *hagioi*, translated "saints." This word basically means "holy ones," i.e., the ones who have been separated or set apart into a special relationship with God. It is used in the NT to describe the body of believers as a whole, not just a select few of the spiritually elite. It refers to the church as a "holy nation," the *ekklesia* that has been called and set apart from everyone else.

II. THE CHURCH IS THE PEOPLE OF GOD

In Peter's words, the church is "a people belonging to God. . . . Once you were not a people, but now you are the people of God" (1 Pet 2:9-10, NIV). This way of describing the church is basic, because it reflects God's original purpose for creation as such. In the beginning God created the human race in his own image in order to have personal fellowship with them in a relationship of intimate love and communion, as he did originally with Adam and Eve in Eden. This purpose was interrupted by sin, which places a barrier between God and man (Isa 59:2). But God was determined to have a people of his own anyway—if not by creation, then by *new* creation (i.e., redemption). Thus, even though the whole human race is God's people in the sense that he is their Creator and Lord, only those who have been called out from the mass of mankind into the church are the people of God in the sense that he originally intended.

God made a step in this direction when he called Abraham out of Haran (Gen 12:1-4) and later a major step when he called the Israelite nation out of Egyptian bondage. He made this promise to Israel: "Then I will take you for My people, and I will be your God" (Exod 6:7). At Sinai he told them, "If you will indeed obey My voice and keep My covenant, then you shall be My own possession among all the peoples" (Exod 19:5). Later he said, "I will also walk among you and be your God, and you shall be My people" (Lev 26:12). See Deut 29:10-13; Jer 30:22; Ezek 11:20; Zech 8:8; 13:9.

Even in the Old Covenant era God was looking ahead to the time when the church, under a new covenant, would be his people in the most intimate of senses (Jer 31:31-34; Zech 2:10-12). In the NT this language is applied to the church: "'I will live with them and walk among them, and I will be their God, and they will be my people'" (2 Cor 6:16, NIV; see Heb 8:10). Even this is but a prelude to the more intimate fellowship of heaven (Rev 21:1-3).

In 1 Pet 2:9 the church is called God's own *peripoiesis*, which literally means "possession, property." The church belongs to God; he owns it. The first image this conjures up is that of the church as *slaves* of God. It is certainly true that we are God's slaves in the sense that he has bought us (1 Cor 6:19-20) and that we owe him our absolute obedience (Rom 6:22; Titus 1:1; 1 Pet 2:16). However, the idea that the church is God's own possession more properly suggests the image of a *family* or household.[2] Paul says, "So then you are no longer strangers and aliens, but you are fellow citizens with the saints, and are of God's household" (Eph 2:19; see Gal 6:10). We occupy neither the slave quarters nor the guest room; we *belong* to God's own family (Rom 8:14-17).

Family relationships form the deepest level of the church's life. God as Father is the head of the family, and every member of the church is his adopted child (2 Cor 6:18). As his children we have the privilege of calling him "Abba!" (Rom 8:15; Gal 4:6-7), an Aramaic word "derived from baby-language" (cf. "Daddy!") and used by adults in the "warm, familiar" sense of "dear father" (Hofius, I:614). In this context Jesus is pictured as the elder brother who shares his inheritance with us (Rom 8:17,29; Heb 2:10-18). The relationship of Christians to one another is that of brothers and sisters; the church is thus a "brotherhood" (1 Pet 2:17).

Because the church is a separated brotherhood, the distinct people and family of God, those who are a part of this family have two major responsibilities. First, Christians must constantly display the distinguishing mark of the church family, which is *love* (John 13:34-35). Of course, we are to show this love toward all people, even our enemies (Matt 5:43-48). But our responsibility toward fellow Christians goes deeper than this. As God's people we must not limit our love for one another to the general *agape* love we owe to everyone; rather, in addition to *agape* we must exhibit family love, a brotherly love, toward one another. Paul commands us to "be devoted to one another in brotherly love" (Rom 12:10). Here he uses words compounded from two other Greek words for love, *philia* and *storge*. The former is used for the affectionate love between friends; the latter, the tender affection among family members. Peter exhorts us to "love [*agapao*] the brotherhood" (1 Pet 2:17), and he tells us specifically to "love as brothers" (*philadelphos*, 1 Pet 3:8, NIV). Hebrews 13:1 (NIV) says, "Keep on loving each other as brothers" (*philadelphia*). The bottom line is that we as God's family must have feelings toward one another that are different from our feelings toward unbelievers.

This leads to the second responsibility we have as a family of believers, namely, we can have *fellowship* only with other members of the household, only with other Christians. We cannot have fellowship—intimate, sharing relationships—with unbelievers. Paul forbids it as being against the very nature of our respective spiritual conditions: "Do not be bound together with unbelievers; for what partnership have righteousness and lawlessness, or what fellowship has light with darkness? Or what harmony has Christ with Belial, or what has a believer in common with an unbeliever?" (2 Cor 6:14-15). This is why God says, "Come out from them and be separate" (2 Cor 6:17, NIV). Fellowship involves a sharing of something in common, but believers and unbelievers at the deepest level have nothing in common. This does not mean that Christians must break off all associations with unbelievers—far from it! It does mean, though, that such associations must have the character of *redemptive friendship* rather than intimate, family fellowship. The latter must be experienced only within the family of God's people.

III. THE CHURCH IS THE BODY OF CHRIST

The church as *the body of Christ* is the third image that sets forth its nature or essence. Christ "is also head of the body, the church" (Col 1:18). The picture this image is intended to convey is that of a human body in all its parts, with the head representing Jesus Christ and the rest of the body from neck to toes representing the church. This head-to-body relationship has three main implications.

First, that the church is the body of Christ means that it is in a relationship of *submission* to Christ, who is its *head* in the sense of "leader, one in authority."[3] This headship-submission relation between Christ and the church is clearly affirmed when Paul says that "Christ also is the head of the church" and "the church is subject to Christ" (Eph 5:23-24). Also, "He put all things in subjection under His feet, and gave Him as head over all things to the church, which is His body" (Eph 1:22-23).

This means that Jesus and Jesus alone is the final authority for all things relating to the church. He exercises this authority through his apostles and prophets (Eph 2:19-20), whose teaching comes to us in the form of the NT Scriptures. Since these writings are in effect the very words of Christ our head (John 16:12-15), they possess the absolute authority of Christ himself. Thus the church is submitted to Christ as its head only to the degree that it is obedient to his Word.

Second, that the church is the body of Christ means that it is the *instrument* through which Christ the head fulfills his *mission* upon the earth. His mission was "to seek and to save that which was lost" (Luke 19:10), to draw all men to himself (John 12:32), and to bring them abundant life (John 10:10) through the power of his death and resurrection. But just as in the human body the plans and purposes devised by the head (the mind) can be carried out only by the other bodily members (e.g., feet and hands), so also the mission of Christ the head can be accomplished only as the members of his body, the church, obey his orders, as in Matt 28:18-20, Acts 1:8, and Rom 10:14-15. "Now you are Christ's body, and individually members of it" (1 Cor 12:27). As we members of the body exercise our Spirit-given talents, the head is carrying out his own purposes through us.

Third, that the church is the body of Christ means that it receives its sustenance and life through Christ the head. Ordinarily in the human body all the food and liquids that nourish and sustain it enter into it through the mouth, which is part of the head. Likewise the church maintains its own life and strength and continues to grow only when it remains in close union and fellowship with Christ its head. We must ever be "holding fast to the head, from whom the entire body . . . grows with a growth which is from God" (Col 2:19; see Eph 4:15-16). The same idea is found in the image of Christ as the vine and individual Christians as branches attached to him (John 15:1-6). Our union with Christ our head is the means by which all the benefits of life and salvation are transferred to us.

IV. THE CHURCH IS THE NEW ISRAEL

The fourth and final thing to understand about the nature of the church is that it is God's *new Israel*, "the Israel of God" in this New Covenant age (Gal 6:16). In explaining this concept we must take account of both the church's continuity and its discontinuity with the Israel of the Old Covenant.

A. The Church's Discontinuity with Israel

It is true that the nation of Israel was the people of God under the Old Covenant, and the church is the people of God under the New Covenant. But the latter is not, indeed cannot be, a simple continuation of the former. This is the case for the simple reason that OT Israel was *before* Christ, and the church is *after* Christ. In a real sense the coming of Christ was a turning point in history that necessitated a change in many aspects of the life of the people of God.

The basic factor in this discontinuity is found in the fundamental purpose for which God chose the original Israel in the first place. The key word is *preparation*. Israel's main (if not sole) reason for her special relation to God was to prepare the way for the first coming of the Christ, the Savior of the world. God chose this nation as a farmer chooses a field for a crop, and he dealt with this nation as a farmer plows and works his field in preparing to sow his seed.

Thus Israel became the context for three elements essential for setting the stage for the coming Messiah. First, Israel was the recipient of the *special divine revelation* through which God explained his purposes and prophesied the Messiah's advent. Focusing this revelation upon a single nation allowed an interconnected canon of sacred literature to be collected (Rom 3:2). Second, this ever-increasing body of revelation was the source of an ever-growing *messianic hope*. The prophecies of Christ's coming kindled within this people a strong expectation and desire; hence when Christ came he was received with some degree of understanding and acceptance. Third, by separating this one nation from all the rest and by giving them the special revelation of his law, God was ensuring that the Messiah would come into a context of relative moral and religious *purity*, in contrast with the idolatry and wickedness of the rest of the world.

Because of her unique role as the means by which God was preparing for the coming of Christ, almost every aspect of the Old Covenant kingdom administration under which Israel lived was specifically designed to enable her to accomplish this purpose. Israel's worship practices, the circumstances of her history, and even her very existence were pointing ahead to a particular event. When this event finally came, all the purposes underlying her special calling and existence were fulfilled, including every aspect of the Old Covenant itself. The special role for Jerusalem, the temple, the sacrificial system, and the levitical priesthood reached its end, both in terms of objective and conclusion.

Because the church as the new Israel exists *after* the first coming of Christ, her covenantal relationship with God and her kingdom administration cannot be the same as that of OT Israel. For example, whereas OT worship (such as the sin offerings) in a veiled way pointed forward to Christ and was fulfilled in him, NT worship (e.g., the Lord's Supper) in an explicit way looks back to and proclaims his already accomplished saving work. The church's role is thus summed up not in the word *preparation*, but in the word *proclamation*. That is, the church exists to proclaim that the Messiah has already come (1 Pet 2:9) and to invite the world to participate in all the blessings of salvation he has provided. This change in covenant administration was announced even in OT times (Jer 31:31-34), and thus the discontinuity between Israel and the church was natural and expected (see Heb 8:7-13; 10:16; Luke 22:20; 1 Cor 11:25).

Another element in the discontinuity between Israel and the church is the contrast between Israel's *exclusivity* or particularity, and the church's *inclusiveness*. God chose Israel as a specific political nation and ordered them to occupy a particular geographical area. This was a necessary condition for their role of preparing for the coming of Christ. But this exclusiveness was only a temporary expedient; it was not intended to be the permanent nature of the people of God. From the beginning God planned that his New Covenant people—the church—would be inclusive, embracing within its borders both Jews *and* Gentiles, indeed, "all the families of the earth" (Gen 12:3; see Gal 3:8,14).

This transition from exclusiveness (Jews only) to inclusiveness (Jews plus Gentiles) was foretold in a general way in the OT itself (see Ps 2:7-8; 145:21). Isaiah 2:2 says that in the Messianic age "the mountain of the house of the LORD will be established . . . and all the nations will stream to it" (see vv. 3-4).[4] In that age "I will pour out My Spirit on all mankind," says the Lord (Joel 2:28). Amos 9:11-12 prophesies the inclusion of the Gentiles, says Acts 15:13-18.

Just as the book of Hebrews clearly teaches that the Old Covenant has been replaced by "a better covenant" (7:22) with "better promises" (8:6) and "better sacrifices" (9:23), so does the book of Ephesians celebrate the transition from the exclusivity of Israel to the inclusiveness of the church (2:11–3:12). The Gentiles are no longer "excluded from the commonwealth of Israel," says Paul, but "have been brought near by the blood of Christ," who "made both groups into one" (2:12-14). This is indeed the great mystery not made clear in OT times, "that the Gentiles are fellow heirs and fellow members of the body" (3:6). This fact is now "made known through the church" (3:10). The olive tree is no longer the same, says Paul in Rom 11:17-24; it contains not only natural branches (believing Jews) but also grafted-in branches (believing Gentiles). See Rom 10:12; Gal 3:26-28; Col 3:10-11.

Israel and the church differ in their *purpose* (preparation vs. proclamation) and in their *scope* (exclusive vs. inclusive). Most significantly, they differ in their very *essence*: whereas OT Israel was basically a physical entity, the church or the new Israel is a spiritual entity (see *GRu*, 143-153).

Though God's dealings with OT Israel certainly involved spiritual blessings and spiritual purposes, the people with whom the covenant was made was a physical nation; and God's interactions with them were mainly on the level of the physical. This is demonstrated by the fact that membership in the covenant people was a matter of physical birth and lineage, regardless of one's spiritual character. Also, the Old Covenant bestowed many material blessings upon the nation of Israel, including the geographical land of Canaan. Worship was centralized in a material temple located in the earthly city of Jerusalem. The enemies whom God used against Israel or from whom he delivered them were physical nations such as the Philistines and the Babylonians.

The New Israel, on the other hand, is a spiritually defined people with whom God deals on a spiritual level. One enters it not by physical birth but by spiritual rebirth (John 1:12-13; 3:3,5; 1 Pet 1:3,23), and its members are "enrolled in heaven" (Heb 12:23). Worship is not limited to nor dependent upon any specific physical location (John 4:22-24). The church is a spiritual temple, and its sacrifices are spiritual (1 Pet 2:5); our Jerusalem is "the Jerusalem above" (Gal 4:26), "the heavenly Jerusalem" (Heb 12:22), not the visible, earthly city. Our enemies are not flesh and blood (Eph 6:12) and our protection and deliverance are from spiritual evil (Matt 6:13; 2 Tim 4:18). The "health and wealth" God guarantees the new Israel are spiritual, not physical. As Paul sums this up, "We are the true circumcision, who worship in the Spirit of God and glory in Christ Jesus and put no confidence in the flesh" (Phil 3:3).

The bottom line is that OT Israel and the NT church are not one continuous people of God. The church is the new Israel, but it is different in many ways from the Israelite nation of old. The new Israel is under a new covenant (Jer 31:31-34; Luke 22:20), is entered a new way (spiritually, not physically), worships in new ways, has a new (Trinitarian) understanding of God, and has a new hope (Christ's *second* coming, not his first). Also, the new Israel has a clear beginning point: the Day of Pentecost, as recorded in Acts 2, when a new Jerusalem and a new Zion were born in the midst of the old.

B. The Church's Continuity with Israel

When God set the Israelites apart from all other nations (Exod 19:5-6), he wanted every one of them to be his people not just on a physical level but on a spiritual level also. His plan and desire were that they would all serve him from the heart, and that when the Messiah came they would all embrace him in joyous faith. Thus his plan from the beginning was never to exclude Israel from his New Covenant people by *replacing* them with the Gentiles, but rather simply to *add* the Gentiles to the Jews. The gospel was always meant to be offered "to the Jew first and also to the Greek" (Rom 1:16). In Paul's olive-tree illustration OT Israel is the root and trunk—i.e., the very basis—of the NT church (Rom 11:17-18).

Thus despite the differences in purpose, scope, and essence that necessitated a change in kingdom administration under the New Covenant, there is a continuity between OT Israel and the new Israel, the church. This continuity is best understood in terms of Paul's statement in Rom 9:6-7, that "they are not all Israel who are descended from Israel; nor are they all children because they are Abraham's descendants." In other words, some Jews chose to remain Jews on a physical level only, especially those who refused to accept Jesus as their Messiah when he came. But other Jews chose to relate to God also on the level of the spirit, especially those who believed in Jesus. The former are the ones broken off from the olive tree (Rom 11:20) when it became the church; the latter are the ones who became the core of the new Israel. Even in OT times this latter group was the "Israel within Israel," sometimes called the "remnant";[5] these are the ones with whom the new Israel is in direct continuity.

What is the inner ground of this continuity between remnant Israel in the OT and the new Israel? It is the unity of God's way of salvation that has existed and been applied in all ages, namely, that sinners are justified by grace through faith in God's gracious promises. This is eminently exemplified in Abraham (Gen 15:6) and has existed throughout God's covenant dealings with his people. This shared faith is what makes us all the children of Abraham (Rom 4:1-25; Gal 3:6-29). The true Israel is and always has been the heart-believers of all ages: "For he is not a Jew who is one outwardly, nor is circumcision that which is outward in the flesh. But he is a Jew who is one inwardly; and circumcision is that which is of the heart, by the Spirit, not by the letter" (Rom 2:28-29).

This inner continuity between Israel and the church is significant, but it does not minimize or annul the points of discontinuity named above. The latter necessarily require many changes in kingdom administration, i.e., in the organization and practices of the church.

C. Avoiding Extremes

It is important to acknowledge both discontinuity and continuity in comparing OT Israel with the church as the new Israel. Only when we do this can we avoid certain serious theological errors. On the one hand, some errors are the result of ignoring the continuity between the old and the new, and drawing too stark a contrast between them. The chief example of this is classical dispensationalism, which posits a nearly absolute dichotomy between Israel and the church. It says that the actual purpose for the first coming of Jesus was to establish an earthly Jewish kingdom. Because the Jews refused to accept Jesus as their Messiah, this step in God's plan has now been postponed until Christ's second coming, when the earthly Jewish (millennial) kingdom will finally be established. The church is just an unrelated temporary expedient, similar to the halftime activities between the two halves of a football game. Such an extreme view is contrary to the true continuity discussed above.

In this original dispensationalism a major point of difference between Israel and the church is the way of salvation. It says that in the OT age obedience to the Law of Moses was the way of salvation; in the present church age salvation is through grace. Sometimes even nondispensationalists are guilty of this error. They think the "law" which is replaced by grace (Rom 3:28; 6:14-15) is simply the Law of Moses. Such an assumption implies that there was no grace under the

Old Covenant, and that anyone saved in that era was saved by Moses' law. Only in the NT era are we saved by grace. Since grace is thus seen as a replacement for one specific law code (the Law of Moses), the tendency is to think of grace as just a new law code rather than a totally different way of salvation, one which in fact has *always* been the only way a sinner can be saved.

Such errors as the above can be avoided by recognizing the continuity between Israel and the church, especially in the matter of the way of salvation.

On the other hand, some serious theological errors are the result of minimizing the discontinuity between OT Israel and the church. The Judaizers in apostolic times were guilty of this. In modern times the most serious example is covenant theology, a method of interpreting Scripture invented by Zwingli as an alternative rationale for infant baptism.[6] This view says that at least since the time of Abraham, God's people have been under just *one covenant*, the covenant he made with Abraham in Gen 12:1-3; 17:1-14. Therefore since that day there has been just *one covenant people*, with OT Israel and the NT church being one continuous entity. This leads to the seriously false conclusion that there has always been just *one covenant sign*, which began in the form of circumcision (Gen 17:9-14) and continues today in the form of baptism. Within this framework baptism is given the meaning of OT circumcision, thus separating it from salvation and interpreting it as simply the sign of belonging to the covenant people. Also, like circumcision, baptism is then seen as being intended for infants.

The point is that this whole system is built on a false understanding of the relation between OT Israel and the new Israel, the church. Specifically, it repudiates the genuine discontinuity between them.

In conclusion we can see how important it is to correctly understand the nature of the church, not only as the new Israel, but also as a holy nation, the people of God, and the body of Christ.

NOTES ON CHAPTER TWENTY-THREE

[1]E.g., Rom 1:7; 8:28; 1 Cor 7:17-24; Gal 1:6; Eph 4:4; 1 Thess 2:12; 5:24; 2 Thess 2:14. See Cottrell, *Romans*, I:83-84, 500-501, 512-513.

[2]In 2 Cor 6:16-18 the concepts of the people of God, the holy (separated) nation, and the church as God's family are all related.

[3]This figurative meaning of *kephale* ("head") is firmly established by all relevant lexicographical and exegetical data. See my monograph, "Headship, Submission, and the Bible," chapters 11–21, on the web site of Council on Biblical Manhood and Womanhood, www.cbmw.org/resources/books/headship.pdf.

[4]See also Isa 19:24-25; 40:5; 49:6; 54:1-3; 60:3; 66:18-23; Micah 4:1-3).

[5]Isa 10:20-22; 11:11,16; 37:32; Jer 23:3; 31:7; Joel 2:32; Micah 2:12; 4:6-7; 7:18; Zeph 3:13.

[6]See Cottrell, "Covenant"; and Cottrell, "Reformed Tradition."

CHAPTER TWENTY-FOUR

THE CHURCH: ITS PURPOSE

We have explained the *nature* of the church as a holy nation, set apart from the rest of the world's population to be God's people, the new Israel. Now we are asking, for what *purpose* has God established the church? What is the function of this "new creation" upon the earth? The answer to this question is the same as our answer to the question of the purpose for God's original creation. That is, the purpose of the church is twofold: first, to display God's *glory* on the earth, and second, to be the means by which he shares his *goodness* with humanity.

To see how the church displays God's glory we will examine its purpose as God's temple and as God's kingdom. To see how God shares his goodness through the church we will explain its purpose as God's fortress and as God's priesthood. (See Cottrell, "Church.")

I. THE CHURCH AS THE TEMPLE OF GOD

The church of Jesus Christ is figuratively called a building. Jesus said he would *build* his church (Matt 16:18); Paul says the church is a "building, being fitted together" (Eph 2:21); Peter says we are "being built up as a spiritual house" (1 Pet 2:5). This spiritual house, the people of God, is no less than God's New Covenant temple. Ephesians 2:21 says this spiritual building is "growing into a holy temple in the Lord." Paul asks, "Do you not know that you"—you, plural; you, the church as a group—"are a temple of God?" (1 Cor 3:16).

The usual purpose for a house is to be somebody's dwelling place. That is exactly what a temple is; in a figurative sense it is God's dwelling place. This was a main purpose of the OT temple, and it is a main purpose of the church today.

The OT describes first the tabernacle and then the temple as "the house of the LORD" and "the house of God" (1 Chr 28:12). God himself called it "My house" (1 Chr 28:6). Jesus called it "My Father's house" (John 2:16). This was true not just in the sense that it *belonged* to him, but that in a real sense he lived in it. This is not true in an absolute sense, of course, as if he lived there and nowhere else. Even Solomon, who built the first temple at Jerusalem, understood this. He said, "But will God indeed dwell on the earth? Behold, heaven cannot contain You, how much less this house which I have built!" (1 Kgs 8:27).

Nevertheless in some real way God did set his presence upon and within the temple. When the original tabernacle was completed, God's visible, cloudlike presence covered it and filled it in the form of a theophany (Exod 40:34-35). When its replacement, the Jerusalem temple, was dedicated, the same thing happened: "The cloud filled the house of the LORD" (1 Kgs 8:10). The people knew that the temple was holy (Ps 79:1), or separate and different from all other such places, because God's presence was there, especially in the innermost sanctum called "the holy of holies" or "the most holy place" (1 Kgs 8:6).

In what ways was God present in his house, his temple? First, the temple was a house for God's *name*. God called it "a house for My name" (1 Kgs 8:18). "My name shall be there," he declared (1 Kgs 8:29). God's "name" stands for all that he is: his sovereign power, his holy character, his gracious love. That the temple was associated with the name of God meant that it was a kind of symbol of the reality of God both for Israel and for the nations (see 1 Kgs 8:41-45). To defile or destroy the temple was to defile the very name of God and challenge his sovereignty.

Second, the temple was a house for God's *Word*. As soon as the temple was built, Solomon ordered the leaders of Israel to place the ark of the covenant within it (2 Chr 5:2). "Then the priests brought the ark of the covenant of the LORD to its place, into the inner sanctuary of the house, to the holy of holies" (2 Chr 5:7). The only things in this ark or chest were the two stone tablets on which God had written his ten commandments (2 Chr 5:10).

Third, the temple was a house for God's *heart*. The Lord declared, "Now My eyes will be open and My ears attentive to the prayer offered in this place. For now I have chosen and consecrated this house that My name may be there forever, and My eyes and My heart will be there perpetually" (2 Chr 7:15-16). Because the people of Israel knew the temple was God's dwelling place, they prayed in it and even *toward* it (1 Kgs 8:29,33,35,38). Jesus called the temple a house of prayer (Matt 21:13). This is why God said that his eyes and ears and even his heart were there, indicating that he would hear his people's prayers and that his heart wanted to answer them.

Finally, it was a house for his *glory*. This especially refers to the cloudlike presence. "The glory of the LORD filled the tabernacle" when it was built (Exod 40:34-35), and the same happened to Solomon's temple (1 Kgs 8:11; 2 Chr 7:1-3). When the people of Israel realized that the temple was a house for the presence of God's glory, their natural response was worship: they "bowed down on the pavement with their faces to the ground, and they worshiped and gave praise to the LORD" (2 Chr 7:3).

Peter says the church is a spiritual house, and Paul makes it clear that it is a house in which God dwells on the earth today. "You also are being built together into a dwelling of God in the Spirit," he says (Eph 2:22). You, the church, are the temple of God, he says, and "the Spirit of God dwells in you" (1 Cor 3:16).

Each individual Christian's body is a temple for the Holy Spirit (1 Cor 6:19), but so is the church collectively, as a body. The Spirit of God dwells among his people. It is true that God is everywhere, and that not even the totality of created space can contain his presence. So in that sense God is present among Buddhists, Hindus, Moslems, and even atheists. But he does not *live* among them; only the church can be called his dwelling place. He lives among us in a special way. This is where it is natural for him to be.

The church is the house for his *name* today. Because he lives in it, his name is on the mailbox, so to speak. Solomon said, "I am about to build a house for the name of the LORD my God" (2 Chr 2:4). Today Jesus is building a house for *his* name; he calls it "My church" (Matt 16:18). This is why the name "church of Christ" or "Christian church" is so appropriate for congregations today.

The church is the house for his *Word* today. The Bible and the Bible alone is the church's only rule of faith and practice. Just as the temple housed the tablets of the ten commandments, so has God written his Word on the very hearts of his New Covenant people (Heb 8:8-11). It is every Christian's responsibility to know and proclaim his Word, and to live by it before the world. The church must continually devote itself to "the apostles' teaching" (Acts 2:42).

The church is the house for God's *heart* today. It is the focus of his love: "Christ also loved the church and gave Himself up for her" (Eph 5:25). This is why the church devotes itself to prayer (Acts 2:42). The Lord's heart is with his people, and he hears them when they pray.

The church is the house for God's *glory*. In the midst of a world that has sunk to the lowest depths of falsehood and decadence, the church should be the one place where the glory of God shines forth. Others should be able to look at the church and *see God* in the world. This is the tragedy of moral lapses among church leaders, and moral mediocrity within the church as a whole.

Recently I drove past a new Mormon temple in a large American city. As a physical structure it was magnificent. My guide told me that the Mormon church had chosen the site very carefully. Their goal was to find the land that had the highest elevation in the area, so that the building would stand out for miles around. Actually this is what God expects, not necessarily of our church buildings, but of the church itself. We should be the visible evidence of the glory of God, as conveyed by our lifestyles and our witness. As Jesus said, we are the salt of the earth and the light of the world. He expects his church to shine the light of God's glory from the highest ground. "Let your light shine before men in such a way that they may see your good works, and glorify your Father who is in heaven" (Matt 5:16).

II. THE CHURCH AS THE KINGDOM OF GOD

The biblical words for "kingdom" (*mam'lakah, mal'kuth, basileia*) have two main connotations. In their primary sense they refer to the *reign* of a king, i.e., his kingly rule or kingship (e.g., Ps 103:19; 145:11-13; Luke 19:12; Rev 12:10; 17:17-18). In a derivative sense they refer to the *realm* over which a king reigns (e.g., Ezra 1:1; Isa 19:2; Matt 24:7; Luke 4:5; 11:17).

These terms apply to God in both senses. In the former sense they refer to his reign, rule, dominion, sovereignty, kingship, lordship: "The LORD has established his throne in the heavens, and his kingdom rules over all" (Ps 103:19, ESV). This is the meaning in Matt 6:33, "But seek first His kingdom and His righteousness." Other texts clearly bear the latter sense, i.e., the realm over which God reigns. This is implied in statements representing the kingdom of God as something one may enter and be a part of, e.g., Matt 5:19-20; 21:31; Luke 18:24-25; John 3:5. This is the sense in which the church is the kingdom of God.

Certainly in one way the entire world is the kingdom or realm over which God reigns, since "his kingdom rules over all" (Ps 103:19, ESV). He is "the God . . . of all the kingdoms of the earth" (Isa 37:16), "a great King over all the earth" (Ps 47:2). He is "the King of kings and Lord of lords" (1 Tim 6:15). However, in the old creation, "this present evil age" (Gal 1:4), not everyone acknowledges the kingship of God. The spirit of rebellion is prevalent (Ps 2:1-3; Luke 19:12). Therefore God's plan is to construct a new creation in the midst of the old, a kingdom in which all the citizens are willing subjects who serve the king from their hearts. OT Israel as such was not this kingdom, since membership therein was based on physical birth, and many individual Jews never became heart-believers (Rom 2:28-29; 9:6). This is, however, exactly what the church (the new, spiritual Israel) is meant to be. It is the body of people not only over whom God reigns, but who also joyfully acknowledge his reign and freely submit to it. This is what makes the church the true kingdom of God in the world today.

As the incarnate Logos, God the Son, Jesus of Nazareth walked among us as the Divine King himself, who came to establish his pure, spiritual kingdom once and for all, as prophesied (Isa 9:6-7; Dan 2:44; 7:13-14). He proclaimed the imminence of this kingdom (Matt 4:17; 10:7; 12:28) and explained its nature as a spiritual entity: "My kingdom is not of this world" (John 18:36); "the kingdom of God is within you" (Luke 17:21, NIV). What is this special spiritual kingdom that Jesus came to establish? It is the church. In Matt 16:18-19 Jesus said, "I will build My church"; he then immediately said to Peter, "I will give you the keys of the kingdom of heaven," apparently equating the church and the kingdom. On the Day of Pentecost Peter proclaimed that the crucified and risen Christ was now reigning from the throne of heaven at God's right hand (Acts 2:34-36), and the kingdom was thus inaugurated with the baptism of three thousand penitent believers (Acts 2:37-42).

Being a part of the church thus means being a part of the kingdom of God, even now. Being saved is equivalent to entering the kingdom: "For He rescued us from the domain of darkness, and transferred us to the kingdom of His beloved Son" (Col 1:13). We are in his kingdom because we have acknowledged or confessed Jesus as Lord or King (Rom 10:9; 1 Cor 12:3). "He has made us to be a kingdom" (Rev 1:6; see 5:10). "We are receiving a kingdom that cannot be shaken," says Heb 12:28 (NIV). The church is not the final stage of the kingdom, of course. The NT speaks of the full inheritance of the kingdom as something still future, referring to our final home in glory (1 Cor 15:50; Gal 5:21; Eph 5:5; 2 Tim 4:18; 2 Pet 1:11).

How does the church's identity as the kingdom of God on earth relate to the church's *purpose*? We must remember that the church consists of those who not only are under God's kingship but who also acknowledge his kingship and submit to it. Hence one of the functions of the church is to bear witness to the dominion and sovereignty of God in Jesus Christ, before the unbelieving world. We do this by our message and by our lifestyle. This is part of the new Israel's responsibility for *proclamation*; our purpose is to bring glory to the King by proclaiming his excellencies (2 Pet 2:9) or declaring his praises (NIV).

III. THE CHURCH AS A REFUGE FROM DEATH

The church exists not only to display God's glory, but also to be the vehicle for bestowing his goodness upon mankind. Specifically, it is the context within which the blessings of salvation are experienced. This is one of the senses in which the church is a structure, a building, a spiritual house. We saw above that the church as a building is a temple or dwelling place for God the Spirit. Here we see that the church as a building is a fortress to which sinners are invited to retreat, wherein they may find safety and refuge from the enemies that "wage war against the soul" (1 Pet 2:11).

Peter says (1 Pet 2:5) that the church as a spiritual house is made of stones, with each stone being an individual person. More specifically, Peter calls the material from which the church is built "living stones." This means that those who become part of the church receive the gift of life; indeed, a major purpose of the church is to be a refuge from death and a source of life.

Whether the world realizes it or not, mankind's greatest enemy is death—death in all its forms. Every unrepentant and unconverted sinner is already in a state of *spiritual* death (Eph 2:1,5). His soul is devoid of true sensitivity toward God and is filled with the decay of sin. *Physical* death likewise starts gripping its ugly fist around us as soon as we come into the world. We know it will crush us; we just do not know when. Most fearful of all is the *eternal* death in the lake of fire that awaits the sinner who is still a sinner when his body dies. Thus the old creation is all but swallowed up by the enemy, death.

Many people ignore this enemy, or they think they have found ways to avoid its vicious and fatal blows. They are like the religious leaders in OT Jerusalem in Isaiah's time, whom the prophet mockingly pictures as declaring, "We have made a covenant with death, and with Sheol[1] we have made a pact. The overwhelming scourge will not reach us when it passes by, for we have made falsehood our refuge and we have concealed ourselves with deception" (Isa 28:15).

People today still create deceptive myths to convince themselves that they have defeated death. This includes those who believe in reincarnation, for example, or those who visit spiritists. The impact of the many reports of "near-death" experiences is to make us comfortable with the prospect of death. Some have had themselves frozen at the point of death, hoping to be revived someday. But what Isaiah said to his contemporaries still applies: when the torrent of death bears down upon us, every lying refuge will be swept away (28:17-19) like a tidal wave smashing a beach umbrella.

At the same time Isaiah gave us this promise from God: "'Behold, I am laying in Zion a stone, a tested stone, a costly cornerstone for the foundation, firmly placed. He who believes in it will not be disturbed'" (28:16). This is no doubt the passage to which Jesus alludes when he says, "Upon this rock I will build My church; and the gates of Hades will not overpower it" (Matt 16:18). *Hades* is the same as *Sheol* in Isaiah 28. It refers to the place of death, the forces of death, the power of death, the domain from whose gates or portals the overwhelming scourge of death bears down upon all men. Jesus is saying, "Let me build you into my church, which rests on the solid rock foundation that God has laid for it in my death and resurrection, and you will find true freedom from the scourge of death. I will make you a *living stone.* You will overcome death in all its forms."

One of the first things that happens when Christ builds us into his church is that we are raised from the dead. The gift of the Holy Spirit (the one who actually inhabits the building) banishes the state of spiritual death, and we become spiritually alive toward God. We also have the promise that our bodies will be raised from the dead one day in a glorious form and that we will **not** be cast into the lake of fire which is the second death.

This is God's promise for as long as we remain *in the church.* The *church*, the spiritual house that Jesus is building, is the only refuge from death. This is one of its main purposes. This is part of the gospel preached to the world in evangelistic work: "When you become a part of the body of Christ, you become a *living stone.* Death has no more power over you!"

The point is that the spiritual fortress called the church is the only sure refuge from death. What makes it a sure refuge is not the strength of the stones themselves (ourselves), but the strength of the *foundation stone* upon which this fortress is built. The tested and costly Rock (Isa 28:16), the solid, fixed Rock *(petra)* upon which Christ is building his church (Matt 16:18), is not Peter (a *petros* or loose stone), but Jesus himself, specifically because of his identity as the Christ, the Son of the Living God (Matt 16:16; see 1 Cor 3:11; Eph 2:20; 1 Pet 2:6-8). As long as we are one of the church's living stones, firmly affixed into the building that rests upon the solid Rock, the tidal wave of death cannot sweep us away.

IV. THE CHURCH AS A HOLY PRIESTHOOD

In 1 Pet 2:5 the apostle says that we as living stones are being built up as a spiritual house "for a holy priesthood." In verse 9 he refers to the church as a "royal priesthood." This means that every church member is a priest. The Protestant tradition has always spoken of the priesthood of all believers, in contrast with the Roman Catholic Church in which only ordained clergyman can function as priests. But what does it mean to be a priest? What do priests do? In what sense does the church function as a priesthood? Peter says that as priests we are meant to "offer up spiritual sacrifices" (1 Pet 2:5).

Sacrifices and offerings played a large role in OT worship and piety. The temple was the location where these sacrifices and offerings were made. Burnt offerings were sacrificed on the altar in the courtyard of the temple, and certain offerings of incense and bread were offered inside the temple itself. Blood from some of the animal sacrifices was offered within the temple, upon the mercy seat in the holy of holies.

One of the major functions of the OT priesthood was to offer these sacrifices up to God on behalf of the people. For example, when an Israelite committed a certain sin, he had to sacrifice a guilt offering to God. In the case of a poor person this could be two young pigeons, one for a sin offering and one for a guilt offering (Lev 5:7-10). Another example is the animals sacrificed on the Day of Atonement. The high priest first killed a bull as a sin offering for himself, then a goat as a sin offering for the people. After each slaying, the high priest took some of the animal's blood into the temple and sprinkled it on and around the mercy seat in the holy of holies (Lev 16:11-15).

What was the purpose of these and other sacrifices? In almost every case the priest offered the sacrifices *on behalf of someone else.* Other people brought their sacrifices to the Lord, as a way of restoring or expressing their communion with him; but the priests offered the animals to God on their behalf. In doing so the priests were mediating between God and the people, bringing them into God's presence and making them acceptable to him. In this sense "the priest shall make atonement for them, and they will be forgiven" (Lev 4:20).

This is the nature and purpose of the priesthood of Jesus Christ, our "great high priest" (Heb 4:14). He offered up to God the sacrifice of himself, in order to make atonement for sinners and make us acceptable in the presence of God.

The work of OT priests and the priestly work of Jesus are the background of Peter's remark that one of the church's functions is that of a holy priesthood. As with the old priesthood, our task and purpose are to bring other people to God. This refers, of course, to *evangelism,* which is one of the main purposes of the church. This is how the church fulfills God's purpose of bestowing the blessings of eternal life upon mankind: we are here to win the world to Jesus Christ. Evangelism is sometimes compared with a harvest, with the church "going forth and reaping" and "bringing in the sheaves" (see Ps 126:6). In the context of 1 Pet 2:5, we could change the song to "bringing in the stones." As Christians we are stone-gatherers. We go forth to collect dead stones (sinners) and lead them to Jesus, who turns them into living stones and builds them into his spiritual house.

How is this purpose carried out in terms of priesthood? As noted, the main function of priests is to offer sacrifices. The Mosaic priests offered physical sacrifices such as goats and pigeons, but Peter says we offer up "spiritual sacrifices." What are these spiritual sacrifices? There are two kinds.

First are the sacrifices of *good words*, with which we bear witness to the power of God's grace, including the personal testimony of how we ourselves have been saved from our sins. In 1 Pet 2:9, where Peter calls the church a "royal priesthood," he says that God gave us that task so "that you may proclaim the excellencies of Him who has called you out of darkness into His marvelous light." This is the "sacrifice of praise to God, that is, the fruit of lips that give thanks to His name" (Heb 13:15).

The point of priesthood, though, is that we do not offer up these sacrifices in private, but rather in the presence of the world. Peter says we are to *proclaim* God's excellencies, or publish them abroad. The Christian priest is thus a trumpet, a newspaper. Without being obnoxious he is always testifying to others. He is always looking for an opportunity to say in some way, "We interrupt this regular daily routine in order to bring you the following announcement: Jesus saves!"

The second kind of sacrifices is *good works*. This includes living a life of holiness before the world. The church after all is a *holy* priesthood. We need to be aware that our holy living is not just to please God but to attract others to him. To this end Peter says we should "abstain from fleshly lusts," and keep our "behavior excellent among the Gentiles, so that . . . they may because of your good deeds, as they observe them, glorify God in the day of visitation" (1 Pet 2:11-12).

The sacrifices of good works also include works of service and benevolence within the community as a whole. As Heb 13:16 says, "And do not neglect doing good and sharing, for with such sacrifices God is pleased." By helping those in need, we show them the love of Christ and draw them to Christ. This is priestly work.

Community service activities by the church draw not only those who are directly helped thereby, but also those who observe what we are doing. Thus Jesus exhorts, "Let your light shine before men in such a way that they may see your good works, and glorify your Father who is in heaven" (Matt 5:16). The point of doing such good works is not to bring praise to ourselves, but to cause others to glorify God and thus to want to surrender to him. This is how acts of Christian love and service become *priestly* work, and serve the purpose of evangelism.

As a priesthood offering up the spiritual sacrifices of good words and good works, the church thus fulfills both of God's main purposes for it, i.e., glorifying his name and attracting others to share in the bounty of his spiritual blessings.

NOTES ON CHAPTER TWENTY-FOUR

[1] *Sheol* in the OT is the place of death, seen figuratively as a great underground abyss or pit. Its NT equivalent is *Hades*.

CHAPTER TWENTY-FIVE
THE CHURCH: ITS ORGANIZATION

When the NT speaks of the church, the *ekklesia*, it does not refer to an organized entity as such but simply to the body of believers who share a common commitment to Jesus Christ. Sometimes when the singular is used ("church," not "churches"), the reference is to the body of believers in general, wherever they may be, without specifying any particular geographical location. This is called the *church universal*.[1] In this sense Jesus says, "I will build My church" (Matt 16:18); and Paul says, "Christ also is the head of the church" (Eph 5:23; see Col 1:18), and, "Christ also loved the church and gave Himself up for her" (Eph 5:25). In 1 Cor 10:32 Paul distinguishes "the church of God" from the Jews and the Greeks, with all three groups together constituting the world's population. See also 1 Cor 11:28; Eph 1:22; 3:10,21; 5:24,27,29,32; Col 1:24; 1 Tim 3:15.

Sometimes the singular form ("church") is used to refer to the totality of believers in a limited geographical area, as when Acts 9:31 speaks of "the church throughout all Judea and Galilee and Samaria." This may be the sense in which Scripture speaks of "the church" in specific cities or metropolitan areas, e.g., "the church in Jerusalem" (Acts 8:1; 11:22; see 5:11; 15:4,22), "the church which is at Cenchrea" (Rom 16:1), "the church of God which is at Corinth" (1 Cor 1:1; 2 Cor 1:1; see Rom 16:23), "the church of the Laodiceans" (Col 4:16; see Rev 3:14), and "the church of the Thessalonians" (1 Thess 1:1; 2 Thess 1:1).[2] At least in some of these areas, such as Jerusalem (Acts 2:41; 4:4; 5:14), it is highly unlikely that the Christians regularly met as a single congregation.

Other biblical references, however, make it obvious that the church universal, even within limited geographical areas, was divided into what we call *local congregations*. This is true for several reasons. First, the NT frequently speaks of *churches*, plural. Sometimes the reference is to "all the churches," wherever located (1 Cor 7:17; 14:33; 2 Cor 8:18; 11:28; see Rom 16:4,16; 1 Cor 11:16; 2 Cor 12:13; 2 Thess 1:4). At other times the reference is to "the churches" in specific areas, including Syria and Cilicia (Acts 15:41), Galatia (1 Cor 16:1; Gal 1:2), Asia (1 Cor 16:19), Macedonia (2 Cor 8:1), Judea (Gal 1:22; 1 Thess 2:14), and specific areas through which Paul traveled (Acts 16:5; see Acts 14:23; 1 Cor 4:17). Second, Paul refers to churches meeting in specific houses: those of Prisca and Aquila (Rom 16:5; 1 Cor 16:19), of Nympha (Col 4:15), and of Archippus (Phlm 1:2). Third, that the church was divided into local congregations is seen from various references to Christians assembling or coming together "as a church" (1 Cor 11:18, literally, "in church"; see also vv. 19,28). When Paul refers to "the whole church" assembling together (1 Cor 11:23), he is undoubtedly referring to a local congregation. Finally, the same conclusion is supported by references to church activities that could take place only on a local level: edifying one another (1 Cor 14:4-5), assisting widows (1 Tim 5:16), and summoning "the elders of the church" for prayer and anointing (Jas 5:14; see 1 Tim 3:5).

Thus we see that the church may be viewed from two different perspectives. On the one hand we may speak of the church in the general or universal sense of all those who are in a saving relationship with Jesus Christ. On the other hand, we may speak of specific local congregations made up of the believers in a limited area who are united together for mutual edification and service. The question of church organization applies to the church in this latter sense.

I. TYPES OF CHURCH ORGANIZATION

The question of church organization is the issue of *church polity*,[3] a term which refers specifically to the system by which the church is governed. Three such systems have come to prevail within Christendom: episcopal, presbyterian, and congregational. These forms of church government differ over how *authority* is exercised in the church.

A. Episcopal

The *episcopal* form of church government takes its name from the Greek word *episkopos*, "bishop, overseer." As we shall see below, in the NT "bishops" and "elders" are just two names for the same office; but episcopal church polity sees them as two distinct offices. While elders are seen as functioning within a single local congregation, a bishop is regarded as a church officer who has authority over a group of congregations called a diocese. Some denominations have a still higher level of authority, where an archbishop has authority over a group of bishops. In this form of church government the authority passes from the top down: the highest authority is Christ, who delegates his authority to the apostles, who pass it along to bishops, who have authority over local ministers or priests, who then exercise authority over their respective congregations. In this system the lower levels usually have no say in the selection of those who rule over them; those occupying the higher levels are appointed either by their peers or by those above them.

This system began to arise in the early second century, as evidenced by the letters of the soon-to-be martyr named Ignatius (*Apostolic Fathers*, 86-118), who was regarded as the bishop of Antioch. Ignatius assumes that the church (or churches) in each city should have a single ruling bishop, to be assisted by elders and deacons (Lawson, 102-105). The development of the system is summed up thus by Hope (32):

. . . In the course of the second century . . . a single bishop became elevated to the spiritual leadership of each local congregation; and he was assisted in his ministry by a corps of presbyters. During the third century, as the Christian Church increased in numbers and in extent, each bishop came to have what was called a diocese—that is, he was the official leader of all the local churches in a particular area. And ever since, the Roman Catholic and Eastern Orthodox churches have been thus ruled by diocesan bishops.

The Roman Catholic church is the most obvious example of episcopacy. Here the pope is seen as having authority equal to that of the apostles. He exercises authority directly over the archbishops, each of whom governs the bishops in an assigned area. Each bishop then rules over the priests in his diocese, with each local congregation being supervised by a priest. The Anglican church (Church of England) and the Episcopal church are similar, except they do not have a level of authority equivalent to the pope. The polity of the Methodist church and of other Wesleyan groups is also episcopal in form, but with only one level of authority above a group of local congregations, namely, a bishop.

The main difficulty with this form of church polity is that it has no biblical basis, either in the form of direct teaching or in the form of approved apostolic precedent. In fact it seems to be in direct contradiction to the biblical equation of elders and bishops (see Acts 20:17,28; Titus 1:5,7), and to the biblical pattern of a plurality of elders in each church.

B. Presbyterian

The second main form of church government is *presbyterianism*, from the Greek word *presbyteros*, "elder." This system is different from the previous one in two major ways. First, no distinction is made here between elders and bishops. The oversight of local congregations is in the hands of elders. Second, in presbyterianism those in authority (the elders) are chosen by the members of the local congregations. In that sense the authority actually begins at the bottom rather than at the top, and is delegated from the congregation to the elders, who rule after the pattern of a representative government.

How do elders govern within this system? In the first place, each congregation selects its own elders from within its membership. Those chosen constitute the "session" (or "consistory" in some groups), which is the local ruling body. A distinction is usually made between *ruling* elders, who take the lead in the governing activity; and *teaching* elders, consisting of the ordained minister or ministers. In the second place, there is another level of authority above the local eldership. It is formed when all the local churches in a given area select representative ruling and teaching elders who form a regional body of elders called the "presbytery" (or "classis" in some groups). The presbytery has ruling authority over all the congregations under its care; it also ordains ministers and as a rule owns the local church property. Most presbyterian-type denominations have one or two levels of representative authority above the presbytery, such as synods and general assemblies, which function largely as courts of appeal concerning decisions made on lower levels.

Groups having this form of church government include, of course, all Presbyterian denominations, as well as most Reformed churches arising from the continental European Reformation.

The presbyterian form of polity is to be preferred over the episcopal, in that it views governing authority as proceeding from the bottom up rather than from the top down, allowing the local congregation to choose its own leaders, who then govern representatively. It is preferred also in that it makes no distinction between bishops and elders, and thus in principle has only one level of authority above the congregation, namely, the elders. The difficulty with presbyterianism, however, is that it proceeds to organize these elders in higher layers of authority which in practice operate hierarchically, very much like an episcopacy. Moreover, this is done with a very tentative biblical basis, specifically, the Jerusalem council described in Acts 15. This council is taken to be a precedent for the regional ruling body called the presbytery.

We must seriously question this interpretation of the Jerusalem council, however. First, the reason this meeting was held in Jerusalem was not because there was a ruling body of elders there, but because most of the *apostles* were there. The local elders assisted the apostles, to be sure (Acts 15:2,6,23; 16:4); but the main authority resided in the apostles. In fact, the ultimate authority in this whole consultation was the Holy Spirit (Acts 15:28), who was guiding the apostles into all truth, as Christ had promised (John 16:13-15). Second, it was not just the apostles and the elders who gave general approval to the decree produced by the council, but also "the whole church" (Acts 15:22). This is not consistent with modern presbyterianism. Third, this council spoke not just with regional authority, but with universal authority; its decision, being apostolic, was meant for all churches (Acts 15:23; 16:4).

We conclude that the central role of the apostles in the Jerusalem council makes this council unique to the first century and nonrepeatable in postapostolic times. It is not equivalent to a modern presbytery. Since the authoritative teaching of the apostles has been inscripturated in the NT, the purpose of the Jerusalem council is now served when local congregations consult the *Bible* when problems arise.

C. Congregational

The third main form of church government is called *congregationalism*. This view agrees with presbyterianism (against episcopalianism) that governing authority proceeds from the bottom up rather than from the top down. That is, the responsibility for making decisions concerning the affairs of a local church lies within the collective membership of that congregation. In most cases many of these decisions will be made by representative local leaders (elders and deacons), but these leaders themselves are chosen by the congregation as a whole (as in Acts

6:3; 15:22) and continue to serve at the will of the membership in general. Groups that have some variation of congregational government are Baptists, Congregationalists, and Christian churches and churches of Christ in the conservative branches of the Restoration Movement.

A key concept for congregational polity is *local autonomy*, or "self-rule." As applied to the church this term means "that a local congregation is independent and self-governing. There is no external power that can dictate courses of action to the local church" (Erickson, *Theology*, 1089). No denominational board or representative tells the congregation what to do. The local church owns its own property, elects it own leaders, chooses its own ministers, and in general makes its own decisions.

The congregational form of church government seems to be most consistent with the way the NT speaks of the church universal being divided into local congregations, as summarized in the introduction to this chapter. The book of Acts speaks often of local churches, and most of the NT letters address the problems and needs of local churches. With the exception of the unique council in Acts 15 (discussed above), there is no reference anywhere in the NT to any kind of governing body that exercises authority either over the church as a whole or over a regional body of churches. The authoritative teaching of the apostles is addressed directly to specific congregations and to the individuals within those congregations. And thus today, the only intermediaries between Christ and local congregations are the apostles and prophets who speak through the pages of the NT (Eph 2:20).

Thus we conclude that congregational polity is the NT pattern for church government. The local congregation is the only governing unit and the only essential, permanent structure within the church universal. In this sense the church universal is thus an aggregate of local congregations. With regard to authority, discipline, nurture, and government as such, the church universal functions through the local congregation. For other purposes, local congregations may and sometimes should voluntarily join together and cooperate for greater efficiency and effectiveness, e.g., in matters of education (supporting colleges, seminaries, and camps) and evangelism (supporting missions and evangelistic associations). This is allowable because autonomy means self-rule, not isolation.

II. THE CHURCH UNIVERSAL

While there is a sense in which the church universal is composed of local churches, it is more appropriate to think of it as being composed of individual Christians. This is seen especially in the various figures by which the church is described as being related to Jesus Christ. The church that Jesus is building (Matt 16:18) is being built living stone by living stone (1 Pet 2:5). Each stone is another believer, being fitted into this glorious structure. The qualities that are expected of the church as the bride of Christ, such as purity (2 Cor 11:2; Eph 5:27) and submission (Eph 5:24), are expressed first of all and primarily in the lives of individual

Christians. Also, in the figure of the church as the body of Christ, each believer is represented as being joined directly to the one body of which Christ is the head (Eph 5:30; 1 Cor 12:12); each is an "individual part" of that body (Eph 4:16). "Now you are Christ's body, and individually members of it" (1 Cor 12:27).

Thus the church, viewed as the totality of the body of Christ, consists of all those who have met the conditions for being saved and thus are under the saving grace of Jesus Christ. I agree with Erickson's "tentative theological definition of the church as the whole body of those who through Christ's death have been savingly reconciled to God and have received new life" (*Theology*, 1044). Membership in the church universal is thus defined in terms of one's personal relationship with Christ, regardless of his relationship to any particular local congregation or any particular form of church government. To say it another way, a person is saved because of his relationship to Christ, and not because of his relationship to any specific group or congregation. This is the sense in which the church is a "communion of saints."

Does this mean that the group or congregation to which a Christian belongs is irrelevant, or that it is irrelevant whether he belongs to any church or congregation at all? Absolutely not! Here we must remember the two aspects of salvation (the "double cure"), justification and sanctification. To be justified or forgiven by the blood of Christ means to be in a saved state and thus to be a member of the church universal, but the justified one is still obligated to pursue sanctification (holiness). And to the extent to which the NT reveals to us the will of God concerning the organization of the church in general and the structure of local churches in particular, the Christian is absolutely obligated to be a part of a congregation that follows this pattern. It is essential for one's sanctification, and thus cannot be a matter of opinion or an irrelevancy.

This biblical distinction between the church universal and local churches is related to the distinction between the *nature* of the church and the *structure* of the church. It is also related to what is sometimes called the distinction between the *invisible* church and the *visible* church. This latter distinction is a valid one, despite the reluctance of some to accept it. There is such a thing as the invisible church, i.e., invisible to man though visible to God. The church universal is defined as all those individuals who are in a saving relationship with Jesus, and God alone knows with certainty who those individuals are. Thus the church is invisible in the sense that its *boundaries* cannot be seen by men, but only by God. Even if we grant that the true visible church must conform to the divinely revealed NT pattern, we cannot simply equate the membership rolls of such churches with the list of those whose names are written in heaven. This is true because many if not all church groups whose structure falls short of God's revealed will nevertheless contain justified believers who are part of the body of Christ (the church universal), though only God knows who all of them are. It is true also because most if not all congregations that are biblically structured have membership rolls that at any given time may contain professed believers who are actually hypocrites and who are thus not a part of the true body of Christ (Matt 13:47-50), though again only God knows who they are. Thus while the church universal is completely visible to God (2 Tim 2:19), its edges or boundaries are invisible to men.

This distinction between the invisible and visible church has implications for the questions of the church's unity and invincibility. Regarding the former, the true unity of the church is on the invisible level rather than the visible. The church universal, since it is made up of all saved individuals, is already "one body" (Eph 4:4). All who are in a saving union with Jesus Christ are already united with one another in the same family and brotherhood; this is true church unity. We may not know the identity of all our brothers and sisters, but our hearts are united nonetheless. Those whose identity we do know may be accepted in warm fellowship, regardless of present differences on the level of the visible church.

Regarding invincibility, Jesus promised concerning his church that "the gates of Hades will not overpower it" (Matt 16:18). This is usually interpreted to mean that, once the church has begun, it will never entirely cease to exist upon the face of the earth. There will always be at least a remnant, a "pilgrim church" existing somewhere. I believe this is a valid conclusion.

The next question, though, is whether this invincibility applies to the church invisible or to the church visible. Many take the latter approach, arguing that the true church has survived since the first century in identifiable communities of faithful believers, even when mainstream Christendom seems to be apostate. As Speiss says, "Jesus promises that the called out ones will prevail, even against the gates of hell (Matt. 16:18). And Jesus' true church has prevailed over the centuries, as little flocks of believers scattered over the face of the earth." They were "continuing in the faith once delivered unto the saints as COMMUNITIES of believers." Books tracing this alleged invincible chain include Broadbent's *The Pilgrim Church* (recommended by Speiss) and Carroll's *The Trail of Blood*.

The problem with this approach is that, in their zeal to discover a true remnant church in every era of Christian history, the advocates of this approach have been forced to identify as such several groups whose basic beliefs are false and even heretical. These include medieval sects such as the Paulicians, the Bogomiles, and the Albigenses, whose dualistic metaphysics caused them to deny the human nature of Jesus, among other things (see *GC*, 61-62). The fact is that the invincibility of the church, in terms of Matt 16:18, cannot be maintained in reference to an unbroken chain of visibly identifiable sects or groups. It is rather to be understood only on the level of the invisible church. From its beginning on the Day of Pentecost a spiritual network of justified believers has continued and will continue to exist, even if all visible forms of the church become corrupt.

III. THE LOCAL CHURCH

Does this mean that the outward, visible structure of the church is unimportant and irrelevant, then? Does it mean that God does not care which type of church organization we choose, or that "one denomination is as good as another"? Again we answer, absolutely not! The outward form of the church *does matter*, and the visible church to which a Christian belongs is directly related to his spiritual growth and maturity (i.e., sanctification). The reason the outward form of the church matters is because God's Word has revealed to us at least a general pattern or structure to which he expects his people to conform. There is a divinely revealed form of church organization that the body of Christ must acknowledge and pursue as it seeks to be pleasing to Christ its Head.

In the first section above we saw that congregational church polity, rather than episcopal or presbyterian, is supported by NT teaching. Regarding structure, the true church has no central earthly headquarters, no denominational organization, no hierarchy of authority outside of and above the local congregation. While so-called parachurch organizations (camps, colleges, etc.) may exist by means of and for the service of local churches, all connections between churches and such groups are purely voluntary. While parachurch groups are not forbidden by Scripture, they are not required by it either; the only essential and proper visible organization of the church as such is the local congregation.

A. Church Membership

We may now ask how an individual becomes a member of the visible church. The moment one receives the gift of salvation, he becomes a member of the body of Christ, the invisible church. But what about membership in the *visible* church, i.e., in a local congregation? How does this take place? A common idea in Protestant Christianity since the time of Zwingli is that a sinner becomes saved and enters the invisible church through an inward spiritual baptism; then that saved person becomes united with the visible church and a member of a local congregation through water baptism. This is incorrect, however. As we have seen, there is only "one baptism" (Eph 4:5), combining both the spiritual and the material aspects. This one baptism, involving both water and Spirit, is the point of time when one enters the *invisible* church (Acts 2:47; see Cottrell, *Baptism*, 96-100). If this baptism is administered in the context of an authentic local NT congregation, then it is also the time when one becomes a member of that local (visible) congregation. If the baptism itself took place outside such a context (e.g., at a retreat, or in a nonbiblical denominational context), then the saved person becomes a member of a local congregation by publicly confessing the faith that he shares with that group, and by voluntarily submitting to its eldership. A change of membership from one congregation to another is accomplished in the same way. A membership roll is kept for each congregation so that the elders may know those for whom they are responsible (Heb 13:17).

The membership of a local congregation, then, consists of those who have been "called out" from the world and have consciously answered that call, who have been sanctified or set apart by the saving blood of Christ (Heb 12:29;

13:12) in Christian baptism, and who have specifically identified themselves with that congregation through confession of faith and submission to its elders. It is obvious that only those who are mature enough to believe, repent, confess, and submit can be members of the church. Infants and young children, even those of believing parents, are not a part of the church's membership and do not need to be, since they are born saved under the original grace of Christ and will remain in that state until they reach the age of accountability.

Is it necessary for a saved person to have membership in a specific local congregation? The answer is yes. Again, salvation involves not only forgiveness of sins (justification) but also becoming a mature Christian through the Holy Spirit's sanctifying work. Though one may be justified and thus go to heaven by being a part of the invisible church alone, he cannot live a life that is pleasing to God without local church membership. As sheep need a shepherd, so do Christians need the guidance and protection of their pastors or elders. As symbiotic organisms need one another, so do Christians need the fellowship and mutual edification that characterizes church life. We need the apostles' teaching, fellowship, breaking of bread, and prayers (Acts 2:42) found in church gatherings. Thus God expects us to "come together as a church" (1 Cor 11:18; see 14:26), and commands us not to forsake "assembling together" (Heb 10:25). He expects us to see ourselves as members of a body where each part depends on all the others (1 Cor 12:4-26) and uses his own gift "in serving one another" (1 Pet 4:10). Anyone who deliberately refuses to affiliate with a local NT congregation is thus openly defying the will of God.

B. Church Leadership

As the head of the church Jesus has final authority over it; but he has mediated his authority through the prophets and apostles, whose inspired teaching constitutes in one sense the very foundation of the church (Eph 2:20). In the first century these apostles and prophets were a direct source of inspired teaching, and thus were the primary leaders of the church in that day. In postapostolic times their teaching comes to us through the written NT; thus the offices of apostle and prophet were temporary and are not filled by anyone in the church today. Christ exercises his authority over the postapostolic church through the written words of the NT.

Does the NT give us any specific teaching about permanent leadership roles for the ongoing church? The answer is yes. This is very important for our understanding of God's will for the structure of the visible church. It is the second major criterion for determining the divinely given organization of the NT church. The first criterion, as we saw, is congregational polity, marked by local autonomy. Now we are saying that the second criterion is adherence to the NT pattern for proper leadership within the local congregation as such.

The NT recognizes two major leadership roles or offices within the congregation, namely, elders (overseers) and deacons. This is seen in Phil 1:1, when Paul addresses his letter "to all the saints in Christ Jesus who are in Philippi, including the overseers and deacons." That these are the two main offices for "the household of God, which is the church of the living God" (1 Tim 3:15) is seen also in the fact that 1 Tim 3:1-13 spells out qualifications for them alone: elders or overseers (1-7), and deacons (8-13).

1. Elders in the Local Church

The main leadership role, the role in which authority resides, seems to be that of the elder. The NT uses three main terms to describe this role: elder (*presbyteros*, e.g., Acts 20:17; 1 Tim 5:17; Titus 1:5; 1 Pet 5:1), overseer or bishop (*episkopos*, Acts 20:28; Phil 1:1; 1 Tim 3:2; Titus 1:7; verb, *episkopeo*, 1 Pet 5:2), and shepherd or pastor (*poimen*, Eph 4:11; verb, *poimaino*, Acts 20:28; 1 Pet 5:2). That these terms are used interchangeably for this one office is seen in Acts 20, which refers to the same group as "the elders of the church" at Ephesus (v. 17) and as "overseers" (v. 28), and says they were called "to shepherd the church" (v. 28). The same thing is seen in 1 Pet 5:1-2, where the apostle says, "I exhort the elders among you" to "shepherd the flock of God among you, exercising oversight." That elders and bishops are the same is also shown by the fact that Titus 1:5,7 uses the words interchangeably. Thus according to these texts, no distinction should be made between elders and bishops/overseers, or between elders and pastors/shepherds.[4]

These terms in themselves show that the elders are the ones who exercise authoritative leadership in the local congregation. The word "elder" as applied to church leaders does not simply have the generic meaning of "an old person." As in the OT, its use is based on the idea that the people of God are a *family*. Israel itself was a patriarchy, a term that means "rule by the fathers," those who are the eldest.[5] "The elders of Israel" are mentioned often in the OT (e.g., Exod 3:16,18; Num 11:16; Deut 21:18-19; 27:1; 1 Kgs 20:7-8; see Matt 21:23). In a similar way, in the NT era the church is a spiritual family, and the elders are the father figures, the ones in the family who have the experience and maturity to exercise spiritual leadership (see 1 Tim 3:4-5).

That the elders are called "shepherds" also reflects their role as leaders. This image, which also has an OT background (e.g., Jer 23:1-4; 50:6; Ezek 34:1-10; Zech 10:3), pictures the people of God as a flock of sheep who need someone to lead and protect them. That the elders are the ones who have this responsibility for God's New Covenant people is seen in Paul's words to the elders at Ephesus (Acts 20:17), "Be on guard for yourselves and for all the flock, among which the Holy Spirit has made you overseers, to shepherd the church of God which He purchased with His own blood" (Acts 20:28). See also 1 Pet 5:1-4, where the elders are exhorted to "shepherd the flock of God." They are the "pastors" to whom Eph 4:11 refers.

This image of the elders as shepherds helps us to understand the full scope of their work. As shepherds they are responsible for *feeding* the sheep, i.e., for making sure that the Christians under their care are being taught the sound doctrine that leads to spiritual maturity (Eph 4:11-16). They must be sure that what is being taught is (a) in sufficient amounts to prevent starvation, (b) of sufficient nourishment to prevent sickliness, and (c) without noxious weeds to prevent poisoning. This is why an elder must be "able to teach" (1 Tim 3:2), which refers more to his knowledge of the truth than to his pedagogical skills. In other words, he must be "holding fast the faithful word which is in accordance with the teaching, so that he will be able both to exhort in sound doctrine and to refute those who contradict" (Titus 1:9; see 1 Tim 5:17; Ezek 34:1-3).

As shepherds the elders are also responsible for *protecting* the sheep from their enemies. These enemies are mainly depicted as false teachers who want to lead the sheep astray from the truth. Ezekiel 34:5 condemns the false shepherds of Israel who allowed their flock to scatter so that they "became food for every beast of the field." In Acts 20:28-31 the apostle Paul warns the elders at Ephesus to "be on guard for yourselves and for all the flock," and to "be on the alert" because "savage wolves will come in among you, not sparing the flock" and "speaking perverse things" (see also Eph 4:11-16; Titus 1:9-11). Thus the feeding and the protecting are two sides of one coin: providing sound doctrine, and protecting from false doctrine.

Shepherds are also responsible for *healing* their sheep. In Ezek 34:4 the shepherds of Israel are condemned for failing to do this: "Those who are sickly you have not strengthened, the diseased you have not healed, the broken you have not bound up." The NT refers to the whole Christian life as a healing process called sanctification; the elders are called to oversee this process. When a lost sheep comes into the flock, it is diseased by sin; the shepherds help it to get well and to reach spiritual maturity (Eph 4:11-16). In Jas 5:14-16 the desire and the quest for physical healing are interwoven with the need for spiritual healing, in which the elders play a significant part (see Ensign and Howe, 60-90).

The word "overseer" (or "bishop") represents one whose work is very much like that of a shepherd, except without the imagery of sheep. An overseer is literally one who *watches over* or *looks after* someone, or one who takes care of or takes oversight of someone. In this sense an overseer is a watcher, a protector, one who gives "protective care" (Beyer, 609-610). The parallel between overseer and shepherd is seen in 1 Pet 2:25, where Jesus is called "the Shepherd and Overseer of your souls" (NIV; ESV). The connection is also seen in Acts 20:28 and 1 Pet 5:2.

That the elders' leadership involves the exercise of authority is seen in 1 Tim 5:17, which says, "The elders who rule well are to be considered worthy of double honor, especially those who work hard at preaching and teaching." The term for "rule" is *proistemi*,[6] a primary meaning of which is "manage, rule, direct, be the head of." The NIV translates it "direct the affairs of" in 1 Tim 5:17. The same term is used in 1 Thess 5:12, the thought of which is parallel to 1 Tim 5:17 and probably also refers to elders: "But we request of you, brethren, that you appreciate those who diligently labor among you, and have charge over you in the Lord and give you instruction." The same term is used for one of the spiritual gifts named in Rom 12:8, "If it is leadership, let him govern diligently" (NIV). In my judgment this is a reference to the eldership, as is "gifts of administration" in 1 Cor 12:28 (NIV). In view of this teaching it is most likely that Heb 13:7 also refers to elders: "Remember your leaders, who spoke the word of God to you" (NIV), as does Heb 13:17, "Obey your leaders, and submit to them, for they keep watch over your souls." The Greek verb in these last two verses is *hegeomai*, "to have the rule over"; it is often used of military commanders or captains of an army (see Matt 2:6, "Ruler").

It seems clear, then, that the elders are meant to have spiritual authority in the church, leading by their teaching (1 Thess 5:12; 1 Tim 5:17; Titus 1:7) and by their example (Heb 13:7; 1 Pet 5:3). In Acts 15:2,4,6,22,23; 16:4 the elders in Jerusalem are pictured as working side by side with the apostles to settle the circumcision dispute; today the elders lead through their knowledge of and application of the apostles' teaching as found in the written Word of God. Such authoritative leadership is not a dictatorship, since the congregation has a voice in the selection of those who lead (Acts 6:3, by analogy), with the help of the Holy Spirit (Acts 20:28) and the church planter (Acts 14:23; Titus 1:5). Also, it should be noted that the NT always depicts local congregations as having a plurality of elders, and not just one elder or bishop or pastor. (See Acts 14:23; 15:2; 16:4; 20:17; Phil 1:1; Titus 1:5; Heb 13:7,17; Jas 5:14.)

2. Deacons in the Local Church

The other major leadership role in the local church is that of deacon. The Greek word is *diakonos*, the basic connotation of which is "servant, helper, one who carries out the will or purpose of another, one who ministers to the needs of others." The NT usually uses it in this generic sense for Christian workers of all kinds, both men and women (e.g., Rom 16:1; Col 1:7; 4:7; 1 Tim 4:6); in such cases the English word "servant" is most appropriate.

But in at least three texts (Phil 1:1; 1 Tim 3:8,12) this word seems to be used for a more or less "official" role of service in the church—"official" in the sense that the individual is selected and appointed by the local congregation to be responsible for a specific task within or on behalf of that congregation (see Acts 6:3). In this case the English word "deacon" is used.

What is the role of deacons in a local church? We must admit that the NT gives us very little data with which to answer this question. The most important clue comes from the word itself, i.e., "minister, servant." Deacons are first of all servants of Jesus Christ, then servants of the local congregation. Their tasks will be determined by the needs existing within the congregation. Though the seven men chosen in Acts 6:1-6 are not specifically called deacons, they are certainly the prototype of deacons. Their relation to the apostles would be comparable to the relation between deacons and elders today. Working under the oversight of the elders, the deacons tend to the many important details of church life so that the elders (like the apostles in the early church) can devote themselves to prayer and to the ministry of the Word. To say it another way, the elders determine policy by studying and applying God's Word, and the deacons help to implement that policy. As Thatcher (58) puts it,

> The association of the deacon with the overseer in both contexts [Phil 1:1; 1 Tim 3] suggests a secondary, technical role, parallel to the relationship between the Twelve and the Seven in Acts 6. Like the apostles, Paul's overseers were responsible for the spiritual and pastoral care of the Christian community; Paul's deacons, like the Seven, presumably possessed the technical skills necessary to the accomplishment of the spiritual vision provided by the overseers. The specific functions and duties of each deacon would vary, depending on the particular service gifts which that individual possessed.

One caution needs to be strongly stated here. In the NT there is nothing comparable to the kind of "church board" that exists in many modern churches. A long-standing tradition in many Christian churches and churches of Christ is for elders and deacons to form one governing body for the congregation, with deacons having authority equal to that of the elders. In this kind of situation, in practice the deacons actually "run the church," since they usually outnumber the elders. This seems to be in direct violation of NT teaching, however, which portrays the elders alone as the ones in authority. A better arrangement, then, is to have a board of elders (always more than one) appointed by the congregation to be the church's spiritual overseers and policy makers, and a board of deacons appointed to assist the elders in carrying out their work.

3. Other Roles of Service

To say that the NT mandates that elders and deacons are the main leadership roles in the church does not rule out other roles of service. A study of the *diakonos* word family in the NT, including *diakonia* ("ministry, service") and *diakoneo* ("to serve, to help, to minister") shows that every Christian should be a *diakonos* or servant of all other Christians (Matt 20:26; 23:11; Mark 9:35; 10:43) and should be involved in some kind of ministry (Eph 4:12). Some categories of ministry are specifically mentioned in the NT, including the ministry of the Word (Acts 6:4), the ministry of the evangelist (2 Tim 4:5), and the ministry of benevolence (Acts 6:1; 11:29; 12:25; Rom 12:7; 15:31; 2 Cor 8:4; 9:1,13). But just because a specific ministry is not mentioned by name does not mean it is forbidden. The NT certainly allows us to design other roles or positions of service according to need, e.g., Sunday school superintendent, Christian education director, church treasurer, church trustee, youth minister, or even senior minister. Any Christian who is carrying out a specific task or is filling a specific role in the church is a *diakonos*, in the general sense of servant.

How does the role of the senior minister (or preaching minister) fit into this picture? Some equate this with the role of *evangelist* in the NT. For example, "An evangelist is synonymous with what we call the 'minister' or 'preacher' of a congregation" (Donley, 248). This is a bit simplistic, however, mainly because our understanding of this role in NT times is not very clear. In fact, the noun "evangelist" is used only three times in the NT (Acts 21:8; Eph 4:11; 2 Tim 4:5). We know that Timothy was commanded to "do the work of an evangelist" (2 Tim 4:5) and that Philip became an evangelist (Acts 21:8), which involved preaching the gospel in Samaria and to the Ethiopian eunuch (Acts 8:4-13,26-40). This is consistent with the verb form of the word, which is used about 54 times in the NT, almost always in the sense of proclaiming good news or preaching the gospel. Thus at the very least an evangelist was one who evangelized in the sense of proclaiming the good news of the gospel of Jesus Christ. In my judgment the modern church function that is closest to the NT role of an evangelist is the missionary, not the senior minister.

The modern-day senior minister or preaching minister certainly "does the work of an evangelist," though. In fact, he also does much more, usually in the areas of teaching, pastoral counseling, and administration. The best understanding seems to be that there is no biblical equivalent to the modern role of senior minister; this role is usually a combination of several legitimate church functions. This does not mean, of course, that the role of senior minister should be abandoned, since NT silence does not imply prohibition. There is nothing wrong with creating a new role by combining several functions into one position. Nor does this mean that this role is unimportant. It has been designed (or perhaps has evolved) to fill an important place in the overall functioning of a NT congregation. The only caution that needs to be voiced is that the senior minister is not "*the* pastor" of the congregation, nor is he automatically even *one of* the pastors (elders). Unless he is qualified and selected to be an elder, he should guard against assuming the role of authority reserved for the eldership.

C. Leadership and Gender

Sincere Christians have serious differences regarding the role of women in church leadership. The egalitarian (or feminist) approach begins with the assumption that God's original creation purpose was for gender to be irrelevant with respect to leadership roles in both the home and the church. One effect of Adam's sin was to replace this equality with a hierarchical relationship where only men may exercise authority and where women must be in roles of submission. One countereffect of the work of Christ, however, was to abolish this sinful hierarchicalism and to restore the original egalitarianism. This conclusion is usually drawn in part from Gal 3:28, which is taken to mean that no gender distinctions should apply to church leadership roles. Qualified women are just as eligible as qualified men to serve as elders, deacons, and preachers.

The other approach to this issue, called complementarianism (or hierarchical-ism), is that God's original intention for the human race, established at creation, is summed up in 1 Cor 11:3, "The man is the head of a woman." The headship/submission relationship did not originate with the Fall, but was only distorted by it. Jesus did not abolish male headship, either in practice or in his redemptive work. Galatians 3:28 addresses the equality of males and females only with re-spect to their access to salvation; it was never intended to apply to the question of role distinctions. The roles of headship and submission are still assigned to husbands and wives respectively (Eph 5:22-24), and women are excluded from roles that involve teaching men and roles that involve having authority over men (1 Tim 2:12).

1. Galatians 3:28

In my judgment this second view is the correct understanding of biblical teaching, and of the two verses that are crucial to the debate.[7] The first of these verses is Gal 3:28, "There is neither Jew nor Greek, there is neither slave nor free man, there is neither male nor female; for you are all one in Christ Jesus" (see Cottrell, "Galatians"; Cottrell, *Gender Roles*, 217-301). The key to understanding "neither male nor female" here is to ask why Paul links these three pairs (Jew/Greek, slave/free, male/female) together in this context. What do they have in common? Why does he mention these three and no more? The context shows that it is a statement about full equality with respect to access to salvation; it is improper to generalize beyond this.

The historical context of Gal 3:28 is the false teaching of the Judaizers con-cerning the nature of salvation; the issue thus is *how to be saved*. The Judaizers were teaching the necessity of circumcision for Gentile converts. Galatians is writ-ten mainly to deny such a necessity: Gentiles do not have to be circumcised to be saved. How does 3:1–4:7 fit into this argument? This is very important: this sec-tion is an explanation of *why* Gentiles do not have to subject themselves to circum-cision or to the Law of Moses in general, in order to receive salvation through Jesus Christ.

The salvation of which Paul speaks is of course salvation through Christ, but it is important to notice how Abraham is brought into the argument (3:8-9,14,16). Salvation through Christ is described as an *inheritance* received from Abraham (3:17-18). This concept of salvation as inheritance is the key to the right under-standing of Gal 3:28. This inheritance, Paul says, is not based on law; it is based on God's promise. That is, it is received not by following the rules of the Mosaic Law and by receiving circumcision, contrary to what the Judaizers were preaching. Rather, receiving the inheritance is a matter of believing the promise (3:18).

Here the metaphor of inheritance enters the discussion. The question is this: under the New Covenant, is "the blessing of Abraham" (3:14) *inherited* accord-ing to the rules of law, or according to the way a promise works? Verse 29 says we are "heirs according to promise." We have received the inheritance, but *how*? Not according to law, but according to promise.

Why does Paul stress this point about inheritance, and the distinction between inheritance according to law and inheritance according to promise? Because *if* we were still going by the Law of Moses, as the Judaizers claimed, *only certain people* would have access to this inheritance. This is true because the Law of Moses, embodying the common practice of the day, limited the inheritance of property to *free Jewish males*. That is, *Gentiles, slaves, and women* ordinarily did not inherit the family property. Some exceptions were introduced later, but according to the rules of the Law of Moses, under normal circumstances the only legitimate heirs were free Jewish males.

But, says Paul, it is different under the New Covenant, the covenant of promise. Technically Jesus alone is the only rightful heir to the Abrahamic promise, a conclusion based on the singular form of the word "seed" in Gen 22:18. But if this is so, how can anyone else become an heir to the promised salvation? The answer is simple: by taking on the identity of Jesus Himself! This is the point of Gal 3:26-27, "For you are all sons of God through faith in Christ Jesus. For all of you who were baptized into Christ have clothed yourselves with Christ." When we identify ourselves with Jesus, we become heirs along with him. In faith and baptism we take on the identity of Jesus himself, i.e., his identity as a *son* and an *heir* (see 4:7). Even though there is only one true seed and one true heir of the Abrahamic promise, if we belong to Christ, then we too are counted as Abraham's seed and *heirs according to promise* (3:29).

This is the only point of Gal 3:28. As far as salvation is concerned, it does not matter whether we are Jews or Greeks, slaves or free men, males or females. The only thing that matters is whether we *belong to Christ*. The rules of inheritance sanctioned by the Law simply do not apply. Herein lies the significance of the three pairs in 3:28. Under the rules of the Law, the "Greek," "slave," or "female" ordinarily would not be eligible to inherit; but in Christ the inheritance is not given according to the rules of the Law, so these distinctions are no longer relevant for salvation.

This, therefore, is the sole significance of Gal 3:28. **Anyone who is one *with* Christ inherits the blessing of salvation. It no longer matters if one is a Jew or a Greek, a slave or a free man, a male or a female. All baptized believers are one *with* Christ, and thereby inherit salvation.** The context shows that the end of this verse should be translated, "one *with* Christ Jesus," not "one *in* Christ Jesus." Paul's point is not that we are all *one with each other* when we are "in Christ Jesus." The point is that, through faith and baptism, when we clothe ourselves with Christ (3:26-27), we take on his identity and become *one with him* and thus share the inheritance with him.

In conclusion, as far as equality is concerned, "neither male nor female" refers only to equal access to the blessings of salvation through Jesus Christ. The context warrants no other conclusion. Those who wrongly assume that soteriological equality requires functional or role equality should read 1 Pet 3:1-7, which clearly shows that equality of salvation (v. 7) does not imply equality of roles (vv. 1-6).

2. 1 Timothy 2:12

The second verse that is crucial to the debate about gender roles is 1 Tim 2:12, "But I do not allow a woman to teach or exercise authority over a man, but to remain quiet."[8] It is true that earlier verses here (vv. 8-9) include some instructions that may be relevant only in first-century culture, but the main instructions (to pray and to wear modest clothing) are timeless principles. That verse 12 belongs in the latter category is seen by its connection with verse 13, where Paul gives the creation order as the *reason* why women may neither teach nor exercise authority over men.

Many egalitarians say that this verse was addressing a specific problem that existed only at that time and only in the Ephesian church; thus Paul was giving a temporary solution to a temporary, local problem. The problem was that certain liberated but as-yet-uneducated women in the church at Ephesus were teaching false doctrine and usurping authority over men in the process. Thus Paul's concern in 1 Tim 2:12 was not that women were teaching and exercising authority over men, but that they were teaching false doctrine in a presumptuous manner. The problem, however, is that this alleged background situation has been fabricated basically out of nothing, for the sole purpose of allowing this verse to be interpreted in a way that is consistent with egalitarianism. That this passage actually has a straightforward complementarian meaning will now be shown, as the verse is explained phrase by phrase.

"But" (de). This first word, the conjunction "but," may seem inconsequential; but it is important because it shows that the content of verse 12 stands in some kind of contrast with verse 11, which says, "A woman must quietly receive instruction with entire submissiveness." Since the two main words in verse 12 are "to teach" and "to exercise authority," it seems obvious that these ideas are meant to contrast with "receive instruction" and "entire submissiveness" in verse 11.

Thus Paul is saying that women must study and learn Christian doctrine and have an understanding of the contents of the Bible, *but* they are not permitted to use their knowledge to teach men or to have authority over men. This knowledge may be used in many other ways, but not this way.

"I do not allow" (ouk epitrepo). This prohibition is very straightforward; it says unequivocally, "I do not allow." This is not just the unbinding opinion of some ordinary male chauvinist; these words are spoken by an apostle of our Lord Jesus Christ, one who was appointed to preach and teach in faith and truth (v. 7). As an apostle, Paul speaks with the very authority of the One who appointed him.

Some try to say that this command is not applicable today because *epitrepo* is in the present tense, which (they claim) means that the prohibition was intended to apply only to the time at which it was spoken, and not to the ongoing church. The present tense, they say, limited the application of the prohibition to that specific era. As one egalitarian says, Paul is simply saying, "I am not presently allowing a woman to teach" (Spencer, 85). Another says, "The present tense . . . has the force of 'I do not permit *now* a woman to teach'" (Bilezikian, 180). (This is part of the view that the temporary problem at Ephesus was uneducated women teaching false doctrine.)

The fact, however, is this: what these egalitarians are saying about the meaning of the present tense of the Greek verb is exactly the opposite of the usual and ordinary way this tense is explained. The present tense actually indicates *ongoing activity*, not limited, temporary activity. Action described in the present tense is temporally open-ended, as in Heb 10:26 ("go on sinning") and 1 John 3:9 ("continue to sin," "go on sinning," NIV). It is no different in 1 Tim 2:12.

"A woman . . . a man" (gynaiki . . . andros). Depending upon the context, the Greek terms used here (*gyne* and *aner*) can mean either "woman" and "man," or "wife" and "husband." Almost every NT translation takes them to mean "woman" and "man" in 1 Tim 2:12, but some contend that they refer to the husband/wife relationship. Paul is simply forbidding wives to teach and have authority over their husbands, they say. The implication is that this verse would not apply to roles within the church as such; it applies only within the home.

How can we decide what these words mean in this text? Since the words as such can have either meaning, the context is the key. In my judgment the context requires the meaning "woman" and "man." In verses 8,9 the same words are used and surely mean "man" and "woman" in general. The same is true of *gyne* in verse 11. Also, in verses 13,14 Adam and Eve are cited to support the prohibition in verse 12. It is true that Adam and Eve were husband and wife, but when first created they were just "the man" and "the woman." Adam represented all *man*kind (in the narrow sense of "man"), not just married men; and Eve represented all *woman*kind, not just married women. As Gen 1:27 says, "Male and female He created them," not "Husband and wife He created them."

We should note also that verse 14 refers to Adam and "**the** *gyne*" (with the definite article), not Adam and "**his** *gyne*" (with a possessive pronoun). We would expect the latter if Paul were thinking of Adam and Eve as husband and wife, i.e., "Adam and his wife." But he does not say this; he says "**the** *gyne*," i.e., the woman. (We can say this confidently because elsewhere in the NT, unless it is clear from the context, possessive modifiers are used with *gyne* and *aner* to specify the meanings "wife" and "husband." See Titus 3:5; 1 Cor 7:2; 14:35; Eph 5:22. But here no such modifiers are used.)

Another main contextual consideration confirms this conclusion, and that is the general context of the entire epistle. In 3:15 Paul informs Timothy that he is writing this letter "so that you will know how one ought to conduct himself in the household of God, which is the church of the living God, the pillar and support of the truth." In other words, he states specifically that his intention is to discuss *church* life, not home life. The fact that the instruction concerning women and men in 2:8-15 is followed immediately by instruction concerning church offices is indicative of this more general focus of the entire letter.

"To teach" (didaskein). The word "teach," from the Greek *didasko*, is in contrast with "receive instruction" in verse 11. It is best to understand the word "a man" to be the common object of both verbs, "teach" and "exercise authority over." Thus "I do not allow a woman to teach a man" is a complete thought that is separate from "I do not allow a woman to exercise authority over a man," as shown below.

What exactly is meant by "teach"? Rengstorf (135) says the Greeks used this word to mean "teaching" or "instructing" in the widest sense, including the imparting of information, the passing on of knowledge, and the acquiring of skills. There is also a nuance of authority, in the sense that the teacher is telling his students what they *ought* to believe or *ought* to do. This is quite different from other kinds of verbal presentations, such as personal testimonies and reports from mission fields.

Since 1 Tim 3:15 specifies that Paul is giving instructions about church life, we conclude that this prohibition applies only within the context of the church. Paul thus forbids women to teach *Christian* men in all functions of the church sanctioned by the elders, including but not limited to public worship. He is not forbidding such things as Christian mothers teaching their sons, or Christian women school teachers having male pupils. Since church life is in view, we also conclude that the prohibition is limited to teaching *Christian doctrine*, or teaching about the meaning and application of the Bible. That is, Paul is forbidding women to give authoritative instruction concerning biblical doctrine to Christian men in any kind of church function.

What about the common egalitarian contention that the teaching Paul is forbidding here is *false* teaching only? There is nothing at all in this verse or in this word to suggest that this is what Paul had in mind. Also, such an idea raises some obvious questions. If Paul's main concern here is *false* teaching, why does he limit his prohibition only to women teaching *men*? It is just as wrong to teach false doctrine to women as to men. Also, if the main concern is false teaching, why does he prohibit only *women* from such teaching? It is just as wrong for men to teach false doctrine as for women to do it.

Thus this prohibition has nothing to do with whether the content of the teaching is true or false. Paul forbids a woman to teach a man (as defined above), period.

"To exercise authority over" (authentein). The meaning of *authenteo* (used only here in the NT) is very controversial. One idea prevalent among egalitarians is that this word in itself has a negative connotation, i.e., that it refers to a kind of authority which in itself is sinful or wrongly seized. This view is perpetuated in

some translations, including the KJV, which says "usurp authority." Other versions use the word "domineer" (Berkeley, Williams, NEB), a practice that of course is objectionable by definition. As one egalitarian says, it means to seize autocratic, dictatorial control (Webb, 2:7).

This conclusion is drawn mainly from one of the meanings of the related noun, *authentes*, which in ancient Greece was sometimes applied to individuals in the negative senses of "autocrat" and even "murderer." Thus, it is concluded, if an *authentes* is "a murderer," then the verb *authenteo* must mean "to commit murder," or at least to exercise violent and dictatorial control over someone. Thus Paul is forbidding women to exercise absolute power over men in a destructive manner; he is not forbidding the exercise of ordinary authority over men.

Others, however, have concluded that the verb *authenteo* does not have this negative connotation, but simply means "exercise authority over" (NASB, ESV) or "have authority over" (NKJV, NRSV, NIV), as most translations render it. In other words, it is not a kind of authority that is objectionable in itself, nor is it necessarily seized ("usurped") in an unlawful manner.

One way to decide the meaning of this word is to examine all the times *authenteo* was used in Greek literature of any kind near the time of the NT. This has been done H. Scott Baldwin. He has identified, examined, listed, and analyzed all the 82 relevant uses of this verb from the first century B.C. to the twelfth century A.D. (see Baldwin, "Word" and "*authenteo*"). He concludes that in every case but two, *authenteo* was used to mean legitimate authority without any kind of destructive connotation such as "domineer." The two exceptions are one use by Chrysostom in A.D. 390, where it means something akin to "usurp authority." The other negative sense comes from the tenth century A.D., where it was used in the sense of "murder." But these examples are too late to help us understand what the word meant closer to the first century. The fact is that every known use of the word in NT times and for several hundred years thereafter refers not to sinful authority but to a valid, positive kind of authority.

If *authenteo* in itself meant a sinful kind of authority, why would Paul again limit his prohibition to women? It would be just as wrong for men to usurp such authority as it is for women. Also, if this were the meaning, why does Paul forbid such domineering only over *men*? Would it not be wrong to domineer over women also?

The only sound conclusion is that Paul is prohibiting women in the church to hold positions of authority over men. The apostleship was such a position; this is a reason why no woman was chosen to the office of apostle. The eldership is such a position; thus 1 Tim 2:12 prohibits women from serving as elders in the church.

"Or" (oude). This simple conjunction linking "teach" and "exercise authority" may seem insignificant, but in fact it is very important for our understanding of the verse as a whole. This is so because some think *oude* links these two verbs together in such a way that they represent just one activity, not two. The idea is

that Paul is saying that it is wrong for a woman to teach men *in such a way* that she usurps authority over them. That is, as long as she is not usurping authority, it is all right for her to teach men. Thus if the elders sanction it, a woman can legitimately teach a mixed adult Bible class or even preach from the pulpit.

This view assumes two things. First, it assumes that the word *authenteo* means "usurp authority," which we have already seen is entirely false. Second, it assumes that the very force of the word *oude* is to link two actions together in such a way that they are inseparable, or in such a way that the one defines the other. One egalitarian has said that its English equivalent is *'n'*, as in such familiar phrases as "nice 'n' easy," "hot 'n' bothered, "eat 'n' run." Thus what Paul is saying is that a woman must not "teach 'n' domineer" over a man, i.e., she must not teach men in a domineering manner.

Is this the proper meaning of *oude*? The answer is no. Köstenberger's study of *oude* ("Sentence") shows that it never connects a positive activity with a negative activity, but always connects either two positive activities or two negative ones. This in itself rules out the suggestion that the two verbs, *didasko* and *authenteo*, form a single idea meaning "teach (positive) so as to usurp authority (negative)." Also, though this conjunction does connect two things or activities that are related, they always remain distinct. It is usually like our combination "neither . . . nor," and sometimes it is equivalent to "not even." Its precise force in 1 Tim 2:12 is probably this: "I permit a woman *neither* to teach a man, *nor* to have authority over a man."

"But to remain quiet" (all' einai en hesuchia). Hesuchia does not mean "be silent" (as the NIV translates it), but to have a quiet demeanor or attitude.[9] Apparently this was an important point for Paul, because he gives the same instruction in verse 11, "Let a woman *quietly* receive instruction." Thus Paul opens and closes this two-verse instruction to women with an emphasis on a quiet spirit. This suggests that the Ephesian women did have a problem that Paul is addressing here, namely, that they were dutifully learning Christian doctrine but were not doing so in quietness and submission (v. 11). Rather, they were seeking to use their knowledge in an improper way, i.e., in teaching and having authority over men. This would explain Paul's emphasis on a quiet, submissive attitude.

3. Practical Applications

How may these conclusions be applied to questions of church leadership today? In my judgment, only two kinds of church activities are prohibited for Christian women by 1 Tim 2:12. The first is *teaching Christian men*, as defined above. Two notes may be added here. One, this verse does not prohibit women from teaching *non-Christian* men, e.g., in an evangelistic situation (see below). Two, exactly when a boy becomes a man is something we may never agree upon. Each body of elders should set a policy on this for their own congregations, without condemning those who disagree. The bottom line is that women are not allowed to teach in any Christian-to-Christian situation where men are in the audience. This applies especially to preaching from the pulpit, and teaching mixed adult Sunday school classes.

The second prohibited activity is *exercising authority over Christian men*. This means that women may not be elders, since this is an office of general authority in the church. This also shows why Jesus chose no women to be apostles.

It should be emphasized that the category of things *not* prohibited by 1 Tim 2:12 is **much** larger than the former. First, this text does not prohibit women from teaching in church contexts where no men are present. That is, they may teach other women (Titus 2:3-5), as well as children of both sexes. If a woman has a gift of teaching and there is not a proper context for the use of her gift, a congregation should seriously consider dividing Bible classes according to gender, thus creating more women's classes.

Second, this text does not prohibit women from witnessing to unbelievers, men or women. Unbelievers are not a part of the "household of God" (1 Tim 3:15) and thus are not excluded by the prohibition. This means that women may participate fully in evangelism and missionary work. In Acts 18:26 Priscilla's "teaching" of Apollos was in fact witnessing to an unbeliever (Apollos had not been baptized into Christ, Acts 18:25; see 19:1-7).

Third, this text does not prohibit women from participating in a worship service, as long as they are not teaching men or exercising authority over men. "Leading" singing is not exercising authority. Giving inspirational testimony is not teaching. Communion meditations, on the other hand, are usually a form of teaching.

Fourth, this text does not prohibit women from being involved in many positions of leadership or administration in the church, where these do not involve teaching men and having authority over men. We should make a distinction between having authority over *people*, and administering *programs* or having responsibility over certain areas of service in the church.

Whether women can be deacons or not cannot be settled by this text. Biblically understood, the office of deacon does not involve teaching men or having authority over men; thus 1 Tim 2:12 does not apply. But a study of other texts suggests that there is no biblical precedent for women as deacons. In Rom 16:1 the use of *diakonos* for Phoebe is best understood in the generic sense of "servant" (see Cottrell, *Romans*, 2:461-464). In Acts 6:1-6 when the apostles gave instructions for choosing the seven protodeacons, they commanded that "seven men" be selected. The word for "men" is *aner*, which specifically means "males."

Does 1 Tim 3:11 refer to deaconesses, as Thatcher (65-66) believes? The question arises in view of the fact that this verse, which appears in the middle of Paul's list of qualifications for deacons (vv. 8,12), refers to *gynaikas* (plural for *gyne*), which can mean either "wives" or "women." Many take this to mean the deacons' wives; others see it as referring to women leaders, if not deacons as such then something equivalent to deacons. The latter is a possibility, but several considerations rule out including the *gynaikas* in the general category of deacons. These are as follows.

(1) The use of the word "likewise" (*hosautos*) in 1 Tim 3:8 and 3:11. In 3:8 this word introduces the deacons as a group different from the elders. Its use in 3:11 suggests that it is here introducing yet another group distinct from the deacons. (This is how the word functions in 1 Tim 2:8-9 and Titus 2:2-6.)

(2) The use of the words *semnotes* and *semnos* in this chapter. *Semnotes* is a noun meaning "gravity, dignity" and is used in 1 Tim 3:4 as a qualification for elders. *Semnos* is the equivalent adjective, meaning "grave, dignified, worthy of respect." It is used in 3:8 as the first qualification for deacons, and is also used in 3:11 as the first qualification for the *gynaikas*. If 3:11 is giving further qualifications for women deacons, why is this adjective (*semnos*) repeated from 3:8? The fact that it and its related noun are used three times in these lists suggests that we have three groups here: elders, deacons, and *gynaikas*.

(3) The use of "deacons" in both 3:8 and 3:12 and *gynaikas* ("women, wives") in 3:11 pointedly distinguishes these women from the category of deacons.

(4) Those who hold that 3:11 refers specifically to women deacons usually say that 3:12 then refers specifically to men deacons. If this were the case, we would expect the word "men" in 3:12 instead of the word "deacons."

(5) If 3:12 states qualifications for men deacons only, then it is required of both elders (3:2) and men deacons that they be "the husband of one wife." Why would it not be equally important that the women deacons be "the wife of one husband"? Even widows who wanted church support had to meet this requirement (1 Tim 5:9). Yet it is not given as a requirement for the *gynaikas* in 3:11. This implies that the *gynaikas* are not women deacons.

(6) The use of the Greek word *gyne* (singular for *gynaikas*) in the sense of "wives" in 3:2 and 3:12 suggests that this is its meaning in 3:11 also. The reason there is no possessive ("their") in 3:11 may be that in this verse *gynaikas* includes both the wives of the elders and the wives of the deacons.

IV. THE RESTORATION OF THE TRUE CHURCH

The belief that the outward, visible structure of the church does matter is at the very heart of all efforts through the centuries to "restore the true church." It is the basic presupposition of the Restoration Movement that began in early nineteenth-century America, the one sometimes called the Stone-Campbell Movement (after its early leaders, Barton W. Stone, and Thomas and Alexander Campbell). Such attempts to restore the church do not apply to the invisible church as such, but to the visible church. The goal is to restore the God-intended organization or structure of the church as it can be seen by the world.

This concept of restoration is based on four suppositions. First, there is a definite pattern for the visible church revealed in the NT. This pattern is not necessarily found in any particular congregation that existed in apostolic times; thus we are not seeking to restore the Jerusalem church, or the Ephesian church, or certainly not the Corinthian church. The pattern rather lies in the overall teaching of the NT, both in its didactic portions and in the recorded practices sanctioned by apostolic approval. Also, the NT pattern for the church is not a massive blueprint, as if every detail were addressed and finalized. The general structure is given, as outlined in this chapter; but many decisions are left to the best judgments of God's people through the ages.

Second, the pattern for the visible church given in the NT is normative for all ages. This is true because of the nature of apostolic authority as that authority was expressed in the first century and as it is embodied in the writings of the NT. Because all Scripture is God-breathed, we conclude that *God has spoken* with regard to church structure. We are not free to rethink the appropriateness of congregational autonomy and the local church organization explained above, and replace them with forms that we might think are better oriented to different times and cultures.

Third, advocacy of restoration presupposes that most modern visible church groups or denominations are not conforming to the pattern for God's church as revealed in the NT. Even if one or a few such groups are close to the NT pattern, the great number and the wide variety of denominations assures that many are not in conformity with the pattern.

Finally, most restoration efforts assume that even if most visible churches fall short of the NT teaching and should be either reformed or abandoned, nevertheless the invisible church is alive and well. In other words, such efforts usually assume that there are individual Christians in all the sects, immersed believers in Jesus Christ who are a part of the body of Christ, the church universal. The hope of restorationism is that all of these Christians will see the importance of banding together within one true visible church structure, thus enhancing spiritual growth (sanctification), brotherly fellowship, and Christian witness to the world. In this sense a restoration movement is a unity movement, seeking to unite all those who belong to the invisible body of Christ in a properly restored visible body.

NOTES ON CHAPTER TWENTY-FIVE

[1] Ordinarily the reference is to all saved individuals presently living on earth, though Heb 12:23 may be using the term to include those Christians who have died and are in the presence of Christ.

[2] See also references to "the church" at Antioch (Acts 11:26; 13:1; 14:27; 15:3), Caesarea (Acts 18:22), Ephesus (Acts 20:17; 20:28; Rev 2:1; and maybe 3 John 6,9,10), and Philippi (Phil 4:15). See Rev 2:8,12,18; 3:1,7.

[3] "Polity" comes from the Greek *polis*, "city, city-state"; cf. *politeia*, "citizenship, state."

[4]The words "overseer" and "bishop" are interchangeable translations of the Greek noun *episkopos*, which is used for elders in the four texts listed above. The word "pastor" literally means "shepherd." In the NT the pastors (plural) of a local congregation are the elders.

[5]See Acts 2:29, "the patriarch David"; Acts 7:8-9, "the twelve patriarchs"; Heb 7:4, "Abraham, the patriarch."

[6]This word literally means "to stand before or in front of." This can mean "to stand before people for the purpose of protecting, aiding, or helping them," or "to stand before people for the purpose of leading, governing, or presiding over them."

[7]I have defended this view in detail in *Gender Roles*, "Headship," "Timothy," "Galatians," "Response," and "Priscilla."

[8]For further discussion of this verse see Cottrell, "Timothy" and "Response." For the best detailed study see Köstenberger, *Women*.

[9]This is different from *sigao* in 1 Cor 14:34, which means literal silence, "do not speak." In that context it is referring especially to the use of the gifts of prophesying and speaking in tongues in the assembly. The subject here in 1 Tim 2:12 is quite different.

CHAPTER TWENTY-SIX
THE CHURCH: ITS ASSEMBLIES

The idea of the church as an assembly is implicit in the very word *ekklesia*, the "called out" ones. In the secular Greek world in NT times this term referred to a public assembly of any sort (as in Acts 19:32,39,41). The *ekklesia* of Jesus Christ consists of those who have been called out from the world for the very purpose of assembling themselves in the presence of God. How the local congregation assembles together is an important part of its identity as the true visible church.

The NT regards such assembling together as a duty that every Christian is obligated and expected to fulfill. Hebrews 10:25 warns us not to be "forsaking our own assembling [*episynagoge*] together, as is the habit of some." The noun used here is a form of the word "synagogue" (*synagoge*), which is used for the church's assembly in Jas 2:2. These words are related to the verb *synago*, a common word meaning "to gather together, to assemble," which is used to refer to the assembling of the church in Acts 14:27; 15:30; 20:7-8; 1 Cor 5:4 (see also Matt 18:20). Another verb used for the church's assembling is *synerchomai*, "to come together" (see 1 Cor 11:17-18,20,33-34; 14:26).

These many NT references to Christians actually assembling together make it clear that this is part of what it means to be a member of the body of Christ. Those who argue, "I can be a Christian without 'going to church,'" are simply resisting God's will. The question arises, however, as to the *purpose* of our meeting together. We generally have many types of assemblies, e.g., Sunday school classes, VBS, Bible study classes, youth meetings, prayer meetings, fellowship dinners, class parties, small group meetings, revival meetings, evangelistic crusades, and of course "worship services" or "church services." Here we are asking, based on biblical teaching, *why* should we be meeting together? What purposes should such assemblies serve?

God's Word pictures believers meeting together for three, and perhaps four, main purposes. In general these represent four kinds of relationships that should or may be experienced in Christian assemblies, by means of activities that are oriented in four directions: believer-to-God activities, or *worship*; God-to-believer activities, or *edification*; believer-to-believer activities, including edification and *fellowship*; and believer-to-unbeliever activities, or *evangelism*.

I. THE BELIEVER-TO-GOD PURPOSE

In a general sense worship is any activity of the spirit or body that is directed toward God for the purpose of honoring and glorifying him. Of course, we may worship God individually in private (Matt 6:5-6), but we also can and should worship him collectively with other believers. Thus a major reason for church assemblies is to worship God together. "In fact," says Grudem, "the primary reason that God called us into the assembly of the church is that as a corporate assembly we might worship him" (*Doctrine*, 1003).

A. The Object of Worship

Jesus declares that those who worship God must worship him "in truth" (John 4:24). This means that the only proper object of our worship is the one true God, the Creator and Lord of the universe and the Redeemer of his people: "You shall worship the Lord your God and him only shall you serve" (Matt 4:10, ESV). Idolatry—the worship of anything other than the true God—is the ultimate wickedness, as well as the ultimate foolishness (see *GC*, 390-419). The Creator-Redeemer alone is *worthy* of worship (Rev 4:11; 5:9).

When Jesus first spoke of worshiping God "in truth," he was talking specifically to the Samaritan woman (John 4:7). The Samaritans' concept of God was based on the earlier portions of the OT (especially the Pentateuch), but was seriously incomplete. Jesus signaled its inadequacy when he said of the Samaritans as a group, "You worship what you do not know" (John 4:22). As in their case, even if one's knowledge of God is partially right (e.g., monotheism and creation), an ignorance of the full revelation of God's nature inevitably leads to distortions and falsehoods and thus to unacceptable worship. Herein is the basic flaw with Muslim religion and worship.

Jesus says that the Father seeks "true worshipers" who will worship him in truth (John 4:23). At the time Jesus spoke these words to the Samaritan woman, the Jews were the ones who met this qualification: "We worship what we know, for salvation is from the Jews" (John 4:22). That is, the Jews worshiped Yahweh as he was revealed in the complete OT. At that point this was acceptable worship.

In this same context, however, Jesus pointed ahead to a time when neither Samaritan nor Jewish worship would be worship "in truth": "An hour is coming when neither in this mountain or in Jerusalem will you worship the Father" (John 4:21). This is a reference to the coming of the New Covenant on Pentecost, when the Old Covenant as such, including its entire system of worship anchored to the temple site in Jerusalem, would become incomplete and obsolete. A more complete revelation of God would be made known to all, including his universal, non-localized presence, his Trinitarian nature, and his redeeming activity through the Son and the Spirit. True and acceptable worship today must be directed toward God in his fullness as he is revealed in the complete NT as well as in the OT.

Thus worshiping God "in truth" means not just worshiping the one true God, but also worshiping him according to the fullness of his revelation of himself. This means that the more we know about God's nature and works, the more rich and meaningful our worship can be. In other words, the more we understand the nature and implications of his attributes, the more specific our praise for him can be. The more we know about his manifold works as Creator, Lord, and Redeemer, the more variety we can experience in our worship activities.

B. The Essence of Worship

In his response to the Samaritan woman Jesus said that true worship must be not only "in truth" but also "in spirit" (John 4:23-24). He probably does not mean "in the Spirit," i.e., the Holy Spirit. Rather, he seems to be referring to the human spirit, the part of our nature God made in his own image specifically for the purpose of enabling us to have personal, spiritual communion with him. To say that our worship must be "in spirit" means that it must begin in our spirits, in the "inward man." It cannot be mere external acts, but must involve a conscious, rational activity of the mind. Indeed, the very essence of worship is an inward attitude of the heart along with specific mental activity directed toward God. One may worship in the spirit alone, and one may worship with the body along with the spirit (see below); but one cannot worship at all unless the spirit or heart is actively involved.

When we worship, then, the object of our thoughts is God. We are concentrating or focusing specifically upon God, perhaps as our Creator, perhaps as our Savior, perhaps as our Lawgiver, perhaps as our Comforter. Worship is an *attitude* of the heart toward God—a consciousness or awareness of his presence, a spirit of reverence or awe in view of his power and glory, an attitude of adoration and love in awareness of his love toward us, a spirit of submission to his law and his will, a sense of peace and joy in contemplation of his grace. Worship is more than an attitude or feeling, though; also, it is more than just thinking *about* God. Worship is also a conscious mental activity in which our heart speaks to God and addresses him in words of love, praise, thanksgiving, submission, and petition. Worship is always an *I-Thou*, person-to-person experience, the conscious and deliberate overflowing of the worshiper's heart in direct communication with the heart of the personal God.

Certain Psalms include worship as words spoken directly to God. An example is Psalm 8, which begins, "O LORD, our Lord, how majestic is Your name in all the earth, Who have displayed Your splendor above the heavens!" (v. 1). Another example is Ps 25:1-2, "To You, O LORD, I lift up my soul. O my God, in You I trust, do not let me be ashamed." Also Ps 84:1-2, "How lovely are Your dwelling places, O LORD of hosts! My soul longed and even yearned for the courts of the LORD; my heart and my flesh sing for joy to the living God." And Ps 92:1,5, "It is good to give thanks to the LORD, and to sing praises to Your name, O Most

High . . . . How great are Your works, O LORD!" And Ps 145:1, "I will extol You, my God, O King, and I will bless Your name forever and ever." See Ps 108:1-6.

Sometimes our worship toward God may take the form of a *declaration* of his works and his excellencies, spoken deliberately in his hearing, for the purpose of making them known to others and thus of motivating and leading others to join with us in such worship. Many praises in the Psalms take this form, e.g., 34:1-3, "I will bless the LORD at all times; His praise shall continually be in my mouth. My soul will make its boast in the LORD; the humble will hear it and rejoice. O magnify the LORD with me, and let us exalt His name together." And Ps 99:1-3, "The LORD reigns, let the peoples tremble; He is enthroned above the cherubim, let the earth shake! The LORD is great in Zion, and He is exalted above all the peoples. Let them praise Your great and awesome name; holy is He." See also Ps 146:1-2; 147–150.

C. The Means of Worship

True worship toward God always involves the conscious mental activity of the heart; and sometimes it is an activity of the heart alone as our thoughts are quietly directed toward our God. This is truly worship "in spirit" (John 4:24) and is reflected in Mary's words in Luke 1:46-47, "My soul exalts the Lord, and my spirit has rejoiced in God my Savior." As Paul says, worship is a spiritual or rational (*logikos*) act (Rom 12:1); i.e., it necessarily involves the mind, the intellect, the spirit.

But Jesus does not say we must worship God in spirit *alone*, i.e., in purely mental activity without the participation of the body. Indeed, true worship often rightly involves the physical side of our nature. As Ps 84:2 says, "My heart and my flesh sing for joy to the living God." This is appropriate and even unavoidable in view of the fact that our authentic human nature includes not only the soul or spirit but also the physical body. God is Spirit and not body, thus our spirits are our proper link with him; but we ourselves are *body* and spirit, and our bodies are a vital *means* by which we worship God. Paul says it thus: "Therefore I urge you, brethren, by the mercies of God, to present your bodies a living and holy sacrifice, acceptable to God, which is your spiritual service of worship" (Rom 12:1).

The Bible frequently pictures worship being offered to God acceptably through bodily means. This is especially true of the mouth (lips, tongue, voice) since our spoken words sound forth the silent thoughts of the heart. As David said, in anticipation of forgiveness, "My tongue will joyfully sing of Your righteousness. O Lord, open my lips, that my mouth may declare Your praise" (Ps 51:14-15). "Shout to God with the voice of joy," says Ps 47:1. David declared, "I will bless the LORD at all times; His praise shall continually be in my mouth" (Ps 34:1), and, "My soul is satisfied as with marrow and fatness, and my mouth offers praises with joyful lips" (Ps 63:5). Hebrews 13:15 exhorts us, "Through Him, then, let us continually offer up a sacrifice of praise to God, that is, the fruit of lips that give thanks to His name." See Ps 26:7; 35:28; 42:4; 63:3; 71:23; 109:30; 119:171-172; 145:21; Isa 57:19.

Even parts of the body that do not directly voice the thoughts of the heart, such as hands and feet, are pictured as means by which we worship God. "O clap your hands, all peoples; shout to God with the voice of joy" (Ps 47:1). "Lift up your hands in the sanctuary and bless the LORD" (Ps 134:3; see Neh 8:6; Ps 63:4). "Let them praise His name with dancing" (Ps 149:3; see Ps 150:4; Exod 3:5; 2 Sam 6:14). Bodily postures of bowing and kneeling are means of worship: "Come, let us worship and bow down, let us kneel before the LORD our Maker" (Ps 95:6). The people of God in Ezra's time "bowed low and worshiped the LORD with their faces to the ground" (Neh 8:6; see 2 Chr 29:30; Isa 45:23; Micah 6:6; Rom 14:11; Phil 2:10).

The means by which spiritual worship is offered to God includes not only our physical bodies but also other appropriate physical items. The Lord's Supper as an act of worship praising Jesus for his saving sacrifice uses the material elements of unleavened bread and the fruit of the vine. Giving as an act of worship acknowledging God as the owner of all things uses pieces of metal (coins) and paper (bills, checks). Physical instruments of music are also used as a part of worship, either to accompany the singing of praises or simply as a means of expressing reverent joy and praise toward God.

In Scripture three main types of musical instruments are represented as means of worshiping God: stringed instruments, variously translated as harps, lyres, lutes, and psalteries; percussive instruments, variously translated as cymbals, drums, castanets, tambourines, and timbrels; and wind instruments, variously translated as trumpets, flutes, pipes, and horns. For example, "David and all the house of Israel were celebrating before the LORD with all kinds of instruments made of fir wood, and with lyres, harps, tambourines, castanets and cymbals" (2 Sam 6:5; see 1 Chr 13:8; 15:28). In 2 Chr 5:11-14, when the presence of the Lord filled the newly built temple, the people worshiped him with cymbals, harps, lyres, and 120 trumpets. The Psalms are filled with such references: "Raise a song, strike the timbrel, the sweet sounding lyre with the harp. Blow the trumpet at the new moon" (Ps 81:2-3). It is good to sing praises to God "with the ten-stringed lute and with the harp, with resounding music upon the lyre" (Ps 92:3). "Praise Him with trumpet sound; praise Him with harp and lyre. Praise Him with timbrel and dancing; praise Him with stringed instruments and pipe. Praise Him with loud cymbals; praise Him with resounding cymbals" (Ps 150:3-5). In the Apocalypse both angelic figures and redeemed individuals are pictured as praising God with harps (Rev 5:8; 14:2; 15:2).

Some, of course, have a strong conviction that musical instruments must not be used in a public worship service. Whatever their reasoning for holding this view, it cannot be that such worship is wrong in itself, since inspired Scripture presents it as appropriate. Using such physical means for worship is proper because we ourselves are physical beings; our bodies, e.g., our hands, are part of who we are. We may worship God with our hands by raising them, clapping them, or playing a keyboard or stringed instrument with them.

D. Acts of Worship in Christian Assemblies

Romans 12:1 suggests that all Christian living is worship offered up to God. Christians must do *everything* "to the glory of God" (1 Cor 10:31), and whatever is done for his glory is surely an act of worship in some sense. Christians are commanded to assemble together, though, and one of the purposes for doing so is to engage in worship together. Here we are asking what *acts* of worship should be included in corporate assemblies.

Strictly speaking, some of the things Christians do in their assemblies are not worship or are not limited to worship, i.e., they are not activities directed specifically and exclusively toward God in interpersonal adoration and communion. Some Christian activities can and indeed do function as worship in this strict sense, however. Most if not all of them can be done as private worship apart from an assembly, but most if not all can and should be practiced by the church when it meets together. The list includes songs of praise, prayer, the Lord's Supper, and the giving of offerings.

Singing praises to God is clearly an act of worship: "Sing praise to the LORD, you His godly ones" (Ps 30:4). "Give thanks to the LORD with the lyre; sing praises to Him with a harp of ten strings. Sing to Him a new song; play skillfully with a shout of joy" (Ps 33:2-3). "Sing praises to God, sing praises; sing praises to our King, sing praises. For God is the King of all the earth; sing praises with a skillful psalm" (Ps 47:6-7; see Ps 101:1; 105:2; 144:9). Paul says one result of being a Spirit-filled Christian is "singing and making melody with your heart to the Lord" (Eph 5:19; see Col 3:16). In heaven the angels and the redeemed sing songs of praise to God and the Lamb (Rev 5:9; 14:3; 15:3).

In Old Covenant times God's people are pictured as singing praises together. "Moses and the sons of Israel" sang a song to the Lord (Exod 15:1). On a special occasion "David and all Israel were celebrating before God with all their might, even with songs and with lyres, harps, tambourines, cymbals and with trumpets" (2 Chr 13:8). Jesus and his apostles sang a Passover hymn (Matt 26:30). Congregational singing is clearly implied in Ps 95:1-2; 100:2; 149:1.

What about the New Covenant age? Actually there is no *clear* NT reference to a Christian assembly engaged in congregational singing, either by command or example. Ephesians 5:19 ("singing and making melody with your heart to the Lord") does not clearly refer to an assembly. Hebrews 13:15 (offering sacrifices of praise) specifically mentions neither singing nor assembling. Acts 16:25 (Paul and Silas singing in prison) is hardly a normal assembly. In 1 Cor 14:15 the singing does seem to be in the context of an assembly, but it does not seem to be congregational (see v. 26). How, then, can we justify congregational singing in church assemblies? For one thing, the NT does not prohibit singing praises to God as an assembled group; silence cannot be taken as a prohibition. Also, in view of the OT precedent, and in view of the appropriateness of musical worship as such, most Christian assemblies rightly include collective songs of praise in their worship time.

The second act of worship properly included in the corporate assembly is prayer. While some prayers (e.g., intercession) have purposes other than worship, some are clearly directed toward God as expressions of the worshipers' praise, submission, and trust. Many of the Psalms may be regarded as such prayers, e.g., Ps 51, 83, 86, 88, 130, 141–143. The early Christians continued steadfastly in prayer, according to Acts 2:42, which seems to refer to assembled activities. In Acts 4, after being arrested and released by the Jewish leaders (vv. 1-23), Peter and John assembled with other Christians for a season of prayer (vv. 23-31). In Acts 12 the church is pictured as assembling specifically for the purpose of prayer, but mainly in intercession for Peter (vv. 5,12). The clearest reference to prayer in a regular assembly is 1 Cor 14:15-17, a passage that implies that one person may "lead" a prayer for the benefit of all.

The third act of worship in the Christian assembly is the Lord's Supper, which is probably "the breaking of bread" in Acts 2:42. The Supper functions in other ways as well, but one of its main purposes is to honor and glorify Jesus Christ for his work of salvation. And even though a Christian might take the emblems of the Supper while alone, it is clearly intended to be a corporate worship activity. Acts 20:7 shows that it was a main reason why the early Christians met on a weekly basis: "On the first day of the week, when we were gathered together to break bread, Paul began talking to them." Though 1 Cor 10:14-22 and 11:17-34 are dealing mainly with problems related thereto, these texts show that the Supper was one of the central elements of the church's corporate life.

I include the time of giving (the collection of tithes and/or offerings) as an appropriate act of corporate worship for two reasons. First, the spirit and the activity of giving were definitely a part of the early church's life (Acts 4:32–5:11; 2 Cor 8:1–9:15). Like the Lord's Supper (Acts 20:7), it was apparently connected with the church's regular first-day-of-the-week assembly, as suggested by 1 Cor 16:1-3. Second, the act of giving is properly considered to be a worship event, even though the money and other gifts that are given may be designated for benevolent or evangelistic purposes. (In a like manner many of the OT worshipers' offerings and sacrifices were used in part to feed the priests who helped to offer them, e.g. Lev 6:14-18; 7:15-16,28-34.) In our giving we are honoring God as the creator and owner of all things, acknowledging him as the source of all our blessings, and confessing our dependence upon him.

How do we know that musical praise, prayer, the Lord's Supper, and giving should be a part of Christian assemblies? The NT does not provide us with a definitive *list* of mandated acts of corporate worship. All those discussed above are individually commanded, but not necessarily in connection with a corporate assembly. The lack of a definitive list and clear commands for corporate acts of worship does not keep us from knowing God's will on this matter, however. His will is made known to us in two ways. First, all four of the acts of worship discussed above are mentioned as being practiced in some form[1] by assembled Christians, apparently with the approval of the apostles (Acts 2:42; 20:7; 1 Cor 14:15; 16:2). Since the apostles were the primary authoritative teachers in the early church, we accept the practice of these acts of worship as perpetually binding upon the church by the authority of apostolic precedent.

The second way we know God's will for corporate worship is through the general teaching concerning God, man, and worship as found in all of Scripture, including the OT. Of course we are under the New Covenant, and the legal requirements of the Old Covenant do not apply to us. However, only a relatively small part of the OT sets forth the law code that applied only to Israel in their Old Covenant existence. Much of the OT describes the relationship that exists between God as God and man as man. This is the case especially with the wisdom literature, such as the Psalms. Most of the OT's teaching about worship transcends covenantal boundaries. For example, the Psalms clearly show that both congregational singing and instrumental praise are appropriate as acts of worship, just because of who God is and who man is. The lack of an express command or clear precedent for such practices in the apostolic churches is not definitive. To think otherwise is to deny the unity of Scripture; it also commits the fallacy of equating silence with prohibition, which is a form of speaking where the Bible is silent.

E. The Time of Corporate Worship

At any time of day, and on any day of the week, it is appropriate for an individual to worship God and also for Christians to assemble together for corporate worship. Here two questions must be briefly addressed, however. First, is it necessary for Christians to reserve one specific day of the week as their special day when assembly is required? Second, if so, what is that day?

Under the Old Covenant given at Sinai the Jews were required to set aside the Sabbath day (the seventh day of the week, Saturday) as a special day: "Remember the sabbath day, to keep it holy" (Exod 20:8). The first reference to Sabbath observance was after the exodus from Egypt and before Sinai, in connection with God's gift of manna (Exod 16:22-30). The purpose of Sabbath keeping was to honor God for redeeming Israel from Egyptian slavery: "You shall remember that you were a slave in the land of Egypt, and the LORD your God brought you out of there by a mighty hand and by an outstretched arm; therefore the LORD your God commanded you to observe the sabbath day" (Deut 5:15). Appropriate Sabbath keeping for the Jews was rest and cessation from labor (Exod 20:8-11; 31:12-17); this was not connected with any requirement to assemble together. The seventh day was chosen for this ritual rest because that is the day God rested from his work of creation (Gen 2:1-3). Thus it was only fitting that this be the day on which the Jews honored him by ceasing from *their* labor (Exod 20:11; 31:17).

It is important to see that Sabbath observance applied only to Israel under the Old Covenant. No one prior to the postexodus Israelites was commanded to keep the Sabbath. Exodus 31:17 specifically says that God established this day as a sign between himself and Israel. Of the ten commandments in Exodus 20, the Sabbath commandment is the only one that is not repeated or taught in the NT.

In fact the NT says that none of the special days designated by the Mosaic law are binding on Christians today, including the Sabbath: "Therefore no one is to act as your judge in regard to food or drink or in respect to a festival or a new moon or a Sabbath day" (Col 2:16). Whether one regards one day as special or regards every day alike is a matter of opinion, says Rom 14:5. Some take this to apply even to the Christian practice of Sunday-keeping, and thus they feel free to substitute Thursday or Saturday assemblies for Sunday assemblies. In my judgment, however, these two texts were intended to be limited to the holy days named in the Mosaic law, including the Sabbath day.

In my own mind I am persuaded that God intends for Christians in this New Covenant age to assemble for worship on a specific day of the week, and that this day is the Lord's Day, Sunday, the first day of the week. I offer three reasons for this view. First, in recorded NT practice there seems to be something special about the first day of the week. This is when the Christians at Troas "gathered together to break bread" (Acts 20:7), providing an occasion for Paul to preach. "On the first day of every week" was also the convenient time for the Corinthian Christians to add a sum of money to the collection being amassed for the poor saints in Jerusalem (1 Cor 16:1-2). These two texts taken together imply that first-day assemblies were a regular practice in at least some parts of Christendom, with apostolic approval.

Second, several early post-NT Christian writers testify that Christians observed the first day of the week as their special day. In the early second century Ignatius ("To the Magnesians," 9) said that Christians were "no longer keeping the Sabbath but living in accordance with the Lord's day, on which our life arose through him" (*Apostolic Fathers*, 95). Later in the second century, in "The Epistle of Barnabas" (15), the writer says that our focus is no longer on the Sabbath or seventh day, but on the eighth day, "which is the beginning of another world. This is why we spend the eighth day in celebration, the day on which Jesus both arose from the dead and, after appearing again, ascended into heaven" (*Apostolic Fathers*, 183). Likewise in the mid-second century Justin Martyr says that "on the day called Sunday" Christians gathered to hear readings from the apostles and prophets, to hear sermons, to pray, to take the Lord's Supper, and to give. "Sunday is the day on which we all hold our common assembly, because it is the first day on which God . . . made the world; and Jesus Christ our Saviour on the same day rose from the dead" ("Apology," 67, p. 186).

These writers are very clear that Christians observed the *first* (or eighth) day rather than the seventh, and they are clear that the *reason* for doing so was because this was the day on which Jesus rose from the dead. This connection between Christ's resurrection and the first day of the week makes it appropriate to call it "the Lord's day" (see Rev 1:10).

The third reason for this view is theological, and it applies specifically to *which* day of the week is special for Christians. As the early Christian writers noted, the *first* day is the day Jesus was raised from the dead. All four Gospels begin their accounts of the resurrection events by saying it was the first day of the week (Matt 28:1; Mark 16:1-2; Luke 24:1; John 20:1). It is only fitting that we honor the Savior on the day when he won his victory.

That the resurrection occurred on the first day of the week is not accidental. The resurrection of Jesus was a monumental event comparable only to the original creation of the world (Rom 4:17). Ever since the Fall of Adam the first creation has been corrupted by sin (Rom 8:20-22) and has been under the reign of death (Rom 5:17). But Christ's resurrection was in fact the beginning of a *new* creation, and a new age. Christians live not in the old creation but in the new (2 Cor 5:17). It is again fitting that the mighty act which *inaugurated* the new creation should occur on the *first* day of the week, and also that the *birthday* of God's New Covenant people, the church, should be on Pentecost—also the *first* day of the week.

The seventh day is counted in terms of the days of the old creation, and everything about seventh-day observance is based on old-covenant realities. But Jesus has begun a new creation and a new covenant; it is these *beginnings* that we celebrate, appropriately on the day that begins the week. When Christians assemble for worship on Sunday they are bearing witness to the world that they are part of this new creation and this new covenant. The essence of Sunday observance is not rest from work, which is an Old-Covenant motif, but lively kingdom activity in celebration of new beginnings. To continue the pattern of Sabbath (seventh-day) observance and Sabbath rest is to deny and negate the cosmic changes wrought by our Lord on *His* day, the day of his resurrection. Sunday is not the Sabbath.

Some attempt to justify Saturday night Christian worship by pointing out that the Jewish Sabbath began at six p.m. on Friday and ended at six p.m. on Saturday. Thus according to the Jewish way of counting days, any assembly after six p.m. on Saturday is technically on the first day of the week. In my judgment the error here is the same as in Sabbath-day observance as such, i.e., the Jewish way or Old-Covenant way is still made normative. We are no longer under the Old Covenant, and no longer under the Jewish system of counting days.

II. THE GOD-TO-BELIEVER PURPOSE

Though worship (believer-to-God activity) is surely the main reason why Christians gather together, it is not the only one. At the beginning of this chapter I suggested that another purpose for assembly is *edification*. To *edify* means literally "to build," as in building an "edifice." In Scripture the church universal is compared to a building being constructed and built up by God (Acts 9:31; 1 Cor

3:9; Eph 2:20-22; 1 Pet 2:5) through Jesus Christ (Matt 16:18). This refers to the ongoing growth of the kingdom as it continues to spread and embrace more and more people (see Matt 13:31-32).

The concept of edification, however, refers not so much to numerical growth of the church in general as to the spiritual maturing of individual Christians in the context of the local church. Thus it can be viewed as a major aspect of the process of sanctification, as empowered by the Holy Spirit through his personal indwelling and through the Spirit-inspired Word. Thus the principal source and force for edification is God himself. By working within our hearts through his Spirit and his Word he builds us up in our faith and strength of character. As such God can accomplish our edification to some degree through the times of our own private spirituality and personal devotions.

The fact is, however, that the process of spiritual maturing cannot be satisfactorily accomplished while one remains in isolation from other believers. In his work of building us up in the faith, God uses all members of the body of Christ to *edify one another*. This then is a major reason why we must not forsake assembling together: we need one another in order to become mature in Jesus Christ. Thus edification as a purpose for the church's assemblies is both a God-to-believer activity and at times a believer-to-believer activity. (The latter will be explained in the next section).

What aspects of Christian assemblies are intended specifically to edify believers? We are told that good physical health is maintained by proper diet and regular exercise. The same is true for spiritual health and growth: we must be properly fed on the sound doctrine of God's Word, and we must regularly participate in spiritual exercises. The former is a major aspect of our Christian assemblies; from the very beginning of the church God's people have continued steadfastly in "the apostles' teaching" (Acts 2:42). Christians today are still built up by feeding on the Word of God as spoken to us through the apostles and prophets.

We have neither apostles nor prophets to address our assemblies in person today, but we do have their written words in the Spirit-inspired Scriptures, which are "profitable for teaching, for reproof, for correction, for training in righteousness; so that the man of God may be adequate, equipped for every good work" (2 Tim 3:16-17). The "word of His grace . . . is able to build you up" (Acts 20:32). This is why a central aspect of our assemblies is the collective hearing of the Word of God, through which God is edifying us all.

This is accomplished by several specific activities involving the Word, including the reading of Scripture. Paul said to Timothy, "Until I come, devote yourself to the public reading of Scripture" (1 Tim 4:13, ESV; see Col 4:16-17; 1 Thess 5:27). He also tells Timothy to devote himself "to exhortation and teaching" (1 Tim 4:13). Today this is accomplished through the preaching of sermons and through Bible school classes, where the meaning of the Word is expounded and applied. It is also done through Lord's Supper meditations, small group Bible studies, and special meetings or seminars.

The other aspect of our assemblies that is designed in part to edify includes the spiritual activities that exercise the soul and make it stronger, namely, prayer, the Lord's Supper, and giving. While each of these activities has a believer-to-God element (i.e., worship), each also has a God-to-believer purpose (and for some, even a believer-to-believer purpose). When we pray, we are not only offering sacrifices of praise to God; we are also learning how to trust and depend upon him more and more as we express to him our thanksgivings and confessions and petitions. The Lord's Supper likewise is both worship and edification. We take the emblems not only as a memorial to honor our Savior, but also as a means of reminding ourselves that his blood is the only reason we are saved. A major purpose of the Supper thus is to strengthen our own faith. Also, the collecting of the offering is not only a time of honoring God as the giver of every good gift, but also a time for God to edify us by weakening the grip of greed and covetousness on our lives.

Thus it seems clear that the Sunday assembly of believers is not *just* a "worship" service. It is surely also a time for personal edification, a time when we are allowing God to speak to us through his Word and to strengthen our souls through the very activities by which we worship him.

III. THE BELIEVER-TO-BELIEVER PURPOSES

While the relationship between God and believers is surely the main focus of church assemblies, it is not the only one. According to the NT, some of the reasons for meeting together involve the relationships of believers to one another. Two such believer-to-believer purposes may be identified: edification and fellowship.

Edifying one another—building each other up—is something we are commanded to do. "Therefore encourage one another and build up one another, just as you also are doing" (1 Thess 5:11). It is true that the power that edifies and strengthens our Christian life comes mainly from God, and that he edifies us largely through his Word. But his Word operates in our lives only through the work of human instruments, first of all through the prophets and apostles who have delivered his Word to us through revelation and inspiration, and then through those who explain and apply these inspired messages to us through preaching and teaching. Thus a main reason Christians meet together is to edify one another through the study of God's Word.

In the apostolic era, before all the NT books were written and distributed, when congregations assembled, the Holy Spirit directly inspired some Christians to deliver divinely revealed messages to the rest of the believers. This involved mainly the spiritual gift of prophecy, along with the gift of knowledge and even the gift of tongues if accompanied by interpretation. In his discussion of this in 1 Cor 14:1-40, Paul emphasizes that the main purpose for these gifts was mutual edification. For example, "One who prophesies speaks to men for edification and exhortation and consolation. . . . One who prophesies edifies the church" (vv. 4-5; see v. 6). "One who speaks in a tongue edifies himself . . . unless he interprets, so that the church may receive edifying" (vv. 4-5; see vv. 13,28). Paul urges Christians to seek gifts "for the edification of the church" (v. 12). He sums it up thus: "When you assemble, each one has a psalm, has a teaching, has a revelation, has a tongue, has an interpretation. Let all things be done for edification" (v. 26).

Even after the entire NT became available and miraculous gifts such as prophecy ceased, God still gave gifts of teaching and preaching to some Christians to enable them to build up the entire church and bring it to a state of collective maturity. Paul explains this in Eph 4:11-16. Through the foundational work of apostles and prophets God delivered his inscripturated Word (Eph 2:20); and through evangelists and pastor-teachers who are equipped to expound his Word, he continues to build up the superstructure of the church (Eph 4:11). Through their combined efforts they accomplish "the equipping of the saints for the work of service, to the building up of the body of Christ" into a state of maturity (Eph 4:12-13). This maturity includes "the unity of the faith, and of the knowledge of the Son of God" (Eph 4:13), and "the growth of the body for the building up of itself in love" (Eph 4:16). Thus through "speaking the truth in love," the whole church grows up (Eph 4:15).

This edification through teaching could be and sometimes is done in a one-on-one situation, but for the sake of efficiency and economy it is usually done when the church comes together. Thus a main reason for assembling together is to edify one another through the public preaching and teaching of the Word of God. This may be done through a variety of activities, such as Sunday school lessons, sermons, and small group Bible studies.

Preaching and teaching the Word are not the only ways believers edify one another, whether publicly or privately. Another way is to speak words of exhortation, encouragement, and comfort to one another. The verb used to describe this activity is *parakaleo*, which suggests the picture of one Christian standing alongside others to aid and encourage them in their quest to grow in Christ. Some have a gift for this (Rom 12:8), and elders are especially told to "encourage others by sound doctrine" (Titus 1:9, NIV); but all are called to do what they can to encourage each other (1 Cor 14:31; 2 Cor 1:4; 1 Thess 4:18; 5:11; Heb 3:13). In Heb 10:25 this activity is specifically connected with the church assembly: "Let us not give up meeting together, as some are in the habit of doing, but let us encourage one another" (NIV). The goal of such encouragement seems to be to "spur one another on toward love and good deeds" (Heb 10:24, NIV).

Another closely related means of edification is *admonishing* one another. The verb used here is *noutheteo*, which means "to instruct, to admonish, to warn." It literally means to "put something in someone's mind," sometimes by making observations and sometimes by giving warnings (Spicq, II:548). Trench says it means "training by word—by the word of encouragement, when this is sufficient, but also by that of remonstrance, of reproof, of blame, where these may be required" (112). Often it seems to have this latter, more stern and serious tone, e.g., "admonish the unruly" (1 Thess 5:14; see 2 Thess 3:14-15). It is our duty to instruct and admonish one another (Rom 15:14; Col 3:16), with this responsibility falling especially upon the elders (1 Thess 5:12). This seems to be the point of 1 Tim 5:20 (though a different Greek word is used): "Those who sin are to be rebuked publicly, so that the others may take warning." See 2 Tim 3:16; 4:2; Titus 2:15.

In seeking to edify one another believers must not overlook Eph 5:19. This verse, which commands us to "sing . . . to the Lord," also exhorts us to "speak to one another with psalms, hymns and spiritual songs" (NIV). Thus we may properly use songs in our assemblies that are not worship in the strict sense of praise being spoken directly to God. Some singing is believer-to-believer activity and is designed to instruct, encourage, and admonish—i.e., edify—one another (see Col 3:16).[2] Abandoning gospel songs because they are judged to be "unworshipful" results in a one-dimensional kind of assembly.

The second believer-to-believer purpose for our assemblies is *fellowship*. This is the familiar word *koinonia*, which refers to a relationship of togetherness among individuals, i.e., a close positive association, a sharing, a partnership, a common participation in something. The fellowship Christians have with one another is both a state and an activity. Because we all have the same fellowship with God through Jesus Christ, "we have fellowship with one another" (1 John 1:7). This is a state of being, i.e., a common identity and an equal participation in the blessings of salvation shared with all Christians—even those we will never meet and know on this earth.

But fellowship is also an activity. The early Christians continued to devote themselves to fellowship (Acts 2:42). This is something we do with and for our fellow believers, and it is one reason why we assemble together. We assemble to share our Christian experience with each other, to share our physical goods with believers in need, and to share our very lives together. It is very important that we see our Christian assemblies as fulfilling this purpose.

Such fellowship is accomplished by several kinds of joint activities. For one thing, just *being together* reinforces in our minds our sense of the unique relationship we have with other Christians (see 2 Cor 6:14-15). Just by sitting together in a service, and by talking with one another before and after services, we experience our spiritual kinship and our relationship of oneness with each other. This sense of fellowship is intensified when we participate together in acts of worship, such as hymns of praise and the Lord's Supper. In fact, though the Lord's Supper is largely an act of communion between God and the worshiper, it also has a dimension of fellowship that binds its participants together. Through our partaking of the bread and the cup, Jesus provides us with a "sharing" (*koinonia*) in the saving benefits of his sacrificed body and blood (1 Cor 10:16). Also, when Christians partake of the Supper together in an act of shared worship, they reinforce their unity with each other: "Since there is one bread, we who are many are one body; for we all partake of the one bread" (1 Cor 10:17). "Communion" is thus not only communion with Christ; it is communion with one another.

Another specific fellowship activity is the giving of tithes and offerings. When *koinonia* is used with the connotation of sharing, it often refers to the sharing of our physical goods with one another. *Koinonia* is used in Rom 15:26 for the "contribution" Paul was collecting for the poor saints in Jerusalem. It is used also in 2 Cor 8:4 ("participation in the support of the saints") and in 2 Cor 9:13. Giving as a fellowship activity is commanded for us all: "And do not neglect doing good and sharing (*koinonia*), for with such sacrifices God is pleased" (Heb 13:16; see Rom 12:13). Even offerings that are used to "pay the preacher" are acts of fellowship (Gal 6:6, *koinoneo*).

Another fellowship activity is intercessory prayer. When Christians come together and share their prayer requests with the group, they are in effect sharing their deepest needs, their very lives, with one another. When prayer is then offered on behalf of those in need, we are all sharing our love and common concern for them.

A final act of fellowship included in Christian assemblies is indicated in Paul's frequent exhortation, "Greet one another with a holy kiss" (Rom 16:16; see 1 Cor 16:20; 2 Cor 13:12; 1 Thess 5:26). A chaste kiss of greeting was part of the culture of the ancient world in general. As a culture-relative practice (like foot-washing), what is binding upon Christians in other and later cultures is not the form of this act, but rather its essence as an act of fellowship and brotherhood. Other cultural expressions having the same meaning will serve the same purpose, e.g., a warm handshake ("the right hand of fellowship," Gal 2:9) or a hug. In the form of such cultural substitutes, acts of greeting are indeed a legitimate part of the public assembly (see Cottrell, *Romans*, 2:480-481).

IV. THE BELIEVER-TO-UNBELIEVER PURPOSE

One final aspect of church assemblies must be addressed, namely, the believer-to-unbeliever purpose. Actually, "purpose" may be the wrong word, for I am not aware of any NT reference to believers organizing an assembly for the express purpose of addressing or relating to unbelievers. In the Book of Acts, when Christians wanted to meet with and evangelize the lost, they went to those places where the latter were already assembled (e.g., Acts 17:1-4,17-19; 18:4). In the NT the only *purposes* for church assemblies seem to be worship, edification, and fellowship.

We do know, however, that unbelievers sometimes were present in the assemblies of local congregations. This is clearly implied in 1 Cor 14:20-25, in the midst of Paul's instructions on the use of miraculous gifts in church meetings. Rightly done, says Paul, speaking in tongues may function as a sign to unbelievers (v. 22). But "if the whole church assembles together and all speak in tongues," in a disorganized cacophony, "and . . . unbelievers enter, will they not say that you are mad? But if all prophesy, and an unbeliever . . . enters, he is convicted by all" and may even be converted (vv. 23-25).

This brief instruction shows two things. First, though unbelievers were welcome to attend church services, the services themselves were not designed specifically to reach out to them. Second, though the services were designed to facilitate the believers' relationships to God and to one another, it was important that the activities of the assembled Christians present a positive witness to any unbelievers who happened to enter.

These observations lead to an important application: the concept of "seeker sensitive services" is valid, as long as this aspect does not dominate and determine the content of regular Christian assemblies. Of course, "evangelistic meetings" can be conducted for the express purpose of reaching out to the unsaved. But the regular weekly meetings of God's people, especially the main Sunday service, must be designed mainly with *believers* in mind, in terms of the first three purposes discussed in this chapter. The expected presence of unbelievers should be taken into account when services are being planned, but in the final analysis it must be regarded as incidental to the assemblies' main purposes.

CONCLUSION

In my judgment, authoritative NT teaching and precedent require local congregations to organize and Christians to attend at least one major church assembly per week, and that on Sunday or the Lord's Day. In view of what has been discussed above, it seems too restrictive to limit it to worship (believer-to-God) activities and to call it a "worship" service. It must also include God-to-believer and believer-to-believer events. The service should be planned in such a way that the participants are aware of these different emphases.

There is no rule, though, that says the people of God can have just this one weekly assembly. Most churches have a Sunday school or Bible school hour, the main purposes of which are usually edification and fellowship. Other kinds of special services are scheduled throughout the year, e.g., V.B.S. for edification and fellowship, youth outings and class parties for fellowship, and prayer services for worship and fellowship. The main point is that every church's leadership must plan its congregational activities so that all the purposes for assembling together are being met.

NOTES ON CHAPTER TWENTY-SIX

[1]We must remember that the only text clearly connecting musical praise with an assembly is 1 Cor 14:15,26; but this does not seem to refer to *congregational* singing.

[2]Hence the validity of such hortatory songs as "Rescue the Perishing," "Count Your Blessings," "Send the Light," "O Zion Haste," "Trust and Obey," "Stand Up, Stand Up for Jesus," and "Onward, Christian Soldiers."

CHAPTER TWENTY-SEVEN
INTERPRETING BIBLICAL PROPHECY

We come now to the last major section of Christian theology, the subject of eschatology. This word is from the Greek adjective *eschatos*, meaning "last" or "final." Used as a noun, the *eschaton* refers to the *end* of something. As a theological term it means the end of time, the end of the world, the end of history. "Eschatology" is the study of what the Bible says about the events surrounding the end time.

Since the end time is in the future from the perspective of the biblical writers, whatever the Bible says about it must be in the form of predictive prophecy. Thus to properly understand eschatology, one must have an understanding of the nature of prophecy as such. The purpose of this chapter is to establish some crucial principles about the interpretation of prophecy and to apply them to certain key prophecies often linked to the end time. Regarding the latter we shall examine OT prophecies concerning two relevant subjects, namely, Israel and the kingdom of God.

I. THE KEYS TO PROPHETIC INTERPRETATION

Before we begin to interpret specific prophecies, we should give some thought to the nature of biblical prophecy as such. Are there any rules or guidelines that must be followed? If so, where do we find them and what are they? The tragic fact is that many approach Bible prophecy without first considering such questions, and thus they construct whole systems of prophetic interpretation that are false because they are based on false presuppositions about the nature of prophecy. In order to avoid this problem I will here identify four basic principles to use in interpreting prophecy, all of which are taken from biblical teaching itself.

A. The OT Was Written for the Sake of the Church

The first principle is that the OT was written for the sake of the church. The Jews as stewards "were entrusted with the oracles of God" (Rom 3:2), preserving and protecting the written OT so that God's New Covenant people may benefit from it. In Rom 15:4 Paul says, "For whatever was written in earlier times was written for our instruction," i.e., for the instruction of the church. This purpose was all-inclusive; "whatever" is in the OT is for our benefit: history (1 Cor 10:1-6), poetry (see Rom 3:9-18), law (1 Cor 9:9-10), types (Heb 9:1-28), teaching

(Rom 4:22-24), and especially prophecy. Even the prophets through whom the prophecies came did not necessarily understand what they meant (1 Pet 1:10-11), but "it was revealed to them that they were not serving themselves, but you," i.e., you who live in the era of the gospel of Christ (1 Pet 1:12). "Yes, for our sake it was written," says Paul (1 Cor 9:10). (See Wilmot, 18-22.)

What does this mean in terms of how we should interpret OT prophecy? It means first of all that the OT Scriptures, including especially their prophecies, were pointing ahead to the coming of Christ, and specifically to his *first* coming rather than his second coming. In giving their prophecies about Jesus, says Peter, the OT prophets were serving us "when they spoke of the things that have now been told you by those who have preached the gospel to you by the Holy Spirit sent from heaven" (1 Pet 1:12, NIV).

Second, it means that God had the church age and the church itself in mind when he was inspiring the OT prophets to foretell the works of the coming Messiah. That all of these things had reference to a coming era when the Jew-Gentile distinction would no longer be relevant was a mystery to the Jews themselves, but the inspired apostles and NT prophets have shown that this was God's plan all along (Rom 16:25-26; Eph 3:1-10). Now when we look at OT prophecy through the eyes of the NT writers, its veiled references to Christ and his church are clearly seen.

This leads to the third point, that for all OT prophecies relating to the Messiah, we should look for their fulfillment first of all in this present messianic age. Since all OT writings were given "for our instruction" and "for our sake," their applications and implications must be meaningful to all who now live under the New Covenant.

B. The NT Often Interprets the OT for Us

The second principle governing the interpretation of OT prophecy is simply the fact that the NT itself often gives us or points us to the proper fulfillment of OT prophecy or the proper counterpart of OT types. As Wilmot says, "What God said in the Old Testament is given His meaning in the New Testament" (15). Not all OT prophecies are interpreted for us in the NT, of course, but enough are so interpreted to give us a fairly clear idea of how to approach the rest.

A few examples will illustrate this point. In the very first OT prophecy God says to the serpent, "And I will put enmity between you and the woman, and between your seed and her seed; he shall bruise you on the head, and you shall bruise him on the heel" (Gen 3:15). In the NT this serpent is clearly identified as Satan (Rev 12:9; 20:2), who is defeated in battle by the power of Jesus Christ (Rev 12:7-11; 20:1-3; see Matt 12:29; Luke 10:18-19), who then shares his victory with his people (Rom 16:20). The very last OT prophecy says, "Behold, I am going to send you Elijah the prophet before the coming of the great and terrible day of the LORD" (Mal 4:5). In the NT this is interpreted as being fulfilled in

John the Baptist: "And if you are willing to accept it, John himself is Elijah who was to come" (Matt 11:14; see Matt 17:12; Mark 9:13; Luke 1:17).

Another example is the way the book of Hebrews interprets the prophetic types embodied in Old Covenant worship and ritual. The high priest was an incomplete forerunner of the perfect high priesthood of Jesus (Heb 7:23-28). The OT sacrifices foreshadowed the one perfect sacrifice of Jesus (Heb 8:3-5; 9:12-28; 10:1-18). The OT tabernacle or temple is "a mere copy of the true one" (Heb 9:24), which is the heavenly throne room where Christ is presently seated at God's right hand "in the true tabernacle, which the Lord pitched, not man" (Heb 8:1-2).

C. Prophetic Language Is Often Figurative

The third main biblical principle that shows us how to interpret prophecy is quite simple: prophetic language is often figurative. To state it negatively, not all prophecy is intended to be interpreted literally.

This principle is specifically rejected by many students of Bible prophecy. For example, Hal Lindsey has declared, "The real issue between the amillennial and the premillennial viewpoints is whether prophecy should be interpreted literally or allegorically" (165). Lindsey himself is committed to the literal approach as applied to such main prophetic themes as Israel, Jerusalem, and David's throne (40, 165). J. Dwight Pentecost also defends prophetic literalism (*Things*, 1-64). He and others who take this view acknowledge that sometimes figurative language is used (ibid., 12-13), but they severely limit its scope where prophecy of the end time is in view.

In opposition to this view and in agreement with the Bible, we note first of all that language in general is not always literal. In ordinary, everyday speech, no one would insist that all statements must be taken literally. Biblical language in general is no different, nor is prophetic language. In fact, in several places we are specifically told that prophets speak in figurative language. In Num 12:6-8 God contrasts the way he speaks to Moses with the way he speaks to most prophets. With Moses he speaks "mouth to mouth" rather than in dreams and visions (as with ordinary prophets), and with Moses he speaks "even openly, and not in dark sayings" or riddles. This clearly means that much prophetic language *is* in the form of "riddles," the English word some translations (e.g., NIV, NRSV) use to translate a Hebrew word meaning "difficult speech requiring interpretation" (Wilson, 107). Hosea 12:10 is a later affirmation of this same characteristic of prophecy: "I have also spoken to the prophets, and I gave numerous visions, and through the prophets I gave parables" (or "symbols," NKJV).

This same point is made in the first verse of the Book of Revelation, which says that Jesus "signified" the contents of this prophetic work by his angel to John (Rev 1:1). This key word is *semaino*, which many versions translate in a generalized way here, i.e., "to communicate, to make known" (NASB, NIV, ESV, NRSV). Its basic meaning, though, is "to communicate through signs or symbols or figures," i.e., "to *signify*," and is so translated in the KJV, NKJV, and ASV. In view of the contents of Revelation, and in view of the OT texts just discussed, this basic (more literal) meaning of *semaino* seems to be justified here. That is, the Book of Revelation, like most OT prophecy, is couched in the language of signs and symbols.

The point is that the Bible itself describes the nature of prophetic language as parabolic or figurative; thus we cannot insist that prophecy must always be interpreted literally. For example, in Mal 4:5, when God says he is going to send "Elijah," this name is surely being used figuratively or as a riddle. When Gen 3:15 prophesies that the seed of the woman will crush the serpent's head, this too is surely figurative language. When Exod 17:6 says that water came from the rock at Horeb, surely Paul is interpreting this figuratively when he says "the rock was Christ" (1 Cor 10:4).

D. Prophecy Is Fulfilled on Different Levels of Reality

While the debate over biblical prophecy usually focuses on the nature of its *language*, this is not really the key issue. A much more significant difference has to do with the nature of the *reality* with respect to which a particular prophecy is intended to be fulfilled. If a prophecy is fulfilled at all, it is fulfilled in reference to some reality. The fact is, however, that there are *different levels of reality*, and regardless of the nature of prophetic language, the key question is, to which level of reality does it refer?

What are these different levels of reality? One possible way to distinguish them is to say that some reality is *physical*, and some is *spiritual*. Using this terminology, the real problem with those who insist that prophecy be interpreted literally is not really the nature of the language as such, but the nature of the reality to which they insist it must be applied. As a general rule, prophetic literalists want to interpret all prophecy as applying to physical realities, rather than spiritual. They usually condemn all attempts to "spiritualize" prophecy. This approach, however, is seriously contrary to the Bible's own interpretation of prophecy, which makes a clear distinction between the different levels of reality and often applies prophecy to the spiritual rather than the physical level. Such a distinction is clearly made, for example, between two kinds of Israel (Rom 9:6), two kinds of Jerusalem (Gal 4:25-26), and two kinds of kingdom (John 18:36).

While I am thoroughly convinced that the Bible speaks of two levels of reality, I am not completely happy with the terminology *physical* and *spiritual*. Some may take these terms to mean that a "spiritual" reality is something completely ethereal or otherworldly, having no presence in this physical world at all. This is not the point, however. For example, Paul's statement in Rom 9:6, "For they are not all Israel who are descended from Israel," clearly shows that even in OT times there were two kinds of Israel, which may be called "physical Israel" and "spiritual Israel." The latter group, however, had just as much physical reality as did the former. What made them different was that the latter had a *spiritual dimension* lacking in the former, i.e., a saving relationship with God. The former group was physical *only*; the latter was spiritual *also*.

Thus if we say that the two levels on which prophecy may be fulfilled are the physical and the spiritual, this does not necessarily mean that the latter has no physical existence. An example is that the prophecy about Elijah (Mal 4:5) was not fulfilled on a physical level only, with a physical "second coming" of the OT prophet. It was fulfilled in a physical person to be sure, i.e., John the Baptist; but John was on a different level of reality in that he represented the spiritual dimension of the Messiah's work.

Because there is still some ambiguity in this set of terms, I will suggest a supplementary approach. From the New Covenant perspective I believe that it may be better to refer to these two levels of reality as *pre-Messianic* reality and *Messianic* reality. The fact is that much OT prophecy was fulfilled in the Old Covenant era itself, i.e., in pre-Messianic times, and almost always on the level of physical reality. However, much OT prophecy is fulfilled only in connection with the coming of the Messiah, in reference to his initial and ongoing work. This latter category represents a different level of reality in contrast with the OT, simply because it is set into motion or brought into existence by the saving work of Christ. Such reality possesses a spiritual dimension that could not have existed in pre-Messianic times. And this spiritual, Messianic reality is the level on which a large portion of OT prophecy is fulfilled.

Thus far I have stated four keys to prophetic interpretation: the OT was written for the church's sake, the NT often interprets the OT for us, prophetic language is often figurative, and prophecy is fulfilled on different levels of reality. My plan for the rest of this chapter is to make two specific applications of these principles, first to Israel in prophecy and then to the kingdom of God in prophecy.

II. ISRAEL IN PROPHECY

The importance of prophecies about Israel, including Jerusalem (Zion) and the temple, cannot be overemphasized. Many are convinced that the Jewish people and the present nation of Israel will be the primary participants in the events surrounding the second coming of Christ. In his immensely popular book, *The Late Great Planet Earth* (173), Hal Lindsey exhorts, "Keep your eyes on the Middle East." Why? Because this is where Israel is, and Bible prophecies that refer to the second coming are all focused on Israel. This view of the prominence of Israel in prophecy has also been illustrated by the recent *Left Behind* fiction series.

The modern interest in Israel in prophecy was reawakened in 1948, when the present nation of Israel was born; and it gained much momentum in 1967, when in the Six-Day War the Israelis regained control of the Old City of Jerusalem and especially the original temple site. The latter event is what prompted Lindsey to write his book, since it was now feasible to think about rebuilding the OT temple of worship on its original location. When Lindsey wrote in 1970, he was convinced that this rebuilding was imminent (45-46), and that all the OT prophecies about Israel and the end time would soon be fulfilled, ushering in the second coming of Christ. He and millions of others are still waiting for all this to happen.

In my judgment this whole approach to the end time is a massive error. The Jews will have no special role in the final events of this age; in fact, they have had no special role in God's plan since their purpose was fulfilled in the *first* coming of Christ (Gal 3:28; Eph 2:11-16; Col 3:11). Why, then, do so many believe Israel will have this central role in end-time events? This error is based primarily on their false view of the nature of prophecy as such, and a failure to see that most if not all prophecy about Israel as a nation has already been fulfilled, either in OT times themselves or in connection with Christ's first coming.

The fact is that those who regard Israel as the focal point of end-time events usually take a literalist approach to prophecy. They not only regard the language of prophecy as always "literal if possible," but also insist on applying it to physical realities. Thus they insist that prophecies about Israel, about Jerusalem, and about the temple must always apply to Israel in its pre-Messianic form of a physical nation, to Jerusalem as the physical city that exists at a specific geographical location in the Middle East, and to the temple as a material edifice built of stones and mortar by human hands.

Now, it is certainly true that some OT prophecy is directed toward the physical nation of Israel. But when this is the case, such prophecy was fulfilled in the OT era itself, in connection with God's dealing with Old Covenant Israel prior to and leading up to the Messiah's first coming. This means that when we see an OT prophecy about Israel (or Jerusalem, or the temple), we should look first of all to see whether it has already been fulfilled in OT history. We should not be surprised to find that many times this is the case, since the main subject of the OT from Genesis 12 to Malachi 4 is the Jewish nation.

This means that one cannot hope to accurately interpret OT prophecy about Israel without a good understanding of OT history. Many are still looking for the fulfillment of many such prophecies because they are not familiar with the main events in the history of physical, pre-Messianic Israel, and thus they do not realize that they have *already* been fulfilled. I have talked with individuals who read OT prophecies about Israel's tribulation, or the rebuilding of the temple, and who assume these prophecies will be fulfilled at some time in the future of modern Israel. They simply do not understand that such prophecies about Israel's return to their homeland and their rebuilding of the temple were fulfilled in OT times.

A brief survey of OT history will make this point clear. The accompanying chart lists a few of the main events in the history of OT Israel, both as they were prophesied and as they were fulfilled, according to the Bible's own testimony.

EVENT	PROPHESIED	FULFILLED
1. Possession of Canaan	Gen 12:7; 13:15-17; 15:18-19; 17:8; 26:3; 28:13	Deut 1:8; Josh 21:43-45; 23:14; 24:28; 1 Kgs 4:21-25; Neh 9:7-8
2. Disobedience and Captivity	Deut 28:15-68; 29:22-29; Josh 23:15-16	2 Kings 24:10–25:21; Lamentations
3. Return to Canaan; Rebuilding Temple	Deut 30:1-5; Isa 2:2-5; Jer 29:14; 30:18; Ezek 20:41; 34:11-14; 37:21-28	Ezra 1:1-11; 6:14-18; Haggai
4. First coming of Christ	Gen 12:3; 26:4; 28:14; 2 Sam 7:11-16	Luke 24:44-47; Acts 13:30-34; 26:22-23; 28:20-23; Rom 9:5

The first event listed here is the possession of Canaan, first promised to Abraham in Gen 12:7 and subsequently repeated to him and to the other patriarchs. The point is that this promise of the land was *fulfilled* when Israel crossed the Jordan River and took possession of Canaan. As the Israelites were about to cross over, Moses said to them, "See, I have placed the land before you; go in and possess the land which the LORD swore to give to your fathers, to Abraham, to Isaac, and to Jacob, to them and their descendants after them" (Deut 1:8). When the conquest was completed, God's promise was fulfilled: "So the LORD gave Israel all the land which He had sworn to give to their fathers, and they possessed it and lived in it. . . . Not one of the good promises which the LORD had made to the house of Israel failed; all came to pass" (Josh 21:43,45).

Some have stumbled at the way the promise is worded in Gen 17:8 where God said that Canaan would be the "everlasting possession" of Abraham's descendants. Some take this to mean that the land of Palestine still belongs to the Jews today and will be their homeland forever. This is an erroneous idea and is based on a faulty English translation of the Hebrew word *'olam*. Though this word sometimes carries the connotation of "eternal," it often means no more than "age-lasting" or "until the end of the age," namely, the OT age.

This is especially true of OT statements about things related to Israel. God's provisions for the life and religion of Israel were not meant to endure forever. Here is a list of some other things about Israel that are described with the same Hebrew word (*'olam*) and which obviously were intended to become obsolete when the Old Covenant ended: circumcision as a covenant sign, Gen 17:13; the Passover feast, Exod 12:24 (see 12:14,17); Sabbath observance, Exod 31:16-17; the Day of Atonement, Lev 16:29,31; the Aaronic priesthood, Exod 40:15; the priests' clothing, Exod 28:43; the priests' portion of the sacrifices, Exod 29:28 (see Lev 6:18); the priests' washings, Exod 30:21; the bread of the Presence, Lev 24:8; the candlestick, Exod 27:21; Solomon's temple, 1 Kgs 8:13 (see 9:3); and the Levites as custodians of the ark of the covenant, 1 Chr 15:2 (see 23:13).

From this list it should be clear that the word *'olam* does not necessarily mean "everlasting." Regarding things having to do with Israel, it means only "as long as the Old Covenant age lasts." Thus Israel's right to claim Canaan as her own possession ended along with all other Old Covenant practices and privileges.

The second main event in Israel's history was their disobedience and ultimate captivity at the hands of the Babylonians, climaxed by the destruction of Jerusalem and the temple around 586 B.C. This event illustrates an important truth about God's promises and predictions in general: they are *conditional*, depending on a satisfactory response by man. Israel was given the land as promised, but it could be kept only on the condition that the people remain faithful. This conditionality relating to the land is clearly set forth in Deut 28:15-68. Here God sets forth in shocking detail the curses that would come upon his people if they did not keep their covenant with him (v. 15). They would suffer all manner of afflictions and tribulations, and in the end "be torn from the land where you are entering to possess it. Moreover, the LORD will scatter you among all peoples, from one end of the earth to the other" (vv. 63-64).

The horrible truth is that Israel did not remain faithful, and thus all the tribulations depicted in Deuteronomy 28 did befall them, as recorded in 2 Kgs 24:10–25:21. A more detailed description of the horrors involved in the destruction of Jerusalem is provided by Jeremiah in his Book of Lamentations. (I knew a man who read Lamentations and assumed it was a prophecy of the tribulation Israel will supposedly suffer just before the second coming of Christ. He simply was ignorant of Bible history.)

The next main event in the history of OT Israel was their return to their homeland and the rebuilding of Jerusalem and the temple. This return was predicted clearly in Deut 30:1-5. After a period of banishment and a season of repentance, "the LORD your God will restore you from captivity, and have compassion on you, and will gather you again from all the peoples where the LORD your God has scattered you. . . . The LORD your God will bring you into the land which your fathers possessed, and you shall possess it." Jeremiah 30:18 says, "Thus says the LORD, 'Behold I will restore the fortunes of the tents of Jacob . . . ; and the city will be rebuilt on its ruin, and the palace will stand on its rightful place.'"

Strangely enough, many think that the numerous prophecies of this event only recently began to be fulfilled, i.e., in A.D. 1948. I once heard a speaker (a Bible college professor) recite a list of the principal events in God's dealing with Israel. He listed several from the OT, such as the exodus, the monarchy, and the Babylonian captivity. Then he skipped directly to the NT age, leaving Israel dispersed until the great "gathering" in 1948! Thus he completely ignored what must be one of the greatest events in Israel's history, comparable only to the exodus itself, namely, their restoration from Babylonian captivity in 536 B.C. In so doing he was able to block out this crucial fact, that the prophecies of Israel's return to their homeland were fulfilled in OT times, not in modern times. The books of Ezra and Nehemiah record how Israel of old returned to their own land, and rebuilt the city of Jerusalem, including the temple.

The final main event in physical Israel's history was the first coming of Christ, prophesied scores of times in the OT, as summed up in God's words to Jacob, "In you and in your descendants shall all the families of the earth be blessed" (Gen 28:14; see Gen 12:3). The first coming of Jesus was the one main event for which Israel was given a special existence in the first place. The promises originally made to the patriarchs were fulfilled in Christ's coming and especially in his resurrection from the dead (Acts 13:30-34). Christ is called "the hope of Israel" (Acts 28:20). Of all the events and blessings for which the Jews could thank God, the climactic one, the "grand finale," was Christ's first coming (Rom 9:1-5).

God's sole purpose for the physical nation of Israel can be summed up in one word: *preparation*. God set this people aside and gave them special treatment solely to prepare for the first coming of Christ. Everything Israel stood for and hoped for was accomplished and fulfilled when that happened. Now that the prepared-for Messiah has come, there is no longer a divine rationale for Israel's separate existence as a nation.

Does this mean that *all* OT prophecies about Israel were fulfilled in OT times, in connection with Israel's role of preparing for the Messiah? No. What it means is that all prophecies about Israel as a *physical, pre-Messianic reality* have been thus fulfilled. But this is not the only "Israel" in God's plan! With the coming of Christ and the establishment of his church, a new kind of Israel was begun.[1] This new Israel is just as literal and just as real as OT Israel, but its identity is not based on physical descent from Abraham and attachment to a specific geographical location upon this earth. Its identity is based rather upon a spiritual relationship with Jesus Christ, and thus it is a spiritual, Messianic entity. This new, spiritual Israel is the *church*. And as far as prophecy is concerned, many of the OT prophecies about Israel, about Jerusalem, and about the temple are in fact prophecies about this *new* Israel, the church; thus they have nothing to do with the modern nation of Israel or with the second coming of Christ as such.

This identification of the church as God's New Covenant Israel is not arbitrary speculation. The NT itself specifically speaks of the church as God's temple, God's Jerusalem, and God's Israel today. In 2 Cor 6:16 Paul says, "What agreement has the temple of God with idols? For we are the temple of the living God," God's dwelling place on earth today. Paul also says, "Do you not know that you are a temple of God and that the Spirit of God dwells in you? . . . For the temple of God is holy, and that is what you are" (1 Cor 3:16-17; see Eph 2:21-22; 1 Pet 2:5). Though it has a physical presence in this world, the church is nevertheless a *spiritual* temple, since its identity as such is based on our spiritual relation to God through Jesus Christ.

The church is also God's true Jerusalem today—a spiritual, heavenly Jerusalem, in contrast with the physical city. Paul makes this very distinction in Gal 4:21-31, where he says Hagar and Sarah represent God's two covenants. The Old Covenant, which proceeded from Mount Sinai, "corresponds to the present Jerusalem," whose children (the Jews) are in bondage (v. 25). The New Covenant, though, corresponds to "the Jerusalem above," which is the mother of Christians who dwell in freedom (v. 26). The former is the "present"[2] Jerusalem in the sense that it belongs to the old creation, to the pre-Messianic level of existence. The latter is the "above" Jerusalem in the sense of "heavenly." In other words, it belongs to the new Messianic level of reality, the new creation begun through Christ's death and resurrection. It is truly the *spiritual* Jerusalem, since its citizens are "born according to the Spirit" and not "according to the flesh" (v. 29).

Hebrews 12:18-24 makes a similar contrast between OT Israel, a physical nation attached to a physical mountain (Sinai); and New Covenant Israel, those who "have come to Mount Zion and to the city of the living God, the heavenly Jerusalem" (vv. 18-22). The latter is specifically identified with "the church of the firstborn who are enrolled in heaven" and with everything spiritual (v. 23). Christians are citizens of this heavenly Jerusalem (Phil 3:20). See references to "the new Jerusalem" in Rev 3:12; 21:2,10.

If the church is God's new temple and God's new Jerusalem, we are not surprised to see it identified in the NT as God's new Israel. The pre-Messianic Israelites took pride in being physically descended from Abraham (Matt 3:9; John 8:33,39; 2 Cor 11:22), but the true Messianic Israel of the new era is composed of those who are related to Abraham *spiritually*. "Therefore, be sure that it is those who are of faith who are sons of Abraham" (Gal 3:7). Jesus Christ is the one true seed of Abraham (Gal 3:16); but all who believe in Christ and are baptized into him take on his identity and become one with him (Gal 3:26-28) and therefore are true descendants of Abraham also: "And if you belong to Christ, then you are Abraham's descendants, heirs according to promise" (Gal 3:29).

The true Israel exists not on the level of the physical but on the level of the spiritual: "For he is not a Jew who is one outwardly, nor is circumcision that which is outward in the flesh. But he is a Jew who is one inwardly; and circumcision is that which is of the heart, by the Spirit" (Rom 2:28-29). This distinction between the true (spiritual) Israel and the false (physical) Israel is also emphasized in Phil 3:2-3: "Beware of the dogs, beware of the evil workers, beware of the false circumcision; for we are the true circumcision, who worship in the Spirit of God and glory in Christ Jesus and put no confidence in the flesh."

In view of this there can be no doubt that Paul is referring to the church when he speaks of "the Israel of God" in Gal 6:15-16: "Neither circumcision nor uncircumcision means anything; what counts is a new creation. Peace and mercy to all who follow this rule, even to the Israel of God" (NIV). The words of ordination originally applied to physical Israel (Exod 19:5-6) now apply to this new Israel, the church: "But you are a chosen race, a royal priesthood, a holy nation, a people for God's own possession" (1 Pet 2:9).

All who accept Jesus as Messiah belong to this Messianic Israel, whether they be Jews by birth or Gentiles by birth. God is no longer interested in this genealogical distinction. "There is neither Jew nor Greek, there is neither slave nor free man, there is neither male nor female; for you are all one in Christ Jesus" (Gal 3:28; see Rom 10:12-13; 1 Cor 12:13; Col 3:11). Those formerly known as Jews and Gentiles are now all part of the same group (Eph 2:11-16); they are all branches on the same tree (Rom 11:17-24).

In view of this abundant and emphatic teaching that the church is God's New Covenant Israel, how can anyone presume to limit OT prophecy about Israel simply to pre-Messianic, physical Israel? Such an approach is not true to the nature of prophetic language, and especially it is not true to the nature of reality as such. The new Israel is just as real as the old one, and in a sense is the true Israel for which the old one was just a forerunner. Thus it is only natural to expect much OT prophecy about Israel, Jerusalem (Zion), and the temple to refer to this spiritual, Messianic Israel, the church.

In fact on several occasions the NT itself applies such OT prophecy about Israel to the church. A main example is Jer 31:31-34, where God prophesies that the Old Covenant will be replaced by a new and different one. The key point here is that God promised to make this new covenant "with the house of Israel and with the house of Judah" (v. 31). I have heard literalists declare that this prophecy has not yet been fulfilled, since God has not made such a new covenant yet with *the house of Israel*, namely, with physical Israel. This well illustrates the absurdity of the literalist approach, since the NT makes it clear that this prophecy has already been fulfilled. Christ has already established this new covenant through the shedding of his blood (Luke 22:20), specifically in fulfillment of Jer 31:31-34 (see Heb 8:7-13; 10:11-18). Thus "the house of Israel" with whom this covenant has been made must refer to the *new* Israel, the church.

Another example of an OT prophecy about Israel, interpreted in the NT as referring to the church, is Amos 9:11-12: "In that day I will raise up the fallen booth of David, and wall up its breaches; I will also raise up its ruins and rebuild it as in the days of old; that they may possess the remnant of Edom and all the nations who are called by My name." Here the "fallen booth [tent, tabernacle] of David" may refer to the Jewish people as such, in their state of being scattered into captivity; or it may refer to the city of Jerusalem as it would be later destroyed by the Babylonians. In any case Amos predicts a restoration and a rebuilding: "Also I will restore the captivity of My people Israel" (Amos 9:14). This passage was quoted by James when he spoke at the Jerusalem council as recorded in Acts 15:13-18. James was especially interested in Amos's reference to "all the nations who are called by My name." This of course refers to the Gentiles, and James says this prophecy is a validation of God's plan to include the Gentiles in the church. Thus he applies this prophecy of the restoration of *Israel* to what was going on at that very time, i.e., to the building up of the *church*. "Here, therefore, we have a clear example in the Bible itself of a figurative, nonliteral interpretation of an Old Testament passage dealing with the restoration of Israel" (Hoekema, *Bible*, 210).

Another prophecy of the restoration of Israel applied to the church (Jews plus Gentiles) is Hosea 2:23; see Rom 9:23-26 and 1 Pet 2:10. Compare also 2 Sam 7:11-16 and Acts 2:29-36.

Would those living in OT times have understood that such prophecies did not apply to physical Israel? Would they have understood the concept of a "spiritual" Israel? Most likely they would not. But neither would they have understood that a prophecy about Elijah (Mal 4:5) would not refer to *their* Elijah, but to a man named John the Baptist. That God's eternal purpose would lead through OT Israel to a new Israel called the church was a mystery until NT times (Eph 3:1-11). Not even the prophets—nor angels themselves—knew what their prophecies would entail (1 Pet 1:10-12). But *we* know, thanks to the NT's own teaching; and according to the point made earlier, the OT was written for the *church's* benefit. Thus there is no excuse for continuing to apply prophecies that have already been fulfilled in connection with Christ's first coming to a fictionalized future scenario related to Christ's second coming.

Does God still have a separate plan for national, physical Israel? Many will say yes. Lindsey expresses this common idea: "For us, as believers, our hope is different from Israel's" (128). But the Bible says no. When God tore the veil of the temple asunder at the death of Jesus (Matt 27:51), he was signifying the end of the special role of the Jews (see John 4:21). There is only "one hope" (Eph 4:4); this one hope is the same for Jews and Gentiles alike. God no longer has a *separate* plan for physical Israel.

God still has a *plan* for the Jews, however: he wants them to become a part of his church, the *new* Israel. The only way that "all Israel will be saved" (Rom 11:26) is if they are grafted back into the original olive tree, which has now become spiritual Israel, the church (Rom 11:17-24).

III. THE KINGDOM IN PROPHECY

Another great theme of OT prophecy is the kingdom of God—that the Messiah will come and set up a kingdom over which he will reign forever. Since the kingdom is often equated with the millennial reign of Christ, it is very important that we understand how to interpret kingdom prophecies as they relate to the end time. Here we will use these prophecies as a second illustration of the proper application of the principles of prophetic interpretation discussed at the beginning of this chapter.

All agree that Jesus of Nazareth is the King who fulfills the prophecies about the kingdom. There is serious disagreement, however, as to *how* these prophecies are fulfilled. Especially, there is disagreement as to the *time* and the *nature* of the kingdom Jesus comes to establish. Many believe that when Christ comes back to the earth in his *second* coming, then he will establish a *physical, political kingdom* in Jerusalem and literally rule over all the peoples of the earth for one thousand years. Others believe that Christ actually established his kingdom when he came the *first* time, and that it is a *heavenly, spiritual kingdom*. The idea is that Christ reigns now from heaven in the hearts of his followers.

What prophecies are at stake here? At this point we can cite only a few of the many that are scattered throughout the whole OT. We call attention first to the promise God made to David, "I will raise up your descendant after you, who will come forth from you, and I will establish his kingdom. He shall build a house for My name, and I will establish the throne of his kingdom forever. . . . Your house and your kingdom shall endure before Me forever; your throne shall be established forever" (2 Sam 7:12-13,16). Some elements of this prophecy may refer to Solomon, but its basic application seems to be Messianic.

Several Psalms are called royal Psalms because they appear to be prophecies of the coming Messiah's kingship. An example is Psalm 2, where the Lord God says, "But as for Me, I have installed My King upon Zion, My holy mountain" (v. 6). Then God addresses the King himself: "Ask of Me, and I will surely give the nations as Your inheritance, and the very ends of the earth as Your possession. You shall break them with a rod of iron, You shall shatter them like earthenware" (vv. 8-9). This King is surely Jesus Christ (Rev 12:5); but is the mountain on which he is enthroned a physical location in Jerusalem, or is it the heavenly Zion of Heb 12:22?

Another example is Psalm 45, which pictures the King riding forth in majesty to receive his bride. He is addressed with words of worship: "Your throne, O God, is forever and ever; a scepter of uprightness is the scepter of Your kingdom" (v. 6).

A final royal Psalm is Ps 110: "The LORD says to my Lord: 'Sit at My right hand until I make Your enemies a footstool for Your feet.' The LORD will stretch forth Your strong scepter from Zion, saying, 'Rule in the midst of Your enemies'" (vv. 1-2). This is an important prophecy because it is quoted or alluded to so many times in the NT in reference to Christ. The reference to "Zion" shows the connection between this Psalm and Ps 2:6.

The well-known Messianic prophecy in Isa 9:6-7 is also a kingdom prophecy: "For a child will be born to us, a son will be given to us; and the government will rest on His shoulders; and His name will be called Wonderful Counselor, Mighty God, Eternal Father, Prince of Peace. There will be no end to the increase of His government or of peace, on the throne of David and over his kingdom, to establish it and to uphold it with justice and righteousness from then on and forevermore." The "throne of David" theme is continued in Ezek 34:23-24, "Then I will set over them one shepherd, My servant David, and he will feed them; he will feed them himself and be their shepherd. And I, the LORD, will be their God, and My servant David will be prince among them." See also Ezek 37:21-28.

The book of Daniel contains several kingdom prophecies, notably Dan 2:44, "In the days of those kings the God of heaven will set up a kingdom which will never be destroyed, and that kingdom will not be left for another people; it will crush and put an end to all these kingdoms, but it will itself endure forever." Also Dan 7:13-14, "I kept looking in the night visions, and behold, with the clouds of heaven one like a Son of Man was coming, and He came up to the Ancient of Days and was presented before Him. And to Him was given dominion, glory and a kingdom, that all the peoples, nations and men of every language might serve Him. His dominion is an everlasting dominion which will not pass away; and His kingdom is one which will not be destroyed."

Also significant is Micah 4:6-7, "'In that day,' declares the LORD, 'I will assemble the lame and gather the outcasts, even those whom I have afflicted. I will make the lame a remnant and the outcasts a strong nation, and the LORD will reign over them in Mount Zion from now on and forever.'" See also Zech 6:12-13, "Thus says the LORD of hosts, 'Behold, a man whose name is Branch, for He will branch out from where He is; and He will build the temple of the LORD. Yes, it is He who will build the temple of the LORD, and He who will bear the honor and sit and rule on His throne. Thus, He will be a priest on His throne.'" See Zech 9:9-10.

What do these prophecies mean? What kind of kingdom is this? When is it supposed to be established? How we answer such questions depends in large part on our understanding of the nature of prophecy as such, and the nature of the reality in which it is fulfilled. Since there are many who insist on taking all prophecy literally and applying it to physical realities only, we are not surprised when they take these kingdom prophecies to mean that the Messiah will come and establish a literal, physical, earthly kingdom for the Jews, headquartered in Jerusalem. In fact, many Jews at the time of Jesus' first coming interpreted them thus. They were "waiting for the kingdom of God," like Joseph of Arimathea (Mark 15:43), but typically they were expecting an earthly kingdom (John 6:14-15). Even the apostles seemed to have this view (Acts 1:6). Unfortunately, however, this was a false interpretation of the kingdom prophecies, and much of Jesus own teaching was devoted to correcting it and explaining the true nature of the kingdom. His remark to Pilate sums up this element of his teaching: "My kingdom is not of this world" (John 18:36).

Nevertheless there are still countless Christians who today take this same approach to the kingdom prophecies. Many of these believe that Christ's original purpose was to establish an earthly kingdom for the Jews; but most of the Jews would not accept him as their King, and thus this plan was postponed until his second coming. This and other views of the millennium agree that the kingdom of God has not come yet; and when it comes, it will be an earthly kingdom marked by physical peace and prosperity for the whole earth. The whole subject of the millennium will be discussed in the next chapter.

One of the most serious problems caused by the literalist approach to prophecy is that it causes many to apply prophecies to the second coming of Christ that were actually fulfilled as a result of his first coming. This is especially true of the OT kingdom prophecies. The fact is that according to NT teaching itself, the wonderful kingdom of God, as prophesied in the OT, *has already been established.* Jesus planned to establish it when he came the first time, and he did not fail. The kingdom has not been delayed until his second coming; it is already present. The key to understanding this is to have the right approach to prophecy as such, as outlined earlier in this chapter. Much prophecy is couched in figurative language, and it is fulfilled in spiritual realities. This is true of our present subject; the kingdom Christ came to establish, and did establish, is heavenly and spiritual, as the following discussion will show.

The establishment of the kingdom of God is one of the main themes of NT teaching, especially the teaching of Jesus. As he said in Luke 4:43, "I must preach the kingdom of God to the other cities also, for I was sent for this purpose." It is significant that this major subject of OT prophecy should figure so prominently in the Gospels. This in itself suggests that the fulfillment of kingdom prophecies was to be accomplished through Christ's first coming. This conclusion is reinforced by the summary of the message of both John the Baptist and Jesus: "The kingdom of heaven is at hand" (Matt 3:2; 4:17).[3] "Is at hand" is the verb *engizo*, which means "to approach, to come near." This is a specific affirmation that the kingdom would soon be established.

"Is at hand" or "is near" is still a bit vague, but two other teachings of Jesus give us a more specific time reference for the establishment of the kingdom. One is that John the Baptist was in a sense the dividing line between the prekingdom era and the kingdom era. In Matt 11:11 Jesus said, "Truly I say to you, among those born of women there has not arisen anyone greater than John the Baptist! Yet the one who is least in the kingdom of heaven is greater than he." And in Luke 16:16, "The Law and the Prophets were proclaimed until John; since that time the gospel of the kingdom of God has been preached, and everyone is forcing his way into it."

The other teaching narrowing down the time of the kingdom's coming is that some who heard Jesus teach would be alive when the kingdom was established: "But I say to you truthfully, there are some of those standing here who will not taste death until they see the kingdom of God" (Luke 9:27). As Matthew 16:28 sums it up, "Truly I say to you, there are some of those who are standing here who will not taste death until they see the Son of Man coming in His kingdom" (see Mark 9:1).

Other texts tell us that the kingdom of God was in a sense *already present* at the time Jesus was upon the earth. One possible affirmation of its presence is Luke 17:20-21, "Now having been questioned by the Pharisees as to when the kingdom of God was coming, He answered them and said, 'The kingdom of God is not coming with signs to be observed; nor will they say, "Look, here it is!" or, "There it is!" For behold, the kingdom of God is in your midst.'" So translated, the words "in your midst" declare the kingdom's presence. However, the same Greek expression could be translated "within you," as in the NIV. Other teachings are less ambiguous, though. After saying that John the Baptist was a dividing line for the kingdom (Matt 11:11), Jesus added these words: "From the days of John the Baptist until now, the kingdom of heaven has been forcefully advancing" (Matt 11:12, NIV). Also, in explaining how he is able to cast out demons, Jesus declares, "But if I cast out demons by the Spirit of God, then the kingdom of God has come upon you" (Matt 12:28).

In what sense could the kingdom of God have already been present during Jesus' earthly ministry? In the sense that *the king himself* was present, walking the earth in the person of Jesus Christ. He was indeed the "son of David" (Matt 1:1; see Matt 9:27; 12:23; 21:9). The magi sought him as "King of the Jews" (Matt 2:2); Nathanael confessed him to be "the King of Israel" (John 1:49). Jesus' triumphal entry fulfilled the prophecy of Zech 9:9, "Behold, your King is coming to you" (Matt 21:4-5). Jesus himself acknowledged before Pilate that he was a King (Matt 27:11; Luke 23:3; John 18:33-37), and Pilate placed a sign on the cross which read, "Jesus of Nazareth, the King of the Jews" (John 19:19).

Without doubt, then, the kingdom of God was already present in some sense since the King himself was present, but this is not the whole story. From the perspective of Jesus' earthly ministry, the decisive inauguration of the kingdom was still in the future, though the *near* future. Jesus' statement that some in his audience would not die until they saw the kingdom of God come suggests that this had not happened yet. Mark's record of this statement shows how this is the case: "Truly I say to you, there are some of those who are standing here who will not taste death until they see the kingdom of God after it has come with power" (Mark 9:1). Though the kingdom was already present in a sense, it had not yet come *with power*, in its fullness. As Matthew 16:28 says, some will not die "until they see the Son of Man coming in His kingdom." This seems to be the same event described in Jesus' statement to the high priest at his trial, "You have said it yourself; nevertheless I tell you, hereafter you will see the Son of Man sitting at the right hand of Power, and coming on the clouds of heaven" (Matt 26:64). "Hereafter" points to a future event.

At this point we may pause and ask, what event could Jesus be referring to here? It sounds a lot like the second coming, at which time many believe Jesus will establish his millennial kingdom, an earthly, political kingdom, over which he will reign from a literal throne in Jerusalem. But this interpretation is inconsistent with two things. One, it does not agree with Jesus' promise that this predicted event would occur before some in his audience had died. Two, it is not consistent with Jesus' own teaching about the *nature* of the kingdom.

Everything Jesus taught about this latter point shows that the promised kingdom would *not* be earthly and political, but would be ethical and spiritual. When questioned by Pilate about his kingship, Jesus plainly said, "My kingdom is not of this world. . . . My kingdom is not of this realm" (John 18:36). Participating in this kingdom is a matter not of political power, but of love, righteousness, and childlike trust. To the man who expressed keen understanding of the love commandments, Jesus said, "You are not far from the kingdom of God" (Mark 12:34). The kingdom belongs to the humble and to those who suffer for righteousness' sake (Matt 5:3,10). One seeks God's kingdom by seeking his righteousness (Matt 6:33). The spread of the kingdom comes not through earthly power but through the Word of God (Matt 13:19; see 13:3-9,18-23). One enters the kingdom only through a childlike spirit (Mark 10:14-15). In one interpretation of Luke 17:21, Jesus specifically says, "The kingdom of God is within you" (NIV), i.e., its presence is not on the physical level but on the level of the spirit.

From the standpoint of Jesus' own earthly ministry, then, the establishment of the kingdom in power and fullness had to be an event in the near future that resulted in the spiritual reign of Christ the King over the hearts of his subjects. The event that obviously fulfills these conditions is the risen Christ's ascension into heaven and his reign in power from God's right hand, an event that began to be formally announced and applied on earth on the Day of Pentecost (Acts 2:33-36).

This understanding of the establishment of the kingdom of God is perfectly consistent both with OT prophecy and with Jesus' own teaching. Prophetic references to the throne of David (e.g., 2 Sam 7:16; Isa 9:7; Jer 30:9; Ezek 34:23-24) are figurative, not literal, in perfect harmony with the nature of prophecy as such (Num 12:8; Hos 12:10). The same is true of prophecies that the Messiah will reign from Zion (e.g., Ps 2:6; Isa 24:23; Micah 4:7), i.e., he reigns from "the Jerusalem above" (Gal 4:26), the nonmaterial "Mount Zion" in "the heavenly Jerusalem" (Heb 12:22). The marvelous prophecy of Christ's enthronement and kingship in Ps 110:1-2 is specifically said to be fulfilled prior to and in preparation for Pentecost (Acts 2:33-36). The great prophecy in Dan 7:13-14, about the Son of Man coming up to the Ancient of Days and receiving a universal, eternal kingdom, likewise is a reference to Christ's ascension and enthronement at God's right hand.

All of Jesus' own teaching points to the same event. His reference to "the Son of Man sitting at the right hand of Power, and coming on the clouds of heaven" (Matt 26:64), is clearly the same event as Ps 110:1-2 and Dan 7:13-14.[4] That some in Christ's audience would see the kingdom coming "with power" (Mark 9:1) is a reference to *Pentecostal* power (Luke 24:49; Acts 1:8). In the forty days between his resurrection and ascension, in preparation for the kingdom era that would begin on Pentecost, Jesus was speaking to his disciples "of the things concerning the kingdom of God" (Acts 1:3). That Pentecost was the birthday of the church is consistent with Christ's equation of church and kingdom in Matt 16:18-19. In his Christian witness in Samaria Philip was "preaching the good news about the kingdom of God" (Acts 8:12). Paul's message to Jews and Gentiles alike was about Jesus Christ and the kingdom of God (Acts 19:8; 20:25; 28:23,31). The redeemed of the present age are members of "the kingdom of His beloved Son" (Col 1:13). We are part of "a kingdom which cannot be shaken" (Heb 12:28), i.e., a spiritual kingdom in contrast with the pre-Messianic covenant as characterized by physical limitations (Heb 12:18-28).

Our conclusion is that the OT prophecies about the kingdom of God, when understood in light of the principles for interpreting prophecy laid down at the beginning of this chapter, are rightly understood as being fulfilled at Christ's *first* coming. They refer to the spiritual kingdom Jesus established when he ascended to his throne at the Father's right hand. As is the case with prophecies about Messianic Israel, the prophecies about the Messianic kingdom have already been fulfilled, and fulfilled on a different level as compared with the pre-Messianic Davidic kingdom under the Old Covenant. In fact, the prophecies about Israel and about the kingdom are both fulfilled in the *same* spiritual reality, the church of Jesus Christ. Just as the church is the true Israel today, so the church is the true kingdom of God. This convergence is seen in Gabriel's prophecy about Mary's virgin-born son, that "the Lord God will give Him the throne of His father David; and He will reign over the house of Jacob forever, and His kingdom will have no end" (Luke 1:32-33).

This is a simple, uncomplicated, biblical way to understand prophecy about Israel and about the kingdom of God. It is also faithful to the NT's own interpretation of such prophecy. This is why the NT warns us not to keep focusing on material realities. The true circumcision, the true Israel, says Paul, consists of those "who worship in the Spirit of God and glory in Christ Jesus and put no confidence in the flesh" (Phil 3:3). Therefore, "Keep seeking the things above, where Christ is, seated at the right hand of God. Set your mind on the things above, not on the things that are on the earth" (Col 3:1-2).

NOTES ON CHAPTER TWENTY-SEVEN

[1]The new Israel is actually in continuity with the spiritual "Israel within Israel" that existed even in OT times (Rom 9:6).

[2]This is the Greek word *nyn*, an adverb that means "now." When used as an adjective, as here, it means "present." When used in this latter sense it often refers to this present age in contrast with the age to come. See Rom 8:18; 1 Tim 6:17; 2 Tim 4:10; 2 Pet 3:7. In 1 Tim 4:8 Paul contrasts this "present" (*nyn*) life with the coming life.

[3]See also Mark 1:15, where Christ's message is summed up as, "The time is fulfilled, and the kingdom of God is at hand." This, compared with Matt 4:17, shows that there is no difference between "the kingdom of heaven" and "the kingdom of God."

[4]See also Eph 1:20-23; Phil 2:8-11; Heb 1:13; 8:1; 10:12-13.

CHAPTER TWENTY-EIGHT
THE MILLENNIUM

O ur next subject in the exposition of eschatology is *the millennium*, a word that literally means "one thousand years." In the context of theology it refers to a thousand-year period that is somehow connected with Christ's second coming. As a specific historical period it is mentioned in only one passage in the Bible, Rev 20:1-7, where the phrase *chilia ete* (Greek for "one thousand years") appears six times. Exactly how this millennium should be understood is one of the most controversial questions in eschatology.

At stake here are a number of points of disagreement, including all the issues discussed in the previous chapter. Governing all the rest is the question of the nature of prophecy: are the things related to the millennium to be understood as literal or as figurative? For example, must we take the number "one thousand" literally, or does it symbolize simply a long period of time? Also at stake are the role of Israel and the role of the church during this thousand-year period. Also, how does it relate to the kingdom of God?

Millennial views also differ greatly on the matter of *timing*: exactly when does the millennium occur? Does it have any connection with Christ's first coming? How is it related to his second coming? How does it fit into the sequence of other end-time events, such as the rise of the anti-Christ, the tribulation, the rapture, and the resurrection of the dead?

The final and perhaps main thing that is at stake is the *nature* of the millennial kingdom. What conditions will prevail upon the earth during this time? If it is a time when Jesus reigns as King, what will be the nature of his reign, i.e., will it be physical or spiritual? Will Christ be physically present on the earth, or will he somehow reign from heaven? Will the earth itself be a paradise? In what sense will Satan be bound?

In contemplating such questions over the centuries, Christian thinkers have delineated four distinct views about the millennium, called postmillennialism, traditional premillennialism, dispensational premillennialism, and amillennialism.[1] In this chapter we will first explain each of these views. Then we will set forth an overview of the Book of Revelation, with an emphasis upon its cyclical structure. Finally, we will explain and defend the meaning of Rev 20:1-6 from an amillennial perspective.

I. VIEWS OF THE MILLENNIUM

Though four clearly defined views of the millennium are usually distinguished, there are variations regarding details within each view. What follows here is a typical representation of each position.

A. Postmillennialism

The first view is postmillennialism, a term that literally means "after the millennium." To say that Christ's second coming is postmillennial simply means that it will happen after the millennium; the thousand-year period of Rev 20:1-6 will precede it. This is one of the newer views, traceable to the writings of Thomas Brightman (1562–1607).[2] It became popular during the nineteenth and early twentieth centuries, being taught by theologians such as Alexander Campbell[3] and B.B. Warfield. The two world wars were a temporary setback for this view, but in the latter half of the twentieth century it has picked up some staunch advocates. See Boettner, *Millennium* and "Postmillennialism"; John J. Davis, *Kingdom*; and Gentry, *Dominion*. The typical view is as follows:

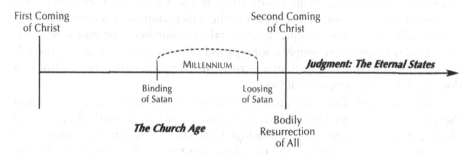

POSTMILLENNIALISM

First Coming of Christ

Second Coming of Christ

MILLENNIUM

Judgment: The Eternal States

Binding of Satan

Loosing of Satan

The Church Age

Bodily Resurrection of All

The unique thing about this view is its belief that the first part of the church age is a period in which the gospel of Christ makes steady progress toward converting the whole world to Christianity. This is the age of conquest during which, through the preaching of the gospel, most people will actually become Christians. This is the gradual "binding of Satan" pictured in Rev 20:1-3. Though the process is slow, it *will* be accomplished; and it will be done not by a miraculous intervention of Christ but by forces now at work in the world, i.e., through obedience to the Great Commission and through the sanctifying work of the Spirit. The kingdom of God will grow, slowly but surely (Matt 13:31-33), until most of the world is won.

Not only is this *supposed* to happen; as postmillennialists see it, it *is* happening. Thus postmillennialism is very optimistic about the world situation, which it interprets as getting better and better all the time. At some point this increasing righteousness will reach a critical mass, and then the millennium will begin. Jesus does not return to the earth; nevertheless he reigns from heaven over the whole world. His reign or kingdom is not earthly or political; he reigns spiritually in the hearts of most of the earth's population. Peace and righteousness prevail. Sin exists, but it is a negligible exception. The visible church will embrace all nations. Satan is truly bound!

This great spiritual progress will naturally be accompanied by material progress as a matter of cause and effect, with the latter being both a by-product and a verification of the former. As Boettner says, "The great material prosperity of which the Bible speaks as accompanying the millennial era will be, to a large extent, the natural result of the high moral and spiritual life of that time" ("Postmillennialism," 130-131). The result is that the whole earth will be a virtual paradise, with optimal social, economic, political, and cultural conditions. Poverty, ignorance, and disease will be eliminated. Wealth will be greatly increased and evenly distributed. The earth will be subdued (Gen 1:28), and even the deserts will blossom with roses.

Again, all this will come about and continue to prevail through forces now operative within mankind and within nature. This millennial era will simply be the second part of the church age. The basic facts of life will be no different from now. People will be born, marry, procreate, and die; the laws of nature will be intact. The good blessings of the millennium will be the same blessings we now enjoy, only on a grander scale.

This heavenly reign of Christ over an earthly paradise will last for an indefinitely long time; the "one thousand years" may be figurative. When it comes to an end, though, Satan will be released again, according to Rev 20:7-9; and there will be a brief resurgence of evil to show just how dreadful sin is and how much it deserves to be punished. This sets the stage for Christ's second coming and the final judgment.

Though the optimism of this view and its emphasis on and confidence in the Great Commission are very appealing, and though its relative simplicity is commendable, and though it rightly identifies the millennium with at least a part of the church age, it must still be rejected for several reasons. First, we may question whether the Bible warrants such optimism regarding the spiritual progress of the world during the church age. Texts such as Matt 7:13-14 and Matt 22:14 suggest that many more will be lost than saved, and it seems arbitrary to apply these statements of Jesus to anything less than the entire church age. Second, though the parables of the mustard seed and leaven (Matt 13:31-33) show that the kingdom of God will greatly increase and be present everywhere, they do not justify the conclusion that there will be a time when almost everyone is saved (see Grudem, *Theology*, 1123). Third, biblical teaching seems to indicate that spiritual conditions will gradually get worse and worse, rather than better and better (see 1 Tim 4:1-3; 2 Tim 3:1-9,13; 2 Pet 3:1-4). In this connection the parable of the wheat and tares (Matt 13:24-30) suggests that both good and evil will coexist in considerable strength until the very end.

Fourth, we must question the alleged cause-and-effect connection between spiritual progress and material progress, with its assumption that increasing material prosperity is a sure sign of increasing spiritual prosperity as well. The many advances of modern science in areas such as agriculture, health care, communication, and transportation are simply not evidence that a spiritual paradise is in the making. In fact, though great spiritual progress has been made since the first century, and though surges of spiritual growth occur regularly in limited contexts in the world, in modern times the conclusion that the world in general is becoming more and more Christian is very questionable. Fifth and finally, this view makes it impossible for Christians throughout most of the church age to expect the imminent, any-moment return of Jesus Christ. If this view is correct, then up to this point everyone would have to say that we know Jesus is *not* coming for at least a thousand years, and probably much longer. Biblical exhortations to "be ready" (e.g., Matt 24:36-51; Luke 12:35-40) lose their urgency.

B. Traditional Premillennialism

Our second millennial view is traditional premillennialism, as distinct from the dispensational premillennialism discussed in the next section. Traditional (historic, classical, posttribulational) premillennialism appeared very early in Christian history, occurring in the second and third centuries in writers such as Justin Martyr, Irenaeus, and Tertullian. It has continued to surface from time to time down to the modern era, and has recently been defended by theologians such as Payne, *Encyclopedia*; Ladd, "Historic Premillennialism"; Erickson, *Theology*, 1226-1231; and Grudem, *Theology*, 1109-1135. The typical view is as follows:

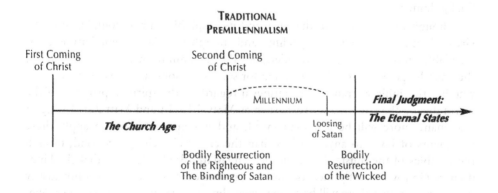

The word "premillennial" means "before the millennium" and signifies that the second coming of Christ will precede the millennium; i.e., the thousand-year reign of Christ will follow his return. While most who defend this view tend to take a literalist approach to prophecy, some are comfortable with applying some prophecies to spiritual realities.[4] Some also take the number "one thousand" to signify a long period of time (Grudem, *Theology*, 1112).

Traditional premillennialism has a distinctive view of the end time and the millennium. Whereas postmillennialism optimistically teaches that the world situation will get better and better during the church age, this present view sees it as getting worse and worse. The church continues to witness, but fails to convert the world. Near the end a period of terrible wickedness arises. The anti-Christ appears and leads the Armageddon assault upon the church, which endures great tribulation and suffering.

At the climax of this assault Jesus Christ visibly returns, destroys the anti-Christ and his hosts, and rescues God's people. Some see this as the time when national Israel is converted *en masse*. Also at this time the "first resurrection" occurs; the dead saints of all ages are raised and given new bodies, while the bodies of the still-living saints are instantly transformed. All the saved are then raptured (taken up) to meet the returning Christ in the air. Christ (with his redeemed ones following) then continues his descent to the earth, where he sets up his millennial kingdom.

It should be remembered that this view is *premillennial* since it says Christ's return will *precede* the millennium, but it is *posttribulational* since it says his return will *follow* the tribulation.

Christ's millennial reign is universal and literal. From his headquarters in Jerusalem, in his glorified body, he rules over the whole earth with his saints, who also have their glorified bodies. Satan is bound and thus is not active on the earth. The curse is removed from nature: deserts blossom, and all animals become herbivorous. The earth is indeed a paradise of universal peace, righteousness, and prosperity. Many sinners remain on the earth during the millennium. Some are converted; but others harbor a spirit of rebellion in their hearts, though they are kept in unwilling outward submission through Christ's rod-of-iron rule.

At the end of the thousand years Satan is loosed for a short time. He leads the unconverted in a brief, violent outburst of sin, resulting in an assault on Jerusalem. Christ defeats him soundly in the Battle of Gog and Magog. This is followed by the "second resurrection," i.e., the bodily resurrection of all the wicked; then come the final judgment and the eternal states.

This historic premillennial view suffers from several difficulties. First, though there are exceptions, most who defend this view are committed to a literalist interpretation of prophecy. Even those who leave some room for spiritual application (e.g., Ladd) still see the kingdom as a literal, earthly rule contrary to what was described in the previous chapter. Second, this view is usually based (at least partially) on a faulty view of the structure of the Book of Revelation. It usually sees the chapters in Revelation as following chronologically one after the other, with Revelation 20 especially following sequentially after Revelation 19. The assumption is that since Revelation 20 (the millennium chapter) comes near the end of the book, the millennium must come near the end of history. In the next main section of this chapter, we will present a more reasonable approach to the Book of Revelation and thus to the millennium. Third, the overall nature of the millennial events as described in Rev 20:1-6 can be understood and interpreted in a better way, as the last main section of this chapter will show.

Fourth, the separation of the final resurrection of the dead into two stages one thousand years apart seems contrary to the biblical teaching of what appears to be a single resurrection involving both the righteous and the wicked. This is especially seen in John 5:28-29, where Jesus says "an hour" is coming when "all who are in the tombs" will hear his voice and come forth, some to a resurrection of life and others to a resurrection of judgment. In other words there are two *kinds* of resurrection, but both occur in the same "hour," as part of a single, unitary event. See also Dan 12:2 and Acts 24:15. Also, we will show in the last section below that the two resurrections in Rev 20 do not refer to two *bodily* resurrections.

Fifth, premillennialism's description of the earth's population during the millennial kingdom presents a number of problems. According to most premillennial explanations, there will be a hybrid population combining the redeemed in their glorified, immortal bodies with the unredeemed in their natural, mortal bodies. If this is still the old, unrenewed earth, as many premillennialists believe, then the glorified saints are in an unnatural environment. But if this is the "new heavens and new earth," as others believe (Grudem, *Theology*, 1112), then the unredeemed are definitely out of their element. Another problem with mixing the saved and unsaved together is that this hardly seems to be an ideal situation for the saved. Even though the wicked are ruled with a rod of iron, their rebellious spirits would surely be a negative element in the environment. This would hardly seem paradise-like for those resurrected saints whose spirits had been residing in the heavenly presence of Jesus since their death. A final problem stemming from the mixture of saved and unsaved has to do with the purpose of the final loosing of Satan, and his mobilization of the unsaved for an attack upon the saved. If the latter are already in their glorified state, such an attack would obviously be futile.

A final difficulty with the premillennial view is the question of the very *purpose* of such a thousand-year interval between the end of this age and the final state of heaven itself. From the standpoint of the redeemed, there seems to be nothing gained by it. Why not just go directly into the final state itself? In this connection Hoekema rightly contends that the NT knows and speaks of only two ages: the present age and the age to come, with one leading directly to the other without an interval or "parenthesis" in between (*Bible*, 185-186).

Our conclusion is that traditional premillennialism is an unacceptable approach to the question of the millennium. It has too many difficulties, and in the end is not the best interpretation of the Book of Revelation and especially of Revelation 20.

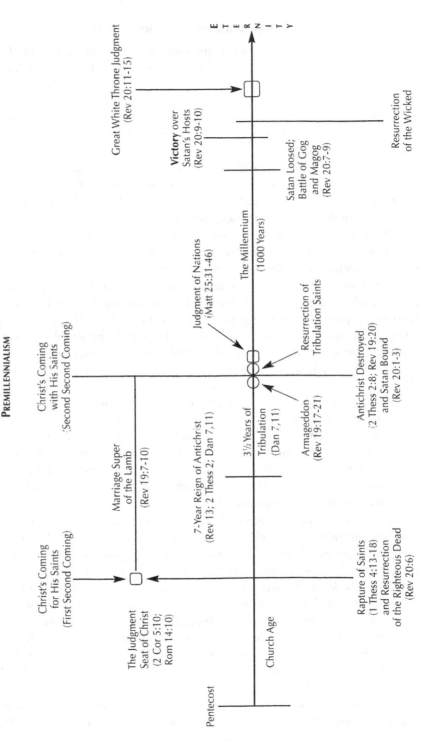

DISPENSATIONAL PREMILLENNIALISM

Pentecost

Church Age

Christ's Coming
for His Saints
(First Second Coming)

The Judgment
Seat of Christ
(2 Cor 5:10;
Rom 14:10)

Rapture of Saints
(1 Thess 4:13-18)
and Resurrection
of the Righteous Dead
(Rev 20:6)

Marriage Super
of the Lamb
(Rev 19:7-10)

7-Year Reign of Antichrist
(Rev 13; 2 Thess 2; Dan 7,11)

3½ Years of
Tribulation
(Dan 7,11)

Christ's Coming
with His Saints
(Second Second Coming)

Judgment of Nations
(Matt 25:31-46)

Armageddon
(Rev 19:17-21)

Resurrection of
Tribulation Saints

Antichrist Destroyed
(2 Thess 2:8; Rev 19:20)
and Satan Bound
(Rev 20:1-3)

The Millennium
(1000 Years)

Satan Loosed;
Battle of Gog
and Magog
(Rev 20:7-9)

Victory over
Satan's Hosts
(Rev 20:9-10)

Great White Throne Judgment
(Rev 20:11-15)

Resurrection
of the Wicked

ETERNITY

C. Dispensational Premillennialism

Dispensational (pretribulational) premillennialism is the newest of the four views, having arisen in the early nineteenth century in the British Isles. Dave MacPherson[5] traces its crucial component, the secret rapture idea, to a feverish vision by a Scottish teenager named Margaret Macdonald in 1830. This idea was almost immediately integrated into the budding dispensational theology being systematized by the early Plymouth Brethren leader, John Nelson Darby. Darby's work has greatly influenced certain circles of evangelical theology to this day, through earlier writers such as W. E. Blackstone, Dwight L. Moody, C.I. Scofield (especially through his *Scofield Reference Bible*), and L.S. Chafer; and more recent writers such as Hal Lindsey, J.D. Pentecost, John Walvoord, Herman Hoyt, and the authors of the *Left Behind* series. (See Clouse, 12-13.) The dispensational approach to the millennium is the most susceptible to sensationalist dramatization and thus is the most widely disseminated and popularly embraced view. A typical version is summed up in the accompanying chart.

Since this view is a form of premillennialism, it agrees with the previous view that Christ's second coming will precede the millennium. But what distinguishes it from the previous view? One of the main differences is that this view has a unique approach to the history of God's dealings with the world in general, an approach that determines its view of the end time. According to dispensationalism world history is divided into at least five and perhaps as many as seven distinct stages or periods ("dispensations"). For our purposes the three main dispensations are the past Mosaic era, the present church age, and the future millennial kingdom. The key to understanding how these are related is to maintain an absolute distinction between Israel and the church. Underlying the entire historical schematic is the literalist approach to biblical interpretation and especially to prophecy, especially as it applies to Israel. As Ryrie says, "Dispensational theology grows out of a consistent use of the hermeneutical principle of normal, plain, or literal interpretation" ("Dispensation," 322).

In the dispensational scheme all the OT prophecies about the kingdom of God were intended to be fulfilled in an earthly kingdom to be established by the Messiah for physical Israel. That was actually the purpose for which Christ came the first time. But when the Jews rejected Jesus as their Messiah, God simply postponed the kingdom until Christ could return to earth in his second coming. Only then would all the OT prophecies about the Jews and their kingdom be fulfilled. In the interim, as a kind of substitute for the kingdom, Jesus established the church. This present church age has no real continuity with either the OT period or with the millennial kingdom yet to come. It has been called a parenthesis in God's real purpose, which has to do with the Jews. It is like the halftime events that separate the two halves of a single football game.

When God is ready to restart his postponed program for the Jews, he will begin the countdown for the second coming of Jesus in a very dramatic way. This could happen at literally any moment, since there are no special conditions that must precede it. What is this dramatic, any-moment event? It is the *secret rapture* of all Christians out of the earth. This coincides with Christ's *first* second coming (second coming #1), which itself will be secret and invisible from the standpoint of earth's normal activities. This event is called the *parousia*, the coming or presence of Christ. All at once, in some unexpected moment, all living Christians will suddenly disappear (evaporate, in a sense) from this world and will instantly receive their glorified bodies. They will then join all previously dead Christians, who have just been raised from the dead in their new bodies in what is called the first resurrection; then all will be taken up together to meet their Savior, who has returned for them to take them up to heaven. All Christians, now glorified, will then stand before the judgment seat of Christ (2 Cor 5:10) for the assignment of their rewards. Then as the bride of Christ they will join their Bridegroom for a seven-year wedding feast (Rev 19:7-9), which takes place in heaven.

What is the purpose of this secret rapture? Why does God suddenly remove all Christians from this world? There are two reasons. First, God has no more use for the church upon the earth. It has served its purpose; the halftime events are over. God is now ready to resume the real game, where the main players are the Jews (physical Israel). Second, the next seven years of earth's history are about to be filled with some of the greatest suffering the world has ever witnessed, most of it the result of Satan's attacks on the people of God. In an act of untold mercy God removes the church from the world just so it will not have to go through the "great tribulation." Thus this view is called *pretribulational* premillennialism.

Concerning these seven years Lindsey says, "There is more prophecy concerning this period than any other era the Bible describes" (33), most of it dealing with the Jews. One blockbuster event follows another: conversion of the Jews (who then evangelize others), the restoration of Jewish worship, the rise of the anti-Christ, the great tribulation, and the Battle of Armageddon. At the climactic point of this battle, Christ returns in his *second* second coming (second coming #2).

This second return of Christ will not be secret; it will be an *apokalypsis* or revelation, and every eye will see him. He will be accompanied by the glorified Christian saints who have been in his presence for the past seven years. With his angelic hosts he will destroy all of Satan's minions and will deliver his people from tribulation. Satan will then be bound, and all Satanic influence will be removed from the earth. The second bodily resurrection will then occur, involving believers who died during the tribulation, plus all OT believers. A series of judgments follows: the newly raised are assigned their rewards; still-living Jews are judged for salvation or damnation, with the saved entering the millennial kingdom; and the still-living Gentiles are judged in the sheep-and-goats judgment, with the sheep also entering the kingdom.

After these preliminaries the millennial kingdom begins. As to its nature, the dispensational view is quite similar to that of traditional premillennialism, except in the former the Jews are given much more prominence. "It will be a *literal* kingdom in every sense of that word" (Hoyt, 79), and Jesus will sit on a material throne and reign over a literal earthly paradise, with the redeemed ruling with him. Since many entered the millennium in their mortal bodies, many children are born during this time. Some are saved; some are not. The latter are kept in outward conformity to God's law through Christ's rod-of-iron rule.

At the end of the millennium Satan will be loosed and will ensnare many of those born during this time. This loosing of Satan thus serves as a final demonstration of the corruption of human hearts. Those thus deceived by Satan launch a final rebellion against Christ's reign in the Battle of Gog and Magog, but they are destroyed by God. Then come the final bodily resurrection and the final judgment day, these involving the wicked only. Then the eternal states begin.

This view of the millennium must be emphatically rejected. Most of the difficulties identified above as applying to traditional premillennialism apply here as well, with some being intensified. The problem of literalism in the interpretation of prophecy is much more pronounced with this view, as is the tendency to sever the end-time events into fragmented parts. For example, whereas the traditional view posits two distinct end-time bodily resurrections, dispensationalists posit three. This latter view also has at least three judgment days; it even has two separate second comings. All this makes the end time unnecessarily and unbiblically complicated.

A serious problem with the dispensational view in particular is that the whole concept of a secret rapture is unbiblical. The details of the origin of this idea in themselves make it problematic (again, see MacPherson, *Cover-Up*). But even apart from this, there simply is no biblical basis for it. There will be a rapture, to be sure, as mentioned in 1 Thess 4:17; but as we shall see below in the chapter on Christ's second coming, the biblical rapture is totally unlike the popular dispensational idea, and in fact shows the whole dispensational picture of the end time to be false.

A very serious difficulty that applies only to this view of the millennium is that it is part of an overall dispensational hermeneutic that is itself unbiblical. It includes an absolute distinction between Israel and the church, and between the kingdom and the church, that is seriously false. It obscures the true preparatory role of Israel in relation to the church, and it demotes the church from its climactic role in God's plan to that of a temporary stopgap.[6] It pictures Christ as failing to accomplish the purpose for which he allegedly came the first time, i.e., to set up an earthly Jewish kingdom; this means that the whole rationale for the millennium is to give Jesus a second chance to get this done.

In my judgment dispensational premillennialism is not just false doctrine; it is *seriously* false and dangerous doctrine (something I do not say about the two previous views). This is a dangerously false view because it is diversionary: the obsession to constantly restructure prophetic application to keep pace with ongoing world events absorbs the attention of many and keeps them from attending to more important spiritual matters. It is dangerously false because it detracts from the glory of Christ's blood-created New Covenant (Luke 22:20) and his blood-bought new people, the church (Acts 20:28). Those who insist on continuing to exalt physical Israel in God's plan are the new Judaizers and are violating every warning of Paul in Phil 3:2-3. A final reason this is a dangerously false view is that it creates a spurious and precarious basis for belief in Christ and his Word. By presuming to declare that contemporary events, especially about Israel, are the fulfillment of myriads of Bible prophecies, dispensationalists are thus tying the accuracy and trustworthiness of God's Word to the fate of modern Israel. Thus it is no wonder that some weaker brethren might be led to say (as I once heard one affirm), "If the nation of Israel is ever defeated or destroyed, I will give up my faith."

We conclude that this view of the millennium, like the two before it, is unacceptable. The inadequacy of each is not just a matter of opinion, but is a conclusion based on biblical teaching and principles. This leaves one final view of the millennium to be considered, the one which in my judgment is required by sound biblical exegesis: amillennialism.

D. Amillennialism

The fourth millennial view, called amillennialism, can be traced back to the fourth and fifth centuries A.D., especially to the writings of Augustine. Through his influence "it became the dominant interpretation in medieval times," and was also embraced by the Protestant Reformers, says Clouse (9-10). It has held its own in competition with the other views even until now. Some major modern defenders include Louis Berkhof, O.T. Allis, and William Hendriksen. See especially William Cox, *Studies*; and Anthony Hoekema, *Bible* and "Amillennialism." Hoekema's work is highly recommended.

The word "amillennialism" literally means "no millennium." This is an unfortunate title, since it suggests that the proponents of this view do not believe in any kind of millennium. This certainly is not the case. Amillennialists believe there is a millennium as taught in Rev 20:1-6; but unlike the previous three views, they do not believe that it entails any kind of physical, earthly rule or paradise. In this view kingdom prophecies are seen as being fulfilled on a spiritual level in terms of spiritual realities. A typical version is as follows:

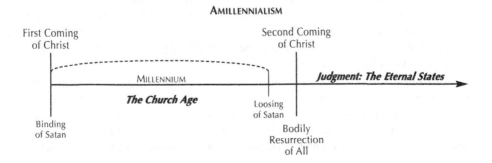

AMILLENNIALISM

First Coming of Christ — Second Coming of Christ

MILLENNIUM — *Judgment: The Eternal States*

The Church Age — Loosing of Satan

Binding of Satan

Bodily Resurrection of All

The amillennial view begins with the unique idea that Jesus established his kingdom when he came the first time. At that point he established his lordship through his death, resurrection, and ascension; and inaugurated his church on the Day of Pentecost. Since then Jesus has been reigning from heaven as Lord over the hearts of his people. Thus the kingdom exists on earth in and through the church, which is the new Israel. This kingdom is spiritual in nature, not earthly or political; and it does not involve a universal material paradise.

The millennium thus is equivalent to the church age, at least up until near its end. All the conditions described in Rev 20:1-6 began to exist when Jesus came the first time, when the church began. Satan was defeated and bound as the result of Christ's redeeming work. The "first resurrection" has likewise been taking place since the Day of Pentecost, though amillennialists disagree as to what this means. These conditions will prevail for the "thousand years," a number that is not literal but is symbolic for a long period of time.

For amillennialists the actual end time is quite uncomplicated. At the end of the church age or millennial kingdom, Satan will be loosed and will launch a concentrated spiritual (not military) attack upon the church (not Israel). This will be Armageddon and "Gog and Magog" combined; and it will be worldwide, rather than focused upon a single geographical area. In the midst of this battle the second coming itself occurs. Christ returns visibly to the earth, destroys the church's enemies, raises all the dead in a single resurrection, changes all the living, takes them all away to a single judgment day, and then inaugurates the eternal states.

Of the four millennial views described here, it is my judgment that the amillennial view has the best scriptural support, as will be explained in the rest of this chapter and the concluding chapters of this book. The rest of this chapter will show that the amillennial view is consistent with the Book of Revelation as a whole and will show that it is specifically taught in Rev 20:1-6.

II. THE BOOK OF REVELATION

To properly understand the Book of Revelation one must remember that the language, imagery, and numbers are basically figurative. As we saw in the previous chapter, the first verse of the book says that God "sent and signified" these things to John, with the word "signified" meaning "communicated in signs and symbols." This makes sense when we understand that Revelation belongs to a category of writing called *apocalyptic literature*, which uses symbolism freely. (See C. Davis, 16-47.) It is important to remember that this applies to numbers, especially to the number "one thousand."

This raises a question: if the language is figurative, is it possible to know what realities the figures represent? In one sense, no. It is not possible to make a specific, one-to-one equation between a particular figure in Revelation (e.g., the beast in 13:1) and one specific individual in the course of world history. The beast represents a certain *kind* of individual or presence in the world. But in another sense, the answer is yes. The one thing that we can know about all these images is this: we can know which ones represent the "good guys" and which stand for the "bad guys." This is all we really need to know to get the point of the book.

This is all we need to know because the one main theme that comes through loud and clear throughout Revelation is that God and God's people will be the ultimate victors over the powers of evil. The Greek word for "victory," *nike*, occurs only once in the NT (1 John 5:4), but its verb form *nikao* occurs 28 times in all. It means "to overcome, to conquer, to triumph, to be the victor." This word is used 17 times in Revelation, and echoes its main message: no matter how bad the circumstances on earth may be, especially for the church, God and his people will triumph in the end. Christ's kingship will prevail, his enemies will be destroyed, and his saints will be delivered. The purpose of this writing is thus to strengthen the faith of Christians, and to give them the patience to endure in the midst of trials and persecutions. Each figure does not have to correspond to just one specific earthly person or movement in order to get this point across.

The real key to a right interpretation of Revelation is a proper understanding of its outline or structure. This issue is intertwined with another, namely, to what period of Christian history does Revelation apply? Several approaches to the book are usually distinguished. One is called the *preterist* view. In grammar this word refers to the past tense, and in our context it refers to the view that everything written in Revelation refers to events that were in the past from the standpoint of its writing at the end of the first century. That is, it refers to the persecution of the church by late first-century Roman emperors such as Nero and Domitian. This means it has no direct application to the bulk of Christian history and no reference to the end time. This is inconsistent with the book's own stated intention to deal with "the things which must soon take place" (1:1; see 1:19), and with its many clear references to the end time.

Another common approach is the *historical* view, which says that the entire book, at least from chapter 4 onward, is a description of the entire scope of church history from Christ's first coming to his second coming. It also says that the book makes just one continuous sweep through the course of history, with the described events happening in unbroken chronological order, in one progressive sequence leading up to the end. This assumes that the figures in the various chapters are intended to represent identifiable persons and events that have appeared or will appear on the stage of world history. Thus to understand Revelation, one must have a good grasp of history, especially the history of the church. This also assumes that the closing chapters of Revelation, especially chapters 20–22, must necessarily refer to the end of history since they are at the end of the book. This tends to support the premillennial view of the millennium. We shall see below, though, that this is an incorrect approach to the book as a whole.

A third approach is called the *futurist* view. It holds that almost all of Revelation (especially chs. 4–22) refers to the events that will happen at the very end of history, specifically in the seven-year period of the "great tribulation" between the secret rapture and Christ's visible return. Like the historical view, it sees the events described as happening in the chronological sequence in which they appear in the book. Thus 19:11-21 refers to the visible coming, 20:1-6 to the subsequent millennium, and 20:11-15 to the last judgment, the judgment of the wicked only. Except for chapters 1–3, the contents of the book have no application to the church age. This view is held mostly by dispensational premillennialists. Its weaknesses will become apparent in the following discussion.

In my judgment the correct approach to the structure of the Book of Revelation is the one called the *cyclical* or *recapitulation* view.[7] It says that the contents of the book (after the introduction in chs. 1–3) form a series of parallel descriptions relevant to the whole of Christian history and the end time. This view has several important characteristics. First, it denies the assumption of the historical and futurist views, i.e., that chapters 4–22 are a single chronological series of events happening in an unbroken sequence. This means that the events of chapter 9, e.g., may or may not follow sequentially upon those of chapter 8; it means that the events of chapter 20, e.g., may or may not follow sequentially upon those of chapter 19. This means that we cannot assume that just because something is described in chapter 19 or in chapter 20, near the end of the book, that it must necessarily occur at the end of history. Instead of this chronological approach, the cyclical view says that Revelation 4–22 is divided into several sections that are *parallel* descriptions of church history and the end time.

Second, each of these parallel units is relevant to the entire sweep of church history from the first coming of Christ to his second coming. This does not mean that each unit necessarily covers the *entire* scope of Christian history. Each has its own perspective, its own focus, its own purpose. One may focus on the entire church age; another may concentrate upon the last days. One may describe events from the perspective of the church, another from the perspective of its enemies.

Third, each segment basically raises the same question, namely, "Who's in charge here?" In its symbolic reference to some aspect of Christian history, each unit of Revelation highlights the conflict between good and evil, specifically between Satan and his forces on the one hand, and God and his people on the other hand. The strength of the powers of evil and their enmity toward the church are emphasized, as is the reality of Christian suffering and tribulation. Thus Revelation is addressed especially to Christians who find themselves to be the objects of persecution, and who ask with pious sincerity, "Who's in charge here? God, are you in control?"

Fourth and most significantly, each of the parallel segments in Revelation ends with the resounding note of *nike*—victory! Christ is pictured as triumphing over Satan and his forces, bringing all his enemies to righteous judgment, and delivering his saints while sharing his victory with them. Like a symphony that develops a single strain or repeats the same musical refrain over and over yet in different ways, so does Revelation echo and reecho this single theme, this one main point several times in different ways: ***Christ is King!***

How do we know that this cyclical view is the correct approach? The key or basic giveaway is the fact that at several places in the book, there are more or less clear references to the same end-time events: the second coming, the final judgment, the eternal states. These events appear not just at the end of the book, but in several other chapters along the way. For example, beginning in 6:1 the opening of the seven seals seems clearly to be a perspective on the church age, but the sixth seal seems to bring it to a climax. Revelation 6:17 declares that "the great day of their wrath has come," in an unmistakable reference to the second coming. This is closely followed by a description of God's people who have already been through a "great tribulation" (7:14) and who are described as being in the same heaven (7:15-17) that is pictured in chapters 21–22. This is followed by the opening of the seventh seal, which clearly brings "a break in the action," as John is given a half-hour rest period until the next unit begins.

Since the end of chapter 7 deals with the final state of heaven, the set of revelations triggered by the blowing of the seven trumpets (chs. 8–11) must take us back into the church age once more. That this unit will also conclude with a perspective on the second coming is seen in the forewarning in 10:7, that the end will happen when the seventh angel sounds: "But in the days of the voice of the seventh angel, when he is about to sound, then the mystery of God is finished." Then in 11:15 when the seventh angel sounds his trumpet, the end does in fact come: "Your wrath came, and the time came for the dead to be judged" (11:18). That the end of chapter 11 brings us to the end of history is confirmed by the beginning of chapter 12, which without doubt refers to the first coming of the Messiah and thus begins a new cycle.

We find the next clear reference to the end time in 14:7, "The hour of His judgment has come." Then in 14:15 comes the message, "The hour to reap has come, because the harvest of the earth is ripe" (see Matt 13:39). The imagery of 14:19-20 can refer to nothing less than hell itself.

This means that a new parallel unit begins in chapter 15. But where is the next clear reference to the end time and judgment? Certainly 20:11-15 (the great white throne judgment) refers to the end, and is followed by a detailed description of the final state of the redeemed (chs. 21, 22). But is there any other end-time reference before this? This is a crucial point for the question of the millennium, for if chapters 15–22 form a single unit, then even in the cyclical view of Revelation, the millennium chapter would follow chronologically upon chapter 19 and would occur near the end and thus would be consistent with a premillennial view of the millennium.

In my judgment, however, it is best to see chapter 19 as forming the end of the fourth cycle of Revelation, and chapter 20 as beginning the fifth and last cycle. The "great supper of God" (19:17) is an image of hell itself, which is shown by the reference to "the wine press of the fierce wrath of God" in 19:15, which is parallel to the reference to hell in 14:19-20. This means that chapter 20—the millennium chapter—begins a new cycle, and thus goes back to encompass the church age. That the imagery of the binding of Satan (20:1-3) is an appropriate description of what happened at Christ's *first* coming is seen in its parallelism with 12:7-9, which is clearly related to the first coming.

In the final analysis this means that the Book of Revelation, after the introduction (chs. 1–3), has five main parallel sections, each of which give a perspective on the church age and ends with the second coming, judgment, and eternal states. See the accompanying chart.

AN OUTLINE OF THE BOOK OF REVELATION
(Introduction: Chapters 1–3)

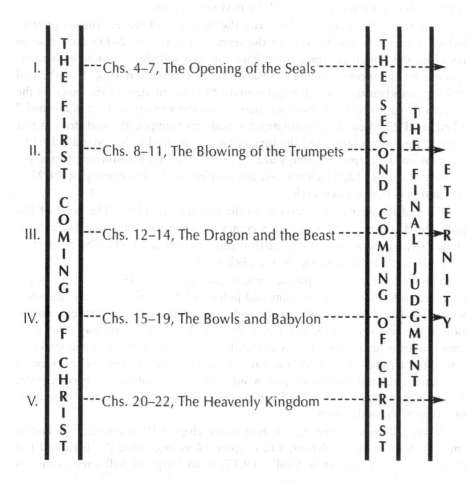

	THE FIRST COMING OF CHRIST		THE SECOND COMING OF CHRIST	FINAL JUDGMENT	ETERNITY
I.		---Chs. 4–7, The Opening of the Seals-------			
II.		---Chs. 8–11, The Blowing of the Trumpets---			
III.		---Chs. 12–14, The Dragon and the Beast----			
IV.		---Chs. 15–19, The Bowls and Babylon------			
V.		---Chs. 20–22, The Heavenly Kingdom------			

Having thus established the overall structure and divisions of Revelation, we are now prepared to go back through it in detail and draw conclusions as to the specific perspectives and applications within the individual segments. We can do this best if we see from the beginning that Rev 20:1-10 embraces the entire church age, from first coming to second coming. This period is then divided into two segments: a long era ("a thousand years," 20:1-6) and a brief era ("a short time," 20:3,7-10). Some of the imagery in the preceding sections may apply to the long era, and some to the short time.

The following are my own conclusions, without detail, as to how the various sections of Revelation should be understood. The first section, the opening of the seven seals (chs. 4–7), is prefaced by a description of the heavenly throne room where these revelations are given to John (chs. 4, 5). These are real-time, real-place events; John sees these things as they happen. Then in 6:1 he begins to see symbolic visions (either in his mind or in holographic images in a gigantic theater) that *represent* realities.

The first seal (6:1-2) is the vision of one on a white horse, which I take to be Jesus at his first coming. The next three seals (6:3-8) represent calamities that befall Christians: physical and economic persecution, and calamitous death. The martyrs for Christ's sake voice the cry of all Christians under persecution: "How long, O Lord, holy and true, will You refrain from judgment and avenging our blood on those who dwell on the earth?" (6:10). They are counseled to be patient (6:11), but John is immediately shown God's answer to the question in the opening of the sixth seal, which presents the second coming and the day of wrath upon God's enemies (6:12-17). Chapter 7 gives a perspective on the final salvation of all the saints.

The opening of the seventh seal (8:1) gives John a real-time 30 minutes to rest and recover, in preparation for the next series of revelations: the seven trumpets. The first four (8:6-13) bring visions of physical judgments from God upon the earth during the church age, to which both believers and unbelievers may be subject, but which specifically seek the repentance of the latter (9:20-21). The fifth and sixth trumpets (9:1-19) describe severe judgments upon the wicked, which I take to refer to the loosing-of-Satan era (20:7-9). Chapter 10, referring to the entire time covered by the six trumpets, describes the limits of human knowledge and opportunity and thus encourages Christians to spread the Word of God while there is still time. Then 11:1-14 describes how the church fares between the comings. In 11:1-6 the two witnesses represent the era of the binding of Satan through the preaching of the Word, and 11:7-10 describes the loosing of Satan where suppression and deceit abound. In 11:11-14 Christians are assured that God will vindicate his people and destroy his enemies. Then the seventh angel sounds its trumpet, and John witnesses the second coming and the promised vindication (11:15-19).

Chapter 12 starts a new cycle, and clearly begins with the birth of Christ (12:1-6). The conflict between Christ and the devil is prominent here. The spiritual warfare in 12:7-10 is a picture of the battle between Christ and Satan that occurred at Christ's first coming, and Satan's decisive defeat accomplished through Christ's death and resurrection. Having lost his battle against Christ, the devil then turns to make war on Christ's people (12:10-17). Chapter 13 describes this latter war in more detail. The two beasts represent, first, the anti-Christian powers that oppose Christianity down through the centuries with physical force (e.g., the Roman Empire, communism, Islam), and second, the anti-Christian religions and philosophies that give a theoretical basis for the evil powers (e.g., idolatry, dialectical materialism, the Qur'an, evolution). Chapter 14 is God's encouragement to believers that they will be delivered (14:1-5) and that the wicked will be brought to judgment (14:6-20). "Here is the patience of the saints" (14:12).

The next segment is chapters 15–19, which describe mostly the extreme wickedness and divine judgment that will characterize the short time when Satan is loosed. In 15:1 the "seven last plagues" are announced, and in 15:2-4 believers are assured that the bowls of wrath will not harm them. After some heavenly preliminaries (15:5-8) John sees the angels pour out the seven bowls of wrath (16:1-21), which I believe symbolize both the Satanic evils and the divine wrath that will characterize the era of Satan's loosing (20:7-9). The seventh plague (16:17-21) reprises the sixth seal (6:12-17) and describes the very end of the loosing-of-Satan period (20:10) from the perspective of the wicked. Chapters 17 and 18 give more detail about the seventh plague and Satan's final defeat, under the imagery of the fall of Babylon (16:19), with all its anti-Christian materialism and hedonism. Chapter 19 then describes heaven and hell under the symbolism of two feasts: "the wedding supper of the Lamb" (19:9), representing heaven; and "the great supper of God" (19:17), representing hell. Every human being will be in attendance at one or the other of these meals, either as a believer enjoying the blessings of salvation forever, or as an unbeliever being treated as carrion by birds of prey. In other words, our choice is to be either the beautiful bride, or buzzard bait.

This leads to the final segment (chs. 20–22), which begins with a symbolic description of a consequence of Christ's first coming: the binding of Satan. This marks the beginning of the church age, which is in fact the era of Christ's millennial kingdom. We will now discuss the content of 20:1-6 in greater detail.

III. THE MILLENNIUM IN REVELATION 20:1-6[8]

What Rev 20:1-6 teaches about the millennium is not unique. Even if this text were not in the Bible, we would still have the concept of Christ reigning over his kingdom between his first and second comings, based on what is taught elsewhere in Scripture (see the previous chapter). Also, the marvelous characteristics ascribed to this thousand-year reign in Revelation 20—the binding of Satan, the first resurrection, reigning with Christ—also are described elsewhere as the realities enjoyed by Christians during the church age. Revelation 20:1-6 simply sums them up and reminds us that the positive spiritual blessings experienced continually by the church far outweigh any negative circumstances that we might have to endure in this life.

As we look more closely at this text, we must remember that the language of Revelation is mainly figurative or symbolic, e.g., "chain," "thousand years," "thrones." Also we must remember that the cyclical nature of the book places the events of 20:1-6 at the beginning of the church age, not at the end of history. Every event described here took place, or began to take place, as the result of Christ's earthly ministry, death, resurrection, and ascension to God's right hand. His thousand-year reign began at that point, and still continues today. *The Millennium is now!*

A. The Binding of Satan

The first three verses of Revelation 20 describe an event that surely sends a thrill through every Christian's heart: *the binding of Satan.* The text says,

> Then I saw an angel coming down from heaven, holding the key of the abyss and a great chain in his hand. And he laid hold of the dragon, the serpent of old, who is the devil and Satan, and bound him for a thousand years; and he threw him into the abyss, and shut it and sealed it over him, so that he would not deceive the nations any longer, until the thousand years were completed; after these things he must be released for a short time.

My strong conviction is that Jesus bound the devil when he came the first time. Many find it extremely difficult to accept this idea, mainly because they hear the words "binding of Satan" and formulate their own idea of what this must mean before they examine the biblical data. If Satan is bound, they think, then there should not be any sin or even temptation on the earth. But sin obviously was not eliminated by Christ's first coming and is still abundant on the earth today. Would one not have to be blind to think that Satan is bound in times like these?

The key to understanding the binding of Satan is to pay close attention to what the Bible actually says about it, not only in Rev 20:1-3 but elsewhere in the NT as well. Regarding the latter we begin with the way Scripture describes the *purpose* of Christ's first coming. Among other things, it is specifically taught that Jesus came to deal with the devil. First John 3:8 says, "The Son of God appeared for this purpose, to destroy the works of the devil." Among Satan's works are falsehood and death (John 8:44; Heb 2:14), but Jesus came "to testify to the truth" (John 18:37; see John 8:31-47). He has already "abolished death and brought life and immortality to light through the gospel" (2 Tim 1:10).

Jesus came not only to destroy Satan's works but to "destroy" Satan himself. Hebrews 2:14 clearly states that Jesus came the first time "so that by his death he might destroy him who holds the power of death—that is, the devil" (NIV). The word rendered "destroy" by the NIV (*katargeo*) does not necessarily mean "to annihilate, to abolish completely." Obviously Jesus did not do this to Satan at his first coming. But the word also can mean "to set aside, to make ineffective, to nullify, to render powerless." This is the better understanding here, as in the NASB: Christ came to "render powerless him who had the power of death, that is, the devil."

Either way this is very strong language. John says Jesus came specifically to destroy the devil's works; Hebrews says he came to render the devil powerless. We must ask, if this is why Jesus came, did he actually accomplish these things or did he fail? Surely it would be blasphemous to say the latter. Therefore we conclude that Jesus destroyed Satan's works and rendered him powerless when he came the first time. This is in effect no different from "the binding of Satan" in Rev 20:1-3. If anything, the language of 1 John and Hebrews is even stronger than that of Revelation 20.

What about the expression, "the binding of Satan"? Does this specific language appear elsewhere in Scripture? The answer is yes. In Matt 12:29 (and Mark 3:27) it is used to describe what Jesus was doing during his first advent. Throughout Jesus' earthly ministry he was already limiting Satan's power, especially through his many victorious encounters with demonic spirits who had taken over people's bodies. By casting out demons Jesus was demonstrating his power over Satan's kingdom; he was winding the chains around the devil's neck.

Jesus made this very claim in connection with an exorcism recorded in Matt 12:22-30 (see Mark 3:22-27; Luke 11:14-23). Here Jesus explains that in casting out demons he is not working *with* Satan, but *against* him. He uses the illustration of a strong man who is holding people captive in his house, and a stronger man who attacks and overpowers the captor and sets the captives free (Luke 11:21-22). As he explains in Matt 12:29, "Or how can anyone enter the strong man's house and carry off his property, unless he first binds the strong man? And then he will plunder his house." By casting out demons Jesus was already in the process of binding the devil (the "strong man") during his earthly ministry.

Jesus also gave his disciples the authority to cast out demons (Matt 10:1). In Luke 10:1-20 he sent out 70 evangelists with similar authority. When they returned, they joyfully reported, "Lord, even the demons are subject to us in Your name" (Luke 10:17). Jesus replied, "I was watching Satan fall from heaven like lightning" (Luke 10:18). Satan's "fall from heaven" here is not his prehistoric, initial sin; it refers to the *defeat* he was experiencing through Christ's power at the hands of the disciples at that very time. This is the same event described symbolically in Rev 12:7-9,

And there was war in heaven, Michael and his angels waging war with the dragon. The dragon and his angels waged war, and they were not strong enough, and there was no longer a place found for them in heaven. And the great dragon was thrown down, the serpent of old who is called the devil and Satan, who deceives the whole world; he was thrown down to the earth, and his angels were thrown down with him.

Again this is not Satan's initial sin, but his defeat at the hands of the Messiah at the latter's first coming (Rev 12:1-6).

The death blow against Satan was struck in the death and resurrection of Jesus (see Gen 3:15; John 12:31-33; Col 2:15). On the eve of his crucifixion Jesus announced his imminent mortal combat with the devil (John 14:30). Through his own death he rendered Satan powerless (Heb 2:14), and through his resurrection the victory was complete. The risen victor declares, "I am the first and the last, and the living One; and I was dead, and behold, I am alive forevermore, and I have the keys of death and of Hades" (Rev 1:17-18). The "keys" here are the same as "the key of the abyss" in Rev 20:1. A key is symbolic of power and authority. Through his death and resurrection Jesus gained power over the abyss—the realm of death, Satan's proper domain; and with that power he both locks Satan himself in the abyss and rescues those who have been held captive there (Heb 2:15). Revelation 20:1-3 thus symbolically represents Christ's present control over Satan and his works, and the consequent limitation of his power.[10]

Some will still be skeptical that "the binding of Satan" has been a reality since Christ's first coming. Again, this is because they have created their own idea of what this should entail, i.e., the earth should be a perfect place, free from sin and filled with righteousness, peace, and prosperity. But this is not how things have been. So how can this be the millennium? How can we accept the idea that Satan is bound now? We can do this if we do not jump to unwarranted conclusions about the results of Satan's binding. Does the Bible actually say that this binding will result in a paradise-like world? No. In fact, Rev 20:3 states very specifically that the single purpose of Satan's binding is "so that he would not deceive the nations any longer."

The question is whether this was actually a result of Christ's first coming, and the answer is yes. Satan's main activity is deception. John 8:44 says, "he is a liar and the father of lies." Revelation 12:9 describes him, prior to his defeat at Christ's first coming, as the one "who deceives the whole world." He is the source of lies, false teachings, false religions, and all idolatry. With the exception of Israel, prior to Christ's first coming the entire world—all nations *as nations*—was totally engulfed in Satan's lies, languishing in darkness (see Rom 1:18-32). But what happened when Christ came? He accomplished the works of redemption, thus defeating the devil and his hosts. The gospel—the good news about the saving power of Christ—is the *gospel truth* that dispels Satan's lies and brings light and life to all the world (2 Tim 1:10).

This is exactly how the risen Jesus described Paul's mission to the Gentiles, i.e., to the *nations*: "to open their eyes so that they may turn from darkness to light and from the dominion of Satan to God, that they may receive forgiveness of sins and an inheritance among those who have been sanctified by faith in Me" (Acts 26:18). This tells us that prior to the preaching of the gospel, the *nations* were in darkness; they were the domain of Satan. But as the gospel has been preached "to all the nations" in obedience to the Great Commission (Luke 24:47; see Matt 28:18-20; Mark 16:15), multitudes "from every nation and all tribes and peoples and tongues" (Rev 7:9) have been delivered from captivity to the devil. In terms of Rev 20:1-3, *the truth of the gospel of Jesus Christ* is the chain that binds Satan, so that he is not able to deceive the nations any longer.

This does not mean that Satan is doing nothing today. He still roams about, like a roaring lion, seeking to devour us (1 Pet 5:8). But Christ has established a safety zone, as it were, a place where Satan has no power. It is the *church*, which is the realm over which Christ reigns in his millennial kingship, a haven from the forces of death (Matt 16:18), and "the pillar and support of the truth" (1 Tim 3:15). Anyone who accepts the truth of the gospel and surrenders to the Lordship of Christ is rescued from captivity to Satan and set free to live beyond the reach of his lying mouth and slashing claws.

The results of Christ's initial binding of Satan are bestowed on individuals. When one makes his choice to follow Christ instead of Satan, the almighty power of Jesus Christ binds the devil in reference to that person's life. Jesus has already bound the strong man as such; when we preach the gospel and convert individuals, we are in effect plundering the strong man's house and carrying off his property (Matt 12:29). Because this has already been done on a worldwide basis, with practically every nation being exposed to Christ's liberating power to some degree, it can no longer be said that Satan is deceiving *the nations*. Therefore, in terms of Rev 20:1-3, he is bound. *The Millennium is now!*

B. The First Resurrection

The second major event that characterizes the millennium, according to Rev 20:4-6, is *the first resurrection:*

> Then I saw thrones, and they sat on them, and judgment was given to them. And I saw the souls of those who had been beheaded because of their testimony of Jesus and because of the word of God, and those who had not worshiped the beast or his image, and had not received the mark on their forehead and on their hand; and they came to life and reigned with Christ for a thousand years. The rest of the dead did not come to life until the thousand years were completed. This is the first resurrection. Blessed and holy is the one who has a part in the first resurrection; over these the second death has no power, but they will be priests of God and of Christ and will reign with Him for a thousand years.

Amillennialists differ in their interpretation of the first resurrection. Some say it refers to something that happens not on the earth, but rather in heaven, and that it happens only to believers who have died, such as martyrs (Hoekema, *Bible*, 230-231). This first resurrection which they experience is not physical but spiritual; it refers to the fact that their souls are now consciously alive in heaven, living with Christ and sharing the blessings and privileges of Christ's millennial reign (ibid., 232-233). As

Grudem sums it up, this view says the first resurrection means "going to heaven to be with the Lord," or coming into the presence of God (*Theology*, 1115).

I strongly reject this interpretation of the first resurrection, and I agree with its critics who say that this is an unusual and unlikely connotation for the words in 20:4-6 that are translated "come to life" and "resurrection" (see Grudem, *Theology*, 1118-1119; Ladd, "Response," 189-191). Here I will explain that the first resurrection is something very different. It refers to a specific event that happens in the life of every Christian convert, an event that happens on the earth but which has eternal consequences. It is the event known as *regeneration*, the resurrection from spiritual death that happens when one is baptized into Christ.

At this point we must look at what is specifically said about this first resurrection in Revelation 20. First, there are two categories of persons who came to life. One is the martyrs beheaded because of their faith; John sees only their disembodied souls (see Rev 6:9). Thus we may conclude that they are in heaven. The second group consists of "those who had not worshiped the beast or his image, and had not received the mark on their forehead and on their hand." This cannot be the same group as the martyrs, for contrary to what is implied in the NASB, there is no parallelism in the Greek phrasing translated "those who had been beheaded" and "those who had not worshiped." The former phrase is a genitive participle and is correctly translated as modifying "souls." The latter phrase, however, is an aorist verb preceded by the nominative plural relative pronoun, *hoitines*, "whoever," which is the subject. That *hoitines* is nominative, not genitive, means that it does not modify "souls," i.e., John does not say that he saw *the souls* of those who had not worshiped the beast. However the latter group is connected with "I saw" at the beginning of the verse, it is a broader category than the martyrs as such, and refers simply to *whoever* is not on Satan's side, whether in heaven or on earth.

Second, the text says that the coming to life in verse 4 is the *first* resurrection, which implies that there is also a *second* resurrection. Verse 5 indicates that anyone not included in the two categories in verse 4, i.e., anyone who does not experience the first resurrection, will experience this second resurrection after the millennium ends: "The rest of the dead did not come to life until the thousand years were completed." One thing should be noted: the text does not say that those who participate in the first resurrection will *not* participate in the second one also. It simply says that some will experience *only* the second resurrection.

Third, those who have a part in the first resurrection will escape the second death (v. 6), which in verse 14 is equated with "the lake of fire," i.e., hell (see 21:8). These are the only ones who are saved from eternal punishment. Thus there seems to be a redemptive power in the first resurrection that is not present in the second. Those who participate in the second resurrection but not in the first are still subject to the second death.

Now we must address the question, exactly what is this "first resurrection" that makes the millennium so attractive? Many assume that since two resurrections are implied, and since we know that one is a bodily resurrection, then the other must be bodily also. The problem, though, is that we have already seen that Scripture seems to speak of only one bodily resurrection event, which includes both the righteous and the wicked. So the two resurrections must be different *kinds* of resurrection. But then the objection is raised, surely two different kinds of resurrection would not be described with the same terminology in the same brief text. But is this a valid assumption?

The fact is that there are two other NT texts that speak of two resurrections, and in each case two different *kinds* of resurrection are in view. One is the spiritual resurrection that takes place only in the soul at the time of baptism; the other is the bodily resurrection that takes place at the end time. One of these texts is John 5:24-29, which clearly speaks of two distinct resurrections that are in sharp contrast with one another. First Jesus says, "Truly, truly, I say to you, an hour is coming and now is, when the dead will hear the voice of the Son of God, and those who hear will live" (v. 25). Then in verses 28-29 he says, "Do not marvel at this; for an hour is coming, in which all who are in the tombs will hear His voice, and will come forth; those who did the good deeds to a resurrection of life, those who committed the evil deeds to a resurrection of judgment."

One contrast here is between the two kinds of death from which we are raised. Verse 25 speaks simply of "the dead," and the second reference speaks of "all who are in the tombs." The latter reference to "the tombs" suggests physical death; the former reference simply to "the dead" is consistent with the concept of *spiritual* death, the condition of every unsaved sinner (Eph 2:1,5; Col 2:13). Also, the former reference implies that not all the (spiritually) dead will actually hear the Son's voice, but those who do hear will live. The second category clearly is universal: "all who are in the tombs will hear His voice, and will come forth."

Another point of contrast is the description of the event of resurrection itself. For the former group, those who hear Christ's voice simply "will live." This is an echo of verse 24, "Truly, truly, I say to you, he who hears My word, and believes Him who sent Me, has eternal life, and does not come into judgment, but has passed out of death into life." These are appropriate ways to describe the spiritual resurrection of regeneration. For the latter category, though, the resurrection is described as *coming forth from the tombs*, which clearly pictures a bodily resurrection.

A final contrast is the different *times* when these two resurrections will occur. For the first one, Jesus says "an hour is coming *and now is.*" That he says both "is coming" and "now is" means that the transition was beginning to occur at that very time. It did not technically begin until Pentecost, but Jesus indicates that its time is already present because everything is poised for it to begin. Of the second resurrection, though, Jesus simply says, "an hour is coming" when it will happen. His description of it in verse 29 is basically eschatological in nature.

It is quite clear, then, that here Jesus speaks of two separate resurrections of two entirely different kinds. It should also be noted that believers will participate in both. This is parallel in every way with Rev 20:4-6.

One other text that speaks of two kinds of resurrection is Rom 8:10-11, "If Christ is in you, though the body is dead because of sin, yet the spirit is alive because of righteousness. But if the Spirit of Him who raised Jesus from the dead dwells in you, He who raised Christ Jesus from the dead will also give life to your mortal bodies through His Spirit who dwells in you." Here clearly verse 10 refers to the spiritual resurrection we experienced at conversion, and verse 11 refers to the bodily resurrection that is yet to come. Again the amillennial understanding of the first resurrection in Revelation 20 is supported.

The first resurrection, then, is a spiritual resurrection, not a bodily one. It is something that Christ made possible through his first coming, and it has been taking place from the beginning of the church age to this very day. It is the same thing the Bible calls being born again or being regenerated. Human beings are both body and spirit (soul), and death affects both. The spirit of a sinner is "dead in sin," and the sinner is also doomed to die physically without the hope of redemptive resurrection. At conversion, though, he is raised from his state of spiritual death into spiritual life; *this is the first resurrection.* See John 5:24; Rom 6:3-4; Eph 2:1,5,6; Col 2:12-13; 3:1; 1 John 3:14. That this occurs in baptism is specifically stated in Rom 6:3-4 and Col 2:12. Along with the rest of the human race, the saved person still awaits the second resurrection, the resurrection of the body. The more important one, though, is the first resurrection; only those who receive this one will escape the second death of hell. Bodily resurrection is no guarantee against the second death, but the spiritual resurrection is. No wonder John says, "Blessed and holy is the one who has a part in the first resurrection"! It is a great blessing, and one that can be experienced *now.* **The Millennium is now!**

C. Reigning with Christ

The third great blessing of the millennial kingdom according to Rev 20:4-6 is that those who take part in the first resurrection also *reign with Christ* for the thousand years. "I saw thrones, and they sat upon them" (20:4). "They came to life and reigned with Christ for a thousand years" (20:4). "They will be priests of God and of Christ and will reign with Him for a thousand years" (20:6). What does this mean?

As we saw in the previous chapter, Jesus Christ is already reigning over the whole earth, and especially over the church, from his heavenly throne. When he ascended into heaven, he was enthroned as King at God's right hand (Ps 110:1; Dan 7:13-14; Acts 2:32-36; Eph 1:20-22; Heb 10:12-13). His kingdom is a spiritual reality; it is not of this world (John 18:36). He reigns now over those whose hearts are surrendered to him.

But the point here is that not only does Christ now reign *over us,* but also, when we are in Christ, we reign *with him* over all our common enemies such as

Satan, sin, and death. In our conversion, says Paul, when God raised us up from spiritual death, he also "seated us with Him in the heavenly places in Christ Jesus" (Eph 2:6; see Col 3:1-4); i.e., even now we are seated on the spiritual thrones of which Rev 20:4 speaks. Concerning the redeemed it is said, "You have made them to be a kingdom and priests to our God; and they will reign upon the earth" (Rev 5:10).

Thus "reigning with Christ" refers not just to some future heavenly glory but also to our Christian experience upon this earth. We already share Christ's victorious power over sin and death. We have spiritual victory, through Christ, over Satan. Satan's power over us as Christians is limited (1 John 4:4; Eph 6:10-17; 1 Cor 10:13; 2 Pet 2:9). The Christian no longer fears Satan's dreaded weapon, death (Heb 2:14-15); death has lost its terror (1 Cor 15:55-57), since we know that there is no longer any condemnation for those who are in Christ Jesus (Rom 8:1).

Satan does not have power over us; we have power over him. This is what it means to "reign with Christ." We are already doing it. *The Millennium is now!*

CONCLUSION

We have explained the binding of Satan, the first resurrection, and reigning with Christ in the context of Revelation as a whole. These are millennial blessings begun by Christ when he came the *first* time. Revelation 20:1-6 does not describe some future paradise on earth. It speaks of what is true now in the life of every Christian. It also speaks of what *could* be true for everyone else now. This depends on whether the church will take the gospel to all the world and share these millennial blessings with all mankind. Like Paul, through the gospel, we can "open their eyes so that they may turn from darkness to light and from the dominion of Satan to God" (Acts 26:18).

To put it another way, Jesus spoke of binding the strong man, who is the devil. Then he spoke of plundering the strong man's house and carrying off his property. His property, his goods, are the captive souls still in his grip. The straightforward facts are these: Christ himself has bound the strong man; but it is the church's job to plunder his house and rescue those whom he still holds captive so that they also may share in the present blessings of Christ's millennial kingdom.

NOTES ON CHAPTER TWENTY-EIGHT

[1]See Clouse, *Millennium*, for succinct presentations of all four views. Some decline to align themselves with any specific view, and facetiously call themselves "pro-millennialists," i.e., whatever it is, they are for it; or "pan-millennialists," i.e., they believe it will all "pan out" in the end.

[2]See Gentry, 296ff., for a thorough history of the subject.

[3]The very name of Campbell's periodical, *The Millennial Harbinger*, reflects this view. Campbell defends it in detail, against premillennialism, in a long series of at least twenty-six articles called

"The Coming of the Lord." The series begins in the January 1841 *Harbinger* (new series, V:1, 5-12), and continues through most of 1843. In the February 1843 issue he says, "I yet expect, a Millennium—a thousand years of a triumphant Christianity, and at no very distant day" (74).

[4]For the latter approach see Ladd, "Premillennialism," 18-29. He says, e.g., "that the New Testament applies Old Testament prophecies to the New Testament church and in so doing identifies the church as spiritual Israel" (23).

[5]See the entire story in his book, *Cover-Up*. He says, "We have seen that a young Scottish lassie named Margaret Macdonald had a private revelation in Port Glasgow, Scotland, in the early part of 1830 that a select group of Christians would be caught up to meet Christ in the air *before* the days of the Antichrist. An eye-and-ear witness, Robert Norton M.D., preserved her handwritten account of her pretrib rapture revelation in two of his books, and said it was the *first* time anyone ever split the second coming into two distinct parts, or stages" (93).

[6]For further critique see Allis, *Prophecy*, and Wyngaarden, *Future*. See Hoekema, *Bible*, chapter 15, "A Critique of Dispensational Premillennialism," especially the bibliographical footnote, 194-195.

[7]See Hendriksen's commentary, *Conquerors*, for a more complete explanation and example of this view.

[8]The view I am presenting and defending here is a form of amillennialism.

[9]The only way this may not be true is if the thousand years have already been completed, and we are now in the "short time" of Satan's loosing—which is a possibility. See ch. 30 below. For our purposes here, we are assuming that we are still in the era of the thousand-year reign (the number, of course, being symbolic for a long period of time).

[10]The angel in Rev 20:1 is probably Michael, the captain of the heavenly hosts. See Rev 9:1; 12:7-9; Jude 9.

CHAPTER TWENTY-NINE
THE INTERMEDIATE STATE

In reference to the Bible's teaching about "last things," a distinction is usually made between the end of the world as such (general eschatology) and the fate of individuals (personal eschatology). The subject of this chapter falls within the latter category. The specific issue is this: Exactly what happens to human beings after they experience physical death? We know that ultimately there will be a resurrection from the dead, a final judgment, and eternity either in heaven or in hell. But what about the interim between the moment of an individual's death and the moment of his resurrection? This is the question of the "intermediate state." In answering it we shall divide the material into two main sections: the *reality* of the intermediate state, and the *nature* of it. In other words, is there such an interim? If so, what is it like?

I. THE REALITY OF THE INTERMEDIATE STATE

A true intermediate state involves the after-death existence of the individual person, who is conscious of his condition, his surroundings, and the passage of time. For believers it involves an awareness of the fact that their salvation is not yet complete, and an anticipation of its still-future consummation. Does physical death usher us into such a state? Though some deny it, in my judgment the Bible teaches that this interim state is a reality.

A. Denials of an Intermediate State

Before we look at the biblical data affirming the individual's interim existence, we will explain why so many deny it and the alternatives they suggest.

1. The Extinction/Re-creation View

The most obvious reason why some reject an intermediate existence is that they deny the reality of the soul or spirit as an entity that can exist separate from the body. Since no such entity exists (they say), and since the entire personhood of the individual is a function of the physical body, when the body dies the person simply ceases to exist. Cooper (107-108) calls this the extinction/re-creation view. That is, when the body dies the entire person is annihilated and becomes nonexistent. Then later, at the time of the resurrection of all people, God will simply re-create each person in his final bodily form. Thus there is an interim *period* between death and resurrection, but no intermediate *state* for individuals.

This is generally the view of those groups or cults that have a materialistic-monistic view of man, i.e., those that deny the existence of a soul or spirit. An example is Jehovah's Witnesses, who have always argued that man has no "immortal soul," a spiritual entity that survives death (*"Let God Be True,"* 66-75). Though they sometimes speak of the state between death and resurrection as a "death sleep" (ibid., 275), it is not a true sleep since no aspect of man continues to exist as the subject of such sleep. (See their publication, *What Do the Scriptures Say about "Survival after Death"?*)

Seventh-day Adventists have a similar view, summed up thus: "The soul has no conscious existence apart from the body. There is no text that indicates that the soul survives the body as a conscious entity" (*Seventh-day Adventists Believe,* 83). When they describe the state of death as "a sleep" and as "a state of unconsciousness" (ibid., 352-353), this is misleading since both sleep and unconsciousness imply the existence of a being or metaphysical entity that continues to exist after the body dies. But this is the very thing Adventists deny. Even the spirit that returns to God at death (Eccl 12:7) is just "the spark of life" or "life principle" shared by human beings and animals alike, they say (ibid., 353).

A Restoration author who holds this view is Curtis Dickinson. As a materialistic monist he denies the existence of a separable soul or spirit (*Immortality,* 7-10). Thus "death is not something that happens only to the body, leaving the 'real you' still alive. The state of death applies to the whole man" (ibid., 10). The only "life after death" is that bestowed via the resurrection of the body ("Gateway," 1-2).

The Christian philosopher Bruce Reichenbach holds a similar view. The Bible, he says, teaches a "monistic anthropology," with "no continuously existing inner self or soul" (180-181). In such a monistic view nothing "survives death" (97); nothing about the individual exists "in objective time between one's death and his re-creation"—a term he prefers to resurrection (176, 181). That is, "the individual human person does not exist during this interim. He ceases to exist at his death, and begins again to exist at his re-creation" (182). "In the interim there is no consciousness, for there is no individual to be conscious" (185). Reichenbach rightly distinguishes this view from soul sleep.

A final example is John Hick, who says the prevailing view of man in many circles is "that he is an indissoluble psycho-physical unity" (i.e., monism), where "there is no room for the notion of soul in distinction from the body; and if there is no soul in distinction from the body, there can be no question of the soul surviving the death of the body." In such a view life after death comes only via resurrection of the body (*Death,* 278). This, says Hick, is Paul's view: a person becomes extinct at death, but God by his power "resurrects or reconstitutes or recreates him" (278-279).

This extinction/re-creation view must be rejected completely, since it is based on a false (monistic) view of human nature. As we have seen in chapter six, man is a dualism of body and soul/spirit. The latter does survive in conscious, disembodied existence after death, as will be seen below. Cooper's book, *Body, Soul, and Life Everlasting*, is a thorough refutation of this false view.

2. The Soul-Sleep View

A second form of the denial of an intermediate state is the view known as soul sleep. According to this idea, the soul does survive death and continues to exist in the interim between death and resurrection, but it exists in a state of unconsciousness or sleep. Thus it has no awareness of its condition, its surroundings, or the passage of time. In the individual's own subjective perception he passes directly from death into the moment of resurrection.

The concept of soul sleep was espoused by many in the sixteenth-century Radical Reformation (including Carlstadt, Westerburg, and many Anabaptists) as a way of counteracting the Catholic doctrine of purgatory (Williams, 24, 104-106). Sometimes called psychopannychism, this view was more precisely labeled psychosomnolence, or "the unconscious sleep of the soul . . . pending the resurrection" (ibid., 582-583).

Martin Luther at times expressed his support for this view. While accepting the dualistic concept of death as separation of soul and body, and the continuing bodiless existence of the soul until Christ's return, he "generally understands the condition between death and the resurrection as a deep and dreamless sleep without consciousness and feeling." With some exceptions, on the Last Day "Christ awakens a man . . . from the sleep of death and only then gives him blessedness." Because of this intervening sleep, the individual does not experience an intermediate state but experiences himself as arriving at the end of the world at the moment of death (Althaus, 414-416).

A modern example of soul sleep is Oscar Cullmann, who says that after death "the inner man . . . continues to live with Christ in this transformed state, in the condition of sleep." This state of sleep gives the dead a different "time-consciousness," thus shortening the interim period for them ("Immortality," 44-45).

From a positive perspective it is good that the soul-sleep view does not deny the biblical (dualistic) view of man, as the previous view does. Also, it tries to take seriously the Bible's many references to death as a kind of sleep. In the OT "he slept with his fathers" was a common way of saying "he died" (e.g., 1 Kgs 2:10; 11:43; 15:24; see Acts 13:36). Daniel 12:2 describes the dead as "those who sleep in the dust of the ground" (see Matt 27:52). When Lazarus died Jesus said, "Our friend Lazarus has fallen asleep" (John 11:11). When Stephen was stoned to death "he fell asleep" (Acts 7:60). Paul speaks of the dead as being in a state of sleep (1 Cor 11:30; 15:6,18,20,51; 1 Thess 4:13-15; 5:10).

Despite this biblical language, the biggest problem with the soul-sleep view is that the Bible also portrays the dead as being in a state of consciousness, as will be seen below (e.g., Luke 16:19-31; Phil 1:23; Rev 6:9-10). In view of this latter teaching it seems best to consider the references to death as a state of sleep to be a euphemistic, figurative way of referring to an unpleasant event. It is an appropriate figure, since from the perspective of the living a dead person's body has the appearance of being asleep. It is also theologically appropriate to call death a sleep, since it is only temporary, in anticipation of an "awakening" at the resurrection; and since from God's perspective he is able to raise the dead to life again as easily as we might arouse a sleeping child (see Mark 5:35-42; John 11:11-14,43-44).

3. The Instantaneous Resurrection View

A third view that denies a true intermediate state is the concept of instantaneous resurrection, or the view that as soon as a person dies he receives his final resurrection body. In other words, there is no period of time in which one exists in an intermediate or disembodied state. Until death one exists in the present body of flesh, but at the point of death he is clothed with his new body.

Some who hold this view may believe in the existence of the soul as a separable spiritual entity (i.e., anthropological dualism); they just believe that the soul is in fact always embodied. Others who hold this view have a monistic concept of human nature. The instantaneous resurrection view enables them to deny the existence of a separable soul and at the same time to affirm that the continuity of personal existence is not interrupted by death. Examples of the latter are Murray Harris (140) and W.D. Davies (317-318).

Some who hold this view, and thus deny an interim *state* or condition of human existence, do not actually deny an intermediate *period* between death and the second coming of Christ. They simply say that individuals do not exist in an "unclothed" state during this time. Their thinking is usually based on a particular interpretation of 2 Cor 5:1-10. An example is Harris, who says that in this text Paul teaches "that between the destruction of this earthly house [body] and the provision of the spiritual house [body] there would be no 'interval of homelessness'" (98-99). Harris still uses the expression "intermediate state," but he is referring to the interim *period* between the individual's death and Christ's return, rather than to a state of disembodiment during this period (133-142).

In my judgment this version of instantaneous resurrection must be rejected as exegetically and theologically unsound. A main problem is its faulty exegesis of 2 Cor 5:1-10, a passage that will be discussed in the next section. Another problem is that this view says that even though believers receive their new bodies at the moment of death, they must still wait for the future return of Christ. However, the NT consistently connects the bodily resurrection of both believers and unbelievers with the second coming of Christ. Erickson (*Theology*, 1188) points out that the severance of the reception of our new bodies from Christ's future return contradicts texts such as John 5:25-29; Phil 3:20-21; and 1 Thess 4:16-17. Cooper says that 1 Thess 4:13-18 teaches that "believers will all be raised at the same time—at the second coming," and he suggests that those who hold the immediate resurrection view must simply reject this text as erroneous teaching (137). He also points out that 1 Corinthians 15 (e.g., vv. 22-23,51-52) connects the resurrection of all with Christ's return (139). In Phil 3:20-21 Christ's second coming and our bodily transformation "share the same future"; the same is true in Rom 8:18-23 (153).

A second version of this instantaneous resurrection view seeks to avoid the problem just discussed by appealing to a qualitative difference between time and eternity. Those holding this version of the view deny not only an intermediate state but also an intermediate period of time between an individual's death and the end-time events of Christ's return, the general resurrection, and the final judgment. When one dies, he simply "goes to sleep" in his old body and immediately "wakes up" in his new body on the Last Day. The supposed distinction between time and eternity (they say) makes it happen thus. Until the point of death we exist in the realm of created time and space, but when we die we "enter eternity" and are thus no longer bound by time. As Norman Anderson puts it, "When we die we pass out of a space-time continuum into a realm where time is merged in eternity; so might it not be true that those who die in Christ are immediately with him, in their resurrection bodies, at the Advent—which, while still future to those of us who still live in time, is to them already a present reality?" (33).

In defending the possibility of this view Emil Brunner says that we need not distinguish between the day of our death, which exists in time, and the day of Christ's return, which exists in eternity.

> Here on earth there is a before and an after and intervals of time which embrace centuries or even millenniums. But on the other side, in the world of the resurrection, in eternity, there are no such divisions of time, of this time which is perishable. The date of death differs for each man, for the day of death belongs to this world. Our day of resurrection is the same for all and yet is not separated from the day of death by intervals of centuries—for these time-intervals are here, not there in the presence of God, where "a thousand years are as a day." (*Hope*, 152)

Because of this difference between "the temporal-earthly and the eternal-heavenly," entering Christ's presence "is not the moment immediately after death. For in the eternal world there is no next moment. In death the world of space and time disappears" (*Hope*, 153). "Perhaps events which lie at a distance from each other in time are not separated from the standpoint of eternity, but simultaneous in the eternal Now" (Brunner, *Dogmatics*, III:393).

In his exposition of 2 Cor 5:1-10 William Baker suggests a similar view. "The absence of an intermediate state" between death and resurrection is understandable if we can see beyond "the time restrictions of human existence," he says. "If God himself is outside of time, unrestricted by it (2 Pet 3:8), just as he is above and beyond the universe itself, why should people after death necessarily remain restricted by it?" (201). We can exclude the need for "a waiting interval or an intermediate state of some kind" between death and judgment, because "time factors lose their relevance at death" (218).[1]

This whole approach to the intermediate state must be rejected because the alleged distinction between time and eternity upon which it rests simply does not exist. First of all, even if there were such a distinction between the eternal God and created time, this would have no effect upon us when we die. This is so because when we die we do not "enter eternity," i.e., we do not enter into the divine (eternal) dimension, but into the dimension of created spirits, the invisible creation in which angels naturally dwell. This is the "heaven" witnessed by John in the book of Revelation as the throne room of God, in which God's presence exists as a permanent spiritual theophany (see ch. 5), and where the risen Christ himself now exists in his glorified human body. This is the realm our spirits enter at the point of death (Rev 6:9-10; 15:1-4; 20:4). It is not an "eternal" realm, but is just as much a part of the temporal creation as is the visible space-time universe in which we live prior to death. In that "heaven" we will still be completely bound by the limitations of time. It is impossible for it to be otherwise for created beings of whatever kind. To think otherwise is to eliminate the distinction between Creator and creature and to deify man.

In the second place, the concept of eternity presupposed by this version of the instantaneous resurrection view does not exist even in God himself. The notion of timelessness or simultaneity usually found in classical theism has absolutely no basis in the Bible (see pp. 74-76; see *GC,* 259-263; *GRe,* 484-486). God himself everlastingly and consciously exists along a time line where before, now, and after are real in his consciousness and experience. So even if at death we were to enter the divine dimension itself (which we do not), we would not enter a timeless sphere where all events are compressed into an "eternal Now."[2]

In this section we have explained and rejected three attempts to deny the existence of an intermediate state: the extinction/re-creation view, the soul-sleep view, and the instantaneous resurrection view. Each of these positions has its own problems, and all of them are inconsistent with the data to be discussed next.

B. The Biblical Affirmation of an Intermediate State

The main reason why most Christians through the ages have held to a concept of an intermediate state between death and resurrection is that the Bible contains abundant testimony supporting such a concept. In this section we shall survey a number of texts that affirm two basic points: first, that individuals continue to exist in a state of *personal consciousness* after death; and second, that they exist in this state as *souls without bodies.*

In 1 Sam 28:11-19 God permitted the prophet Samuel to speak to King Saul, even though Samuel was dead (v. 3). The fact that he conversed with Saul implies his continuing conscious existence. His visual appearance (the medium described him as "an old man . . . wrapped with a robe," v. 14) does not necessarily reflect the state of his existence at this point, for this was probably a form given to him by God for this one occasion.

The appearance of Moses and Elijah at the event of Christ's transfiguration (Matt 17:3) is similar. They conversed with Jesus, showing their continuing conscious existence. The visible form seen by Peter, James, and John again may not necessarily correspond to their condition on the "other side," but neither does it suggest that they had already received their new glorified bodies (contra Baker, 201). Noncorporeal angelic spirits have visible forms (Rev 4:4-8; 8:2; 22:8), suggesting that our own souls in themselves have forms that image our bodies. That Moses and Elijah appeared "in glory" (Luke 9:31) means only that they were reflecting the glory of the transfigured Christ (Matt 17:2; Mark 9:2-3; Luke 9:29,32), not that they possessed glorified bodies. (See Cooper, *Body*, 122-124.)

In Matt 10:28 Jesus exhorts, "Do not fear those who kill the body but are unable to kill the soul; but rather fear Him who is able to destroy both soul and body in hell." This does not speak directly of the intermediate state, but it clearly shows that the soul is separable from the body and that it continues to exist apart from the body after physical death.

Luke 16:19-31 tells the story of the rich man and Lazarus, both of whom died and continued on in conscious existence in what is obviously an interim state (Cooper, 124-125). To dismiss the significance of this passage as "a parable, a fictional story" (Baker, 201) misses the point. Certainly all of Jesus' parables are fictional in that they do not refer to any specific individuals or historical events, but every parable reflects a *realistic situation* (e.g., a wedding feast, a lost sheep, sowing and harvesting), not a fantasy world. Even if Lazarus and the rich man were not real people, the circumstances pictured in the story must reflect the reality of the afterlife; otherwise Jesus has misled us (contra Cooper, 126). Thus at the very least Jesus is here confirming the fact that the dead exist in a conscious interim state. The reference to bodily parts (eyes, finger, tongue—vv. 23-24) does not imply the actual possession of bodies, since (as noted above) even our spirits have a form similar to our bodies.

Luke 23:42-43 records the thief's prayer, "Jesus, remember me when You come into Your kingdom!" and Jesus' reply, "Truly I say to you, today [Friday] you shall be with Me in Paradise." This text suggests both consciousness and disembodiment after death. The very concept of Paradise implies a state of blessing (Hoekema, *Bible*, 103), but how can it be a blessing if it is not consciously experienced? Also, that Jesus promised the thief he would be *with* Jesus that very day implies conscious existence, excluding soul sleep, "for what would be the point of saying these words if the thief after death would be totally unaware of being with Christ in Paradise?" (ibid.).

Jesus' promise to the thief also shows that existence in Paradise is a state of disembodiment. This is suggested by the fact that Christ himself in Paradise would be in a disembodied state, since his resurrection would not occur until Sunday. Hence the thief would also be in a disembodied condition in Paradise.

Shortly after his promise to the thief and just before he died, Jesus, "crying out with a loud voice, said, 'Father, into Your hands I commit My spirit'" (Luke 23:46). In Acts 7:59 Stephen made a similar remark as he was being stoned to death: "Lord Jesus, receive my spirit!" These texts show that the spirit continues to exist after the death of the body. In view of the promise Jesus had just made to the thief, in Luke 23:46 he must have meant that his own spirit would now be existing in a state of conscious fellowship with the Father, even as the thief would be in fellowship with him. The fact that both Jesus and Stephen refer only to their spirits suggests that their spirits would be existing in this state of fellowship apart from their bodies.

In Phil 1:21-24 Paul declares that he is happy "to remain on in the flesh" for the sake of serving Christ in this life; but as far as his own personal desires are concerned, he would much prefer "to depart and be with Christ, for that is very much better." As he sums it up, "For to me, to live is Christ and to die is gain" (v. 21). The close grammatical connection between *departing* and *being with Christ* shows "that the moment he departs or dies, that very same moment he will be with Christ," not asleep or nonexistent (Hoekema, *Bible*, 103-104). "For how could soul-sleep or nonexistence be 'far better' than the present state, in which he does have conscious, though imperfect, fellowship with Christ?" (ibid., 104).

A very important text for understanding the intermediate state is 1 Thess 4:13-18. Here Paul says that living Christians should not grieve for Christians who "are asleep," for when Jesus returns "God will bring with Him those who have fallen asleep in Jesus." At that time "the dead in Christ will rise first. Then we who are alive and remain will be caught up together with them in the clouds to meet the Lord in the air." This text shows us two significant things about the intermediate state. First, dead Christians are now in the presence of Christ, since at his second coming he will *bring them with him* (v. 14). This simply confirms the conclusions already drawn from Luke 23:42-43; Acts 7:59; and Phil 1:21-24. (We have already seen that the depiction of death as sleep does not imply a state of unconsciousness.) Second, when Christians die and enter the presence of Christ, they remain in a disembodied state until the second coming, which is a later event. Verse 15 clearly states that the time of Christ's return is the time when "the dead in Christ will rise," i.e., will receive their resurrection bodies. This text thus rules out the instantaneous resurrection view.

In Heb 12:22 we are told that every Christian is an inhabitant and citizen of Mount Zion, the city of the living God, the heavenly Jerusalem (see Phil 3:20). The full citizenship of this spiritual domain includes "myriads of angels," plus all members of the "church of the firstborn," plus "God, the Judge of all," and "Jesus, the mediator of a new covenant" (Heb 12:22-24). Most significantly for our present purpose, the circle of fellowship in which every Christian participates includes "the spirits of the righteous made perfect" (v. 23). This phrase confirms the reality of an intermediate state. "The righteous" refers to all saints, OT and NT. "Made perfect" refers to their full sanctification, which is guaranteed only at death; thus the phrase describes saints who have already died. That they are referred to only as *spirits* is clear proof that after death they exist in a disembodied state, as unclothed spirits awaiting their resurrection bodies. That these righteous spirits are part of the total citizenry of the heavenly Jerusalem, linked together with angels, the church on earth, God the Father, and Jesus Christ, implies that they are fully existent and fully conscious, and in full fellowship with all the others.

Another text is 1 Pet 3:18-20, which says that after Jesus was put to death he was "made alive in the spirit, in which also He went and made proclamation to the spirits now in prison, who once were disobedient." This is a notoriously difficult passage, but it seems to confirm an intermediate state in two ways. First, it speaks of Jesus (in his human nature) as being "alive in the spirit" in the brief time between his death and resurrection. His human spirit was separated from his body (see Luke 23:46) and was able both to have fellowship with dead saints in Paradise (Luke 23:42-43) and to announce his victory over sin and death to the lost in Hades. Second, "the spirits now in prison" probably refers to the wicked dead; and the phrase shows that in death they exist only as spirits (without bodies), and that they are conscious since they are the audience for Christ's proclamation.

That the spirits of the wicked dead are now "in prison" may be explained by 2 Pet 2:9, which says that "the Lord knows how to rescue the godly from temptation, and to keep the unrighteous under punishment for the day of judgment." The phrase "for [*eis*, unto, until] the day of judgment" shows that Peter is referring to the unrighteous in their state of death because he says their condition persists all the way up to the judgment day. That they are conscious is seen by the fact that they are experiencing punishment. This punishment must be an interim experience since it precedes the final judgment (Hoekema, *Bible*, 102). What Peter says here is consistent with Jesus' description of the condition of the rich man in Hades (Luke 16:19-31).

One of the clearest references to the intermediate state is Rev 6:9-10. Here John says he "saw underneath the altar the souls of those who had been slain because of the word of God, and because of the testimony which they had maintained; and they cried out with a loud voice, saying, 'How long, O Lord, holy and true, will You refrain from judging and avenging our blood on those who dwell on the earth?'" Those described here are certainly disembodied spirits who are fully conscious and who are experiencing the passing of time in anticipation of the final day. That these are the souls of *the dead* is specifically stated (vv. 9,11). That they are souls only and not embodied persons is clear from John's specification that they are the *souls of* those persons who had been martyred. He is not saying that he saw simply some persons, but rather the *souls* of those persons. That they are conscious is seen in their awareness of their condition, and in their question-answer exchange with the Lord (vv. 10-11). That they are in the flow of time with the judgment day being still in the future is seen in their question, "How long?"

Some say this picture of the intermediate state of the dead is not real and literal, but is just a symbolic vision presented to John's mind. This objection fails to make the proper distinction in the book of Revelation between the reality of the heavenly throne room itself (e.g., chs. 4, 5), and the symbolic revelations made known to John while he was there. The souls and the altar under which they rested are part of the former. Other references to the altar show that this is the case: 8:3,5; 9:13; 14:18; 16:7. The altar is real, and the souls are real (see Rev 20:4).

In reference to the intermediate state the most significant text is 2 Cor 5:1-10. A main issue Paul seems to be addressing here is an anxiety about death that leads some to desire to continue in this present earthly existence as long as possible. To make the prospect of death less threatening, Paul makes two main points. First, in verses 1-5, he assures us as Christians that even though our earthly body must die, it will surely be replaced by an eternal, heavenly body. He makes this point by combining the figures of living in a house or tent, and wearing clothes. At present we are clothed with an inferior kind of house or dwelling, but after death we shall be clothed with one that is far better. Second, in verses 6-8, Paul eases our fear of death by assuring us that the circumstances we shall enter then are far better than the ones that prevail while we exist in our present bodies. Specifically, "while we are at home in the body we are absent from the Lord." Speaking for himself Paul declares that he would much prefer "to be absent from the body and to be at home with the Lord." This is the same sentiment as Phil 1:21-23. Here as there, he suggests that in the intermediate state we shall be very much aware of our condition and our surroundings.

According to some, however, this is the very issue at stake in the exegesis of this text; i.e., does it actually teach the existence of an intermediate state, or does it in fact deny it? Some take the latter view, interpreting the text in terms of instantaneous resurrection. The specific issue is whether the new, postdeath body (house, dwelling) is received immediately at the point of death, or whether there is a delay and thus a period of time during which we exist in an intermediate, disembodied state, a state of "nakedness."

In my judgment Paul is affirming the latter. He says that we know a new and better house awaits us after death. In fact, we long for it, because we know we will leave this present house behind at death, and we do not want to be homeless, or naked (vv. 1-3). In fact, "while we are in this tent, we groan, being burdened, because we do not want to be unclothed but to be clothed" (v. 4). Now, at this point we must ask this question: *If the instantaneous resurrection view is correct, why does Paul say, "We groan, being burdened"?* If the new body is to be immediately received, if there is no state of "nakedness," then there is no reason to groan; there is no burden to be borne! But Paul says, "We groan, being burdened, because we do not want to be unclothed but to be clothed." The only reason or justification for the groaning is that Paul knew this "being clothed" would not happen immediately; he knew that we shall indeed have to endure an interim state of nakedness.

Nevertheless we can still face death cheerfully and confidently, because we know that we shall eventually receive the new body (v. 5), even though an unnatural state of disembodiment will intervene. Also, if we simply compare our present state of bodily existence with the expected intermediate state of temporary bodilessness, the latter is still preferable because in it we shall actually see the Lord (v. 7) and be in his presence (v. 8)!

In conclusion this text is quite consistent with all the others surveyed above. They all combine to teach that the inner man, the soul/spirit, the seat of personhood, survives the death of the body and continues to exist in a state of consciousness and in a state of anticipation and expectation of the future day of judgment. There is indeed an intermediate state.

II. THE NATURE OF THE INTERMEDIATE STATE

In the first section of this chapter we have sought mainly to establish the *fact* of an intermediate state by briefly examining most of the relevant biblical passages. In so doing we have already encountered numerous details about the *condition* of the soul as it exists in the interim period between death and resurrection. Our purpose here is to systematize this data and to address certain related questions and issues.

A. The Condition of the Soul

What will existence in the intermediate state be like? When we die, falling asleep to this world and awakening in the next, what will we experience? While certain aspects of our condition will depend on whether we are saved or lost, some characteristics of the interim life will be shared by all who die.

1. Bodilessness

The main common characteristic is *bodilessness*; i.e., our souls or spirits will exist without a physical body to be used as a means of expression. This is an unnatural state for human beings, since we were created to be an eternal, harmonious combination of body and spirit. The death of the physical body and its severance from the soul are the consequences of sin. But even though bodilessness is an unnatural state for human beings, it is not an impossibility. All the traits of personhood as such are inherent in the soul. Thus even in the state of bodilessness we retain our full personality and the same personal identity that we had prior to death. We should remember that angels are bodiless spirits by nature, and they are persons in every respect.

The fact that we will be bodiless in the intermediate state is consistent with the fact that the "heaven" into which we are translated at death is not our final destination but is the invisible, spiritual creation, the realm of created angelic *spirits*. By its very nature this is not a normal environment for *bodily* existence. Rather, it is a realm where disembodied existence is natural (Christ's resurrection body being an exception). Our resurrection bodies will be suitable for our final abode, the new heaven and new earth (Rev 21:1), which does not yet exist. Thus it makes sense to be bodiless while we are in the spiritual universe, and to postpone the reception of our new bodies until our final abode has been prepared.

Though in the intermediate state we will exist as bodiless spirits, this does not mean that we will be without form and substance. Spiritual essences (e.g., angels) are invisible to and undetectable by our physical senses; but in their own realm (the invisible universe) they are substances with shape and consistency. Just as angelic beings have specific forms, so our own bodiless spirits have or will have forms that probably as a rule will mirror the forms of our earthly bodies (see 1 Sam 28:11-19; Matt 17:3; Luke 16:19-31). We will not be just amorphous energy fields or nonspatial disembodied minds capable only of mental experiences and activities (contra Habermas and Moreland, 117-119). As beings of spiritual substance we will exist in spiritual space and be capable of interaction with everything else existing therein.

We must remember that this state of bodilessness is an *intermediate* state; it is only temporary. As bodiless souls it will be natural for us to exist in this interim in the spiritual universe; but bodilessness itself is not natural for us as human beings. At Christ's return our souls will be given new bodies suitable for the new heaven and new earth, and we will be completely restored to wholeness. But we do not receive these new bodies until that time, and thus we should not think of our deceased friends and loved ones as already existing in their new bodies.[3]

2. Consciousness

A second characteristic of the intermediate state shared by all is *consciousness*. The description of death as a kind of sleep applies only to the dead person's relation to his former physical life. To those of us still alive a dead body has the appearance of being asleep, and the one who has died is now asleep to this world. But in its disembodied state in the spiritual universe, the soul of the deceased person is fully alive and fully conscious of its surroundings.

Many of the texts describing the intermediate condition, as discussed above, picture its participants as being in a state of consciousness. Samuel (1 Sam 28:11-19), Moses and Elijah (Matt 17:3), the rich man in Hades (Luke 16:19-31), and the souls of the martyrs under the heavenly altar (Rev 6:9-11) are all described as speaking and conversing with others. Jesus' promise to the thief that he would "be with" Christ (Luke 23:42-43), and Paul's desire to die and to be "at home with the Lord" (2 Cor 5:8) or to "be with Christ" (Phil 1:23), make sense only if there is a conscious awareness of being in the presence of Christ. "The spirits of the righteous made perfect" (Heb 12:23) form one part of a larger circle of those with whom every Christian is in fellowship; the others in this circle (angels, the church, the Father, Jesus—Heb 12:22-24) are all personal, conscious beings. The "spirits now in prison" (1 Pet 3:19) consciously heard Jesus speak to them. Thus the biblical testimony supporting the fact that we will be conscious in the intermediate state is quite overwhelming.

One thing we will be conscious of is the passing of time. Samuel told Saul of an event that would happen the next day (1 Sam 28:19). Jesus' death was still future to Moses and Elijah (Luke 9:31). The rich man in Hades contemplated a possible future event, i.e., that his five brothers might also be condemned to Hades when they died—which had not yet happened (Luke 16:27-31). Second Peter 2:9 implies that the wicked dead know that the judgment day is still future. In Rev 6:9-11 the souls of the martyrs want to know how much longer it will be before their deaths are avenged. As we noted above, creaturely existence is never timeless, whether it be in the visible creation or in the invisible creation. Thus unless we are alive at the time of Christ's return, we can expect a period of waiting for the final day to arrive.

3. Torment or Bliss

Bodilessness and consciousness as such are experienced by everyone in the intermediate state, but the content of consciousness will differ depending on whether one is saved or lost. The texts discussed above state quite clearly that some will be in torment while others are in bliss. The references to the former are few but conclusive. The rich man in Hades "lifted up his eyes, being in torment," declaring "I am in agony in this flame" (Luke 16:23-24). Without being specific 2 Pet 2:9 pictures the lost as being kept "under punishment." In 1 Pet 3:19 their punishment is depicted as being "in prison." This suffering is ongoing and unabated (Luke 16:24-25); yet it must not be equated with the final state of hell itself, since the judgment day is still in the future (2 Pet 2:9). It is simply a foretaste of hell, a prelude to eternal punishment, but nevertheless terrifying in itself.

The interim bliss of the redeemed, on the other hand, is delightfully desirable. It is not yet perfection, especially since it is a time of "nakedness" (2 Cor 5:1-5), or a time when the soul exists unnaturally without a body. Yet compared with our present existence it is much to be preferred (2 Cor 5:8; Phil 1:21-23). In describing this state prior to his resurrection, Jesus spoke of it as "Abraham's bosom" (Luke 16:22), which to the Jews would have represented the apex of comfort and contentment. In this Messianic era the glory of the intermediate state for Christians is that they are *with Christ*, in his very presence, in intimate fellowship with him. From our present perspective we perhaps cannot picture in our minds all that is entailed in this, but we know that it must be far more delightful than anything we can imagine.

Though Christians enter a state of bliss after death, we should not think that this means we have nothing more to look forward to. We must remember that the intermediate state is still an incomplete state in which we are without bodies. As Hoekema says, "This state of existence is provisional, temporary, and incomplete. Because man is not totally man apart from the body, the central eschatological hope of the Scriptures with regard to man is not the mere continued existence of the 'soul' (as in Greek thought) but the resurrection of the body" (*Bible*, 95). Thus even in our intermediate bliss we will still be existing in hope and anticipation of the final day when we will receive our new bodies and be allowed to enter our final home where we shall also be "with Christ" (1 Thess 4:17).

One implication of the fact that the intermediate state will be either torment or bliss is that we will know as soon as we die whether we are saved or lost. We will not have to wait for the judgment day to find out where we will spend eternity. What, then, is the purpose of the final judgment? This question will be addressed in chapter 31.

B. The Location of the Dead

Our next question has to do with the *location* of those existing in the intermediate state. Where are they? Exactly where do we go when we die? Can such questions even be answered? What does the Bible say?

We begin with a look at the biblical concept of Sheol or Hades. Sheol is a Hebrew word that occurs about 65 times in the OT; Hades is its Greek equivalent. In the LXX Hades is used to translate Sheol in all but three of its occurrences. In the NT Hades is used only ten times (eleven for those who accept the Western text of 1 Cor 15:55, e.g., the KJV). What do these words mean? The main point is that they are always connected with death; Sheol/Hades is the state of death, the place of death, the realm of death. For this close connection see Ps 18:5; Prov 5:5; Isa 28:15; Rev 1:18; 6:8; 20:13-14.[4]

In the OT Sheol is commonly pictured as a place beneath the earth's surface into which the dead enter: "Sheol from beneath is excited over you to meet you when you come" (Isa 14:9). It is compared with the idea of a pit or abyss dug into the depths of the earth or at the bottom of the sea (Ezek 28:8). Cooper says, "It is 'the Pit,' reached by going into the earth, usually through the grave. It is the great subterranean chamber into which all graves eventually merge" (54). David praised God for delivering him from death thus: "O LORD, You have brought up my soul from Sheol; you have kept me alive, that I would not go down to the pit" (Ps 30:3; see Ps 28:1; 88:1-7; Isa 14:15; 38:18; Ezek 26:19-21; Amos 9:2). In Num 16:30-33 Dathan, Abiram, and their households "went down alive to Sheol" when the earth opened up and swallowed them.

Are we to conclude from such teaching that Sheol/Hades, the place of the dead, is located literally somewhere below the earth's surface, in the bowels of the earth? Not necessarily. The key point is that in biblical cultures (as in most cultures) the language of height and depth is used to communicate the qualitative concepts of good and bad, superior and inferior, positive and negative, honorable and vile, desirable and undesirable. In this sense God and heaven are always pictured as "up" or "on high," not in a literal spatial sense but figuratively to indicate superior value, rank, and esteem (*GC*, 217-222). In a similar way death and the place of death are pictured as being "down" in the "lowest depths," at the very opposite of heaven (e.g., Deut 32:22; Job 11:8; Prov 9:18; 15:24; Isa 14:13-15; Ezek 26:20; Amos 9:2; Matt 11:23). The main conclusion to be drawn from such language is that Sheol/Hades, the place of the dead, and death itself are negative and undesirable, a fate to be feared and dreaded, a threat, an enemy.

Merrill (6) sums up the negative light in which Sheol is depicted thus:

> As a personification, *sheol* is a fearsome enemy. With ropes (2 Sam 22:6 = Ps 18:4[5]) it drags its victims down (Job 24:19) into its very mouth (Ps 141:7). It is a cruel despot (S of Songs 8:6), capable of carrying out its evil designs because of its irresistible power (Ps 89:48[49]). Jonah, though in the belly of the fish, metaphorically saw himself also to be in the belly of Sheol (Jonah 2:2[3]).

This negative quality is reinforced by the references to the gates or bars of Sheol/Hades, by which it is pictured as a kind of prison waiting to ensnare us (Job 17:16 [ESV]; Isa 38:10,18; Matt 16:18; see Ps 9:13). But again, such language is mainly figurative or symbolic of the dreadfulness of death in all its aspects.

What, then, do these words tell us about the *location* of the souls of the dead? Here we must note that the terms are sometimes used in a general sense, and sometimes in a specific sense. Regarding the former, Berkhof's insight is on target: "The words *sheol* and *hades* do not always denote a locality in Scripture, but are often used in an abstract sense to designate the state of death, the state of the separation of body and soul," and sometimes the power of death or the danger of death (685). In this sense Sheol/Hades can refer simply to the inevitable event of death (e.g., Gen 37:35; 42:38; 1 Sam 2:6; Prov 30:15-16), or it can be personified as an enemy to be feared (e.g., Isa 5:14; 28:15,18; Matt 16:18). Of this general use of Sheol/Hades Hoekema says, "When we think of Sheol in this way, we must remember that both the godly and the ungodly go down into Sheol at death, since both enter the realm of the dead" (*Bible*, 96).

There are times, however, when the terms Sheol and Hades seem to be used in a more specific sense, indicating specific locations into which the dead enter. A proper understanding of Sheol/Hades as the place of the dead in this sense requires us to accept the biblical, dualistic view of man as a combination of body and spirit. When we approach the subject with this understanding, it becomes obvious that sometimes Sheol and Hades are used to refer to *the grave*, which swallows up the *bodies* of those who die, righteous and wicked alike.

On the question of whether Sheol/Hades ever refers to the grave, there are two extremes. One is that these words *always* refer to the grave. This is the view of many who see man as body only, such as Jehovah's Witnesses (e.g., *"Let God Be True,"* 88-93). See also *Seventh-day Adventists Believe*, which says that Sheol and Hades "generally refer to the grave where the dead—both righteous and wicked—await, in a state of unconsciousness, the resurrection" (369). Dickinson says of Sheol, "It was a common enough term to the Hebrews, simply referring to the grave" ("Gates," 1). The other extreme is that Sheol/Hades *never* refers to the grave. An example is Robert Morey, who says that "Sheol cannot mean the grave" (75), nor can Hades (82-83).

Both extremes are wrong. On the one hand (contra Morey), in some texts Sheol/Hades clearly means the grave. In its sense of "the place of the dead," Sheol/Hades is the place beneath the surface of the earth where dead bodies are buried. As such, both the righteous and the wicked enter into Sheol/Hades, the enemy which captures and devours every member of Adam's race. In this way even for the righteous death seems to be the victor, since the grave swallows us all and turns our bodies back to dust (see Ps 89:48;[5] 116:3; 141:7; Isa 38:10). In this sense Sheol/Hades is something to be dreaded and feared, something from which we all long to be delivered and redeemed (Ps 49:14-15; 86:13; Hos 13:14). As such it is equivalent to Abaddon, or destruction (Job 17:13-14; 26:6; Prov 15:11; 27:20), since in the grave the body is dissolved. This is the light in which Ps 16:10 must be understood: "For You will not abandon my soul to Sheol; nor will you allow Your Holy One to undergo decay."[6] In Acts 2:27,31 Peter cites this as a prophecy of the resurrection of Jesus' body from the tomb, whereby "He was neither abandoned to Hades, nor did His flesh suffer decay." This refers only to Christ's body as buried in and raised from the grave (Sheol/Hades), not to the state or activity of his spirit between his death and resurrection.

On the other hand (contra monists) in some texts where Sheol/Hades refers to a specific location, it does *not* refer to the grave as the receptacle of the *body* but to the place to which the *spirits* of (some of) the dead are taken, where they will exist in their intermediate (bodiless, conscious) state until Christ's return. Since Sheol/Hades is the place of the *dead*, only the souls of the *wicked* are put into Sheol/Hades in the sense of the waiting place for disembodied souls (see Job 24:19; Ps 9:17; 31:17; 55:15; Prov 9:18; 23:14; Isa 14:13-15; Matt 11:23). The souls of the righteous do not enter Sheol/Hades, since their souls are not in a state of spiritual death but have been made alive through God's resurrection power (Eph 2:5-6; Col 2:12-13). Thus we should not think of Sheol/Hades being occupied by the souls of the righteous and the wicked alike (Ps 49:14-15; 86:13; Prov 15:24).

As the place where the wicked abide until judgment, Sheol/Hades is seen as an enemy or captor in all its terror. In Jesus' story of the rich man and Lazarus, only the rich man (personifying the wicked in general) is said to be in torment "in Hades" (Luke 16:23).

In both of its specific meanings, (1) the grave as the receptacle of the bodies of all men, and (2) the intermediate dwelling place for wicked souls, Sheol/Hades is mankind's enemy, a foul force conquered by the redeeming work of the crucified and risen Christ (Rev 1:18) and from which we find refuge in the church (Matt 16:18). In the end it will be finally destroyed in the lake of fire (Rev 20:14).

Where, then, do the souls of the righteous go when separated from the body at death? Their destiny is never called Sheol or Hades. They are described as being in Abraham's bosom (Luke 16:23), in Paradise (Luke 23:43), "at home with the Lord" (2 Cor 5:8), and under the heavenly altar (Rev 6:9). We may refer to this simply as Paradise (see 2 Cor 12:4), which should not be considered as just one section of Hades.[7] Righteous souls have been "made perfect" (Heb 12:23), and that includes being made fully alive in a spiritual sense. They no longer have the stench and penalty of spiritual death about them, and thus are not proper citizens of Hades. The righteous are "in Hades" only in the sense that their *bodies* are in the grave.

Some construct charts to visually depict the intermediate state as related to what precedes it and what follows it. Here is my suggested chart, which reflects the body/soul dualism of human beings:

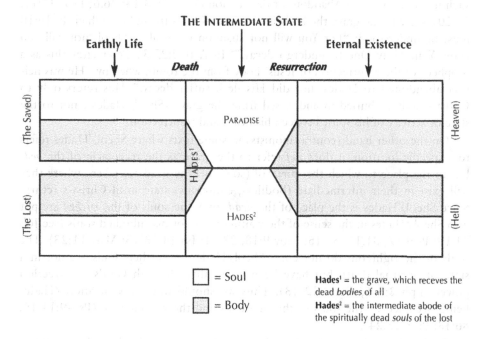

We still have not answered the question of the *location* of Paradise and Sheol/Hades, in the sense of the abode of dead spirits. Do we know where they are? The Bible does not address this in any detail, but from what it does say about the intermediate state we can draw the following tentative conclusions. First, neither Paradise nor Sheol/Hades is located in our physical, visible universe. Jeremias wrongly interprets the NT when he says that it teaches "that Hades lies at the heart of the earth" (148). Of course, Sheol/Hades in the sense of the grave is located in the earth, but this is not the case for Hades as the abode of the souls of the wicked dead.

Where, then, are Sheol/Hades (in the latter sense) and Paradise located? The answer seems to be that they are in the *invisible universe* (Col 1:16), the part of God's creation designed specifically for spiritual beings, i.e., angels. We know nothing of the "geography" of this spiritual universe. As a metaphysically different kind of world, it is a distinct dimension that intersects our own but is invisible and inaccessible to us. It is not part of our physical space, but has its own kind of spiritual space, occupied by spiritual stuff, including the spiritual essences of angels. One aspect or part of this spiritual universe is the throne room of God, into which John was transported for his wonder-filled revelations (Rev 4:1-3). This throne room section of the invisible universe is called "heaven" (Rev 4:2), because that is where the presence of God is manifested to the angels. This is not the same as the pure essence of God, the divine dimension itself, which no created being can enter or experience. Nor is it the "heaven" where the righteous will spend eternity. That will be the new heaven and new earth, i.e., the new universe, provided for us after the day of judgment (Rev 21:1).

I conclude that what we call Paradise, i.e., the place where the souls of the righteous dead exist in their intermediate state, is equivalent to or at least adjacent to this heavenly throne-room district of the invisible universe. This conclusion is based on two facts. First, John saw the souls of at least some of the righteous dead under the altar of this heaven (Rev 6:9). Second, when we die our souls will be in the presence of Christ (2 Cor 5:8; Phil 1:23), and Christ himself in his glorified human existence is presently in this heavenly throne room (Acts 7:55; Rev 3:21; 5:6,13). When we die, our souls will awaken in that blessed place.

But where is Sheol/Hades, the place into which the souls of the wicked are ushered at death? Based on the above, I infer that this too is a part of the invisible universe, a distant or nether region far from the presence of God and the glorified Christ, perhaps adjacent to the place called Tartarus occupied by some fallen angels (2 Pet 2:4). It is a place of darkness (Job 17:13), gloom, and suffering, without light and without hope.

We must remember that both Paradise and Sheol/Hades, as parts of the present invisible universe, are temporary; they are the *intermediate* state of human souls, not their final state. In this I disagree with Erickson, who says "it is likely that these are the very places to which believers and unbelievers will go after the great judgment" (*Theology*, 1189). In chapters 32 and 33 we will explain why this is not the case.

III. QUESTIONS AND QUALIFICATIONS

We conclude this chapter by addressing a few related questions. First, is the doctrine of an intermediate state somehow bound up with the false concept of an "immortal soul" found in many pagan systems? If so, does this not undermine and negate the significance of the resurrection of the body? This kind of challenge is usually heard from those who deny the existence of the soul as such, and who usually also deny the reality of eternal punishment in hell. In response, it is true that the pagan concept of an immortal soul is a false idea. It assumes that the soul is inherently and immutably immortal, that it *must* survive the death of the body because it is by nature indestructible. Those who hold such a view usually discount the significance of the body and look favorably upon death as the time when the immortal soul gains release from its encumbrance. The idea of that liberated soul later being resurrected (re-bodied) is interpreted as a step backward.

This entire scenario is, of course, pagan to the core and must be rejected out of hand. The point here, though, is that this view has *absolutely nothing* to do with the biblical concept of the intermediate state. Those who attempt to tie them together miss the point entirely, and come dangerously close to slander or bearing false witness. As we saw in the chapter on the nature of man, human souls are created entities and are thus subject to annihilation or nonexistence. That they do survive death and exist without bodies in an intermediate state is simply a matter of God's decision and decree. Their continuing existence is in no way dependent on the alien concept of an inherently immortal soul.

Second, is there a difference between the intermediate state of saints who died prior to Christ's resurrection, and the intermediate state of all saints after his resurrection? Some think so. This is a concept known as the *limbus patrem*, the "limbo of the fathers." In this phrase the "fathers" are the OT saints, and the "limbo" is the bland, neutral state of death (Sheol) in which they existed, as in a kind of prison or holding pen, prior to Christ's redeeming work. The theory is that they could not be fully saved until their actual redemption was historically accomplished through Christ's death and resurrection. Christ's preaching to the spirits in prison (1 Pet 3:19) is taken to be his announcement that their long wait is now over, and they may now join him and the Father in Paradise. Ephesians 4:8 is taken to be the triumphal entry of these once-captive OT saints into heaven with the risen Christ at his ascension.

In my judgment this whole concept is false. OT saints were fully justified, fully forgiven; in fact, Abraham is used in the NT as a model for someone justified by faith (Rom 4; Gal 3). There is no reason to assume that the souls of OT saints had to wait to enter the presence of the Father in the throne room of the invisible universe. Christ's assured redemptive work was being applied already (see 2 Kgs 2:11; Matt 17:3; Luke 16:25). The "spirits in prison" in 1 Pet 3:19 are the souls of the *wicked* dead, not the righteous dead. The "host of captives" symbolically pictured as trailing behind Christ at his ascension (Eph 4:8) are not *released* captives, but newly conquered captives, Satan and his demonic hosts as bound by the chains of the gospel. They are the King's spoils of victory.

A third question is whether unbelievers have an opportunity to accept God's grace after they die. When Christ preached to the spirits of the wicked dead during the time between his death and resurrection (1 Pet 3:19), was he giving them a chance to believe in his atoning death and be saved? There is no reason to assume this is so. The word used for Christ's preaching here is not *euangelizo*, "to preach the gospel, evangelize," but simply *kerysso*, "to announce, proclaim." Hebrews 9:27 is quite decisive: "It is appointed for men to die once and after this comes the judgment." In other words, there is nothing that will happen after we die that can change the outcome of our judgment. As 2 Cor 5:10 says, our final recompense will be based on what we have done *in this body*, during our physical lives.

Fourth, is there any contact between the spirits of those who have died, and those who are still on the earth? On two occasions recorded in Scripture this seems to have happened: the spirit of Samuel talked with King Saul (1 Sam 28:15-19), and the spirits of Moses and Elijah talked with Christ (Matt 17:3). But both of these events are clearly miraculous exceptions. In Jesus' story of the rich man in Hades, Abraham forcefully refuses the rich man's request to send a messenger from the dead to warn his brothers about the agony of Hades (Luke 16:27-31). Most significantly, God's Word decisively forbids all attempts to contact the spirits of the dead. Such attempts are called spiritism, which is unconditionally condemned in Lev 19:31; 20:6,27; Deut 18:9-12 as something hated by God. Those who think they are in contact with the spirits of the dead are being deceived either by a phony "medium," or by demonic spirits pretending to be departed human spirits.

Fifth, how does the biblical teaching on the intermediate state relate to the Roman Catholic doctrine of purgatory? We should note first that in Catholicism purgatory has nothing to do with Hades. Only the spirits of the lost go to Hades, and only the spirits of the saved go to purgatory. All who are in purgatory will eventually be in heaven. It is a step toward heaven, not hell. It is an instrument of salvation, not condemnation. The idea is simply this, that many if not most saved people when they die still have some remains of sin that have to be worked off or purged out of their system. This may include some vestiges of sinfulness, or even some temporal penalties for minor sins that were not fully forgiven in this life. Hence the need for a proportionate period of redemptive suffering to be endured before one is worthy of heaven.

This doctrine must be rejected as inconsistent with the biblical teaching on the intermediate state. The main Catholic proof text for purgatory is not even in the canonical Bible; it is in the Apocryphal book of 2 Maccabees (12:42-45).[8] Every canonical Scripture that pictures the state of believers in the afterlife portrays them as experiencing joy and bliss in the very presence of God or Christ. There is no text whatsoever that depicts a period of suffering for the saved. Also, no text suggests any kind of distinction among saved saints on the other side of death. All are depicted as "spirits of the righteous made perfect" (Heb 12:23).

Most significantly, though, the doctrine of purgatory must be rejected because it contradicts the biblical doctrine of grace, especially the doctrine of full forgiveness through the saving blood of Christ. In Jesus, *all* penalty for *all* sins is forgiven; "there is now no condemnation for those who are in Christ Jesus" (Rom 8:1). The doctrine of purgatory is based on the idea that *something we do* can cancel out some of the punishment we incurred through our sins. Nothing could be further from the truth.

NOTES ON CHAPTER TWENTY-NINE

[1]Another example of this view is Davies, 317-318. For further examples see Berkouwer, *Return*, 38-46. He says, "In many theological circles there is considerable sympathy for this notion of the 'abolition' of time" (41).

[2]See Berkouwer, *Return* (38-46) for an excellent critique of the false notion of "timeless eschatology" (44).

[3]A church newsletter included this statement in the death notice of a handicapped member: "We will miss [him] in our services but rejoice that he now has a new body perfect in every respect." This is incorrect. Though his present bodiless spirit does not reflect his earthly handicap, he will not have his perfect *body* until the day of resurrection.

[4]The KJV translates Sheol as "hell" 31 times, and Hades as "hell" in every passage but one. This is seriously misleading, since the English word "hell" almost always connotes the eternal punishment of the wicked that begins only after the final judgment. However, Sheol and Hades are used only of the interim state, never for the final state. We cannot draw inferences about the latter from their use.

[5]In Ps 89:48 it is important to see that in the phrase "his soul," the word "soul" is being used in the sense of "person, individual." The word *nephesh* is often used in this sense in the Psalms.

[6]Again, it is important to take "soul" here in the sense of "person, individual, self"; i.e., "my soul" means "me, myself." See Ps 30:3; 86:13. The two clauses in Ps 16:10 are thus equivalent, being an example of Hebrew parallelism.

[7]Contra Morey, 86. When the Hades of departed spirits is divided into two sections, one for the righteous and one for the wicked, some refer to the latter section as Tartarus, a word found only in 2 Pet 2:4. There is no reason, however, to connect this term, state, or place with the souls of human beings. In 2 Pet 2:4 it is applied only to angels. It is possible that it refers to a place comparable to Hades, but its inhabitants are (some) fallen angels, not fallen men.

[8]For a discussion of purgatory's alleged support from the canonical Scriptures, see Grudem, *Theology*, 818-819.

CHAPTER THIRTY

THE SECOND COMING OF JESUS

The last three chapters have all dealt with material usually called "eschatology," i.e., a study of the last or final things; but we are just now getting to the actual *last things*. That is, we are ready to discuss what the Bible says about the second coming of Jesus. As we have already seen, there is considerable confusion among Christians as to which events were related to Christ's first coming, and which are related to his second coming. This is due in part to a confusion as to how to interpret prophecies about both comings and the time in between. We have addressed these issues above, and have already dealt with certain subjects that some still wrongly associate with the second coming, such as the establishment of the millennial kingdom, the binding of Satan, and the first resurrection.

Thus when we come to the subject of the second coming, the scenario is not nearly as complicated as some think it is. As we shall see, the events related to Christ's return are actually quite straightforward. Here we will present them under three simple headings: events preceding Christ's second coming, the second coming itself, and events accompanying his coming.

I. THE PRECURSORS OF CHRIST'S RETURN

Because our Christian hope is inseparably intertwined with Christ's second coming, Christians throughout the church era have eagerly awaited this event and have been very interested in any indications that it might occur at "any moment now." Thus much attention has been given to the so-called "signs of the times," i.e., the signs that his coming is near. In this section we will examine what the Bible says about these signs or precursors of the end.

The discussion of the subject today is dominated by the dispensational premillennial view of prophecy, the view which teaches that events surrounding the nation of Israel are the main focus of prophecy and the key to the end times. This view says that the countdown to the end will begin when all Christians suddenly disappear from the earth in the "secret rapture." When this happens only seven years will remain until Christ's visible return, and during these seven years the Jews will be the main focus of world attention and of God's own plan. These seven years will include what some call "the great tribulation" and "the Battle of Armageddon."

This Christian Israelicentric fervor began after Israel became a nation in 1948 and regained control of the temple site in 1967. These events led Hal Lindsey to write his influential book, *The Late Great Planet Earth*. In it he says (32-34),

> Some time in the future there will be a seven-year period climaxed by the visible return of Jesus Christ. . . . There is more prophecy concerning this period than any other era the Bible describes. . . . This period will be marked by the greatest devastation that man has ever brought upon himself. Mankind will be on the brink of self-annihilation when Christ suddenly returns to put an end to the war of wars called Armageddon.

At the beginning of the 21st century this fervor is at its highest, thanks to the wildly successful line of fictional books by Tim LaHaye and Jerry Jenkins called the *Left Behind* series, beginning in 1995 with the publication of *Left Behind*. Seven years later (2002) the tenth book in the series, *The Remnant*, has appeared. With total sales approaching 40 million copies, this phenomenon has warranted a cover story in *Time* magazine ("Apocalypse Now," July 1, 2002).

During these past several decades Lindsey, LaHaye, and countless other prophecy buffs have constructed detailed scenarios of the seven years between the rapture and the return, based on their own assumptions of how to interpret prophecy. The details are drawn piecemeal from all over the Bible, since "the pieces are scattered in small bits throughout the Old and New Testaments," says Lindsey (33). Each interpreter has his own unique twists, and the details are adjusted constantly to take account of the changing political fortunes of the relevant nations; but the overall picture remains about the same. The following scenario is typical, gleaned from various sources (especially Lindsey) and probably already out of date:

> The stage for Christ's return will be set by Israel's return to its homeland, Palestine (Ezek 36:24,28; 37:21-22). The temple will be rebuilt upon its original site (Zech 6:12ff.; Ezek 41–46). The ancient Roman Empire will be revived, consisting of the European nations (Dan 7:23). This will be headed by the antichrist (Rev 13:1ff.), who will make a pact with Israel (Dan 9:27). This will be followed by three and one-half years of peace and prosperity for Israel. Many conversions will take place through the ministry of the Jewish remnant.
>
> Suddenly the antichrist will break the covenant and set himself up as God in the temple (Matt 24:15; 2 Thess 2:4). This begins the three and one-half year period of tribulation and war, leading to the Battle of Armageddon (Matt 24:15-21). The "king of the south" (Arab nations) invades and attacks Israel (Dan 11:5-6,40). The "king of the north" (Russia, Gog leading Magog) pushes in upon Israel from above (Ezek 38:14-16), then continues on and overwhelms the Arab nations, too (Dan 11:42-43). At this point God intervenes and destroys Gog (Ezek 38:18-22; 39:6), rescuing Israel, but only temporarily.
>
> What follows is the climactic "mother of all battles, WW III, "the last great war of mankind" (Lindsey, 71). Two hundred million Chinese soldiers (the "kings from the east") march overland toward Israel (Rev 9:14-16; 16:12-16),

while the antichrist marches toward Israel with a European army. These two gigantic armies meet at a specific area of geography in Israel known as Armageddon (Rev 16:16). Here, amid fierce fighting and great destruction, many Jews are converted (Zech 13:8-9). Then just as Israel is about to be completely overwhelmed, Christ returns, lands on Mt. Olivet, rescues believing Jews and annihilates the enemy (Zech 14:1-4, 12). Now the millennium can begin.

This is the kind of thing many Christians think of when they hear the term, "the Battle of Armageddon." But we must ask the question, *is* this the kind of scenario that will precede Christ's coming? Is this the picture prophecy paints for us? My answer is an emphatic *no*. It is true that the end of the age can be described in terms of conflict and warfare, but it is warfare of a totally different kind.

We must remember God's own rules for interpreting prophecy. God tells us in Num 12:6-8 and Hos 12:10 that he speaks through the prophets in riddles and parables: signs and symbols, figurative language, physical pictures representing spiritual realities. We have already seen how this is true of prophecies about Israel, the kingdom, and the millennium. Now we will see how it also applies to the Armageddon-type material; i.e., the graphic and gory descriptions of great military conflicts are God's symbolic way of picturing our spiritual warfare (e.g., Ezek 38:14-16; Dan 11:40–12:1; Eph 6:12).

The Armageddon armies are not necessarily engaged in political and military conflict, but in spiritual battles: the enemies of Christ, his church, and his truth rise up and attack him and his people and his Word. This will happen not just in one small geographical location in the Middle East, but throughout the earth. And it happens to some degree not just for a brief three and one-half year period, but throughout the whole history of the church. There is some biblical basis for believing that a concentrated spiritual attack upon the church will happen near the end, however, as a precursor to the second coming. We can call this concentrated assault "Armageddon" if we like, as long as we remember its *spiritual* nature and its *worldwide* scope. The following is my understanding of how this spiritual warfare will intensify and what we can expect to take place shortly before this blessed event of Christ's return.

A. The Relevant Texts

Several NT texts must be considered together as we attempt to discern what the world will be like just before the end. We begin with Rev 20:7-9, which speaks of the time just before the end when Satan will be loosed. Earlier we saw that the binding of Satan (Rev 20:1-3) occurred as a result of Christ's *first* coming, and that the "thousand years" (the millennium) refers symbolically to the entire scope of the church age—or rather, *almost* to its entire scope. The exception is at the very end, because Rev 20:3 says that after the thousand years of Satan's binding, "he must be released for a short time." The length of time is not stated;

it is simply to be a *short* time relative to the *long* period of Christian history. This short time is described thus in verses 7-9:

> When the thousand years are completed, Satan will be released from his prison, and will come out to deceive the nations which are in the four corners of the earth, Gog and Magog, to gather them together for the war; the number of them is like the sand of the seashore. And they came up on the broad plain of the earth and surrounded the camp of the saints and the beloved city, and fire came down from heaven and devoured them.

It is important to see that this describes something that will happen just before the return of Jesus Christ, which is symbolized by the fire that came down from heaven. In some way (see 2 Thess 2:11) God will allow Satan one last campaign of deception and falsehood in opposition to the gospel of Christ. This deception is worldwide; he will "deceive the nations" of the whole earth. The deception is preparatory for launching a deliberate war on "the camp of the saints and the beloved city." This is not physical Jerusalem, but "the Jerusalem above" (Gal 4:26), "the heavenly Jerusalem" (Heb 12:22), which is the church. The planned attack is not localized (e.g., against just one nation), but takes place "on the broad plain of the earth." This may well represent one last period of "great tribulation" for God's people, a time of extreme spiritual warfare. However, the main attack never takes place; Christ returns while his people are "surrounded," and Satan's army is destroyed before he can destroy the church.

A group of relevant texts are the verses in John's letters that refer to the antichrist, a figure that most people associate with the end time. In 1 John 2:18,22 the apostle says, "Children, it is the last hour; and just as you heard that antichrist is coming, even now many antichrists have appeared; from this we know that it is the last hour. . . . Who is the liar but the one who denies that Jesus is the Christ? This is the antichrist, the one who denies the Father and the Son." Also, "Every spirit that does not confess Jesus is not from God; this is the spirit of the antichrist, of which you have heard that it is coming, and now it is already in the world" (1 John 4:3). Finally, "For many deceivers have gone out into the world, those who do not acknowledge Jesus Christ as coming in the flesh. This is the deceiver and the antichrist" (2 John 7). These are the only biblical references that specifically use the term "antichrist."

The first thing we notice about these texts is that they are not just about the last days. There is not just one person called the antichrist; antichrists and the spirit of antichrist seem to be a characteristic of every era of the church. Apparently anyone who espouses and teaches false doctrine about Jesus Christ is an antichrist. In John's day this applied especially to those who, under the influence of a dualistic philosophy such as Gnosticism, denied the full human nature of Jesus. Thus the antichrist is associated with deception and false doctrine in any era.

One thing that John says does relate the antichrist phenomenon to the second coming, however. This is his statement (1 John 2:18) that since many antichrists have appeared, "from this we know that it is the last hour." Some think John's "last hour" refers to the entire church age between Christ's first and second comings, but in my judgment he is referring to the last hour or last days of the church age itself. Was he then asserting that Jesus would come during his lifetime or shortly thereafter, and was he thus mistaken? No. John does not actually say that it is "*the* last hour," since there is no definite article in the Greek. Thus it is likely that he is saying that the presence of antichrists shows that it is "a last-hour kind of time" (Summers, 134). This means that he does indeed associate the spirit of antichrist with the last days, and it implies that the time just before Christ's return will be rampant with false, antichrist doctrine. When combined with 2 Thess 2:1-12 it warrants the expectation of an individual who will be the ultimate antichrist as a precursor of the end.

The next relevant text, then, is 2 Thess 2:1-12. Here Paul is discussing "the coming of our Lord" and "the day of the Lord" (vv. 1-2), and he says "it will not come unless the apostasy comes first, and the man of lawlessness is revealed, the son of destruction, who opposes and exalts himself above every so-called god or object of worship, so that he takes his seat in the temple of God, displaying himself as being God" (vv. 3-4). This "man of lawlessness" may be a specific person or just a certain kind of person; I take him to be the former and see no reason not to identify him as the ultimate antichrist.

At the time Paul wrote this letter he said that this man of lawlessness was being restrained, "so that in his time he will be revealed" (v. 6). "For the mystery of lawlessness is already at work; only he who now restrains will do so until he is taken out of the way" (v. 7). This corresponds to John's remark that the spirit of the antichrist is already in the world (1 John 4:3), but here we see that it is being restrained, i.e., its power is being limited (as in the binding of Satan, Rev 20:1-3). The one who restrains this lawlessness is God himself, and he will do so *until he withdraws his restraint* (which is the best understanding of v. 7b).

It is this withdrawing of the restraint upon lawlessness that marks the beginning of the end: "Then that lawless one will be revealed whom the Lord will slay with the breath of His mouth and bring to an end by the appearance of His coming; that is, the one whose coming is in accord with the activity of Satan, with all power and signs and false wonders, and with all the deception of wickedness for those who perish, because they did not receive the love of the truth so as to be saved" (vv. 8-10). The parallel with Rev 20:7-9 is obvious. The lawless one is empowered by Satan, whom God has loosed; and his antichrist campaign ends abruptly when Christ appears and slays him with the breath of his mouth (the devouring fire from heaven, Rev 20:9; see 2 Thess 1:7).

The emphasis here is on falsehood and wickedness. This "lawless one," the antichrist figure, embodies these traits and encourages them in others. God allows this to happen, withdrawing his restraint in accordance with the loosing of Satan in Rev 20:7-9: "For this reason God will send upon them a deluding influence so that they," the followers of the lawless one, "will believe what is false, in order that they all may be judged who did not believe the truth, but took pleasure in wickedness" (2 Thess 2:11-12).

Another text is Rev 16:12-16, the one passage that mentions a so-called "Battle of Armageddon." John saw this symbolic vision when "the sixth angel poured out his bowl on the great river, the Euphrates; and its water was dried up, so that the way would be prepared for the kings from the east" (v. 12). As we have seen, for the most part the various visions given to John in the book of Revelation are a series of symbolic glimpses of the conflict between God and Satan that is carried out upon the earth between Christ's two comings. Some references are to the church age in general. In my judgment, though, the seven bowls of wrath in Revelation 16 have a special intensity and represent what will happen during the "short time" when Satan is loosed. Thus the Armageddon scene pictured here does indeed refer to the end time, and is parallel to Rev 20:7-9.

John's vision shows that this will indeed be a time of great Satanic activity, as represented by the "three unclean spirits like frogs" that proceed from the mouths of the dragon, the beast, and the false prophet (Rev 16:13). These are the "spirits of demons, performing signs" (see 2 Thess 2:9). The purpose of these signs is to "deceive the nations" (Rev 20:8), to "go out to the kings of the whole world, to gather them together for the war of the great day of God, the Almighty" (16:14). This is the same scenario described in Rev 20:8. The "great day of God" is clearly the second coming of Christ, as verse 15 shows. When these armies have been recruited by Satanic deception, "they gathered them together to the place which in Hebrew is called Har-Magedon" (v. 16). This is equivalent to the surrounding of the camp of the saints in Rev 20:9.

It should be carefully noted, however, that the armies gathered at Har-Magedon (Armageddon) never get to launch an all-out attack against their target. Just as in Rev 20:9 and 2 Thess 2:8, the second coming of Christ destroys these armies. This destruction is pictured in the outpouring of the seventh bowl of wrath (Rev 16:17-21), which describes the cataclysmic destruction of "Babylon the great" (another symbol for God's enemies, parallel to the armies of the kings in Rev 16:12-16). Thus the impending "Battle of Armageddon" never actually takes place.

In this connection we should also take account of Rev 17:1-19:6, which is simply an expanded version of the same event represented in 16:17-21. It gives more insight into the evil conditions of the world just prior to Christ's return. The character of Babylon is that of a harlot, steeped in wickedness especially of a sexual nature, along with a materialistic lust for earthly riches (Rev 17:1-5; 18:9-19). Also emphasized is Babylon's antitheistic, antichristian stance, carried to the point of outright attacks upon Christians (17:3,6,14; 18:24). Her Satanic purposes end in destruction, however: "These will wage war against the Lamb, and the Lamb will overcome them, because He is Lord of lords and King of kings" (Rev 17:14).

The next passage is Matt 24:1-35 (with parallels in Mark 13:1-32 and Luke 21:5-33). This is part of the so-called "Olivet discourse," and is notoriously difficult to interpret since in it Jesus seems to refer to two distinct events, i.e., the destruction of Jerusalem and the end of the world. The former is definitely included, since Jesus initiates the discourse by declaring that the Jews' temple would be torn down, stone by stone (vv. 1-2). When the disciples question him about this, they seem to add the latter event as well: "Tell us, when will these things happen, and what will be the sign of Your coming, and of the end of the age?" (v. 3).

Deciding which part of the discourse (Matt 24:1-35 only) refers to Jerusalem's end and which to the world's end is the difficulty. Some say the whole section refers to Jerusalem's destruction and none to Christ's second coming (Chouinard, 416-417). Others say the whole section refers to Jerusalem's destruction *and* to the end of the world, because these are literally the same event.[1] Others divide the material into separate sections and refer some to Jerusalem and some to the second coming.[2]

In my judgment this discourse does refer to the two distinct events, but it is impossible to be dogmatic about the division of the verses. In fact, I do not believe Jesus intends for us to divide the material thus. I believe rather that these events are to be viewed together, as one might look through a powerful telescope at two mountaintops that are aligned but are actually separated by a considerable distance. The foreshortening effect of the telescope causes us to see the features of the two mountaintops as mingled together. This is a technique called "prophetic foreshortening" (see Hoekema, *Bible*, 130), and it is often found in the OT in prophecies that mingle, e.g., the restoration of the Jews from Babylonian captivity and the first coming of Christ (as in Ezek 36:22-36).

This passage is more than just two random events blended together, however. The events in view have an inherent connection in the sense that one is a symbolic paradigm of the other. That is, the destruction of Jerusalem and the events leading up to it are in many ways parallel to the second coming and its precursors. Thus the description of the one is not sharply distinct from the other, and at times the language seems to apply to both events. At other times, however, the language seems unique to one or the other, though we cannot always clearly discern the dividing line between the general and the specific.

With this approach to the discourse in view, it would seem that the precursors to Christ's return listed here are basically the same as in the other texts discussed above. In the context of international conflict and natural disasters (Matt 24:6-8), there will be personal suffering: "Then they will deliver you to tribulation, and will kill you, and you will be hated by all nations because of My name" (v. 9). While this applies to events leading up to the destruction of Jerusalem (see vv. 15-22), the reference to "all nations" shows that it must also apply to the time before the second coming (see v. 29). Another precursor, perhaps to both but especially to the second coming, will be rampant false teaching resulting in apostasy (vv. 4-5,10-11). Verse 24 says, "For false Christs and false prophets will arise and will show great signs and wonders, so as to mislead, if possible, even the elect" (see 2 Thess 2:9). The false doctrine will be accompanied by an increase in lawlessness (v. 12).

Two other texts, both from the Pastoral Epistles, should be mentioned as speaking specifically of what to expect just before the end. One is 1 Tim 4:1-2, "But the Spirit explicitly says that in later times some will fall away from the faith, paying attention to deceitful spirits and doctrines of demons, by means of the hypocrisy of liars seared in their own conscience as with a branding iron." Here the main emphasis again is on the deceiving work of Satan and his demons. Their deception succeeds even in causing some Christians to fall away; this is the apostasy that must precede Christ's return (2 Thess 2:3). The other text is 2 Tim 3:1-9, which emphasizes the excessive wickedness that will precede Christ's coming. Here Paul says that "in the last days difficult times will come" (v. 1); then he gives a long list of specific sins that will abound in those days (vv. 2-7). By comparing the instigators of such wickedness with Pharaoh's sorcerers, Jannes and Jambres (vv. 8-9), he alludes to their connection with Satan and his demons—a point that is explicit in most of the other texts.

In my judgment these are the main passages upon which we should concentrate to gain some insight into the time leading up to the second coming of Jesus. There is a remarkable unity and parallelism among them, which will become even more clear in the next section.

B. The Nature of the Last Days

Here we will try to summarize and systematize the data found in the series of texts just discussed. We should remember that in the main course of church history Satan is bound (Rev 20:1-3) or is under divine restraint (2 Thess 2:6-7). A time will come, however, when this restraint will be removed and Satan will be loosed, but just for a "short time" leading up to Christ's return (Rev 20:3,9). We do not know how long this period will last; we know only that it will be relatively short in contrast with the "thousand years" of the church age.

What will this period be like? The main point is that it will be a time of intense *spiritual* battle. Images of military armies and battles and physical destruction are for the most part figurative of spiritual warfare. Paul has clearly stated that "our struggle is not against flesh and blood, but against the rulers, against the powers, against the world forces of this darkness, against the spiritual forces of wickedness in the heavenly places" (Eph 6:12). The role of the demonic in the end-time struggle was emphasized in most of the relevant texts above. What this means is that we cannot predict the arrival of the end just by monitoring international political and military developments. These may be related (see Matt 24:7); but they are secondary, not primary. The main precursors of the second coming are movements and developments in the realm of ideas and in the realm of everyday character and behavior, all satanically inspired.

I see three main characteristics of the end time emerging from the texts presented above. First and primarily, it will be a time of great *falsehood*. This is consistent with the fact that Satan will be unusually active, and with the fact that Satan's main strategy has always been deception. Thus in terms of spiritual warfare, this era will be marked by a battle for our *minds*. This theme is present in all the relevant texts. When Satan is loosed he goes forth to "deceive the nations" once more (Rev 20:8). False Christs will arise (Matt 24:5,24), and perhaps an ultimate antichrist. The antichrist is one who denies the truth about Jesus (1 John 2:21-22); antichrists are by nature deceivers (2 John 7). The man of lawlessness will foster apostasy and false religion (2 Thess 2:3-4); his coming will be marked by "false wonders" and deception (2 Thess 2:9-10; see Matt 24:24). Those who follow him neither love the truth nor believe the truth; instead they "believe what is false" (2 Thess 2:10-12). The Armageddon adversaries of the church have been seduced by demonic signs and wonders (Rev 16:14), "paying attention to deceitful spirits and doctrines of demons" (1 Tim 4:1). The end will be heralded more by what is happening in university classrooms, the communications media, and even religious assemblies than by developments in Middle Eastern politics.

The second main characteristic of the end is that it will be a time of great *wickedness*. In warfare terms it will be a battle for our *wills*. Satan has always been a master of temptation, and the temptations of the end time will be unprecedented. This theme is present in many of the texts discussed above. It is especially strong in 2 Thess 2:1-12, where the antichrist figure is actually described as a man of *lawlessness*[3] (v. 3; see Matt 24:12), the *lawless* one (v. 8). Lawlessness is equated with sin in 1 John 3:4, "Everyone who practices sin also practices lawlessness; and sin is lawlessness." One of the main purposes of the lawless one's Satanic deception is to open the door to guilt-free sin (2 Thess 2:10), so that those who reject the truth can take pleasure in wickedness (2 Thess 2:12). Babylon the great (another figure for the Armageddon armies) is filled with immorality (Rev 17:1-5; 18:3). Paul's list of the sins that will fill the "last days" is long and explicit (2 Tim 3:1-7). Thus the presence of sin in the end will be so intense and so pervasive that many will just take it for granted and accept it as normal. This means that for Christians the temptation to accept such wickedness and even participate in it will be both subtle and powerful.

The last precursor emerging from the relevant texts is *persecution*, which may at times take the form of a battle for our *lives*. The texts make it clear that during his period of loosing Satan's deception of the nations is not an end in itself, but in fact is a means to amassing an army that will launch a war against God's people (Rev 20:7-9). This is called "the war of the great day of God" (Rev 16:14). It is wrong to think that such persecution must be in the context of some great military conflict, carried out with physical weapons of destruction. Satan's war may take the form of social ostracizing, emotional bullying, intellectual ridicule, and economic injustice, all directed against Christians just because they are Christians ("because of my Name," Matt 24:9). It may also take the form of extreme physical attacks, such as slavery and martyrdom (Matt 24:9). John saw the harlot Babylon "drunk with the blood of the saints, and with the blood of the witnesses of Jesus" (Rev 17:6). Even if we reject the literalistic military Armageddon scenarios of many modern prophecy buffs, we must not overlook the reality of a many-faceted assault that will be directed against God's people at the end.

C. Deliberate Ambiguity

We may raise the question of whether we are presently in this "short time" of the loosing of Satan. Our answer depends to some degree on *how long* we interpret this "short time" to be. Relative to the "thousand years" of the church era (now nearing two thousand actual years), the "short time" might encompass as much as 100 or 150 years. In terms of falsehood, the rise and/or spread of false religions and philosophies in the Western world in the nineteenth and twentieth centuries is historically unprecedented, e.g., communism, evolutionism, materialism, cults, liberal theology, humanism, existentialism, pragmatism, process philosophy, occultism, and relativism in general. Even if we shrink the "short time" to 25 or 50 years, many old lies have acquired new forms and greater intensity within this time. For example, the New Age Movement as a westernized form of pantheistic Hinduism has arisen within the last few decades; as has postmodernism as just the most recent form of relativism; Islam has replaced communism as the most militant opponent of Christianity.

In terms of wickedness, the same analysis may be made. Even within the shorter perspective we can identify unprecedented lawlessness in the form of open rebellion against authority, the "new" morality, the public display and shameless approval of sin in the media (especially television), government-supported abortion, Internet pornography, acceptance of immodesty and even nudity, apathy toward divorce, gay liberation, widespread approval of self-serving lying and cheating, feminism, multiculturalism, and a generally hedonistic mentality.

In terms of persecution, in the twentieth century we witnessed a suppression of and attacks upon Christianity on a widespread basis, first by communistic regimes and more recently by fundamentalist Islamic governments. Such attacks are growing in other cultures, especially among the Hindu population in India. In some areas Christians are physically attacked and enslaved. The social persecution of Christians and the suppression of the Christian message is common in America under the guise of "separation of church and state." The media almost consistently ridicule Christian values and the Christian lifestyle, depicting believers either as hypocrites or as wimps and losers.

Can we say, then, that we are in the last days? My answer: *perhaps; perhaps not.* This answer will seem like a cop-out to many, but I can explain it thus. In my judgment the signs or precursors that the Bible associates with the end time are *deliberately ambiguous.* That is, the concepts of falsehood, wickedness, and persecution are general enough to allow any Christian living in almost any era of the church to survey the world situation and identify certain circumstances that seem to him to be obvious fulfillments of these requirements. This would apply even to a numerical marker such as "666" (Rev 13:18). Thus we are encouraged and even intended to search for indicators of the imminence of Christ's return, and it is possible if not likely that these are actually present today. But the same was true for Christians in the second, and in the seventh, and in the sixteenth centuries, indeed, in any period of church history. All are encouraged to look, and all may find reason to draw the same conclusion many are drawing today: Christ's return must be imminent!

Thus, because of this deliberate ambiguity, Christians in every era can take an "any moment" approach to the second coming. But at the same time, in no era including our own can we be dogmatic about the time of Christ's return. We should never say, "Jesus *is* coming soon." Rather, we should always say, "Jesus *may* come soon."[4] Thus we must always act and live as if the end will come at any moment. But the ambiguity of the precursors, and our inability to interpret world circumstances infallibly and dogmatically, mean that we may be wrong in our interpretation and that our generation may pass without Christ's return. Still, we have neither embarrassed ourselves nor discredited the Christian hope, and we have been able honestly to obey Christ's exhortation, "Therefore be on the alert, for you do not know which day your Lord is coming. . . . For this reason you also must be ready; for the Son of Man is coming at an hour when you do not think He will" (Matt 24:42,44).

How then may Christians prepare for his coming? Since we know the end will involve much deception and falsehood, we can be ready for it only by knowing, believing, and loving the truth (see John 8:32; 2 Thess 2:10,12; Eph 6:14). Since we know it will involve much wickedness, we can be ready for it by depending totally on the power of the Holy Spirit to keep us morally strong (1 John 4:4), and we must get in the habit of practicing righteousness now (Eph 6:14). Since we know it will also involve persecution, we must learn simply to trust God's power and promises no matter what our circumstances (Rom 8:28; Eph 6:16). And we can take comfort in knowing that Christ will ultimately be victorious, destroying all his (and our) enemies at his coming (2 Thess 1:7-10; 2:8; Rev 19:11-21; 20:9).

II. THE EVENT OF CHRIST'S RETURN

Scripture definitely affirms that "Christ . . . will appear a second time" (Heb 9:28). His second coming is one of the most clearly and frequently attested events in the NT (see Erickson, *Theology*, 1192-1194). Jesus promised, "I will come again and receive you to Myself" (John 14:3). At his ascension the attending angels promised, "This Jesus, who has been taken up from you into heaven, will come in just the same way as you have watched Him go into heaven" (Acts

1:11). His return will be the next main event in God's plan for the world, and it is the main event of the end time as such.

A. The Unity of His Coming

Christ's return is mentioned in many passages and is described in many ways (see the next section), but in the final analysis there is only one event that can be called "the second coming." There is a sense in which Christ came to his people on the Day of Pentecost (Matt 10:23; 16:28); but this is not the second coming mentioned in Heb 9:28, which was still future when that letter was written. The second coming will have major events preceding it (the precursors discussed above) and major events accompanying and following it (see the next section), but the coming itself is a single, onetime event.

The main reason for emphasizing this point is that the dispensational premillennial view of Christ's return splits the event into two stages separated by seven years, and applies some biblical data about his coming to the first stage and other data to the second stage. For example, this view says that the first stage is Christ's invisible return "for his saints," when they are raptured out of the earth prior to the tribulation. The second stage is his visible coming "with his saints," when he destroys the Armageddon hosts and sets up his millennial kingdom. This division of his coming into two parts results also in a proliferation of resurrections and judgments. This means that the expected sequence of end-time events is unnecessarily and unbiblically complicated.

We have already seen why the dispensational view of the millennium is wrong, and in the next section we will see that the whole idea of a secret second coming involving a secret rapture is wrong. There is simply no reason to divide the second coming into stages. There will be one coming, in one moment of time. (See Erickson, *Theology*, 1197-1199.)

B. The Terminology of His Coming

It is generally agreed that there are three main Greek words used in the NT to refer to Christ's coming: *epiphaneia*, *apokalypsis*, and *parousia*. William Cox adds a fourth, *hemera*, the word for "day" (*Studies*, 118-119). The word *epiphaneia* is from the verb *epiphaino*, which means "to show, to appear, to become visible." It is used six times in the NT, once for Christ's first coming (2 Tim 1:10) and five times for his second coming (2 Thess 2:8; 1 Tim 6:14; 2 Tim 4:1,8; Titus 2:13). It is usually translated "appearance" or "appearing." In ancient Greece the term was used to describe the appearing of a deity for the purpose of rendering divine assistance in time of trouble. In the NT it denotes the appearing of the divine King of kings, whose arrival is heralded by a trumpet (1 Cor 15:52; 1 Thess 4:16).

The second term is *apokalypsis*, which means "a revelation, an uncovering, a laying bare."[5] It is used specifically for Christ's return four times. Paul says we are "awaiting eagerly the revelation of our Lord Jesus Christ" (1 Cor 1:7). Peter exhorts Christians to "fix your hope completely on the grace to be brought to you at the revelation of Jesus Christ" (1 Pet 1:13). He adds that at "the revelation of His glory" we will greatly rejoice (1 Pet 4:13). See also 2 Thess 1:7. Though the term in not used in Rev 6:12-17, this text well represents the concept of the second coming as a revelation, as it pictures the lifting of the curtains on this final drama: "The sky was split apart like a scroll when it is rolled up" (v. 14). What is connoted by this term (as well as by *epiphaneia*) is that Christ's second coming will be in stark contrast with his first coming, where his divine nature was "veiled in flesh" and his glory was cloaked in humiliation (Phil 2:6-8). Even though he now reigns in power from God's own right hand, his majesty is still hidden except to the eyes of the heart (Eph 1:18-23). But on the day of his return, his true glory and majesty and power will be openly and undeniably revealed to all.

The third term is *parousia*, which can mean either "coming" (in the sense of arrival) or "presence." In the Greek world this word was often "used technically for the visit of a ruler or high official," and was especially applied to "the helpful *parousia* of the gods" (Oepke, 859-860). Thus it is most appropriate as a term for Christ's return and is used 17 times in the NT in this connection, most often being translated "coming."[6] For example, In 1 Thess 3:13 Paul prays that the Lord "may establish your hearts without blame in holiness before our God and Father at the coming of our Lord Jesus with all His saints." James 5:7 says, "Therefore be patient, brethren, until the coming of the Lord." This word emphasizes the fact that Christ will return in order to be present with us, to be in our midst, personally and visibly, with the consequence that "we shall always be with the Lord" (1 Thess 5:17).

William Cox (118-119) says that the word "day" (Greek, *hemera*) should be added to the list of NT terms that refer to the second coming. It is in fact used of this event even more often than *parousia*. Cox lists 25 passages with nine different expressions such as "the day of the Lord," "the day of Jesus Christ," "the day of God," "that day," "the last day," and "his day," all referring to the second coming (118).

It is important to remember that all of these words refer to the same event; there is only one "day of our Lord Jesus Christ" (1 Cor 1:8), which is at the same time his *parousia*, his *epiphaneia*, and his *apokalypsis*.

C. The Manner of His Coming

The question of the *manner* of Christ's second coming is this: exactly what will it be like? (See Hoekema, *Bible*, 171-172.) First we note that his coming will be *personal*. The risen Lord himself, the same person who was here during his incarnate ministry, will come back to this earth. It will not be just the coming of his spirit or Spirit; it will not be just the triumph of his teachings in the world. At his ascension the angels told his disciples that "this Jesus," the same one "who has been taken up from you into heaven," is the one who will return (Acts 1:11). "The Lord Himself will descend from heaven," says Paul (1 Thess 4:16).

Second, his return will be *visible*. In this sense it could also be described as literal, bodily, physical, and even audible. This is opposed to all those who say that the second coming will be hidden or secret, or that it will result in just a spiritual presence. That his coming is an appearing (*epiphaneia*) and a revelation (*apokalypsis*) underscores its visibility. Hebrews 9:28 says Christ "will appear a second time," i.e., will become visible, will be seen just as he was the first time. He "will be revealed from heaven" (2 Thess 1:7). Titus 2:11-13 implies that his second coming will be an appearing just as much as his first coming was (Hoekema, *Bible*, 171-172). As the disciples "were gazing intently" while Jesus was ascending into heaven, the angels said to them, "This Jesus, who has been taken up from you into heaven, will come in just the same way as you have watched Him go into heaven" (Acts 1:11). The implication that his second coming will be visible is inescapable. Revelation 1:7 clearly says, "Behold, He is coming with the clouds, and every eye will see Him, even those who pierced Him, and all the tribes of the earth will mourn over Him." This same language is used in Matt 24:30: "All the tribes of the earth will mourn, and they will see the Son of Man coming on the clouds." Emphasizing Christ's resurrection body, 1 John 3:2 says that when He appears, we will be like Him, because we will see Him just as He is." See also Col 3:4; Heb 9:28.

Surely such teaching rules out all claims that the second coming was or will be somehow just an invisible, spiritual presence of Christ, a view espoused by liberalism (Berkhof, 705) and preterism. A representative of the latter view, John Noe, says, "We need to wean ourselves from the idea that the Presence of Jesus, who is God, must be visible or somehow material" (*End Times*, 199). Dispensational premillennialism says that the "first" second coming, the one that is supposed to result in the secret rapture according to 1 Thess 4:16, is itself secret and invisible. But the coming portrayed in that text is a literal, physical, eminently public event: "For the Lord Himself will descend from heaven with a shout, with the voice of the archangel and with the trumpet of God." Three distinct sounds will be heard: Christ's own voice uttering "a cry of command" (ESV) or "a loud command" (NIV)—see Matt 13:41; 24:31; the voice of an archangel—see Rev 11:15; and a trumpet—see Matt 24:31; 1 Cor 15:52.

In the third place Christ's coming will be *sudden* or unexpected. Matthew 24:27 compares it with the instantaneous abruptness of a bolt of lightning: "For just as the lightning comes from the east and flashes even to the west, so will the coming of the Son of Man be" (see Luke 17:24).[7] The comparison of his coming with the coming of a "thief in the night" (1 Thess 5:2) also emphasizes this point: "But be sure of this, that if the head of the house had known at what hour the thief was coming, he would not have allowed his house to be broken into. You too, be ready; for the Son of Man is coming at an hour that you do not expect" (Luke 12:39-40; see Matt 24:43; 2 Pet 3:10; Rev 3:3; 16:15). The suddenness of his coming will be due in part to our preoccupation with ordinary things (Matt 24:37-41), and in part simply to the fact that the exact time of his coming is unknown: "But of that day and hour no one knows, not even the angels of heaven, nor the Son, but the Father alone" (Matt 24:36; see 25:13; Mark 13:32-33; Luke 12:40). This is the basis for the many biblical exhortations to be alert and to be ready for the time of his coming: "For this reason you must be ready; for the Son of Man is coming at an hour when you do not think He will" (Matt 24:44; see Luke 12:40). "Take heed, keep on the alert; for you do not know when the appointed time will come" (Mark 13:33; see 13:34-37; Matt 25:13).

A final point is that Christ's coming will be *triumphant* and glorious. He will return "on the clouds of the sky with power and great glory" (Matt 24:30). He will come "in His glory, and all the angels with Him, then He will sit on His glorious throne" as Ruler and Judge of the universe (Matt 25:31). He will be "revealed from heaven with His mighty angels in flaming fire, dealing out retribution to those who do not know God and to those who do not obey the gospel" (2 Thess 1:7-8). This includes a final, miraculous victory over all his enemies (2 Thess 2:8; Rev 20:9-10), and a celebration of adoring worship from his people, as he comes "to be glorified in His saints on that day, and to be marveled at among all who have believed" (2 Thess 1:10).

What will be the human response to such a glorious event? This depends upon our present relationship to Christ as Savior and Lord. The wicked—those who have not obeyed the gospel (2 Thess 1:8)—in great fear will try to flee and hide (Rev 6:15-17), but this will be futile. God's people, on the other hand, will welcome his coming with rejoicing (1 Pet 4:13).

D. The Time of His Coming

The final aspect of Christ's coming to be discussed here is the *time* of this event. It is indeed his "second" coming (Heb 9:28), in the sense that it is the only time he will come in a personal, visible way similar to his first coming. His coming in his kingdom on the day of Pentecost (Matt 16:28) was a different kind of coming, as was his coming in A.D. 70 at the destruction of Jerusalem, if this event did indeed involve some kind of "coming" of Christ. His *second* coming, in the manner described in the previous section (personal, visible, sudden, and triumphant), is yet in the future.

What can we say about the time of this second coming? The main point is that *we cannot know the time.* This point is stated very specifically in the texts mentioned above in connection with the suddenness of Christ's return. Jesus clearly said that we do not know the day nor the hour (Matt 24:36,42; 25:13; Mark 13:32-33; Luke 12:40). Even though there are specific precursors that will precede his coming, the identity of these is ambiguous enough that we can expect the Parousia at any time yet cannot be dogmatic about it. When Jesus said that we cannot know the day nor the hour, he was not leaving open the possibility that we might know the month or the year or the century of his coming. The same ambiguity applies to these time references. We simply cannot say that Jesus will come on a certain day or even in a certain year. Would-be prophets have embarrassed themselves by attempting to predict specific dates for Christ's return. Early Jehovah's Witnesses said it would happen in 1914 (Gruss, *Speculation*, 20-58). Herbert Armstrong said it would happen in 1975 (1-30). Edgar Whisenant said the secret second coming accompanied by the rapture would take place on September 12, 1988 (see his book, *88 Reasons Why the Rapture Will Be in 1988*). These and all other predictions have invariably turned out to be wrong.

In connection with the time of Christ's return, questions are often raised as to the meaning of NT statements that say, from the perspective of the NT writers themselves, that the day of his coming is *imminent* or very near. In some passages Jesus says his coming will occur while some in his audience were still alive (Matt 10:23; 16:28; 24:34; Mark 9:1; 13:30; Luke 9:27; 21:32). Other passages say the second coming is "near" or "at hand" (Rom 13:11-12; Phil 4:5; Jas 5:8-9; 1 Pet 4:7), or that it will happen "quickly" or "soon" (Rev 22:7,12,20). See Heb 10:37. How may we understand such references?[8]

First, some of these texts do not refer to the second coming as such, but to events in which Christ "came" in a different sense. My conviction is that Matt 16:28 (see 26:64); Mark 9:1; and Luke 9:27 refer to Christ's ascension and enthronement as a prelude to Pentecost. This is why Jesus could say some would still be alive when this took place. It is possible that Matt 24:34; Mark 13:30; and Luke 21:32 refer to the destruction of Jerusalem in A.D. 70, another "coming" which would also be within the lifetime of some in the audience. These texts can be understood in other ways, though. Jesus says, "This generation will not pass away until all these things take place." Hoekema says "this generation" refers not to those chronologically contemporary with Jesus, but to "the rebellious, apostate, unbelieving Jewish people, as they have revealed themselves in the past, are revealing themselves in the present, and will continue to reveal themselves in the future." He shows how the word "generation" (Greek, *genea*) was often used in the Gospels in such a qualitative sense (*Bible*, 116-117). (Both the NASB and the NIV give the alternate translation "race," i.e., the Jewish race, in the margin.) If taken in this sense Matt 24:34 and its parallels could be taken as referring to the second coming without difficulty.[9]

But why do other texts picture Jesus' return as "near" or "soon"? The best understanding of such statements is that they are being made from God's own perspective, not man's. The apostle Peter addresses this very question and gives this very answer in 2 Pet 3:3-9. He says that mockers will call attention to "the promise of His coming" (v. 4), and will demand to know why there has been so long a delay. The key point in Peter's answer is this: "But do not let this one fact escape your notice, beloved, that with the Lord one day is like a thousand years, and a thousand years like one day" (v. 8). From the perspective of eternity, what may seem a long time to us is still "soon" or "near." Wayne Jackson gives an OT example: "Obadiah . . . foretold the final day of earth's history. Concerning that event, he said: 'For the day of Jehovah is *near* upon all the nations . . .' (vs. 15).

This cannot refer to some local judgment, for 'all nations' are to be involved. And yet, the event is depicted as 'near'" (3). Haggai 2:6-7 is another example, referring to something that would happen "in a little while" but which happened no sooner than the coming of the New Covenant (Heb 12:26-28).

One might ask, even from God's perspective, why would Christ's second coming be described as "near" to his first coming? The answer seems to be that once Christ has come the first time and set up his kingdom (the church), the *next main event* in God's plan is indeed the *second* coming of Christ. And in view of the deliberate ambiguity of the precursors, that's how we must regard it as well. Indeed, his coming is near, perhaps at "any moment."

One other issue regarding the time of Christ's coming must be discussed, namely, the issue of preterism. The prefix "preter-" means "beyond," and in a grammatical context it refers to the past, as in "past tense." In eschatology "preterism" is the view that, from our perspective, everything related to the second coming of Jesus is *in the past*. Now, most theologians agree that some events that can be called eschatological are in the past, e.g., the resurrection of Jesus. The view I am presenting here is usually qualified as full, consistent, hyper, or radical preterism. Advocates of this view include James S. Russell, David B. Curtis, John Noe, Max King, and John Bray.

The dominant version of preterism says that everything—*everything*—associated with the second coming of Jesus happened in A.D. 70, in connection with the destruction of Jerusalem as an act of judgment on OT Israel. This includes the antichrist, the man of sin, the second coming of Jesus, the rapture, the resurrection, and the judgment day. Everything predicted in Matthew 24 and in the book of Revelation (which preterists date c. A.D. 65) was fulfilled at that time.

The only way to affirm this, of course, is to say that many of the prophecies were fulfilled not literally or visibly but spiritually. Jesus' return was not visible (Noe, *Top Ten*, 29-43). Curtis says that when Christ came (in A.D. 70), "he literally, yet spiritually, gathered those that were alive to be caught up in the kingdom with Jesus Christ, and Jesus Christ spiritually returned with the believers to the earth, to ever be with them. This was a spiritual event that was visibly manifest in the destruction of Jerusalem" ("Rapture"). The "resurrection of the dead" happened in A.D. 70 when Christ emptied Hades and took the saved to heaven in "heavenly" bodies; they will experience no further resurrection (Noe, *Delusion*, 59-86). The old "heaven and earth" was the world of Old Covenant Judaism; in A.D. 70 it was replaced by a new "heaven and earth," or the New Covenant world (Noe, *End Times*, 223-264). The world we now live in will never be destroyed; it will just continue on without end, with its death and evil enduring forever (ibid., 41-66; Noe, *Top Ten*, 51-52).

A basic rationale for the preterist view is the desire to take seriously the various biblical texts that speak of Jesus' coming as "near" and as happening "soon." Since God's Word never lies, all these texts must have been literally fulfilled within a short time after they were written. At stake is the trustworthiness of God's Word (Noe, *End Times*, 99-109; Curtis, "Inspiration"). And since some of the "imminent return" texts seem to refer to the destruction of Jerusalem in A.D. 70, we can then conclude that all references and events related to the second coming were fulfilled at that time.

At this point I will offer a brief critique of the preterist view. First, it is to be commended for wanting to take the Word of God seriously in every respect. Also, it is to be commended for understanding that much biblical prophecy is figurative, or that it is fulfilled spiritually in spiritual realities rather than in physical realities. Because of this insight preterists are able to offer thoughtful critiques of dispensational premillennialism; see Noe's book, *Shattering the 'Left Behind' Delusion*.

However, I conclude that preterism pushes the spiritualization of prophecy to an extreme. Denying the visible components of the Parousia, including Christ's own presence (see above), the attending angels, and the resurrected and transformed bodies of the saints, simply cannot be reasonably squared with the biblical data. The "spiritual bodies" of those who are raised are much more like the physical bodies we have now than the spiritual essences of angels (see below). Jesus speaks of the resurrection as people coming forth from their tombs (John 5:28-29). The more we spiritualize our resurrection bodies, the more we must spiritualize Christ's own resurrection, in view of the correspondence between them (Phil 3:20-21; 1 John 3:2). Curtis's point about 1 John 3:2 illustrates this. He says that "we will see Him just as He is" means we will see him spiritually, not physically; i.e., we will see him as loving, kind, gentle, and merciful ("Rapture").

I also conclude that preterists are in many ways guilty of the same kind of errors found in dispensationalism. Especially, just as dispensational premillennialists tend to apply many prophecies to the second coming that were actually fulfilled in the first coming, so do preterists wrench many prophecies and statements away from what happened at the first coming and likewise apply them to their version of the second coming. Here are some examples:

(1) Union with Christ in death, burial, resurrection, and enthronement (as in Eph 2:6-7; Col 2:12-13; 3:1-3) were not fully experienced until the "rapture" occurred in A.D. 70 (Noe, *Delusion*, 105-111). Thus "post-A.D.-70 Christians have a tremendous advantage over pre-A.D.-70 Christians. After A.D. 70 we have the fullness of salvation-resurrection reality" (ibid., 87).

(2) According to preterists, A.D. 70 was a key date for the establishment of the kingdom. Noe says the only kingdom the NT knows about is the one "Jesus announced and ushered in during His earthly ministry, and consummated in 70 A.D." (*Top Ten*, 47-48). This ignores the significance of Christ's ascension and its connection with Pentecost as the key events for the establishment of the kingdom (Dan 7:13-14; Matt 10:23; 16:28; Acts 2:32-36).

(3) Preterists say the destruction of Jerusalem was necessary for us to know that Christ's atonement and thus our own salvation are complete. He had "to ap-

pear 'a second time'"—i.e., in A.D. 70—"to show that his sacrifice had been accepted." Otherwise "we can't know for sure if our sins are fully forgiven" (Noe, *End Times*, 192). This gives the destruction of Jerusalem—an event not even recorded in Scripture—the evidentiary significance the Bible gives the resurrection (Rom 1:4; 4:25; 1 Cor 15:12-19).

(4) One of the most serious examples is the idea that the Old Covenant and the role of Judaism in God's plan were set aside not at the time of Christ's death but at the destruction of Jerusalem in A.D. 70. This is seen in Curtis's statement that "the old covenant was taken away in A.D. 70" ("Rapture"). Noe says, "After the destruction of Jerusalem and the Temple, all separation between God and his people was thereby removed" (Noe, *Delusion*, 104). This in effect denies the reconciling power of the blood of Christ, and Paul's specific teaching that the blood of Christ had already brought both Jews and Gentiles near to God at the time he wrote Ephesians 2:11-22, for "through Him we both have our access in one Spirit to the Father" (Eph 2:18). The Old Covenant was fully set aside (Matt 27:51) and the New Covenant established (Luke 22:20) when Christ died. A.D. 70 had nothing to do with it.

I will sum up this point with the general critical observation that preterism is guilty of magnifying and exalting a very limited historical event, one that has a relatively marginal significance in Scripture, to the status of a cosmic redemptive event with eternal significance. The centrality and gravity bestowed upon the A.D. 70 destruction of Jerusalem is completely out of proportion to its treatment in the Bible. Yes, Jesus' Olivet discourse addresses Jerusalem's fate, but even then most of his teaching about this event is in the form of instructions to his followers on how to understand it and cope with it and be saved physically from its horrors. For the Jews themselves it is described simply as "days of vengeance" (Luke 21:22). The awesome universal saving significance attached to it by preterists is without any biblical foundation, and is completely unlike the global event which the Bible pictures the second coming to be (e.g., Matt 24:30; Acts 17:31; Rev 1:7; 6:14-17).

It should also be noted that the biblical texts that refer to the second coming as "near" or happening "soon" do not require that Christ's return be within the lifetime of those contemporary with Jesus, as preterists claim. Earlier in this section we showed how all these texts are perfectly consistent with a still-future Parousia.

Wayne Jackson refers to this radical preterism (the "A.D. 70 doctrine") as "quite heretical" and "radically unorthodox" (2, 5). I agree that it is, both in content and in method. Regarding the latter it reminds me of a book I saw several decades ago called *I Found an Elephant in the Bible*. I do not remember what caused the author to begin looking for an elephant in the Word of God; but once he began looking for it, he found it literally everywhere. For preterists A.D. 70 is the elephant.

III. EVENTS ACCOMPANYING CHRIST'S RETURN

A. The Destruction of His Enemies

Several events will accompany Christ's return. The first is the destruction of his and the church's enemies in an act of divine vengeance. Paul tells us that "the Lord Jesus will be revealed from heaven with His mighty angels in flaming fire, dealing out retribution to those who do not know God and to those who do not obey the gospel of our Lord Jesus" (2 Thess 1:7-8). John saw a symbolic representation of this aspect of Christ's coming in Rev 19:11-16, in which Christ as a victorious King comes riding forth on a white horse with his angelic armies to "strike down the nations" (v. 15).

The immediate result of this retributive aspect of his coming is the physical death of at least the most militant of the hosts of evil, including the man of lawlessness (or antichrist), "whom the Lord will slay with the breath of His mouth and bring to an end by the appearance of His coming" (2 Thess 2:8). Slain with him will be all the armies recruited for the Armageddon assault upon the church (Rev 20:9). Whether all the wicked will suffer physical death at this point is uncertain, but it is a possibility (see 2 Pet 3:7).

This is an aspect of Christ and of his coming that is often ignored, especially by those of a pacifistic bent who want to think of Jesus as only a gentle, nonviolent, nonresisting Lamb. We must remember, though, that wrath is just as inherent in God's nature as love, and so also in the Son of God. This side of his nature will be clearly visible on that day, when the unrighteous from every class and nation will see him revealed in all his wrath and cry out to the mountains and rocks, "Fall on us and hide us from the presence of Him who sits on the throne, and from the wrath of the Lamb; for the great day of their wrath has come, and who is able to stand?" (Rev 6:16-17).

B. The Resurrection of the Dead

The second event accompanying Christ's return will be the resurrection of all the dead, including those who have just perished by "the breath of His mouth." This is the *one and only* bodily resurrection. Some views of the end time separate the resurrection of the righteous from the resurrection of the wicked by 1,000 years (traditional premillennialism) and some by 1,007 years (dispensational premillennialism), but the Bible says they will happen at the same time. Some have misunderstood 1 Thess 4:16, "The dead in Christ will rise first," thinking this is distinguishing the resurrection of "the dead in Christ" from that of the wicked dead. But this is not Paul's point. The wicked dead are not part of this discussion. Paul is comparing *only* the resurrection of dead believers with the transformation of living believers: the *dead* in Christ will rise before the *living* in Christ are changed.

In other passages, though, it is clear that the one resurrection includes both saved and lost. Daniel 12:1-2 speaks of "a time of distress" at which "many of those who sleep in the dust of the ground will awake, these to everlasting life, but the others to disgrace and everlasting contempt." Acts 24:15 declares that "there shall certainly be a resurrection of both the righteous and the wicked." In each case only one resurrection is mentioned, and it includes the saved and the unsaved together.

John 5:28-29 says the same thing: "An hour is coming, in which all who are in the tombs will hear His voice, and will come forth; those who did the good deeds to a resurrection of life, those who committed the evil deeds to a resurrection of judgment." Here the resurrection is distinguished according to kind, but not time. "An hour" is coming—a single hour—when Christ will call *all* the dead to life, possibly with the "cry of command" in 1 Thess 4:16 (ESV). *All* the dead will hear His voice and come forth at the same time. There is but one bodily resurrection.

Revelation 20:4-5 does speak of a "first resurrection" as compared with an implied second resurrection. We have already seen, though, that this first resurrection is the spiritual resurrection that occurs when one is baptized into Christ (Rom 6:3-11; Col 2:12-13). John 5:24-25 refers to this first or spiritual resurrection in which only believers participate, while John 5:28-29 speaks of the second or bodily resurrection experienced by all.

It is important to see that the wicked dead are resurrected at the second coming, just as the righteous are. They do not remain in the disembodied state in which they existed in Hades. They will receive new bodies that will be retained throughout eternity in hell (Matt 5:29-30). It is likewise important to understand that these bodies are not like the bodies that believers will receive. They are in no sense redeemed bodies; they are not the product of Christ's redemptive work and are not patterned after Christ's own glorified resurrection body. We are not told what they will be like. Daniel 12:2 says the lost will come back from the grave "to disgrace and everlasting contempt," and John 5:29 says it is "a resurrection of judgment." Isaiah 66:24 may symbolize their loathsome nature: "For their worm will not die and their fire will not be quenched; and they will be an abhorrence to all mankind." The main point is that the disembodied souls of the wicked will be reunited with a kind of body that is appropriate for their state of eternal punishment.

The resurrection of the righteous, on the other hand, *is* the direct result of Christ's redeeming work; and the day of Christ's return will be the day of "the redemption of our body" (Rom 8:23). Our spirits have already been redeemed, initially dying and rising with Christ in baptism (Rom 6:3-4; 8:10) and being perfected at our physical death (Heb 12:23). The latter event ushers our perfected spirits into the presence of Christ in Paradise (2 Cor 5:8; Phil 1:23), where they remain until the second coming. Then at his coming, "God will bring with Him those who have fallen asleep in Jesus" (1 Thess 4:14). In other words, when he returns, our redeemed spirits accompany him and are sent on down to the earth to be rejoined with redeemed bodies.

What will these new bodies be like? These questions are asked in 1 Cor 15:35:

"How are the dead raised? And with what kind of body do they come?" For one thing the new body will not be the same as the body that died (vv. 36-41), which probably means it will not have the same kind of molecular makeup as our present bodies, much less the very same atoms and molecules. The event of resurrection will not be the restoration and reanimation of rotten corpses and scattered atoms, reconstituted into bodies that burst through the surface of the earth. It will be more in the nature of another act of *ex nihilo* creation, as God gives us a totally new kind of bodily material, adapted to our eternal home rather than to this present earthly one. We will simply be "resomafied." This is the sense in which our bodies will be "transformed" (Phil 3:21).

This does not mean we will have a completely different kind of *shape*. Our bodies will be like Christ's glorified body (Phil 3:21), and when Stephen saw Christ in his new body he readily identified him as the human Jesus (Acts 7:54-60).[10] Thus we have every reason to believe that our new bodies will have the same form as the bodies with which God endowed the human race in the beginning. This implies that in our new bodies we will maintain the same recognizable identities we now possess; hence we will know each other in heaven. We do not know how this applies to infants and children, but we may speculate that God will give to those who die young a body comparable to what their matured earthly bodies would have been.

What more does 1 Corinthians 15 tell us about our new bodies? Some general characteristics are described in verses 42-44, in terms of the contrast between our old bodies and our new ones: "It is sown a perishable body, it is raised an imperishable body; it is sown in dishonor, it is raised in glory; it is sown in weakness, it is raised in power; it is sown a natural body, it is raised a spiritual body." What can we learn from this?

The first contrast is between perishable and imperishable. The present body is corruptible; it can perish. That is, it is subject to disease and decay and destruction. It is marked for death and decomposition; it is a mortal body composed of atoms that can be separated and scattered. The resurrection body, however, will be imperishable or incorruptible. It will not be subject to decay or destruction: "The dead will be raised imperishable . . . . For this perishable must put on the imperishable, and this mortal must put on immortality (1 Cor 15:52-53). This means that the new body will not be subject to disease and death. "But when this perishable will have put on the imperishable, and this mortal will have put on immortality, then will come about the saying that is written, 'Death is swallowed up in victory. O death, where is your victory? O death, where is your sting?'" (1 Cor 15:54-55). Whereas the old body was marked for death, the new body is characterized by life and immortality. "What is mortal will be swallowed up by life" (2 Cor 5:4), and "there will no longer be any death" (Rev 21:4).

The second contrast is between dishonor and glory. Adam's and Eve's original bodies may have been somewhat more "glorious" than post-Fall human bodies; we do not know. Some people work to keep their bodies in top physical condition, but in this fallen world they always come to an inglorious end. As the body grows old it accumulates aches, feebleness, and signs of decay; and in the grave there is nothing honorable about it. The new body, however, is "raised in glory," in "conformity with the body of His glory" (Phil 3:21). This is a wonderful promise for those whose bodies have been ravaged by genetic defects, diseases, or accidents. In their new bodies the blind will see and the lame will walk. Every physical defect will be corrected, because salvation means that we shall be redeemed from every result of sin; and physical defects are ultimately the result of sin. The redemption effected by Christ affects the whole person, soul and body. God will remove not only the sin-stains on the soul, but the marks on the body caused by sin as well.

The next contrast is between weakness and power. Our present physical frame is certainly weak; at best it is capable only of limited tasks. It cannot work long without becoming weak and tired. Its weakness increases near the end of life, frailty and helplessness finally giving way to death. But such will never be the case with the new body, which is "raised in power." All traces and causes of weakness will be gone. "It will be equal to all the requirements of the eternal life. It will never grow weary; never become exhausted; never have to fail because of lack of strength" (Hough, 73).

The final contrast is between a natural body and a spiritual body. The present body is called a natural (*psychikon*) body because it is suited to this natural world. It has the nature and characteristics of the *psyche*, in the sense of the animal life shared by both man and animals. That is, man's natural body belongs to this physical environment. "But if there is a natural body, there is also a spiritual body" (1 Cor 15:44). The difference between the two is that of adaptability to their intended environments. Our present body is an "earthly tent," but our new body is "a building from God, a house not made with hands, eternal in the heavens" (2 Cor 5:1). It is a spiritual body because it will be perfectly adapted to the more spiritual environment of heaven, the new order of nature in which it will live.

We must not assume that because the resurrection body is called "spiritual," it will have no form or substance. As Vos says, "This adjective *Pneumatikon* express-es the quality of the body in the eschatological state. Every thought of immateri-alness, or etherealness or absence of physical density ought to be kept carefully removed from the term" (*Eschatology*, 166). The spiritual body should not be equated with the substance of angels, who are by nature nonbodied spiritual essences designed for the invisible creation. Our new bodies will not be designed for "heaven" in that sense, but for "heaven" in the sense of our eternal home in the new heavens and earth (Rev 21:1). They will be "spiritual" bodies; but they will still be *bodies*, as distinct from our spirits, and will be visible and solid compo-nents of the renewed visible universe.

The most important point is that our new bodies will be patterned after the glorified body of Jesus Christ: "Just as we have borne the image of the earthy

[Adam], we will also bear the image of the heavenly [Christ]" (1 Cor 15:49). Paul says we are eagerly awaiting the return of our Savior, "who will transform the body of our humble state into conformity with the body of His glory" (Phil 3:21). Even though we do not know exactly what this is like, "we know that when He appears, we will be like Him, because we will see Him just as He is" (1 John 3:2). This is the point of Rom 8:29, which says we are predestined to be "conformed to the image of His Son, so that He would be the firstborn among many brethren." The "image of His Son" here is the glorified body he received as "the firstborn from the dead" (Col 1:18), to which our bodies will ultimately be conformed as those subsequently adopted into God's family (Rom 8:23).

We must remember that Christ's glorified body is not the same as the body with which he came out of the tomb and in which he appeared to his followers (except Paul). He retained his old body for evidential purposes, and received his new body only at his ascension (see Cottrell, "Faith"). Thus 1 John 3:2 says, "It has not appeared as yet what we will be." Hence we should not use the Gospel accounts of Christ's resurrection appearances to give us information about the nature of our own new bodies.

The resurrection of the body is a unique element in Christian faith and hope; it is foreign to the pagan concept that only the soul has value and survives forever, while the body is expendable if not an outright curse (see Acts 17:31-32). In the Bible the resurrection of the body is a basic doctrine (Heb 6:1-2) and an essential part of our salvation. This is because our authentic human existence is a wholistic combination of spirit and body; we are not what God created us to be without our bodies. The pagan idea of the immortality of the soul is completely unsatisfactory. The resurrection of our glorified bodies, to be united with our made-perfect spirits (Heb 12:23), will give us an eternally perfect existence.

C. The Transformation of the Living

The third event accompanying Christ's return will be the *transformation* of the bodies of those who are alive at that time. If any of the wicked remain alive after Christ's initial judgment of physical death upon them at his coming, they will be included in this event of transformation. If so, their present bodies will simply be miraculously replaced with bodies like the resurrection bodies of the wicked described above. Scripture is silent on this point, though.

The Bible does speak of what will happen to believers who are alive at the Parousia. Without having to experience physical death, their present physical bodies will be transformed into (replaced by) the glorified, eternal, perfect models equivalent to those received by resurrected believers. The dead are raised first (1 Thess 4:16), and then comes the transformation described in 1 Cor 15:51-52, "Behold, I tell you a mystery; we will not all sleep, but we will all be changed, in a moment, in the twinkling of an eye, at the last trumpet; for the trumpet will sound, and the dead will be raised imperishable, and we [who are still alive] will be changed."

The result of this resurrection of all the dead and the immediate subsequent transformation of all the living is that the surface of the earth is now quite filled with all the members of the human race who have ever lived. They stand there, the righteous and the wicked mixed together, with the revealed Christ still suspended in the air (1 Thess 4:17). Then comes the final great event that accompanies Christ's return: the *rapture*.

D. The Raptures

The concept of the rapture is one of the most controversial and most misunderstood aspects of eschatology. The word "rapture" as such does not appear in Scripture. It is the equivalent, though, of the word for "caught up" in 1 Thess 4:17, which in this context simply means "the physical act of snatching away or taking up." (Sometimes we use the word "rapture" to mean a state of sublime feelings, but that has nothing to do with the rapture associated with Christ's coming.)

The most common view of the rapture is that taught by dispensational premillennialism, as popularized by the Scofield Reference Bible, Hal Lindsey, and the *Left Behind* novels. This view is quite specific and quite dramatic. It is usually called the *secret* rapture, i.e., it is secret in the sense that it takes place in the invisible, spiritual realm. The return of Jesus that results in the rapture is not visible to the world in general. No one except the raptured will see him or know he is there. Also, when believers are raised and transformed, their physical bodies disappear from this world and their new bodies just appear in the spiritual world, totally unseen by those left behind. This instantaneous disappearance is the only thing noticed by the unraptured.

According to this view only believers are involved in this secret rapture and the resurrection that precedes it. The general bodily resurrection of the unsaved is delayed until after the tribulation and the millennium. Also, this view says that the purpose of the secret rapture is to remove believers from the earth during the time of the "great tribulation," which will conclude the seven-year period that begins immediately after the rapture and is climaxed with the Battle of Armageddon.

In my judgment this view is mistaken in practically every sense. The Bible presents a totally different view of the rapture, indeed, one that makes the entire dispensational interpretation of the end time impossible.

We affirm that the Bible does teach that there will be a rapture. Many assume that the rapture is a concept peculiar to the dispensational view. Thus they think that those who reject this view also reject the idea of a rapture. This is not so. There will be a rapture, but not the *secret* rapture described above. In 1 Thess 4:17 Paul speaks specifically of our being "caught up," i.e., raptured, to meet the Lord in the air. But it is clear from this passage itself that the return of Jesus and its accompanying rapture can hardly be a secret. The Lord "will descend from heaven with a shout, with the voice of the archangel and with the trumpet of

God, and the dead in Christ will rise first. Then we who are alive and remain will be caught up together with them in the clouds to meet the Lord in the air" (1 Thess 4:16-17). The idea of secrecy is totally contradicted by the array of sounds that are calculated to draw attention to Christ's presence; they are an audible announcement to the whole earth that the Lord has come.

The point of the rapture is simply that when Christ comes, all believers, after being either raised or transformed, will be taken up to meet him in the air at some point in his descent from heaven. But contrary to the dispensational view, there is nothing secret or invisible about it.

Another aspect of the Bible's rapture teaching also contradicts the dispensational view. This aspect, which is practically unnoticed among Bible students of all stripes, is that there are actually *two* raptures, one for the wicked and one for the righteous. And the most surprising fact of all is that *the wicked are raptured first.*

In 1 Thessalonians Paul does not comment on the rapture ("taking up") of the wicked, but other passages do. The parable of the tares in Matt 13:24-30 is especially clear. Here Jesus pictures the wheat and the tares (weeds) as growing together "until the harvest; and in the time of the harvest I will say to the reapers, 'First gather up the tares and bind them in bundles to burn them up; but gather the wheat into my barn'" (v. 30). The tares go first.

Someone may say, "So what? That's just a parable." Yes, but Jesus himself has given the meaning of the parable in Matt 13:37-43. The field is the world, and the harvest is the end of the age. The tares are the wicked, and the wheat represents the righteous. The reapers are angels (vv. 38-39). "So just as the tares are gathered up and burned with fire, so shall it be at the end of the age. The Son of Man will send forth His angels," and they will gather the wicked out from among His kingdom (i.e., rapture them) and take them ultimately to judgment (vv. 40-42). The righteous will be left behind, standing alone in their glorified bodies (v. 43). Only then will occur the rapture described in 1 Thess 4:17, as the company of the redeemed are lifted up to meet the Lord in the air (see Matt 24:31).

But does not Jesus say that two men will be working in the field, and one will be *taken* while the other is left behind? and that two women will be grinding at the mill, and one will be *taken* and the other left behind (Matt 24:40-41)? Yes, but *which one* is taken, and *which one* is left behind? The uncritical assumption is that the righteous is the one taken, and the wicked the one left behind. But Jesus' point is actually the opposite, as a simple comparison with the analogous event of the flood clearly shows. In the preceding verses Jesus says "the coming of the Son of Man will be just like the days of Noah," when unbelievers were preoccupied with ordinary things, "and they did not understand until the flood came and took them all away; so will the coming of the Son of Man be" (Matt 24:37-39). Here it is clear that those "taken away" by the flood are the wicked. Since the Son's coming will be "just like" this, we have to conclude that those "taken" at that time will also be the wicked. It has simply been mistakenly assumed that those taken are the saved. The saved are actually the ones left behind, but only for a brief time. Almost immediately after the rapture of the wicked (Matt 13:41), the rapture described in 1 Thess 4:17 will occur.

What, then, is the state of things on earth after the rapture (or raptures)? It is left *totally empty* of human occupants, dead or alive, saved or unsaved. This raises the question of the purpose of the rapture: *why* is everyone raptured out of the earth? It should be obvious that it has nothing to do with escaping some kind of "great tribulation," as many think. Rather, the purpose of the rapture is to empty the world, the physical universe, for the great renewing fire described in 2 Pet 3:10-13. This will be discussed in the next chapter.

NOTES ON CHAPTER THIRTY

[1] See the discussion of the view called "preterism" on pp. 541-543.

[2] In his commentary on Luke (338) Mark Black says Luke 21:5-24 (equivalent to Matt 24:1-22) refers to the fall of Jerusalem, while Luke 21:25-33 (equivalent to Matt 24:23-35) refers to the second coming.

[3] One manuscript tradition for 2 Thess 2:3 reads "man of sin" instead of "man of lawlessness" (see KJV, NKJV).

[4] This is one reason I speak of the "precursors" of his coming rather than the "signs" of his coming. A precursor is simply something that comes before or precedes something else, and which may or may not function as a sign of the latter.

[5] Thus the book of *Revelation* is sometimes called the *Apocalypse*.

[6] The word has been Anglicized so that in English discourse the second coming is often called the Parousia.

[7] This statement is not meant to imply that Jesus' appearance at his second coming will necessarily be in "the eastern sky."

[8] See Hoekema, *Bible*, 111-127, for a good discussion of this.

[9] Hoekema well says, "The insistence that these passages require a Parousia within the generation of those who were contemporaries of Jesus is clearly at variance with Jesus' own disavowal of the knowledge of the time of his return" (*Bible*, 113).

[10] John's visions of Jesus in the book of Revelation were highly symbolic (Rev 1:12-16; 5:6).

CHAPTER THIRTY-ONE
THE FINAL JUDGMENT

W e now begin to consider the final things related to the "final things," namely, the last judgment and the final states of heaven and hell. In this chapter we will deal with various aspects of the final judgment.

The reality and certainty of the final judgment are clear themes of Scripture. Popular wisdom says only two things are certain: death and taxes. The Bible's two certainties are slightly different: "It is appointed for men to die once and after this comes judgment" (Heb 9:27). We have God's word on it, from both the OT and the NT. "For God will bring every act to judgment, everything which is hidden, whether it is good or evil" (Eccl 12:14; see Ps 96:13). The resurrection of Jesus Christ is the guarantee of judgment: God "has fixed a day in which He will judge the world in righteousness through a Man whom He has appointed, having furnished proof to all men by raising Him from the dead" (Acts 17:31). The "eternal judgment" is one of the foundational teachings of the Christian faith (Heb 6:1-2).

Where will the judgment be held? Some have assumed that it will take place on this earth, immediately following Christ's return. Cox (147) says the saints are raptured "to meet the Lord in the air . . . for the purpose of escorting him to the earth. The Lord, upon coming to the earth 'with his saints,' will immediately inaugurate the general and final judgment." I disagree. When Jesus returns he will leave his place beside the Father in the invisible universe and come into our dimension and into our sight. When the raptures (plural) occur, both the righteous and the wicked will be taken away, not only from the surface of the earth but from the visible universe altogether. This universe will be completely emptied of human occupants. Everyone (including Christ) will pass through the dimensional barrier into the invisible universe, where God's presence is manifested to the angels and where the glorified Christ joins him once again upon his throne. This is the throne before which all will be gathered in order to be judged (Matt 25:31; Rev 4:2; 20:11).

I. THE UNITY OF THE JUDGMENT

How many end-time judgments will there be? Those who accept the dispensational premillennial (secret rapture) view distinguish at least three judgments of human beings, and sometimes more. J.D. Pentecost has a total of four: (1) the "judgment seat of Christ" (2 Cor 5:10), which occurs just after the rapture to assign rewards to believers (*Things*, 219-226); (2) a judgment upon Israel (Matt 25:1-30) just after Christ's visible return and prior to the millennium (ibid., 413-415); (3) the judgment upon the living Gentiles or nations (Matt 25:31-46) immediately after the judgment upon Israel (ibid., 415-422); and (4) the great white throne judgment (Rev 20:11-15), which applies only to the unsaved dead (ibid., 423-426) and occurs after the millennium.

Contrary to this, I agree with the amillennial view that there will be just one judgment associated with Christ's second coming. Christ will return, all the dead will be raptured from the earth and brought before God's throne, and the judgment will take place, to be followed immediately by the final states. Scripture always refers to a single "day" or time of judgment, not several days or times. First John 4:17 speaks of believers' confidence "in the day of judgment." Jesus is able to safeguard all that we "have entrusted to Him until that day" (2 Tim 1:12). In Matt 7:22 Jesus describes some of the futile appeals of the lost "on that day" (see 2 Thess 1:10). Romans 2:5 speaks of "the day of wrath and revelation of the righteous judgment of God" (see Matt 11:22). Jesus says, "He who rejects Me and does not receive My sayings, has one who judges him; the word I spoke is what will judge him at the last day" (see 2 Pet 3:7; Jude 6). In all these references a single day of judgment is in view.

Matthew 25:31-46 pictures this one judgment day as being sandwiched between the one second coming of Jesus and the eternal states. "When the Son of Man comes in His glory" he separates the individuals of all nations into two groups, the saved on his right hand and the lost on his left hand. As soon as the separation has been made and explained, the wicked are sent away to their eternal fate (vv. 41,46), and the righteous to eternal life (v. 46). There is no mention of a millennial interval. Matthew 16:27 likewise associates the judgment of "every man" with the second coming (see 2 Tim 4:1), and Rev 11:18 says all will be judged at the same time: "And the nations were enraged, and Your wrath came, and the time came for the dead to be judged, and the time to reward Your bond-servants the prophets and the saints and those who fear Your name, the small and the great, and to destroy those who destroy the earth" (see 1 Cor 4:5).

There is only one final day of judgment.

II. WHO WILL BE THE JUDGE?

Who will be the Judge before whom we stand on the day of judgment? Scripture clearly speaks of "God, the Judge of all" (Heb 12:23), and of "God's righteous judgment" (2 Thess 1:5). Paul speaks of standing "before the judgment seat of God" (Rom 14:10). That this refers to God the Father is seen in Matt 18:35; 1 Pet 1:17; 2:23. However, it is also clear that the Judge before whom we will stand is Jesus Christ, God the Son. Jesus has told us that "not even the Father judges anyone, but He has given all judgment to the Son" (John 5:22). The Father "gave Him the authority to execute judgment, because He is the Son of Man" (John 5:27). In Matt 25:31-46 it is clearly the Son of Man who sits on the throne and judges the nations. Thus we will stand before "the judgment seat of Christ" (2 Cor 5:10), "who is to judge the living and the dead" (2 Tim 4:1; see 4:8).

How must we understand this? The answer seems to be that even though God the Father has the inherent authority to judge, he has delegated this authority to the man Jesus Christ, who is also God the Son. Paul explains that the Father "has fixed a day in which He will judge the world in righteousness through a Man whom He has appointed," namely, Jesus Christ (Acts 17:31; see 10:42). "God will judge the secrets of men through Christ Jesus" (Rom 2:16). Thus it seems that God the Father will judge us only in the sense that he will occupy the judgment throne alongside God the Son, to whom he has delegated the authority and prerogative to do the actual judging.[1]

III. THE OBJECT OF THE JUDGMENT

On the day of judgment, exactly what will be judged? The answer seems to be that on that day, *all* the works of *all* people will be judged. God is described as the "Judge of all" (Heb 12:23). When Heb 9:27 says that "it is appointed for men to die once and after this comes judgment," no exceptions are made. God is ready to judge "the living and the dead" (1 Pet 4:5; see 2 Tim 4:1), "both the righteous man and the wicked man" (Eccl 3:17); he will "judge the world" (Rom 3:6); "all the nations will be gathered before Him" (Matt 25:32). "We will all stand before the judgment seat of God," says Paul. "So then each one of us will give an account of himself to God" (Rom 14:10,12). In 2 Cor 5:10 also he says, "We must all appear before the judgment seat of Christ."

We readily accept the idea that the wicked will be judged (Jude 14-15), but some have been misled to think that the righteous will not go through the judgment. Sometimes John 5:24 is interpreted to mean this: "Truly, truly, I say to you, he who hears My word, and believes Him who sent Me, has eternal life, and does not come into judgment, but has passed out of death into life." This is a false understanding of this verse, though. The word for "judgment" (*krisis*) often means a *negative* judgment, i.e., "condemnation." The NIV gives the correct sense: whoever hears and believes "will not be condemned" (see Rom 8:1). But as for the judgment event as such, the universal references noted above ("all," "each one," "the world") clearly include believers. This is especially true of Romans 14:10 and 2 Cor 5:10, where Paul uses first person plural ("we"), including himself and all Christians. In Matt 25:31-46 the sheep are judged along with the goats. Certainly, "the Lord will judge His people" (Heb 10:30). See Jas 3:1; 1 Pet 4:17.

Exactly what aspects of our lives will be judged? The answer seems to be, *every one of them*. The Bible puts a lot of emphasis on the fact that we will all be judged according to our *works*, according to what we have done in this life.

Solomon in 2 Chr 6:30 expresses the expectation that God will "render to each according to all his ways." This language is repeated numerous times in the OT. For example, God "pays a man according to his work" (Job 34:11); he will "recompense a man according to his work" (Ps 62:12). God says, "I, the LORD, search the heart, I test the mind, even to give to each man according to his ways, according to the results of his deeds" (Jer 17:10). In the OT see also Prov 24:12; Eccl 12:13-14; Isa 59:18; Jer 32:19; Ezek 33:20.

The NT repeats this truth many times. Jesus says that when he returns in glory he "will repay every man according to his deeds" (Matt 16:27). Paul says that "the righteous judgment of God" means that he "will render to each person according to his deeds" (Rom 2:5-6). "We must all appear before the judgment seat of Christ, so that each one may be recompensed for his deeds in the body, according to what he has done, whether good or bad" (2 Cor 5:10). The Father "impartially judges according to each one's work" (1 Pet 1:17). The Messiah promises, "Behold, I am coming quickly, and My reward is with Me, to render to every man according to what he has done" (Rev 22:12). In the NT see also Matt 12:36-37; 25:31-46; Acts 10:34-35; 1 Cor 3:13; Eph 6:8; Col 3:25; Rev 2:23; 20:12.

Special emphasis is put on the fact that even our secret or hidden deeds will be made known, and even the thoughts and motives of our hearts. "God will bring every act to judgment, everything which is hidden, whether it is good or evil" (Eccl 12:14). Secret piety will be rewarded (Matt 6:4,6,18) and secret sins revealed (Luke 12:2), since "God will judge the secrets of men" (Rom 2:16). When the Lord comes he "will both bring to light the things hidden in the darkness and disclose the motives of men's hearts" (1 Cor 4:5). See 1 Tim 4:14-15.

By what standard will our works be judged? Quite simply, by the standard of "the revealed will of God" (Hoekema, *Bible*, 259), whether it be that which is known only through general revelation (Rom 1:18-32; 2:14-15) or that which is known through special revelation also, i.e., the teachings of Scripture. This standard will be applied to everyone in the same way. Each person will be judged impartially by whatever light is available to him, i.e., in accordance with his conscientious response to available light. This makes it clear that God as a righteous judge is judging impartially, "for there is no partiality with God" (Rom 2:11). Peter stated it thus: "God is not one to show partiality, but in every nation the man who fears Him and does what is right is welcome to Him" (Acts 10:34-35). See Eph 6:8-9; 1 Pet 1:17. Indeed, "His judgments are true and righteous" (Rev 19:2).

IV. THE PURPOSE OF THE JUDGMENT

It is important to understand the *purpose* of the judgment day. One thing is clear: its purpose is *not* to determine who will be saved and who will be lost. The omniscient God does not need a final examination of each person's records in order to make such a decision. In fact he foreknew everyone's life history even before the foundation of the world, and had already predestined believers to heaven as a result (Rom 8:29). But even from man's standpoint, a judgment day is not needed for this purpose. Even before we die, believers in a sense are already judged; in the act of justification God is saying, "No penalty for you!" (see Rom 8:1,31-39; Phil 3:9-10; 1 John 4:17; Jude 24). Those who are thus saved by grace are supposed to have an assurance of their saved status. Also, at the point of death a saved person enters the bliss of Paradise and a lost person enters the torment of Hades. At the second coming itself, after the resurrection and transformation, the human race is transported to the scene of the judgment in two waves, the wicked first and then the righteous. Thus the decision as to who is saved and who is lost has already been made before the judgment itself begins.

So what is the purpose of the judgment? For one thing, this event is the occasion for the first formal *separation* of the entire company of the saved from the entire host of the lost. While living upon the earth, the saved and the lost are mingled together (Matt 13:30,47-49). They are separated at death, but at the resurrection are intermingled again. Then the two-stage rapture functions as a prelude to the final judgment, as one band of angels pluck away the lost (Matt 13:41) and deposit them on the Judge's left hand (Matt 25:33), while another group of angels rapture the saved (Matt 24:31) and deposit them at the Judge's right hand (Matt 25:33). Here at the judgment scene, for the first time, a complete and final separation occurs.

This will also be the occasion for the first public *proclamation* of the fate of each individual. When one enters his specific intermediate state at death, this is primarily a private experience. But at the final judgment scene Jesus says to the saved in the presence of all, "Come, you who are blessed of My Father, inherit the kingdom prepared for you from the foundation of the world" (Matt 25:34). Likewise he says to the lost, "Depart from Me, accursed ones, into the eternal fire which has been prepared for the devil and his angels" (Matt 25:41; see 7:23).

One could say, however, that such separation and proclamation are not really *necessary*, i.e., that the final states could be ushered in without them. Thus there must be some deeper purpose for the judgment day, whereby something may be accomplished that God considers to be very important if not necessary. What might this be? The answer may be summed up in one word: *vindication*. The public examination of every person's deeds will vindicate God's decision regarding each person's eternal destiny. As mentioned above, it will demonstrate God's righteousness and impartiality in judgment. No one will be able to accuse God of being unfair, nor have any basis for complaint about his fate. Everyone will be "without excuse" (Rom 1:20; 2:1); every mouth will be closed (Rom 3:19). God will be glorified in his justice because it will be made clear that those who are lost are getting what they deserve, and he will be glorified in his grace because it will be made clear that those who are saved are getting the opposite of what they deserve. "What is therefore central on the day of judgment is not the destinies of individuals but the glory of God" (Hoekema, *Bible*, 254).

This same rationale for the judgment applies also to the fact that a final judgment according to works will demonstrate God's righteousness in assigning specific degrees of reward and punishment to those who are judged. That different degrees of punishment will be meted out to the lost seems to be the point of Luke 12:47-48, "And that slave who knew his master's will and did not get ready or act in accord with his will, will receive many lashes, but the one who did not know it, and committed deeds worthy of a flogging, will receive but few. From everyone who has been given much, much will be required; and to whom they entrusted much, of him they will ask all the more." Concerning the hypocritical religious leaders of his day Jesus said, "These will receive greater condemnation" (Luke 20:47). He also said that it will be "more tolerable" for some than others "in the day of judgment" (Matt 11:22-24). This is true because some commandments have greater significance than others (Matt 22:36-40), some sins are worse than others (Matt 23:23), and some people have more opportunity than others (Matt 11:22-24).

The same applies to degrees of reward. In Jesus' parable of the nobleman and his stewards ("the parable of the pounds"), one steward is rewarded by being given authority over ten cities, and another by being given authority over five cities (Luke 19:17-18). In 1 Cor 3:12-15 "the quality of each man's work" will be tested as with fire. The works of some are equated with gold, silver, and jewels; these pass the test and result in a reward. The works of others are compared with wood, hay, and straw; these fail the test, resulting in salvation without rewards. Greater responsibility results in "stricter judgment" (Jas 3:1), implying variable rewards. See also Matt 5:19; 6:19-21; 18:4; 2 Cor 9:6; see Grudem (*Theology*, 1144) for other related texts.

What determines the degree of reward or punishment? Nothing other than the individual's works; this is a main reason for the examination of each person's deeds. Such an examination requires not only the analysis of our good works, but also the full exposure of our sins (Eccl 12:14; 2 Cor 5:10). Some believers mistakenly think that their sins will not be brought out on that day, based on Ps 103:12 and Jer 31:34 (see Heb 8:12; 10:17). The latter texts say that under the New Covenant God "will remember their sins no more." These texts do not mean, though, that the omniscient God literally forgets about our sins and never mentions them at the judgment; they mean that, thanks to the blood of the New Covenant, he will *never hold them against us again.* They will never condemn us, not even on the day of judgment. But they *will* be displayed.

But why is this necessary? Again, from God's perspective it is not necessary; because of his total knowledge of every aspect of our lives, good and bad, he is perfectly able fairly to assign degrees of reward to the saved and degrees of punishment to the lost without a public examination of their works. But again, the issue is the vindication of the righteousness of God. By judging us according to our own works, God's impartiality again is demonstrated; and the degrees of reward and punishment assigned to all are shown to be utterly fair.

We must remember that everyone who reaches heaven will be saved by grace; admission to heaven as such is not related to the extent of one's labor in the kingdom (Matt 20:1-16). Also, in heaven no degree of reward is literally deserved (Luke 17:10). That God determines to assign such rewards is also a matter of grace, and the various degrees of reward experienced by individual believers are determined by a fair examination of each one's works. What we are not told, however, is exactly how these various degrees of reward are assigned and experienced. Many think it will have to do with our relative subjective capacities to enjoy the blessings of eternal life (Hoekema, *Bible*, 264), rather than with differences in our external environment.

V. JUSTIFIED BY FAITH, YET JUDGED BY WORKS?

We have seen that even the saved will be judged according to their works, including their evil deeds (2 Cor 5:10). This raises a serious question, namely, how is this consistent with the fact that we are *justified by faith* apart from a consideration of works, good or bad (Rom 3:28)? If we are justified by faith, how can we be judged by works?

That there is no conflict here can be seen in several ways. First, we have just noted that believers, though justified by faith, are judged by works in order to determine or at least publicly expose the basis for the degree of their rewards. Second, "the intimate connection between faith and works" (Hoekema, *Bible*, 261) warrants a display of one's works as objective evidence of the presence of subjective faith. "Faith must reveal itself in works, and works, in turn, are the evidence of true faith" (ibid.). This again is a matter of the public vindication of God's judgment, since he himself does not need to review our works in order to determine whether or not we have faith.

Third, it may be that in the many passages which speak of judgment according to works, the term "works" and its equivalents are being used not in the technical Pauline sense of "any response to the law of the Creator" but in the more general sense of "what we do," as in John 6:28-29. Thus when Scripture says that a man will "be recompensed for his deeds in the body, according to what he has done" (2 Cor 5:10), "what he has done" may well include making a positive response to the gospel, including believing and repenting. Indeed, if God's revealed will is the standard by which we are judged, his revealed will ("the word I spoke," John 12:48) includes both law and gospel. Where the final judgment is concerned, our examined "works"—"what we do"—will include our responses to both. Those who have rejected the gospel or who have never heard it will be judged only according to what they have done in response to law (Rom 2:7-10), but those who have accepted the gospel will be judged according to their response to this aspect of God's revealed will. In each case the judgment is in terms of what one has done.

Finally, a close examination of the judgment scene as described in Rev 20:11-

15 shows that there is no conflict between justification by faith and judgment according to works. This passage says:

> Then I saw a great white throne and Him who sat upon it, from whose presence earth and heaven fled away, and no place was found for them. And I saw the dead, the great and the small, standing before the throne, and books were opened; and another book was opened, which is the book of life; and the dead were judged from the things which were written in the books, according to their deeds. And the sea gave up the dead which were in it, and death and Hades gave up the dead which were in them; and they were judged, every one of them according to their deeds. Then death and Hades were thrown into the lake of fire. This is the second death, the lake of fire. And if anyone's name was not found written in the book of life, he was thrown into the lake of fire.

This text seems to say there will be two stages through which all will pass at the final judgment. The first is a judgment according to "the books"; the second is a judgment according to "the book of life" (v. 12). When John says "the books were opened," this refers either to the books in which all men's works are recorded, or to the books that contain the standard by which these works will be judged. In either case, judgment by "the books" is a judgment according to deeds, a judgment to which everyone is subjected (vv. 12-13).

What is significant, though, is that this works-judgment based on "the books" is not the final word in the judging process. Rather, the final determination of each person's fate is based on judgment according to "the book of life," indeed, the *Lamb's* book of life (Rev 13:8; 21:27). The idea seems to be that, after the first phase of the judgment, the one according to works, *no one* is found to be worthy of entrance into heaven. But when the Lamb's book of life is consulted, it is found that some have not trusted in their works but have accepted God's offer of grace; these and these alone are admitted into heaven, not on the basis of their works but on the basis of the blood of the Lamb. But "if anyone's name was not found written in the book of life, he was thrown into the lake of fire" (v. 15). In the final analysis this and this alone determines who will be in heaven and who will be in hell.

The purpose of the first stage (judgment according to works, even for believers) has been explained above. But here we may note one more benefit of requiring believers to confront all their works, even their sins, before the final and fully expected verification of their salvation is announced from the book of life. As a result of this full disclosure and remembrance of our works at the very threshold of heaven, it will be made perfectly plain that the *only* reason we are saved for eternity is because of God's infinite grace and mercy. God's own mercy is thereby glorified, and we will enter heaven with hearts that are overflowing with gratitude and praise to the Redeemer.

NOTES ON CHAPTER THIRTY-ONE

[1]There is also a sense in which believers themselves will "judge the world" and even "judge angels" (1 Cor 6:2-3; see Rev 20:4), but it is not explained how this will be. See Erickson, *Theology*, 1208.

CHAPTER THIRTY-TWO

HEAVEN

Immediately following the day of judgment, the two groups are taken to what will be their final and eternal abodes. The saved are escorted to what we call "heaven," and the lost are cast into what we usually call "hell." These are the eternal states, the eternal destinies of all mankind.

This chapter deals with the subject of heaven, about which there is considerable speculation and a lot of misunderstanding. Hoekema asks, "Are we to spend eternity somewhere off in space, wearing white robes, plucking harps, singing songs, and flitting from cloud to cloud while doing so?" (*Bible*, 274). Popular piety often pictures heaven thus, but such a picture is far from biblical, as we shall see.

I. DO WE GO TO HEAVEN WHEN WE DIE?

All Christians look forward to "going to heaven"; this is one of the main things that make death (and often life itself) bearable. It is a main element in our "blessed hope" (Titus 2:13). But what does it mean to go to heaven? Do we go to heaven when we die? The answer actually depends on what is meant by the word "heaven." This word occurs hundreds of times in the Bible,[1] and it is used in several different senses.

A. The Cosmological Heaven

The term "heaven" often refers to that part of the cosmos (the visible universe) that is not the earth. Erickson (*Theology*, 1233) calls this its *cosmological* sense. Thus the terms "heaven" (singular or plural) and "earth" are frequently combined to represent the entire universe, e.g., "In the beginning God created the heavens and the earth" (Gen 1:1; see Exod 20:11; Ps 115:15; Isa 42:5; Matt 5:18; Heb 1:10: Rev 10:6).

Since from our earthly perspective the rest of the universe always seems to be above our heads, in the Bible "heaven" is used for any aspect of the universe that is above us or overhead. It refers to the air where birds fly (Gen 1:20; Matt 6:26; 8:20). It refers to the atmosphere where clouds exist (Ps 147:8) and whence come rain, snow, and hail (Josh 10:11; Deut 11:11,17; Isa 55:10; Acts 14:17). It also refers to the sky as such, the firmament or expanse where the heavenly bodies are (Gen 1:8,14-17; 26:4; Ps 19:1; 33:6; Matt 16:2-3; Acts 2:5; Col 1:23). In this last sense Christ will appear in the heavens, i.e., in the sky, when he returns (Matt 24:29-31; 26:64; Acts 1:1-11; see Rev 6:13-14).

B. The Theological Heavens

The term "heaven" is also used in what we may call a *theological* sense, because of its connection with God (*theos*). God and heaven are so closely related that heaven (in this sense) may reasonably be defined as "wherever God is," or "the dwelling place of God." In fact, when the Bible uses the word in this theological sense, it refers to two different heavens that presently exist.

One heaven is the *divine dimension* itself. In this sense heaven is not a place where God dwells but is actually the equivalent of God. When used thus, as Erickson notes, "'heaven' is a virtual synonym for God" (*Theology*, 1234). Because of this identity Scripture can use the phrases "kingdom of God" and "kingdom of heaven" interchangeably. God is "the God of heaven" (Ezra 1:2; Neh 1:4-5). We can speak of our Father who is "in heaven" (Matt 5:16,45; 6:1,9; 7:11,21). In this sense God looks upon us "from heaven" (Deut 26:15; Ps 14:2; 33:13; Isa 63:10); he hears "from heaven" (1 Kgs 8:30; 2 Chr 7:14); he speaks "from heaven" (Matt 3:17; John 12:28); he gives signs "from heaven" (Matt 16:1; Luke 11:16). In this sense John's baptism is "from heaven," i.e., from God (Matt 21:25); we sin "against heaven," i.e., against God (Luke 15:18); and our names are recorded "in heaven," i.e., in the mind of God (Luke 10:20; Heb 12:23). Also, this is the sense in which at his first coming Christ "descended from heaven" (John 3:13; see 3:31; 6:38,41-42,50-51,58).

The other theological heaven is the *divine throne room* located in the invisible universe, in the spiritual cosmos where angels dwell.[2] This is the sense in which angels are "in heaven" (Matt 22:30; 24:36; Rev 5:13). This is why they come "from heaven" when they visit our universe; God sends them to us from his presence as messengers (Matt 28:2; Luke 22:43; Rev 20:1). This is the place to which they return when they go back "into heaven" (Luke 2:15).

This is the heaven John entered after he saw "a door standing open in heaven" and was invited to go through it (Rev 4:1). He saw immediately that "a throne was standing in heaven; and One was sitting on the throne" (Rev 4:2). This was God himself (Ps 11:4; Matt 5:34; 23:22) in the spiritual theophany by which he permanently manifests himself to the angelic world. Because of this theophany Jesus says that the "angels in heaven continually see the face of My Father who is in heaven" (Matt 18:10). Because it is located in a part of the spiritual world, his throne room is thus a *place* within that universe. This place is called heaven, precisely because God's presence is there. In this sense it is his "abode."

This is the "heaven" that Jesus entered when he was received or carried "up into heaven" (Mark 16:19; Luke 24:51; see Acts 1:11). At the present time, in his glorified human body, Jesus is seated in this heaven upon the heavenly throne at God's own right hand (Acts 2:34; 3:21; 7:56; Eph 6:9; Heb 8:1; 9:24; 1 Pet

3:22). This is also the heaven from which he will return at the time of his second coming (1 Thess 1:10; 4:16; 2 Thess 1:7).

At times in Scripture the cosmological "heaven above" and the theological heavens seem to be conceptually merged, in the sense that the latter are also depicted as being spatially located somewhere above us, among or beyond the stars. Thus in a figurative sense God is pictured as *looking down* from heaven: "He looked down from His holy height; from heaven the LORD gazed upon the earth" (Ps 102:19; see Deut 26:15; Ps 14:2; 53:2). Also, men are pictured as *looking up* to God in heaven: "To You I lift up my eyes, O You who are enthroned in the heavens!" (Ps 123:1; see Mark 7:34). Jesus "descends" from heaven both at his first coming (John 3:13; 6:38) and at his second (1 Thess 4:16). Though this directional language should not be taken literally, this merging of the two concepts of heaven does mean that at times the phrase "heaven and earth" includes the invisible universe as well as the visible (e.g., Matt 28:18; 1 Cor 8:5; Eph 1:10; 3:15; Col 1:16,20; Jas 5:12; Rev 5:3,13).

C. To Which Heaven Do We Go?

Our original question was, do we go to heaven when we die? The answer is yes, those who are saved do go to heaven at the moment of death. But now we must ask, *which heaven?* And even more importantly, will this be the heaven in which we will spend eternity?

To which heaven do we go? Obviously we do not go to the cosmological heaven, the one filled with stars and clouds. Nor do we go to the first theological heaven explained above, i.e., the divine dimension itself. Heaven in this sense is simply not accessible to created beings, not even to angels. This divine dimension is not a place, not even a spiritual place; it is God himself in his uncreated, invisible, immortal glory. This leaves only one option, namely, the second theological heaven described above, the divine throne room located in the created invisible universe. When we die, our disembodied spirits will be transported into this spiritual heaven, to rest in the presence of God until the time of the second coming.

What we are talking about, of course, is the *intermediate state* discussed in a previous chapter. The "heaven" to which we go when we die is indeed the heaven where God is seated on his throne and surrounded by angels. *But this is not our final state, our final heaven.* This is only our temporary, intermediate state, what Gilmore calls "Intermediate Heaven" (107). A serious point of confusion is that many people assume that this heaven is the one we will inhabit for eternity. *This is not the case.* At the second coming our spirits leave this heaven to accompany Christ in his second coming to this earth (1 Thess 4:14), where our spirits are then resomafied, or reunited with new bodies—glorified resurrection bodies. Then we all return to the throne room-heaven for the final judgment. Once that is completed, then we are ready to be transported to our final destiny, our eternal home: *the new earth.* This will be a kind of heaven, since God's presence will be there (see below), but it is not the heaven to which we go when we die. In fact, it does not even exist yet.

II. THE NEW HEAVENS AND THE NEW EARTH

At the time of the raptures, first the wicked and then the righteous are transported from this world into the divine throne room. Then two great events will take place simultaneously. One is the final judgment, which is carried out in the spiritual universe. The other is the cosmic holocaust described in 2 Pet 3:10-13, when the now-empty physical universe is renewed by God's cleansing fire. The very purpose of the raptures is to allow this second event to take place, so that God can prepare the final and eternal home for his redeemed people.

God first revealed his plan to create a new universe in Isa 65:17-25. He says, "For behold, I create new heavens and a new earth; and the former things will not be remembered or come to mind" (v. 17). The description that follows no doubt contains some symbolic imagery, e.g., the references to death (v. 20), childbearing (v. 23), and animals (v. 25). The overall picture, though, is of a paradise-like environment that will be a source of everlasting joy (v. 18).[3] The eternal nature of this new heavens and new earth is also emphasized in a similar prophecy given through Isaiah: "'For just as the new heavens and the new earth which I make will endure before Me,' declares the LORD, 'so your offspring and your name will endure'" (Isa 66:22).

In the NT the apostle Peter alludes to these prophecies when he speaks of the ascended Christ, "whom heaven must receive until the time for restoring all the things about which God spoke by the mouth of his holy prophets long ago" (Acts 3:21, ESV; see Matt 19:28). In Rom 8:19-22 the apostle Paul speaks in more detail about the coming day when the present universe will be set free from the curse that has permeated and corrupted it since sin entered it as recorded in Gen 3:1-19. Paul says,

> For the anxious longing of the creation waits eagerly for the revealing of the sons of God. For the creation was subjected to futility, not willingly, but because of Him who subjected it, in hope that the creation itself also will be set free from its slavery to corruption into the freedom of the glory of the children of God. For we know that the whole creation groans and suffers the pains of childbirth together until now.

This fallen universe is here personified as eagerly expecting "the revealing of the sons of God," which refers to the bestowing of our anticipated resurrection bodies at the Parousia. Why this eager expectation? Because the day our bodies are redeemed (Rom 8:23) will be the day when the universe itself is redeemed. This will be a cosmic redemption through which the heavens and the earth will participate in "the freedom of the glory of the children of God." Not just our bodies, but the universe itself will be changed into a glorified state.

How will this take place? Peter explains that it will happen when "the day of the Lord will come," a day "in which the heavens will pass away with a roar and the elements will be destroyed with intense heat, and the earth and its works will be burned up" (2 Pet 3:10). "All these things are to be destroyed in this way," he says; i.e., "the heavens will be destroyed by burning, and the elements will melt with intense heat!" (2 Pet 3:11-12). This sounds punitive but is ultimately purgative since it is the means to the cosmic redemption of which Paul spoke, for "according to His promise [Isa 65:17-25; 66:22-23] we are looking for new heavens and a new earth, in which righteousness dwells" (2 Pet 3:13).

It is possible that the old universe will be literally destroyed in the sense of annihilated (see Ps 102:26), necessitating an act of *ex nihilo* creation as the origin of the new heavens and new earth. Most agree, though, that the fire is one of renovation and purification, like a piece of metal being heated to a molten state, allowing its dross to be removed and its purified matter to be recast into a new shape (Heim, *Jesus*, 179). Hoekema (*Bible*, 280-281) gives four reasons why Peter means renewal rather than annihilation. One, the word for "new" (*kainos*) means "new in nature or in quality," not new in the sense of "totally other." Two, Paul in Rom 8:19-22 speaks of a universe longing to be liberated from corruption, not replaced. Three, the continuity between our old and new bodies is an analogy of the old earth being made new. Four, if God has to annihilate this present cosmos, then his original purpose for it will have been thwarted and Satan will have won a victory. Grudem agrees with Hoekema's final conclusion (*Theology*, 1160-1161), as does Gilmore (83). C.S. Lewis (*Miracles*, 155) says that the picture is "not of unmaking but of remaking. The old field of space, time, matter, and the senses is to be weeded, dug, and sown for a new crop. We may be tired of that old field: God is not."

Out of the fiery furnace, says Peter, come *new heavens*. This refers not to the invisible universe with its divine throne room, but simply to the cosmological heavens, i.e., the stars and galaxies of outer space. How much actual renewing is required for these we do not know. Also emerging from the fire is a *new earth*, an updated, deluxe model of the orb on which we now dwell. This new earth will be our literal home for all eternity.

God gave John a vision of this new universe: "Then I saw a new heaven and a new earth; for the first heaven and the first earth passed away" (Rev 21:1). What John sees in this vision will happen immediately following the final judgment (Rev 19:11-15). As he stands gazing upon this new world the apostle says he "saw the holy city, new Jerusalem, coming down out of heaven from God, made ready as a bride adorned for her husband" (Rev 21:2). To John this new Jerusalem had the appearance of a city (Rev 21:10-21) descending from the heavenly throne room to settle upon the new earth. This city represents the redeemed saints of all ages, who are transported from the judgment event in the invisible universe back into this visible universe, which is now being reopened after being "closed for renovations."

We must emphasize that this renewed creation is a real space/time universe, and the earth on which we will dwell is a solid, bodily place located in the space of this universe. It is a place perfectly coordinated with and adapted to the nature of our (and Christ's) new glorified bodies. We will be perfectly at home in this new environment. Thus will Jesus' promise be fulfilled, that the meek and gentle "shall inherit the earth" (Matt 5:5). OT Israel's possession of the "promised land" was but a symbolic type of the fact that Abraham and his spiritual seed "would be heir of the world" (Rom 4:13), i.e., the entire new universe.

That the new universe is a real space/time world means that, as with all created being, time will exist just as it does now, moment succeeding moment and event following event. Gilmore is wrong to say that "in heaven time is no more" (279); his view of "heaven as everlasting present" and of "stand-still" time (156-162) is artificial and unnecessary. The only thing temporally different about life on the new earth (i.e., "in heaven") is that time will *never end* (see Grudem, *Theology*, 1162). What this means is that heaven is not the elimination of time itself, but the elimination of *time limitations*. No more deadlines! No more expiration dates! No more having to quit before the job is done! No more "I just ran out of time"!

If this is beginning to sound a lot like a kind of paradise, well, it is!—as the next section shows.

III. THE QUALITY OF LIFE ON THE NEW EARTH

What will life be like on the new earth, i.e., in our eternal heaven? It will indeed be "the Paradise of God" (Rev 2:7), with all the positive connotations that word includes. Perhaps the biblical word that most accurately describes it is "glory" (*doxa*). True glory is inherent only in the nature of God; it is the totality of his greatness and the majesty of all his perfections as they are manifested and as they shine forth for all to see. But through his power and wisdom, when God works his mighty works of creation and redemption, the glory that is inherent within him is imparted to his creatures so that his own glory shines in and through them. As applied to the new creation and especially to the new earth, we may say that it will be *glorious* in that it will radiate an aura of grandeur, power, brilliance, splendor, majesty, beauty, purity, and dignity that will fill us with awe and cause us simply to praise God.

When Christians think of heaven they think of glory and sometimes call it "glory land" (as in "I've got a home in glory land that outshines the sun"). We also anticipate our own existence there as an experience of glory: "When, by the gift of His infinite grace, I am accorded in Heaven a place, just to be there and to look on His face, will through the ages be glory for me" (Charles H. Gabriel). Scripture speaks of heaven as glory (Rom 2:7,10; Eph 1:18; Heb 2:10; 1 Pet 5:10). Christians are filled with "the hope of glory" (Col 1:27; see Rom 5:2; 8:18; 2 Cor 4:17). We will have bodies of glory (Rom 8:21; 1 Cor 15:43; Phil 3:21) and crowns of glory (1 Pet 5:4). When John saw the new Jerusalem coming down to the new earth, he saw it as "having the glory of God" (Rev 21:4), since "the glory of God has illumined it" (Rev 21:23).

Thus when we ask what life will be like in our eternal home the answer truly is, "O that will be glory for me!" This is true in several respects.

A. Glories of Our Physical Life

I have no qualms about speaking of the new heavens and new earth (as well as our new bodies) as physical or material, since they will be a new version of the visible creation. However, I do not expect their material stuff to be constructed according to the same principles and patterns of atomic physics found in this present world. I believe that one result of the recreating process of 1 Pet 3:10-12 will be a new kind of material stuff, one that is not subject to breakdown and decay. It will, however, be *material stuff.* Also, I see no reason to think the new earth will be radically different from our present earth in terms of soil and water, and plant life such as trees and flowers (Rev 22:1-2).[4] We may think of it as something like the prefall earth, or this earth with the curses of Genesis 3 removed (Rev 22:3); but it will be much more, e.g., a worldwide Eden or an eternal millennium-type kingdom.[5]

The physical glory of the new earth will be manifested in various ways, especially in its *beauty.* John's main description of the new world is limited to "the holy city, new Jerusalem," which came down to the new earth (Rev 21:2-4; 21:10–22:5). This city is identified as "the bride, the wife of the Lamb" (Rev 21:9), meaning that its inhabitants are the redeemed saints. Also we must recognize that the physical descriptions may be symbolic of presently hidden realities. Thus we cannot be dogmatic in our conclusions. Still, if John's description of the city has any physical application at all, it is that the new earth will possess a beauty that can be expressed only in terms of precious jewels, pure gold, and majestic size (a cube 1,500 miles on each side).

Some of the most striking aspects of the physical life and environment of the new earth have to do with what will *not* be there. One, there will be no darkness, "no night there" (Rev 21:25; 22:5), "for the glory of God has illumined it, and its lamp is the Lamb" (Rev 21:23). Thus there is no need for the sun or moon or for lamps (Rev 21:25; 22:5). That there is no darkness means we will have nothing to fear and nothing to hide.

Two, there will be no danger there, nothing to threaten our peace and safety. This is symbolized in God's promise that on the new earth, "the wolf and the lamb will graze together, and the lion will eat straw like an ox; and dust will be the serpent's food. They will do no evil or harm in all My holy mountain" (Isa 65:25). This is also the reason why "there is no longer any sea" on the new earth (Rev 21:1); to the ancients the sea was a source of jeopardy and peril.

Third, there will be no physical discomfort in heaven: no hunger, thirst, or excessive heat (Rev 7:16) and no pain (Rev 21:4). These are representative of discomforts of all kinds.

Fourth and most significantly, "there will no longer be any death" (Rev 21:4). In earlier prophecy God suggested that in the new universe death will simply be irrelevant (Isa 65:20,22), but in his more complete and final revelation he indicates that it will be removed altogether. The curse of death as Adam's legacy upon the race (Gen 2:17; 3:19) will be gone. Those in resurrection bodies "cannot even die anymore" (Luke 20:36).

Stated positively, the greatest physical glory of heaven is the everlasting, never-ending life that will be bestowed upon us. Even now we have the spiritual aspect of that life, but then it will empower our bodies as well (Rom 6:23; 8:10-11). An environment where life reigns instead of death is marked by the presence of "springs of the water of life" (Rev 7:17; 21:6), "a river of the water of life" (Rev 22:1,17), and the tree of life in a variety of forms (Rev 2:7; 22:2,14). We will live forever in imperishable, immortal bodies (1 Cor 15:42,53-54) that are not subject to pain or discomfort.

What about activities that give us physical pleasure in our present lives, i.e., eating, drinking, and sex? This question is neither irrelevant nor irreverent, for these are normal and good activities in this life. Concerning eating and drinking, in Rev 19:7-9 heaven is represented as a wedding feast; and Isa 65:21 says, "They will also plant vineyards and eat their fruit." The water of life and the tree of life suggest that eating and drinking will still be natural. Revelation 7:16 says there will be no hunger or thirst there. Is this because we will always have all we want to eat and drink, or simply because eating and drinking will no longer be necessary? If the latter is the case, then the tree of life and the water of life are just symbols of "never-ending and totally satisfying refreshment by the Spirit" (Gilmore, 116). There really is no biblical basis for ruling out literal eating and drinking, however.[6]

We do have a biblical reason for thinking there will be no sexual relations in heaven, though. Jesus' answer to the Sadducees' question in Matt 22:23-33 implies that husband-wife relationships of all kinds will be transcended in heaven: "For in the resurrection they neither marry nor are given in marriage, but are like angels in heaven" (v. 30). Since sexual relations are intended for marriage only, this seems to exclude them from our new-earth relationships. This does not mean, however, that our new bodies will necessarily be genderless (see Lewis, *Miracles*, 165-166; Gilmore, ch. 13, "Sex in Heaven?").

Erickson raises the question, "If there is to be no eating nor sex, will there be any pleasure in heaven?" He rightly answers "that the experiences of heaven will far surpass anything experienced here," as indicated by 1 Cor 2:9 (NIV), "No eye has seen, no ear has heard, no mind has conceived what God has prepared for those who love him" (*Theology*, 1239-1240). Gilmore (84) says it well: "Glorified bodies will, doubtless, involve glorious action and enormous enjoyment. It would seem that some form of the pleasures of sight, sound, touch, and (less so) taste will be part of the new earth."

B. Glories of the Heart and Mind

The greatest glories of heaven will no doubt be those of the inner life, including those that affect our intellectual and emotional states. From a negative perspective the most significant of these will be the complete absence of sorrow. Revelation 21:4 says that "there will no longer be any mourning"; nor will there be any crying, for "He will wipe away every tear from their eyes" (see Rev 7:17). Concerning the new earth "there will no longer be heard in her the voice of weeping and the sound of crying" (Isa 65:19).

This raises the question of whether we will retain any memories of our life on this earth, since for many of us it seems that this is a life of "constant sorrow." In view of the fact that there will be no sorrow in heaven, we must conclude that God wipes away not only our tears but also any memories that would cause such tears. These are part of "the former things" that "will not be remembered or come to mind" in the new life (Isa 65:17); "the first things have passed away" (Rev 21:4).

On the other hand we cannot think that our entire memories of our former lives will be erased, since a main part of one's personal identity will be his remembrance of his relationship with Jesus Christ during this present life. As Gilmore says (316), "In the life of the resurrected righteous, it appears our memories of God's grace on earth will continue, revive, sharpen, and be part of the impetus behind praising God." So in the final analysis we conclude that we will have very good memories of this life (probably even better than the ones we now have!), but that God will erase from them whatever might cause us sorrow.

This gives us reason to believe that we will remember and recognize members of the saved community that we knew in our old lives. Indeed, Gilmore (329) speculates that this will be one of the main causes for joy and laughter in heaven, namely, reunion with loved ones separated from us by death (see Luke 6:21).

This leads to a consideration of one of the main glories of the heart in heaven, namely, constant joy. Everything that happens in heaven, as already discussed above and yet to be discussed below, is a source of happiness and joy. Concerning the new earth God says in Isa 65:18, "But be glad and rejoice forever in what I create; for behold, I create Jerusalem for rejoicing and her people for gladness." Sometimes the word *makarios* in the Beatitudes (Matt 5:3-11) is translated "happy" instead of "blessed."[7] Either way the joys of the new earth are the ultimate fulfillment of the Beatitudes. "The pure will see God, the poor will possess the imperishable, the persecuted will have losses restored, the deprived will have immediate access to all parts of the renovated earth" (Gilmore, 113). No wonder there is joy!

Another glory of the inner life in our new-earth existence will be the many activities in which we will be engaged. This could have been discussed under the glories of the physical life, but I choose to include it here because activity is as much a state of the mind as it is bodily exertion. It is true that we may think of eternal life as in some sense a state of *rest*, just as the promised land was a gift of rest for the Israelites (see Heb 3:18–4:11). But this is rest from toil and mental stress, not rest from activity, nor even rest from work. Adam and Eve had plenty of work assigned to them before sin's curse turned it into toil (Gen 3:17-19). With the curse removed from the new earth, we can engage once more in a variety of activities without toil and stress.

Thus we should note that heaven will not be rest in the sense of an absence of productive activity; it will not be just "endless rows of hammocks" (Gilmore, 176). Nor will our only activity be singing praises to God, as is perhaps some angels' prerogative (Rev 4:8), since what angels do is not necessarily what we will do. In fact, on the new earth we will not be rubbing shoulders with angels, because they will still be in their own invisible universe while we are in our new visible one.

Nor should we expect to be bored with our heavenly activities, even though we will be engaged in them forever. A main reason for this is that our new life will be one of endless challenges to grow in our knowledge and understanding not only of God but of the new universe. Being finite even in our new bodies, we will never have "perfect knowledge" (contra Erickson, *Theology*, 1235). There will be a new universe to probe and to explore, indeed, to conquer, in reference to its potential for science and the arts. Here we will finally be able to do justice to the original cultural mandate (Gen 1:28) wherein the human race was commanded to subdue and rule over the earth. When Rev 5:10 says that the saved will be "a kingdom and priests to our God; and they will reign upon the earth" (see Rev 21:24; 22:5), this does not mean that we will rule over *people*, but over the *new universe itself.*

Gilmore sums this up well: "Heaven, if anything, is perfected action: doing more, doing it better; and having more space in which to do it. We contend that heaven is pell-mell, reflective exploration and not occupied with immobile contemplations" (73). "Adventures in the kingdom of heaven await the ransomed church" (84). The new universe "requires a magnificent full-scale active life in the habitation, use, and governing of the new earth by those who are part of the blissful eternal state" (87). But if one *wants* to rest, he will surely be able to do so!

C. Glories of the Spirit

Surely the greatest glories of our eternal life in heaven will be those of the spirit, those that have to do with what are sometimes called morality and religion. While everything about our heavenly life will be God-oriented and thus "religious," some of it will be more directly so. That is the aspect of new-earth existence we are dealing with here.

Without question the most unspeakably marvelous glory of our life on the new earth will be the fact that *God himself will be present there.* When John saw the new Jerusalem descending to the new earth, he also "heard a loud voice from the throne saying, 'Behold, the dwelling place of God is with man. He will dwell with them, and they will be his people, and God himself will be with them as their God'" (Rev 21:3, ESV). The heavenly city contains no temple, "for the Lord God the Almighty and the Lamb are its temple" (Rev 21:22); "the throne of God and of the Lamb will be in it" (Rev 22:3). This does not refer to the omnipresence of God; nor does it mean that the immortal, invisible essence of God, who "dwells in unapproachable light" (1 Tim 6:16), will become visibly present to us. Nor does it mean that God will no longer be manifesting his presence to the angels in the spiritual throne room. What it means is that in the new earth God will establish a new throne room and will provide redeemed saints with a permanent theophany, similar to the one with which he will continue to bless the angels. In this way the pure in heart will see God forever (Matt 5:8); "they will see His face" (Rev 22:4). Herein will be the source of our greatest joy: "In Your presence is fullness of joy; in Your right hand there are pleasures forever" (Ps 16:11; see 27:4).

One advantage we will have over the angels is that the resurrected Christ, the Lamb of God, will no longer sit on God's throne in their presence, but will move to the new throne room on our new earth. Indeed, "the Lamb in the center of the throne will be their shepherd" (Rev 7:17); it is "the throne of God and of the Lamb" (Rev 22:1,3).

The fact that God will manifest his presence on the new earth is the reason why we call it "heaven." Hoekema well says, "Since God will make the new earth his dwelling place, and since where God dwells there heaven is, we shall then continue to be in heaven while we are on the new earth" (*Bible*, 274). From that point on, then, there will actually be *three* "theological" heavens: the divine dimension itself, the divine throne room in the angelic realm, and the divine throne room on the new earth. Since God's presence is what makes the new earth a true heaven, we can say that as far as our eternal state is concerned, we do not "go to heaven," but heaven comes to us.

Because God's very presence will be made visible to us, and because Christ himself is there, the most enticing and the most satisfying of our heavenly activities will be to worship and to commune with them with a consistency and a fervor that may now seem impossible. Revelation 7:9-10 pictures the multitude of the redeemed standing before the throne and before the Lamb, singing praises to God and the Lamb. This will not necessarily be constant, but it will be regular.

Another spiritual glory of the new earth will be the complete absence of sin and everything caused by sin. Our redeemed spirits will already be fully sanctified and spiritually perfected in their intermediate state (Heb 12:23), and our new bodies will contain none of the residue of sin that infected the old ones. Thus in our final state we will be as spiritually pure and beautiful as a holy bride dressed for her wedding: "It was given to her to clothe herself in fine linen, bright and clean; for the fine linen is the righteous acts of the saints" (Rev 19:8). We will live forever in a completely glorified state, unable to sin again (Habermas and Moreland, 150-151). Our environment will also be completely sinless, since the purifying fire of 2 Pet 3:10-12 completely cleansed the old earth of all the effects of sin that had corrupted it. The result is "a new heavens and a new earth, in which righteousness dwells" (2 Pet 3:13). John's vision of the new earth assures us that no sinners will be present there (Rev 21:8,27; 22:15). All its residents will have hearts of gold, which is more important than harps of gold or streets of gold.

Finally we may mention the spiritual glory of getting to know all of God's saints from all ages and all parts of the globe. The 144,000 in Rev 7:4-8 probably represent symbolically the total saved from OT Israel, while the Christians from the NT era are represented in Rev 7:9 as "a great multitude which no one could count, from every nation and all tribes and peoples and tongues." Here unity and diversity are combined in a way that provides an opportunity for unlimited fellowship.

We conclude this chapter on heaven by noting that this glorious new earth and indeed new universe will be the ultimate fulfillment of God's original purpose for creating "the heavens and the earth" in the first place (Gen 1:1). This will be the final phase of the "kingdom of heaven" promised in the Beatitudes (Matt 5:3,10). Herein we will find and eternally explore all the treasures we have stored up "in heaven" (Matt 6:20); herein lies the final installment of our inheritance "reserved in heaven" (1 Pet 1:4; see Matt 5:5; Eph 1:13-14), the long-awaited fulfillment of Jesus' promise, "Rejoice and be glad, for your reward in heaven is great" (Matt 5:12). Perhaps it will all be summed up in the word "bliss": "a bliss of love, of *koinonia* in the Spirit, of reunion, of praise and worship, of the joy of being with Christ, and perhaps of some form of divine service" (Wirt, 11).

NOTES ON CHAPTER THIRTY-TWO

[1]In the OT the main term *shamayim* occurs about 400 times; in the NT *ouranos* appears 273 times.

[2]This is not a dimension of our own space/time universe, contra Grudem (*Theology*, 1159). It is a separate, differently dimensioned universe.

[3]See Hoekema, *Bible* (201-203), who shows that this is *not* a prophecy of some temporary, old-earth millennium. See also Gilmore, 363-393.

[4]Whether there will be animals there is not known. Isa 65:25 is probably symbolic of the absence of danger. See Gilmore, 130-133.

[5]Hoekema suggests that the kind of earth that millenarians expect to last for only 1,000 years in many ways will actually be the nature of the eternal new earth (*Bible*, 201-206, 275-276).

[6]The fact that Jesus ate after his resurrection (Luke 24:43) tells us nothing about our new-earth bodies, since Jesus did not have his glorified resurrection body until his ascension.

[7]E.g., J.B. Phillips' translation; and *Good News Bible: Today's English Version*.

CHAPTER THIRTY-THREE

HELL

This chapter attempts to set forth the Bible's teaching about the eternal abode or state of the wicked, which is usually called hell. Two guidelines are in order for such a study. First, in some translations of the Bible, not all references to hell are actually referring to the eternal destiny of the wicked. For example, the English word "hell" is used 54 times in the KJV, but only 12 of these apply to our subject. Forty-one are incorrect translations of *Sheol* and *Hades*; and one is *Tartarus*, the temporary abode of some fallen angels (2 Pet 2:4). The twelve uses that properly refer to hell are translations of the Greek word *geenna*, usually written Gehenna.

Second, the biblical teaching about hell is not limited to the twelve verses that specifically refer to Gehenna. References are varied and numerous. Perhaps surprisingly, many of them are in the Gospels. Blanchard (128) points out that "of 1870 verses recording words which Jesus spoke, thirteen per cent are about judgement and hell. Jesus spoke more about these two topics than about any other." Also, "of about fifty parables Jesus told, more than half of them relate to God's eternal judgement of sinners."

Hell is a subject that we deal with reluctantly, and one we would rather not think about at all. In fact, God himself would prefer not to deal with it, since he is "not wishing for any to perish" (2 Pet 3:9) but "desires all men to be saved" (1 Tim 2:4). However, it is God's own righteousness that makes hell a reality, and it is our determination to uphold his righteousness and the authority of his Word that now leads us into this final study.

I. THE REALITY OF HELL

To anyone who accepts the full inerrancy and authority of Scripture, the reality of hell is not an issue. The Bible clearly teaches that at the final judgment the human race will be divided into two groups, one destined to spend eternity in heaven and the other condemned to eternal hell. Jesus sums up this truth, that the wicked "will go away into eternal punishment, but the righteous into eternal life" (Matt 25:46). Some will spend eternity in the heavenly city, the new Jerusalem; others will end up "in the lake that burns with fire and brimstone, which is the second death" (Rev 21:1-8).

The world is full of people who deny the reality of hell, however. One major group, of course, are the secularists or materialists who deny the existence of life after death in any form. In this sense human beings are regarded as no different from animals and insects; when they die their consciousness simply ceases to exist and their bodies return to dust. There is no hell, but no heaven either.

A second major approach to the denial of hell is found among some who accept the reality of the afterlife for all people. This is the view called *universalism*, which says that all people, even the most wicked, will eventually be drawn to God and be saved. This means that everyone will spend eternity in heaven; there will be no need for hell. Salvation will be universal.

In the context of Christianity the first significant universalist was Origen (A.D. 185–254). He did not actually deny the reality of hell, though. He said sinners will spend time there, but all will ultimately pay their debt of punishment and will be taken to heaven. Thus hell exists but serves a purgatorial or redemptive purpose. All will finally be saved, even Satan and his demons. This view was declared heretical at the second Council of Constantinople (A.D. 553).

In modern times a considerable number of true universalists arose in various contexts (Nicole, 35). In the U.S. these included New Englanders John Murray (1741–1815) and Hosea Ballou (1771–1852), to whom the Universalist church is usually traced. This group merged with the Unitarian church in 1961. Their views were originally based largely on a false view of the universal atonement of Christ (e.g., Rom 5:18-19).

In more recent times other (sometimes well-known) theologians have espoused universal salvation. William Barclay (*Creed*, 239) has said that if God is truly the God and Father of Jesus Christ, then "we may dare to hope that when time ends God's family will be complete," since he is surely "a Father who can never be content when even a single child of his is outside the circle of his love." Emil Brunner (*Hope*, 182) says,

> That is the revealed will of God and the plan for the world which He disclos-es—a plan of universal salvation, of gathering all things into Christ. We hear not one word in the Bible of a dual plan, a plan of salvation and its polar op-posite. The will of God has but one point, it is unambiguous and positive. It has one aim, not two.

We stress that one cannot believe such a view while accepting the full authority of the full canon of Scripture. A few individual verses can be given a universalist slant when taken out of context, but so interpreted these would be in conflict with other teachings of Scripture. For example, John Hick says that 1 Cor 15:22, Rom 5:18, Rom 11:32, and Eph 1:10 teach universalism, whereas Romans 9 and 2 Thess 1:8-9 teach the opposite. "Thus one can quote Paul on either side of the debate" (*Death*, 247-248). Hick himself opts for universalism: "We must thus affirm the ultimate salvation of all mankind, and the faith in which we affirm this is that in which we have affirmed God's saving love and sovereign power" (ibid., 259).

In the end we must reject all such universalist views as contrary to a true understanding of the nature of Scripture in general and of its alleged universalist texts in particular (see Blanchard, 189-208).

II. THE NATURE OF HELL

Most Bible believers agree that hell is real, but there is considerable discussion as to its nature. What is hell like? To answer this question we must begin with a look at the many biblical images that are applied to it.

A. Images of Hell in the Bible

The first image of hell is that of a *garbage dump*. This is the image portrayed by the term properly translated as "hell," namely, *Gehenna* (Matt 5:22,29,30; 10:28; 18:9; 23:15,33; Mark 9:43,45,47; Luke 12:5; Jas 3:6). This word refers literally to a small valley (called Hinnom in Bible days) just south of Jerusalem. It was an abomination to the Jews because it had been used for child sacrifice and idol worship (Jer 32:35) in the days of King Ahaz (2 Kgs 16:3) and King Manasseh (2 Kgs 21:6). Placed under God's curse (Jer 7:30-33; 19:1-6), the Valley of Hinnom came to be used as a garbage pit, "a public rubbish dump in which all the offal and filth of Jerusalem was poured. Later, the bodies of animals and even the corpses of criminals were flung there and left to rot or to be consumed by the fire that was kept constantly burning to dispose of the stinking mass of garbage" (Blanchard, 41). This is the image that would leap immediately into the minds of those who heard Jesus declare that the wicked would be cast into Gehenna. To them it was the ultimate symbol of abomination and ruination.

Related to this is the image of hell as a place where *worms* (i.e., maggots) are eternally gnawing away at one's flesh. Jesus refers to those who are cast into hell (Gehenna), "where their worm does not die, and the fire is not quenched" (Mark 9:47). Here Jesus is echoing God's curse upon those who do not occupy the new heavens and new earth (Isa 66:24).

This leads to the most common image of the final state of the wicked, namely, *fire*. Gehenna as a garbage pit was itself a place of unending fire and smoke, which led Jesus to speak of "the unquenchable fire" of hell (Mark 9:43), the place where "the fire is not quenched" (Mark 9:48). We should not assume, though, that the concept of hell as a place of fire is derived from the Gehenna image. It is based rather on the common idea that God's wrath is like a raging fire (*GRe*, 276-277). This is a common OT theme, e.g.: "Upon the wicked He will rain snares; fire and brimstone and burning wind will be the portion of their cup" (Ps 11:6). "'For behold, a day is coming, burning like a furnace; and all the arrogant and every evildoer will be chaff; and the day that is coming will set them ablaze,' says the LORD of hosts" (Mal 4:1). Indeed, "our God is a consuming fire" (Heb 12:29).

Thus it is no surprise that fire is the dominant image for hell since it is a common way of representing God's wrath. Hell is called "the hell of fire" (ESV, Matt 5:22; 18:9; see Jas 3:6); "eternal fire" (Matt 18:8; 25:41; Jude 7); "unquenchable fire" (Matt 3:12; Mark 9:43); "the furnace of fire" (Matt 13:42,50); "the lake of fire" (Rev 20:14-15) and "fire and brimstone" (Rev 14:10; 19:20; 20:10; 21:8). When most people think of hell, they think of fire.

Hell is also pictured as a place of *darkness*, indeed, "outer darkness" (Matt 8:12; 22:13; 25:30) and "black darkness" (2 Pet 2:17; Jude 13). This reminds us that one of the plagues upon Egypt was "a darkness which may be felt," a "thick darkness" (Exod 10:21-23). This is the opposite of heaven, where there is no night (Rev 21:25; 22:5).

The last image is that of *separation from God* and from the presence of the Savior. On the day of judgment Jesus will say to the wicked, "Depart from Me" (Matt 7:23; 25:41; Luke 13:27). They will be "thrown out" of God's eternal kingdom (Luke 13:28; see Rev 22:14-15), thrown out into "outer darkness" (Matt 8:12; 22:13; 25:30). In these last passages the verb is *ekballo*, "to drive out, cast out, throw outside." The concept of "outer" darkness refers to the darkness that is *outside*, indeed, "*the darkness farthest out*" (AG, 279), i.e., farthest away from the God who is Light (1 John 1:5). Paul says the wicked "will pay the penalty of eternal destruction, away from the presence of the Lord and from the glory of His power (2 Thess 1:9).

B. Literal or Figurative?

What are we to make of these images? Shall we take them literally? Will the restored bodies of the wicked be literally gnawed by maggots while they writhe in flames in sightless darkness? Some say yes. John Walvoord defends "the literal view" of hell in a book on *Four Views on Hell*. He says, "The frequent mention of fire in connection with eternal punishment supports the conclusion that this is what the Scriptures mean" ("View," 28). It is significant, though, that he ties this to dispensational premillennialism's commitment to interpret all prophecy literally. Calling this "the crux of the matter," he declares, "Those who accept a literal view of hell do so largely because they accept a literal view of prophecy" ("Response," 78-79). Earlier we pointed out the weaknesses of such a view of prophecy.

The more common approach among evangelicals is to say that most of these figures should be taken metaphorically or figuratively. This is Crockett's view in the book just mentioned: "Hellfire and brimstone are not literal depictions of hell's furnishings, but figurative expressions warning the wicked of impending doom" ("View," 44). One reason usually cited for this view is that literal fire and literal darkness seem incompatible (ibid., 59). Another reason is that hell is actually created for spirit beings (fallen angels, Matt 25:41). What kind of literal fire could afflict both angels and embodied men? (ibid., 61). Leon Morris says that "Scripture uses symbolic terms of necessity to refer to realities beyond the grave." Given the wide "variety of terms, it is unwise to press one as though that gave the complete picture" ("Punishment," 370).

If the language is symbolic, what does it symbolize? Here we cannot be dogmatic. Blanchard suggests that the "worm" image represents the sinner's conscience, whose nagging and gnawing will be "infinitely greater in hell" than on earth (143-145). Crockett mentions the idea that the fire of hell "might be better understood as a terrible eternal burning within the hearts of the lost for God, fire that can never be quenched" ("View," 61). Linton says the language points mainly to "an existence of loss." Hell "is defined by the good things that are lacking— light, hope, love, purpose, beauty, joy" (13).

Perhaps the most attractive view is that the only literal image is that of separation from the Father, the Son, and the Spirit for eternity, and that all the other images are ways of emphasizing the suffering that this will cause. Erickson well says, "If there is one basic characteristic of hell, it is, in contrast to heaven, the absence of God or banishment from his presence. It is an experience of intense anguish, whether it involve physical suffering or mental distress or both" (*Theology*, 1242).[1] In *The Great Divorce* C.S. Lewis offers a picture of hell as "the grey town" in perpetual twilight "with its continual hope of morning" which never arrives (17, 24, 38). In it are "the cold and the gloom, the lonely, lonely streets" where even the people live "millions of miles" from each other (19, 116).

C. A Place of Suffering

It is generally agreed that whatever these images may symbolize, "the reality will be worse than the symbols" (Hoekema, *Bible*, 273). Pinnock says, "If fire is the biblical image, something terrible must be meant by it, even if it is a metaphor" ("Response," 37). As Blanchard remarks, "Even if we can prove that hell's 'fire' and 'worm' are metaphorical we shall not have removed one iota of their horror or terror" (141).

The point is that whatever these images represent, hell will be a place of *suffering*. There will be weeping and gnashing of teeth[2] (Matt 8:12; 13:42,50; 22:13; 24:51; 25:30; Luke 13:28), which shows conscious suffering (Grudem, *Theology*, 1148). It seems impossible to exclude some kind of physical suffering, since the wicked will be given bodies and will be cast into hell body and soul (Matt 10:28). The main point, though, seems to be mental suffering, such as "the bitterness of remorse and hopeless self-condemnation" (Hoekema, *Bible*, 268). Habermas and Moreland think "the pain suffered will be due to the shame and sorrow resulting from the punishment of final, ultimate, unending banishment from God, his kingdom, and the good life for which we were created in the first place. Hell's occupants will deeply and tragically regret all they lost." Hell's flames "depict human shame, punishment, sorrow, and anguish" (159-160). Paul calls it "tribulation and distress" (Rom 2:9), with tribulation possibly referring to bodily afflictions and distress to the accompanying inward or mental anguish and torment.

Hell is real, and its suffering is real. Whatever its nature, it is worse than physical death (Matt 10:28; 18:6; Heb 10:28-31), indeed, worse than nonexistence itself (Matt 26:24). However, even though this suffering can be nothing but punitive or retributive, i.e., God's righteous curse upon the wicked because they deserve it, we must not think of God as actively torturing those in hell. As Habermas and Moreland put it, "There will indeed be everlasting, conscious, mental and physical torment in various degrees according to the life people have lived here on earth. But the essence of that torment is relational in nature: the banishment from heaven and all it stands for" (170).

III. THE ETERNALITY OF HELL

There is no question that hell is eternal; Dan 12:2 says the wicked are raised up to "everlasting contempt," and Matt 25:46 says they go away from the judgment "into eternal punishment." In both verses the punishment of the wicked is as eternal as the salvation of the redeemed. There is much debate, though, as to what the eternality of hell really means. The issue is whether the lost experience conscious suffering for eternity, or whether at some point they are annihilated for eternity. The traditional view says the former. The language of eternality is taken to mean that the lost exist eternally in hell in full awareness of their abysmal surroundings.

In support of this traditional view of hell's eternality, Dan 12:2 calls it an experience of "disgrace and everlasting contempt." Its fire is eternal (Matt 18:8; 25:41; Jude 7); it is a place of "eternal punishment" (Matt 25:46), "eternal destruction" (2 Thess 1:9), and "eternal judgment" (Heb 6:2). The word used in these NT verses is *aionios*, which is also used to describe "the eternal God" (Rom 16:26) and "the eternal Spirit" (Heb 9:14). It is used 44 times in the phrase "eternal life," and also describes our eternal dwellings, house (body), glory, salvation, redemption, inheritance, and kingdom. Wherever it is used it always refers to eternity—sometimes to eternity past, but mostly to eternity future. This is surely its intended meaning when it refers to hell.

The related word *aion* is also used for eternal punishment. This word sometimes has a limited meaning, as when it refers to a specific age or era. But when it is the object of the preposition *eis* ("unto"), the phrase means "unto the age, forever." It is used thus in Jude 13 for the "black darkness" that "has been preserved forever." If the darkness is preserved forever, it must be intended to be experienced forever. The phrase is intensified when the word *aion* is repeated, i.e., "unto the ages of the ages," translated "forever and ever." This is the phrase used in Rev 14:11, which says that the smoke from the fire and brimstone that torment the wicked "goes up forever and ever; they have no rest day and night." To say that it is just the *smoke* that goes on forever and not the torment itself is shown to be false by the addition of "they have no rest day and night." The same phrase, "forever and ever," describes the torment of Satan, the beast, and the false prophet in Rev 20:10. Morey says, "It would make no grammatical sense whatsoever to use such metaphors if the punishment is not endless in duration"

(143). Both forms of the phrase using *aion* ("forever" and "forever and ever") are used many times in the NT to refer to our eternal life (e.g., John 6:51,58; 1 John 2:17; 2 John 2; Rev 22:5), and even to God himself. To say they mean anything less when referring to eternal punishment is completely arbitrary. Leon Morris agrees: "The concept of endless duration could not be more strongly conveyed; the use of these expressions for the eternity of God shows conclusively that they do not mean limited duration" ("Punishment," 369).

Other considerations support the concept of eternal punishment. For example, when Dan 12:2 refers to the destiny of the wicked as "everlasting contempt," we understand that they cannot be the objects of contempt for eternity unless they actually exist for eternity. John 3:36 says, "He who does not obey the Son will not see life, but the wrath of God "remains on him" (NIV). The present tense, indicating continuing action, is significant. Hoekema asks, "If the wrath of God remains upon such a person, to what conclusion can we come than that the punishment involved is everlasting?" (*Bible*, 269). Also important is the parallel between the fates of the righteous and the wicked in Dan 12:2 and especially in Matt 25:46. The former receive eternal life, and the latter eternal contempt and punishment. The parallelism must mean that the contempt and punishment received by the wicked is as eternal as the life received by the righteous. The eternal punishment of Matt 25:46 is the eternal fire prepared for the devil and his angels (Matt 25:41), and Rev 20:10 shows that this eternal fire is intended to be a place of eternal suffering (see Dixon, 88-91). Also, that the fire of hell is described as "unquenchable" (Matt 3:12; Mark 9:43,48) is best understood as implying eternal suffering. If such language does not mean endless suffering, there is absolutely no reason to use it at all. This is the natural way to apply it (see Hoekema, *Bible*, 268).

The fact is, however, that many evangelicals today are denying the eternal suffering of the wicked and are espousing a form of annihilationism. This is the view that at some point God will simply cause the wicked to cease to exist, period.[3] Unlike universalism, this view does not necessarily involve a rejection of biblical authority.

There are three main versions of annihilationism. One is the view that the wicked are annihilated at death, a view held by Jehovah's Witnesses. Actually the Witnesses say that everyone is annihilated at death, but the irretrievably wicked will be denied any sort of resurrection from the dead. Thus they are extinct forever. The righteous are raised from the dead, however; and so are the less culpable unbelievers. The latter are given a second chance during the millennium, but if they fail this time, they are again annihilated and will be forever extinct.

Another view is that the wicked are annihilated after the day of judgment. They are raised from the dead and subjected to the final judgment; then they are cursed with eternal nonexistence. An example of this view is Seventh-day Adventism. Their view is this: "Immediately upon their sentencing, Satan, his angels, and his human followers receive their punishment. They are to die an eternal death," which is their "total destruction" (*Seventh-day Adventists Believe*, 369).

A third view of annihilationism, the one most commonly held among evangelicals, says that the wicked are extinguished only after they have spent a period of time in the hell described above. How long this conscious suffering will endure will depend upon the seriousness of one's sins. After this time of "equitable punishment" is over, the individual is annihilated (Boatman, 34-35, 102).

A main example is Edward Fudge, whose work *The Fire That Consumes* is an exhaustive attempt to explain and defend this view. Like many others he prefers to call this view *conditionalism*, meaning that immortality (eternal existence) is conditional and that some will not meet those conditions. Fudge defines the view thus: "The term 'conditionalist' is used for the view that the wicked will suffer conscious punishment precisely measured by divine justice but that they finally will perish in hell so as to become totally extinct forever" (xvi). He grants that some texts imply "degrees of punishment in proportion to light spurned and opportunity neglected" (190). This "period of conscious pain" does not last forever, though, for sinners "will eventually be destroyed forever, both body and soul" (202).

Another example is Clark Pinnock, who has also written extensively in defense of this view. He is mostly concerned to establish the ultimate annihilation of the wicked, but he does concede that there *may* be a period of equitable punishment before this: "Maybe there will be a period of punishment before oblivion and nonbeing" ("View," 154). "Before oblivion, there may be a period of suffering, but not unendingly" (ibid., 157). This is Pinnock's attempt to account for "possible degrees of punishment" (ibid., 154).

Here we will briefly consider several arguments used by annihilationists. First, in order to reconcile the many references to *eternal* punishment with extinction, they say that annihilation *is* eternal punishment, because it is final and lasts for eternity. It is an eternal punish*ment*, not an everlasting punish*ing*, i.e., not an eternal conscious suffering but eternal nonexistence. The biggest problem with this explanation is that it does not do justice to the parallelism between eternal *punishment* and eternal *life* in Matt 25:46. It limits the former to an eternal result while granting that the latter is an eternally experienced state, thus destroying what appears to be an intended symmetry. Also, some annihilationists say "eternal" (*aionios*) does mean eternal when applied to God, since he is immortal. But when used of mortal people or perishable things, "it means as long as the person lives or the thing exists" (*Seventh-day Adventists Believe*, 370). Such an argument begs the question, however, and in the end makes the term mean nothing at all. That is, to say that a thing is eternal would mean no more than to say it will last as long as it will last. Surely there is more content in the word than that. Also, if this limited meaning of "eternal" were true, it would rule out eternal life as well as eternal suffering, since both are asserted of mortal human beings.

A main argument used by annihilationists is that certain biblical language applied to the damned can be interpreted only as annihilation. They are referring to the terminology of death and destruction. For example, "the person who sins will die" (Ezek 18:20). "The wages of sin is death" (Rom 6:23). The lake of fire is "the second death" (Rev 21:8). God will "destroy both soul and body in hell" (Matt 10:28). Sinners "pay the penalty of eternal destruction" (2 Thess 1:9). Sin plunges men "into ruin and destruction" (1 Tim 6:9). Their "end is destruction" (Phil 3:19). "Destruction will come upon them" (1 Thess 5:3). Those who do not repent will "perish" (Luke 13:3,5). God "is able to save and to destroy" (Jas 4:12). The fire of God's judgment is "a fire which will consume" (Heb 10:27; see Mal 4:1-2). All such words, says Dickinson, "mean to *end life*, or cause it to *cease to be*" (*Immortality*, 22).

In my judgment, such claims are excessive and do not fairly represent the relevant biblical terminology. Besides the concept of death as such, the main terms that refer to the "destruction" of the wicked are *olethros*, *apollymi*, and *apoleia*. The main point is that, even if these words can convey the concept of annihilation, this is not their *only* connotation and not even a principal one. For example, the fate of the wicked is called "death." But one cannot argue for annihilation from this word or concept as such, since in Scripture death often describes the state of an existing being, i.e., the sinner's state of spiritual death (e.g., Matt 8:22; Luke 15:24,32; Eph 2:1,5; 1 Tim 5:6). Blanchard argues that the essence of death is separation: alienation, not annihilation (71, 227-228).

The same applies to the other words. *Olethros*, the term referring to sinners' eternal "destruction" in 2 Thess 1:9 (see 1 Thess 5:3), can mean ruin; death; loss (as loss of money); and corruption, as corruption of character, as in 1 Tim 6:9. The connotation of annihilation is not inherent in the word. This is also true of the common verb *apollymi* and its noun form *apoleia*. These words are often translated "destroy, perish, destruction"; but to assume that "destroy" is equivalent to "annihilate" is totally unwarranted. The words also have connotations such as ruin, kill, lose, spoil, and waste, without any hint of annihilation. For example, when wineskins are "ruined" (Matt 9:17), they are not annihilated. The "lost" sheep of the house of Israel (Matt 10:6) are not annihilated. When the Pharisees sought to "destroy" Jesus (Mark 3:6), they were not thinking of annihilating him. When a woman "wasted" perfume on Jesus (Mark 14:4), she did not annihilate it. When the sheep, the coin, and the boy were "lost" (Luke 15:4,6,8,9,17,24,32), they were not annihilated. When thieves "destroy" (John 10:10), they do not annihilate. When one "destroys" a brother through bad example (Rom 14:15), he does not annihilate him. When the flood "destroyed" the world (2 Pet 3:6), it did not annihilate it.

It should be obvious that to argue from these words to annihilationism is a very weak argument. In Hoekema's judgment, *apollymi* in the NT "never means annihilation" (*Bible*, 269). Blanchard (239) agrees:

To insist that *apollumi* and *apoleia* must refer to annihilation is absurd, as they never do so when applied to things other than human destiny. There is not a single occasion in the New Testament when *apollumi* refers to anybody or anything passing out of existence. Trying to make it mean so when it is used in connection with the destiny of the wicked is therefore pointless. The word simply does not bear that meaning.

When applied to the eternal fate of the wicked, such terms refer to the loss or destruction of all meaning, peace, value, and usefulness. They signify that the lost have brought upon themselves an eternal existence that is the very opposite of God's intended purpose for human beings. Everything that matters about them is truly lost; they are "wasted" in every sense of the word. But they are not annihilated.

It is also argued that the frequent use of the metaphor of fire implies extinction of the wicked, since the purpose and inevitable result of *fire* is to *consume* in the sense of annihilate. This argument fails, however, in view of Exod 3:2 and Dan 3:19-27 (see Blanchard, 230-231). Also, the common word for "consume" (Heb 10:27) almost always refers to the ordinary act of eating food. In eating, the food is not annihilated but swallowed. The fire of hell consumes the wicked not by annihilating them but by swallowing them up and engulfing them into its misery.

We conclude that none of the "death and destruction" terms imply that hell's punishment is annihilation.

Another argument used by annihilationists has to do with the nature of man. The assumption is that the concept of eternal suffering is dependent upon the inherent immortality of the human soul. Specifically, the belief that the soul by nature cannot not exist requires that it spend eternity *somewhere*. Since it would not be appropriate for the wicked to spend eternity in heaven, God is forced to create an eternal abode suitable for them, i.e., hell. But, say the annihilationists, the concept of an inherently immortal soul is antibiblical, being derived from pagan philosophy. Therefore the idea of the eternal suffering of the wicked is false. In fact, they say, if this pagan idea had not been accepted by postbiblical Christian thinkers, the idea of hell as eternal suffering would never have arisen. For example, Boatman refers to "the doctrine of the innate and irrevocable immortality of the human soul, and corollary postulate: the doctrine that the unredeemed shall be endlessly tormented in hell" (101; see 51-52). Pinnock likewise cites the unbiblical hellenistic belief in the immortality of the soul as "the real basis of the traditional view of the nature of hell" ("View," 147). See also *Seventh-day Adventists Believe*, 371-372.

It is true that the concept of the inherent immortality and hence indestructibility of the soul is an unbiblical, pagan idea. The soul is a created entity and is susceptible to annihilation in the same way as any other created being is. Also, it may be true that some Christian thinkers have tied this false idea of the soul to the idea of hell as eternal conscious suffering. But to conclude from this that the latter idea is therefore false is a *non sequitur* of the greatest magnitude. The bottom line is this: the doctrine of hell as eternal conscious suffering is *in no way dependent* on the false notion of an immortal soul. The souls of the wicked, along with their restored bodies, exist forever *because God wills it*, period. Disproving the inherent immortality of the soul in no way disproves the eternal conscious suffering of the wicked. The argument is at best irrelevant and at worst misleading.

Another main argument for annihilationism is based on the nature of God; this will be discussed in the next section.

Before we turn to that, I will mention here a few problems and inconsistencies related to annihilationism. One is that to many people, annihilation does not sound like much of a punishment (see Grudem, *Theology*, 1150-1151). Pinnock does his best to make its prospect sound worthy of weeping and gnashing of teeth ("View," 165), but he is not convincing. This may be one reason why many annihilationists also believe in equitable punishment, i.e., a variable period of time spent in actual conscious suffering before nonbeing kicks in. The problem then arises, which is the actual penalty for sins: the equitable conscious suffering, or the annihilation? What makes this a problem for annihilationists is that the main arguments for their view all point to annihilation itself as the actual punishment for sins, e.g., the argument that the words for death and destruction *mean* annihilation, and the argument that Matt 25:46 means eternal punish*ment* in terms of annihilation and not eternal punish*ing* in terms of suffering. But the introduction of a preannihilation period of suffering seriously compromises such arguments. It creates ambiguity as to the identity of the real penalty for sin and as to the purpose for annihilation. For example, on the one hand Boatman calls annihilation "the ultimate punishment" (32), but then speaks of the likelihood that the wicked will "be put out of their misery" through annihilation (81). Even Pinnock says that God will not inflict endless punishment on sinners "but will allow them finally to perish" ("View," 143). To "allow" them to perish sounds as if it is a blessing, not a penalty.

This leads to another problem, especially for the equitable-punishment annihilationists: if each one is condemned to a period of conscious suffering based on what his sins deserve, when he gets to the end of that period, why is he not then taken to heaven (a la Origen) rather than annihilated? For example, Boatman speaks of the postsuffering annihilation of the wicked thus: "God ultimately withdraws from them whatever life support system(s) He may have used to sustain them in hell until His justice could be satisfied" (35). But if his justice is thereby *satisfied*, why the annihilation? Especially, how can the annihilation then be considered as *punishment*? See Blanchard, 223.

One very serious problem with annihilationism is that it stands in direct opposition to the biblical doctrine of the substitutionary atonement of Jesus Christ. This is the doctrine that whatever punishment is due to the sins of all mankind according to the just judgment of God, Jesus suffered that penalty in our place. Some annihilationists argue that since Jesus is not suffering eternally in hell, therefore hell cannot be eternal suffering. We have already shown, though, that because of his *infinite divine nature* Jesus was able to suffer the *equivalent* of eternity in hell for all people in a finite time. The real problem with the atonement, though, is not for those who hold the traditional view of hell but for annihilationists. If Jesus truly intended to suffer the penalty for our sins in our place, and if that penalty is annihilation, then Jesus should have been *annihilated forever*. Nothing of the sort happened, though. After being dead for three days, Jesus was raised from the tomb. Even during those three days nothing about him was annihilated (see Morey, 102). There is simply no way to reconcile any form of annihilationism with the biblical doctrine of the atonement.

We conclude that the case against annihilationism is strong, and that the annihilationist's case against the traditional view of hell is weak. The next section will add more to this latter point.

IV. HELL AND THE NATURE OF GOD

A final question about the doctrine of hell as eternal suffering is whether it is consistent with the Bible's teaching about the nature of God. The opponents of the doctrine charge specifically that it contradicts the goodness and love of God, the justice of God, and the sovereignty of God.

A. Hell and God's Love

Universalists insist that a retributive hell of any sort is contrary to the nature of God as a God of love. Nels Ferré says, "No worthy faith can ever attribute eternal hell to God, . . . whom we meet in Christ as eternal and almighty love" (24). Annihilationists also use this argument. For example, Adventists reject eternal torment because "it would detract from the attribute of love as seen in the character of God" (*Seventh-day Adventists Answer Questions on Doctrine*, 543). It contradicts God's goodness and boundless mercy, says Pinnock ("View," 149, 151). Words such as cruelty, sadism, and torture chamber abound in such criticism.

In response we may say first of all that if this criticism were valid at all, then it would apply not only to the traditional view but also to some extent to equitable-punishment annihilationism. If love is all that matters, then why allow for even a *temporary* "torture chamber" for sinners? In Blanchard's view (222), if love is all that counts, annihilation itself should give way to universalism, since "it would seem to be more merciful for God to save people than to obliterate them."

Our main response to this objection, though, is that in fact God's love is not the only aspect of his nature that must be taken into account in the matter of the eternal destinies of mankind. Love is one side of God's moral nature (1 John 4:8) but not the only one. God is equally a God of holiness and wrath (Heb 12:29), a God of both kindness and severity (Rom 11:22), a God who both saves and destroys (Jas 4:12). Because of his nature as love God wants to save sinners and has done everything divinely possible to do so; but when free-will creatures rebel against his holiness and reject his love, his righteousness requires his wrath to be poured out upon them. We cannot ignore the latter side of God's nature. He is a God who says, "Vengeance is Mine, I will repay." Indeed, "it is a terrifying thing to fall into the hands of the living God" (Heb 10:30-31). It is significant that Pinnock rejects "vengeance and vindictiveness" as "totally out of keeping with the love of God." Endless suffering "would be punishment just for its own sake. Surely God does not act like that" ("View," 153). Obviously Pinnock has blinded himself not only to a large part of the Bible's teaching about God, but also to logic itself. That is, what could be more of a "punishment for its own sake" than annihilation?

B. Hell and God's Justice

Our point is that God is just as much a God of holiness as he is a God of love. Heaven is the final outworking of his love; hell is the final outworking of his holiness. The response of holiness to sin is wrath (see, e.g., Isa 63:1-6; Rom 2:5,8; 2 Thess 1:7-9; Rev 14:9-11,19-20), and hell is the just and righteous expression of God's wrath toward unrepentant sinners.

Critics of hell argue, though, that hell as eternal suffering violates God's justice in the sense that it is not a just and righteous expression of his holy wrath. This is alleged to be true in two ways. First, if all sinners suffer in hell forever, then this is unfair to those who were just minor rebels against God as compared with the Hitlers and Stalins of the world. But if each sinner is punished for only a finite period of time according to what his own particular sins deserve, and then annihilated, then fairness and justice are preserved. In response, one could argue that annihilation as the ultimate punishment for sins is also unjust, since its consequences are the same for all sinners. Our main response, though, is that fairness and justice are preserved in eternal suffering for all sinners if the suffering has different degrees of intensity based on each one's works.[4]

A more serious criticism is that eternal conscious suffering is contrary to justice since no *finite* act deserves *infinite* punishment. Pinnock says, "It is too heavy a sentence and cannot be successfully defended as a just action on God's part. Sending the wicked to everlasting torment would be to treat persons worse than they could deserve." He adds, "It would create a serious disproportion between the sins committed in time and the resulting suffering experienced forever" ("View," 152). The usual reply to this is that there is an element of infinity in every sin because every sin is committed against the infinite God (Erickson, *Theology*, 1247). As Dixon says, "There are no small sins against a great God" (84; see 81-85). Walvoord comments, "If the slightest sin is infinite in its significance, then it also demands infinite punishment as a divine judgment" ("View," 27). Habermas and Moreland say it thus: "If people reject an ultimate God who is the greatest being that could possibly exist, then an ultimate judgment where one pays with one's life in a final, irrevocable sense is just" (173). According to David Wells, "If God is as good as the Bible says he is, if his character is as pure, if his life is as infinite, then sin is infinitely unpardonable and not merely momentarily mischievous. To be commensurate with the offense, God's response must be correspondingly infinite" ("Punishment," 42). Actually, God has provided two infinite responses to sin: the infinite sacrifice of Christ on the cross, and infinite suffering in hell.

Pinnock believes that such an explanation as this is superficial ("Response," 39; "View," 152) and chooses to reject it. In my judgment, though, we must allow God to determine what is just and not try to dictate to him (Job 33:13; Rom 3:5-6; 9:19-20).

Two other considerations are relevant. First, God does not send anyone to hell arbitrarily. He gives us all free will to obey his laws; sin itself is our choice. Then he provides us with salvation from sin and hell through Jesus Christ; refusing to accept this salvation is our choice (see Matt 23:37). Thus no one can say that he is suffering the eternal consequences of his sin without warning and contrary to his own will. Second, we must allow for the reality of *degrees* of punishment to vindicate God's justice in the end. We do not really know just how the difference between "many lashes" and "few lashes" (Luke 12:47-48) will be experienced. The eternal punishment of some will be "more bearable" for some than others (Matt 10:15, NIV). The justice of God will ensure that no one's punishment is more than he deserves.[5]

C. Hell and God's Sovereignty

A final challenge to hell as eternal suffering is that such an idea is contrary to God's sovereign control over his universe, and especially contrary to his stated purpose of bringing all things together under the lordship of Jesus Christ. Has not God promised (Phil 2:10-11) that every knee will bow to Christ and every tongue confess him as Lord? Has he not promised (1 Cor 15:28) that "all things" will become subject to him? Has he not declared (Eph 1:10) that "all things"— "things in the heavens and things on the earth"—will be brought under the headship of Christ? Has he not promised (Col 1:20) "to reconcile all things to Himself"? Has he not said (Rev 21:5), "Behold I am making all things new"? But, says the critic, if throughout eternity somewhere in God's universe there must still exist a dark corner where wicked men and angels are undergoing punitive torment, how can God claim to have worked out his purpose and kept his promises? Pinnock complains that this would be an "everlasting cosmological dualism," and that "the new creation turns out to be flawed from day one" ("View," 154). This is unacceptable, say the Adventists, because there would still be "a plague spot in the universe of God throughout eternity, and would seem to indicate that it is impossible for God Himself ever to abolish it" (*Seventh-day Adventists Answer Questions on Doctrine*, 543).

Two comments are in order. First, God's sovereign power and control over his creation are shown just as much by his just punishment of sinners as by his salvation of believers. This criticism would be valid only if sinners were able to evade God's justice and escape eternal suffering for their sins. Some knees will bow to Christ voluntarily; some will be forced to bow contrary to their will. But God's sovereignty is shown in both cases. As Blanchard says, "God will be glorified as greatly in hell as he will in heaven; he will reign as completely in one place as in the other" (221).

Our second comment is that hell will not mar the beauty and perfection of the new creation, because it will not be a part of the new heavens and new earth, the renewed visible universe. It is not now and never will be somewhere in the bowels of the earth; nor will it be in some "dark hole" in the outer space of the new creation, where only righteousness will dwell (2 Pet 3:13). Will it have any "location" at all, then? Yes, I believe so. But we must remember that hell is in its primary purpose "prepared for the devil and his angels" (Matt 25:41), whose torment we know is eternal (Rev 20:10). I conclude, then, that hell will be located in a place primarily compatible with the being of fallen angels. Thus it will be either in some part of the space of the invisible creation (where Hades now exists), or in some specially created dimension of its own. We need not fear that it will interfere in any way with God's sovereign reign over the new creation which will be our glorious and eternal home.

Notes on Chapter Thirty-Three

[1]On the other hand, Blanchard says the fire may symbolize God's *presence* in hell, i.e., his presence as a God of wrath, as a consuming fire. Sinners will be separated only from God's love and grace (158-162).

[2]Blanchard (156) thinks the "gnashing of teeth" actually represents anger—at God, at the devil, at oneself (see Job 16:9; Acts 7:54).

[3]Some forms of annihilationism are called "conditional immortality," but the distinction is not important for our purposes. See Grudem, *Theology*, 1150; Erickson, *Theology*, 1244-1245.

[4]This is parallel to the idea that degrees of *reward* have nothing to do with differing lengths of time spent in heaven. The rewards are equal in duration (i.e., eternal) yet different in intensity.

[5]We should note that a judgment-day annihilation cannot do justice to the biblical teaching about degrees of punishment; nor can the equitable-punishment version do so, if annihilation is indeed the main or ultimate punishment.

BIBLIOGRAPHY OF WORKS CITED

This bibliography includes all works cited in the text and footnotes of this work. Citations include a minimum of information, usually the author's name and an abbreviated title (in **bold print** below) if necessary. This list gives full titles and bibliographical data.

Albrecht, Mark, and Brooks Alexander. "Thanatology: Death and Dying," *Journal of the Spiritual Counterfeits Project* (April 1977).

Allis, Oswald T. *Prophecy and the Church*. Philadelphia: Presbyterian and Reformed, 1945.

Althaus, Paul. *The Theology of Martin Luther*. Tr. Robert C. Schultz. Philadelphia: Fortress Press, 1966.

Anderson, Neil. *The **Bondage Breaker***. Eugene, OR: Harvest House, 1993.

Anderson, Norman. *Issues of Life and Death*. Downers Grove: InterVarsity, 1977.

"Apocalypse Now," *Time* (July 1, 2002), 40-48.

Apostolic Fathers. See Holmes, Michael W., ed.

Armstrong, Herbert W. *1975 in Prophecy!* Revised ed. Pasadena, CA: Radio Church of God, 1957.

Arndt, William F., and F. Wilbur Gingrich. *A Greek-English Lexicon of the New Testament and Other Early Christian Literature* [**AG**]. 4th ed. Chicago: University of Chicago Press, 1952.

Arnold, Clinton E. *3 Crucial **Questions** about Spiritual Warfare*. Grand Rapids: Baker, 1997.

——————. *Powers of Darkness: Principalities and Powers in Paul's Letters*. Downers Grove, IL: InterVarsity, 1992.

Atkins, Anne. *Split Image: Male and Female after God's Likeness*. Grand Rapids: Eerdmans, 1987.

Augustine, Aurelius. "Against Two **Letters** of the Pelagians." *The Works of Aurelius Augustine, Vol. XV: The Anti-Pelagian Works, vol. iii*. Ed. by Marcus Dods. Tr. by Peter Holmes and R.E. Wallis. Edinburgh: T. & T. Clark, 1876. Pp. 237-371.

——————. "A Treatise on **Rebuke** and Grace." *The Works of Aurelius Augustine, Vol. XV: The Anti-Pelagian Works, vol. iii*. Ed. by Marcus Dods. Tr. by Peter Holmes and R.E. Wallis. Edinburgh: T. & T. Clark, 1876. Pp. 69-117.

——————. "A Treatise on the Gift of **Perseverance**." *The Works of Aurelius Augustine, Vol. XV: The Anti-Pelagian Works, vol. iii*. Ed. by Marcus Dods. Tr. by Peter Holmes and R.E. Wallis. Edinburgh: T. & T. Clark, 1876. Pp. 171-235.

——————. "A Treatise on the **Merits** and Forgiveness of Sins." *The Works of Aurelius Augustine, Vol. IV: The Anti-Pelagian Works, vol. i*. Ed. by Marcus Dods. Tr. by Peter Holmes. Edinburgh: T. & T. Clark, 1872.

Aulen, Gustaf. *Christus Victor: An Historical Study of the Three Main Types of the Idea of Atonement*. Tr. by A.G. Hebert. New York: Macmillan, 1951.

Baillie, John. *The Idea of Revelation in Recent Thought*. New York: Columbia University Press, 1956.

Baird, William. *The Corinthian Church: A Biblical Approach to Urban Culture*. New York: Abingdon Press, 1964.

Baker, William R. *2 Corinthians.* The College Press NIV Commentary. Joplin, MO: College Press, 1999.

Baldwin, H. Scott. *"Authenteo* in Ancient Greek Literature." Appendix 2 in *Women in the Church: A Fresh Analysis of 1 Timothy 2:9-15.* Ed. by Andreas J. Köstenberger et al. Grand Rapids: Baker, 1995. Pp. 269-305.

_____ . "A Difficult **Word**: *authenteo* in 1 Timothy 2:12," In *Women in the Church: A Fresh Analysis of 1 Timothy 2:9-15.* Ed. by Andreas J. Köstenberger et al. Grand Rapids: Baker, 1995. Pp. 65-80.

Balz, Horst, and Gerhard Schneider, eds. *Exegetical Dictionary of the New Testament [EDNT].* 3 vols. Grand Rapids: Eerdmans, 1990ff.

Barclay, William. *New Testament Words.* Philadelphia: Westminster, 1974.

_____ . *The Plain Man Looks at the Apostles' Creed.* London: Collins, 1967.

Barth, Karl. *The Doctrine of the Word of God: Church Dogmatics [CD I],* I/2. Tr. by G.T. Thomson and Harold Knight. Edinburgh: T. & T. Clark, 1956.

Beam, Joe. *Seeing the Unseen.* West Monroe, LA: Howard Publishing, 1994.

Beasley, Thomas. "Unity and Doctrine," *Christian Standard* (5/29/83).

Behe, Michael. *Darwin's Black Box: The Biochemical Challenge to Evolution.* New York: The Free Press, 1996.

Berkhof, Louis. *Systematic Theology.* Grand Rapids: Eerdmans, 1941.

Berkouwer, G.C. *Divine Election.* Tr. by Hugo Bekker. Grand Rapids: Eerdmans, 1960.

_____ . *The Return of Christ.* Tr. by James Van Oosterom. Grand Rapids: Eerdmans, 1972.

Best, W.E. *Justification before God (Not by Faith).* Houston: South Belt Assembly of Christ, n.d. [1973].

Bettenson, Henry, ed. *Documents of the Christian Church,* 2nd ed. London: Oxford University Press, 1963.

Beyer, Hermann W. *"Episkeptomai,"* etc., *TDNT,* II:599-622.

Bietenhard, Hans. "Satan, etc." (part), *NIDNTT,* III:468-472.

Bilezikian, Gilbert. *Beyond Sex Roles,"* 2nd ed. Grand Rapids: Baker, 1985.

Bishop, Jim. *The Day Christ Died.* New York: Pocket Books, 1959.

Black, Mark C. *Luke.* The College Press NIV Commentary. Joplin, MO: College Press, 1996.

Blaikie, Robert J. *"Secular Christianity" and God Who Acts.* Grand Rapids: Eerdmans, 1970.

Blakely, Fred O. *The Apostles' Doctrine.* Vol. I, revised ed. Highland, IN: Author, 1957.

Blanchard, John. *Whatever Happened to Hell?* Durham, England: Evangelical Press, 1993.

Boatman, Russell E. *Beyond Death: What the Bible Says about the Hereafter.* Florissant, MO: Author, 1980.

Böcher, Otto. "diabolos," *TDNT,* I:297-298.

Bockmühl, Klaus. "Theology as Servant," *Christianity Today* (2/27/76).

Boettner, Loraine. *The Millennium.* Philadelphia: Presbyterian and Reformed, 1957.

_____ . "**Postmillennialism**." In Clouse, ed. *Millennium,* 117-141.

_____ . *Studies in Theology,* 3rd ed. Grand Rapids: Eerdmans, 1953.

Borland, James A. *Christ in the Old Testament.* Chicago: Moody, 1978.

Bowman, Richard. "Words and Their Meanings." *Disciple Renewal* (August 1987): 9-11.

Boyd, Gregory A. *God of the Possible: A Biblical Introduction to the Open View of God.* Grand Rapids: Baker, 2000.

_____. *Oneness Pentecostals and the Trinity: A Worldwide Movement Assessed by a Former Oneness Pentecostal.* Grand Rapids: Baker, 1992.

Broadbent, E.H. *The Pilgrim Church.* London: Pickering and Inglis, 1931.

Brown, Colin. "**Guilt**," etc. (part), *NIDNTT*, II:137-140.

_____, ed. *The New International Dictionary of New Testament Theology [NIDNTT].* 3 vols. Grand Rapids: Zondervan, 1975-1978.

Brown, Harold O.J. *Heresies.* Garden City, NY: Doubleday, 1984.

Brown, William Adams. *Christian Theology in Outline.* New York: Charles Scribner's Sons, 1906.

Bruce, F.F. *The Epistle of Paul to the Romans.* Tyndale New Testament Commentaries. Grand Rapids: Eerdmans, 1963.

Brumback, Carl. *God in Three Persons.* Cleveland, TN: Pathway Press, 1959.

Brunner, Emil. *The Christian Doctrine of Creation and Redemption: Dogmatics*, Vol. **II**. Tr. by Olive Wyon. Philadelphia: Westminster, 1952.

_____. *The Christian Doctrine of the Church, Faith, and the Consummation: Dogmatics*, Vol. **III**. Tr. by David Cairns and T.H.L. Parker. Philadelphia: Westminster, 1962.

_____. *The Christian Doctrine of God: Dogmatics*, Vol. **I**. Tr. by Olive Wyon. Philadelphia: Westminster, 1950.

_____. *Eternal Hope.* Tr. by Harold Knight. Philadelphia: Westminster Press, 1954.

Buchanan, James. *The Doctrine of Justification.* Edinburgh: T. & T. Clark, 1867; reprint, Grand Rapids: Baker, 1955.

Bultmann, Rudolf. "Pisteuo," etc., *TDNT*, VI:174-228.

Buswell, J.O. Jr. *A Systematic Theology of the Christian Religion,* 2 vols. Grand Rapids: Zondervan, 1962, 1963.

Byrum, Russell. *Christian Theology.* Anderson, IN: Warner Press, 1925.

Calvin, John. "A **Defence** of the Secret Providence of God." *Calvin's Calvinism.* Tr. by Henry Cole. Grand Rapids: Eerdmans, 1956. Pp. 207-350.

_____. "A **Treatise** on the Eternal Predestination of God." *Calvin's Calvinism.* Tr. by Henry Cole. Grand Rapids: Eerdmans, 1956. Pp. 1-206.

Campbell, Alexander. "An Address on **Colleges**." *The Millennial Harbinger,* series IV, vol. IV:2 (February 1854); reprint, Joplin, MO: College Press, 1970. 25:61-79.

_____. "Address on **Demonology**." *Popular Lectures and Addresses.* Nashville: Harbinger Book Club, reprint of 1861 ed. Pp. 379-402.

_____. *The Christian System.* Nashville: Gospel Advocate, 1974 reprint.

_____. *A Debate between Rev. A. Campbell and Rev. N.L. Rice on . . . Christian Baptism.* Lexington, KY: A.T. Skillman & Son, 1844.

_____. "Essay on **Man**," No. 1. *The Christian Baptist*, VI:1 (Aug. 4, 1828); reprint, Joplin, MO: College Press, 1983. Pp. 463-464.

_____. "**Instinct**, Soul, and Spirit." *The Millennial Harbinger,* series V, vol. I:5 (May 1858); reprint, Joplin, MO: College Press, 1970. 29:290-291.

_____ . Letter III "To '**Paulinus**.'" *The Christian Baptist*, IV:10 (May 7, 1827); reprint, Joplin, MO: College Press, 1983. Pp. 336-338.

_____ . "'**Response**' to a letter entitled 'Remarks on the Bible.'" *The Christian Baptist*, VI:5 (Dec. 1, 1828); reprint, Joplin, MO: College Press, 1983. P. 499.

_____ . "The Three **Kingdoms**." *The Christian Baptist*, IV:11 (June 1, 1829); reprint, Joplin, MO: College Press, 1983. Pp. 557-558.

_____ . "The Whole Work of the **Holy Spirit** in the Salvation of Men." *The Millennial Harbinger*, II:7 (July 4, 1831); reprint, Nashville: Harbinger Book Club, n.d. II:290-297.

Carroll, James Milton. *The Trail of Blood*. Lexington, KY: American Baptist Publishing Co., 1931.

Carson, D.A. *Exegetical Fallacies*. Grand Rapids: Baker, 1984.

Charnock, Stephen. *The Existence and Attributes of God*. Grand Rapids: Kregel reprint, 1958.

Chouinard, Larry. *Matthew*. The College Press NIV Commentary. Joplin, MO: College Press, 1997.

Christian, C.W. *Shaping Your Faith: A Guide to Personal Theology*. Waco: Word, 1973.

Clark, Don. "A Custom of Cruelty." *Christian Standard* (3/22/69): 104:3-4.

Clark, Gordon H. *Biblical **Predestination***. Nutley, NJ: Presbyterian and Reformed, 1969.

Clouse, Robert G., ed. *The Meaning of the Millennium: Four Views*. Downers Grove, IL: Inter-Varsity, 1977.

Colwell, E.C. "A Definite Rule for the Use of the Article in the Greek New Testament." *Journal of Biblical Literature* (January 1933): 52:13.

Cook, Stuart D. "Making Jesus Central." *Christian Standard* (4/19/67): 116:35-36.

Cooper, John W. *Body, Soul, and Life Everlasting: Biblical Anthropology and the Monism-Dualism Debate, 2nd ed.* Grand Rapids: Eerdmans, 2000.

Corson, John D. "Faith Alone Involves Obedience, Too!" *Christian Standard* (10/2/77): 126:5-6.

Cosgrove, Mark. *The Amazing **Body Human***. Grand Rapids: Baker, 1987.

Cottrell, Jack. "1 **Timothy** 2:12 and the Role of Women." 3 parts. *Christian Standard* (1/10/93): 4-6; (1/17/93): 4-6; (1/24/93): 4-6.

_____ . "1 Timothy 2:12 and the Role of Women: The Meaning of **Galatians** 3:28." *Christian Standard* (1/31/93): 4-6.

_____ . "1 Timothy 2:12 and the Role of Women: **Priscilla**, Phoebe, and Company." *Christian Standard* (12/12/93): 4-5.

_____ . "1 Timothy 2:12 and the Role of Women: **Response** to My Critics." 3 parts. *Christian Standard* (11/21/93): 5-6; (11/28/93): 4-6; (12/5/93): 4-6.

_____ . *Baptism: A Biblical Study*. Joplin, MO: College Press, 1989.

_____ . "Baptism according to the **Reformed Tradition**." *Baptism and the Remission of Sins: An Historical Perspective*. Ed. by David W. Fletcher. Joplin, MO: College Press, 1990. Pp. 39-81.

_____ . "The Biblical **Consensus**: Historical Backgrounds to Reformed Theology." *Baptism and the Remission of Sins: An Historical Perspective*. Ed. by David W. Fletcher. Joplin, MO: College Press, 1990. Pp. 17-38.

_____ . "The **Church**: The House of God." In *Christ's Victorious Church: Essays on Biblical Ecclesiology and Eschatology in Honor of Tom Friskney.* Ed. by Jon A. Weatherly. Eugene, OR: Wipf and Stock, 2001. Pp. 7-17.

_____ . "**Covenant and Baptism** in the Theology of Huldreich Zwingli." Ph.D. diss., Princeton Theological Seminary, 1971.

_____ . "**Faith**, History, and the Resurrection Body of Jesus." *The Seminary Review* 28 (December 1982): 143-160.

_____ . *Faith's Fundamentals: Seven Essentials of Christian Belief.* Cincinnati: Standard Publishing, 1995.

_____ . *Feminism and the Bible.* Joplin, MO: College Press, 1992.

_____ . "The **Gender of Jesus** and the Incarnation: A Case Study in Feminist Hermeneutics." *Stone-Campbell Journal* 3 (Fall 2000): 171-194.

_____ . *Gender Roles and the Bible: Creation, the Fall, and Redemption.* Joplin, MO: College Press, 1994.

_____ . "**Headship**, Submission, and the Bible." www.cbmw.org/resources/books/headship.pdf.

_____ . "Historical and Contemporary Perspectives on **Inerrancy**." *Restoration Forum VI.* Joplin, MO: College Press, 1988. Pp. 70-97.

_____ . "The Nature of the Divine **Sovereignty**." *The Grace of God, the Will of Man.* Ed. by Clark H. Pinnock. Grand Rapids: Zondervan, 1989. Pp. 97-119.

_____ . *Romans.* 2 vols. The College Press NIV Commentary. Joplin, MO: College Press, 1996, 1998.

_____ . *Solid: The Authority of God's Word.* Joplin, MO: College Press, 1991.

_____ . *What the Bible Says about God the Creator [GC].* Joplin, MO: College Press, 1983.

_____ . *What the Bible Says about God the Redeemer [GRe].* Joplin, MO: College Press, 1987.

_____ . *What the Bible Says about God the Ruler [GRu].* Joplin, MO: College Press, 1984.

_____ . "Will the Real Seventh Day **Adventist** Please Stand Up?" 3 parts. *The Lookout* (8/20/78, 8/27/78, 9/3/78).

Cox, William E. *Biblical Studies in Final Things.* Nutley, NJ: Presbyterian and Reformed, 1977.

Craig, William. *The Existence of God and the Beginning of the Universe.* San Bernardino, CA: Here's Life Publishers, 1979.

_____ . *Reasonable Faith: Christian Truth and Apologetics,* rev. ed. Wheaton, IL: Crossway Books, 1994.

Cranfield, C.E.B. *A Critical and Exegetical Commentary on the Epistle to the Romans.* 2 vols. The International Critical Commentary, new series. Edinburgh: T. & T. Clark, 1975, 1979; 1990/1994 printing.

Crawford, C.C. *Survey Course in Christian Doctrine.* 4 vols. Joplin, MO: College Press, 1962, 1964.

Crockett, William, ed. *Four Views on Hell.* Grand Rapids: Zondervan, 1992.

_____ . "The Metaphorical **View**." *Four Views on Hell*. Ed. by William Crockett. Grand Rapids: Zondervan, 1992. Pp. 43-76.

Crouch, Owen. "The Tree of Knowledge of Good and Evil." *Christian Standard* (5/17/81).

Cullmann, Oscar. *The **Christology** of the New Testament*, rev. ed. Tr. by Shirley C. Guthrie and Charles A.M. Hall. Philadelphia: Westminster, 1959.

_____ . "**Immortality** of the Soul or Resurrection of the Dead: The Witness of the New Testament." In *Immortality and Resurrection*. Ed. by Krister Stendahl. New York: Macmillan, 1965. Pp. 9-53.

Curtis, David B. "**Inspiration** and the Second Coming of Christ." www.lvcm.com/preterism/inspiration.htm, accessed 7/18/02.

_____ . "The **Rapture**—Physical or Spiritual?" www.lvcm.com/preterism/rapture.htm, accessed 7/18/02.

Davies, W.D. *Paul and Rabbinic Judaism*. London: SPCK, 1955.

Davis, Christopher A. *Revelation*. The College Press NIV Commentary. Joplin, MO: College Press, 2000.

Davis, John Jefferson. *Christ's Victorious **Kingdom***. Grand Rapids: Baker, 1986.

Denton, Michael. *Evolution: A Theory in Crisis*. Bethesda, MD: Adler & Adler, 1985.

DeWelt, Don. *Romans Realized*. Joplin, MO: College Press, 1959.

DeWolf, L. Harold. *A Theology of the Living Church*. New York: Harper & Brothers, 1953.

Dickason, C. Fred. *Angels, Elect and Evil*. Chicago: Moody, 1975.

_____ . *Demon **Possession** and the Christian*. Chicago: Moody, 1987.

Dickinson, Curtis. "**Gateway** to Life." *The Witness* (August 1974): 1-2.

_____ . "The **Gates** of Hades." *The Witness* (November 1978): 1-2.

_____ . "How Traditional **Theology** Neutralizes the Gospel." *The Witness* (June 1982): 1-2.

_____ . *What the Bible Teaches about **Immortality** and Future Punishment*. Alamogordo, NM: Author, 1984. (Earlier title: *Man and His Destiny*.)

Ditmanson, Harold. *Grace in Experience and Theology*. Minneapolis: Augsburg, 1977.

Dixon, Larry. *The Other Side of the Good News*. Wheaton, IL: Victor Books (Bridgepoint), 1992.

Dodd, C.H. *The Bible and the Greeks*. London: Hodder & Stoughton, 1935.

Donley, Jeffery R. *What the Bible Says about Basic Theology*. Joplin, MO: College Press, 1988.

Dunn, James D.G. *Romans 1-8*. Word Biblical Commentary. Vol. 38. Dallas: Word, 1988.

Eddy, Mary Baker. *Science and Health with Key to the Scriptures*. Boston: The Christian Science Publishing Society, 1906.

Edwards, James. "Testing the Spiritualities." *Christianity Today* (9/12/94).

Ensign, Grayson; and Edward Howe. *Counseling and Demonization: The Missing Link*. Amarillo, TX: Recovery Publications, 1989.

Erickson, Millard J. *Christian Theology*, 2nd ed. Grand Rapids: Baker, 1998.

_____ . *The Evangelical **Mind** and Heart*. Grand Rapids: Baker, 1993.

_____ . *How Shall They Be Saved? The **Destiny** of Those Who Do Not Hear of Jesus*. Grand Rapids: Baker, 1996.

Ferre, Nels F.S. "Universalism: Pro and Con." *Christianity Today* (3/1/63): 24.

Fowler, Gene S. "Why Do People Die?" *Christian Standard* 125 (10/24/76): 9-10.

"**Freud** and Death." *Time* (7/17/72).

Fudge, Edward William. *The Fire That Consumes: A Biblical and Historical Study of Final Punishment.* Fallbrook, CA: Verdict Publications, 1982.

Gardner, Lynn. *Christianity Stands True: A Common Sense Look at the Evidence.* Joplin, MO: College Press, 1994.

Gasson, Raphael. *The Challenging Counterfeit.* Plainfield, NJ: Logos Books, 1970.

Geisler, Norman. *Creating God in the Image of Man? The New "Open" View of God: Neothism's Dangerous Drift.* Minneapolis: Bethany House, 1997.

_____ . *Philosophy of Religion.* Grand Rapids: Zondervan, 1974.

Gentry, Kenneth L. Jr. *He Shall Have Dominion: A Postmillennial Eschatology.* Tyler, TX: Institute for Christian Economics, 1993.

Gilkey, Langdon. *Maker of Heaven and Earth.* Garden City, NY: Doubleday Anchor, 1965.

Gilmore, John. *Probing Heaven: Key Questions on the Hereafter.* Grand Rapids: Baker, 1989.

Greenlee, John. "Back to **Basics**." *Christian Standard* 128 (8/5/79): 15-16.

_____ . "Theological **Roots**." *Christian Standard* (4/3/77).

Gregory of Nyssa. "An Address on Religious Instruction." *Christology of the Later Fathers.* Ed. by Edward R. Hardy. Library of Christian Classics. Vol. III. Philadelphia: Westminster, n.d.

Gresham, Charles. "**Creeds**, Statements of Faith, Practical Wisdom." *The Restoration Herald* (March 1991): 1, 4, 8.

_____ . "The **Goodness** and Severity of God." *The Restoration Herald* (November 1987).

Gromacki, Robert. *The Virgin Birth: Doctrine of Deity.* Nashville: Nelson, 1974.

Grotius, Hugo. *A Defence of the Catholic Faith Concerning the Satisfaction of Christ.* Ed. by Frank H. Foster. Andover: Warren F. Draper, 1889.

Grudem, Wayne. *Bible Doctrine: Essential Teachings of the Christian Faith.* Ed. by Jeff Purswell. Grand Rapids: Zondervan, 1999.

_____ . *Systematic Theology: An Introduction to Biblical Doctrine.* Grand Rapids: Zondervan, 1994. *(added)*

Gruss, Edmond C. *Apostles of Denial.* Grand Rapids: Baker, 1970.

_____ . *The Jehovah's Witnesses and Prophetic Speculation.* Nutley, NJ: Presbyterian and Reformed, 1972.

Guillebaud, H.E. *Why the Cross?* 2nd ed. London: Inter-Varsity Fellowship, 1946.

Gundry, Robert. *Soma in Biblical Theology.* Grand Rapids: Zondervan, 1987.

Habermas, Gary R., and J.P. Moreland. *Immortality: The Other Side of Death.* Nashville: Thomas Nelson, 1992.

Harris, Murray. *Raised Immortal: Resurrection and Immortality in the New Testament.* Grand Rapids: Eerdmans, 1983.

Hayes, Howard A. "Another Tragic **Divorce**." *Christian Standard* 123 (6/16/74): 7-8.

Heim, Karl. *Jesus the World's Perfecter.* Tr. by D.H. van Daalen. Edinburgh: Oliver and Boyd, 1959.

Hendriksen, William. *More Than Conquerors: An Interpretation of the Book of Revelation*. Grand Rapids: Baker, 1977 printing.

Hick, John. *Death and Eternal Life*. San Francisco: Harper and Row, 1976.

_____ . *Evil and the God of Love*. New York: Harper & Row, 1966.

Hobbs, A.I. "Conversion: What Is It, and How Produced?" *The Old Faith Restated*. Ed. By J.H. Garrison. St. Louis: Christian Publishing Co., 1891.

Hodges, Zane. *Absolutely Free! A Biblical Reply to Lordship Salvation*. Grand Rapids: Zondervan, 1989.

Hoekema, Anthony. **"Amillennialism."** In *The Meaning of the Millennium: Four Views*. Ed. by Robert G. Clouse. Downers Grove, IL: InterVarsity, 1977. Pp. 155-187.

_____ . *The Bible and the Future*. Grand Rapids: Eerdmans, 1979.

_____ . *Created in God's Image*. Grand Rapids: Eerdmans, 1986.

Hofius, Otfried. "Father." NIDNTT I:614-621.

Holmes, Michael W., ed. *The Apostolic Fathers*, 2nd ed. Tr. by J.B. Lightfoot and J.R. Harmer. Grand Rapids: Baker, 1989.

Hope, Norman V. "Presbyterians and Bishops." *Presbyterian Life* (5/1/67): 32-33.

Horn, Robert. *Go Free! The Meaning of Justification*. Downers Grove, IL: InterVarsity, 1976.

Hough, Robert Ervin. *The Christian after Death*. Chicago: Moody, 1947.

Houston, James. *I Believe in the Creator*. Grand Rapids: Eerdmans, 1980.

Howden, William D. "Death Belongs to You." *Christian Standard* (4/19/81).

Hoyt, Herman A. "Dispensationalism Premillennialism." In *The Meaning of the Millennium: Four Views*. Ed. by Robert G. Clouse. Downers Grove, IL: InterVarsity, 1977. Pp. 63-92.

Hume, David. *Dialogues Concerning Natural Religion*. Ed. by Norman Kemp Smith. Indianapolis: Bobbs-Merrill, 1947.

Irenaeus. *The Demonstration of the Apostolic Preaching*. Tr. by J. Armitage Robinson. London: S.P.C.K., 1920.

Jackson, Wayne. "The Menace of Radical Preterism." *Christian Courier*. www.christian courier.com/feature/august99.htm, accessed 7/18/02.

James, William. *Pragmatism*. Cleveland: World/Meridian, 1955.

Jastrow, Robert. *God and the Astronomers*. New York: Warner Books, 1980.

Jenkins, David. *The Glory of Man*. New York: Scribner's, 1967.

Jeremias, Joachim. *"hades."* TDNT I:146-149.

Johnson, Philip. "Modest Ambitions." *Books and Culture* (September/October 1995).

Josephus. **"Wars** of the Jews." *The Works of Flavius Josephus*. Tr. by William Whiston. Philadelphia: Henry T. Coates, n.d. Pp. 498-707.

Justin Martyr. "The First **Apology** of Justin." ANF I:159-187.

Kaiser, Christopher B. *The Doctrine of God: An Historical Survey*. Westchester, IL: Crossway Books, 1982.

Kantzer, Kenneth. "The Communication of Revelation," *The Bible: The Living Word of Revelation*. Ed. by Merrill C. Tenney. Grand Rapids: Zondervan, 1968.

Kelly, J.N.D. *Early Christian Doctrines*, 2nd ed. New York: Harper & Row, 1960.

Kenneson, Philip D. "There's No Such Thing As Objective Truth, and It's a Good Thing, Too." *Christian Apologetics in the Postmodern World*. Ed. by Timothy R. Phillips and Dennis L. Okholm. Downers Grove, IL: InterVarsity, 1995. Pp. 155-170.

Kittel, Gerhard. "*ainigma.*" *TDNT* I:178-180.

Kittel, Gerhard; and Gerhard Friedrich, eds. *Theological Dictionary of the New Testament* [*TDNT*]. Tr. and ed. by Geoffrey W. Bromiley. 10 vols. Grand Rapids: Eerdmans, 1964-1976.

Knowles, Victor. *Angels and Demons*. Joplin, MO: College Press, 1994.

Köstenberger, Andreas J. "A Complex **Sentence** Structure in 1 Timothy 2:12." In *Women in the Church: A Fresh Analysis of 1 Timothy 2:9-15*. Andreas J. Köstenberger et al., eds. Grand Rapids: Baker, 1995. Pp. 81-103.

Köstenberger, Andreas J., et al., eds. *Women in the Church: A Fresh Analysis of 1 Timothy 2:9-15*. Grand Rapids: Baker, 1995.

Kübler-Ross, Elisabeth. *Death: The Final Stage of Growth*. Englewood Cliffs, NJ: Prentice-Hall, 1975.

_____ . *On Death and Dying*. New York: Macmillan, 1970.

Kushner, Harold. *When Bad Things Happen to Good People*. New York: Schocken Books, 1981.

Ladd, George Eldon. "An Historic Premillennial **Response**.," In *The Meaning of the Millennium: Four Views*. Ed. by Robert G. Clouse. Downers Grove, IL: InterVarsity, 1977. Pp. 189-191.

_____ . "Historic **Premillennialism**." In *The Meaning of the Millennium: Four Views*. Ed. by Robert G. Clouse. Downers Grove, IL: InterVarsity, 1977. Pp. 17-40.

_____ . *A Theology of the New Testament*. Grand Rapids: Eerdmans, 1974.

Laidlaw, John. *The Biblical Doctrine of Man*. Edinburgh: T. & T. Clark, 1905.

Lake, Kirsopp. *The Religion of Yesterday and Tomorrow*. Boston: Houghton, 1926.

Lamar, J.S. "The Ground of Man's Need of Salvation, or Sin and Its Remedy." *The Old Faith Restated*. Ed. by J.H. Garrison. St. Louis: Christian Publishing Co., 1891.

Lamont, Corliss. "The Crisis Called Death." *The Humanist* (January-February 1967).

Lang, J. Stephen. "Condensed Christianity." *The Lookout* (3/5/89).

Lard, Moses. *Commentary on Paul's Letter to Romans*. Cincinnati: Standard Publishing, n.d.

Lawlor, George L. *When God Became Man*. Chicago: Moody, 1978.

Lawson, John. *A Theological and Historical Introduction to the Apostolic Fathers*. New York: Macmillan, 1961.

Leith, John H. *Creeds of the Churches*, 3rd ed. Atlanta: John Knox Press, 1982.

"*Let God Be True*," rev. ed. Brooklyn: Watchtower Bible and Tract Society, 1952.

Lewis, C.S. *The Great Divorce*. New York: Macmillan, 1963.

_____ . *Miracles: A Preliminary Study*, 2nd ed. New York: Macmillan, 1960.

Lindsey, Hal. *The Late Great Planet Earth*. Grand Rapids: Zondervan, 1970.

Linton, Calvin D. "The Sorrows of Hell." *Christianity Today* (11/19/71): 12-14.

Lovett, C.S. *Jesus Wants You Well*. Baldwin Park, CA: Personal Christianity, 1973.

Luther, Martin. "The Babylonian **Captivity** of the Church." *Three Treatises*. Philadelphia: Fortress Press, 1960. Pp. 123-260.

_____ . "The Holy and Blessed **Sacrament** of Baptism." Tr. by Charles Jacobs and E.T. Bachmann. *Luther's Works,* American Edition, Vol. 35. *Word and Sacrament, I.* Ed. by E.T. Bachmann. Philadelphia: Muhlenberg Press, 1960. Pp. 29-43.

_____ . "The **Large Catechism**." *The Book of Concord.* Tr. and ed. by Theodore Tappert et al. Philadelphia: Fortress Press, 1959. Pp. 257-461.

MacArthur, John. *Romans.* 2 vols. The MacArthur New Testament Commentary: Chicago: Moody, 1991, 1994.

MacPherson, Dave. *The Incredible Cover-Up.* Medford, OR: Omega Publications, 1980 reprint of 1975 ed. by Logos International.

Macquarrie, John. *Principles of Christian Theology.* New York: Scribner's Sons, 1966.

Maurer, Christian. "*hypodikos.*" *TDNT* VIII:557-558.

Maury, Pierre. *The Christian Understanding of Man.* London: Allen & Unwin, 1938.

McDonald, H.D. *Theories of Revelation: An Historical Study, 1860–1960.* Grand Rapids: Baker, 1979.

McDowell, Josh. *New **Evidence** That Demands a Verdict.* Nashville: Thomas Nelson, 1999.

McGarvey, J.W. "**Justification** by Faith." *Lard's Quarterly* (January 1866): III:113-129.

McGarvey, J.W., and Philip Y. Pendleton. *Thessalonians, Corinthians, Galatians, and **Romans**.* Cincinnati: Standard Publishing, n.d.

McGavran, Donald. "That the Gospel Be Made Known." *Theology, News and Notes* (June 1985): 10-11. Used by permission.

Menninger, Karl. *Whatever Became of Sin?* New York: Hawthorn Books, 1973.

Merold, Ben. "Christ Challenges Our Brotherhood." *Christian Standard* (10/9/94).

Merrill, Eugene H. "*Sh'ol.*" *NIDOTTE* 4:6-7.

Metzger, Bruce M. "The Punctuation of Rom. 9:5." *Christ and Spirit in the New Testament.* Ed. by Barnabas Linders and Stephen Smalley. Cambridge: University Press, 1973.

Milligan, Robert. *Exposition and Defense of the Scheme of Redemption.* St. Louis: Bethany Press, n.d.

Mollenkott, Virginia. *Women, Men, and the Bible,* rev. ed. New York: Crossroad, 1988.

Moo, Douglas J. *The Epistle to the Romans.* The New International Commentary on the New Testament. Grand Rapids: Eerdmans, 1996.

Moreland, J.P., and David Ciocchi, eds. *Christian **Perspectives** on Being Human.* Grand Rapids: Baker, 1993.

Moreland, J.P., and Scott B. Rae. *Body and Soul: Human Nature and the Crisis in Ethics.* Downers Grove, IL: InterVarsity, 2000.

Morey, Robert A. *Death and the Afterlife.* Minneapolis: Bethany House, 1984.

Morris, Desmond. *The Naked **Ape**: A Study of the Human Animal.* New York: Delta, 1967.

Morris, Leon. *The Apostolic **Preaching** of the Cross,* 2nd ed. Grand Rapids: Eerdmans, 1960.

_____ . "Eternal **Punishment**." *Evangelical Dictionary of Theology.* Ed. by Walter A. Elwell. Grand Rapids: Baker, 1984. Pp. 369-370.

_____ . "God's Way Is **Grace**." *Christianity Today* (3/16/62).

_____ . *I Believe in **Revelation**.* Grand Rapids: Eerdmans, 1976.

_____ . *The Wages of Sin: An Examination of the New Testament Teaching on Death.* London: Tyndale Press, 1955.

Moser, K.C. *The Way of Salvation.* Delight, AR: Gospel Light, reprint of 1932 ed.

Mounce, Robert. *Romans.* The New Testament Commentary, Vol. 27. Nashville: Broadman & Holman, 1995.

Murphy, Ed. *The Handbook for Spiritual Warfare,* rev. ed. Nashville: Thomas Nelson, 1996.

Murray, John. *Collected Writings of John Murray, Volume Two: Select Lectures in Systematic Theology.* Carlisle, PA: Banner of Truth Trust, 1977.

_____ . *The Epistle to the Romans,* 2 vols. New International Commentary. Grand Rapids: Eerdmans, 1959, 1965.

Nash, Donald. "*God* Fully Pardons." *Christian Standard* 143 (7/24/94): 10-11.

_____ . "Living Under **Law**." *The Lookout* (10/20/94): 15.

Nash, Ronald H. *Is Jesus the Only Savior?* Grand Rapids: Zondervan, 1994.

Nee, Watchman. *The Spiritual Man,* 3 vols. Indianapolis: Christian Fellowship, 1968.

Nicole, Roger. "Universalism: Will Everyone Be Saved?" *Christianity Today* (3/20/87): 32-39.

Noe, John. *Beyond the End Times.* Bradford, PA: Preterist Resources, 1999.

_____ . *Shattering the Left Behind Delusion.* Bradford, PA: International Preterist Association, 2000.

_____ . *Top Ten Misconceptions about Jesus' Second Coming and the End Times.* Fishers, IN: Prophecy Reformation Institute, 1998.

Norris, Frederick. "Jesus Is Lord." *Envoy* (January 1977): 1.

Nygren, Anders. *Agape and Eros.* Tr. by Philip S. Watson. Philadelphia: Westminster, 1953.

Oepke, Albrecht. "*parousia, pareimi.*" *TDNT* V:858-871.

Packer, J.I. *Knowing God.* Downers Grove, IL: InterVarsity, 1973.

Paley, William. "**Natural Theology**." *The Works of William Paley,* new ed. Philadelphia: J.J. Woodward, 1841.

Palmer, Edwin H. *The Person and Ministry of the Holy Spirit: The Traditional Calvinistic Perspective.* Grand Rapids: Baker, 1974.

Paragein, Stan. "No Creed but Christ." *Christian Standard* (8/18/74).

Paxton, Geoffrey J. *The Shaking of Adventism.* Grand Rapids: Baker, 1977.

Payne, J. Barton. *Encyclopedia of Biblical Prophecy.* New York: Harper and Row, 1973.

Pentecost, J. Dwight. *The Glory of God.* Portland, OR: Multnomah, 1978.

_____ . *Things To Come: A Study in Biblical Eschatology.* Grand Rapids: Zondervan, 1964 reprint of 1958 ed.

Peterson, Robert; and Martha Peterson. *Roaring Lion.* Denver: OMF Books, 1989. (Earlier title: *Are Demons for Real?*)

Pinnock, Clark. "The Conditional **View**." *Four Views on Hell.* Ed. by William Crockett. Grand Rapids: Zondervan, 1992. Pp. 135-166.

_____ . "**Response** to John F. Walvoord." *Four Views on Hell.* Ed. William Crockett. Grand Rapids: Zondervan, 1992. Pp. 36-39.

_____ . *A Wideness in God's Mercy.* Grand Rapids: Zondervan, 1992.

Pinnock, Clark, et al. *The Openness of God: A Biblical Challenge to the Traditional Understanding of God*. Downers Grove, IL: InterVarsity, 1994.

Piper, John. *The Justification of God: An Exegetical and Theological Study of Romans 9:1-23*, 2nd ed. Grand Rapids: Baker, 1993.

Pohle, Joseph. *God: The Author of Nature and the Supernatural*. Ed. by Arthur Preuss. St. Louis: B. Herder, 1912.

Portalie, Eugene. *A Guide to the Thought of Saint Augustine*. Tr. by Ralph J. Bastian. Chicago: Henry Regnery, 1960.

Ramm, Bernard. *The Christian View of Science and Scripture*. Grand Rapids: Eerdmans, 1956.

_____ . *Special Revelation and the Word of God*. Grand Rapids: Eerdmans, 1961.

Reese, Gareth. "The Faith That Saves." *New Testament History: Acts*. Joplin, MO: College Press, 1976. Pp. 598-610.

_____ . *New Testament History: Acts*. Joplin, MO: College Press, 1976.

Reichenbach, Bruce. *Is Man the Phoenix? A Study of Immortality*. Washington, DC: University Press, 1978.

Rengstorf, Karl Heinrich. "*Didasko,*" etc. *TDNT* II:135-165.

Ridenour, Fritz. *How to Be a Christian without Being Religious*. Glendale, CA: Regal Books, 1967.

Robbins, John W. "The Sagan of Science." *The Trinity Review* (September-October 1988): 4-5.

Roberts, Alexander, and James Donaldson, eds. *Ante-Nicene Fathers [ANF]*, 10 vols. Grand Rapids: Eerdmans reprint, 1978.

Robertson, Scott. "The Holy Spirit according to 1 Corinthians 12:13." *The Seminary Review* (December 1977).

Rondet, Henri. *Original Sin*. Staten Island: Alba House, 1972.

Ross, Hugh. *The Creator and the Cosmos*, 2nd ed. Colorado Springs: NavPress, 1995.

Russell, Jeffrey Burton. *The Devil: Perceptions of Evil from Antiquity to Primitive Christianity*. Ithaca, NY: Cornell University Press, 1987.

Ryrie, Charles C. "**Dispensation,** Dispensationalism." *Evangelical Dictionary of Theology*. Ed. by Walter A. Elwell. Grand Rapids: Baker, 1984. Pp. 321-323.

_____ . *So Great Salvation: What It Means to Believe in Jesus Christ*. Wheaton, IL: Scripture Press, 1989.

Samples, Kenneth. "The Recent Truth about Seventh-Day Adventism." *Christianity Today* (2/5/90): 18-21.

Sanders, John. *No Other Name: An Investigation into the Destiny of the Unevangelized*. Grand Rapids: Eerdmans, 1992.

Sartre, Jean-Paul. "The Wall." In *Existentialism from Dostoevsky to Sartre*. Ed. by Walter Kaufmann. Cleveland: Meridian Books, 1956. Pp. 223-240.

Saucy, Robert L. "Theology of Human Nature." *Christian Perspectives on Being Human*. Ed. by J.P. Moreland & David Ciocchi. Grand Rapids: Baker, 1993.

Sayers, Stanley. "Life after Death." *Gospel Light* (September 1983).

Schaff, Philip, ed. *The Creeds of Christendom*, 4th ed. 3 vols. New York: Harper & Brothers, 1919.

Schrenk, Gottlob. "*grapho*, etc." *TDNT* I:742-773.

Seneca. *The Stoic Philosophy of Seneca.* Ed. by Moses Hadas. Garden City, NY: Doubleday Anchor, 1958.

Seventh-day Adventists Answer Questions on Doctrine. Washington, DC: Review and Herald, 1957.

Seventh-day Adventists Believe . . . A Biblical Exposition of 27 Fundamental Doctrines. Washington, DC: Ministerial Association, General Conference of Seventh-day Adventists, 1988.

Shank, Robert. *Elect in the Son.* Springfield, MO: Westcott Publishers, 1970.

Skard, Bjarne. *The Incarnation: A Study of the Christology of the Ecumenical Creeds.* Tr. by Herman E. Jorgensen. Minneapolis: Augsburg, 1960.

Smith, Stephen M. "**Kenosis**, Kenotic Theology." *Evangelical Dictionary of Theology.* Ed. by Walter A. Elwell. Grand Rapids: Baker, 1984. Pp. 600-602.

Sontag, Frederick. "Anthropodicy and the Return of God." *Encountering Evil: Live Options in Theodicy.* Ed. by Stephen T. Davis. Atlanta: John Knox, 1981. Pp. 137-151.

Spencer, Aida B. *Beyond the Curse: Women Called to Ministry.* Nashville: Thomas Nelson, 1985.

Spicq, Ceslas. *Theological Lexicon of the New Testament*, 3 vols. Tr. and ed. by James D. Ernest. Peabody, MA: Hendrickson, 1994.

Spiess, Tim. "Come Out from among Them and Be Separate!" www.john14-6.org/Separate.htm.

Sproul, R.C. *Grace Unknown.* Grand Rapids: Baker, 1997.

_____ . *The Holiness of God.* Wheaton, IL: Tyndale House, 1985.

Stacey, W. David. *The Pauline View of Man.* New York: Macmillan, 1956.

Stälin, Gustav. "*orge*, etc." (part). *TDNT* V:419-447.

Stauffer, Ethelbert. *New Testament Theology.* Tr. by John Marsh. London: SCM Press, 1955.

Storms, C. Samuel. *The Grandeur of God.* Grand Rapids: Baker, 1984.

Stott, John. *Romans: God's Good News for the World.* Downers Grove, IL: InterVarsity, 1994.

Strong, Augustus H. *Systematic Theology*, 3 vols. in 1. Valley Forge: Judson Press, 1962 reprint of 1907 ed.

Summers, Ray. *The Life Beyond.* Nashville: Broadman, 1959.

Tanner, Jerald; and Sandra Tanner. *The Changing World of Mormonism.* Chicago: Moody, 1980.

Taylor, James. "Born of a Virgin." *Christianity Today* (12/18/64).

Tertullian. "On **Baptism**." *ANF* III:669-679.

_____ . "A **Treatise** on the Soul." *ANF* III:181-235.

"**Thanatology**: Death and Modern Man." *Time* (11/20/64).

Thatcher, Tom. "The Deacon in the Pauline Church." In *Christ's Victorious Church: Essays on Biblical Ecclesiology and Eschatology in Honor of Tom Friskney.* Ed. by Jon A. Weatherly. Eugene, OR: Wipf and Stock, 2001. Pp. 53-67.

Thieme, R.B. Jr. *Origin of the Soul.* Houston: R.B. Thieme, Jr., Bible Ministries, 1983.

Thiessen, Henry. *Introductory Lectures in Systematic Theology.* Grand Rapids: Eerdmans, 1949.

Thompson, Fred P. "Fundamentalism and the Restoration Movement." *Christian Standard* (11/16/75).

Tillich, Paul. *Systematic Theology*, 3 vols. in 1. Chicago: University of Chicago Press, 1967.

Torjesen, Karen; and Leif Torjesen. "Inclusive Orthodoxy: Recovering a Suppressed Tradition." *The Other Side* (December 1986).

Trench, Richard Chenevix. *Synonyms of the New Testament.* Grand Rapids: Eerdmans, 1958.

Trueblood, David Elton. *General Philosophy.* Grand Rapids: Baker, 1976 reprint of 1963 ed.

Unger, Merrill F. *Biblical Demonology.* Wheaton, IL: Scripture Press, 1967.

_____ . *What Demons Can Do to Saints.* Chicago: Moody, 1977.

Van Dusen, Henry P. "The Significance of Jesus Christ." *Liberal Theology: An Appraisal.* Ed. by David Roberts and Henry P. Van Dusen. New York: Charles Scribner's Sons, 1942. Pp. 205-222.

VanGemeren, Willem A., ed. *New International Dictionary of Old Testament Theology and Exegesis [NIDOTTE],* 5 vols. Grand Rapids: Zondervan, 1997.

Van Rheenen, Gailyn. *Communicating Christ in Animistic Contexts.* Grand Rapids: Baker, 1991.

Vos, Geerhardus. *Biblical Theology.* Grand Rapids: Eerdmans, 1948.

_____ . *The Pauline Eschatology.* Grand Rapids: Eerdmans, 1952.

_____ . *The Self-Disclosure of Jesus.* Ed. by Johannes Vos. Grand Rapids: Eerdmans, 1954.

Wainwright, A.W. *The Trinity in the New Testament.* London: S.P.C.K., 1962.

Walvoord, John. "The Literal **View**." *Four Views on Hell.* Ed. by William Crockett. Grand Rapids: Zondervan, 1992. Pp. 11-28.

_____ . "**Response** to William V. Crockett." *Four Views on Hell.* Ed. by William Crockett. Grand Rapids: Zondervan, 1992. Pp. 77-81.

Ware, Bruce A. *God's Lesser **Glory**: The Diminished God of Open Theism* Wheaton, IL: Crossway Books, 2000.

Warfield, B.B. "The Biblical Doctrine of the **Trinity**." *Biblical and Theological Studies.* Ed. by Samuel G. Craig. Philadelphia: Presbyterian and Reformed, 1952. Pp. 22-59.

_____ . "The Chief Theories of the **Atonement**." *The Person and Work of Christ.* Ed. by Samuel G. Craig. Philadelphia: Presbyterian and Reformed, 1950. Pp. 351-369

_____ . "The Divine **Messiah** in the Old Testament." *Biblical and Theological Studies.* Ed. by Samuel G. Craig. Philadelphia: Presbyterian and Reformed, 1952. Pp. 79-126.

_____ . "The **Emotional Life** of Our Lord." *The Person and Work of Christ.* Ed. by Samuel G. Craig. Philadelphia: Presbyterian and Reformed, 1950. Pp. 93-145.

_____ . "The New Testament Terminology of '**Redemption**.'" *The Person and Work of Christ.* Ed. by Samuel G. Craig. Philadelphia: Presbyterian and Reformed, 1950. Pp. 429-475.

Warren, Virgil. *What the Bible Says about Salvation.* Joplin, MO: College Press, 1982.

Watson, Philip S. *Let God Be God!* Philadelphia: Fortress Press, 1947.

Webb, Joseph M. "Where Is the Command to Silence?" 2 parts. *Christian Standard* (5/21/89): 4-6; (5/28/89): 7-8.

Wells, David. "Everlasting **Punishment**." *Christianity Today* (3/20/87): 41-42.

_____ . *No Place for **Truth**.* Grand Rapids: Eerdmans, 1993.

_____ . *The Person of **Christ**.* Westchester, IL: Crossway Books, 1984.

Wenger, J.C. *Introduction to Theology.* Scottdale, PA: Herald Press, 1954.

What Do the Scriptures Say about "Survival after Death"? Brooklyn: Watchtower Bible and Tract Society, 1955.

Whisenant, Edgar. *88 Reasons Why the Rapture Will Be in 1988.* Nashville: World Bible Society, 1988.

Whitcomb, John C. Jr. *The Early Earth.* Grand Rapids: Baker, 1972.

Wiley, H. Orton, and Paul Culbertson. *Introduction to Christian Theology.* Kansas City, MO: Beacon Hill Press, 1946.

Williams, George Huntston. *The Radical Reformation.* Philadelphia: Westminster, 1962.

Wilmot, John. *Inspired Principles of Prophetic Interpretation.* Swengel, PA: Reiner Publications, 1975.

Wilson, Gerald. *"chidad." NIDOTTE* 2:107-108.

Wirt, Sherwood Eliot. "Destination Heaven." *Christianity Today* (8/12/77): 10-12.

Wolff, Richard. *The Last Enemy.* Washington, DC: Canon Press, 1974.

Wood, Leon J. *The Holy Spirit in the Old Testament.* Grand Rapids: Zondervan, 1976.

Woodbridge, John. *Biblical Authority.* Grand Rapids: Zondervan, 1982.

Wuest, Kenneth S. *Romans in the Greek New Testament for the English Reader.* Grand Rapids: Eerdmans, 1955.

Wyngaarden, Martin J. *The Future of the Kingdom.* Grand Rapids: Baker, 1955.

Yancey, Philip. "How Dirty Jokes and the Fear of Death Prove There Is a Heaven." *Christianity Today* (3/2/84): 78.

Young, Edward J. *Studies in Genesis One.* Phillipsburg, NJ: Presbyterian and Reformed, 1973.

_____ . *Thy Word Is Truth.* Grand Rapids: Eerdmans, 1957.

Young, Richard. *Intermediate New Testament Greek: A Linguistic and Exegetical Approach.* Nashville: Broadman & Holman, 1994.

Zwingli, Huldreich. "Of Baptism." *Zwingli and Bullinger.* Library of Christian Classics, vol. 24. Ed. and tr. by G.W. Bromiley. Philadelphia: Westminster Press, 1953. Pp. 129-175.

Subject Index

Scripture Index

Scripture Index